THE ANCHOR BIBLE

MATTHEW

INTRODUCTION, TRANSLATION, AND NOTES

BY

W. F. ALBRIGHT

AND

C. S. MANN

Doubleday & Company, Inc.
Garden City, New York

ISBN: 0-385-08658
Library of Congress Catalog Card Number 77–150875
Copyright © 1971 by Doubleday & Company, Inc.
All Rights Reserved
Printed in the United States of America
First Edition
Third Printing

PREFACE

At a time when the Anchor Bible was still supposed to consist of concise, one-volume paperbacks, the editors invited Professor W. D. Davies to prepare commentaries on Matthew and Mark. He accepted, but pressure of other work kept delaying him until he finally decided—presumably because of the steadily increasing length of the published contributions—that he would have to give up the assignment. We were greatly disappointed, but fortunately Dr. C. S. Mann of London and Baltimore had just finished collaborating with the senior editor on the unfinished commentary on Acts left by the late lamented Johannes Munck. We agreed to collaborate on the Matthew commentary.

We owe special thanks to the junior editor, Professor David Noel Freedman, for reading the manuscript and pointing out weaknesses in the original treatment.

We owe a deep debt of gratitude to Dr. Leona Running, of Andrews University, Michigan, for much invaluable help at various stages of the preparation of this work, and not least in the final editing of the typescript.

For much too long a time the course of New Testament scholarship has been dictated by theological, quasi-theological, and philosophical presuppositions. In far too many cases commentaries on NT books have neglected such basic requirements as up-to-date historical and philological analysis of the text itself. In many ways this preoccupation with theological and metaphysical interpretation is the unacknowledged child of Hegelianism. To this should be added the continuing and baleful influence of Schleiermacher and his successors on the whole treatment of historical material. The result has often been steadfast refusal to take seriously the findings of archaeological and linguistic research. We believe that there is less and less excuse for the resulting confusion in this latter half of the twentieth century.

Closely allied with these presuppositions is the ever present fog of existentialism, casting ghostly shadows over an already confused landscape. Existentialism as a method of interpreting the New Testament is based upon a whole series of undemonstrable postulates of Platonic, Neo-Platonic, left-wing scholastic, and relativistic origins. So anti-historical is this approach that it fascinates speculative minds which prefer clichés to factual data, and shifting ideology to empirical research and logical demonstration.

In this commentary we have endeavored to take the words of Matthew's gospel seriously and to see behind them a whole cultural, legal, and spiritual tradition growing around the belief that Israel was the chosen people of God and that the coming of the Messiah was the fulfillment of God's revelation of himself to men. This is the conviction with which the nascent Christian community met the world of its day, both Jewish and Greek, and there is no understanding of our NT sources unless the conviction that Jesus was the promised Messiah is treated seriously. We have, therefore, taken considerable pains to place the Jesus of the gospels firmly against his own background, making full use of all the evidence now available—historical, archaeological, and linguistic. For example, we have insisted that it is absolutely necessary to take seriously Greek historical sources such as Josephus and Eusebius, both of whom are now being vindicated as careful historians by independent discoveries. This is particularly true of the discoveries at Masada, Qumran, Chenoboskion, and Ugarit (the last-mentioned may seem anachronistic to NT scholarship, but it has done more to demonstrate the accuracy of Eusebius' use of such sources as Philo Byblius than any other discovery of modern times). Similarly, in spite of steadfast refusal on the part of some writers to give credence to the discoveries at Qumran as illustrating the New Testament, the cumulative results of Qumran studies so far have more than vindicated the tentative conclusions drawn by some of the first writers in the field.

Of almost equal importance for the NT scholar have been the epoch-making discoveries in Palestinian archaeology since the beginning of this century. We now possess a great deal more information about social and cultural conditions in Palestine in the time of Jesus than was dreamed possible seventy years ago.

In preparing this volume we have drawn especially on the results of Qumran research and other recent discoveries in the area of early Jewish sectarian studies as well as on the critical rehabilitation of early Christian historians. Thanks to this material, we have been able to determine the kind of Aramaic spoken by Jesus to an extent never before remotely approached. As a result we have resumed the research of the senior author on the original Aramaic form of the proper names of the New Testament, begun nearly fifty years ago and continued intermittently since then. This particular research has proved to have implications far beyond those originally envisaged. We do not believe that any *substantial* part of our present gospel text was first *written* in Aramaic, though the possibility of such a composition cannot be ruled out entirely. Research on the proper names has led to recognition of the extraordinary importance of the Syriac recensions for better understanding of the gospels.

It is doubtful whether this commentary would ever have been written at all without the highly original investigations carried on by the late Abram Spiro, of Wayne State University, on the importance of the Samaritans in NT tradition. This particular collaboration began with the joint study of some *pēsher* (commentary) fragments of Qumran while the senior author was in Detroit in April 1964. It led to a prolonged and voluminous correspondence between us, in which the junior author joined soon after his arrival in this country in July 1965. Dr. Spiro's untimely death put an end to this fruitful co-operation, but a mass of manuscript material is preserved, the most important of which was condensed by the authors of the present volume into a long appendix to Johannes Munck's Anchor commentary on Acts. In our opinion, Spiro's work is revolutionary in its importance for proper understanding of early Christian tradition in the book of Acts, and it casts a bright light on the parallel gospel tradition. We must rank Spiro's contributions to the understanding of the New Testament on a par with the Qumran and Chenoboskion discoveries and the new knowledge about the development of Aramaic dialects. We gratefully dedicate this volume to his memory.

W.F.A. and C.S.M.

CONTENTS

CONTENTS

TRANSLATION AND NOTES

PRINCIPAL ABBREVIATIONS

1. PUBLICATIONS

BA	Biblical Archaeologist
CBQ	Catholic Biblical Quarterly
ET	Expository Times
IB	The Interpreter's Bible, 12 vols., New York and Nashville: Abingdon Press, 1951–57
ICC	International Critical Commentary
IDB	The Interpreter's Dictionary of the Bible, 4 vols., New York and Nashville: Abingdon Press, 1962
JBL	Journal of Biblical Literature
NovT	Novum Testamentum
NTS	New Testament Studies
1QH	Qumran Hymns of Thanksgiving
1QS	Qumran Manual of Discipline
RB	Revue Biblique
StB	H. L. Strack and P. Billerbeck, *Kommentar zum Neuen Testament aus Talmud und Midrasch*, 6 vols., Munich: Beck, 1922–61
StEv	*Studia Evangelica.* Papers from the Oxford International Congresses of NT Studies, published at Berlin, Akademie-Verlag
TNTS	*Twelve New Testament Studies*, by John A. T. Robinson, London: SCM, 1962
TS	Theological Studies
TWNT	*Theologisches Wörterbuch zum Neuen Testament*, eds. Gerhard Kittel et al., Stuttgart: Kohlhammer, 1933–
ZNW	Zeitschrift für die neutestamentliche Wissenschaft und die Kunde der älteren Kirche

2. Versions

AB	The Anchor Bible, 1964–
KJ	The King James, or Authorized Version of 1611
LXX	The Septuagint
MT	Masoretic Text
NEB	The New English Bible, 1961, 1970
RSV	The Revised Standard Version, 1946, 1952

3. Other Abbreviations

Ar.	Arabic
Aram.	Aramaic
Gr.	Greek
Heb.	Hebrew
NT	New Testament
OT	Old Testament
Syr.	Syriac
TB	Talmud Babli
TY	Talmud Yerushalmi

INTRODUCTION

I. THE GOSPEL AND THE CANONICAL "GOSPELS"

A

The four books in our New Testament which are called the "gospels" stand alone, in that there is no other material by which to judge them.[1] This is not to say that they are a wholly new literary form, but rather that the material they discuss is not to be found paralleled anywhere else. It is true that during the centuries after the events recorded in the New Testament, the apocryphal gospels and various Gnostic compilations of sayings attributed to Jesus were composed. But an examination of the materials so collected, and a comparison of them with the canonical gospels of the New Testament, reveals that these later compositions were slanted to a form of belief about the person and work of Jesus which finds no expression in the pages of the New Testament.

The designation of Matthew, Mark, Luke, and John as "gospels" has grown out of a convention. The New English Bible (NEB) provides the general title "The Gospel" for all four books, and then a subheading for each one, as: "according to Matthew." *The* Gospel is the proclamation in the ministry of Jesus that through him the reign of God is being declared to men who are ready to receive it: it is the good news of man's incorporation into this reign, this kingdom, through the remission of sin. "Good tidings," or "to convey good tidings," is a common enough expression in the Dead Sea scrolls: *the* Gospel, *the* proclamation, came about at a decisive moment in history when God uttered once-and-for-all his good news through Jesus, his "Word." The Gospel shows us that God's promise to Israel was fulfilled at a midpoint in history, that everything which God promised in his dealings with the people of the Old Covenant was summed up in his Anointed Servant, the Messiah Jesus. This Gospel presupposes and grows out of the Old Testament,

[1] Cf. recently U. E. Simon, "The Problem of the Biblical Narrative," *Theology* 72 (1969), 588 ff.

and there is no understanding of the books of the New Testament without the books of the Old. (Even a cursory examination of Paul's letters, especially Romans and Corinthians, shows how much knowledge of the Old Testament the Apostle demanded, even if the majority of his converts were non-Jews.) When we speak of the books of the Old Testament, it is well to remember that the Jewish canon of Hebrew Scripture was fixed long before the early rabbinic scholars gave it formal expression at Jamnia toward the end of the first century A.D.

If we come to Matthew's interpretation of the Gospel expecting chronologically arranged history, we shall be disappointed. It is exceedingly difficult, if not impossible, to reconcile the two nativity narratives of Matthew and Luke; we have to assume that these represent two sources, or two traditions. The Great Instruction, which in Matthew is said to have taken place on a mountainside, is said by Luke to have been delivered on the plain; moreover, Matthew uses this account to include a whole block of teaching found in quite different contexts in the other gospels.

If we come to the gospels expecting to find biography in the modern sense, we shall again look in vain. There was little real interest in scientific biography in the ancient world—Plutarch is an exception—and Matthew provides us with no biographical material between the infancy and the beginning of the Baptist's ministry. Almost all the elements that a modern reader would demand of a biography are lacking. Matthew has two principal interests: the fulfillment of God's purposes in and through Jesus, and how this fulfillment will find expression in the community which Jesus founded. In addition to Matthew's concern with themes rather than with history, the most cursory inspection of this gospel would reveal that—from the purely historical point of view—it devotes a disproportionate amount of space and attention to the narrative of the passion.

This concentration on the passion and the resurrection of Jesus provides us with a clue to the purpose of a written gospel. Although it is possible to reconstruct something of the earthly life, and even the ministry, of Jesus from the letters and from Acts (and we have to remember that the letters of Paul were all written prior to the gospels), obviously there was a further need felt to make the record as clear and authentic as possible. There were, for example, phrases in Paul's letters which were open to misinterpretation or misuse by such as the nascent Gnostic sects (cf. the Apostle's use of "the wisdom of God" in I Cor i 24). In addition, there must have been considerable anxiety among Christians lest all the original twelve disciples should die before the process of sifting and control had been completed. The four gospels were not written for people to whom Jesus-Messiah was outside experience; those outside the Christian community were not the intended audience for the gospels, however much the availability of those writings may now persuade us to the contrary. Belief in the passion and resurrection of Jesus, and in their saving effects, is central to the gospels; for the evangelists the passion was central to the interpretation of those events. References to the life and ministry of Jesus in the letters are central to practical questions of Christian living— God's will is ascertained by prayer and study of the Lord's teaching (I Cor vii 10, 17, 25), and behavior at the Eucharist is determined, or should be, by what the Eucharist is (I Cor xi 23 ff.; II Cor viii 9; Gal iv 4; I Pet iii 12 ff.).

Certainly there were differences of emphasis in the early Church on the ministry of Jesus. Jewish Christians might be acutely sensitive about the role of Jesus as Lawgiver, while Gentiles might be much more aware of Jesus as the harbinger of salvation (a popular concept in the world of that time). We must be careful not to see these two points of view as contradictory—all too often the contrast between these roles has been hopelessly exaggerated. There is equal concern for "salvation" in the material allegedly from the source(s) called "Q," and lawmaking is not a Jewish prerogative. The two strands might appear to present divergent traditions, but both are to be found throughout the gospels and in the New Testament generally; they present us with a rounded picture of the whole scene. If we expect to discover traces of divergent tradition in the gospels, with the simplicity born of our modern habit of encapsulating everything, we shall find merely our own notions of what we think the divergent traditions ought to have been. It has been debated often enough in the past precisely how far it is correct to regard the gospel of John as "anti-Jewish," or how far Matthew's composition is the most "Jewish" of the four gospels. This is hopelessly simple. It supposes that Jews in the first century possessed a homogeneity which we now know to have been wholly lacking. It also fails to recognize that the *omission* of polemical material (e.g., against the Sadducees) may be due to the fact that after A.D. 70 the Sadducees had ceased to exist as a force at all.

Why were the gospels written?

The infant Christian community demanded that oral tradition be rightly evaluated to avoid misunderstanding, in the knowledge that the original disciples would soon be dead and the Community faced with the need to have more or less fixed patterns for recalling God's redemptive act in Jesus. There were other factors at work, too. We know from the evidence of both archaeology and secular writers that conditions in Palestine after A.D. 60 were fraught with uncertainty and pending civil strife, and that in these years (even before the fall of Jerusalem in A.D. 70) thousands of people left the country. In such a situation, it is understandable that only Christians would feel the need to record and preserve the earliest oral memories of the ministry of Jesus and its culmination.[2]

Because of the nature of the Gospel proclamation, the original oral repetition of the story of Jesus and his teachings did not satisfy the early Christians for long. It was of the essence of the Gospel— supremely exemplified in Matthew and in Paul's teaching—that all Israel's experience had been gathered up, fulfilled, in Jesus. But how, and in what manner, had it all been fulfilled? If the earliest Christians had the Old Testament as scripture, and presumably followed the old synagogue pattern of reading and prayers, then it is obvious that the Gospel had to be put into a form in which it could be similarly used. We know from Paul's letters (cf. Col iv 16) that he was able to order his letters to be read aloud in his convert-congregations, and we may infer from this that during worship there was teaching by the apostles and elders. It is only logical to assume, therefore, that there was pressure to have on record an authentic account of what Jesus had said and done, and the better to show Christianity's roots in Israel.

[2] For a thorough examination of the place of oral tradition in the early Christian community, the reader is referred to the following invaluable works by Birger Gerhardsson: *Memory and Manuscript*, Acta Seminarii Neotestamentici Upsaliensis, XXII, 1961, and *Tradition and Transmission in Early Christianity*, Coniectanea Neotestamentica, XX, 1964. (Both are published by Gleerup, Lund, and Munksgaard, Copenhagen.) The author's work perhaps makes oral transmission too rigid, but it is a very valuable corrective to the view that the gospel material was almost a free compilation of the early community.

It is possible to reconstruct the approximate process of transmission from oral to written form. There is a disproportionate amount of attention, from the standpoint of strict biographical interest, paid to the passion, death and resurrection of Jesus, which indicates the degree of importance attached to these saving events in preaching and teaching, and they must have been among the first parts of the Gospel written down. Matthew's use of OT quotations has led many to infer that the earliest written documents in the Christian tradition may have been collections of pieces from the Old Testament, and this view has been heavily reinforced by the discovery of just such collections (though not of course Christian ones) at Qumran.[3] The manner in which the gospel material took final shape can be deduced from yet another characteristic of the finished product. Each pericope (a Greek word indicating a small block of material) in the gospels is self-contained, and is meant to convey some specific teaching, usually with no chronological or topographical indication of its place in the scheme of the Lord's ministry. Thus, for example, it is possible that the story of the Syro-Phoenician woman (Mark vii 24 ff.) may have been recalled originally in answer to the question: "How did Jesus deal with those outside Judaism?"

It is not easy to determine whether the pericopae as we now have them are identical with those same small blocks of material as they existed in oral tradition. For example, Mark ii 13 ff. (=Matt ix 9 ff. and Luke v 27 ff.) places the call of Matthew after a time of teaching, whereas Matthew and Luke both place it after a healing. Each evangelist tells the story differently, and we are in no position to determine which evangelist to follow here—but all three (Matt ix 10; Mark ii 15; and Luke v 29) have the same note of location. On the other hand, the healing of the centurion's slave in Matt viii 5 and Luke vii 1 ff. takes place in different places in the two gospels. If we assume that the pericopae were self-contained originally and implied some lesson, or sought to convey a truth,

<hr/>

[3] On the so-called "testimonies" from Qumran see: J. M. Allegro, "Further Messianic References in Qumran Literature," JBL 75 (1956), 174–87; *idem*, "Fragments of a Qumran Scroll of Eschatological *Midrāšîm*," JBL 77 (1958), 350–54; *idem*, "A Recently Discovered Fragment of a Commentary on Hosea from Qumran's Fourth Cave," JBL 78 (1959), 142–47; William R. Lane, "A New Commentary Structure in 4Q Florilegium," JBL 78 (1959), 343–46; Joseph A. Fitzmyer, "'4Q Testimonia' and the New Testament," TS 18 (1957), 513–37.

then if a pericope could only be understood in the context of a whole passage, it is quite likely that some editing took place.

The spread of the Church's work among Gentiles also served to dictate the formation of the gospels. The *diatribē* was a well-known literary form (Luke's Acts has been thought by many to belong to this category). It is unfortunate that the word has such pejorative undertones in modern usage, for the Gr. *diatribē* meant "propaganda," or better, "essays to persuade." There were obviously urgent questions to be answered among Jews, such as, "If Jesus was the Messiah, then why did he suffer an ignominious death?" Greek converts would have to be shown why a divine figure, especially one called "God's Wisdom" (I Cor i 24), had allowed himself to undergo the torture and death normally reserved for criminals. The very length of the passion narratives in all four gospels has led many scholars to argue the existence at a very early stage of a kind of catechist's manual, which was used to provide tested and approved answers to such questions.

It has occasionally been said (notably by Papias as early as A.D. 130) that the gospels were committed to writing because the apostles had begun to die. This doesn't seem very plausible, however—the gospel of Luke was composed by a man who had not known the Lord at all, and his Acts suggests that he was writing in a time when most of the apostles were already dead. The suggestion has also been made that the writing of the gospel was encouraged as the expectation of an early *parousia* (a manifestation of the presence again in visible form of the Risen Lord) faded; hence the needs of posterity had to be considered. The expectation of the parousia, however drastically reinterpreted (as, for example, by Paul), never did fade completely, but it was to remain a part of the faith of the writers.

In the light of the interpretations current in popular and semi-popular literature, it is of capital importance to note the appeal of the gospel to the educated classes. There is enough evidence from pagan classical writers to show that libraries were not uncommon among educated people. Luke's two-part work of gospel and Acts is plainly addressed to a man who did not need to have allusions spelled out for him. Evidently, Luke's material, addressed as a kind of "apologia" to a Greek patron, deals with the relationship of Christianity (of which his patron has heard) to Judaism.

It has been suggested that the pattern of the four gospels is in some sense dictated by liturgical considerations, or that the framework went back to an original pattern that either reflected the Jewish synagogue lections and the Jewish feasts, or was ordered according to the demands of early Christian worship. This theory further maintains that it is possible to determine, from the gospels themselves, the patterns of readings used by the primitive Church. However, we have no contemporary information about the lectionary patterns of the first-century synagogue, and Justin Martyr's record that the "memoirs" of the apostles were read at the Eucharist might equally well be applied to their letters.

It may be asked how far early Christian theology has either distorted, or been responsible for the arrangement of, the material which we now have, collected in the four gospels. Occasionally, the question is asked in a way which suggests that the inquirer is thinking of theology in terms of the developed Christology of the councils of Nicaea (A.D. 325) or of Chalcedon (A.D. 451). In any discussion of the gospels, one must remember that "faith" for the writers of the New Testament meant trust in the mighty acts of God through Jesus, with all that these acts implied about the intervention of God promised in the Old Testament. This kind of theological outlook has been provided by the Qumran discoveries with a good deal of control evidence bearing on the New Testament. Theology has indeed determined the framework of the four gospels, in the sense that there has been massive concentration on the central events: the passion and crucifixion.

The gospels have interpreted the material as well. For all the differences in precise chronology, John and the other three gospels agree that the passion must be seen in the light of the commemoration of God's deliverance of his people in the Passover rite. And we must read the gospels remembering the OT way of treating history. The books of the Old Testament view the escape of Israel from Egypt as a mighty act of God's intervention (cf. Exod xiv–xv; Pss cxiv–cxv), though the ascertainable facts might suggest only a disorganized and fearful group making its way by moonlight across the Sea of Reeds. So with the crucifixion: to Roman soldiers it was a routine execution; to the priestly party an end to a sordid little disturbance; to Paul and the NT writers generally it was the instrument of man's freedom from bondage, an event that will have repercussions right into eternity. In United States history, the incident at Harpers Ferry centered around John Brown seemed minor at the time, but we have seen how its implications exploded; this is the case again and again in the Bible. It is important to beware of using the stick of "distortion" in order to beat the evangelists when no other evidence is available.

Occasionally, endings—and even beginnings—appear to have been lost, elided, or misplaced from many of the gospel stories. For example, Mark i 29–31 has no apparent ending, and vs. 32 has been added to fit, while Mark iii 1–6 ends with an account of Jesus' enemies plotting against him—a circumstance which does not fit our notions of how the story should end (cf. ii 21–22, xi 23–24). When it is obvious that some of the stories have been rearranged or collected into blocks, with the original meanings perhaps lost in the change—or at any rate misplaced (cf. Matt v 25 ff. and Luke xii 58 ff., and this commentary ad loc.)—it is well to remember that the writers' interest centered in the Lord's mighty works, and that teaching was secondary.

Though the use of OT text seems central to Matthew's concern —and we will have more to say about this below—it is important to note that in the final analysis no one reason governs the arrangement of Matthew's material. We can say only that Matthew appears to have been influenced most by the theological idea of fulfillment. Most important in the written gospels is the proclamation of God's declaration of himself and his will in his Messiah Jesus, crucified, risen, and glorified. Around such a proclamation, there is—as one should expect—a great deal of variation in emphasis. Mutual agreement in detail would be suspect; and this we do not have.

B

In view of the interest excited by the discovery of parts of a library at Nag Hammadi in Egypt, including what has come to be called the "Gospel of Thomas," it is important to determine precisely what is, or is not, a canonical gospel. It is simplest to answer the question by means of a negative, and to delineate what is *not* a gospel. (At the same time, documents such as Thomas ought not to be rejected out of hand because they may conflict with what has already been declared to be canonical.)

As rooted in historical circumstance as the Apostles' Creed shows the Christian faith to be (*sub Pontio Pilato*), we have every right to expect a written Christian source, with the oral sources embedded in it, to manifest an awareness of history, and to place Jesus both politically and religiously in the framework of the history and circumstances of his time. Any document, therefore, which claims to be a "gospel," but which actually consists of teaching or exhortation which is wholly detached from the Jesus whom we know historically from the four canonical documents, is not a gospel in any recognized canonical sense.

In the light of what we know of developments after the recorded events of the four gospels and the Acts, it may be better to stress another very important and definitive matter, the passion of Jesus. Paul tells us plainly that the cross and all that it implied in the early preaching and teaching was abhorrent to Jew and Gentile alike (I Cor i 23–24). Many people who might have been regarded as promising material for the infant Church must for this reason have rejected Christianity, whether sophisticated Greek intellectuals or passionately nationalist Jews. The development of the Gnostic movements came to show very early that there were those who were offended by the concept of the deity trafficking with mortal flesh (cf. I John iv 1–7). Therefore a need arose to accommodate the scandal of incarnation and passion to some modes of dualist thought, and the whole of John's first letter is witness to the fact that in spite of acute differences there was a common "proto-Gnostic" vocabulary in which debate could be conducted. We have already called attention to the very high proportion of the four gospels' narrative devoted to the passion. Any Christian document (or any document purporting to be Christian) that, compared with the canonical documents, plays down the central element of the passion in Jesus' life and ministry must be held suspect.

Paul stresses one theme more than any other in his letters: the supremacy of grace, that unmerited free relationship with God which he avows characterizes the man "in Christ." Though Paul's letters were written before the gospels, they nevertheless are theological interpreters of the oral tradition, and the apostle's emphasis on the supremacy of grace is echoed by its emphasis in the canonical gospels. We know from Paul's letters to Corinth and to Colassae—not to mention the evidence of John's letters to other parts of Asia Minor—that the early Christians often were tempted to consider other parts of Christian doctrine more important. Plainly, there was a good deal of exaltation of human progress, human reason, human achievement, all at the expense of the primacy of grace. No warnings in our gospel traditions are more frequently given, or more sharply worded, than those which condemn boasting, however "spiritual." This concern with grace, then, is yet another criterion by which to judge anything that comes to us as presumed teaching from the lips of Jesus and his apostles.

Matthew constantly stresses the element of "fulfillment" (which we shall examine in Part IV of this Introduction), and all four gospels in varying ways and degrees (followed later by Acts) emphasize the ministry of Jesus as the consummation of the prophecy of the Old Testament. That is to say, the four gospels indissolubly link the Old Testament and the revelation in Jesus. It was this relationship between the ministry of Jesus and the Old Testament that caused Marcion's teaching (second century) to founder and be condemned. His teaching, like that of many later "biblical" heresiarchs, was founded on a desire to make a clear repudiation of the "God of the Old Testament," variously presented as a cruel or a creator-God (as distinct from the true God), but in all the varying interpretations someone wholly other than the Father of Jesus. Many Gnostic systems, beginning with the followers of Simon Magus and Nicholas (cf. Acts viii 10; Rev ii 7) in one way or another sought to make the creation of matter itself the work of a lesser deity, with which the true God would have had no alliance. Hence, it was emphatically necessary, in any of these attempts to interpret the New Testament, that a decisive break be made with the Old Testament; and this break between New and Old Testaments was another negative criterion which the Church applied in assessing material laying claim to apostolic authorship or authority.

Closely connected with this concern for the Old Testament as necessary preparation for the acceptance of God in Jesus was the Church's consciousness of herself as the people of a "new covenant." A look at any concordance will show the New Testament's emphasis upon the adjective "new": following the ministry of Jesus, there is a new creation, a new man, a new life, a new age, a new covenant—in fact, the last book in the New Testament asserts that all things are being made new. But nowhere does the New Testament claim that there is a new Israel, a new people of God: rather, the Church is the inheritor of ancient promises, direct descendant of the people of ancient Israel, heir to the covenants made with the patriarchs. A new covenant is established in the blood of the Messiah's cross, but all our documents (especially the tract called "the epistle to the Hebrews") insist that this new covenant, sealed in blood as was the Exodus covenant, is essentially one with the older history of Israel, a new covenant for which that older history was a preparation. For any understanding of the NT faith this insistence on "covenant" is vital; it also explains the exclusion of much material which the Church refused to recognize as canonical scripture. Thanks to the work first of G. E. Mendenhall, followed more recently by H. B. Huffmon, it is clear that "covenant" in the Old Testament (and, *pari passu,* in the New Testament) describes an arrangement in which a sovereign Lord lays down the conditions under which he is prepared to accept the vassalage of, and afford protection to, those who seek his aid and wish to enter his dominion. Moreover, as Huffmon has pointed out, the Hebrew word "to know" is often to be interpreted in this convenantal sense, as demonstrating that God acknowledged, or "recognized," Israel as his, and Israel acknowledged the sovereignty of her Lord. From man's side—that is, from Israel's side, in this context—no conditions could be attached to this acknowledgment, for all the conditions were laid down by her superior, the Lord.

In this concept of "covenant," we have another test for any material which seeks, or sought, to be an authentic "gospel" handed down by an apostle. Again and again the Pauline letters—themselves a commentary, in a very real sense, on the Gospel proclamation—emphasized that man is saved only through the sacrifice of Christ consummated in blood; anything seeking to make this basis for salvation conditional is false to the Gospel. According to Paul, faith, that humble acceptance of what God has done for man in Jesus, is itself a gift of God; any pretense that human wisdom or any other achievement can substitute for faith is founded simply on human pride and arrogance. There are many indications in Paul's letters to Corinth and Colossae, and in the first Johannine letter, that certain people claimed a kind of esoteric wisdom or access to divine secrets denied to the generality of Christians. No doubt this kind of pseudosophistication must have been very disruptive to the life of the Christian community, and at the same time threatening to that direct dependence upon God which "covenant" implies. Indeed, this kind of attitude to "lesser breeds without the law" could, and frequently did, lead to an assumption of superiority in the sphere of moral conduct too. The apostle Paul is our principal witness to this phenomenon in early Christian experience.

At this stage we must briefly examine the background of the Gospel of Thomas, and some of the reasons which led the Church to reject, almost instinctively, such material as at best speculative, at worst heretical. The library (for such it appears to have been) of manuscripts discovered at Nag Hammadi (300 miles south of Cairo, 150 miles north of Aswan, near the ancient Greek monastery of Chenoboskion) included this "Gospel of Thomas." Works that begin with some formula such as "These are the secret words which the living Jesus spoke" are usually late, and are associated with a specific kind of literature. But the Gospel of Thomas cannot be placed so neatly into such a category. It consists of 114 sayings attributed to Jesus, with very few dialogues, no narrative, and a bare minimum of incident. Furthermore, there are no links between the paragraphs. The discovery is important because collections of sayings ("logia") are often thought to have existed before there was any attempt to set down a consistent gospel narrative. (We know, for example, from Acts xx 35, of at least one saying of Jesus that is not included in the four canonical gospels.) The age which produced Thomas is a little hard to determine, but the Coptic agrees with some third-century Greek fragments from Oxyrhyncus, which proves that the Gospel of Thomas goes back to the third century, and maybe earlier.

Opinions in the scholarly world about the document have varied. R. M. Grant (whose work is listed at the end of this part) dismisses Thomas as an example of how Gnostics understood, or rather misunderstood, Jesus and his Gospel. For Grant, the whole compilation witnesses to the very early perversion of the Christian proclamation. Professor G. Quispel, on the other hand, prefers to see in Thomas an independent and early gospel tradition, which even has traces of an Aramaic source-tradition lying behind it. Between these two positions, which might reasonably be described as the two poles of scholarly argument, Bertil Gärtner has it that Thomas does indeed contain some old material, but so overlaid with later material that it is hard to know how to define and limit it. If this section is not to become far too long and technical, we must content ourselves with merely giving some of the more significant links between Thomas and the canonical gospels, pointing out where the significant differences lie.

There is a good deal of material in Thomas that is very reminiscent of the canonical gospels; equally, there is material that is
completely characteristic of Gnostic teaching, in its emphasis on
salvation through knowledge, in its contempt for the body, and in
its use of vocabulary with Gnostic shades of meaning ("light,"
"unity," "rest").

Occasionally, there are passages in Thomas which are very close
to the synoptic material, passages which could even be abridged
versions of that material. There are parallel passages which are
longer than their synoptic counterparts, and these might be expansions, or material from which the canonical material has been
abridged. There can be no certainty on this point. In addition,
there are wholly new parables, along with some sayings which
seem to be composed of a regrouping of canonical material. For
example, the parable of the Sower (Thomas ix) has features which,
Quispel argues, are primitive, while the parable of the Tares
(Thomas lvii) looks very much like an imperfectly remembered
version of Matt xiii 24 ff. (the dialogue between the lord and the
servants has been cut to one speech in Thomas).

There is one feature in Thomas which is interesting in that it
bears out the contentions of C. H. Dodd, made as long ago as
1935 (*The Parables of the Kingdom,* London: Nisbet; New York:
Scribner). This is Thomas lxv, the parable of the Wicked Husband-
men (Mark xii 1 ff., and parallels). In the Thomas version, there
are but two servants and a son—which was the original basis of
the story, according to Dodd's theory. This kind of feature in
Thomas argues for an early origin, and perhaps earlier than the
tradition enshrined in our synoptic gospels. There is, of course, no
proof of this, and we ought to beware of subscribing automatically
to the suggestion that what is shorter must necessarily be more
primitive.

Expansion of the parable material in the canonical gospels is a
far more difficult consideration. Thomas lxiv (Matt xxii 5 ff.) provides us with a moral ending far more concerned with good manners
than with response to the eschatological hope of the early Church, in
favor of more mundane considerations in a continuing community.
But so stated this makes the gospel material far too static and rigid, incapable of adaptation to the changing needs of the community as
it moved into and faced the challenges of a Greek environment.
Jeremias has pointed out that within the synoptic gospels there was

an observable movement from eschatology to other interpretations in the parables. The confrontation of Israel with Jesus' assertion that the times were fulfilled in him is the keynote of most of the parables as they were originally delivered, but this kind of confrontation would have to be reinterpreted for those who were outside the covenants when the Gospel first came to them.

At the same time, there are interpretations of synoptic parables in Thomas, or lessons read into them, which can only be described as pale and insignificant beside the accounts which the canonical gospels provide. Such, for instance, is the treatment accorded to Matthew's "Agree with your opponent quickly" (Matt v 25): in Thomas this becomes an injunction not to go to law. Here again a note of caution is necessary. We have Paul on record as expressing surprise that Christians in Corinth found it possible to reconcile Christian faith with litigation against their fellows (I Cor vi 1–8); and it is at least possible that what we have in Thomas is a simple statement which may owe more to Paul than to Matt v 25.

There is material in Thomas which could be looking back to sayings from the ministry of Jesus which have not otherwise been preserved—for example, the parables of the Lost Meal and the Attacker proving his strength (Thomas xcviii). The first of these may be genuine, as several scholars have argued; the second is far more uncertain, involving a man trying his strength against a fortified wall with no weapon but a sword. By and large, however, although we cannot with certainty say that the reinterpreted material in Thomas is Gnostic, there is reason to believe that his reinterpretation would have been acceptable to Christians who were in touch with Gnostic thinking. Thomas xlviii has a saying about two people agreeing together in one house, and then saying "Be moved" to a mountain: as a result of their agreement, the mountain is moved. Though this looks at first sight like a combination of two sayings (Matt xviii 19 and Mark xi 23), the meaning provided by the combination in Thomas is radically different from that of the synoptic gospels. There *is* a saying about agreement between two people, but it results in our canonical sources in a promise of answered prayer, while the removal of a mountain (in Luke a sycamore tree) is the reward of faith, and has nothing to do with unity between two people. It would be hazardous to impose theological concepts on the material in Thomas, where we have as yet no controlling parallel evidence. Nevertheless, Thomas shows an interest in "unity"—a common Gnostic interest—and has nothing to say about faith nor of prayer.

There are inconsistencies in Thomas which suggest that it may have been written during the period when incipient Gnosticism was fast becoming consciously opposed to the Christian majority view, while still using large amounts of NT material. Knowledge is evidently for Thomas the one desirable goal, the one inestimable treasure. There are parables in our canonical sources which speak of the Kingdom as a treasure to be found: in Thomas (cf. cxi) the goal of search is self-knowledge. We must suppose that this was a major preoccupation of the writer (or compiler); the Kingdom is to be found in self-awareness (cf. xviii, xlix, l, lxvii, lxxxiv). If the writer is uninterested in the facts of Jesus' life, it is rash to suggest that he is saying that salvation is merely to be possessed by knowing a secret, or that the significance of Jesus lies precisely in his being custodian of secrets now known to men. But it is true that this enigmatic collection of sayings seems to suggest that there is in all men the truth of their own being, which can be revealed by learning the meaning of the "secret words." The life hidden within man must be sought, often at the cost of suffering and rejection, but the essential point to notice in Thomas is that this life is already in man—there is no marred image to be restored, no radical change in man's being (repentance) necessary as a prerequisite for God's action upon the soul. This life (variously described—cf. xxiv, l, lxi, lxxvii, xc and also iv, xii, lxxiv, cviii) is dormant in man and must be sought (ii, xxiv, xcii, xciv), if necessary through suffering (lviii, lxviii, lxix) and rejection of the material world (lxxx). It is difficult to escape the conclusion that what we have here is a scheme of salvation which—to use the modern phrase—is a "do-it-yourself" challenge to human striving.

And if there is no interest in the life and ministry of Jesus, there is an equal lack of interest in a future Event at the end of Time. There is no future Kingdom, such as we find in Matthew; rather, for Thomas (iii) the kingdom is "within you, and it is without you: if you know yourselves, you will be known." Similarly, the "rest" of the dead (li) has come already, but "you know it not." Though there are two sayings in Thomas which suggest (xxi, ciii) a need for awareness of an approaching time of judgment, they must be balanced against sayings which declare (e.g., xviii, lxvii) that the Kingdom will not come as an act of God in the affairs of men, but may be discovered by self-knowledge, by self-discipline.

Another feature should be noticed here: the suggestion in Thomas is that the Old Covenant was a spurious revelation of God's purposes. Circumcision is rejected (liii), prophecy is repudiated (lii), and Jesus is represented as attacking the threefold duty of prayer, fasting, and the giving of alms (vi, xiv, civ). It is just possible the Gospel of Thomas contains, along with all known Gnostic writings, elements of anti-Jewish polemic. Considering the New Testament's unanimity about the continuity of the New Covenant from the Old, and in light, too, of the controversy which centered around Marcion's editing of the New Testament scriptures, these negative elements in Thomas are very serious.

We do not intend to draw any particular conclusions about the origin, provenance, date, or purpose of Thomas, since we are at this stage without adequate parallel material or evidence. It might, however, be appropriate to give a brief list of the most commonly held views about the Gospel of Thomas:

(1) Thomas was composed by means of excision and conflation from two existing documents, a Jewish-Christian gospel ("according to the Hebrews") which was known to Jerome and is now lost, and another, far more Gnostic document ("according to the Egyptians") known to Clement of Alexandria and also lost.

(2) Thomas was a thoroughly polemical work, composed by a Gnostic, containing enough orthodox Christian material to secure an audience, but nevertheless written with a single religious and theological end—namely, the Gnostic one.

(3) It is possible to hold, as do some accomplished scholars in this field, that Thomas was compiled at a time when rigid distinctions had not yet been drawn between what was orthodox and what was specifically and undeniably Gnostic. In this view, Thomas is a rather haphazard collection of sayings—some imperfectly remembered, some interpreted by homiletics, some deliberately gnosticizing, and some written with the aim of encouraging spiritual perfection.

There are features in Thomas which argue against its being a unified collection of sayings. In many places we have good reason to think that the author or compiler was in fact relying on oral tradition, however much this may have been colored by his own interpretations or embellished from sources already departing from strictly NT standards. Joseph A. Fitzmyer (whose important contribution to the study of Thomas is listed below) argues that Thomas' work can be correctly called a gospel on the grounds that a collection of sayings would have been accepted without question by the early Church as being a proclamation of the good news in some form. Fitzmyer's contention is a useful reminder that we often assume far too easily that Christian faith in the century following the apostolic period had been already so far codified that there was a fully recognizable, organized, and coherent body of teaching which could be called "orthodox"; and that, correspondingly, beyond the periphery of this body of teaching there was an equally recognizable Gnosticism. This assumption makes the development of Christian belief far too simple. Not only did oral tradition, with an attendant danger of speculative interpretation being added to it, last longer in some places than in others, but even the written sources themselves were in a fluid state. By the middle decades of the second century, men had begun to rally round the canonical gospels as we have them now, and the position of the episcopate as the guardian of that tradition was becoming established. In this early period there was a large area of controversy over the admissibility of parts of our present New Testament (especially the Apocalypse), and some material of pre-apostolic date was often used as though it was canonical Scripture. In such circumstances, it was comparatively easy for anyone with a cause to serve and a case to plead to utilize oral tradition, written sources, or homiletic material to further his own ends. We need not suppose that this was always done with evil intent: the asceticism of the Gospel of Thomas in regard to property, sexual morality, and worldly involvement has many parallels with the canonical NT, and it is perhaps no accident that the document came to light near a settlement of early Christian hermits.

Christology, and the later definitions of the councils, could not have become the momentous matters they were in the third and fourth centuries without the intervention of the technical terms of Greek philosophy. But the process of codification and definition was immeasurably helped by an awareness on the part of the Church of the need to determine what was canonical Scripture, and what was interpretation.

SHORT BIBLIOGRAPHY ON THE GOSPEL OF THOMAS

Doresse, J. R. *Les Paroles de Jésus.* Paris: Librairie Plon, 1959.

Fitzmyer, J. A. "The Oxyrhynchus *Logoi* of Jesus and the Coptic Gospel according to Thomas." TS 20 (1959), 505–60.

Gärtner, Bertil. *The Theology of the Gospel according to Thomas.* Translated by Eric J. Sharpe. New York: Harper / London: Collins, 1961.

Grant, R. McQ., and D. N. Freedman. *The Secret Sayings of Jesus: The Gnostic Gospel of Thomas.* With a translation of the gospel by William R. Schoedel. New York: Doubleday, 1960.

Guillaumont, Antoine, H.-C. Puech, G. Quispel, W. Till, and Yassah 'abd Al Masih. *The Gospel according to Thomas.* New York: Harper / London: Collins, 1959.

Montefiore, Hugh, and H. E. W. Turner. *Thomas and the Evangelists.* Naperville, Ill.: A. R. Allenson / London: SCM, 1962.

Unnik, W. C. van. *Newly Discovered Gnostic Writings: A Preliminary Survey of the Nag-Hammadi Find.* Translated from the Dutch by H. Hoskins. Naperville, Ill.: Allenson / London: SCM, 1960.

Wilson, R. McL. *Studies in the Gospel of Thomas.* London: Mowbray, 1960.

II. MATTHEW IN RELATION TO
THE SYNOPTIC GOSPELS

What has come to be known as the "synoptic problem," studied with great determination during this century, concerns the relationships which may be found among the first three gospels, with the implied suggestion that it may be possible through such study to arrive at more or less firm conclusions about the temporal order of the three documents.

It is generally agreed that: (1) there was a period of oral transmission, in which stories about Jesus, incidents from his life and ministry, and collections of examples of his teaching were passed on by teachers to members of the community; and (2) it was the passion narrative that first took definite form as a result of constant repetition (though it is less generally held that this was the first part of our present gospels to have reached definitive form in writing). It is sometimes asserted, on the basis of what appear to have been collections of a similar character at Qumran, that the first Christians early developed a series of "testimonies" from Scripture (the Old Testament) which were thought to bear directly or indirectly on the life and ministry of Jesus the Messiah.

The commitment to writing of the sayings of Jesus and of reminiscences about his work may not have been urgent while the apostles were alive and Jesus' early return was expected by many; but it was not long after this that the pressures for a permanent record began to grow. Conditions in Palestine in the middle years of the first century were marked by years of considerable crisis (to put it mildly), and large numbers of people (including Christians who were invaluable in keeping the memory of Christ alive) were already leaving the country. Simultaneously there was a rapid spread of false teaching about Jesus, his person and his work. Had Simon Magus been a minor figure, and his influence small, it is unlikely that Luke would have wasted so much time and costly writing material on setting the record straight. Apart from the testimony of the early Fathers about the malign influence of Simon, we have the witness of the Johannine letters to the emergence of a threat to the integrity of the Gospel—docetism, the claim that the Word of God, the Logos, in Jesus only *appeared* (Gr. *dokein,* "to appear") to be in human flesh. This clothing of the Logos in a make-believe body, in the (deceptive) person of Jesus, was not without its attraction to the Greek mind, whose Hellenistic gods were only too human and often smaller than life-size. Any serious-minded person might be forgiven for scoffing at yet another manifestation of divinity in human form, especially one disgracefully executed. Docetism, this denial that the Word of God had truly appeared in human form, was also a theological refuge for many Jews who were attracted to Christianity, but to whom the notion of a crucified Messiah was abhorrent. In time, this teaching, along with many other features, was to find classic expression in what has come to be called "gnosticism." Whatever may eventually prove to have generated the complex of movements and ideas that is loosely titled Gnosticism, it could never have become more than one minor field of speculation among many, had not the Gospel asserted that in Jesus a divine-human figure had entered the realm of man and the field of human history. The early Christian community's awareness of the dangers inherent in movements like the one provoked by the religious genius of Simon Magus was enough to guarantee their careful attention to source material for a long time to come.

Oral Tradition

Though the role of oral tradition can be exaggerated, it seems generally true that the memory of words and stories is better in the ancient East than in the modern West. Yet even in the West today, anyone familiar with oral folklore and often-repeated rural tales in remote country villages will testify to the resistance of such stories to erosion or accretion. There are normally too many interested and informed auditors for embellishment to pass unnoticed. One of us was brought up in circumstances where the nightly retelling of old village stories, some more than two centuries old, was commonplace; he can testify to rigid controls on the intrusion of extraneous matter—"You've left that bit out . . . you've no right to add that. . . ." Jesus himself, like most early rabbis, relied on the tenacity of oral tradition, especially in the parables.[4] Some of the differences in the gospel narrative are best understood as small—and normally unimportant—details which differed in the memories of those who passed on the stories. (For example, James and John's *mother* asks a favor in Matt xx 20 ff., where Mark x 35 ff. has the disciples themselves ask; Mark xi 33 is in direct discourse, in contrast with Matthew's reported speech in xxi 27.) There are, however, some details of agreement or difference which can best be understood as based on oral tradition: the gospels agree and disagree on points which we find unimportant, and differ where we expect unanimity; for example, in the accounts of the feeding of the multitudes, the texts differ about the kind of basket used to gather fragments, and, more seriously, the gospels do not agree about the nature of the resurrection-body of Jesus.

A Common Literary Source?

Matthew and Mark agree against Luke on several occasions, and Mark and Luke agree against Matthew on others. Either Matthew or Luke, it would appear, is following Mark on one occasion or another, in detail. The common order of events appears to be that of Mark, though Matthew deserts this order far more frequently than does Luke, in order to group his special material under subject headings. There is a common framework of incidents—John the Baptist, his preaching and mission, the baptism of Jesus, the temptations, the call of the twelve, the Galilean ministry, healings leading to controversy, Peter's confession, predictions of the passion, the final journey to Jerusalem, the passion and the resurrection—and this framework seems to come from Mark.

From this, it was possible for some early scholars to conclude that Mark was an abbreviation of Matthew (or Luke?), which was generally the view of the early Church, and especially of Augustine. In consequence of that view, Mark was seldom used in the early Church. It is now accepted by a great many NT scholars that Mark provided Matthew and Luke with a common source, to which they added their own special traditions, along

---

[4] A recent article—"The Oral Tradition that Never Existed," by Howard M. Teeple, JBL 89 (1970), 56–68—is useful as a summary of views which are, or have been, propounded on oral tradition in the gospels. Unhappily, the author makes no mention at all of Rabbinic oral tradition. Enough is now known to make such an omission a fatal flaw in his argumentation.

with the traditions which they found (according to this theory) in another body of tradition ("Q," from the German *Quelle,* "source"). It cannot be too strongly emphasized that this theory is *not* the *assured* result of critical scholarship, and some recent critics have pleaded for the priority of Matthew's gospel or even Luke's, both in time and in source material. Moreover, it is only necessary (as some have suggested) to posit that Luke had read Matthew before compiling his gospel—and not the other way around—to dispense with the mysterious "Q" altogether. (A note appended to this section attempts to take a fresh look at the "Q" hypothesis.) Under the "four-document hypothesis," it has generally been assumed that Luke and Matthew both had independent access to the material found in the "Q" tradition and wrote independently of each other. This thesis was brilliantly criticized by Austin M. Farrer, in his contribution "On Dispensing with Q" to *Studies in the Gospels: Essays in Memory of R. H. Lightfoot,* ed. D. E. Nineham, Naperville, Ill.: A. R. Allenson / Oxford: Blackwell, 1955.

Mark has only about fifty verses that are unique: i 13, ii 2, iii 20–21, iv 26–29, v 3–6, vii 1–4, 31–37, viii 22–26, ix 49, xii 29, xiv 51–52. It has been suggested that there was an "earlier edition of Mark," of which our present gospel is an expansion. The difficulty with this theory is that it is hard to separate expansions, or insertions, and there are unique details in Mark which have every indication of being a part of the original. (It is Mark, for example, who tells us that Jesus was asleep during the storm on the lake, who fixes the time of the feeding of the five thousand by informing us that there was green grass—i.e., it was spring—and who provides us with the family background of Simon of Cyrene, presumably because *these men* were known to his readers.)

To complicate the precise relationship among the documents as we know them, there is what is termed the Great Omission in Luke (i.e., the narrative covered by Mark vi 45 – viii 26), which occupies Luke ix 51 – xviii 14. In this material, Luke omits all the material covered by the Markan tradition, from the feeding of the five thousand to Peter's confession. Furthermore, this Lukan material is set in a kind of travel diary recording a very odd route—a route so strange that it provides commentators with much occasion for debate. Jesus is seen as traveling outside Galilee, and the

only Markan note to assist us here is the evangelist's remark that
Jesus left Galilee in order to be away from Herod Antipas, since
the hour of decision had not yet been reached. All this raises
questions: Did Luke omit this Markan material because the healings
in Mark vi 45 – viii 26 were paralleled elsewhere in his own tradition? Or does Luke's omission mean that he did not know the
Markan tradition? Certainly it is simpler to assume the latter rather
than to contend that, once Mark's gospel had been written, it was
a necessary vade mecum for the other two evangelists. Whatever
may be the answer to this question, it is true that Matthew,
unlike Luke, appears to follow the Markan framework at this
point in his narrative.

Three commonly cited arguments in favor of Markan priority
are: (1) the retention of three Aramaic expressions, as against
only one in Matthew, (2) an almost unconscious change in the
later gospels to a more reverential attitude toward Jesus, and (3)
the fact that only once in Mark is Jesus addressed as "Lord."
None of these arguments is very strong, however, since the characteristics used in (1) and (3) might be accounted for by the audience
to whom the gospel was addressed, and (2) might indicate (on the
part of later writers) a more leisured composition of their material.
Moreover, though the supply of eyewitnesses may have been small
when the oral tradition was committed to writing, there was undoubtedly disagreement over details in the tradition, with all sides clamoring
for pride of place: Markan priority does not solve the question of
dependence—it merely makes an assertion about temporal priority.
Care in the assessment of oral tradition, given a restricted number
of reliable eyewitnesses, would almost certainly produce some degree
of agreement, both with regard to chronology and to the way in which
blocks of narrative were put down.

The more critically the material in the three synoptic gospels
is examined, the harder it is to determine precisely what—if any—
dependence there was of Matthew and Luke on Mark, or in what
way—if at all—Matthew or Luke were dependent on each other.
There are, for example, twenty agreements of a verbal character
between Matthew and Luke against Mark. Were Matthew and
Luke working independently, and not using Mark, at these points?
The word "agreements" is overdrawn, for there are variant readings

between Matthew and Luke, even when they coincide against Mark. The tendency in copying is to assimilate—and it would be a bold man who went on record as preferring Matthew or Luke in a secondary role. (Some of the agreements of Matthew and Luke against Mark: Matt xvii 17 and Luke ix 41=Mark ix 19; Matt xiii 10 and Luke viii 9=Mark iv 11; Matt ix 20 and Luke viii 44=Mark v 27; Matt xiv 1 and Luke ix 7=Mark vi 14; Matt xxvi 68 and Luke xxii 63=Mark xiv 65; Matt xxvii 40 and Luke xxiii 35= Mark xv 30.)

Both Matthew and Luke have material peculiar to themselves, notably the nativity narratives (where each is plainly independent of the other's tradition). There are, however, sayings and incidents common to both evangelists but not found in Mark. It has been held by many that we have here a common "source," Q (referred to above), which accounts for about two hundred verses common to Matthew and Luke. There is, however, no hard evidence for this assumption other than the literary desk-work of continental scholars who may (or may not) have been acquainted with the manner in which oral tradition, for all its diffusion among various groups, can effectively and consistently preserve a story. No doubt "Q" is a useful kind of symbol, provided we remember that it *is* only a symbol, and not the name of an exactly determined, homogeneous body of tradition. "Q" is useful, for example, in categorizing sayings of Jesus that exist in doublets in Luke, in one instance in a Markan context (e.g., Luke xi 33=Luke viii 16; Luke xii 8= Luke ix 23), and in the other in a non-Markan context but an argument for a single body of tradition drawn upon by both Matthew and Luke is difficult to sustain.

The two hundred verses which comprise the non-Markan material common to both Matthew and Luke consist of sayings of Jesus, short discourses, an account of John the Baptist's mission and preaching, and the story of the baptism and temptations of Jesus. Scholars who have been most vigorous in their championship of "Q" are not agreed as to whether this material originally contained a passion narrative. This non-Markan material contains elements that may have been collected in convenient "testimony" form at an early stage, in order to answer specific questions Christians might be presumed to have asked. The only miracle contained in this material is, significantly, the healing of the centurion's servant—

which may indeed have provided a stock answer to questions
about Jesus' attitude to Gentiles. This "Q" material too has a
good deal of information on John the Baptist, his preaching, and—
again significantly—the account of the messengers from John in
prison, leading to Jesus' eulogy of John, which would have been of
great interest to former followers of the Baptist.

But a far more important question is connected with this "Q"
block of tradition than that of priority, or possible use by Matthew
and Luke independently. What light does this material shed upon
Jesus' own account of what he had come to do, upon his own
understanding of his ministry? We know something from Acts of
the content of the primitive Christian community's preaching, but
was this an unwarranted series of inferences from poorly understood
facts? The record of the sayings of Jesus in the "Q" material is
clear: the primitive teaching begins with the ministry of John, whom
Jesus (in this material) regards as standing at a mid-point in a
crisis of the history of Israel—belonging to the old order, yet able
to see the advent of a time of fulfillment. After John's ministry,
there is something wholly new, but still conceived in OT terms:
Jesus has a "baptism to be baptized with" before his mission
to send fire upon the earth can be accomplished (Luke xii 49).
Jesus has his death and passion already in view in this tradition,
and it is interpreted as a "day of the Lord" (cf. Luke xvi 16)
and a day of the outpouring of the Spirit. Even allowing for the
massive insights of Paul, there is no warrant for the once-popular
liberalism intended to drive a wedge between the (alleged) simplicity of the teaching of Jesus and the (again alleged) later Greek
sophistications of Paul.

Whatever may be the truth of the matter with regard to the
Q-tradition, there are references in the New Testament to collections
of sayings (cf. 1 Thess iv 5—Thessalonians may be the earliest
Pauline letter—and I Cor vii, where Paul makes a careful distinction between the teaching of Jesus and other, non-canonical
teaching). The "Q" theory as a source-hypothesis is not as popular
now as it once was, and it is impossible to reconstruct "Q" as a
document. There may well have been a number of "little gospels,"
using OT texts and allusions, as indeed there are certainly references
and allusions to such texts in oral teaching in the time of the
apostles. There may equally well have been fairly standardized

collections of testimonies and stories, sayings and reminiscences, for purposes of missionary work. We know from Clement of Alexandria (ca. A.D. 200) that there was a good deal of fluidity in the state of the source material, even as late as the beginning of the second century. He quotes a saying as though it belonged to canonical Scripture, and on another occasion gives the same saying in a different form, attributing it to the "Gospel to the Hebrews" (the saying is now known to us from the Gospel of Thomas—lxxx 15–19—and the Oxyrhynchus papyri—Pap. Ox. 654b). On the other hand, there is the testimony of Irenaeus of Lyon (130?–?202) in his *Adversus Haereses* (I. 1. 15) that the Valentinians (a Gnostic sect) were guilty of conflating and even altering canonical material. Sayings, or collections of sayings, may have flourished for some time, but our present four canonical gospels reached their present status very early and it was against these four documents that the authenticity of sayings was judged. The fact that only four gospels are known to us (as noted earlier, Jerome was acquainted with the Gospel to the Hebrews, but this is now lost to us) may emphasize the fact that conditions in first-century Palestine were such that firsthand witnesses were few.

The supposition of an original gospel in Hebrew or Aramaic makes the problem of the relations among the synoptic gospels far more susceptible to rational explanation. The suggestion has been made, and recently repeated, that such an Aramaic or Hebrew source lies behind *all our gospel* traditions. If such a theory turns out to be true, the entire discussion of who depended on whom will be irrelevant. What does appear to emerge from a fresh examination of the evidence, in the light of conditions known to have existed in Palestine and the Near East in the first century, is that the oral tradition became relatively fixed at a very early stage, while the chronology of Jesus' ministry was paid little mind.

With all this in view, we might turn to the words of Papias (bishop of Hierapolis, ca. 130) as they were recorded by Eusebius of Caesarea (bishop of that city, ca. 320) in his *Historia Ecclesiastica* (III. 39). Papias is reported to have written:

The Elder used to say this also: Mark became the interpreter of Peter and he wrote down accurately, but not in order, as much as he (Peter) related of the sayings and doings of Christ.

For he was not a hearer or a follower of the Lord, but afterwards, as I said, of Peter, who adapted his teachings to the needs of the moment and did not make an ordered exposition of the sayings of the Lord. And so Mark made no mistake when he thus wrote down some things as he related them; for he made it his special care to omit nothing of what he heard, and to make no false statement therein. . . . So then Matthew recorded the sayings [Gr. *logia,* which can mean "discourses"] in the Hebrew tongue, and each interpreted them to the best of his ability.

Papias, whom Eusebius first dismisses as a man of "weak intellect" and then later reconsiders, is reported by Eusebius to say that he took very great care to discover from those who had known the disciples, and especially from John the Elder[5] precisely what each "living and abiding voice" had to say of the acts and words of Jesus. Perhaps bemused by Eusebius' first verdict on Papias, perhaps for other preferred reasons, NT scholars have dismissed the testimony of Papias nearly out of hand. Papias had, however, one inestimable benefit denied to his denigrators—he happened to live closer in time and place to centers of Christian missionary activity, to people who had heard the disciples, and to Jesus himself. It was fashionable at one time to qualify the testimony of Irenaeus of Lyon against the Gnostics with the suggestion that he was too biased an observer to be heard uncritically; now the discoveries at Chenoboskion in Egypt have materially confirmed all that the good man said. Irenaeus, whom we now know to have been careful about his sources, evidently believed the work of Papias bore out his own received traditions—and Irenaeus had been a close follower of Ignatius of Antioch, who had known the Apostle John.

All in all, *if* we allow due weight to the testimony of Papias—and of those who came after him—and *if* also we posit an original block of Hebrew/Aramaic tradition, or even an original Aramaic collection of sayings and reminiscences about Jesus, then some problems regarding the sources of our gospels become at once clearer and simpler. Certainly Papias' description deals faithfully with the very disjointed and almost breathless character of Mark's gospel.

[5] On "John the Elder" see C. Stewart Petrie, "The Authorship of 'The Gospel according to Matthew': A Reconsideration of his External Evidence," NTS 14 (1967), 15–32, and our view, below, Part XIII, Appendix A.

The various episodes, often strung together with the Gr. *euthus* ("immediately"), seldom identified by chronological notes, do indeed give the impression of being self-contained homiletic notes, faithfully drawn from the oral tradition, with details which betray the hand of a participant in the events (for example, "green" grass at the feeding of the five thousand), but with little attempt to present the kind of consistent narrative we might have looked for in a biography. Readiness to admit the evidence of Papias agrees with C. C. Torrey's view that there is an Aramaic/Hebrew original behind both Matthew and Mark. Moreover, this view is consistent with Streeter's account of what Luke did with Mark —that is, throughout his gospel, Luke alternates large blocks of Markan and non-Markan material, careless about fitting his own tradition into a Markan framework or chronology (cf. B. H. Streeter, *The Four Gospels* [London: Macmillan, 1924], pp. 165 ff.). However, this does not necessarily assume that Luke had access to Mark as he compiled his gospel, for Streeter's "alternate-block" thesis could allow for Luke's treating an Aramaic/Hebrew gospel just as easily.[6]

There is more to be said in favor of an original Aramaic/Hebrew gospel than this, however. Again we refer to Streeter: he described Mark's gospel as a ". . . shorthand account by an impromptu speaker, with all the repetitions, redundancies and digressions which are characteristic of living speech. And it seems to me most probable that his Gospel, like Paul's epistles, was taken down from rapid dictation by word of mouth" (p. 163). This is, in effect, no more and no less than was indicated by Papias.

But it is a wholly different matter to suggest that Mark's gospel lies behind Matthew—or Luke, for that matter. For this implies that a *Roman* gospel, mainly composed in the fashion indicated by Streeter, and largely homiletic in character, was the germ of wholly fresh Palestinian traditions. This we find wholly unacceptable, for it nearly compels the belief that, rumor having reached Jewish Christians of a collected volume of sayings and deeds of Jesus, a reception committee made haste to meet the boats as they arrived from Italy, in the hope that Mark's work would finally enable them to write down the Palestinian oral tradition. Such a theory ignores

[6] Cf. E. P. Sanders, "The Argument from Order and the Relationship between Matthew and Luke," NTS 15 (1968–69), 249–61.

the extreme tenacity of oral tradition in rural areas, which as we have seen exists even in twentieth-century America. (It was, after all, in *this* century that some descendants of Scottish immigrants in North Carolina were discovered to have preserved a pre-Reformation hymn to the Blessed Virgin Mary.) Whole phrases, or series of words, appear in Matthew and Luke to parallel exactly words and phrases in Mark; but this is not positive proof that Matthew and Luke depended on Mark—though it is more than likely that both evangelists were glad to have independent (and, at one remove, apostolic) confirmation of their own traditions.

It has sometimes been urged that the "sayings" which Papias asserts were compiled by Matthew in Hebrew are best understood as being related to the material which is commonly designated "Q." It is not in the least necessary, we think, to suppose that there was a *single* block of material on which both Matthew and Luke drew. The vitality of oral tradition, the varying emphases cherished by various groups in the early Church, the care that was taken (to which the Johannine letters bear witness) to ascertain from reliable sources precisely what did happen in the public and private ministry of Jesus, the urgent need felt to preserve Christ's teachings in writing in the face of the difficult times—all these will have led to more than one tentative collection of oral material.

Far too much work on the synoptic problem has been done on the tacit assumption that the making and dissemination of books in the first century was almost akin to the limited, hand-set editions published by private presses in our own time. We may underrate the literacy of the first century—and most people do—but there is enough classical evidence to show that the dissemination of written material was a considerable project even if the author was fortunate enough to have a wealthy private patron. Luke's Theophilus may have been such a patron, and Mark may have been a middle-class Jew with property, but the early Church in general was not made up of wealthy men who could assist in publishing. In any case, if we are to assume (with most NT commentators) that Mark's gospel was written ca. 65, its date almost rules it out as a serious contender for being the basis of (at least two) other Palestinian gospels. Traditions, wherever and under whatever conditions they were collected and committed to writing, will have been most carefully husbanded. Simple explanations may yet prove correct, and Mark and Matthew may represent two quite separate collections of tradition; it is only a failure to take tradition itself seriously that has driven many to assume the existence of almost a multitude of copies of written gospels on which the evangelists could exercise scissors and paste.[7]

[7] The reader who is interested in pursuing this matter of synoptic relationships further must not expect to arrive at any easy conclusions. Some recent articles only serve to demonstrate how complicated the discussion is at present. Not even the most elaborate of modern statistical methods does more than underline the uncertainty of arriving at firm conclusions simply on the basis of documentary evidence. Cf. in this connection A. M. Honoré, "A Statistical Study of the Synoptic Problem," NovT 10 (1968), 95–147. Similarly, attempts to arrive at new solutions of the relationship between Matthew and Luke only serve to emphasize the relative poverty of the "Q" hypothesis: cf. R. T. Simpson, "The Major Agreements of Matthew and Luke against Mark," NTS 12 (1965–66), 273–84.

III. THE "Q" MATERIAL IN THE SYNOPTIC GOSPELS

One of the difficulties facing a NT student is that of determining precisely how scholars use the term "Q" for the underlying source(s) of all material common to Matthew and Luke but not found in Mark. Some writers have concluded that this common material was at one time or another in a single document, which can be reconstructed with a fair degree of accuracy. Other writers use the term "Q" for this material without ever stating what kind of source(s) they suppose Matthew and Luke to have used. The hypothesis that Matthew and Luke drew their common non-Markan material from a single document seems far too narrow to us. All that can be said with any safety is that behind the "Q" material there appears to lie gospel material which may belong to many different traditions, written and oral. The material as it is found in our present gospels of Matthew and Luke overlaps, and verbal identity is not as common as the documentary hypothesis might lead us to think. There has been a good deal of rearrangement, regardless of whether Matthew or Luke was written first.

When Matthew and Luke are following the same historical framework as Mark, the degree of agreement between them is high, notably when they are reporting the words of Jesus. This near identification when reporting the sayings is what we would have expected, and in some cases the agreement is so close that we may reasonably posit a common source.

In some cases, however, the agreement is so slight that, though we may suppose Matthew and Luke to have had access to different versions of the same tradition, the visible modifications in the material are puzzling. Assuming the homogeneity of "Q," the changes are anomalous and only cease to be odd when we rid our minds of the suggestion that "Q" is a single source. It is worth examining some of the "changes" in "Q," if that is what they are.

(1) Luke vi 29 has a story of the theft of a coat, which Matthew changes (Matt v 40) into a lawsuit. Is it not far easier to suggest an independent tradition of the saying rather than an alteration? Jesus, in common with all teachers, must often have used the same illustrations, and it would be unusual not to find in the gospels stories that were similar in wording, but different in meaning.

(2) In Luke xi 44 Jesus charges some with being like graves. The same charge is made in Matthew xxiii 27, but with different emphasis, and a totally different didactic purpose. Streeter (*The Four Gospels,* pp. 253 ff.) suggested that the form of these stories in Matthew has been conflated with Matthew's own peculiar material. But it is far simpler to say that both Matthew and Luke had independent and variant traditions here.

(3) In one of the longer "Q" sections (Luke vi 20–26), a collection of Beatitudes and Woes, we are faced with a major piece of editing on the part of Matthew—assuming, that is, that Matthew had seen Luke, and also had access to the same "Q" material as Luke. Luke's collection of Beatitudes and Woes in his chapter vi is an entity, but it is odd that Matthew (who on the "Q" theory made a whole chapter, xxiii, out of a few sayings of Luke against the Pharisees, Luke xi 37–46), apparently did not know *this* collection of woes.

(4) Protagonists of the "Q" theory assert that material about John the Baptist, and the sayings of Jesus concerning the Baptist, were to be found in this source. The sayings about John in Luke xvi 16 and Matt xi 12 f. do not bear this out. Manifestly, they come from different sources.

(5) If Luke xiii 23–24 is from the hypothetical "Q," then Matthew vii 13 demonstrates minimal agreement at this point.

(6) There is striking dissimilarity to be found in the two accounts of rejection in the judgment. For Luke (xiii 25 ff.) those who are cast out are people who had heard Jesus and eaten with him. Matthew, however (vii 21 ff.), makes of these people men who were so closely identified with the Messianic community as to have been prophets and exorcists. It is true that these two categories of people may overlap; nevertheless, there is far closer identification with Jesus in Matthew than in the so-called "Q" material in Luke. More likely, these represent two disparate traditions.

(7) Far from Matthew's having made use of "Q" material, it is

perhaps possible to find one place where he certainly did not. Matthew xvi 2 is omitted by some good Greek manuscripts, and it is to be presumed that a later scribe, noticing the lacuna, supplied the missing material from Luke xii 54 f.

(8) If the common assumption holds, that Matthew not only had access to Mark but had also read Luke, then in a good many instances an equally good case can be made for Luke's having read Matthew. Luke thus might be the editor, not—as is usually assumed—Matthew. For example, it would be hard to say which of the two was responsible for apparently emphasizing the soil and the seed in Matthew xiii 1 ff. and Luke viii 4 ff., rather than the sower, as in Mark iv.

(9) If we admit that Matthew's additional comment on the sign of Jonah (Matt xii 40) came from a source which he knew and Luke did not, then it is possible that Luke read Matthew's version, recognized that the Matthean comment did not fit the context, or the original meaning of Jesus' use of the sign, and omitted it.

In relation to this version, it may be said that many minor variants in the use of the "Q" material between Matthew and Luke can be ascribed to varying translations of the original. But we must add that scholars are not agreed upon the degree of Aramaic, Hebrew, or Greek underlying our gospel sources. The examples given above are outstanding variants that must somehow be explained by any theory which postulates a "Q" source. It is, we contend, far simpler to suppose that both Matthew and Luke used their own sources than to assume that one evangelist saw the other's work and proceeded to some radical editorial revision. Though recent discoveries about the melting pot, assimilative character of ancient Syria-Palestine have been a great help in attempting to unravel the various languages used to compose the gospels, the new discoveries have also increased the difficulty of asserting with conviction precisely which of three languages might have been used in any parts, or the whole, of original gospel fragments—Greek, Hebrew, or Aramaic.[8]

[8] In Part XIII below it will be shown that the Aramaic personal and place names preserved in the Greek gospel tradition were in virtually every instance correctly transmitted by the Syriac recensions, dating in their extant text to the second–fifth centuries A.D. Where there is a marked divergence in form, the Syriac is nearly always to be preferred.

If "Q" (whether oral or written) was a source in the sense of being a block of recognizable, homogeneous gospel material, complete in outline, then something of the *order* of this source should have been found in Matthew and Luke. But this is not the case, as we can see by looking at a larger block of "Q" material.

About half of the verses in Matthew's Great Instruction appear also in Luke—that is, "Q." But of these fifty plus verses supposedly from "Q," Luke includes a mere twenty-five in his "Sermon on the Plain." Beyond this, sayings in one context in Luke are found in a wholly different context in Matthew, and the "Q" sayings in Matthew are widely scattered through Luke, between chapters xi and xvi. Matthew's saying about coming to terms with an opponent are put by Luke in an apocalyptic context (Matt v 25=Luke xii 57 f.). The Lord's Prayer, put by Luke in his chapter xi—an apocalyptic context—is by Matthew placed in his great block of teaching material. If Matthew has edited and rearranged Mark and "Q," and done this in the light of Luke, then his methods are at best unconventional. For if "Q" was a recognizable single entity, and Matthew also had access to Luke as well as to Mark, would he have separated the two verses of Luke xi 33–34, inserted them at different points in his own gospel, and in the process changed the meaning of the verses?

In very broad terms, the suggestion that Matthew knew and used "Q" together with Mark and Luke might stand. The accounts of John the Baptist, his ministry, and his baptism of Jesus (Luke iii 2–22=Matt iii 7–17), the temptation narrative (Luke iv 1–13= Matt iv 1–11), and the first instructions to disciples (Luke vi 20–49 =Matt v 1–7, 27)—all these come in the same historical order in Luke and have broad affiliation with each other. But when the story of the centurion's servant has been told (Luke vii 1–10=Matt viii 5–13) the two gospels begin to diverge. Luke includes John's questions to Jesus from prison, in vii 18–35, while Matthew postpones them until xi 2–19. The same thing is true of other material which has commonly been attributed by derivation to "Q." The questions on discipleship are found in Luke ix 57 – x 24, and in Matthew in two places—viii 19–22, ix 37 – x 14; the discussion of "signs" comes in Luke xi 14–32, and in Matt xii 22–45. Matthew leaves the polemic against the Pharisees (Luke xi 39–52) to almost the end of the ministry. All these examples occur in quite different contexts and are arranged in different chronological order. In fact, as soon as Mark's order is deserted, Luke and Matthew begin to diverge. As a single, ordered source, oral or written, "Q" will not stand.

Much of the trouble with "Q," then, has been the confidence with which some scholars have sought to reconstruct it as a *single document*. But even when this has been done, the contents of this hypothetical source are much what any oral *tradition* might have been expected to contain, outside the passion narrative: John the Baptist, his ministry, and preaching, his baptism of Jesus and the subsequent temptation story; selected instructions by Jesus; John's place in the divine purpose and his subsequent fate; questions on the meaning of discipleship, signs authenticating the ministry, the disclosure of Messiahship, and preparation for the last acts of the ministry, with warnings about persecution. All that an examination of the "Q" material in Matthew and Luke seems likely at this stage to produce is evidence that more than one source was employed by all three evangelists.

IV. THE OLD TESTAMENT BACKGROUND
OF MATTHEW'S GOSPEL

There have been many hypotheses about how Matthew arranged his material, and the text of the gospel can be interpreted to justify most of them.[9] However, nearly all hypotheses have failed to do justice to one feature of the gospel as it appears to us, and that is Matthew's apparent conflation of two originally distinct traditions: (1) a missionary's vade mecum, mostly narrative in form, with illustrative material drawn (where helpful) from (2) the bulk of the private teaching Jesus gave to his disciples. This feature of Matthew's gospel we propose to consider below in Part XIII, Authorship and Chronology.

A

As Matthew discovered the need to explain the person of Jesus in order to encourage the development of Christian awareness, it might be suggested that his Christology dictated the framework of his gospel. For the sake of completeness, such a Christological framework is given here. Although it is viable and does full justice to the conservative Jewish background of Matthew, based wholly on Scripture, we do not find it entirely satisfactory. The analysis offered further below has the advantage of taking full account of

[9] Unimpressive attempts have been made to find some kind of OT numerology in Matthew, as though a common formula ending each of five sections (vii 28, xi 1, xiii 53, xix 1, xxvi 1) automatically provides us with a NT Pentateuch. This, the suggestion of B. W. Bacon (*Studies in Matthew,* London: Constable / New York: Holt, 1930), is unlikely because of the difficulty of finding any parallel to Leviticus. Austin M. Farrer's *St. Matthew and St. Mark* (London: A. & C. Black, 1954) goes so far as to propose a Matthean Hexateuch, apparently forgetting that this combination of OT books was purely a nineteenth-century invention. There is no limit to similar possibilities. Why not a "Genesis" in ch. i, an "Exodus" in ch. ii, a "Numbers" in chs. iii and iv, and so on? Most artificial numerology is obviously ludicrous.

the hermeneutic background of the gospel; we suggest it is the framework chosen and used by the author. The Christological framework would develop in this fashion:

(1) Up to the Petrine confession, the covenant people is called to relive its OT experience. The prologue makes the Messiah the Son of David (i 6, 17) and the Emmanuel quotation (i 23=Isa vii 14) in the Isaian context promises such days for God's people as they have never known before. The Micah passage (ii 6=Mic v 2) comes from a whole context in which the future ruler is depicted feeding his flock like a shepherd. So, too, with the return from Egypt: Israel, *the* child of the Lord, is called again from the land of slavery (Hos xi 1; Exod iv 22).

(2) This broad theme of reliving the OT experience is marked again at the baptism and temptation narrative. The beloved of Isa xlii 1 (Gr. *agapētos,* as in the Transfiguration narrative of Matt xvii 5) is reminded of his vocation to fulfill all righteousness (Matt iii 17). The temptation narrative (which will be discussed in its context) is cast in terms of Israel's time of trial in the desert. Here the narrative *encapsulates* Israel in the person of Jesus, and subjects him to the testing of covenant-loyalty in Deuteronomic terms.

(3) The (miscalled) Sermon on the Mount, or Great Instruction —which was private instruction for the inner circle of the disciples— with its strong emphasis on the law underscores the unique character of Israel's law, represents Jesus as compelling the errant community to return to the fundamentals of all law. So far, conceding the degree of authority attributed to Jesus (vii 28–29) and also incidental assertions of his relationship with God which close the instruction (vii 21), there is nothing which marks off the ministry as being more than largely a recapitulation of Israel's history, though admittedly in high relief.

(4) The next part of the ministry significantly changes this, though it is possible to see this change in scriptural terms, too. Chapter viii introduces the term "The Man" (vs. 20) for the first time *in a context of suffering.* This appears to be an old tradition, in which "The Man" who fulfills a destiny of suffering could only be introduced when the ground was properly prepared for him. The "Servant Songs" of Isaiah were used in iii 17, but

this was in a far different role from that indicated in viii 20.[10]
There is now an atmosphere of crisis about the ministry, almost
as though history had suddenly leaped from the united people of I
and II Samuel to the turbulence of Isaiah and Jeremiah. The
Son of Man dispenses divine pardon (ix 6 ff.) and excites charges
of demonic alliance (ix 34), meanwhile providing for his small
community (x 5, 16, 23).

(5) The same picture carries through chapters xi to xv, with
The Man asserting his vocation and demanding allegiance to his
message—and to his own person (xi 19, xii 8, 15). This is heavily
underlined in private to the disciples (x 16–42), while all the
time those who may at first have expected Jesus to fulfill Messianic
expectations of their own devising were driven to find explanations
of his exorcisms in a conspiracy with Satan (xii 22). The lines
for and against his person and ministry are drawn harder and
firmer, and the community of Israel, along with Jesus, begins to
reach crisis point. At xii 32 Jesus heightens the prophetic insistence
upon the validity of his message by asserting his familiarity with
the inmost secrets of God's "council" (a well-known concept in
the Old Testament). This had already been done privately (xi
25 ff.), when the signs of the imminent reign of God had been
apparently rejected.

(6) From xii 38, provoked by a demand for a sign, Jesus (in
Matthew's tradition) reinterprets the covenant with Israel in a
series of parables (xiii 1–51). The report of John's death causes
him to withdraw. The die is now cast, and Jesus gives the crowds
a foretaste of the Messianic banquet (xiv 13–21: there is apparently
a repetition of this at xv 34–39, a sign of the great significance
attached to this incident). Chapters xv through xvi 4 provide in
miniature a summary of the mission of the Servant, wholly misunderstood (xv 1–2, 12; cf. Isa liii 1), yet with a mission even
beyond Israel (xv 21–28; cf. Isa xlix 6). Though the signs of the
age to come are misunderstood, yet the disciples are put to the
test, and xvi 13–20 marks the watershed of the gospel. The Petrine
confession is followed immediately in the present Matthean tradition
by the first prediction of the passion (xvi 21–23), the call to believers to identify with The Man in suffering, and the transfiguration.

---

[10] See NOTE ad loc. In the kind of scheme here under discussion the
change to The Man as suffering is important. However, our own view of
the framework of Matthew does not depend on such a change. Cf. NOTES
on xvii 12, 23, xx 17–19, 28.

From this point on, the gospel narrative is concerned with the inevitable movement toward the cross. The Petrine confession in Matthew (not, as in Mark and Luke, the transfiguration) marks the midpoint.

This sketch of the way in which Matthew treats the events prior to Caesarea Philippi seems to indicate a tradition that is (a) Galilean, (b) controlled exclusively by rigidly scriptural standards, and (c) wholly uninfluenced by speculative messianism from sectarian or other sources. The narrative which follows chapter xvi, containing as it does the eschatological material, then develops very differently. The combination of the two traditions in this gospel suggests an editor and compiler of great ability, and—considering the smoothness of the whole—of no small theological skill.

B

Another device—well known to Jewish rabbinical writings, and also found in Proverbs—derives from oral tradition, and is faithfully followed by Matthew: it involves the use of numbers in teaching.[11] This phenomenon has been observed before—notably by W. H. Allen (*The Gospel According to St. Matthew*, ICC, Edinburgh: T. & T. Clark / New York: Scribner, 1907), and is listed here again because it throws light on the processes of oral tradition and transmission.

Two is a conveniently memorized number. In Matthew, we have two demoniacs (viii 28), two blind men (ix 27, xx 30), and two false witnesses (xxvi 60). The number three is most frequent in Matthew, and always appears in blocks of material in which the proximity of the three integers is easy to recall. There are three temptations (iv 1–11), three examples of righteousness (vi 1–18), three prohibitions (vi 19–vii 6), three injunctions (vii 7–20), three healings together (viii 1–15), three miracles demonstrating the authority of Jesus (viii 23–ix 8), another three of restoration (ix 18–34). There is a threefold "fear not" (x 26, 28, 31), and a threefold answer to questions on fasting, interwoven with the three complaints of the Pharisees (ix 14–17, ix 1–17). The disciples are warned of three types of persons unworthy of Jesus (x 37–38), and there are three sayings about "little ones"

11 This is emphatically not numerology, but a familiar and successful pedagogical device.

together (xviii 6, 10, 14). There are three parables on sowing
(xiii 1–32), three of warning (xxiv 43 – xxv 30), and three
prophetic parables (xxi 28 – xxii 14). The three questions in the
Passion narrative (xxii 15–40) highlight the Messianic mission,
and in a sense summarize the whole controversy about Jesus'
ministry in easily remembered form, whether they were all asked
in one day or not. It is difficult to see any numerical contriving
in the historical "threes" of the passion narrative (three prayers in
Gethsemane, xxvi 39–44; three denials of Peter, xxvi 69–75; and
the three questions of Pilate, xxvii 17, 21, 22–23) because that
narrative would not demand such artificial memory aids as seem
to have been applied to other material.

Five and seven are equally well known as mnemonics (the
Talmudic *Ethics of the Fathers* has seven signs of a scholar and
seven of a sluggard); in Matthew the number seven is well represented: seven demons (xii 45), the sevenfold pardon (xviii 21–22),
seven brethren (xxii 25), seven loaves (xv 34), seven baskets
(xv 37), and seven "woes" (xxiii 13–30). There seems little
doubt that number schemes such as these were made an intentional
part of the structure of the gospels to aid early evangelists in their
teaching.

C

The attempts to find some structure in Matthew's gospel were for
the most part made before the discoveries at Qumran. Now, however, we have a large corpus of material to illustrate at firsthand
the methods of at least one kind of biblical interpretation in the
first century B.C. This is pre-eminently the case with the Essene
commentary on Habakkuk (1QpHab), which at first sight makes
comments on the prophetic text that appear unrelated to the text
itself. For example, Hab i 11 reads: "The wind then sweeps on
and passes: and they make of their strength their god." The Qumran
commentary has this to say: "Interpreted (this concerns) the commanders of the Kittim, who, on the counsel of the guilty house,
pass one in front of another; one after another their commanders
come to lay waste the earth. . . ." Despite the apparent discrepancy
between prophetic text and sectarian commentary, principles of
interpretation are involved. We give here the principles as seen by

W. H. Brownlee ("Biblical Interpretation among the Sectaries of the Dead Sea Scrolls," BA 14 [1951], 54–76).

(1) Everything written by the ancient prophet had a hidden eschatological meaning.

(2) Since the prophet often wrote cryptically, the meaning may have to be ascertained through a forced or abnormal construction of the biblical text.

(3) The prophet's meaning may be discerned through the study of textual, or orthographic peculiarities in the text—that is, the meaning may turn upon special readings in the text.

(4) A textual variant may also assist interpretation.

(5) The application of a verse may be determined by analogous circumstances or allegorical propriety.

(6) For full understanding, more than one meaning may be attached to the prophet's words.

(7) Sometimes the prophet so concealed his meaning that recourse must be had to synonyms for the words used.

(8) Sometimes the hidden meaning may have to be discovered by a rearrangement of the letters the prophet actually used, or by substituting similar letters for one or more of those found in the text.

(9) Sometimes the prophet's meaning may be arrived at through dividing a word into two or more parts and expounding the parts, while at times the prophet may have concealed his meaning by abbreviation.

(10) Other passages of scripture may illuminate the prophet's original meaning.

Brownlee's survey was in 1951 an important contribution to our understanding of an interpretation of the Old Testament contemporary, or near contemporary, with the New Testament. But though Brownlee's study was quoted with some approval by Krister Stendahl (*The School of St. Matthew and Its Use of the Old Testament* [Lund: Gleerup, 1954], especially pp. 143 ff.), such definitive statements about sectarian hermeneutics were then premature. Since 1954 we have seen the Qumran version of most texts of our present Old Testament. (Esther alone remains unrepresented.) With far more confidence than was possible ten years ago, we can assert that the idea of a *fixed* text of the Hebrew of the Old Testament is later than the NT period. The sectarians of Qumran did not deliberately change the received Hebrew text in accordance with

their own preconceptions—far from it. In fact, the Greek text
of the Old Testament (LXX) derives from Hebrew originals which
were often more reliable than the present Hebrew text (MT).
Further, since much written work was copied from memory or
from dictation (as illustrated by manuscripts from Qumran), the
possibilities of misunderstanding are great. Some obscurities in
the present Hebrew text of the OT, in both words and meanings,
have been illuminated by the Qumran remains. So far as Matthew's
gospel is concerned, therefore, we should not rely too much upon
variations from the LXX text in Matthew's quotations from the Old
Testament. To this extent, points (2) to (4) in Brownlee's listing
given above are of merely peripheral interest. But points (8) and
(9) as we have given them above are capable of seriously misleading us in understanding hermeneutics in both Old and New
Testaments: pursued to their logical conclusion, Brownlee's suggestions could lead to an interpretation of Scripture similar to the
fanciful identification of various Elizabethan dramatists with William
Shakespeare. It must be added, however, that Brownlee's final
point is still very important: it might be used as a text for this
section of our examination of the structure of Matthew.

In his *Hellenism in Jewish Palestine* (New York: Jewish Theological Seminary of America, 1950), Saul Lieberman comments: "The
early Jewish interpreters of Scripture did not have to embark for
Alexandria in order to learn there the rudimentary methods of
linguistic research. Although they were not philologists in the modern
sense of the word they nevertheless often adopted sound philological
methods." Lieberman goes on in his chapter on "Rabbinic Interpretation of Scripture" to outline the significant developments introduced into scriptural interpretation by Hillel the Elder. Interpretation of the Law had been a somewhat formless discipline before
the first century of the Christian era, but the impact of systematic
Alexandrian hermeneutics upon rabbinical study was profound. As
Lieberman observes: ". . . it was the Greeks who systematized,
defined and gave definite form to the shapeless mass of interpretations" (p. 62). This interplay between Greek orderliness in interpretation, and the practice of Hillel the Elder and his school in the
interpretation of secular legal documents, has been discussed by
David Daube in a series of articles (cited by Lieberman). The
somewhat vague conventions of allusion and analogy were given
precise formulation by Hillel as follows: (1) inference from the

lesser to the greater, (2) inference by analogy between equal propositions, (3) constructing a family of regulations from a single biblical instance, (4) a similar procedure to the former, but based on two instances, (5) argument from the particular to the general, and inferring the particular from the general, (6) interpretation by means of a similar passage, and (7) derivation of meaning from context.[12]

The New Testament contains interesting contrasts between the somewhat loose methods of *midrash* (exposition or homily) on the one hand, and the more precise methods of *halakah* (legal material with commentary) on the other. Midrash is the method of Matthew, while *halakah* is exemplified in Paul's custom of applying precise norms of interpretation to words and phrases. Paul, especially when examining the central themes of the Gospel, was capable of using the older homiletic method of interpretation (cf. I Cor x 1–5; II Cor iii 7–18), but in general his hermeneutical method follows Hillel, with precise attention to words and meanings (cf. I Cor ix 8–10, x 23–30), particularly in the extended treatment of the Law in Romans and Galatians. There is no ground today, apart from a desire to dissociate Paul from Judaism, upon which to deny that he was a pupil of Gamaliel (Acts v 34).

The OT quotations in Matthew are a vital key to understanding the author's methods, and also his background and possible identity. Characterized by a framework of OT quotations, Matthew's subject matter, considered in the context of those quotations, accords far better with the *pēsher* (commentary) models of Qumran than does the later interpretive method of Paul.[13] C. H. Dodd, in his *According to the Scriptures,* London: Nisbet, 1952; New York: Scribner, 1953, made a strong case for considering the OT quotations in their original context as a key to understanding the gospel author's use of them. (Dodd's work, however, met with a remarkably cool reception from critics and reviewers alike; that the work appeared too soon for proper evaluation of the Qumran material as it bears on the New Testament hardly justifies this neglect.)

To assert, as has been done more than once, that Matthew's

[12] A full discussion of these Middôth of Hillel can be found in Hermann L. Strack, *Introduction to the Talmud and Midrash* (Philadelphia: Jewish Publication Society of America, 1959), especially pp. 93 ff.

[13] On the characteristics of *pēsher* commentary method see the list drawn up by Brownlee (BA 14 [1951], 54–76), as well as Stendahl, *School of St. Matthew,* pp. 183 ff.

quotations must be assessed as "proof texts" is a waste of time.[14] Verse divisions are a relatively modern device, of which both the Old and New Testaments were wholly devoid in the early Christian era. The notion of a "verse" was foreign to hermeneutics—Pauline, Matthean, or any other kind. "Proof texts," with the ensuing barren controversies they have engendered down the years, would consequently have puzzled any NT writer. Not only would the whole context of a cited passage have to be searched—if indeed a gospel author wished to discover what we call a "verse"—but the whole context would usually be known by heart. Contemporary Judaism shows innumerable instances of this in practice, and some writers on the New Testament might well have drawn warning and controlling evidence from it.

Here is the structure of Matthew's narrative, as we came to examine it.

Prologue (Matt i–iii)

The evangelist's account of the annunciation to Mary is linked with the familiar formula "to fulfill what was written . . . ." Here it is Isa vii 14, and the most striking feature about the Emmanuel prophecy in Isaiah is the promise of the exercise of God's initiative in the face of the faithlessness and vacillation of men. For Isaiah, the promised child is a token of the end-time (Isa vii 17–25), a time of testing and also of calling to trust. The later uses of "sign" in this gospel are significant: one sign has been given—another will not be (cf. Matt xii 39, xvi 4).

Closely allied with the thought of the birth of Jesus as a God-given sign is the quotation with which Herod's advisers in ii 5–6 reply to the king's question. Royal anxiety for a dynastic future, secular calculation—neither can stand against the whole prophetic context of Mic v, with its promise of national upheaval until the birth of him who is to stand and feed his flock in the strength of the Lord. But this birth, and the promise of a future ingathering of the dispersed, followed by lasting peace, is to be accomplished at great cost: the denial of all the secular and religious aids (including sorcery) upon which Israel has hitherto relied. For God's people, as well as for their enemies, judgment is near.

[14] "Proof texts": the practice of attempting to establish theological teaching by reference to often arbitrarily selected texts.

The verse concerning the son in Hos xi 1 (Matt ii 15) carries with it the implications which we have seen at work (cf. Part I above) in Matthew's Christology: Jesus relives the spiritual experience of Israel in leaving the bondage of Egypt for freedom. All the emphasis in Hos xi is on the close relationship which Israel, God's son (cf. Exod iv 22), enjoyed with God at that time. Jesus in his obedience is to relive, and reverse, Israel's dallying with temptation in the wilderness.

This thought of the Exodus, and of the grace which Israel might have found in the betrothal time of the desert wanderings, is not far removed from the ideal in the next quotation in Matthew (ii 18=Jer xxxi 15). The testing and proving which inevitably follow God's initiatives also bring suffering, and the innocent are as likely to be struck down as the guilty. The whole of Jeremiah's chapter xxxi is concerned with the hope of return held out to Israel by God's promise: those who have survived the sword will find grace and eternal love in the wilderness—a consideration which the evangelist cannot possibly have overlooked. Again there are references (as in the Micah passage) to God's shepherding of his scattered people. To Ephraim in the north (the prophet's own country) and to Judah in the south, the promise of healing and restoration is held out. God's sifting and judgment (Jer xxx 28) will be followed by his planting and building. Above all, there is at the end of Jer xxxi the promise of the New Covenant. Considering the importance which the New Covenant has in no less than five texts of the New Testament (Matt xxvi 28; Mark xiv 24; Luke xxii 19—the longer text; I Cor xi 25; Heb xii 24), this circumstance, in the face of Matthew's knowledge and use of the Old Testament, cannot possibly be considered pure accident or coincidence.

Baptism and Temptation (Matt iii 1 – iv 11)

Matthew's quotations from Jeremiah come, as we have seen, from a chapter which spoke unequivocally of Israel's experience in the desert, and here in this section the theme is renewed.

Matthew links the ministry of John the Baptist with Isa xl, which opens with the promise of pardon and restoration near at hand (1–2), heralded by an unidentified messenger in the desert. Here there is a link with John's gospel, in which all that the Baptist claims to be is a voice (John i 23; cf. Isa xl 3 and Matt iii 3).

Second Isaiah's prophecy, from which Matthew draws his quotation, refers again, as does Jer xxxi, to the divine initiative (cf. Isa xl 10 ff.) and recalls the shepherd theme of Micah (Isa xl 11; cf. Mic v 4). The whole chapter in the prophet emphatically asserts the unfailing will of God, who will brook no rivalry from idols. Perhaps Matthew's report of John's ax of judgment (iii 10) is a reflection of the prophet's scorn for idolatry (Isa xl 18 ff.). Whether or not this is so, John's charge to those who come to him is wholly that of Isa xl 21–31: those who have come to hear the prophet have no excuse for ignorance, and the privilege of election-covenant avails nothing in the face of the call to repentance.

The baptism of Jesus pinpoints the total identification of Jesus with his own people—he must, as must Israel, fulfill all the demands God makes of his people (iii 15). (It is significant that Matthew here represents Jesus as hearing of John's mission while still in Galilee; this may have some bearing on the author's origins.) The occasion of the baptism is marked by divine approval (iii 17), again in OT terms. Like the quotations concerning the flight to Egypt, this refers to the "chosen" ("beloved") status of God's son. There is here the ambivalence that characterizes the use of "the righteous" in Enoch xxxviii, moving as it does between "the Righteous (One)" and the "righteous (ones)" who are his followers. But the reference in iii 17 is not merely one of status concerning Israel, which Jesus represents, or of Jesus himself, but a direct hint from Isa xlii of the nature of the mission of the "chosen," the "beloved" of Matt iii 17. The mission of the servant in Isa xlii is followed by the conditions which God's act demands in that mission (xlii 5–9). The servant, the chosen, is a covenant bearer, a light and release both to Israel and the Gentiles, and the harbinger of new things (cf. Isa lxi, the first verse of which is quoted by Jesus in the synagogue sermon account at Luke iv 18). The concluding part of Isa xlii changes the meaning of servant from an individual to the whole people: God now gives his servant-people an opportunity (which they have hitherto not heeded) to repent and be restored to divine favor.

The temptations, which we shall discuss in the commentary proper, again look to the spiritual history of Israel, and are seen primarily against the background of Israel's wilderness-testing. This has been brilliantly demonstrated by John A. T. Robinson, "The

Temptations," in *Twelve New Testament Studies* (abbr. TNTS), London: SCM, 1962.

The Ministry (*Matt iv 12–25*)

This short section provides the occasion for an OT statement of the meaning of the ministry, and is characterized by a quotation from a "messianic" context in Isaiah (ix 1–2). Here again we notice Matthew's interest in the north, in Galilee. Joy at the birth of the future ruler (Isa ix 6–7) is offset by the thought of the rebellious nature of those with whom God must deal, and part of the Isaianic text speaks—as does the gospel itself in the later discourses—of the sifting and choosing which God performs (Isa ix 13–16). For the evangelist, the rejection of the divine calling by those who ought first to have heeded it (Isa ix 15) must have been a poignant reminder of Jesus' later controversies with Israel's leaders. In the meantime, the work of building the new ruler's kingdom (Isa ix 7) begins with the first selection of the immediate circle of disciples (Matt iv 18–22), in the restoration presaged in Jeremiah (Jer iv 23–31), and, most important, in the private instruction given to the disciples on the nature of the kingdom (Matt v–vii).

The Ministry (*Matt viii–ix—Healings and Questions*)

It is significant that the whole complex of healings (viii 1–22, 28–ix 8) and the stilling of the storm (ix 23–27) should center upon the quotation from Isaiah (Isa liii 4) and a reminiscence from that book (Isa xlix 8–13), the first as commentary by Matthew, and the second implicit in Jesus' interpretation of his work. Isaiah xlix is concerned, as are so many of the OT texts that Matthew considers, with the restoration, national or spiritual, of Israel, while Isa liii (which the evangelist uses as the keystone of the whole section) speaks of the means by which God will accomplish restoration. This is in full accord with what we have written below (Part X) on miracles: all disorder and chaos in God's creation is inimical to the divine purpose and must be overcome. This, at the most crucial point of all, will bring the beloved Son to the final trial of strength at the Passion. But at this stage of the ministry the Servant bears man's burdens by the work which

he must do to confront the dominion of Satan. But the very signs
which proclaim God's reign, and in which that reign is demonstrably
embodied, bring only misunderstanding—a theme which Matthew
records Jesus as illustrating in a quotation from Hosea (vi 6—cf.
Matt ix 13, xii 7). Both Jesus and Matthew were surely familiar
with Hosea, the prophet who earnestly longed for Israel's return
to God in penitence (vi 1–3), but who also knew that the prophets
had been ignored (vi 4–5) and that the people had broken the
covenant and dealt in treachery, despite God's judgment (vi 7–10).
When they have opportunity to learn and to repent, their only
response is to lie. They are too blind to see their own wrong
(vii 9) and indeed oppose the work of restoration by accusing it of
collusion with evil (Matt ix 34). Here is another significant link
with John's gospel: the fourth evangelist is emphatic that this charge
of collusion with evil (John ix) is the highwater mark of opposition
to Jesus. But through all faithlessness, God's love is unchanging
(Hos vi 1–3), and Jesus' mission is once more described in terms
of his shepherding his people (Matt ix 35–37; cf. John x; Mic v).

In a real sense, Matthew's chapter x, which is private instruction
to the disciples, follows through the theme of Hos vii—the disciples
must not expect any better treatment than has been, or will be,
accorded to Israel's king.

The Baptist (Matt xi)

Jesus' identification of John as the promised messenger of God's
act, as we now have that identification in Matthew's tradition, is
periodically the subject of investigation by NT scholars, the more
so in that Matthew's quotation of Malachi at xi 10 is not a
quotation from the Septuagint—as it stands, it appears somewhat
closer to Exod xxiii 20—and the declaration by Jesus that John
was "Elijah" has increased the attention paid to the last two chapters
of Malachi. Perhaps the most persuasive attempt in recent years to
examine the whole idea of a "coming Elijah," who was to prepare
the way for a day of the Lord, has come from Robinson, whose
book TNTS has already been mentioned. The article in that collection, "Elijah, John and Jesus: An Essay in Detection," argues
that John the Baptist had cast Jesus in the role of an *Elijah
redivivus,* did not at any time see himself in that role (cf. John i 21),
and sent his message from prison because he was puzzled that

Jesus did not seem to be playing the part John had anticipated. Moreover, Bishop Robinson contends, there is a clue which we miss in this incident, for the simple reason that we know the end of the story, and therefore accept without question the equation John=Elijah, and Jesus as the "Coming One." This, the author contends, is mistaken, and John's question "Are you the Coming One?" was addressed to Jesus out of doubt that Jesus might not, after all, be the Elijah-who-was-to-come. Though we do not share his view, Robinson's article set us thinking again about the precise way in which the Malachi quotation did, or did not, fit into what we are convinced was Matthew's mode of composition.

There is no reference to Elijah in the Qumran literature so far discovered, where we might have expected it. More significantly, there is no suggestion in the extracanonical books of Enoch that there was any expectation of a coming Elijah to prepare for the Messiah. Granted that there was some such expectation in the time of Jesus (to which John i 21 and Josephus bear witness), the lines were not so finely drawn as Robinson's article might suggest. Our research into the ancestry of "the Righteous One" of Acts vii 52 has convinced us that there were varied expectations, any two or more of which might coalesce. Moreover, there is good NT evidence that the Messiahship of Jesus, his Sonship, was declared after his resurrection (Acts ii 36; Rom i 4); in that event, there is but *one* coming of the Messiah, The Man, and that is the coming *to* the Father in the sense of Dan vii 13.

There is one other factor to be reckoned with—the ending of Malachi (iv 4–5). That ending appears to us to come under the heading that was once described as "euphemistic liturgical appendices," and it (in spite of all absence of textual variation) may not be more than a later appendage, even though it did give rise to the Elijah-expectation. (It should be noted that this ending is certainly older in the Hebrew than ca. 135 B.C., by which time the prophets had been translated into Greek, according to Sirach's grandson. It certainly appears in that translation.)

We came to the following conclusions: (1) John the Baptist's question in Matthew xi 3 might have referred to one of a number of "expected" personages, not excluding the prophet of Deut xviii 15; (2) textual variation, when the text had not been finally fixed, is not as important as we might think at this remove of time, and the similarity of possessive personal pronouns between Matt xi 10 and Exod xxiii 20 does not alter the fact that the messenger of xi 10 does not *guard* (as he does in Exodus) but *prepares* the way: Matthew's quotation, however loose to modern eyes, is from Mal iii 1; (3) the whole context of what follows in Matt xi 11–24 is *pēsher* on Mal iii. In other words, there is no substantial difference between the way Matthew treats this OT quotation and the way the remaining quotations are treated. The whole context of Jesus' teaching about the Baptist must be seen in the light of the whole context of Mal iii–iv. We gain the impression from this important passage in Matt xi 11–24 that a lot of discussion—public discussion—of the role of the Baptist occurred at this point. Matthew may have taken his Malachi quotation out of the context of a whole homiletic interlude on the precise place of John in the plan of salvation. If this is so, then Jesus' continued insistence on the manifestation of judgment in John's preaching, and in his own ministry, would have reminded his hearers of the Elijah passage at the end of Malachi. But Jesus dismisses the matter as inconsequential: syntactically, the Greek reads (in loose translation), "If you are interested in having someone fill the part of Elijah, if that kind of speculation interests you, then John is Elijah."

Controversy I (Matt xii)

So far as teaching, as distinct from self-declaration, is concerned, the visit of John's messengers marks an important step in the story of Jesus' ministry. It is as though the clarification of John's role left Jesus free to define more clearly his own ministry as well. Matthew's gathering of an unspecified total number of healings (xii 9–14, 15–16, 22–23) and the subsequent controversy with the Pharisees around Isa xlii 1–4 illustrates well the point we have already made—that the "fulfillment" texts must be seen in total context, both of the OT passages in question and also of the gospel. This quoted passage brings us once more to the "servant" theme of Second Isaiah. For all the opposition to his work and his message, the Servant will not be discouraged (Isa xlii 4), still less will he cast aside as useless the apparently hopeless (xlii 3). The covenant-vocation of Israel itself is recalled (xlii 5–7) as that vocation was willed by God (xlii 8–9)—a vocation which Jesus personifies in his healing of the blind demoniac (Matt xii 22; cf.

Isa xlii 7). God will not concede his sovereignty, will not give his glory to another (Isa xlii 9), and for that reason Jesus challenges his critics' ascription of his ministry to the Lord of Lies (Matt xii 24, 25–28). Those who should lead Israel are deaf and blind to God's call (Isa xlii 18–20; cf. John ix 40–41), but the new things of God's act must be proclaimed, whether men understand or not (Matt xii 30–37; cf. Isa xlii 9).

Parables (Matt xiii)

The parables which Matthew records for us are concerned with man's response to the covenant-promises of God. The promises may directly concern the disciples in their preparation by Jesus for the advent of the Kingdom he proclaims, or they may concern the leaders of the Israel of the Old Covenant, face to face with the demands of that Kingdom. The parables themselves are discussed more fully in another part of this Introduction. But the disciples' questioning of this method of teaching brings another "fulfillment" passage; again from Isaiah (Matt xiii 14–15; Isa vi 9–10; cf. Mark viii 18; John xii 39–40). In Matt xiii the parables are grouped around the theme of final judgment on the Messiah's community, Israel and the Church, and their import is intimately bound up with the prophetic question: "How long, O Lord?" (Isa vi 11–13), and with the promise in reply of a faithful remnant. So too, with the second "fulfillment" quotation in this chapter (xiii 34=Ps lxxviii 2): the whole history of Israel, for all God's declaration of himself, has been one of rebellion and failure to hear, and the motif of refusal and rebellion suitably concludes the Matthean chapter (xiii 53–58). It is not without significance—in the light of what we have emphasized above—that Ps lxxviii ends with a reference to God's shepherding of his people.

Controversy II (Matt xv 1–20)

It is possible that the anti-Pharisaic tone of parts of Matthew's gospel may have much to tell us of the background of the author; this section of the gospel, however, in recording the dispute between Jesus and the Pharisees, does not use the "fulfillment" formula, but (like Mark vii 6) speaks of Jesus quoting from Isaiah (Matt xv 8–9=Isa xxix 13). The section begins and ends on an anti-Pharisaic note, with a significant healing of a non-Israelite between the two passages. But we suggest that the quotations of Isaiah by Jesus, considering the nature of the material in Isa xxix, may provide us with a clue to the way in which Jesus regarded his own mission; they may also indicate that some of Matthew's "fulfillment" quotations come not from the author, but from Jesus himself. The extensive use of Isaiah in Matthew, and the choice by Jesus of a passage from Isaiah for a synagogue sermon (Isa lxi; cf. Luke iv 18–19)—of which there are echoes in Matt xi 5—is an indication which we think may be of importance.

Isa xxix deals, as does so much in the first part of that book, with the grim story of Israel's faithlessness, especially as it is manifest in those from whom faith was most of all demanded. The chapter begins with a lament over the capital of Judaism, and although promise is held out of God's visitation on behalf of Jerusalem, the main burden is of refusal to hear God's word (Isa xxix 9–12; cf. Matt xv 1–6). In the last analysis, rebellion is precisely an attempt to make God an object to be manipulated (Isa xxix 15–16), and this is Jesus' charge against his critics (Matt xv 12–14, xvi 1–4). Between the two parts of the account of controversy are, first, incidents of healing which parallel the Isaianic prophecy (Isa xxix 18–19) and secondly, the evangelist's second tradition of the proleptic Messianic banquet (Matt xv 32–39). If Isa xxx be included in the whole complex of the context, then the refusal of faithful allegiance to the Lord of the Covenant is even more heavily emphasized.

With the acknowledgment of Jesus' Messiahship by Peter at Caesarea Philippi, Matthew reaches the climax of the first part of the ministry, as we have noted. The necessity of being guided from this point on by the historical tradition dictates to the author a far less contrived arrangement of material. (Jesus' quotation of Gen i 27 at Matt xix 5, which belongs at this point in the sequence of the gospel, will be discussed in the commentary.)

There are two points to be noticed: first, from this point onward, Matthew is far more free with his use of the term "The Man" (eighteen times, as compared to only nine before xvi 20); second, the OT quotations draw on the Psalms for the first time—a Messianic psalm (quoted by Jesus) is used only when the issues are no longer in doubt.

The Passion Narrative (*Matt xxi–xxviii*)

The first quotation used in this second part of the gospel is from Isa lxii 11 and Zech ix 9 (Matt xxi 5). Here again, the passage from Isaiah must be read in total context. The salvation which God has appointed has been proclaimed, and prepared for (Isa lxii 10–11). Redemption has been promised for a desolate people, but (continuing the context) Isa lxiii speaks of the loneliness of the messenger of this salvation, and the unique character of God's saving love for his people. Zech ix 9, on the other hand, speaking of a triumphant and victorious king, of apocalyptic trumpets of joy, rests all confidence of victory and the release of prisoners on the blood of the covenant (Zech xi 11–12). This mention of the covenant recalls the previous quotation from Jer xxxi at the outset of this gospel, and it looks also to Jesus' words at the Last Supper as recorded by the three synoptic gospels. Messianic salvation does not rest upon military strength (Zech ix 10), and while there is indeed freedom from captivity (Zech ix 11) it is from the captivity of sin that Jesus brings release. There would appear to us to be some grounds for thinking that it is upon these conflated contexts from Isaiah and Zechariah that Matthew hangs the whole passion narrative.

Matthew xxi 13 has another quotation from Isaiah, again by Jesus. Bearing in mind what was said above about the total absence of verse divisions, Isa lvi is an enlightening commentary on Jesus' mission as he saw it himself. Reaching beyond the boundaries of Israel, God's act gathers not only the dispersed of Israel, but also "others not yet gathered." And the end of the chapter returns again to the shepherd theme, together with another constant prophetic theme—the failure of those whose responsibility it had been to provide for God's people (Isa lvi 11–12). Later in the same chapter (Matt xxi 16) Jesus cites Ps viii, and though the immediate context concerns the salutations of children, the whole psalm is concerned with the dignity of man's estate before God, and—by implication—the almost infinite degradation of man when he refuses or rebels against his God-given vocation. Again the Psalms are used in xxi 42, and Jesus uses words which evidently became a *locus classicus* for the early Christians (Ps cxviii 22; cf. Acts iv 11 and I Peter ii 7). To read this psalm quotation is to be aware of the inevitability of such attention to Ps cxviii, concerned with celebrating God's acts of salvation. Linked with Isa liii and lxiii in vss. v–xiii, it constantly repeats the emphasis on vocation in the Servant Songs, and all in all provides one of the best commentaries in the psalter on the Messianic vocation of Jesus. In the same way, the quotation by Jesus of Exod iii 6 (Matthew xxii 32) focuses attention—in the context of that chapter of Exodus—upon God's saving act, the deliverance of Israel from Egypt. It is not necessary to labor the point that Paul frequently uses Exodus themes in order to emphasize the greater, permanent salvation effected by God in Jesus.

Jesus' challenge to his critics in Matt xxii 44, quoting from Ps cx (vs. 1), appears at first sight to be an assertion of Davidic messiahship. (Plainly there was a strong tradition of Davidic origin in Jesus' family, and humanly speaking it must have contributed appreciably to the growth of his sense of vocation.) But it is difficult to sustain the view that Jesus was here asserting that Messianic claim—perhaps all along we have been unconsciously led to suppose that he was doing so by the presence of the legitimizing genealogies in Matthew and Luke, which insist upon Davidic descent. It seems far more likely that the tenor of this short exchange between Jesus and his opponents was that Jesus rejected mere Davidic messiahship as too confining: it was open to serious misunderstanding for one thing. And far more important, messiahship had been reinterpreted by Jesus in quite other directions. During the process of compiling the gospels as we know them, questioning of members of Jesus' family would reflect this kind of speculation: some Christians would accept, and others reject as irrelevant, the Davidic claim.

If there is, as our Bible margins suggest, an allusion to Gen ix 6 in Jesus' reply to Peter (Matt xxvi 52), then the context of Gen ix emphasizes once again in this Matthean tradition the supreme importance of covenant, and the total obligation of man to fulfill the conditions of covenant. The final OT quotation from Jesus in Matt xxvii 46, his last words, is familiar; and Ps xxii as meditative commentary on the dereliction of the Passion is apposite.

Matt xxvii 9, compounded as it is of Jer xxxii 6–15 (cf. xviii 2–3) and—more particularly—Zech xi 12–13, is not a fixing of geographical location of the field bought by the rewards of Judas' treachery, not a recollected coincidence of thirty silver pieces, so much as commentary upon the treachery of those who should have shepherded Israel. It throws into high relief the infamy of one who had been called to shepherd the new Messianic Community, and had failed his calling.

This part of our Introduction was completed too early to take fully into account the recent work of Robert H. Gundry (*The Use of the Old Testament in St. Matthew's Gospel,* Novum Testamentum Supplement, XVIII, Leiden: Brill, 1967). The reader with technical competence in Hebrew and Greek is strongly recommended to use Gundry's work, since it provides the best recent study of the material. We would not subscribe, however, to some of the author's points of view. Notably, we dissent from his position that Matthew's use of quotations cannot be held to relate the evangelist to any particular tradition of interpretative method.

V. THE DISCIPLES

If we assume that Mark wrote his gospel soon after the middle of the first century, any evaluation we make of the other gospels, and of Mark himself, must take into account the state of affairs in Palestine in the years after A.D. 60. As previously pointed out, the extremely unstable social and political conditions of the times were causing Jews and Christians alike to flee the area.

It would be hard to exaggerate the sense of foreboding that overshadowed life in Palestine in the middle years of the first century of our era. The Nabataeans ceased to be a threat after A.D. 60, but up to that time, there was always the fear of border raids, some of them severe, with the inevitable ruthless Roman suppression and pacification. Strife among the quarreling sects of Judaism inevitably involved the Christians—they were, after all, suspected of being pacifists during the Jewish War, and provided warring sectarians with a common enemy. The archaeological evidence is plain enough from this period, and bears out the essential truth of Josephus' account in his *Jewish War*.

Not only was civil strife in the air long before the war of A.D. 66–70; we have also to take into account the sectarian interests that must have impinged upon the early Christian communities, either in sympathy or in enmity. Internecine warfare between the various sects was becoming common. The incident recorded by Luke (Acts viii 9–24) which centered around Simon Magus was clearly of interest to Luke and to his readers. What later came to be known as Gnosticism was already spreading,[15] and Christians had to protect the gospel narrative against false testimony and false impressions. The ease and frequency of travel in the first century meant people were scattering; and the dispersal of Jerusalem Christians after the death of Stephen made much more difficult the task of correlating the apostles' in-

[15] Cf. *The Acts of the Apostles*, AB, vol. 31 (New York: Doubleday, 1967), Appendices VII and VIII.

formation for written transmission. Acts records the death of James, John's brother, and the consequent search for Peter to subject him to a similar fate. James' death must have driven home the necessity of committing oral tradition to more permanent form before all firsthand witnesses died. In view of all this, we should perhaps avoid speaking of "sources" as though there was an un-limited supply of those who would be able to testify accurately to the events of the Lord's ministry and passion.

But how many people knew all the teaching of Jesus—was it confined to the Twelve, or did the crowds who followed him hear all of it? The answer we find to this question will color all our thinking about the manner in which our gospels were compiled. From the gospels themselves, we know that Jesus taught whole crowds on occasion. But to assume that all the teaching recorded in the gospels was so widely disseminated would mean that the same crowds had followed Jesus on his journeyings, and that wit-nesses from them provided many sources of information. We have already drawn attention to the social factors after the early sixties, if not before, that would have made it very unlikely that such a large entourage could constantly accompany Jesus. And there is the additional factor that the gospels clearly distinguish between teaching given to a wide circle of hearers and that given to the restricted circle of the disciples. (That we shall have occasion to qualify this to some extent in the case of Luke's gospel in no way invalidates the distinction.)

The four gospels may thus have been composed in a far shorter period than has often been supposed, and the amount of reliable material to be drawn upon may not have been so great as has sometimes been thought.

With all this in mind, it has seemed worth while to look again at the use which is made in the New Testament of the term "disciple," with special reference to Matthew's gospel. The back-ground of the word is clear enough, though it is well to remember that in Jewish and early Christian usage the term had much closer definition than it tends to have in modern English. Although the Heb. *talmîd* occurs but once in the Old Testament (I Chron xxv 8), it enjoys wide distribution in post-biblical Jewish literature. It is never used of a mere adherent (which the English *disciple* often tends to denote), but of a learner who constantly practices that which he learns. The Hebrew verb *lāmad* (from which *talmîd* is derived) is relatively common in the Old Testament. Another noun derived from it is used in an important connection in Isa viii 16; there the prophet, deserted by most of the people, entrusts his message to faithful disciples, urging them to make it effective. This meaning is important for the sense in which Jesus "makes disciples" and entrusts to them the proclamation of the Kingdom.

It is well to remember the finer definition of "disciple" not only in discussing the restricted use of the term in Matthew and Mark, but also in connection with those who are called "disciples of John" (cf. Mark ii 18 ff.; Luke xi 1; Matt xi 2; and Mark vi 29) and the "disciples of the Pharisees" (Mark ii 18; Matt ix 14 and xxii 16). We know from the evidence of Acts that many continued to follow the Baptist's way of life, even though they were isolated from other "baptist" groups in Palestine, and the term "disciples of the Pharisees" would indicate those who were being instructed in, and who were assimilating, the teachings and practices of the Pharisees.

In Mark's gospel, the singular "disciple" is never used. The singular does occur in Matt x 24 f. (=Luke vi 40), x 42, with reference to the disciple as the emissary of his Lord. In Luke the singular is found at xiv 26 f. (though not in the Matthean parallel x 37 f.) and xiv 33, again with reference to the disciple as in close relationship to Jesus. There is no reference to a particular disciple. In John's gospel, the singular is used fifteen times, usually with reference to "the disciple whom Jesus loved." Both in Matthew and in Mark, the disciples are few enough to be gathered in a house, or in a fishing boat (cf. Mark vi 25, ix 28), and Mark carefully distinguishes between the crowd and the disciples. In Mark viii 34, immediately following a prediction of his passion, the Lord calls the crowds to him, with the disciples, and speaks to them about suffering as a certain consequence of discipleship, and about willing endurance as a prerequisite of discipleship. The whole context plainly indicates a situation in which Jesus outlines to his hearers the price that must be paid by those who would stand in the same intimate relationship with himself that was shared by the Twelve.

Similarly, common rumor might suggest (Mark vi 15) that John the Baptist was Elijah, or that Jesus was, but it is only in private, with the twelve disciples, that Jesus acknowledges the identification of John with the Elijah who was to come (Mark ix 11 f.). With the disciples there was no risk of misunderstanding, no fear of his own ministry being misinterpreted in terms of revolutionary strife.

We are not immediately concerned with the parables, but it is germane here to point out that it is only by a perversity of scholarship that Jesus can be represented as teaching about his Messiahship and his understanding of his own mission publicly and to large crowds. Only by treating Mark's repeated phrase "into the house," or "in a house" as a stylistic device is it possible to avoid the conclusion that Jesus reserved his innermost thoughts and his self-awareness for his chosen company, which journeyed with him throughout his ministry. Mark records occasions when Jesus withdrew into a house to explain matters privately to the Twelve (Mark vii 17, ix 28, x 10), and the same writer preserves for us the tradition of Jesus interpreting his own parables in private (iv 10, 33).

Matthew agrees with Mark's tradition in all this; Matt ix 10 indicates a small company at table in a house (cf. ix 19), and x 10 ff. makes the explicit statement that Jesus spoke to his disciples "plainly." In xv 1–10 there is a crowd listening to Jesus, but in vs. xi it is the disciples whom Jesus calls to him for further conversation of a private nature. The disciples alone are admitted in xvi 21 to the secret of the forthcoming passion, and xxiii 1 makes the twelve disciples quite distinct from the crowd.

The use of a verb in Matt xxvii 57 to describe Joseph of Arimathea may indicate a slightly wider use of the noun "disciple," but it is also possible that the evangelist here used the verb form precisely in order to avoid a noun which for him had specialized meanings. In that case, the translation would be: ". . . a rich man of Arimathea, named Joseph, who had been taught by Jesus." In the same way, Matt xxviii 19 would have to be rendered "teach all nations," rather than "make disciples of all nations." The verbal form of Matt xiii 52, bearing in mind its context, might very properly be translated by a phrase which gave the narrower meaning of "disciple": "the scribe who has been made a disciple of the kingdom . . ."

It has sometimes been contended that there are two exceptions to Matthew's precise delineation of "disciples" in terms of the Twelve—viii 21 and v 1. However, in v 1 it is clear enough that Jesus, having seen the crowds, *withdrew* with the disciples. In viii 21, it is one of *the* disciples (the definite article is used), not simply "a disciple."

If the usage of Mark and Matthew is clear, Luke's interpretation of the term "disciple" is at first glance wider, more inclusive, and apparently much less precisely defined. However, we hope to demonstrate that Luke's apparent divergence from the use of the other two synoptists is deliberate, and may have its origin in Acts rather than in his gospel. John likewise has other uses for the term than do Matthew and Mark.

It would appear from Acts xix 1, 4 that Luke uses the word "disciple" to indicate the half-instructed, which would not be faithful to the Hebrew sense of "well-instructed," and might approach the common English meaning of "adherent." But Luke is perfectly well aware that there was private instruction to the inner group of the Twelve—cf. x 23, xii 1. If one examines all the occurrences of the word "disciples" in the Lukan passages which are said to be derived from "Q," then not only do they manifestly not concur with Matthew in similar context, but they exhibit what appears to be a confusion of usage. Acts uses "disciples" as an equivalent for "believers" (vi 1, 2, 7, ix 1, xi 26, xviii 23, xix 1, xxi 4, 16), while the derivative verb "to make disciples" is used in xiv 21. Only once in Acts is the word used in a narrower sense—ix 1, "the disciples of Jesus"—indicating that Luke has for purposes of his own changed the original meaning, or rather put it aside in favor of something far wider in scope.

The "Q" passages in Luke where "disciples" occurs are strikingly dissimilar from Matthew. In Luke vi 20, Jesus is apparently speaking to a crowd, while in Matthew this is private discourse with his twelve chosen ones. In Luke this is so public a sermon that in x 23 the evangelist adds a note to the effect that Jesus turned to his disciples and spoke privately; in Matthew the whole discourse is of a private nature. Luke xii 1 begins what is presumably a private discourse—"to his disciples first"—but we have the crowd in xiii 1–21, and then Luke finds it necessary to revert to the previous character of the teaching in vs. 22. Luke xiv 25 ff. seems to suggest a separation between the crowds and the disciples, where the crowds are told of the conditions of discipleship. The warnings about the rich man in xvi 1 are addressed to "the disciples," but here it seems to be indicated that some Pharisees too heard this (xvi 14). Luke's version of the teaching about temptation (xvii 1) has the "apostles" asking (xvii 5) "Increase our faith"—Matthew has "the disciples" at this point. There is no ambiguity in Luke's xviii 5, where it is the Twelve who are indicated by the formula "the disciples." However, Luke makes the crowd which greeted Jesus on his entry into Jerusalem a crowd of his disciples, much as Luke reports a great crowd of his disciples at vi 17. (KJ at vii 11 mistranslates as "many of his disciples," where Luke plainly distinguishes between the crowd and the disciples.) When Luke comes to the passion narrative, his usage is governed by the tradition, and "disciples" in xx 45, xxii 11, 39, 45 indicates the Twelve as distinct from the rest.

In John the same wide application of the term "disciples" that we have seen in Luke is to be found (cf. iv 1, vi 60 ff., viii 31). There is recognition in John, too, that the term mainly covered a smaller circle—xiii 5, xviii 1, xx 19, 30. In any evaluation of the evidence which we have so far covered, full recognition must be given to the terms "the Twelve," and "the twelve disciples," which are widely distributed in the four gospels, with Mark using the term "the Twelve" more frequently than the others.

Luke's use must be briefly examined here. It is clear that Luke (and John, too) was well aware that there was a whole area of teaching that was inaccessible to the crowds gathered around Jesus, at any rate during his ministry. Matthew agrees with Mark's pattern, and carefully separates teaching given to the Twelve from public utterances of Jesus. It seems more than likely that Luke's usage is dependent on that in Acts. If it is remembered that, for Luke, the central figure in Acts is the Apostle Paul, we may arrive at an explanation that will cover what we have seen. While Paul is the central figure in Acts, his mission to Gentiles is also a principal feature. But Paul, it will be remembered, had occasion to defend his claim to apostleship in his letter to Galatia, and based his claim on having seen the risen Lord. Yet if the qualifications outlined in Acts i 21 ff. were to be valid, then the term used in the Markan tradition to describe those who had been privy to Jesus' teaching all through his ministry (that is, "disciples") could not easily be applied to Paul, except proleptically. (There is some recognition of this in Paul's first letter to Corinth, where he affirms that he received the Church's Eucharistic tradition "from the Lord," which can only mean the rest of the apostles—I Cor xii 23 ff.) It is therefore likely that Luke diverged from the Markan tradition, broadening "disciples" to embrace all believing Christians. If this interpretation is correct, then what we have in Luke vi 17, and above all in Luke xix 37, is the evangelist seeing the post-resurrection community in prolepsis—both listening to, and confessing faith in, Jesus as Lord and Messiah. This would be equally true of John's use in vi 60 ff., where the heavenly origin of Jesus is questioned, which John recognizes as an even more serious offense to docetic belief, in one of his letters (I John ii 18 ff., iv 1–6).

Bearing in mind the unsettled situation in Palestine in the years after the events recorded in the gospels, coupled with the uncertainties attaching to the perhaps uneasy existence of the Church as an enclave within Judaism, and the realization that the original twelve disciples were growing older, we may be better able to re-evaluate the dates at which we assume the first oral traditions of the gospel to have been committed to writing. However much Luke and John may have extended the term "disciple" to include the early believers (an extension, incidentally, which the early Christian writers also followed), it is clear that few heard *all* the teaching of Jesus throughout his ministry. It was therefore imperative that all available material should be sifted and tested against known sources and parallel controls, that hearsay evidence from casual listeners be balanced against the testimony of the original disciples, and that interpretations from the known, tested evidence be balanced against the known traditions of the continuing community. It's hardly surprising that as a result there are conflicts of dating, timing, and even topography. It is astonishing that with the prevailing conditions in Palestine known to be what they were, it has so often been assumed that Jesus did a great amount of public teaching of which only a selection survives; likewise that with the plain testimony of the first Johannine letter before us, some can still assume that the infant community felt no need to evaluate its records of the ministry of Jesus, and that dates as late as the end of the first century can still be suggested for any of the four gospels.

We shall have occasion to mention an important essay on "disciples" by Moses Aberbach in the course of the COMMENT on §82 (ch. xxiii).

VI. THE KINGDOM:
THE MAN AND THE MESSIANIC COMMUNITY

Considerable controversy has attended discussion among NT scholars as to whether eschatology (consideration of the "last things," or the "end of the age") in the gospels and the epistles is "realized" (i.e., conceived as having already broken in upon men with the life, death, and resurrection of Jesus), or whether the end of the whole temporal process is yet to come, at a time determined only by God, not yet revealed. There is much material for both sides of the argument in the New Testament, and after some thirty years, there is still no real agreement among scholars as to how, if at all, the two views can be reconciled.

Matthew's gospel is especially interesting for this discussion. The evangelist combines a very strong "futurist" eschatology on the one hand with stern notes of judgment arising from the ministry of Jesus on the other.

We shall not deal here with the parables except to note in passing that they, too, have Matthew's characteristic conjunction of community-interest with eschatology.

It is not merely that Matthew's work, in the Great Instruction, manifestly inspired a very early Christian document (*The Didache*) to provide a concept of what would be demanded of those who sought to enter the Kingdom (cf. the false prophets in Matt vii 15 ff. and xxiv 4 ff.). The whole discourse, from v 3 to vii 21 ff., with its emphasis on the breaking in upon men of God's act in inaugurating the Kingdom, still includes quite precise directions for the conduct of the continuing community which Matthew's gospel assumes throughout; we may cite the sayings about prayer and fasting in Matt vi. The false prophets, to whom we have called attention already and who were a matter of much concern to Paul and the early Church, are gathered into the context of the Great Instruction, reappearing in an eschatological context in chapter xxiv.

In fact, Matthew's combination of the eschatological with the

ecclesiastical begins with the ministry of the Baptist. Here is none
of the apparent hesitation with which the gospel of John treats John
the Baptist, and it is noticeable that Matthew identifies John with
the Christian community in a way which is not wholly true of the
other gospels. Indeed, Matthew unites the Baptist's proclamation
with that of Jesus (iii 2; cf. iv 17). The first proclamation (iii
3) is bound up with an OT quotation which speaks of preparing the
way for God's act, but the second (iv 15 f.) links the announcement
of the Kingdom's coming with OT citations which demand the notion
of fulfillment. Again, John's baptism is said by this gospel to be "for
repentance" (iii 11) and not "for the remission of sin" (cf. Mark
i 4), which indirectly bears testimony to Matthew's interest in re-
serving the privilege of baptismal *forgiveness* for the future Christian community. John's strictures against those who come to him
claiming a privileged status through the Chosen People (iii 7 ff.)
are found in similar form on the lips of Jesus in vii 15 ff.

In Mark's gospel, the confession of Peter at Caesarea Philippi is
a turning point, linked as it is with the first prediction of the passion
(Mark viii 27 ff.). It is equally pivotal in Matthew, though for
different reasons. In Matthew, the confession of Peter is linked with
the saying about the Church, and Peter's function in it (Matt xvi
13–23). This is followed, as it is in Mark, by the first passion-
prediction (Matt xvi 21 ff.); by the private warning to the Twelve
on the meaning of the discipleship to which they were called, and
by the account of the transfiguration—all of which is equally true
of Mark (Matt xvi 24–xvii 8; cf. Mark viii 31–ix 8). But after
Matthew parallels Mark's account of the meaning Jesus attaches to
the ministry of John—and we have already seen that Matthew places
John in the context of both the ministry of Jesus and the continuing
community—the evangelist begins to develop interests of his own.
The story of the epileptic boy (Matt xvii 14 ff.) clearly, in the
private saying to the disciples, anticipates a community beyond the
resurrection. Whatever its original meaning, the story about the
temple tax in xvii 24 ff. betrays Matthew's concern for, and interest
in, institutions. (Incidentally, it may also hint at the provenance of
this gospel.) But above all, it would seem that the Petrine confession
in Matthew serves to introduce a whole section on the management
of the affairs of the infant community (Matt xviii).

A continuous thread runs through most of Matthew's material—
a thread of concern for the right ordering of the community founded

by Jesus. Jesus gives injunctions as the disciples depart from him in x 5–15. The rules laid down for missionary activity, which Matthew confines to Israel (x 5), are followed by precepts which could only apply in the time after Jesus' ministry was ended (x 16–23). This wider application of missionary principles is placed by Mark at the very end of the ministry. Yet even here there is a combination of the theme of judgment, and the "last things," with the other Matthean theme of the Church as the post-resurrection community (cf. Matt x 28–33). A saying which Mark places in the context of the feeding of the five thousand (Mark vi 34) is in Matthew linked with missionary work (Mark ix 37–38; cf. Luke x 2). There will be no "apostolate," no workers "sent" into the field, until there has first been prayer for the harvest and the field workers (ix 38 – x 5). It must be remembered here that in the Old Testament, the theme of the harvest is familiar in pictures of the last judgment (cf. Isa xxiv 13; Joel iii 13; cf. Mark iv 29; Rev xiv 15, 18–19), of which perhaps the classic expression is to be found in Isa lxiii. The task which the missionary charge outlines in Matt x 7–8 is to proclaim the kingdom, heal the sick, and raise the dead— charges which Luke significantly places in an eschatological context, and uses of Jesus himself (Luke vii 32). Matthew identifies the proclamation of Jesus with the proclamation of the disciples. The subordination of the disciple to the Lord (however much the disciple's message may be identified with his Lord's) belongs rather to the theme of the community than to signs of the "last times," but here again Matthew combines his themes. The preaching of the Kingdom, which is the task of the community, will be authenticated by "signs" (x 8 ff.), yet these signs are themselves indications of "the end."

It is indeed difficult to make any rigid distinction in Matthew between material that might be described as specifically eschatological, and material that is more concerned with ecclesiology. For example, the material which Matthew places at the end of his chapter x (vss. 40 ff.) follows sayings which spell out the price which must be paid by those who embrace the cause of Jesus, and in Matthew's arrangement both sayings and ending equally well apply to signs of "the end" and to the post-resurrection community. The Markan equivalent of Matthew's x 40–42, however, is clearly in an eschatological context (Mark ix 37 ff.).

Matthew appears to say that the community of disciples (and, by anticipation, the Church; cf. xvi 16 ff.) embodies all the marks of the proclamation of the Kingdom, with accompanying signs of verification, and also that the community must bear all the marks of living, here and now, in an "end-time" which in the present is not fully consummated. If this interpretation is correct, it is just what Paul urged upon the Corinthians, a doctrine which has passed into the vocabulary of Christian spirituality as "detachment" (cf. I Cor vii 17–31). This is in part borne out by Matthew's use of the story about disputed precedence among the Twelve. Mark (ix 34) links it with a prediction of the passion, but Matthew places it in the context of his material about the conduct of community affairs (xviii 1–4) and of a block of sayings about mutual pardon. But even here, the note of the "last things" is not absent, and the direct simplicity of the child, which must characterize the disciple, is linked with sayings about temptation (xviii 7–10).

In similar fashion, Matthew's material skillfully links the discipline of the community with stories designed to emphasize that there is to be no claiming of privilege (xx 1–16) and with the story about the question addressed by the mother of the two sons of Zebedee (xx 20–27), which makes the same point. This story is followed, as it is in Mark, by the man who asked that his sight be restored (Matt xx 29–34; cf. Mark x 46–52), as though this was the one necessary lesson (cf. John ix 39–41). Israel often misunderstood her vocation as God's beloved people, which led her to think that she was immune from process before the divine tribunal. Matthew's use of material insists that the community of Jesus must not make similar mistaken claims (xx 1–16; xxi 33–41; xxii 1–14).

We find similar interests at work in the Matthean woes against the Pharisees (xxiii 1–36). The community seems not yet free of the ties which bind it to Judaism; to that extent the whole section is "dated and addressed," yet there is consideration given to the later community and its affairs (vss. 8–12). The chapter ends on a note of impending doom, with the final verse bearing witness to the difficulty of finally separating "realized" and "futurist" eschatology.

Further evidence that the Church was identified with a suffering Judaism is provided by chapter xxiv, and it is most likely that this state of affairs had come to pass by the middle of the first century A.D. when the community was beginning to break up. In addition to that, sectarian Judaism was gradually being removed from the main body, and it did not need great prescience to see signs of an approaching end to national and religious life as it was then conducted. There is no need to labor the fact that chapter xxiv is thoroughly Jewish with its list of natural disasters on a cosmic scale, its false messiahs and false prophets, and the final salvation of the elect, culminating in the impending presence (parousia) of The Man. This consideration has been urged often before, and the already published material from Qumran amply illustrates it from near-contemporary sources—apart, that is, from the figure of The Man. But this is not a uniform picture in Matthew: rather, the evangelist once again combines material, in order that a purely eschatological discourse might also serve his interest in nourishing the Messianic community in the post-resurrection period. There are, for example, in chapter xxiv injunctions to watchfulness (vss. 36, 42–44, 45–51), and the same warning is found at xxv 13. The latter is set in a context which will serve equally well the interests of both futurist eschatology and a continuing community.

There is, then, in Matthew a close association of an expectation of the parousia with instructions for the disciples. We shall examine in the final section Matthew's treatment, and reinterpretation of, the judgment theme. We have already called attention to the insistence by Matthew that the call to discipleship, whether to the original number of the Twelve, or to the larger community of the Church, does not imply immunity from judgment. This is demonstrated in the attitudes which, in context, characterize two examples of delay in the advent of the Lord's presence. The disciple, whether one of the original number, or a member of the infant Christian community, may not use the privilege of election to presume upon his Lord (xxiv 48); and at the same time, any delay in the "end" is a test of the way in which the lessons of discipleship have been assimilated (xxv 1–3). Here are two interpretations of the "end," or rather two ways of regarding a possible tardiness in the final decision of the "end": in one, any lack of watchfulness on the part of the disciple is condemned; in the other, delay in the "end" is regarded as a trial of vigilance. The two attitudes or interpretations should not be regarded as mutually exclusive. From whatever tradition they may have come all are constantly under judgment.

The specifically Jewish strain in Matthew's gospel is nowhere more clear than in his separation of the community of believers into the "elect" and the "many" or "the rest." It is important here to keep in mind what has been said above about the necessity of vigilance, that the call to discipleship does not confer unquestioned privilege. Significantly, for Matthew the title "disciple" remains in force beyond the resurrection—the teacher-pupil relationship never ends. Matthew—and here he would appear to agree with Luke, who uses the term "disciples" for those who committed themselves to the infant community—identifies "the Kingdom" which Jesus proclaimed with the community. For that reason, those who are called "disciples" are the foundation of the Kingdom, and to them is given the authority of "binding and releasing" (cf. xvi 19, xviii 18). But at the End those who have been called will not necessarily be of the number of the "Elect." "The righteous" who will shine like the sun (xiii 43) and who will be at the Father's right hand (xxv 31, 37) will not automatically include all "the disciples." It is the "elect" who will be called by angels on that "day" (xxiv 31). For Mark, there is a separation already made between those who have accepted the ministry of the Messiah, and those who have rejected it (Mark xii 1 ff.), but Matthew very plainly makes this theme of election-rejection dependent on the End-time. There may well be here an element of conscious rejection of the separatism of such rigorist sects as Qumran, which were confident that the End would declare the sectaries to have been all along the chosen of God. Cf. NOTE on xx 28. Luke's treatment of the parable of the wedding feast is well known (Luke xiv 15–24); Matthew reopens the already established verdict of the story in terms of the Last Things (Matt xxii 1–14). More than this: Matthew's gospel asks the disciples whether they are in fact the people producing the fruits of the kingdom (Matt xxii 11, xxi 43).

There is in Matthew no facile identification of the Church with the elect. It is true that for the evangelist the community of believers, the Church, *is* the kingdom of The Man (cf. xiii 36 ff.), but this by no means implies a complete identification with those who, as the elect, will enter the Kingdom of God at the last. Certainly there is a difference of theological emphasis, and it is important that we see it for what it is. There is no tension between a "realized" eschatology and a "futurist" eschatology in Matthew's treatment of his material. John emphasizes the element of the "realized," in seeing the "last hour" supremely in the concluding acts of the ministry of Jesus (cf. John xii 23 ff., xiii 31), and John—in common with Mark and Luke—presents the judgment largely in terms

of the confrontation between the Messiah and those who by previous
tradition had received the vocation to prepare for the Coming One.
Matthew does stress this element (in xxvi 64 he heightens the
Markan xiv 62 to ". . . after this you will see The Man seated at
the right hand of power"—cf. Luke xxii 69). But for Matthew,
identifying the Kingdom as he does with the community, judgment
means God's declaration at the End-time, since the decisions called
for by the ministry of The Man have been made.

All these considerations are strikingly confirmed by the manner
in which the evangelist converts secret instructions to a chosen few
(Mark xiii 1–4) into a body of teaching that is cosmic in scope
(Matt xxiv, xxv). The beginning of the "woes" of Mark xiii 3–8
is not followed (as it is in Mark) with a warning of what the community must endure at the hands of the synagogue (Mark xiii 9 ff.),
but with a prophecy of what the community will endure at the hands
of all peoples (Matt xxiv 9 ff.). Indeed, the evangelist sees in the
community itself the signs of the End-time (xxiv 10 ff.), though he
adds the condition that the gospel of the Kingdom must first be
preached throughout the world.

If there is, therefore, a very developed ecclesiology to be found
in Matthew, it would be a gross disservice to the evangelist to see in
his arrangement of material any suggestion that Matthew so identifies the Church with the Kingdom of The Man that all who enter
that Kingdom are *ipso facto* numbered among the elect who will
finally inherit the glories of the Father's reign.

Allied with these considerations, there is the very large element
of reward and punishment in Matthew that has often distressed
Christians. It has been urged from time to time that the whole idea
of rewards and punishments is far removed from the kind of disinterested service the ministry of Jesus emphasized. With this in
mind, we have chosen to deal with this question elsewhere in the
main body of the commentary. (Cf. NOTES on ch. vi, §§22–26.)

VII. THE KINGDOM:
THE MAN AND THE FATHER

It is necessary to exercise a good deal of care at this point in fixing the limits of what may rightly be said about the term "Son of Man" in the time of Jesus. It is important not to read into the NT material a developed Christology which that material will not bear. The term itself, in Hebrew or Aramaic, is best understood as either "Man" in generality, or "The Man" as a representative of some kind (which latter is the use depicted in Ezekiel, for example). Plainly, a wealth of tradition, or speculation, had accrued to the term between Daniel and Enoch, but we do not now have material that would show us the lines of development. Jesus' usage (in the Markan tradition) appears to indicate an identification of Jesus with mankind, first in humble approach to God, then as recipient of God's gracious gift, and finally as standing between man and God in redemptive activity. Jesus' use of the term provoked questioning; that is clear from John xii 23–24, and its omission from the New Testament outside the gospels apart from Acts vii 56—cf. Rev. i 13 and xiv 14—indicates a reluctance to use a term which, in the Judaism of the Dispersion, would not have had the same nuances it carried among the speculations of semisectarian Judaism in Palestine.

All the Markan sayings about the "Son of Man" are found in Matthew; in addition, both Matthew and Luke apparently used some sayings from a common tradition. Two such Son of Man sayings are found only in Matthew (x 23, xix 28); both appear to illuminate Matthew's understanding of the term, and will be examined in due course.

Two interpretations of the "Son of Man" concept in Matthew (xii 41, xxv 31) are much expanded from the context in which they are found in Mark. In xiii 41 Matthew adds apocalyptic material, coupled with the assertion by Jesus that The Man will send *his* angels and sift the wicked from *his* Kingdom. The Man is presented

to us in Matthew as though Jesus were speaking of another person
—yet we know that, for the evangelist, the coming Son of Man is
identical with Jesus (cf. xiii 37). Matthew, in his own tradition,
never combines the two functions of Jesus and Son of Man. Jesus,
who preaches on earth, and brings men into the Kingdom ("sowing
the seed"), is Son of Man; at the same time, the coming Man who
will be Judge in his own Kingdom is Jesus himself. The evangelist's
own special contribution is based on considerations other than those
of Mark.

Not only, apart from the Markan material,[16] is there no indication in Matthew of the concept of The-Man-in-his-humility; in this
gospel The Man is taken to mean a sovereignty which is true even
when the Son's Kingdom is understood as a temporary institution
awaiting the Kingdom of the Father. The sons of the Evil One who
have been planted in The Man's Kingdom have been planted by the
Evil One himself—but the sons of the Kingdom have been planted
there by Jesus himself as The Man (xiii 6 ff.). This is not all. Temporary though the Son's Kingdom is, The Man's judgment at the
End, by which he will sift the children of the Kingdom from the
children of evil, will be confirmed by the Father (xiii 41–43). The
Father will then establish, by incorporating the sons of The Man's
Kingdom into his own Kingdom, that Jesus always acted with full
authority. We have in this interpreted parable of the landowner
no longer the warnings of a landowner against an impatience which
would ruin the crops (xii 29), but warnings of the impending judgment of The Man against the time of the End. In effect, men are
being asked whether, as members of the Kingdom of The Man, they
will be numbered among the elect in the *Father's reign*. In this
interpreted parable, Matthew seems to have made what he could
out of two traditions (two parables?), spoken at different times,
and made both serve a single end.

In Part VI on The Man and the Messianic Community we saw
that the dominion of The Man is the community. The community's
Lord, The Man, will send his angels to implement the findings of the
judgment. In Matthew's handling of the sayings of Jesus, this is the
only occasion on which Jesus is spoken of as judge. It is noteworthy that Paul appears to have taught this conception of a dual
Kingdom also. In I Cor xv 24–28, we have a picture of the Son's
Kingdom, after the destruction of all opposing earthly rule, being

---

[16] This material we believe to be later editorial intrusions, which we shall
examine in proper context (cf. commentary on xvii 12, 22 ff.).

delivered up to the Father. Paul, in addition to Matthew, sets limits on the reign of the Son—"he must reign, until he has put all his enemies under his feet."

Matthew's treatment of the Sower in xiii 18 ff., for all its apparent connection with xiii 37, places the emphasis on the goodness and integrity of the seed rather than on the Sower. Yet, even when attention is drawn to this apparent inconsistency in the two passages, there is in both cases an emphatic assertion of The Man's universal dominion, both as teacher and judge.

In a slight, but not irrelevant, digression we might review some of the steps which in later ages of the Church led to the formulation of the doctrine of the Trinity. It is clear from what has been said that Matthew draws directly on the traditional ideas of The Man-to-come when he combines—albeit inconsistently—two functions of The Man, first as Sower with complete authority, and then as Judge-to-come. The Man is Lord also of the community on earth, a theme developed by Paul in his concept of the Church as the Body, with The Man its Head. He is Lord, too, in his function of removing from his dominion the sons of the Evil One. But though Lord, he is not conceived by Matthew as Ruler of the Church on earth—he is not, that is to say, the Lord acting *in* the Church. This is a concept which Luke and John single out in their two gospels and in the Acts, in dealing with the Spirit. There are two poles in the material which Matthew treats—the time of the teaching ministry of Jesus, calling men and placing them in the Kingdom, and also the time of the coming judgment, a sifting which will deliver over the elect into the Father's Kingdom. In Matthew's gospel, the intermediate stage, though it is the subject of much teaching and provision for the future, is not represented as being the particular concern of The Man—he is Lord, but not Ruler. The Man's Kingdom is one which asks its adherents to have faith in, and commitment to, both Jesus and his sayings. Those who hold fast to this faith and belief will be confirmed in their allegiance by The Man, and at the End will be taken into the Father's Kingdom. Presumably, it was the role of The Man in the synoptic gospels, coupled with the role of the Messiah as seen in John and Luke's conception of the Spirit-in-the-Church (which was John's understanding too), that gave impetus to the formulations which were composed in the centuries after the apostolic age. (Certainly all these conceptions are present in our earliest liturgical texts.) Not until all four gospels, together with Paul's letters, had become established would the application of Greek analytical methods to the transmitted material bring together into creedal formulation the reactions of the NT writers to the material which they had received.

It has been pointed out by Joachim Jeremias (*The Parables of Jesus* [London: SCM, 1963], p. 142) that there is a change from Matt xxv 31 ff., where the evangelist deals with the judgment of The Man, to vss. 34–41, where the judge is named as "king," and those summoned before him are represented as calling him "Lord." Jeremias suggests that Matthew has adapted xxv 30 as an introduction to the whole section, and this seems to be borne out by the interplay between xix 28, xvi 27, and xxv 31, all of which speak of The Man summoning to judgment. The judge declares in xxv 31 ff. that he himself is either well- or ill-used in the persons of the least of his brethren, and so demonstrates the unity of The Man with the humblest. In Mark viii 38 and Luke xii 8 The Man acknowledges as his own those who have maintained allegiance to Jesus by word and deed. In the parallel account in Matthew this test of allegiance is absent, for the very good reason that it is Jesus who describes the judgment, who identifies the tests of judgment with the humility of his own Messianic work and ministry.

We now pass to an examination of the use which Matthew makes of the "Son of Man" material which he shares with Mark, and will proceed to suggest the possible ground for Matthew's use of the Markan tradition.

On one occasion only does Mark (xiii 26 ff.) put a "Son of Man" saying in an apocalyptic context. In Matthew's parallel version there is a subtle change (xxiv 30 ff.): what is seen is the standard of The Man, certainly to be identified with The Man's cross. This sign is a judgment, not only (as in Mark) an ingathering of the elect. (The relation between Matt xxiv 30 ff., and Rev i 7 and Dan vii 13 will be discussed in the commentary proper.) Furthermore, additionally emphasizing The Man's judicial function, Matthew alone has the Son of Man sending "his" angels (cf. Mark xiii 27), and that with the apocalyptic trumpets (cf. Psalms of Solomon xi 1 and I Cor xv 52).

Matthew's tradition also modifies the crucial Mark xiv 62. In Mark, the acknowledgment by Jesus of his claim to be Messiah and Son of God is followed by an assertion of the impending coming of The Man. Matthew, however (xxvi 64), by the use of the particle *plēn* ("more than that") at the beginning of the sentence, makes a decisive break, and considerably modifies what follows: "More than that—from now on, you will see The Man seated at the right hand of power and coming on the clouds of heaven." Matthew uses the term "from now on" (*ap'arti*) at xxiii 39 and xxvi 29, and in neither case can the phrase have any other than the plain meaning "from now on." Here, then, the evangelist provides us with his understanding of the exaltation of the Son—a glorification which is closely in line with the Johannine identification of the glory of Jesus with his being lifted on the cross. In this fashion Matthew closes the ministry of Jesus: the time for choosing or rejecting that ministry is ended, and everything now looks to the eschatological coming of The Man. No longer are the titles Messiah or Son of God acknowledged; instead there is only the sovereignty of The Man.

There is a significant change from the Markan tradition (viii 31) at Matthew's xvi 21. Mark recalls the saying of Jesus that The Man must suffer. (The Greek here is important—*dei pathein*—and the English "must" is to be given its full import.) Matthew drops the title—in this context, the *Messiah* must suffer, but not The Man. Similarly—and significant in the light of what will be later said about Matthew's understanding of the tradition—Matthew has at xvi 13, "Who do men say that The Man is?" (Cf. xvi 15). Here again, The Man is a title of dominion.

Having used the saying in Mark viii 38, in another context, at x 32 Matthew uses the last part of the saying just as Mark records it, but with a meaning which is governed by the preceding material. Mark's use acts as summary of a section on discipleship, while in Matthew it is the familiar pattern of the coming of The Man, conceived as pertaining to the judgment which the Son will execute upon his own dominion. The community, the Church, is established through the Petrine confession (xvi 18 ff.) and that community is immediately warned that all its members must prepare for suffering (xvi 24–26), but neither suffering, nor membership in the community, constitutes an indelible privilege: The Man will judge men according to their deeds in and through the community (xvi 27). This, as we have already had occasion to emphasize in Part VI above, is wholly in keeping with the tradition which Matthew embodies in his gospel. Furthermore, Matthew's significant contribution to the complex concept of The Man is that he preserves elements in the teaching of Jesus which are closely allied to to have emphasized eschatology. Striking parallels between the Discourses of Enoch and the *Hôdayôt* (Thanksgiving Psalms) of Qumran now make it virtually certain that this part of Enoch—like the *Hôdayôt*—is of second-century B.C. date. Together with the "Son of Man" figure in Dan vii 13, this bears directly on our understanding of Matthew's tradition.

In Enoch The Man is pre-existent (xlvii 2), and as Messiah he is also Son of God (cv 2): he is a judicial figure, possessing righteousness, vindicating the righteous, and judging men according to their deeds (xlv 3, xlvi). The Messianic figure in Enoch—variously called The Man (principally), the Elect One, and the Righteous One (by implication, usually)—has been categorized by R. H. Charles, and his division of the material is the one followed here. (Incidentally, Charles shows that the demonstrative "this" preceding "Son of Man" in the Ethiopic, is clearly only to be translated by a definite article, and the Greek demonstrative itself was so used on many occasions. Hence, the NT phrase *ho huios tou anthropou* is no new construction, nor ill-derived from the original—cf. Enoch xlvi 4, xlvii 2, lxii 9, 14, lxiii 11, lxix 26, 27, lxx 1, lxxi 1). In the Enoch *mesâlê,* the Son of Man is first Judge, then Revealer, and third Champion and Ruler of the righteous. As Judge, he has righteousness (xxxviii 2, xxxix 6, xlvi 3, liii 6; cf. Pss xlv 4–7, lxxi; Isa xi 3–5), wisdom (xlix 1, 3, li 3), and power (xlix 3, lxii 6). He illuminates the realms of sin and righteousness (xlvi 3, xlix 2, 4), raises the dead (li 1, lxvii 5) and will judge all men (li 2, lv 4, lxi 8, lxii 2, 3, lxix 27). It is his function to vindicate and reward the righteous (xxxix 7, xlvii 4, 7, li 5, lii 6, lxii 7, 8, 14, 15). Charles calls attention to the following significant parallels between Enoch and the Matthean tradition: Enoch lxii 5 (Matt xix 28), xl 9 (Matt xix 29), liv 4, 5 (Matt xxv 41); and xxxviii 2 (Matt xxvi 24)—all of them in various ways concerned with the dealings of the Son of Man with both the righteous and unrighteous.

But even apart from references (which are in all four cases almost verbally identical) the parallels in ideas between Enoch and Matthew are far too close to be dismissed. To be sure, we can assume (as does H. E. Tödt, *The Son of Man in the Synoptic Tradition,* tr. from the 2nd German ed. by D. M. Barton, Philadelphia: Westminster Press / London: SCM, 1965) that the Son of Man material is "prophecy after the event," incorporated into the gospel material by the evangelists (from the community?) in the light of the passion and resurrection of Jesus, but this is a hazardous assumption at best. The sayings which incorporate the expression "Son of Man" in the synoptic gospels are firmly set in their contexts, and are therefore part of the tradition which belongs to possible early collections of the sayings of Jesus. Another factor has already been noted—a possible *removal* by Matthew of one such expression where it did not agree with the tradition which he knew. We can make excisions and emendations on the basis of our own theological preconceptions, or on our own evaluation of what Jesus could, or could not, have said—presumably, according to taste, either as a simple quasi-peasant itinerant Jewish preacher, or as the initiator of a somewhat odd amalgam of features of Judaism with semi-intellectual "Gnosticism." But the picture of first-century Judaism now open to us is far too involved, far too charged with theological awareness, for any such evaluation not to be slightly foolish.

Mark and Luke preserve for us a tradition of sayings from Jesus about The Man in the humility of an earthly ministry, consummated in a passion and death which the words of Jesus at the Last Supper interpreted as redemptive. Matthew's tradition presents another picture altogether. Many scholars have felt that the two pictures are contradictory, but in the face of present evidence, it is far more correct to say that the synoptic gospels are two sides of a single coin, and that the gospels provide us with a confluence of traditions fully articulate and widespread in the time of Jesus.

The notion of a semidivine figure coming to assist mankind in a quasi-redemptive role was known to the Babylonians as Atrakhasis the Man, before 1600 B.C. The Suffering Servant of Isaiah, whether an idealized figure, a collective for a group in Israel, or Israel itself, is seen not only as performing a redemptive function, but also (especially Isa liii) as sharing in the divine purposes, and as receiving honor from the hand of God. Similarly, all the "Son of Man" addresses in Ezekiel are used by the prophet almost as a title for one who represents God to Israel, and Israel to God. "Son of Man" in Daniel and Ezekiel are our principal written sources in Israel; what manner of apocalyptic speculation went to the making of the fully developed concept in Enoch, in the intervening period, we do not at the present time know. But that the synoptic gospels contain at one and the same time a cloud-rider after the fashion of Baal in the Canaanite epics, and also a redemptive figure marked out for suffering, should not surprise anyone familiar with the literature.

Our final suggestion in this examination of the material in Matthew could be expressed by saying that the real clue to the evangelist's tradition is to be found in Dan vii 13. We must note carefully that the cloud-rider ("on" the clouds, with LXX, and not "with" the clouds, as in the extant Aramaic text), one who is *truly* The Man, comes *to* the Ancient of Days.[17] There is but *one* coming, and it was this coming which, misunderstood, first produced the vocabulary of a *second* parousia in the early post-NT writers. What we appear to have in Matthew is an understanding which proceeds *from* the ministry of Jesus (where the Markan material is intrusive), through resurrection-exaltation, looks to the kingdom of The Man as identified with the continuing community, and then bids men fix their gaze on that End when that kingdom (which The Man will summon to judgment) will be given up by the Son to the Father, whose kingdom will be for eternity. The Man's "coming" in Matthew is properly to be understood of that coming spoken of by Paul in I Cor xv, where The Man delivers up to the Father his own kingdom, which will indeed be the End, and the time of judgment.

With this consideration in mind, we pass in review the "Son of Man" sayings in Matthew. He reflects the Markan tradition of

[17] On any showing, Dan vii 13 is of outstanding importance for the concept of The Man as it appears in the gospels and Acts. But recent study has convinced us that the existing translations of that crucial passage are wholly misleading. In contrast with the designation of the prophet in Ezekiel as "The Man"—i.e., a figure of authority in his relationship with Yahweh and his people—translations of Dan vii 13 have customarily rendered the phrase as "one like a son of man." This translation is generally seen as an attempt to do justice to the Aramaic but with a misunderstanding of the Greek. Whether it can stand must now be questioned.

To begin with, the *hōs* of LXX had, of course, no accent mark, and a choice had therefore to be made between the word as adverb of manner and as a supposed relative or demonstrative. Our present translations all opt for the latter dubious usage. Professor James H. Oliver of Johns Hopkins University, who has an extremely wide and exact knowledge of Greek usage in all periods, has examined the passage carefully and states unequivocally that the ordinary English translation is not acceptable Greek of any known type. We therefore propose that the English translation read: "And behold on the clouds of heaven how The Man was coming!" This does full justice to the Greek and also to the Aramaic if we assume that there was haplography of two letters before the *k* following the word "heaven." The *yodh* and *aleph* at the end of "heaven" should have been followed by *aleph, yodh,* and the *kaph* which still stands, but the second *yodh* and *aleph* were accidentally dropped. The Aramaic word *'eyk* is common also in Ugaritic and Hebrew; note several occurrences in Lamentations, e.g., i 1, "How lonely sits the city that was full of people!" (RSV).

sayings, demonstrating the earthly ministry of Jesus, in viii 20, xi 29, xii 40 (doubtfully), xvii 12, 22, xx 18, 28. At the same time, this Son of Man, in Matthew's tradition, exercises authority and brings salvation (healing): ix 6 (especially), xii 8, xiii 37, xviii 11. He knows and reveals the things of God: xi 27, and in his passion is delivered over to the will of men: xvii 22, xx 18, xxvi 2, 24, 45. But always, the Son of Man is master of events, and his own interpreter of his own share in those events, just as the Messiah is in John's gospel (cf. Matt xx 28, xxvi 64). There is no "adoptionist" suggestion in Matthew saying that Jesus becomes Son of Man, for this he always is, *vide* xvi 13, xvii 9, even in the rejection and humility of the passion. But the definitive element in Matthew is that of the glory of the Son of Man, in his own kingdom, and the instances of its use (x 23, xii 32, xiii 41, xvi 27, 28, xxiv 27, 30, 37, 39, 44, xxv 13, 31, xxvi 64) are all best understood of the Son's coming *to* the Father. This, we suggest, is particularly the case with x 23. We need not infer that the coming of the Son of Man will be so early as to limit the expectation of the End to the horizon of Israel: if this were so, the Gentile mission of xxviii 19 ff. would be nugatory, and contrary, too, to the material which Matthew drew upon from sources other than his own tradition. The saying comes in a context of provisions for a continuing community girded for persecution (x 17 f., 19 f., 21) and of incorporated apocalyptic sayings. The sayings look to a time— to predict which in those days required no particular prescience— when the end of the Jewish state would have taken place long before the Gospel had been extensively preached there. Long before the Son of Man's presentation of his kingdom to the Father, evangelization of Jewry as then understood would be out of the question.

In sum, it would appear that in Matthew there is an understanding of the role of the Son of Man similar to that of the Messiah in John's gospel, summoning men to take sides in the face of the proclamation of the Kingdom, and then bidding those men to look to future judgment as well as present decision. Secondly, we may find a possible explanation of Matthew's dual-role Son of Man in his manifestly Jewish background. Mark and Luke may have found the Son of Man's humility and his voluntary redemptive suffering so striking as to be difficult to accommodate with a tradition which spoke of the Son of Man's glory. It is evident that Matthew found both ideas wholly congenial to patterns of thought with which he was familiar.

There is a very full discussion of recent writing on the subject of the "Son of Man" sayings in I. H. Marshall, "The Synoptic Son of Man Sayings in Recent Discussion," NTS 12 (1965–66), 327–51.

VIII. THE KINGDOM: THE KINGDOM OF HEAVEN

Matthew's understanding of the reign of The Man must be carefully distinguished from his interpretation of material which deals with the reign of the Father (see Parts VI and VII above). We have had occasion to emphasize that in Matthew there will be two judgments in the End-time: that which The Man will execute upon the continuing community, the Church, which is properly The Man's Kingdom, and is in Matthew conceived of as temporary, and the judgment which the Father will execute upon all men, accepting The Man's judgment upon his own Kingdom. We have also seen that Matthew's tradition is rightly understood against a specifically Jewish background which looks to the Son of Man imagery of Enoch and Daniel. In that imagery, we suggested that it was of prime importance to take seriously the *one* "coming" of the Son of Man to the Father; allied with this consideration there were important links between the Matthean tradition and the Johannine concept of the Messianic reign being inaugurated through the passion, crucifixion and resurrection. (There appears to be an important link here, too, with Pauline thought, as expressed in Rom i 1–4, where the "Sonship" is said to be declared by the resurrection.)

Matthew's use of his sources is very clearly exhibited in the care with which he uses the word "kingdom" and its qualifying possessive genitives. Before examining the material Matthew preserves for us, we suggest that no problems are solved by the mere assertion that whoever cast our present gospel of Matthew in its final form resorted to "editing" in favor of clarifying or emphasizing some theory of his own, or some theory of a group to which he may have belonged. We are not in possession of any certain information about such a group, and any assumption of "editing" is based in the last analysis upon nothing more solid than a priori assumptions of our own. What, to the contrary, we *do* have (and in this respect we are far more richly blessed than our predecessors) is a large amount of solid information about first-century Judaism. The more carefully the present information about that Judaism is studied, the more foolish appear many of the assertions made by an earlier generation about what Jesus and his apostles "could" or "could not" have said. The manifold variety of Messianic speculation in the century before Jesus and contemporary with him is sufficient to let the commentator allow the material to speak for itself.

Consistently, Matthew's gospel uses the phrase "Kingdom of the heavens" (or, as it is in most translations, "Kingdom of heaven"). The care with which Matthew differentiates the "Kingdom of heaven" from the "Kingdom of the Father" wherever it is found in his tradition suggests that we approach this distinctive Matthean use cautiously. In only one instance does Matthew concur with Markan tradition—at iv 17 (Mark i 15); elsewhere, the evangelist makes use of his own tradition. We shall later suggest that if Matthew did have access to Mark (which is impossible to prove), then he deliberately changed the Markan use in favor of his own tradition, *precisely because he believed his own tradition to be superior and closer to the sense in which Jesus had spoken of the Kingdom.*

There are other examples in Matthew of "Kingdom" phrases: *the* Kingdom (iv 23, ix 35, xiii 19) in cases where the meaning is unlikely to be misunderstood; *his* Kingdom, or The Man's Kingdom (vi 33, xiii 41, xvi 28); the Kingdom of the Father (vi 10, xiii 43, xxvi 29). "Kingdom of God" occurs in Matthew only five times, at iv 17—cf. "Kingdom of heaven" at iii 2—xii 28, xix 24, xxi 31, xxi 43. Matt xviii 6–9 has no reference at all to the Kingdom, where Mark ix 47 does have it, and at xiv 25 Matthew apparently knew of no Markan tradition of references to the Kingdom at the Last Supper, for he does not incorporate the Markan material at this point.

Matthew's gospel begins—so far as public proclamation is concerned—with John's call, and then Jesus', to repentance, "for the kingdom of heaven is almost here." This, as background to the remainder of this section, is of paramount importance: at hand, invested with an air of great urgency, is not the Father's Kingdom of the End, but The Man's Kingdom. Whether Matthew has deliberately changed John the Baptist's proclamation here is uncertain, the preaching of Jesus as represented by the evangelist is completely in line with all the other ways in which he asserts the distinction between the two Kingdoms.

Matthew's treatment of the way in which men are to enter The Man's Kingdom betrays the same care in arrangement of material, the same meticulous differentiation of vocabulary, that characterizes his "Son of Man" material. The Beatitudes—which, as Joachim Jeremias has pointed out, are "gospel" applying to members of the community, and not a universal ethic—twice (v 3, 10) declare the conditions under which men in the Kingdom (of The Man) are to live. Matthew's strong ecclesiological interest, his care to record all that he knew of the sayings of Jesus about the continuing community, his interest in what Jesus came to fulfill—all these are found in his pericope about the Law in v 19–20. The Man's Kingdom, the "Kingdom of heaven," will have little attraction for those who in libertarian notions of freedom, or in antinomian reaction against their own past, throw aside all restraint. (The Apostle Paul had much to say of this to his converts.)

The Pauline teaching which is normally designated as "justification by faith," that childlike acceptance of God's gracious gift, undeserved and incapable of being merited, is found in Matthew, too. Men cannot enter into the Kingdom of heaven, into The Man's realm, by mere assertions of allegiance (vii 21): it is only the child—and the childlike—who can accept as wholly unmerited what is offered as a gift (xvii 1, 3, 4, xix 14). Those who would enter the Kingdom of heaven must have a faith that knows it can merit nothing, and must also be prepared to renounce quite legitimate human aspirations (xix 12). The call to sacrifice and the certainty of persecution both make the possession of wealth a positive obstacle in the path of the would-be neophyte (xix 23–24).

The comparisons the parables make between the twin worlds of nature and men on the one hand, and the Kingdom on the other, emphasize the miraculous growth of that Kingdom (xiii 31), The Man's dominion over it (xiii 24), the cost of discipleship (xiii 44), and xiii 45 perhaps is intended to demonstrate the costliness of the Kingdom's inauguration to The Man. This Kingdom, which awaits the judgment of The Man, is not the Kingdom of the righteous—it contains both bad and good (xiii 47) and will so remain until the judgment of the End (xviii 23 ff., xxv 1 ff.). Those who are trained and commissioned to preach the message of this Kingdom (x 7 ff.)

know the mind of its Lord (xiii 11), and, instructed as they are, produce for the household of God all manner of treasure (xiii 52).

Two figures intimately connected with The Man's "Kingdom of heaven," one as forerunner and the other as its leader, are subjects of comment. John the Baptist, great though he was, suffered and was martyred before the inauguration of the Kingdom. In that sense, not having witnessed God's gracious act in The Man, he is less than the latest neophyte in that Kingdom (xi 12). In the main body of the commentary we will discuss the difference between Matt xi 12–15 and Luke xvi 16, but an editorial comment ("from the time of John the Baptist to this moment") seems to appear, followed by Jesus' words on impending and inevitable persecution: the Kingdom will suffer violence at the hands of men, who will seek to quell the dominion of The Man. Peter, whose confession of the Messiahship of Jesus gave the community strength at the crisis-point of the ministry, is given the care of this continuing community (xvi 19)—a tradition which also finds expression in another form in John (xxi 20 ff.).

The continuity of the Kingdom of heaven with the previous history of Israel (a theme heavily emphasized in Paul's letter to the Romans) is pointed out in the sayings of Matt viii 5 ff. Those who bow their necks to the yoke of the service of this Kingdom, whether Jew or Gentile, will inherit the promises to the patriarchs (viii 11); those who refuse, not willing to accept God's gracious gift, will be cast out, even though professed allegiance counted them among the sons of the Kingdom (viii 12). Similarly, the continuity of the community, the Kingdom of The Man, with the community of Israel does not confer upon the Jew any privilege or pre-eminence (xx 1 ff., xxii 2 ff.); those who, late or early, enter that Kingdom are equal recipients of God's gift. Of more than passing interest, in the light of what has so far been said here and in Part VII on the "Son of Man," is the fact that the first condemnation of the Pharisees and scribes in xxiii 13 is based on their inability to comprehend what Jesus offers to all men: rejecting the Kingdom of The Man, they fight against it, too.

The remaining instances of Matthew's use of "kingdom," with its varying qualifying genitives, support these contentions. We have the same emphatic separation of the two Kingdoms in xiii 43, the recognition of another Kingdom (that of the Father) in xxvi 29, while iv 23, ix 35, and xiii 19 have no need of any qualification—

what is under discussion is the Son's Kingdom, just as men are bidden to pray for the advent of the Father's reign in vi 10 (i.e., are to look to the End-time as goal). For Israel, acceptance of the message proclaimed by Jesus must understandably have been a matter of great difficulty, as the teaching that the Son's Kingdom was open to all meant an end to what they imagined was their privileged relationship with God. Rejection of Jesus' proclamation, however, was heinous; we ought not to miss the significance of Matthew's careful record in xii 28. Failure to recognize that the focus of Jesus' ministry was the battle against evil, with all its attendant redemptive implications, was to bring upon oneself the final judgment of God's Kingdom, the judgment of the Father—for along with rejection of the ministry of Jesus went rejection of his Kingdom. In xxi 31 the evangelist has "Kingdom of God" where we might have expected "Kingdom of heaven." But—cf. commentary below—the use here is consistent with the evangelist's purpose. The question is not that of entrance into the Messianic Community on the part of those who are still unbelievers, but of entrance into the Father's Kingdom.

Matthew's use of the word "kingdom" elsewhere in the Gospel can be handled more easily. That there was very early some doubt as to the differences between Matthew and Mark is evidenced by the variations at vi 33, though it is plain even in the manuscript variations that it is the Father's Kingdom which men are to seek as the goal of their lives. The *finality* of the Father's Kingdom, as distinct from that of the Son of Man, has been stressed above.

There is one final reference to be noted—Matt xvi 28. This occurs in a context which marks out the path of suffering and denial of self which is the lot of the disciple. Though xvi 27 gives us the familiar pattern of The Man's future judgment upon his own people, this is followed by the saying that there are "men standing here who will not taste death before they see The Man enter upon his reign." Mark ix 1 has "before they see the kingdom of God come with power" (RSV). The distinct use which Matthew makes of the Kingdom of The Man here had prompted some to ask whether the evangelist, or his source, expected an early end to the world order, in the lifetime of some who heard this saying. Some have asked whether, granted that the saying is authentic, Jesus was himself a mistaken visionary (which was the view of Albert Schweitzer). It is not necessary to return an affirmative to either alternative. (To "taste death" was a common Jewish expression [cf. John viii 52; Heb ii 9], and hence we are dealing with a saying which is part of Jewish life in the time of Jesus—the saying need not be denied to Jesus solely on grounds of dating.) Matthew's use of his sources here shows some interesting divergence from the Markan tradition. To begin with, Matthew does not have Mark's "and he said to them," which prefaces the Markan version; instead, he firmly links this saying with what has gone before—that is, with the saying about judgment in The Man's Kingdom. Furthermore, Matthew uses the Greek participle *erchomemon*, "coming," for Mark's *elēluthuian;* in Mark it is the *Kingdom of God* which men will see, while in Matthew it is *The Man* coming in his Kingdom. We have contended elsewhere (fn. 17) that Daniel vii 13 is the clue to Matthew's tradition about the "coming of The Man," and it is possible to see the same concept at work here. In the trial scene of Matthew's passion narrative, Jesus declares that the by-standers will *see* The Man coming on the clouds, already in the seat of power. This can only rightly be understood—as we have seen—in the light of the Johannine tradition that Jesus spoke of his passion and his resurrection as his glorification, his enthronement; the numerous occasions on which Jesus (in John's gospel) speaks of his "coming" to the Father can only refer to the glory of his resurrection-exaltation. To this must be added the further Johannine tradition that the community was established in the Spirit immediately following the resurrection (a tradition which, incidentally, Luke's account in Acts ii in no way contradicts). It seems reasonable to suggest, therefore, that Matthew here records a saying which anticipates the Son's coming to the Father, with a Kingdom, a community, already in being at the time of the resurrection.

This analysis may firmly place Matthew in a first-century Jewish tradition that understood the sayings of Jesus far more clearly than did Mark or Luke—an understanding which the evangelist shares with John. If so, some very interesting questions are raised about the precise relationship between Matthew's tradition and that of John, and a very fruitful field of inquiry is suggested in the exploration of common elements of thought in Matthew, John, and Paul.

IX. JESUS AND THE LAW

No other NT document represents Jesus upholding the Law so extensively as the gospel of Matthew. Jesus confirms the Law in v 17–19, xxiii 1 ff. If this were all—and some writers on the New Testament have apparently been persuaded of this—then we would expect the Judge in the End-time in Matthew's gospel to hold court on the basis of the Law (cf. xxv 31 ff.); his granting or withholding mercy on the basis of the Law would be sufficient ground for acquittal or condemnation.

A massive concentration on the theme of Law in Matthew, however, seriously disturbs the whole balance of the work, and would succeed in removing Jesus' discussion of the Law from the context of the Kingdom he proclaimed. Whatever prominence the Law holds in this gospel, the concern of the Kingdom in all the gospels is soteriological, and interest in the Law is subordinate to this overriding consideration of salvation effected by Jesus.

The element of the soteriological apart, it is right to call attention to one vital concern shared by the Israel of the Sinai Covenant and the Messianic Community which Jesus proclaimed: the relationship of the individual to the community, whether of Israel or of the Church. For Israel under the Old Covenant, as for the Church under the New, the paramount concern was not whether Israel or the Kingdom was a vaguely identifiable disposition of mind or heart, but whether men did or did not belong to Israel or the Kingdom. Individuals may have been aware of being members of Israel or of a proclaimed Kingdom, but it is the people, the community, who stand under the Covenant and the judgment of God. The individual in either community attains the salvation of God as a member of a covenant-community. The attitude of Jesus to the Mosaic Law must be seen against the background of the Covenant; likewise, discussions of the ethical demands of the NT writings are pointless without reference to the community in which those demands are to be met.

It is necessary to emphasize here, too, the element of "fulfillment" in Matthew's gospel, for it has a direct bearing on our subject. The evangelist combines his concept of Jesus establishing the Law with his understanding of the person of Jesus. The teaching of Jesus given to the inner circle of his disciples is supplemented by references to the Law, to its foundation in the purposes of God at creation (cf. xix 4, 8), but he himself fulfills the purposes of the Law (v 17, xxiii 23). To follow mercy, righteousness, and faith is precisely that total *lack* of concern for the things of self which exceeds the righteousness of scribes and Pharisees (cf. v 20): the righteousness demanded by Jesus is based on allegiance to the principles on which the Law was based, and also (and vitally) on allegiance to his own ministry and person.

The very terms in which Jesus proclaimed the Kingdom's advent —OT terms, intimately bound up with the whole concept of covenant-obligation—carried with them the implication of an organization through which the new Covenant-community expressed its allegiance. (The unfortunate and inaccurate contrast often drawn between the idea of a community on one side, and a "religion of the spirit" on the other, is examined carefully in B. C. Butler's *Spirit and Institution in the New Testament,* London: Mowbray, 1961.) Given the need for some means of identifying the membership of a community, there is a corresponding necessity to legislate for that community's life: the Corinthian letters of Paul together with the Johannine letters eloquently testify to this need. The gates of the New Jerusalem in the Apocalypse, it has been pointed out, are always open but that same Jerusalem also has walls. It is quite misleading to imply that the freedom secured for men by Jesus (according to the Apostle Paul) was meant to issue in an undifferentiated enthusiasm, free of all restraint by common discipline.

Matthew's gospel clearly demonstrates that Jesus' life also points out the path of discipleship. Mercy—"covenant-loyalty"—which Jesus teaches as the very heart of the Law (ix 13, xii 7), which he commends to the disciples (v 7, xviii 33), and by which standard the world will be judged (xxv 31 ff.), is what Jesus himself demonstrates in his dealings with men, even the most insignificant of his brethren (xi 28–30). Allegiance to one who acts in such a way demands similar conduct from anyone who professes that allegiance: the disciple must exhibit the humility that characterizes his Master. There is no new Law, but neither is there simply a reiteration of the old Law's precepts; Matthew's gospel presents a new frame of reference—allegiance to the interpreter of the Law, whom Jesus claims to be, an allegiance in covenant-loyalty and faith. But allegiance proves nothing (cf. xxv 40), the imperative is the conduct which allegiance implies.

More than one commentary has suggested that the misnamed "Sermon on the Mount," particularly that part of it known as "The Beatitudes" (x 3–12), was deliberately meant by Jesus to be a superior declaration of the divine will in contrast with an (implied) "lower" revelation under Moses. Such interpretations are more suggestive of outworn theories of "degrees of inspiration" than of serious scholarship. Without the Law there would have been no Gospel: *ex nihilo nihil fit* is valid today as it was in the Middle Ages: without the Covenant of Sinai and the election of Israel there is no understanding of the Gospel. We can say with considerable emphasis that Jesus' attitude to the Law was positive, that he accepted the rightful place of those who taught the Law as God-given (xxiii 3), even in one instance accepting the extension of the law of tithe (xxiii 23). But while affirming the validity of the Law up to the time of its "fulfillment," he rejected the proliferating oral tradition, increasingly fostered by the Pharisees and eagerly seized upon by the scribes.

Matt v 17 records Jesus as saying that he came to "establish," "fulfill," "sum up" (*plērousai*) the Law. David Daube (*The New Testament and Rabbinic Judaism,* The Jordan Lectures, 1952 [London: Athlone Press, 1956], pp. 60 ff.) gives the meaning as "uphold," translating the Heb. *qiyyem.* But the Syriac and the Aramaic would be far more faithfully rendered by "establish" in the sense of "give firm foundation to," while "uphold" in the context would provide the unhappy sense of "defend." The Aramaic can also tolerate the meaning of "resurrect."

In discussing specific examples of Jesus' treatment of the Law in Matthew three things must be borne in mind:

(1) Jesus conceived of his own mission in terms of Israel alone (xv 24–26; the parallel Mark vii 27 is no different), regardless of whatever exceptions might be made in particular cases of healing, or in directions to disciples as to their own missions. It is true that

the abrogation by God of exclusive privileges of election is plainly indicated by the sense of some of the parables, but the keeping (or not) of the Law was not a burning issue until the mission to the Gentiles was begun in earnest.

(2) Jesus' appeal to the Law and his understanding of the demands of God upon the covenant-people is cast, significantly, in terms taken from Deuteronomy (cf. the temptation narrative, and see also Mark xii 29 and parallels, Deut vi 4). That book is not only Law and commentary on Law, it also sharply and frequently emphasizes the compassionate love of God both in the choice of Israel and also in qualifying that choice's provisions for maintaining Israel's unique inheritance.

(3) Whatever lessons the parables may carry about the overconfident reliance of Israel on the mere privilege of choice, Jesus' appeal both in the parables and in his teaching on the Law is to the divine initiative which formed Israel, which act gave the Law its sanctions. As such, the teaching of Jesus is cast in a prophetic mold.

To take up the last point, we are guilty of an alarming simplicity with respect to the evidence of rabbinic form if we suppose that the Matthean formula "It was said by the ancients . . . but I tell you . . ." is tantamount to an abrogation of the Mosaic Law. Cast though it may be in a prophetic and not in an academic/rabbinic mold, it was nevertheless a well-known interpretative device. Daube (*New Testament and Rabbinic Judaism,* p. 58) calls attention to the rabbinic formula "I might hear (understand) . . ." (i.e., literally) "but you must say . . ." (i.e., "the essential meaning is . . ."). This formula—as Daube points out—is certainly as old as the New Testament. It was a well-established convention in the time of Rabbi Ishmael (first part of the second century A.D.) and therefore had a far longer oral history. (The whole of Daube's chapter 7 is extremely useful in illuminating this point.)

Jesus' attitude to the Law has run a whole gamut of comment, some of it theological (and having to do with his Messianic dignity, or even consciousness of divinity), some of it frankly reminiscent of nineteenth-century liberal humanitarianism. Nearly all the commentaries ignore the salient fact of the background and upbringing of Jesus as a loyal and devoted son of Israel. His appeal was not to any new interpretation of the Law, still less to an interpretation propounded by himself, any more than the strictures of Amos, Micah, or Jeremiah can be held to urge any new interpretation of the Law. Jesus' appeal is firmly against new interpretations, in particular those proliferating from the oral tradition of the Pharisees, and arising from the new application of Greek hermeneutics to Jewish law. Jesus' appeal is always to real meanings, real interpretations, to foundations. The whole force of the discussion about duty to parents in Matt xv is directed against new interpretations imposed by legislation. Similarly, in the celebrated passage about divorce (xix 4), the significant phrase is *ap' archēs,*—xix 4, 8: "from the beginning, at the foundation of things." Moses is not being condemned for his legislative work; on the contrary, it is *Israel* which stands condemned for having wrung from the lawgiver a concession which was rooted in human sin.

It is appropriate to consider here Paul's understanding of the "law," as one trained in the rabbinic tradition of Hillel by Gamaliel.[18] The apostle does use *nomos* (=law) in a sense which any Greek would have understood, in the sense of a principle of life itself— that is, natural law. This sense, which we might translate as "the foundation of all good order," is used by Paul at Rom vii 23 and viii 2, and there are certainly instances where *nomos* in his writings would do violence as an equivalent of the Heb. *tôrah* (cf. Rom iii 27, vii 23, 25; viii 2). H. L. Strack and P. Billerbeck, *Kommentar zum Neuen Testament aus Talmud und Midrash* (abbr. StB), 5 vols. (Munich: C. H. Beck, 1922–55), ad loc., maintain that the whole argument of Rom ii 14–15 is foreign to rabbinic Judaism. All this is simply to say that for Paul the Jew, the *primary* meaning of *nomos* would always be *tôrah,* yet once LXX had used the word *nomos* (=the law of a community; cf. Eph ii 15), then Paul could use expressions which covered whole areas of ideas that *tôrah* could not easily sustain. By what steps he came to find in *nomos* a wider sense for *tôrah,* which *contained* "commandments put out as decrees" (Eph ii 15) we are not told; attention has already been called to the way in which Jesus appealed to the Law as an expression of underlying purpose, sustaining principle. It may be that Paul grasped the flexibility of this concept and in his penetrating way saw its implications for his own theological writings. At the same time he is aware of the way in which "law" had come to mean interpretations which

---

[18] See W. D. Davies, *Paul and Rabbinic Judaism* (London: SPCK, 1948), especially p. 66; cf. *Acts,* AB, vol. 31, Appendix VIII.

were not commandments. In Rom iii 10–18 he provides us with a combination of quotations from Isaiah and Psalms, adding that "whatever the Law says it addresses to those who are subject to it." A quotation from Isa xxvii 11 he designates as "written in the Law" (I Cor xiv 21). Obviously, both examples are outside the legal material of the Old Testament, but the point to be made is that rabbinic usage specifically sanctioned such an extension of the meaning of *tôrah* (cf. StB, on John x 34; Rom iii 19; I Cor xiv 21).

Granted such an extension of *tôrah* did include the prophetic writings, it is important to see just how the process began, and eventually came to include oral case law discussion which in turn hardened into positive precept. It is a truism of social and psychological processes that the more consciously a battle is taken up against influence and environment, the more likely it is that such influence and environmental factors will be assimilated—a phenomenon known to psychology as the "law of reversed effort." Some interesting illustrations of this tendency can be seen in the history of Judaism in the NT period, both orthodox and sectarian. The Essene Manual of Discipline (1QS) for example, contains the nearest approach in early Judaism to a creed. Presumably, even when consciously warring against Greek influence in the second century B.C., the Essenes unconsciously assimilated some of the Hellenistic concern for such statements. The climate of the times was heavily in favor of such Greek fondness for abstract generalizations.

Similarly, in orthodox Judaism the influence of Hellenism was deep and lasting even when that influence was being most fiercely contested. So far as we know at present, the Essene material at Qumran contains not a single Greek loan word; the Mishnah is full of them (cf. Liebermann, *Hellenism in Jewish Palestine*). No doubt the process was gradual, but in the field of hermeneutics the change can be seen in the NT material itself. The Qumran commentaries and Matthew's gospel are midrashic, using a sermon-style of exposition and explanation. The method was known to Paul, and he used it (e.g., I Cor x 1–5; II Cor iii 4–23); but his own training had been at the hands of those deeply influenced by the exacting discipline of Greek hermeneutics, and his concern is in the main with the precise meaning of words and phrases. Philo found it possible to allegorize the Law (though this was a wholly Greek phenomenon), and Jews in the Dispersion lived in the midst of city-societies that had been open to Stoic and mid-Platonic thinking for generations.

Even Galilee, nearer to the center of orthodox Judaism, was surrounded by Greek cities and was thoroughly cosmopolitan.

We should bear all of this in mind as we examine the passage in which Jesus is commonly thought to have been most sweeping in his condemnation of those concerned for the Law. Some have maintained that the passage implies a wholesale condemnation of the Law in favor of something to be promulgated by himself.

In this connection nothing is more important than the condemnation of the scribes and Pharisees in Matt xxiii 13. Though various translations have been offered for the phrase which opens each particular condemnation, the KJ will serve to give the general sense rendered by most translators: "Woe unto you, scribes and Pharisees, hypocrites!" "Hypocrites" is simply the Gr. *hupocritēs,* and such has been the influence of translation that two results have followed: (1) the assumption that the Greek precisely denotes one self-consciously playing a part, an actor, whose whole way of life and even convictions may be at variance with the role in which he is cast, or in which he has cast himself; and (2) that the "hypocrisy" or play acting of the scribes and Pharisees so castigated casts a doubt on the continued validity of the Law in the mind and teaching of Jesus. We have rejected the translation "hypocrite" in this commentary because it is merely the Greek word, and its primary meaning in Greek is not "actor." (The linguistic evidence from the remainder of the New Testament is set out in an appendix, below.)

According to context, our translations of *hupocrisis* (Matt xxiii 28, RSV "hypocrisy") and *hupocritēs, hupocritai* (Matt vi 2, etc., RSV "hypocrite," "hypocrites") are varied, but as the appended note demonstrates, all are based on an understanding of the words as denoting an overscrupulous, pettifogging concern with the minutiae of law.

An interesting link with LXX usage is found at Matt xxiii 28— the equation of *hupocrisis* (the only example of this word in Matthew) with lawlessness (*anomia*). It is not necessary to be well acquainted with moral or ascetical theology to be aware that scrupulosity is rightly condemned as sin, and also that what is ostensibly concerned with a punctilious observance of law inevitably becomes *self*-concerned. In this way the function of law is lost, or at best hopelessly obscured as the ego overcomes social concern. Furthermore, as Paul indicated, law as an end in itself, divorced from the relationships with God and man which are its real concern, becomes an intolerable burden. Doubtless "hard cases make bad law," but an overweening legalism which fails to take proper cognizance of particular circumstances, time, and persons, infallibly produces the attitude of mind which Jesus condemned in the Pharisee lawyers.

Far and away the most prevalent form of *hupocritēs* to be found in Matthew is *hupocritai*. We have in chapter vi rendered the plural by "overscrupulous" (vi 2, 5, 16). The exact, punctilious observance of every possible legal prescription and custom, written and unwritten, in the realms of prayer, fasting and almsgiving would tend to produce (and, Jesus charges, did produce), not an offering of self to God, but an exhibition of legal rectitude to those who saw it. At vii 5 the translation is "Casuist!" We realize that casuistry is important in any system of moral theology. It is emphatically no prerogative of seventeenth- and eighteenth-century Jesuits, still less of the Roman Catholic Church, but in popular estimation it almost always bears a pejorative meaning similar to that now enjoyed by the adjective "apocryphal." Here at vii 5 there is enough of the pejorative sense to indicate Jesus' impatience with the legalism which is aware only of failure of observance in others. At xv 7 we have elected to use the colloquialism "Shysters!" which connotes a total disregard for the purpose of the Law while ostensibly paying reverence to it. The incident which provoked Jesus' exclamation in xxii 18 seemed again to demand "You casuists!" for here the aim of a supposedly harmless question was to bring a charge of lawlessness against him.

Matthew xxiii, which contains no fewer than seven passages where *hupocritai* is used (vss. 13, 14, 15, 23, 25, 27, 29), ought to demonstrate to the thoughtful the reverence in which Jesus held the Law of his fathers. Not infrequently, and especially in homiletics, critics have not seen this, and have instead depicted Jesus as condemning the Mosaic Law. We have already called attention to the manner in which Jesus protested against later oral glosses and interpretations imposed on the Law, and chapter xxiii underlines that contention. In this chapter we have translated the familiar opening words of the "seven woes" (vs. 14) by "Away with you, you pettifogging Pharisee lawyers!" Jesus' criticism is not directed against the Law, or against case law and casuistry as such—John viii 1–11, whatever its historical background, does represent Jesus as dealing with a particular "case"—but against that willful disregard for the purpose of the Law, against that misuse of law which supposes that all human experience is ultimately capable of being subject to legislation. The fate of the slave in xxiv 51, whose final destiny lies with the "timeservers" (our translation), is fitting end to the career of one who judged that he could take the law into his own hands.

Here we must pay some attention to conflicting legal approaches to the observance of the Law in the time of Jesus. The differing outlooks of the two great legalists Shammai and Hillel had in the course of half a century hardened into schools of interpretation, often in violent opposition to each other. Both schools had followers among the lawyers, and both gave rise to large amounts of oral law and legal tradition which the "scribes" (lawyers) were only too anxious to write into precise legislation. Despite the more humanitarian attitude of Hillel and his followers, the increasing application of Greek hermeneutics among them gave impetus to a heightened awareness of words and meanings. For both schools the continued existence of the secular state and a sacrificial cultus centered in Jerusalem provided a field in which the possibilities for the growth of legalism were almost unlimited.

We have called attention to the prophetic tradition in which Jesus stood. Standing in that tradition revering the Law and the Covenant enshrined by that tradition, Jesus could be moved to anger at manipulations of the Law. The OT prophetic record is too well known to need recapitulation. When Jesus protested that the Sabbath was God's gracious gift to man, and not an institution intended to dominate man's life (Mark ii 27), he spoke from the prophetic tradition, from conviction that men under the Covenant should be free from self-concern to serve God. While it is true that there is a saying similar in character to Mark ii 27 attributed to Rabbi Simeon ("To you the Sabbath is given over, and you are not given over to the Sabbath"), R. Simeon speaks toward the close of the second century A.D., and it may be doubted whether the saying of either Jesus or R. Simeon would have been acceptable in the inflamed state of opinion before A.D. 70.

For Paul, Jesus as Messiah was the "end," the goal, of the Law (Rom x 4) and Jesus himself regarded the Sabbath as peculiarly appropriate to God's gracious acts performed through himself. A new community was being forged and a Kingdom proclaimed, and therefore the true function of the Law was being declared. So far from being abolished by the proclamation of the Kingdom, it was being championed. But the Law was also to bring men to the Messiah (Gal iii 24). What the Mosaic Law could become when regarded as not merely custodian but father, mother, family and even life itself, Paul the ex-Pharisee testifies eloquently in both his Roman and Galatian letters.

The Mosaic Law, and the demands of the Gospel, apply only to those whose allegiance is claimed either by circumcision or baptism. No doubt Christianity, through its periodic missionary activity, has manifested a greater awareness of responsibility to those beyond its borders than has Judaism. But nothing in Christian history has been more reprehensible than attempts by Christians of *all* persuasions to impose a universal code of ethics supposedly derived from the Christian faith. In this respect the champions of "situation ethics" are no better than proponents of the Roman Inquisition or European and American Puritanism. By the use of the "parable" from case law, coupled with a use of "love" in a non-covenantal sense, the more vocal members of the "situation ethics" school are doing no more—and emphatically no less—than did the Reformers, Catholic and Protestant alike, in the sixteenth and seventeenth centuries. Christian morality may be based on a longer historical experience than were—say—the ethical systems of Confucius or Aristotle, but to attempt to impose Christian standards in a desperate attempt to prove their "relevance" is precisely the kind of unscrupulous behavior castigated by Jesus.

N.B. A recent article (Kenzo Tagawa, "People and Community in the Gospel of Matthew," NTS 16 (1970), 149–63, is of considerable importance for the discussion above, in its examination of the position of the Gentile in Matthew's gospel.

Appendix

Hupokrisis, Hupokritēs, Hupokrinesthai

This appendix is the result of the study of possible translations of the Greek term *hupokritēs* (pl. *hupokritai*) in Matthew, with the implications of such translations for study of Jesus' attitude to the Law (see above). This appendix is intended to present the evidence on which the study was based.

The English translation (or rather, transliteration) *hypocrite,* and the associated *hypocrisy,* carry a minatory meaning which most users of the word think that they fully understand. It is assumed that a "hypocrite" is one who consciously plays a part, an actor, one who may (out of whatever motives) adopt an attitude which is at variance with his own convictions. In short, it is taken for granted that the later Greek sense of "actor" for *hupocritēs* is the sole meaning in the New Testament, indicating (in this view) that Jesus intended to execrate the Pharisees in general as "two-faced," saying one thing but meaning (for themselves) something quite different. While this sense of the word prevails in popular (and academic) circles, Jews can justifiably complain that the gospels consistently misrepresent the Pharisees.

We contend that the Greek verb *krinein* and its derivatives (especially *hupokrinesthai*) are all primarily concerned with interpretation. It was in later Greece, when interpretation became more and more identified with the stage, that *hupokritēs* meant "actor." It would seem that both *apokrinesthai* and *hupokrinesthai* have a basic common meaning, both concerned with correct recitation, but with a slight shift in meaning in Attic Greek for *apokrinesthai* in the direction of "answer," and in Ionic toward the meaning of "recite actor's lines." However, this latter meaning could not be solely concerned with a correct text, since a variation in text almost invariably carries with it a change of emphasis or even interpretation.

The verb *krinesthai* originally meant—in Homer—"to interpret (dreams)" (*Odyssey* 19. 535, 555) and it is only in later times that it came to mean "playing an actor's part." The intermediate sense, through which the later meaning developed, was that of reciting, interpreting, answering (dialogue). It is true that such recitation, interpretation, and answering of questions initially had to do with the epic poetry of Greece, but it is important to remember that "to play a part" was a derived, not a primary meaning. (References are too numerous for the scope of this commentary, but they may easily be consulted in H. G. Liddell and Robert Scott, *A Greek-English Lexicon,* 9th rev. ed. by H. S. Jones and others, Oxford University Press, 1940, and in the relevant article of TWNT [Vol. VI, ed. Gerhard Friedrich, 1969].) Something of the initial meaning of the word may be discerned in the confusion attending *hupokrinesthai* and *apokrinesthai,* partly because of a similarity of prefixes: in the

New Testament *apokritheis eipen* is common for "he answered," following the Attic Greek *apokrinesthai,* where it is normal in this sense.

However much we may have succumbed to pejorative connotations in our English transliteration of *hupokritēs,* we are still accustomed to using the English word "critical" and its congeners in a more or less neutral sense. The Gr. *kritikos* is similarly neutral, implying a capacity for discernment. We may even carry the sense a step further and speak of someone as "hypercritical," intending to convey the idea that a person is given to fine, hairsplitting distinctions, but we do not at the same time accuse such a person of "being a hypocrite" in our modern sense. We suggest only that his faculty of discernment is carried too far for ordinary purposes. The Gr. *krinein* hardly needs comment here: it meant "to judge, to evaluate"—normal activities of one who undertook to interpret Greek epic poetry, whether this had to do with individual words, or with allegorical meanings attached to various passages.

Thus *hupokritēs* came to mean one who declaimed or recited Greek poetry or drama, especially Homer. In this sense *hupokritēs* occupied somewhat the same position as the reciter of epics, saga, and folk tales in Scandinavian and Celtic cultures, not to mention the Greek rhapsodist or the Arab *rāwī* (cf. Plato *Timaeus* 72B; Lucian *Somnium* 17 et al.). But the reciter of the Homeric poems, which were sacred literature to the ancient Greeks, also had to be an interpreter (cf., e.g., Timaeus Sophista). Only in a secondary sense did *hupokritēs* stress that the interpreter was also an actor or was consciously playing a part (cf., e.g., Plato *Republic* 373B.) So also the adjective *huperkritikos,* though not found in LXX or New Testament, also designates a skilled declaimer, or one with good natural diction (cf. Aristotle *Rhetoric* 3. 1. 7; *Poetics* 19. 7, 27. 6). The metaphorical use—as of one pretending to be something other than he is—cannot be documented before the second century A.D.

With this material as background we now turn to the use of the words in question in NT, with such material from LXX as serves to illuminate NT use.

First there is *hupokrinesthai.* An interesting case is to be found in R. H. Charles's treatment in *Apocrypha and Pseudepigrapha* of Ecclus i 29. Accepting the original Hebrew reading of *penê* ("in the presence of") instead of *pî* ("in the mouth of"), we have "do not be overcritical in the presence of men, but be careful what thou sayest."

There are examples of the verb in II Macc v 25, vi 21, 24. Apollonius in v 25 fills the role of a "man of peace," and this is the nearest we come in biblical material to *hupokrinesthai* as "playing a part." Far more instructive are the examples of vi 21, 24. Eleazar, an aged scribe, is asked to interpret, to demonstrate, a fine point of law. He is asked to provide meat of his own choice, to consume it as though it were pork, thus seeming to render obedience to the royal decree and at the same time save himself and his people. It is *not* that (vi 21) the old man is asked to play a part—though that would follow as a result of his action—but that being skilled in the Law, he might satisfy the letter of the Law while at the same time satisfying the legal demands of his interrogators. Evidently they were well assured that however hairsplitting the interpretation might be, Eleazar's compliance would produce the maximum satisfaction for both sides. It is the kind of hairsplitting legal scrupulosity (*hupokrisis*) which the old man rejects in vi 24–25. It is not "deceit" (NEB) or "dissimulation." That *hupokritēs* and allied forms have to do with this kind of legal interpretation is clear from Ecclus xxxii 15 and xxxiii 2: the man who truly seeks the Law, who does not hate it, will find it a strength and support. But the *hupokritēs,* the man whose keeping of the Law is characterized by scrupulosity, is in a wholly different case. Using the Law for his own purposes, he becomes enmeshed in its provisions, stumbles over it (xxxii 15), and in the end is as unstable in his opinions as a ship in a storm (xxxii 2). These examples from the Greek Ben Sira are of considerable importance, since they date from the late second century B.C. (Unhappily, the Hebrew text of the passages in question is obscure.)

In two versions of LXX we have examples of *hupokrisis* in addition to II Maccabees. Aquila and Theodotion, as well as Symmachus, use the word in Isa xxxii 6, where the fool plots *hupokrisis*. Interestingly, the received text of LXX reads "iniquity," or "lawlessness." Nothing breeds disrespect for law more easily than a suggestion that it can be manipulated to serve a number of varying or even contradictory ends. One version of LXX provides us with *hupokritai* instead of the received "robbers" in Hos vi 9. The suggestion is presumably that Israel's religion had become so corrupt that manipulations of its Law were tantamount to robbery.

Job provides some interesting examples. Elihu's speech in xxxiv 30 speaks of the dangers lying in wait when a ruler is *hupokritēs* (Heb. *ḥānēf,* translated "godless" in RSV, and "impious" by Marvin

H. Pope in *Job,* AB, vol. 15). Under such a ruler, all respect for law would come to an end. The same speaker, in further developing the theme of the lawless ruler, uses *hupokritēs* again in xxxvi 13.

The Heb. *hānēf* seems to be a particularly poor foundation upon which to build. *Ḥānēf,* "blasphemous, wicked," also appears in the Dead Sea Manual of Discipline (1QS) with synonymous words; it is rendered by *hupokrisis* in three Greek versions (Aquila, Symmachus, and Theodotion) at Isa xxxii 6, and the word appears to carry moral rather than legal implications. The word does appear in a specifically legal context in Dan xi 32 (early second century B.C.) in speaking of the enemy who seduces, persuades to apostasy, those who violate the Covenant. The use made of both noun and verb in Jeremiah is normal in character and has to do with covenant law only in context. Daniel xi 32, when speaking of the "godlessness" (*hanûphāh*) in the land, equates the state of affairs with treachery. Jer iii 9 and xxiii 11 (where the word *hānēf* is used) argue that the wickedness of the land is a result of the flagrant pursuit of heathen rites.

We may also here adduce the evidence from Arabic and Syriac. The Syr. *nāsĕbai b-appei,* a "respecter of persons," used as a translation of *hupokritēs* in the New Testament, is the lawyer or judge who manipulates the law for a person. Prima facie, the Arabic is less tolerant of this kind of interpretation, and *hanîf* (a loanword from Hebrew through Aramaic) denotes the true believer, the truly orthodox Muslim. It is certainly true that the scrupulously orthodox can on occasion be capable of some impressive legal hairsplitting. Unless the Heb. *hānēf* at a later stage carried with it some such concern for scrupulous observance it is hard to see how the Arabic derivative could have achieved its meaning. The statement in Winckler's article (TWNT, VI, p. 563, n. 25) that *hanîf* means "heathen" in Arabic is contrary to all Muslim belief and usage from the Quran (Koran) onwards, and is based on a misunderstanding of the Arabic Muslim meaning. It would make Abraham—described as *hanîf* in the Quran —into a heathen, whereas to Muslim Arabs Abraham was the friend of God, the ancestor of all Arabs, as well as the first true believer. Other usages of words from the triliteral stem are loan words from Syriac, where the words are used of pagans.

We now turn to NT evidence outside Matthew's gospel. Conveniently, we may begin with Paul. His charge against Peter in Gal ii 3 is that Peter's vacillating conduct arose simply from casuistry (*hupokrisis*), a casuistry which was not called into play until the situation in Antioch was complicated by the arrival of Jewish Christians from Jerusalem. The apostolic condemnation in I Tim iv 2 deals with the sort of casuistry (*hupokrisis,* RSV "pretensions") which attempts to make universal rules out of occasional or voluntary ascetical practices. Two other examples of *hupokrisis* outside the gospels deal with the same theme. James v 12 is in fact an example of the word divided into its two elements; the warning against surrounding plain statements with a mass of qualifications and oaths is paralleled in Matt v 37. The letter adds the warning "lest you fall into casuistry," or "lest you fall under judgment"— the words will tolerate either sense. I Peter ii 1 links *hupokrisis* with malice and guile. The RSV translation here is "insincerity," which in the context is just barely possible.

The uses of *hupokrisis* in the gospels are revealing. Mark xii 15 represents Jesus, in the dispute about the poll tax, as being wholly aware of the casuistry which would fasten for polemical purposes on any statement he made. (The parallel in Matt xxii 18 uses "malice" of his questioner's attitude, and we have translated *hupokritai* by "You casuists!") The Lukan version speaks of his questioners' "craftiness"—frequently, indeed, the mark of the casuist. Luke xii 1 speaks of Jesus warning his disciples against the hyperlegalism of the Pharisees, though the parallels in Matthew and Mark do not have the word *hupokrisis*. In Matt xxiii 28 Jesus emphatically links the casuistry of the scribes and Pharisees with lack of respect for the Law—a usage to which we have already called attention.

In the gospels there is one example of *hupokrinesthai*. In Luke xx 20, Jesus' critics sent spies who represented themselves as men simply concerned for a declaration of his attitude on a point of law, but in reality casuists ready to manipulate his reply in order to provide an opportunity for persecution.

We now turn to the familiar *hupokritēs* (plural *hupokritai*). As a transliteration of the Greek, "hypocrite" was known in English at least as early as the *Ancren Riwle* ("Rule for Anchoresses") of the thirteenth century, where it means a dissembler; "the false ancress is an hypocrite" answers to our modern usage. The only use of "hypocrite" in English throughout the Middle Ages was ecclesiastical, and we have no evidence for its use *before* the thirteenth century. "Hypocritical" is apparently sixteenth century: the example which comes nearest to the translation we defend comes from an Act of Parliament of Henry VIII, mentioning "the hypocritical and superstitious religions among us." A letter of 1711 also speaks of one who "in King Edward's time hypocris'd and comply'd with the Reformations."

All in all, the direct transcription of the Gr. *hupokritēs* has obscured the real attitude of Jesus to the religion of his own time, and has at the same time been responsible for great misunderstandings of the Pharisees.

Mark has but one example of *hupokritēs,* vii 6 (=Matt xv 7) and the translation "You casuists!" precisely fits the context. Luke vi 42 (=Matt vii 5) comes as the conclusion of warning that there is a casuistry so concerned with rectitude in others that it cannot see its own shortcomings. Luke xii 56 is in a similar category: the casuists castigated there are so busily engaged in quite minor "cases" (which are here the indications of fair or foul weather) that the really dramatic signs of the times wholly escape them. They cannot see the wood for the trees. In the final example (Luke xiii 15), we have rendered the parallel in Matt xv 7 "shysters"; this sense is equally demanded by the Markan parallel (vii 6). Here again we have an example of case law which has been allowed to run riot, and in so doing has obscured the very nature of law itself.

If all that we have tried to demonstrate is true, then granted the "Jewishness" of Matthew's gospel, it is no surprise that the word *hupokritēs* should be so frequently used in that gospel. One example of *hupokritai,* the plural, in Matthew (vi 2, 5, 16) is very near the Greek of "those who demonstrate or interpret." To charge those who are condemned in this chapter with being "hypocrites" in the usual English sense is to miss the point. It was not that these people were consciously acting a part which did not correspond to their own inner convictions, but that they were parading their own scrupulousness in public. This is the reverse side of casuistry: not merely an attempt to legislate for all possible contingencies, but setting up a self-conscious example, and thus bringing the service of God into contempt.

In Part X of the Introduction we hope we have established Jesus' reverence for the Law of Moses as a declaration of the will of God, and that he demanded of his disciples—Jews like himself— that they pay reverence to those charged with the duty of teaching that Law (Matt xxiii 2). This is followed in the same chapter with the most stringent denunciations against misuse of that duty, and (coupled with examples from case law) the most numerous occurrences of *hupokritai* (Matt xxiii 13–32). In this instance we have translated the word by "you pettifogging Pharisee lawyers," since the phrase "Pharisee lawyers" throughout the seven "woes" includes both scribes and Pharisees. It is abundantly clear from the context that Jesus is impatient with the disciples of both Hillel *and* Shammai. In spite of the greater flexibility of interpretation associated with the name Hillel, the advent of Greek hermeneutical methods could often mean that the school of Hillel was every bit as exacting in the requirements of the Law as that of Shammai. The *middôt* (to which reference has been made in Part IV above) provided a logical foundation upon which legal speculation could, and did, proliferate. No matter that the schools of Shammai and Hillel were often opposed to each other: both could, and did, provide an atmosphere in which legal hairsplitting made the Law less and less an expression of man's responsive loyalty to God and God's gracious gift to his people, but at the same time more and more a matter of uncertainty. The agricultural peasant, dealing every day with all forms of nature, organic and inorganic, was driven to exasperated near-contempt for the legal directives that interfered with his livelihood. The city dweller, too, in daily contact with those from outside the borders of Israel, must often have developed scorn for a discipline which made finer and finer distinctions of observance so long as the national state and sacrificial cultus remained intact. The final example of *hupokritai* in Matthew (xxiv 51) we have translated by "timeservers." Those who manipulated law brought it into contempt and deserved to be numbered with the ungodly.

Outside the gospels, but of outstanding importance as evidence for our position in this appendix, is the *Didache* (Teaching of the Twelve Apostles), which—following J.-P. Audet in his 1958 edition and commentary (*La Didaché,* Études Bibliques, Paris: Gabalda)—we date about the third quarter of the first century A.D.

The words *hupokrisis, hupokritai* occur in various contexts, and —as Audet observes in his study of the work—the words do not carry condemnation on moral grounds. Didache viii 1 refers to *hupokritai* who diverged from the traditional days of fasting (Wednesday and Friday) in favor of other days (Monday and Thursday), while viii 2 simply repeats the injunction of Jesus in Matt vi 5. Didache ii 6, in a discussion of the "way of life," forbids *hupokrisis* along with other sins of self-seeking, sins which display a flagrant disregard for the rights of others. So too in Didache iv 12: the believer must disdain all *hupokrisis* and everything else which is displeasing to the Lord. There is inherent improbability in Winckler's suggestion (TWNT, VI, p. 569) that the *hupokritai* in Didache are Jews. It seems plain that the author or compiler of Didache was calling attention to the dangers inherent in a situation where some Christians were trying to demonstrate their spiritual superiority by using extraordinary fast days. We seem to be in the presence of a controversy over calendrical usage, such as characterized the dispute of the Essenes with orthodox Judaism about the dates of feasts (implications of which can be found in the New Testament), or the later controversy in the Church about the date of Easter. The dissidents are not being accused of "hypocrisy" or moral turpitude in our modern sense. Their self-conscious rectitude, whether or not it was derived from sectarian practice, plainly constituted a threat to the unity of the Christian community. This seems to be the burden of the injunctions of Didache ii 6 and iv 12. Once more we are in the presence of a legalism which can find some justification for its interpretation of law or custom, and in the process of doing so adopt—albeit unconsciously—an attitude of superiority.

Our treatment of the words which head this appendix was done independently of Winckler's work in the TWNT, but we have checked some points from it, as we have indicated. It is necessary to indicate our disagreement with some of the conclusions which Winckler draws from the rabbinic writings. His assertion (TWNT, VI, p. 563, n. 26) that Rabbi Eleazar used *ḥānēf* in the sense of "heretic" must be contested: it is the legal oppressor, not the heretic, who is compared with a menstruous woman. Similarly with Rabbi Benjamin in the same note: what is under discussion by that rabbi is the legal casuist who oppresses people. Although Winckler—in our view—correctly estimates the evidence from the classical and Hellenistic sources, he quite fails to assess the contribution made by the Jewish concept of law when dealing with LXX.

X. MIRACLES IN MATTHEW

The Old Testament proclaims, without argument (since it knew nothing of Greek logic), what has come to be called "theism." This is most often expressed in such terms as "the living God," the personal, active, overruling Lord of heaven and earth. Throughout the Bible, Old Testament and New, God is conceived as the only and original source of power, from whom all authority is derived. In the biblical view, there are no limitations to God's power; with him all things are possible. Here, however, it is necessary to insist that one of the marks which distinguished the Hebrews from the rest of mankind was the assumption—and in the face of national corruption, the insistence—that God's power is not arbitrary or a matter of whim like that of Poseidon, for example, but is always a declaration of a will that can never be anything but holy and righteous. The God of Israel was also unique in another way. While there was nothing particularly distinctive about seeing God as the Lord of nature—most divinities in the Middle East were nature gods, some of them crudely so—it *was* a unique insight to see God as the sole Lord of history. (It is important to remember at this point that for all the emphasis on God's rule over the events of human history, Israel came to understand this crucial concept through her own experiences during the Exodus from Egypt, an event which for all succeeding generations left an indelible mark on the biblical record.) In the Old Testament there was never any question as to whether or not the Lord of nature and of history could perform "mighty wonders"; the Exodus alone was sufficient proof. For the New Testament, which inherited Israel's faith, the outward sign of the delivering power of God was the raising of Jesus from the dead. In both cases, Exodus and Resurrection, God acted from outside human history, and yet within its framework. The Exodus was not simply an event in history—it was enshrined in the Passover Feast, itself no mere commemoration but a pledge for the present and the explanation of the future. Similarly the Resurrection, commemorated at Easter and on each Sunday, was not merely a past event in history—it was the wellspring of all Christian faith and hope.

It is only with this understanding of the God of Israel as an active, all-powerful God of history that we can go on to discuss the miracles with any meaning. For the biblical writers, miracles are interventions by divine power in the affairs of men, especially when considered as the means by which God declared himself and his purposes to men. In biblical times, the absence of any such concept as "the laws of nature" (as developed by Francis Bacon and his successors) made it necessary to use some such term as "sign" to denote extraordinary happenings beyond ordinary human experience.

Far too much attention has been focused on the miracle narratives by exponents of the "form criticism" school. Bultmann maintains that the stories were told to emphasize the superior status of Jesus as a wonder-worker, a thaumaturge; he finds the origin of the stories in the quite common Hellenistic miracle stories (cf. Rudolf Bultmann, *Study of the Synoptic Gospels,* in *Form Criticism,* ed. and tr. F. C. Grant [London, 1934], pp. 36 ff., and Chicago: Willett, 1934). One difficulty with this view is the exaggerated form in which the similarity is usually stated. Another is that the Hellenistic wonder-workers in question are, so far as we know, post-Christian in date. Still another difficulty comes from the assumption that Greek religion and mythology were already being accepted by Jews en masse during the late pre-Christian and early Christian periods.

In his *Die Geschichte der synoptischen Tradition,* 2d ed. (Tübingen: Vandenhoek & Rupprecht, 1931), pp. 236 ff. and 247 ff.), Bultmann recommends that we consider that both Greek and Jewish "wonder stories" arose in the same atmosphere, and so *pari passu* did the gospel miracle narratives. Bultmann holds that faith, as Jesus demanded it, was not faith in him as a person (though Bultmann prefers to speak of a "faithful adherence to the preaching of Jesus"), but simply trust in him as a wonder-worker. The writers of our gospels, and the oral tradition underlying them, according to Bultmann, were simply concerned to demonstrate the proofs of Jesus' supernatural powers.

To accept such an interpretation, it would be necessary to find an explanation for the total absence of any appeal in the rest of the New Testament to the factor of miracle in any *explanation* of the person of Jesus. And how to account for the way in which the evangelists play down the element of wonder in the stories? The NT writers never use the words *teras, terata* (wonder, wonders) alone to describe the miracles of Jesus and the apostles: they always qualify the words with *semeion, semeia* (sign, signs), and indeed in John, only the word "sign" is admissible.

Substantially, Bultmann's position is also that of Martin Dibelius (*From Tradition to Gospel,* tr. from the rev. 2d ed. of *Die Formgeschichte des Evangeliums* by the author and B. L. Woolf [London: Nicholson, 1934], pp. 70 ff.; New York: Scribner; 1934). Dibelius has it that the miracle narratives in the New Testament belong to a class he calls *Novellen* and not only assumes that these stories belonged to a well-known genre, but also provides us with a totally unattested class of "storytellers" in the primitive Church whose function it was to collect from Jewish and Gentile sources stories of heroes and gods whose exploits could be assimilated into the story of Jesus, in order to improve his public image (p. 96).

Neither Dibelius nor Bultmann seem able to agree on *which* miracle stories are intended merely as "wonder-tales" and which are "paradigms" (narratives with an important "pronouncement" embodied in them). Before accepting their conjectures, the reader should note that there is a total lack of historical evidence for the motives imputed to the NT writers, and should consider several other vital factors as well.

(1) One of the few things that is certain about the universe as we now know it is the total *un*certainty of any firm statement of invariable cause and effect. It is not even certain how far we are justified in speaking of "invariable sequence." Only the most unsophisticated among us can any longer pretend that miracles, in whatever sense understood, "cannot happen."

(2) Perhaps far more serious—from the standpoint of the biblical student—is the downgrading of the Old Testament which the view of Bultmann and Dibelius involves. Dibelius is certain that the miracle stories were simply "tales" and not intended for incorporation into sermons on salvation. But the Old Testament is abundantly clear that what our English Bibles call God's "mighty acts" are in the majority of cases a declaration of his overruling providence

in caring for his elect people—individuals are seldom the object of miracles in the Old Testament. The Hebrew words commonly translated by *teras* (wonder) and later by the Latin *miraculum* (hence the English "miracle") do not have the kind of connotation commonly evoked by the word "miracle" in modern English. Generally speaking, the OT words designate "signs," in the same sense in which the prophets used symbolic acts designed to effect what they portrayed (cf. II Kings xiii 14–19; Jer xxvii–xxviii). In no case are these signs used for self-aggrandizement, but always as manifestations of the overruling purposes of God.

(3) A premise underlying much modern writing on miracles holds that because there is nothing which cannot ultimately be proved or disproved by rational understanding, then miracles in the sense of God's overruling of the natural order *cannot* happen. Conservative Christians may well have brought this attitude upon themselves by relying too heavily on the value of miracles as proof of, for example, the divinity of Jesus. The result has been, in much Christian apologetic, a disastrous cleavage between the preaching of the kingdom by Jesus on the one hand, and the necessity of dealing with the gospel miracle stories on the other. The evidential emphasis on miracles has been much used since the seventeenth and eighteenth centuries, but it belongs essentially with belief in the fixity of the natural order, and belief in a doctrine of immutability in the so-called laws of nature. This emphasis had no place in the minds of the NT writers, for whom miracles might be expected daily, and for whom miracles were no necessary sign of divinity. Paul can attribute miracles to the forces of evil (II Thess ii 9), in the gospels the Pharisee community can be represented as casting out devils (Matt xii 27; cf. Luke xi 19), and the disciples of Jesus are puzzled by their own inability to exorcise a demon (Mark ix 28; Matt xvii 20). Jesus himself emphatically rejects the view that miracles are needed as evidence of his own status (Mark viii 11–12 and parallels).

(4) Both Bultmann and Dibelius suggest that the whole framework for the miracle stories is such that they exactly fit the formal pattern of Hellenistic wonder-stories, and are therefore like them in lack of credibility. This framework is said to be (a) a description of the condition of the patient, with attendant detail; (b) a description of the cure together with the words (if any) of the wonder-worker; (c) the admiring comments of the bystanders to-

gether with the behavior of the former sufferer. In view of the nature of stories of healing, similarity in form is to be expected. But such comparisons offer little or no basis for the evaluation of the content of the story itself. Parallels are not hard to find in the claims made for patent medicines during the past century.

The task of interpreting the miracles is of supreme importance in view of the fact that they loom so large in the gospels. John records only seven, but in the majority of cases they are the points upon which important blocks of teaching are built (cf. especially John vi). The miracle narratives should not just be accepted as they stand and then "spiritualized" away. For all the service that Alan Richardson's *Miracle-Stories of the Gospels* (New York: Harper / London: SCM, 1941) rendered, it must be agreed with James Kallas (*The Significance of the Synoptic Miracles,* London: SPCK, 1961) that Richardson is so intent on discovering homiletic and religious meaning in the narratives that one is left wondering precisely how far the *events* recorded any longer have validity. As Kallas (p. 4) rightly observes, Richardson so allegorizes Mark's two feeding stories that the events are of small moment. The blind man at Bethsaida is summarized in the words "whether [he] was a historical person or not is a secondary question" (Richardson, p. 86). Richardson has on many occasions done great service to NT scholarship, particularly in exposing the frequent pretensions of some whose hold on historical evidence is slender at best; but we are unlikely to find satisfactory explanations in his work for the integral connection which the gospels make between Jesus' proclamation of the reign of God and the signs by which that preaching was accompanied.

Raymond E. Brown points out that "the miracle was not primarily an external guarantee of the coming of the kingdom; it was one of the means by which the kingdom came" (*New Testament Essays* [Milwaukee: Bruce, 1965], p. 171). It is important to see miracles in the gospel narrative in the setting of Jesus' proclamation of the Kingdom: miracle is not an appendage, a verifying after-thought; it is, on the plain statement of Jesus himself, bound up with the announcement of the reign of God (cf. Matt xii 22–30; Luke xi 14–23). For Jesus, the characteristic of his healings was the manifestation of the warfare between God and Satan, good and evil, light and darkness.

This concern with the conflict between God and Satan is important, as there is perhaps nothing which has fascinated men more than the problem of the origin of evil. To deny the existence of evil in men is consummate folly, but when we have said that all the faculties of man's being are shot through with potentialities for evil we are no nearer solving the question of its origin. It may be that we are not likely to arrive at anything which is better for popular use than the personalized and concrete "Satan."

The task of understanding the miracles is not made easier by taking a superior attitude toward the (supposed) simplicity of a first-century belief in a personalized, concrete evil. It is true that the figure of Satan was a latecomer in Jewish thinking, but by the dawn of the NT era that figure had come to occupy a very important position. The NT picture of sharply divided dominions (cf. especially I John v 19), epitomized by the teaching and practice of Jesus himself (cf. Mark iii 22 ff. and also Mark i 24), is a faithful mirror of the kind of language which is now so familiar to us from the Dead Sea scrolls. For Jesus, the casting out of devils was an essential part of his ministry, which had itself begun with Jesus throwing down the gauntlet in OT terms in the temptation narrative. This narrative will be discussed in its proper place. Here it is sufficient to point out that where the Old Testament sees God's "mighty acts" as primarily focused on and conveyed through a people, the gospels see them as initially channeled through one person, Jesus. For Jesus, the exorcisms and healings were a direct indication of the assertion of the reign of God (Matt xii 28), even though after a ministry of such signs (Luke xiii 32) it must have seemed that the victory lay temporarily with the enemy (Luke xxii 53).

The OT writers do not divide man into body, soul, and mind; "salvation" in the OT is the "saving" of the whole man—deliverance from evil, of whatever kind. Healing, casting out of devils is an assertion of order against chaos, the reign of God over the dominion of darkness. Kallas (*Significance of the Synoptic Miracles*, p. 64), and Arthur Gabriel Hebert (*The Throne of David: A Study of the Fulfilment of the Old Testament in Jesus Christ and His Church* [London: Faber, 1941], pp. 143 ff.; New York: Morehouse, 1941) before him, emphasize the eschatological character of the healings which Jesus performed on the Sabbath, asserting the creative character of God's work.

What have often been called the "nature miracles" (such as the stilling of the storm in Mark iv 37 ff.) can equally be seen as a demonstration of the order of God's dominion against the disorder and chaos which can and does threaten men. As Raymond Brown points out (*New Testament Essays,* pp. 175–76), the restoration of order to God's creation is a constant theme of OT prophecy, especially in the Isaianic collection.

It is possible that some of the miracles as now recorded may originally have been parables. The incident of the coin in the fish's mouth (Matt xvii 24–27) is perhaps easier to understand if this was originally a parable which changed its form in the course of transmission, its meaning now lost. There is certainly no suggestion that Peter did catch a fish with a coin in its mouth.

Attention has already been directed to what OT scholars have labeled "prophetic symbolism." To this category would appear to belong the miraculous catch of fish (Luke v 10 emphatically does give this meaning), the blasting of the fig tree (Mark xi 12 ff. and 20 ff.), and possibly also the walking on the water (Matt xiv 22–33; cf. Gen i 2). If indeed the nature miracles, or some of them, were prophetic signs, then they share with similar signs in the Old Testament the purpose of proclaiming to men the gracious will of God and the sovereignty of his rule.

Some mention must be made of the element of faith, which finds so prominent a place in the narratives. If in the past miracles have been stressed in order to lead men to faith in God, this concern is not paramount in the gospels. There, it is man's faith which causes God to respond with his saving act (cf. Matt xv 28; Mark ix 24; Luke v 20; etc.), because such trust in God is witness to a humility which accepts God's sovereign rule. Lack of faith can put obstacles in the way of open declaration of that rule (cf. Matt xvii 19–20). Jesus declares that wholeness, "salvation," has been brought to the sufferer through that sufferer's faith (cf. Luke viii 48, xvii 19, xviii 42).

It is worth while to add one comment at this stage. We are still accustomed in common speech to refer to the extraordinary as "miraculous" and our vocabulary is full of such phrases as "miracle of endurance," "miracle of modern surgery," or we speak of the "miraculous mind of a Newton" (or whomsoever we choose). Yet there are those who assert that miracles came to an end at the close of the apostolic period—this in spite of John xiv 12 and the accounts of signs performed by the apostles in the early days of the Church (Acts iii 1–10). Either the understanding of miracle shared by the authors of this commentary differs radically from that held by those who make the assertion, or those who make it are holding to views about the physical world which cannot be sustained by the present evidence. Much will in any case depend upon the share which we are prepared to allow to human apprehension and understanding in our appreciation of the extraordinary.

Note. This part, X, has intentionally not considered the terms which John's gospel uses in dealing with miracle. It seems better to leave all such considerations to the author of the commentaries on the Johannine books, and confine attention here to the synoptic gospels. The reader is referred to Raymond Brown's Introduction in his first volume of *The Gospel According to John, i–xii,* AB, vol. 29, New York: Doubleday, 1966. When reference was made to Brown's excellent study of miracles in his *New Testament Essays,* we discovered that the treatment given to miracle there not only closely resembled our own approach, but there was even what might appear to the reader to be verbal similarity. However, our first inclination to rewrite this section was more than outweighed by our satisfaction that three commentators of different confessions had found common ground on this sensitive question.

XI. PARABLES IN MATTHEW

One popular definition of parable describes it as "an earthly story with a heavenly meaning." This is a woefully thin description for a form of teaching that angered Jesus' critics so. However well adapted to modern homiletic concerns, the parables in the gospels were directed to asking fundamental questions about spiritual issues in the time of Jesus.

We have used the phrase "the parables in the gospels" advisedly. In order to recognize the importance of the parable as a tool of instruction, it is essential to know something of the history of this device. So far as we know at present, Jesus was the first person to use this method of teaching extensively. The form had already been established; what Jesus did was to take it and make such wide and varied use of it that he gave the parable as a method of teaching renewed vitality. In fact, he perfected the form so well that Christians were reluctant to use it thereafter, knowing they could never be as effective as he was. In addition to hesitation about using a form brought to such perfection by Jesus, the influence of Paul—who did not use the device—was probably important. Paul was more familiar with exposition that examined the precise meanings of words and phrases. Whatever the experience of his earlier life, it seems unlikely that the homiletic exposition of law would have appealed to him. This older homiletic method of exposition continued to be used by the rabbis, especially by Rabbi Aqiba (ca. A.D. 80–130).

The parables of Jesus have manifested an astonishing viability in interpretation. In a wide variety of homiletic circumstances, they have stood the test of constant reapplication and reinterpretation in the light of changing religious and social conditions. Sometimes, a parable causes difficulty because of the dissimilarity between the common assumptions shared by the parable and its inaugural audience and the social customs of its later readers. Most of the difficulty, for example, which is felt about the story of the unjust steward (Luke xvi 1–8) arises from twentieth-century ignorance of the laws which governed trading practice at that time.

The parable is found as a form in the Old Testament, but it is not used very extensively. Nevertheless, its use and the manner of its use—together with some consideration of the persons represented as using it—prompted us to certain conclusions. The first genuine parable in the Old Testament is the hypothetical case presented by Nathan to David (II Sam xii 1–6), and is sharply distinguished from allegory or fable. Fables are usually animal stories that point up a moral, and are primitive in form and content, however well adapted for continuing use. Allegory—essentially a Greek device—is generally rooted in mythology; the identification between an idea or object and its symbol is easy. The rise of allegory was the concomitant of the development of philosophical thinking in the Greek intellectual revolution of the seventh–fourth centuries B.C. II Sam xii 1–6, wholly unlike the fable of the trees in Judg ix 7–15, presents a hypothetical legal case, with a possible issue of guilty or not guilty. David understood it as a specific legal issue which was being presented to him, and his reaction was to set the appropriate penalty. The high incidence of what has been called "covenant lawsuit" in the prophets has been examined carefully by a number of first-class scholars, following the lead of G. E. Mendenhall (*Law and Covenant in Israel and the Ancient Near East*, Pittsburgh: The Biblical Colloquium, 1955). But it now seems clear from present evidence that the Israelite prophets may well have been what can loosely be called "jurists": men concerned with, versed in, and consulted upon, aspects of civil law, as distinct from ceremonial law, which was the concern of the priests.

The expression "civil law" demands careful explanation and limitation, in the face of the division of our own law into categories of law which deal with civil, criminal, property, and ecclesiastical jurisdiction and the like. The function of the prophets, we believe, was to look after the moral and social behavior of the covenant-people of Israel, comprehending all the facets of law which we divide into separate departments. Leaving to priests matters of ceremonial and cultic law, what did concern the prophets was what may with justice be called "prophetic covenant-law"—a pragmatic, empirical approach to the day-to-day living of Israel, as a people and as individuals, living by God's will. It was a homiletic exposition of law, composed of official case law and later custom, embracing every facet of life lived under the Old Covenant. Civil case law, apodictic moral law, criminal law, commercial law, land tenure—all came under the purview of these men whom hitherto we have mainly regarded as simply vehicles of God's revelation. Yet the clues were at hand, had we looked for them, and one of them is to be found in H. W. Fowler's *A Dictionary of Modern English Usage* (2d ed., revised by Ernest Gowers [Oxford University Press, 1965], p. 558). Fowler wrote: *"Allegory* (uttering things otherwise) and *parable* (putting side by side) are almost exchangeable terms. The object of each is, at least ostensibly, to enlighten the hearer by submitting to him a case in which he has apparently no direct concern, and upon which therefore a disinterested judgement may be elicited from him, as Nathan submitted to David the story of the poor man's ewe lamb. Such judgement given, the question will remain for the hearer whether Thou art the man: whether the conclusion to which the dry light of disinterestedness has helped him holds also for his own concerns."

The prophets claimed an intimate acquaintance with the previous decisions of God (cf. Amos iii 7; Jer xxiii 18, 22, and see also I Kings xxii 19 ff.; Job i 6 ff.), and it is at least possible that their apparently easy access to the royal courts of Judah and Israel—and even before that in the united monarchy—indicates a highly privileged place in the national structure. Something of this nature is necessary to explain the immunity of, for example, Micaiah ben Imlah (I Kings xxii) in spite of his disdain for royal authority; of Elijah, whose persecution was largely instigated by Jezebel, (with Ahab's reluctant acquiescence); and of Jeremiah, when the nobility hesitated to dispatch him out of hand because of his unpatriotic preaching. As early in the prophetic history as Samuel, the prophet (although raised in cultic circles in Shiloh) seriously contended for the superiority of the prophetic office, and also apparently made serious attempts to elevate that office to the total exclusion of the priesthood. (For the importance of Samuel in the history and development of prophecy, cf. W. F. Albright, *Archaeology, Historical Analogy, and Early Biblical Tradition,* The Rockwell Lectures, 1962 [Louisiana State University Press, 1966], pp. 42 ff.) Even after the Babylonian Exile, and before apocalyptic had sharply illuminated the conflict felt between the overt and the hidden in the will of God, the prophets Haggai and Zechariah used their office to chide the returned exiles for not rebuilding the temple. They plainly felt that molding responsible opinion was part of their prerogative.

The emergence of men professionally trained in law, who did not depend for their effectiveness on homiletics to emphasize the demands of covenant-law, meant the gradual disappearance of the prophetic order from Israelite society. It is worth noticing, however, that the fate of the desecrated altar stones in 1 Macc iv 46 still apparently depended on possible future prophetic advice. The ascendancy of professional teachers of the Law—the beginnings of the process can be seen in Ezra—meant that by the time of the ministry of Jesus the teachers of law had abandoned the parable as a means of instruction.

Two final references from the Old Testament will suffice here. A parable illustrative of the use of case law or legal process can be seen in Isaiah v, which is cast in poetic form. It points a case, presented at the beginning in metaphorical terms, concerning the rights of an owner to dispose as he sees fit of an unproductive vineyard. From vs. 8 onwards, the hypothetical case is changed to a formal charge, and the figurative illustration is made concrete: Israel is guilty of covenant disloyalty, both toward God and man, and the penalty is exile. Psalm lxxviii rehearses Israelite history as "parable" (vs. 2, Heb. *māshāl*); the tenor of the psalm is an indictment of Israelite rebellion against covenant-law.

This study will confine its remarks on textual and allied problems in the parables as recounted by Matthew to comparisons with parallel material in Mark and Luke. One difference in the way in which transmitted material is handled by two of the evangelists can be usefully demonstrated from Matt v 25 ff. In the Matthean context, the passage occurs in that part of the Great Instruction which deals with the Law, whereas in Luke (xii 58 ff.) it appears in a section concerned with the crisis produced by the coming of The Man. In Luke we have a warning about the urgency of the situation in which Israel finds herself—one in which time is short, and the decision to accept or reject a "day of the Lord" (epitomized in Jesus) must be made quickly. The context in Luke reinforces the sense of urgency. Jesus' opponents are castigated for failure to read the signs of the times (xii 54–56), they have been warned that the delay in the householder's coming to cast up his accounts is apparent only (xii 41–48). The saying is significantly followed by the warning that the fate of the Galileans may be theirs as well (xiii 1–5), like that of the unproductive tree (xiii 6–9). So far this is straightforward; the man called to account is God's Israel, about to be put to the test for failure to understand the nature of the challenge which is posed by the ministry of Jesus. It must be said that in the context of Luke chapters xii and xiii, this parable makes very good sense. Yet this is not quite as neat and ordered, and not quite so obvious, as perhaps our summary has made it. Assuming the above interpretation to be correct, not only does Luke's version cast Jesus in the role of accuser (which is explicitly denied in John v 45), but the language employed is—to say the least—violent, and the accuser is depicted as dragging the defendant by the scruff of the neck. If we add to this the close relationship between Jesus and the Father which is assumed all through the synoptic gospels, then we have the odd circumstances of accuser and judge being in league together.

Matthew's version puts the saying in a wholly different context. In Maithew, the language is not only less forceful, but the exhortation appears to be designed as reinforcement of the lesson of charity emphasized in v 21–24, and no amount of manipulation will produce anything like the Lukan confrontation between Jesus and Israel. It appears that we have, in Matthew, the *ending* of a parable, the substance of which has been lost, but which was remembered as being important enough to be cited frequently. It is probable that the original parable, of which only the ending remains, was some kind of story with the "accuser" as a Satan-figure after the manner of Job, or Rev xii 10. The Greek words employed by Matthew and Luke, and by the Apocalypse, all indicate such a figure—a "prosecutor" or "adversary." We are in this instance uncertain of the aetiological motif of the saying, but the use which Jesus made of the parable as a teaching form was so perfect that we can almost with certainty rule out any question of expansion of the original materials—contraction is far more likely.

We have spent some time on this example because it illustrates three things. First, it emphasizes the care taken to preserve the oral tradition, though different strands of the tradition might be found at variance as to the precise origin of an individual item in that tradition. Secondly, it underlines the possibility that we are employing an altogether too modern technique by positing another source to explain seeming documentary dependence for material common to Matthew and Luke, but not found in Mark. Thirdly, not only do similar items of the tradition appear in different contexts in the synoptic gospels, but the wording is often so markedly different as to demand—on the "documentary" theory—an almost unlimited number of hypothetical sources.

THE PARABLE AUDIENCE

Jeremias, in his *Parables of Jesus* (pp. 33 ff.), calls attention to the changes which one finds in the synoptic gospels from one kind of audience to another. For the detailed examination which Jeremias gives, the reader must be referred to his invaluable work. In the scope of this Introduction, we can only hope to indicate some of the ways in which we find the change of audience significant.

As we have already seen (in Part V, above), the word "disciple" in Luke's tradition refers to the life of the continuing community, and no sharp distinction is drawn in the use of the word in Luke between the inner circle of the disciples and the crowds who followed Jesus on some occasions. Accordingly, where the Matthean tradition ascribes the parable of the lost sheep to the private instruction of the inner circle of disciples (Matt xviii 1), in Luke (xv 3–7) the parable is addressed to Jesus' opponents. (Mark agrees with Matthew in making a distinction between public and private teaching. In Mark the saying about salt—ix 50—is addressed to the disciples, while in Luke—xiv 25—it is a "public" saying.) It should be noted in passing that the Johannine tradition attributes "shepherd" sayings to the opponents of Jesus (John ix 40, x 6, 16 ff.). If we are correct in assuming the quasi-legal background of "parable," then the interpretation of "covenant" was common ground to friends and foes alike.

In this particular instance the "lost sheep" *may* be an errant member of the community of the New Covenant or (in the Lukan context) the Gentile for whom under the Old Covenant little concern was shown. Which interpretation came first we have at present no certain means of knowing. Jesus may himself have used the parable in different contexts; but the possibility ought not to be ruled out that Jesus told the story and invited comment and interpretation from his audience—a method of eliciting response which was introduced by Socrates. Some such explanation may underlie Mark iv 10 describing the parables of vss. 21–32 as addressed to the disciples, while later stating (vss. 33–34) that they were addressed to a general audience. Matthew (xiii 34 f.) is in agreement with the second of the Markan statements.

Something of the "audience-history" of the parables may be historically preserved in the Gospel of Thomas (xxxiv) where the saying about the blind leading the blind stands alone. In Matthew (xv 14) it is directed against the Pharisees, whereas in Luke (vi 39) it is a solemn warning to a general audience. In Matt xv 12–14 the saying appears in some private questioning by the disciples about ritual cleanliness, and arises out of the opposition of the Pharisees, a context where Mark is without the saying. Luke places it (vi 39 ff.) in his version of the Great Instruction.

No amount of attempted harmonization will dispel the uncertainties attaching to other sayings in the category of parable, where two different audiences are envisaged for the same saying. Such is the case in Matt vii 16–20, where the lessons to be derived from the tree and its fruit are expounded to the crowd as well as to the disciples, and in another instance to the Pharisees (xii 33–37; cf. Luke viii 16, xi 13—the lamp on its stand). It must be said, however, that in the case of sayings of a non-legal and metaphorical character, we are not dealing with the more extensive material of parable proper. Illustrative sayings are far more likely than parables to have been used on more than one occasion.

The assumption by Jeremias (among others[19]) that a process is discernible by which parables originally addressed to the crowds were later attributed to private teaching begs all manner of questions. First, the Lukan use of the word "disciple," to which attention has already been called, makes any Lukan evidence very hard to apply to this issue. Secondly, allowing that the evangelists felt free to choose material from accessible traditions, such choice would certainly have influenced them in the placing of this highly versatile parable material in what appear to us to be wholly disparate settings. Once again, if we are correct in seeing parable as a quasi-legal device, then the appearance of the same kind of "case" in more than one situation ought to be no matter for surprise. Thirdly, it is difficult to know what exactly Jeremias means when

---

[19] Cf. especially H. Montefiore, "A Comparison of the Parables According to Thomas and the Synoptic Gospels," NTS 7 (1960–61), 220 ff.

he states (of the parable of the lost sheep) that it "had lost its original *Sitz im Leben,* and had been transformed by the Church into hortatory material, a phenomenon of frequent occurrence" (*Parables of Jesus,* p. 43). Of what persons did the Church consist in this statement? Are the evangelists being considered innocent victims of later editors who were more preoccupied with congregational disputes than with the Kingdom of God? Was, or was not, Matthew (or any other evangelist, for that matter) a member of the "Church" under discussion? If for Jeremias the "Church" under consideration is held to be later than the milieu depicted in the NT books, then when did this transformation of parable from "proclamation" to "sermon" take place? There seems to be some Hegelian analysis at work here: (a) *thesis,* a parable of direct kerygmatic content, addressed either to a public or private audience; (b) *antithesis,* the same material, with some or all of its original meaning eroded by being placed in a different context by another writer; (c) *synthesis,* later ecclesiastical tradition which not only accepts (b), but transforms both it and (a) by making of them a community sermon.[20]

Having established that the parable was primarily a literary form arising from case law, we should point out that any legal statement or judgment, particularly of a constitutional character, is liable to appear and to be quoted in a multitude of situations and at different periods. In that case, statements as to the temporal priority of one gospel over another, based simply on parable material, do not really have much meaning.

In the light of our discussion of "parable" as quasi-legal in origin, the word "rabbi" as applied to Jesus is obviously important. The rabbi was and is still in conservative circles, an expositor and interpreter of case law. It has periodically been stated that the title "rabbi" in the gospels is an anachronism, that it came into use only after the destruction of the temple in A.D. 70, and some have gone so far as to argue that the title was actually unknown at the time of Jesus. However, the term is applied to Jesus no fewer than fourteen times in Matthew, Mark, and John, and both Mark and John preserve the even more honorific *rabbouni,*

[20] For a reasoned critique of the operation of Hegelian dialectic in F. C. Baur and his successors down to the present, see Johannes Munck, *The Acts of the Apostles,* pp. xxx ff.; cf. also W. F. Albright, *History, Archaeology and Christian Humanism* (New York: McGraw-Hill, 1964), pp. 272–84, for an analysis of Bultmann's philosophical presuppositions.

transliterated into English as "rabboni." (The term is caritative, rather in the tradition of calling the Czar of Russia "Little Father" before 1917.) While it is odd that the gospels should have gone out of their way to preserve a Jewish title at a time when missionary enterprise was already directed toward Gentiles, archaeology has disproved the claim that the title was anachronistic. The late E. L. Sukenik ("A Jewish Tomb on the Mount of Olives," *Tarbiz* 1 [1930], 140–41) reported the finding of an ossuary, quite certainly Jewish, on which the name of the deceased was matched by the description of him as *didaskalos* (Greek for "teacher," and the word used by Matthew and Mark to render the Hebrew "rabbi"). The question was examined later by Herschel Shanks ("Is the Title 'Rabbi' Anachronistic in the Gospels?" *Jewish Quarterly Review* 53 [1963], 337–45).

THE MATTHEAN TRADITION

Matthew's arrangement of parable material falls into three sections. The first deals with the Kingdom in broad outline; the second becomes more detailed, making application of the covenant principles; the third reflects Jesus' decision to go to Jerusalem for the last time. The parable material begins in Matthew at a significant point in his tradition. It first appears at the end of a period of instruction for the Twelve, at a point where Jesus' ministry has been questioned by John, and follows directly upon a charge against Jesus of collaboration with the powers of evil. With Jesus' demand to know who was genuinely of his community (xii 46 ff.), there appears to be a break with the synagogue, and the stage is set for decisive proclamation of the nature of the Kingdom. It is unlikely that John was the only one with questions, and so Matthew xiii begins with a public statement of the characteristics of the Kingdom.

The Nature of the Kingdom (Matt xiii 1–52)

Verses 3–8: *The Parable of the Sower* (Mark iv 3–8; Luke viii 5–8). This parable is noteworthy in that it occurs also in the Gospel of Thomas (ix), where it is embroidered with extra detail (e.g., a worm which destroys crops). The story of the sower fittingly opens this section on the kingdom, for the "case" which it presents looks to the End-time, to the harvest (a common eschatological motif). In spite of an interpretation offered later in the chapter (vss. 18–23), the story does not indicate whether the Sower is the Father or The Man. The primary emphasis is on the harvest itself, the miraculous end (in an age innocent of knowledge of plant biology) of the laborious task of sowing. It is impossible to determine with certainty whether in its first use Jesus intended in this parable to equate the harvest with his own preaching, and thus the winnowing-time with Israel's long history, or whether he saw this apparently misunderstood and ill-rewarded preaching as merely the sowing, with the harvest identified with a future judgment.

NT scholarship has emphasized the folly of allegorizing the parables, of attempting to see in each detail some identifiable feature of Christian proclamation, or some equation of this person or that with the Father or The Man. Such allegorizing, it is suggested, is the work of the primitive Christian community (as, e.g., in the interpretation offered in Matt xiii 18–23, 37–43) and was quite foreign to the mind of Jesus. This kind of supposition, based as it is on an ignorance of the allegorizing of detail in inter-testamental Jewish literature, has been assailed by Raymond Brown in his perceptive "Parable and Allegory Reconsidered" (in *New Testament Essays,* pp. 259 ff.).

Too frequently, commentators of various allegiances, having nothing in common but form criticism, assume without further argument that varying interpretations of parables in one gospel or another (or in different contexts in the same gospel) are the work of "the Church," or "the community," conceived as a body almost inimical to the pristine purity of the proclamation of Jesus. Some go so far as to determine which was the original interpretation of Jesus and which the result of later ecclesiastical thought. In this respect, the "Sower" parable is a *locus classicus* for all such commentators. If what we have said above on the nature of parables is correct, then the very flexibility of "case law" is sufficient to account for the use *by Jesus* of the same basic "case" or parable in different contexts, and with varying interpretations.

Verses 10–13: *Why Parables?* (cf. Mark iv 10–12; Luke viii 9–10). The parable of the sower having ended, the question posed by the disciples in vss. 10 ff. is natural enough. But a clearer answer is demanded than that commonly assumed—that Jesus deliberately veiled his teaching about the Kingdom in obscure allusions. Certainly in the political climate of his own time the unqualified use of the word "kingdom" would have been an invitation to armed revolt, with all the mundane entanglements which Jesus' own utterances explicitly excluded (cf. John xviii 36). We make the following two suggestions:

(1) Our examination of the distinction made in Matthew's tradition between private and public teaching is reinforced by Jesus' reply at this juncture. Direct, and even extended, teaching about the nature of the Kingdom can be given to the disciples, because they have been trained in their association with Jesus to examine afresh all their preconceptions about that Kingdom. Even here, however, Jesus employed "cases" in parables, easily remembered, so that the implications would not later be missed (cf. here J. Vincent, "Did Jesus Teach his Disciples to Learn by Heart?," StEv, III, No. 2 [1964], pp. 105–20). For those who came to Jesus expecting or demanding either a revolutionary or a wonder-worker, a different approach was necessary. Such people had to be given the opportunity to examine *their* preconceptions by means of "cases," parables, and encouraged to draw their own conclusions from them. It is worth noting that the important saying of Jesus at Matt xiii 11 has been preserved by all three synoptic gospels. Small wonder, too, that the Pharisees (xv 12) were angered by a use of case law which put them in the wrong.

(2) The disciples were given access to the prior decisions of the Father (xiii 11, 16–17); they were able to learn a great deal about the nature of the Kingdom from the parables because their faith was strong. But for those coming to Jesus who were unbelievers, often hostile or curious, the parables were a testing ground. For them the parables either obscured the Kingdom—in which event it was at least not misunderstood—or they provided an opportunity for opposition to the reign of God to declare itself openly. For some, the parables gave pause in which hesitation might change to faith. It is clear that in the Matthew tradition parables have a decisive function similar to that of the signs and the discourses in the Johannine tradition.

Verses 24–30: *The Weeds in the Field* (cf. Mark iv 26–29). Bearing in mind the functional distinction between the "Kingdom of Heaven" as the Messianic Community and the "Kingdom of the Father" as future event in Matthew, this parable discusses the proclamation of the Kingdom by Jesus.[21] If parable in the Old Testament began as case law connected with the Covenant, and both the rabbis and Jesus continued that use, then we are right in looking for an explanation of the Covenant in this parable, seen against the background of Jesus' proclamation. The first parable describes the sower sowing in good soil on the one hand, and indifferent and poor soil on the other; the second also sees the seed as good, but when growing, inextricably mixed with weeds sown by an enemy. Between the two parables comes the private reply to the disciples' question. Both the weeds in the second parable, and the indifferent and poor soil in the first, are to be seen as the opposition to Jesus' proclamation, an opposition which is in the end infidelity to the Covenant which all his teaching implies or assumes. That the second parable is capable of being used, and later was perhaps almost exclusively used (cf. I Cor v 4) as warning against overhasty judgment, or overzealous disciplinary action, in no way militates against this interpretation. It is entirely possible that *both* interpretations derive from Jesus. A comparison of this passage with Mark iv 26–29 will illustrate the great flexibility of the parable form. In spite of a similarity of wording with this Matthean example, Mark stresses the miraculous growth of the proclaimed Kingdom.

Verses 31–32: *The Mustard Seed* (Mark iv 30–32). The emphasis is not on the future size of the Kingdom compared with its insignificant beginnings, but on the purpose of God which assures its growth. The thought is echoed in Acts xiii 41, quoting Hab i 5: The scoffers and the opponents are reduced to silence before the miracle of divine intervention.

Verse 33: *The Leaven* (Luke xiii 20–21). Again we have a concentration on the overruling purpose of God, similar to that found in the preceding example.

Attention has already been called to the quotation from Ps lxxviii, which is here inserted by the evangelist to explain Jesus' teaching methods. The parables are concerned, as is the psalm, with God's choice of Israel, and with the extension of that Israel into the Kingdom which Jesus proclaimed. In these days which led up to the inauguration of the New Covenant as in the time of the Sinai Covenant, there are the faithless who cannot see the

---

[21] Matthew uses the phrase "Kingdom of God" only once (at xii 13), for which see commentary, ad loc.

purpose of God. For them, the "cases" embodied in the parables are a hindrance to understanding just as they are valuable assistance to the faithful who see, and who therefore understand (cf. Mark xiii 51, and also—for links between this theme and John's gospel— G. L. Phillips, "Faith and Vision in the Fourth Gospel," in *Studies in the Fourth Gospel,* ed. F. L. Cross, London: Mowbray, 1957. For an examination of Phillips' theme, cf. Brown, *John, i–xii,* Appendix I [3]).

Verses 44–46: *The Treasure in the Field.* Whether this saying expresses God's mercy and condescension in seeking man (cf. John iii 16), or—more probably—the joy of the disciples in having found the secret of the Kingdom, hidden from the faithless, either interpretation demonstrates the costliness of the Kingdom. Jesus must give himself completely and the disciples no less: the disciple must match his teacher's effort. The "fine pearl" of vss. 45–46 makes the same point. For Jesus and for the disciples, the claims of the Kingdom are absolute.

Verses 47–50: *The Net.* This parable fittingly closes the chapter, for it anticipates the End-time, the harvest, the gathering in of all kinds, good and bad, Jew and Gentile, when final judgment will be made. The saying also had an immediate meaning regarding the circumstances under which it was told: criticism of those admitted to the fellowship of the Kingdom, to discipleship, is an encroachment upon the prerogatives of the Lord of the harvest.

The Community (Matt xviii 12–14, 23–35)

The second grouping of parable material follows a significant part of the narrative (xiii 53 – xvii 27), in which Matthew deals with an increasing tension between Jesus and his critics. Jesus runs into disbelief in his own countryside (xiii 53–58), the execution of John the Baptist compels his withdrawal, and he faces the challenge to faith and understanding in the rehearsal of the Messianic Banquet (xiv 13–21). The circle of disciples draws closer to him in the face of increasing opposition on the part of the lawyers (xv 1–20), and in response to the demand for a sign (xvi 1–4), Jesus warns against the teaching of the Pharisees and Sadducees (xvi 5–12).

The confession of Jesus' Messiahship by Peter (xvi 13–20) is a decisive point in the Matthean record. It is immediately followed

by the first intimation of the coming Passion and death of the
Master, and a plain warning to the disciples of the cost of their
allegiance.

The vision on the mountain (xvii 1–9) completes a narrative
in which Jesus has made clear statements and Peter, speaking for
the rest, has acknowledged his mission. Jesus here begins, in
Matthew's scheme, to outline some of the "cases" with which the
infant community must soon be concerned.

Verses 12–14: *The Lost Sheep* (Luke xv 3 ff.). In the Matthean
tradition, the case of the lost sheep appears to follow directly
from Jesus' statement about the care members of the covenant-
community must have for each other. The Lukan version places
the parable more firmly in the context of the community which
grows out of the Israel of the Old Covenant. The following parable
of the prodigal son (Luke xv 11–32) may be interpreted as dealing
with the duty of reconciliation within the Kingdom of the Messianic
community. It seems to apply to the need, crucial in the infant
Church, to bring together the adherents of the Sinai Covenant
who had never strayed from the Father on the one hand, with
Gentiles, who seek pardon and reconciliation along with Jews, on
the other, in the community of the New Covenant.

It is hoped that the discussion of parables below will illustrate
our central contention—that the parable was a literary device which
grew out of interpretation of covenant-law. We do not dispute
the legitimacy of parable-interpretation in the later Church, and we
have no wish to minimize the flexibility of the parables of Jesus,
especially in homiletic context. Very plainly, when Jewish Christianity had all but disappeared, and tension between Gentile and Jew
in the Church was a thing of the past, the interpretation of parables
would undergo considerable change. We are concerned, however,
to point out that the movement of the church into an *exclusively*
Gentile milieu was not so early as often supposed. (For example,
the first Corinthian letter, with its Semitisms and OT allusions,
ought to give pause to any assertion that most of Paul's converts
were already Gentile.)

We believe that many commentators on the parables bring to
their study an unconscious background of homiletic interpretation
which belongs to the post-Jewish history of the Church. In doing
so they tend to find a development in the material which may not
in fact be there. We suggest that the parable material, whether

dealing with relations between individuals or with ethnic groups, is best understood *in the New Testament context* as concerned wholly with the impact which the community of a new covenant must make on the thinking of those to whom Jesus first addressed the parables.

Verses 23–35: *The Unmerciful Servant*. This parable is found only in Matthew, and pursues the theme of forbearance and forgiveness in the community of the Kingdom. Whatever remission the disciples have received will be canceled in the End-time if they do not exercise the same mercy that has been bestowed upon them.

The Covenant (Matt xx 1–16, xxi 28–41, xxii 1–14, xxiv 45–51; xxv 1–13, 14–30). Knowing well the implications of his decision to go to Jerusalem for the last time, Jesus—in Matthew's arrangement—can be more specific about the meaning of his teaching. However reinterpreted in later commentary and homiletic, the parables in this section are crisis parables, reflecting the compulsion under which both Jesus and his opponents acted, from their conflicting understanding of the Covenant.

xx 1–16: The Workers in the Vineyard. Israel could claim, with justice, that she had borne the burden of God's revelation to the world for many centuries, with all the obligations of a Law associated with the Covenant. (For the Law as "burden," cf. Acts xv 28.) While from time to time Israel had by conquest and assimilation added other groups to the people, long before the ministry of Jesus Israel was a highly self-conscious ethnic entity, proud of its separation, expectant of privileged treatment by God for having been the keeper of his word. But the proclamation of Jesus, though addressed to the people of the Covenant, did not exclude the Gentile world. (Cf. here the important monograph of Joachim Jeremias, *Jesu Verheissung für die Völker*, the Franz Delitzsch Lectures for 1953 (Stuttgart: Kohlhammer, 1956) in the English translation by S. H. Hooke, *Jesus' Promise to the Nations*, London: SCM / Naperville, Ill.: Allenson, 1958). In Matthew's version Jesus clarifies his point by speaking of a vineyard—substitute for Israel in the prophetic literature and in the Psalms. Moreover, the phrase "Kingdom of heaven," used to denote the Messianic community of Jesus, clearly indicates that he is talking about the admission of those who have not borne the burden; they will be judged equally with those who have.

xx 28–32: The Two Sons. This parable is prompted by the

question of the chief priests and elders about Jesus' authority, which Jesus counters with a searching question of his own about the authority of John. Jesus demands a plain commitment, for or against the authenticity of John's calling. His questioners refuse and so Jesus recounts this parable and the next, the two being closely linked. "Son," as an appellation of Israel, is common in the Old Testament; this is the sense here. Those who would be most zealous in claiming the title of "son" were the most culpable in their lack of response to John: the outsiders, the "non-observants," had repented.

Verses 33–41: *The Vineyard* (Mark xii 1–9). Here again we have the familiar figure of the vineyard for Israel. The accusation and verdict in the parable is that Israel has failed in its commitment to the Covenant, and in the death of Jesus would fail even more grievously. Accusation and verdict are followed by a judgment that the Kingdom will henceforward be given to others. This parable illustrates very strikingly what has aptly been called the "covenant lawsuit in the prophets" (cf. article of that title by H. B. Huffmon, JBL 78 1959), 285–95. Undoubtedly this parable looks to the inauguration of a new Covenant.

xxii 1–10: *The Wedding Invitations* (cf. also Matt xxv 10; Rev xix 7 ff.). This parable reinforces the point of the last one, and again emphasizes God's freedom of action. God's choice of Israel in no way bound him permanently; faithlessness on Israel's part, her rejection of a summons by God, would lead to repudiation. This is no more than OT prophetic teaching; but linked here with controversial questions about John's authority and Jesus' own proclamation of the Kingdom, such a consideration would have been hidden from his critics by the blindness of their own opposition.

It is necessary here to add that nothing which has been said above is meant to imply a permanent rejection by God of his ancient people, still less that the judgments pronounced by Jesus against his critics and opponents are to be taken (as they have been, unhappily, in the past) as valid judgments against the entire institution of Judaism. Paul's statement should be recalled here: "Has God cast off his people? By no means!" (Rom xi 1). The apostle readily admitted his error in persecuting the Church, after his conversion, and saw that it was sin. But at no time did he say that his actions had been insincere, motivated by a perverse disregard of truth or desire of gain. Many of Jesus' critics were pious men, and continued to be devoted servants of the Law, and of the Giver of that Law, long after the events of the passion, death and resurrection of Jesus. We are not entitled to question their sincerity, even though Christian belief in Jesus as Messiah would compel us to hold that they were mistaken about Jesus and his message.

Verses 11–14: *The Wedding Garment.* This is in all probability an incomplete parable, for which no parallel exists in the other gospels. Its ending is perhaps unsatisfactory to us because we have no precise knowledge of the social customs pertaining to weddings in the time of Jesus, or of the garments which guests were expected to wear. (A rabbinic parallel does exist for this parable, however, on which cf. Jeremias, *Parables of Jesus,* pp. 131, 187. Here a king sent invitations to a wedding, but did not specify the time. The wise dressed themselves for the wedding, while the foolish went on working, and when the summons finally came the foolish ones were not admitted. This rabbinic parable comes almost certainly from Rabbi Yohanan ben Zakkai about A.D. 80, and may have had a long oral tradition before being committed to writing.) As it stands in the gospel, the parable carries the clear warning that mere knowledge of the Kingdom's advent is not enough—there must also be response to the proclamation, and people must prepare themselves.

xxiv 45–51: *The Slave Set Over the Household* (Luke xii 42–46). The homiletic flexibility of the parable in later circumstances must not distract our attention from its proper place in Matthew's framework. (In somewhat different circumstances, it has the same function in Luke's account.) Jesus anticipates his "coming," which particularly in the Matthean context is likely to mean his passion and death, when he enters the Father's glory. Worth underlining here is the connection with the Johannine vocabulary of the passion: the "day," the "hour," the "knowledge" reserved to the Father, all familiar to us from John, are to be found preceding this parable in vss. 36–44. This parable is a challenge to his hearers, to the Israel of his time: his people must be on their guard lest they miss the significance of the "coming." In other words, it underlines and emphasizes the warning to "this generation" in vs. 34, and looks forward to the "from now on" of xxvi 64. All the "signs" demanded of him have already been given, if men had but looked. There remains only the hour, the time of his coming to the Father in death, and the Father's acceptance of that death in the resurrection. It is Jesus' hearers who will be on trial, not Jesus. Those who have been set over the Lord's household are indeed in a perilous position.

xxv 1–13: *The Waiting Maidens.* This is clearly another parable of warning, again with the motif of a wedding celebration. Israel's role as the Lord's bride is a commonplace of OT thought. This parable is concerned with the impending inauguration of the New Covenant, and the sealing of it in blood: the new community will then be espoused to its Lord. Some will be ready and waiting for the sign of the bridegroom's coming, but judgment awaits those who—though summoned—fall asleep when the time of the espousals has arrived. No excuses can help an Israel that has been taught to read the signs of his coming, and then fails to recognize them.

Vss. 14–30: *Faithful and Unfaithful Slaves* (Luke xix 12–27). This parable fittingly closes the Matthean cycle. At the end of the parable Jesus makes abundantly clear his own role as the Father's deputy in judgment. The parable states the basis of that judgment—use or misuse of the gifts of God. In varying degrees, all members of the Covenant-community of Israel had been richly endowed by God (cf. Rom iii 1–4), and since the endowment is of God's free gift, failure to respond to God's calling is without excuse. Those who fail to respond will find themselves stripped even of their first endowment (cf. v 29, and also xxi 43, xxiv 1–2).

It should be evident that the parables of Jesus are not the simple and artless teaching forms they have commonly been assumed to be. They are neither simple instructions to an infant Messianic Community nor merely concerned with the controversies between Jesus and his opponents (conceived of as sections or factions of Judaism). If we are to appreciate and understand the parables fully, it is imperative that we set aside our own traditional homiletic interpretations *and* Jesus' immediate controversies, and see the parables in the context of a living tradition of case law.

Two final comments should be made.

(1) Given a heightened awareness of the centrality of "covenant" in OT thought, resulting from the attention paid to the prophets (especially Jeremiah) in the intertestamental period, it ought to be no surprise to discover the principle of case law applied

by Jesus to life under covenant. Jesus' use of case law was not so new that his critics did not recognize its force; it was the directness and simplicity of Jesus' method which made it so distinctive.

(2) Any consideration of the role of "covenant" in the teaching of Jesus, whether implicitly through the form of parable, or explicitly at the Last Supper, must raise again in acute form the long discussion about just how aware Jesus was of his own mission and authority. It seems likely that any reflection on covenant by Jesus would mean he had considered the implied claim that any "New" Covenant must have God as author, and the OT requirement that it be sealed in blood. If this contention is valid, then Jesus must have known the inevitable cost of his own ministry at the very outset of his public teaching.

XII. THE MESSIAH IN MATTHEW

It would be wholly out of keeping with what we have seen of the nature of a "gospel" to find in it a fully developed Christology. There is nothing in the New Testament approaching "ontology"—that which is concerned with the being, essence, or nature of a person or thing. Even the Pauline letters, interpretative and reflective though they are, are not systematic theological works. The person of Jesus in Paul's letters is not so much discussed as implied, and the meaning of his mission and works is never discussed over-all, but rather applied only on an individual case basis.

There was a tendency in the years before 1945 to discuss NT Christology in a mathematical fashion, and to talk of a "high" and "low" Christology depending on the precise elements of a divinity of Jesus thought to be ascertainable in every part of the New Testament. This was understandable in an age which assumed that Messianic expectation was comparatively simple in character in the period before Jesus. The discoveries at Qumran have changed all that, though, and we now have valuable control evidence on Messianism in the century before the birth of Jesus. It is now clear that the ancestral lines of the Messianic titles of the New Testament are widely diverse, with disparities and similarities existing side by side with contradictions in emphasis. Indeed, it is only now that one such title, known to us hitherto from Acts vii 52 (and one doubtful additional use in Matthew)—*ho dikaios,* the Righteous One—is beginning to disclose its line of development. It is in fact doubtful whether Christology would ever have made much progress before the end of the NT period, had not Paul used the phrase: "Jesus is Lord."

It is possible to find some rough guidelines to Christology in the gospels, but we should remember that any scheme which we construct in order to examine the NT material is a scheme which we impose on the material, and not necessarily a conscious production of the NT writers. With that caution in mind, it is fair to look at the gospels in the light of what they have to say about Jesus' involvement in God's act of deliverance. In precisely what way is Jesus involved—as central figure, or as herald in a more immediate sense than was true of John the Baptist; and if he was the central character in the proclamation, was this centrality that of a major prophet (i.e., as *interpreter* of the will of God in major events) or was Jesus the one and only *agent* of God in the acts themselves? Here we find some variation in the NT material.

For example, Mark's account of the transfiguration (Mark ix 2–13) leaves room for question, in spite of "This is my Son, the Beloved One." We have to wait for Matthew's account of the entry into Jerusalem to have the transfiguration account put into perspective. This Jesus is indeed Messianic King (Matt xxi 1–9), and Matthew sees all this in the light of Israel's expectation, even if this King is about to suffer and die. Similarly, Mark raises the question of authority in the matter of Jesus' treatment of the Sabbath, but Matthew closes the question with an assertion of Jesus' dominion over the Sabbath (cf. Mark ii 23–28, Matt xii 1–8); and Matthew's tradition omits Mark's saying that the Sabbath is made for man. Here there is no doubt as to the centrality of Jesus in God's act, God's declaration of himself. Mark's use of the term "Son of Man" received further definition in Matthew's tradition. Mark does not identify, or appears not to identify, Jesus with the Son of Man in viii 38, but the parallel Matthaean version (Matt x 32–33) does. This occurs in a context of judgment. Judgment, in the Old Testament, is God's prerogative, and the prophets are interpreters or heralds of his judgment; Matthew makes it plain that Jesus himself claims the prerogative, and is not merely its herald or interpreter. So, too, with the healing of the paralytic in Matt ix 1–8: here, Jesus acts not as judge but as restorer, as the *agent* of salvation, and God's saving act is declared through Jesus as its principal, and not as its herald. Matthew either omits, or does not know, Mark's question about who is able to forgive.

The nearest approach to philosophical analysis in Matthew's treatment of the person of Jesus is his account of an incident which Mark covers in x 17–18. In Mark, the questioner is told by Jesus to explain his use of the term "good" as a description of

Jesus. Matthew poses the question quite differently: "Why question me about what is good? . . ." In Matthew, the adjective "good" is omitted before the word "Teacher" (xix 16–17).

There may be other clues to Matthew's Christology in his treatment of the continuing Messianic Community, the Church. Matthew's understanding of the person of Jesus is bound up, and springs from, the understanding which the Twelve—and later the community—had of their relationship to Jesus. Some of this was examined in our section on the Church and the End (Introduction, Parts I–III), but it is germane to our discussion to remark that Matthew emphasizes the continuing presence of Jesus with his people in the matter of future rewards (Matt x 40, xviii 5, 20, xxviii 20). If so, the relationship of Jesus to the community, conceived as permanent, must inevitably raise questions about the relationship of Jesus to the Father. If we bear in mind the identification of the Son of Man with Jesus in Matthew, we shall be in a better position to appreciate what he is saying when he places Jesus in the center of the picture of judgment in x 32–33 and xvi 27 (where the angels are *his;* cf. Mark viii 38).

We can now examine the use the evangelist makes of the Messianic titles which he applies to Jesus. Their justification, to Matthew, lies in the usage of the Old Testament, but it must not be supposed that the OT evidence is either uniform or simple. Moreover, for Matthew the Church embodies the proclamation of the Kingdom after the resurrection, and it is this interest in the community of believers that shapes the evangelist's understanding of Jesus as Inaugurator of the Kingdom.

Matthew's gospel alone describes the community of the Messiah as Church, *ekklēsia,* the *qehal Yiśrā'el* or *qehal Adonai* of the Old Testament (Matt xvi 18, xviii 17). Incidentally, in the Greek, the use of *ekklēsia* does justice, too, to the notion of the Church as the assembly of the freeborn (cf. Matt xvii 26). This community, which is the Son of Man's kingdom (xiii 41) and to whose members (through the Twelve) he has entrusted the secrets of that Kingdom (xiii 11), whose members have already seen and heard what the Old Testament looked in vain to see and hear (xii 16–17), is described by various metaphors to show its importance (v 13–16). But the relationship of the community to the Founder chiefly occupies Matthew's attention; this relationship is used occasionally to introduce Messianic titles. Although the Messiahship and function of Jesus is seen in OT terms, and the Twelve are known by a name that echoes OT and rabbinic usage (see "Disciples," in Part V above), there is enough flexibility in Matthew to have made his work the preferred gospel of the primitive Church. Jesus is the King-Messiah, sent to the lost sheep of the house of Israel (xv 24); yet he is also, as raised from the dead, the one who has all authority in heaven and earth, through his disciples summoning all to discipleship (xxviii 19). As the Son of Man coming to the Father (xxv 31 ff.; cf. Dan vii 13–14), he will judge all men (xxv 31 ff.).

Matthew's Christology has undertones which may be missed unless examined carefully. Part V of this Introduction dealt with "Disciples" as a technical term, and as a term which reveals something of the sources of the gospels. In Judaism, the disciple might hope to attain to the status of teacher (and, in later Judaism, to be ordained to that title and function), but Matthew makes it clear that those who come to Jesus remain in the status of disciples (xxiii 8 ff.), as men called to sacrificial service. Similarly, Jesus' disciples may ask questions, but there is no discussion; any such give-and-take relationship is out of the question, and discussion in our gospels is represented as taking place only between Jesus and his enemies. The disciples are witnesses to a Person, not guardians of a tradition (cf. Isa xliii 10, 12), and the fact that Matthew can use the word "disciple" after the resurrection testifies to the status of the Twelve in relation to the Lord (Matt xxviii 19). In Luke's Acts it is clear that the term "disciple" is applied to the generality of believers, and no longer to the inner circle of Jesus' followers. Matthew's continued use of the word after the resurrection heavily underlines the complete dependence of the inner circle on Jesus for their mission to Israel and beyond it. In Matthew, the calling and commission of the disciples (iv 18 ff.) precedes the teaching of Jesus, which emphasizes that the Twelve are witnesses to a proclaimed Kingdom (x 7) and to the Herald and Agent of that Kingdom (cf. John xv 16). With this preface we may now turn to the use which Matthew makes of the specifically messianic titles.

The Gr. *kurios,* which can with equal accuracy, according to context, be translated "Lord" or "Sir," is indeed ambivalent in Greek, but Matthew's use of it is clear. The relationship of disciple to Master underlies his use of *kurios:* the slave is not above (or superior to) his lord (x 24), and in his own household, in his own community, Jesus is Master, is Lord. It is significant that Matthew does not allow the disciples to use the term "Teacher," or "Rabbi," presumably because he felt it to be too familiar, though he allows it to the Pharisees and to strangers. Mark uses "Teacher" in the addresses of the disciples (cf. Mark iv 38, ix 5, 38, x 35, xiii 1). Luke does the same, though he changes Mark's term to a Greek one which is more readily understood by Greek readers (Luke v 5, viii 24, 45, ix 33, 49, xvii 13). Matthew's tradition is consistently "Lord" (cf. Matt viii 25 and Mark iv 38; Matt xvii 4 and Mark ix 5; Matt xx 33 and Mark x 51). It is necessary to be cautious here. We have already seen that *kurios* is ambivalent in meaning, and can be employed both as an address to deity or to royal authority, but also as polite address to equals or superiors. It is true that there is the solitary use of *"the* Lord" (*ho kurios*) which Matthew (xxi 3) uses of Jesus alone (cf. Mark xi 3). But it must be added that *kurios* is used of master and lord in respect of slaves and property, of superior and inferior (cf. Matt xiii 27, xxi 30, xxv 11, 20, 22, 24). One might plead that all Matthew has done is to make uniform the varied usages of Mark. But it is hard to escape the conclusion that Matthew deliberately meant his use of *kurios* to indicate a term of majesty, if not divinity.

Matthew has two principal uses of the term "Lord" (*kurios*).

(1) It is used of Jesus in his activity toward men in various situations, especially in healing—i.e., "salvation": viii 2, 6, 8, 25, ix 28, xiv 30, xv 22, 25, xvi 22, xvii 4, 15, xviii 21, xx 30, 33, xxvi 22. We should take care not to concentrate on the "healing" aspect of those restored to health to the point of forgetting that for those who witnessed such events, the healing was only part of the "salvation" of the whole man.

(2) More importantly *kurios* is applied to Jesus as the Judge of the time to come: vii 21 ff., xxv 11, 37, 44.

There is no better illustration of the way in which *kurios* is used of majesty than in the story (Matt xxiv 45 ff.) about the landowner who delays his return; a story which is an illustration of the saying: "Watch [for] you do not know on what day your Lord is coming" (xxiv 42).

By itself, the name "Jesus" (Heb. *Yēshū'* for older *Yōshū'*) has no known Messianic meaning, and the name was very common at the beginning of our era. But in the Old Testament, Moses' successor is the agent of God in leading his people into the Promised Land, and it is this connection with God's saving activity that Matthew would appear to emphasize. The first verse of Matthew's gospel seems to lay stress on the unique claim of this particular "Jesus" to bear the name, for the reason that he alone will save God's people —from sin (i 21).

Jesus uses the title "prophet" of himself (xii 41, xiii 57), and popular sentiment accords him the title (xvi 14). Like the prophets Jesus speaks with authority (vii 28, xxi 11, 46). This fits in with our original contention, that under this kind of title Jesus is regarded as central to God's saving activity and is here on earth as its major herald. There is nothing in the term "prophet" to indicate by itself a highly developed Christology. In the thought of the time, there was often no clear distinction between the Messianic figure and his forerunner.

It might have been expected that Matthew, with his interest in OT fulfillment in Jesus, would have laid greater emphasis on the Isaian "Suffering Servant" motif. (The sheer quantity of material written on this topic in technical and semitechnical works on the Old Testament is by now nearly overwhelming, and there seems to be no clear way in which the "Servant Songs" of Isaiah can be categorized as applying to an ideal Israel, or a representative of Israel. At times, both ideas appear to be present.) In fact, though there is only one quotation from Isa liii in Matthew (viii 17), and though the title "Servant" occurs but once, at Matt xii 18, it is probably safe to say that many of the "Son of Man" sayings in Matthew can be read with the figure of the Suffering Servant in mind. In Matthew, as in the other gospels, only Jesus uses the title "Son of Man." John xii 34 is the only exception. The possible shades of meaning in the Servant Songs are matched by those which attach to "Son of Man" in OT and subsequent usage. Variously, "Son of Man" in Hebrew and Aramaic can be used to designate "a man," "the man," "Man" (in general), or (as in Daniel and Enoch) "The Representative Man." This last use parallels Paul's use of the figure of First and Second Man in I Cor xv. Even where usage would appear to dictate a single interpretation, the result is inconclusive. For example, the term "Son of Man" occurs nearly eighty times in Ezekiel, and can well bear the vocative meaning "O man," yet in the contexts where it is most often employed, it is

addressed to a prophet standing in close relationship to God as
herald of God's purpose for Israel. It appears, therefore, to have
possessed an honorific meaning, or even to have been a title of
dignity. At the same time, it bears testimony to the subordinate role
of the prophet in relation to the Lord whose message he proclaims.
For Jesus himself, in Matthew's gospel, the designation combines
both the humility of the ministry—and thus far the subordination of
the Son to the Father—and the majesty of the Son of Man in judgment (cf. Matt viii 20 and xxv 31). This title is the subject of
our Introduction, Part VII, above.

"Son of David" (rejected as a title in Matt xxii 41 ff.) is used as
a title of honor and dignity in the genealogy (i 1), through the
ministry (ix 27, xii 23, xv 22, xx 30, 31, xxi 9, 15), but always by
others. The evangelists all reject the title, save for Matthew's first
use of it in his prologue. Some believed the Coming One would be
of the lineage of David, but Matthew's treatment of Jesus-Messiah
cannot be summarized in a single line of thought or development.
In Israel's midst is "something greater" than the temple (xii 6),
than Jonah or Solomon (xii 41 f.), something greater than king,
prophet, or priest. It is in this greater sense that we must examine
Matthew's use of the title "king": "King of the Jews" (ii 2, xxvii 11,
29, 37), "King of Israel" (xxvii 42), "your King" (xxi 5) and "the
King" (xxv 34, 40), and "his kingdom" (xvi 28) all have a for-
ward-looking, eschatological sense, reaching beyond the ministry and
the Passion.

The title of "Messiah" (Gr. *Christos*) as "king" is in fact far more
common in John's gospel and in the Pauline letters than it is in the
synoptic gospels. And as the faith spread into a more and more
Hellenized world, it ceased to be a title and became a proper name,
"Christ." In Matthew, apart from i 1, all the uses of "Christos" are
with the definite article—"the Messiah." It is used most after the
confession of Peter in chapter xvi, where—with the predictions of
the Passion—*the* crisis in the Messiahship of Jesus can be said to
have finally broken. The picture is not simple; from material in
the Dead Sea scrolls, we know that the lines of speculation and
development around Messianic expectation were very diverse.

We have seen so far that Matthew presents a varied picture of
Jesus. This much, however, is clear: according to our present evidence, the Messiah in Israel had normally been considered purely
human, though with very marked qualities and attributes.

We must now consider Matthew's use of the title "Son." In the Psalms, the anointed king (the "Messiah") is spoken of as God's son in an adoptive sense (e.g., Pss ii 7, lxxxix 26–27), but in Matthew the idea of Jesus as a son is so intimate that it marks him off from his contemporaries completely. Jesus is "God's Son" in the mouth of the tempter, (iv 3, 6) "Son of the living God" in Peter's confession (xvi 16), "my Son, the Beloved One" at the baptism and the transfiguration (iii 17, xvii 5), or "my son" simply, in the words of scripture (Pss ii 15, xc; Hos xi 1) as meaning that he embodies Israel. The use of "Son" in the Psalms would suggest a Messianic title, but taken in conjunction with Matthew's use of "Lord," "Son" suggests far more than a leader of great moral and dynamic qualities. The accusations that Jesus is usurping and exercising divine authority (ix 3, xxvi 65) are assumed to be true in xi 25–30. Here a relationship with the Father, a "Christology," is assumed which far outstrips any known Messianic expectation. Whatever may be the origin of the baptismal formula in xxviii 19, it depends on an intimacy of relationship with God which is already foreshadowed in xi 25 ff. It appears inescapable that the Jews rightly interpreted many of the sayings of Jesus as carrying an implication that God was his Father, in a manner not shared by others—in fact in a manner unique to Jesus. A study of the implications of the sayings of Jesus, especially of those in which he speaks of his Father, leaves the reader of the New Testament with precisely the same impression that Jesus' opponents had; it is hard to avoid the conclusion that Jesus meant to convey the fact of a unique relationship which he had with God, a relationship moreover which implied deity. John's tradition states the clear implication of Matthew's gospel in the words "I and the Father are one (John x 30)." It is worth examining all the passages in which Jesus refers to the Father, either with reference to the disciples or to himself. We see that there is always a careful separation made between the two relationships, to which again the gospel of John bears testimony.*

The predictions of the passion, and the New Covenant inaugurated on the eve of the passion, will be discussed in their proper context in the commentary. But attention is called to them here because a

---

* Cf. now the important recent article: F. Charles Fensham, "Father and Son as Terminology for Treaty and Covenant," in *Near Eastern Studies in Honor of William Foxwell Albright,* ed. Hans Goedicke (Johns Hopkins Press, 1971), pp. 121–35.

mere examination of titles, Messianic or quasi-Messianic, is of little value unless they are seen against the scriptural background, interpreted at the time of the acts of the one to whom the titles are applied.

There is a very good examination of the difficulties attendant on any discussion of messianic hope in the time of Jesus by M. de Jonge ("The Use of the Word 'Anointed' in the Time of Jesus," NovT 8 [1966], 132–48). It is recommended to the reader with some knowledge of Hebrew and Greek. See also J. C. O'Neill, "The Silence of Jesus," NTS 15 (1969), 153–67, with special reference to the "Messianic secret."

XIII. AUTHORSHIP AND CHRONOLOGY

A

Not only are there clear differences between John and the synoptists as to the length of the ministry of Jesus, together with puzzling discrepancies in the chronology of the final week of that ministry (assuming uniform calendrical usage): there are also striking difficulties in setting up a chronology which relies wholly on the synoptic gospels. The manner in which Matthew groups his material in whole blocks of teaching, together with the way in which Luke's "travel diary" is employed to introduce teaching, makes any attempt to outline a chronology of Jesus' ministry almost impossible. Such considerations, together with a paucity of detail in other directions, make anything like a "life" of Jesus, in a modern biographical sense, impossible.

It is commonly supposed that the lack of any but fragmentary information about the early life of Jesus is due to the lateness of the gospels, written down after almost all information about his early life had by that time disappeared. It is often suggested that nothing had happened; Jesus is supposed to have lived as an apprentice and assistant carpenter with a life so quiet that there was nothing to record until the vacuum was filled by the miracles of the non-canonical gospels. Below it will be pointed out how drastically the almost complete break in the continuity of Christian life in Palestine affected the tradition. Nearly all the relatives and contemporaries of Jesus had died, so that it may have proved impossible to describe his early life meaningfully. But this is still an inadequate explanation. In our opinion, the only satisfactory alternative is that Jesus was so completely absorbed by his sense of mission that he seldom said anything about his childhood and youth, even to close associates.

Other features in our gospels are hard to accommodate to modern biographical ideas. Not only is there complete silence about Jesus' life between his birth and the beginning of the ministry (except for one incident recorded by Luke), but both Mark and John begin their accounts with the ministry—John after a theological prologue, Mark after a brief announcement of great theological significance. This is not all. The passion narratives in all four gospels, from a purely biographical standpoint, are out of all proportion to the rest of the material (Mark's passion is about a third of the whole work). This can be understood only when we realize that the purpose of the writers was chiefly theological—that is, to lead up to the passion of Jesus and in the process make clear what was the purpose of that passion, and its consequences for the Messianic Community.

The differences between John and the synoptists in the traditions they record are not confined to the chronology of the final week of the ministry. The synoptists record a ministry mainly in Galilee, of a duration impossible to determine, whereas John's record says little of Galilee, emphasizes Samaria, and records a ministry in Judea which the others do not. That Matthew knew of a ministry in Samaria seems plain from x 5 (on which see our NOTE in the commentary), and Luke refers to Jesus as expecting to be received in Samaria (Luke x 51–52). Acts records the missionary activity of the early Jerusalem community among the Samaritans. Evidently there are whole areas of ministry in the life of Jesus of which we read almost nothing in our present gospels.

The baptismal ministry of John, together with the words which he employed to carry out and to further that ministry, make almost inevitable the conclusion that John spent his early and formative years among Essenes, and in all probability at Qumran. (Cf. here Jean Daniélou, *The Dead Sea Scrolls and Primitive Christianity,* tr. from the French by Salvator Attanasio, Baltimore: Helicon, 1958; W. H. Brownlee, "John the Baptist in the New Light of Ancient Scrolls," in *The Scrolls and the New Testament,* ed. Krister Stendahl, New York: Harper, 1957; London: SCM, 1958; Robinson, "The Baptism of John and the Qumran Community," in TNTS; et al.) To this we must add the fact that Jesus was, at a crucial point in the ministry, little known in Nazareth, previously described as his home. Nazareth was then a mere village; no building remains of this period have yet been found, and it is nowhere mentioned by Josephus. From Luke iv 22 and John vi 42 we learn that only comparatively few of the people of Nazareth knew Jesus by sight. In the former passage the Greek clearly means, "Isn't this the son of Joseph?" In the latter we read, "Isn't this Jesus, the son of Joseph?" (Translation of Brown, in his commentary *John, i–xii,* §24.) In view of the implied statement in Matthew, Luke and John (see commentary below on Matt xiii 55), it seems that he had been away for a relatively long time.

The three synoptic gospels all mention a stay of forty days in the wilderness while he was undergoing severe temptations from the devil. It may safely be inferred that he was well acquainted with the desert and had spent a good part of his early manhood in the Dead Sea Valley and Arabia (which at that time meant the land of the Nabataeans). We have interesting parallels which do not prove, but certainly suggest, that he spent much more time in the desert than we are told. When Paul spent three years in Arabia (Gal i 17–18) (including Damascus, which at that time was also under the Nabataeans), we can scarcely separate his stay there from a desire to walk in the Master's footsteps. Taken alone, this phase of Paul's life might be purely coincidental, but as has been pointed out by a number of recent writers (especially Daniélou, cf. above), John the Baptist grew up in the desert, presumably with the Essenes (cf. COMMENT on §7, iii 1–12). This was probably a fairly widespread practice among pious Jews who were not too happy about the temptations of the city. Josephus, who came from a noble Jewish family closely associated with the Hasmonean priest-kings and who, like Jesus, had received a good legal education before he was fifteen, spent three years in the desert according to his own statement in the *Life.* Part of this period was spent with the Essenes, but most of it was spent with an ascetic named Bannus, probably an ex-Essene. His description of the latter's mode of life in the desert reminds one very closely of the manner of life of John the Baptist, who also dressed in skins and lived on whatever he could find. Unfortunately Josephus does not tell us just what Bannus' teachings were, but we may safely suppose that they were not too remote from those of the somewhat earlier John the Baptist. It is true that Josephus was a little younger than Paul and at least thirty years younger than Jesus, but it is clear that his stay with Bannus did not influence him against John the Baptist, whom he mentions favorably in *Antiquities* XVIII.v.2. Among the points which Bannus had in common with the Essenes was his practice of frequent ablutions with cold water; like John he lived on what he could find in the desert. This practice was doubtless much more frequent than the cases mentioned might suggest. The tradition of spiritual purification by living in the desert was very old in Israel. It is, for example, found especially in the traditions of Moses and Elijah, both of whom went into the desert to commune directly with God.

We must then ask what contact Jesus had with John in his early years for both to be represented in Matthew as presenting the same proclamation (cf. Matt iii 2, iv 17). From that point, we must also ask what John the Baptist assumed Jesus had in common with himself when sending messengers from prison with his bewildered questionings. In the light of the teaching of Jesus as that teaching is preserved for us in the gospel according to John, it seems hard to avoid the conclusion that both John the Baptist and Jesus had spent some part of their adult years in close contact with the Essenes, and presumably at Qumran. It is plain that by the time John began his ministry he had abandoned the somewhat vague messianic expectations of the Essenes for the emphatic pronouncement that the Kingdom was at hand.

The duration of the ministry of Jesus—not to mention that of John the Baptist—is impossible to determine from our gospels. A range of dates is provided for the birth of Jesus both by Matthew (ii 2, 22) and more exactly, though without independent verification, by Luke (ii 1–2). Those who may wish to pursue the very vexed questions about possible dates for the birth of Jesus may with considerable profit refer to Jack Finegan's *Handbook of Biblical Chronology* (Princeton University Press, 1964), especially pp. 215 ff. It is Luke who dates the beginning of John's ministry and then goes on to say that Jesus was "about thirty years old" when he began *his* ministry. In effect, all we have is a range of dates from the birth in the days of Herod the Great (37–4 B.C.) and Augustus (31 B.C.– A.D. 14) to a *terminus ad quem* in the time of Pontius Pilate, prefect and later procurator of Judea (A.D. 26–36). On the gospel evidence, therefore, Jesus at the end of his ministry could have been anywhere from thirty-six to forty years old, accepting the controlling dates of Archelaus the Tetrarch (4 B.C.–A.D. 6) and the high priesthood of Caiaphas (A.D. 18–36). The duration of the public ministry of Jesus appears to cover little more than a year in the synoptic gospels, whereas the Johannine tradition has three celebrations of Passover in the course of the ministry. Early church tradition (Eusebius, Epiphanius, etc.) assumes a ministry of two or three years.

The gospels were not intended to be biography in any sense in which we understand the term, and it is impossible to reconstruct the ministry with anything approaching precision. Apart from the fact that each evangelist arranged his material so as to suit his particular method of presentation, we are dealing with material which combines private instruction to the inner circle with public preaching and teaching, along with other activities such as traveling and healing. The disciples came from very different backgrounds, and it is clear that some came from sectarian circles (John, disciple of John the Baptist, Simon the Zealot, and Matthew the Pharisee). In this latter case, if the ministry was not to be wholly compromised, then there was need for sustained teaching and understanding. Not only so, but the careful distinctions made in Matthew and Mark, and also in John, between private instruction and public teaching are often obscured by critical NT scholars. There are many reasons for this, not least of which is the manner in which the universal availability of the gospels to us, in every language, has obscured their necessarily limited availability in the period when the traditions were first committed to writing.

There are other considerations, too. The first, and perhaps the most important, is the extremely compact character of much of the material which we now have. We assume far too readily that in some sense the gospels were intentionally compiled not only for the continuing Messianic Community but also for remote posterity. Aside from any possible limits on such an enterprise which may have been dictated by convictions in some circles that Jesus would soon return in glory, many of the allusions in the gospels are only now becoming clear to us. For example, with the sectarian material already available (most manuscripts are still unpublished) we are now far nearer to an understanding of such terms as "Son of Man" than has been the case for many centuries. Yet we must assume that such expressions were used by the evangelists without explanation on the simple ground that those who made use of their work were perfectly familiar with the theological content and interpretation of the terms. The second consideration concerns the extent to which we assume our gospels to have been addressed to Gentile Christians. (Note in this connection the knowledge of Judaism which Paul obviously expected of his converts in Corinth.) It is not simply that recent research and archaeological discovery have called attention to the relative size and importance of Jewish colonies in the Dispersion (e.g., at Sardis)—we must re-examine the assumption commonly made that the Pauline letters (to use but one example) were addressed to congregations which were mainly, if not wholly, Gentile.

Enough evidence exists (which we are publishing elsewhere)[22] to demonstrate that passages such as the Aramaic in I Cor xvi 22 were at quite an early date seriously misunderstood in the process of transmission in the Greek text. Equally serious has been the fate of such passages as Matt x 5, 34, 40–41. These particular examples are discussed in the commentary proper, but it is interesting to note when, and how, during the transmission (or translation), such misunderstandings arose. It is also of the highest importance to emphasize that in their original form they would have been quite clear to one familiar with the Jewish speech and milieu in which the sayings were first uttered.

What we appear to have in Matthew's gospel is a kind of teacher's guide, a collection of blocks of material from the private instruction of Jesus to the inner circle, together with other material from public teaching, and the whole assembled in a rather loose chronological framework. It is here that our difficulties multiply. How long were the periods of private teaching, as compared with those of public preaching? Our own suggestion is that after the ministry of John and the baptism of Jesus (where, on the Johannine evidence, some of the future disciples first met Jesus), there was an extended period of private itinerant teaching and instruction with the inner circle. But it is plain that this period was interspersed with occasional sermons, times of withdrawal, and isolated acts of healing. That this period gave rise to questioning, prompted either by enthusiastic indiscretion of some disciple, or by sheer curiosity among the hearers of Jesus, may account for much of the growing hostility during the ministry. The sermon at Capernaum recorded in Luke iv 16–22 reads in context like Jesus' response to a challenge.

In the synoptic gospels the confession of Peter and the transfiguration together represent a watershed in the ministry. We may not be too far wrong in supposing that it was there that the large-scale public ministry began. The opposition to Jesus which had already been aroused by occasional acts of healing, and the claims implicit in them (cf. Mark ii 1–12), together with trenchant criticism of

[22] W. F. Albright and C. S. Mann, "Two Texts in I Corinthians," NTS 16 (1970), 271–76.

abuses in interpreting the Law, now had opportunity to crystallize. From the transfiguration onwards the gospel narrative is one of increasing tension and of progression to what Jesus regarded as the inevitable end of his ministry.

If this is so, and the evangelists shaped their material in such a way that we are easily led into finding a quasi-biographical framework which never existed in the period of oral transmission, then how reliable are the recorded traditions, and what chronological indications are there of dating in our sources? Except in Scandinavia, it is doubtful whether systematic analysis of the oral tradition in the New Testament has been taken with anything approaching adequate seriousness by NT scholars. The importance of that tradition has been repeatedly stressed by Harald Riesenfeld (cf. "The Gospel Tradition and Its Beginnings," in *The Gospels Reconsidered*, New York: Humanities Press / Oxford: Blackwell, 1960); by Anton Friedrichsen (cf. "Jesus, St. John and St. Paul" in *The Root of the Vine*, ed. A. G. Hebert, London: Dacre Press, 1953), and by Stendahl (cf. *The School of St. Matthew*). There can be no doubt at all that the tenacity of oral tradition in the interpretation of Jewish law was extremely great, and recent discoveries have emphasized its antiquity (see Solomon Gandz, *The Dawn of Literature, Osiris IV*, Bruges, 1939; and W. F. Albright, *From the Stone Age to Christianity: Monotheism and the Historical Process*, 2d ed. [Johns Hopkins Press, 1957], pp. 64 ff.). We now know, thanks to the work of such scholars as Louis Finkelstein, J. Weingreen, Manfred Lehmann, and many others (much of whose work has not yet been published) that oral tradition in pre-Talmudic Jewish sources, are often extraordinarily accurate even as far back as the Exilic period or earlier. The data contained in our rabbinic sources of the second century A.D. and later are proving to be reliable for earlier times than generally believed. The sayings of the leading Jewish teachers of the intertestamental and NT periods were preserved with remarkable tenacity for centuries after their original date. It has been shown again and again that the methods of teaching employed by Jesus are extremely close in their character to those of the early rabbis. It has also been shown that mnemotechnic devices—for instance, the arrangement of sayings of Jesus according to key words—were well known in rabbinic times and go back to high antiquity. The structure underlying many of the NT *logia* can be paralleled most closely in *Pirqê Abôth* (*Sayings of the Fathers*).

Archaeological research confirms the statements of Josephus and others as to the widespread devastation of Jewish Palestine during the prolonged struggle which began about A.D. 66 and ended in A.D. 73 with the fall of Masada. Not a single synagogue is known to have survived, though synagogues were rebuilt on the same or a neighboring site, as at Capernaum and especially at the Hot Springs of Tiberias (*Ḥammātā d'Tiberia*). The Jewish population of Palestine was greatly reduced by pagan massacres, internecine fighting, and slaughter by the Roman armies. Very large numbers of Jews were carried off as slaves. Christians were regarded as traitors by Jews and as Jews by pagans. The result was an almost complete interruption of Christian life in Palestine for a generation, if not longer. According to the well-known tradition preserved by Eusebius (whose accuracy has been strikingly vindicated by Ugarit and Chenoboskion), the Christians fled from Jerusalem to Pella in the eastern Jordan Valley. Pella was in an exposed location, open to pagan and Jewish reprisals, so it is in the highest degree improbable that it was more than a temporary refugee camp for fugitives who were planning to move on to safer places in Syria and Mesopotamia. The great break in the continuity of Palestinian tradition about A.D. 66–73 was stressed by W. F. Albright in *The Archaeology of Palestine* (Harmondsworth: Penguin Books, 1949), pp. 240 ff., and in *The Background of the New Testament and Its Eschatology: Studies in Honour of Charles Harold Dodd,* eds. W. D. Davies and David Daube (Cambridge University Press, 1956), pp. 155 ff.

It thus seems clear that the period of relative calm envisaged by so many NT scholars for the production of the four gospels during the last third of the first century A.D. never existed—least of all among the refugees from Palestine. We may reasonably assume that some Jewish Christians fleeing from Palestine took with them fixed oral traditions, especially those underlying the so-called "Q" source, which we believe to have been orally transmitted before it was included in our gospels of Matthew and Luke. Once outside of Palestine, and scattered in all directions, the refugees found it necessary, for the preservation of the oral tradition, to put it into writing and publish it as fast as possible. Where the four gospels were written becomes a matter of relative indifference, as long as we recognize that they must have been composed in substantially their extant written form no earlier than the late 60s and no later than the 70s or early 80s.

We do have, as it happens, an important and almost entirely neglected body of evidence for the tenacity with which the oral tradition about Jesus was preserved during this extremely difficult period of almost complete discontinuity in the life of Palestinian Christians. This consists of the proper names, including both personal and place names, found in the four gospels and preserved in the Syriac version. The Syriac tradition has been strangely disregarded; it was generally rejected even by such authorities as Dalman and Lagrange. If we examine the Syriac recensions of the gospels carefully, we find that the most important recensions —the Vetus Syra (second or third century), the Peshitta (about fourth century), and the Syro-Palestinian lectionaries (about fifth century)—agree almost throughout in the form of proper names. This agreement does not hold, however, in a few obscure place names which have not yet been identified with certainty by modern scholars.

That proper names are of exceptional importance for the relation of oral and written tradition, especially in cognate dialects, has been stressed particularly by E. Y. Kutscher, in a German article on Mishnaic Hebrew in *Rocznik Orientalistyczny* 26 (1964), 33–48, on the great value of proper names in fixing the relations between recensions in different Aramaic dialects. The only other way in which we can explain some of the phenomena which we list here is by the incredible supposition that native scholars were somehow trained in modern philological method and sent from Syro-Mesopotamian monasteries on fact-collecting expeditions to Palestine. Since no such notion is conceivable, our only other solution is to suppose that the names were carried from Palestine, embedded in pre-gospel tradition by Aramaic-speaking Christians who found refuge in Syria and Mesopotamia.

In some cases, of course, no problem is involved, since names like *Yôḥanān* (John), *Shim'ôn* (Simon), *Maryam* (Mary), *Martā* (Martha) could not have been forgotten. There is a striking parallel between the names found on Jewish ossuaries in the neighborhood of Jerusalem, dating from the last century of the Second Temple (30 B.C.–A.D. 70), and the names occurring in the gospels. We find roughly the same proportion of Greek and Hebrew names among them as in the gospels: not only such names as John, Simon, Mary, and Martha, but also such names as *Shalôm* (Salome)—all very common in this period. However, there are also names which are not so obvious. For instance, Bartholomew has not generally been recognized as containing the patronymic which is well attested as *Tlmy,* the normal transcription of Greek Ptolemy, in Nabataean and South Arabic inscriptions, as well as in rabbinic sources (see commentary on x 3). Since we already have so many Greek names among the disciples of Jesus, such as *Andreas, Philippos,* and *Kleopas* (for the very common Greek name *Kleopatros*), there is nothing surprising about this. But we also have names such as *La'zar* (Lazarus), which appears in the same spelling in the ossuary inscriptions as a shortened form of "Eleazar." It is not self-evident that Alphaeus, which looks superficially like Greek *Alpheus* (with which it used to be connected) should appear in Syriac as *Ḥalfay,* also the short name of Rabbi Ḥalaftā (who flourished toward the end of the first century). This Jewish name meant "compensation." An epithet like *Boanergēs* is correctly transmitted in Syriac as *benay regesh* (*rigshā*), "sons of noise." One suspects that the curious Greek form is a corruption, resulting from confusion with some such word as Doric *boa,* Attic *boē,* "loud cry."

The place names are, however, more significant than the personal names, since place names seldom wander as personal names do so easily. Here we have such clear cases as Bethsaida "house of fishing/hunting" spelled with *ṣade,* and Capernaum, which is well known from Jewish sources as *Kephar Naḥūm* (village of Nahum). Bethany appears in the Syriac recensions as *Beth-'anyā,* which (as pointed out by Albright in the *Annual of the American Schools of Oriental Research* 4 [1924], 158–160) is a shortened form (with haplography) of older *Beth-'ananyah,* mentioned as Ananiah (*'Ananyah*) in Neh xi 32. An equally obvious case is Bethesda, which is spelled in all Syriac recensions *Beth-ḥisdā* or *-ḥasdā.* This is a normal transcription from Aramaic into Greek, and the name was common in later times, usually in the alternative form *Ḥisdai/Ḥasdai,* short for biblical *Ḥasadyahu.* This obviously correct identification, which shows that Aramaic tradition had accurately preserved the name of the long-since destroyed Pool of Bethesda, has been abandoned by some scholars since the publication of the copper strips from Qumran, where a name *Beth-eshdatain* was erroneously read in the official publication by J. T. Milik with M. Baillet and R. de Vaux of *Les 'Petites Grottes' de Qumran,* Discoveries in the Judaean Desert of Jordan, III (Oxford University Press, 1962), p. 297. Beth-eshdatain was promptly identified by Milik with Bethesda, though the word itself

is otherwise wholly unknown and fails completely to yield a satisfactory meaning. Besides, the context was completely misunderstood
by Milik; we must read with J. M. Allegro (*The Treasure of
the Copper Scroll* [New York: Doubleday, 1960], p. 53) and
D. N. Freedman, *Beth-ashwaḥayn*, "the house of the two reservoirs."
In our opinion there can be no doubt whatever about the correctness
of this reading, though a few obscurities remain in the following lines.
The word for "underground reservoir" which occurs in Hebrew inscriptions and texts from the ninth century B.C. to the second century
A.D., was pronounced *ashwaḥ,* later *ashôaḥ;* it appears in the name of
the town *Shôḥîn* of the Talmud (*Asochis* of Josephus) in central
Galilee. In this case the poor hand of the carver is responsible for
the mistake, but the editor's poor paleography and philology have
served us ill. Where the place itself was located we do not know,
probably in Jerusalem. In any event, this cannot possibly be the
Bethesda of the gospel of John, the only plausible form of whose
Aramaic name has been correctly transmitted by all the Syriac
recensions.

One of the most stubborn of all place names in the gospels is
Gethsēmane. Because of its great importance in the passion narrative, which was almost certainly the first part of the gospels to be
written down, there can be no reasonable doubt that the form of
the name would be correctly transmitted in Syriac. The Greek form
Gethsēmane, spelled at the end variously with *epsilon-iota, iota,*
or *ēta,* was almost certainly influenced by the Greek verbal form
sēmanei, meaning "he will show" or "he/it will show/mean." But the
Syriac recensions have *Gedsīmān* (*Gessēmānīn* in the Syro-Palestinian lectionaries) and *Gessēmani* in some Greek manuscripts). G.
Dalman, *Orte und Wege Jesu* (Gütersloh: Bertelsmann, 1924),
p. 340, gave up his earlier explanation of the name as "oil press,"
following long-standing conventional ideas, and preferred to render
"wine press of signs" or "wine press of omens." But we cannot
disregard the Syriac recensions, because *Gedsīmān,* etc., makes no
sense at all as a corruption of an original *Gethsīmān.* More important, however, is the fact that there is no real evidence at all for
the supposed meaning "oil press" for the name in question, since
gath is nowhere used in the Bible or in Aramaic literature in the
sense of oil press, if we except two very doubtful rabbinic passages
alluded to as possibilities by Dalman. On the other hand, the word
gad, gaddā, "good luck," is exceedingly common in Aramaic as well

as in Hebrew-Phoenician in the same sense. It must originally have been the personal name of the owner of the place, in which case he would bear a name of pagan origin which could well be borne by a Jew; "The (astrological) omen(s) is/are (my) good luck." There are many parallels; a good one is the Aramaic name *Naḥash-ṭāb,* which appears in Aramaic and South Arabic, and in Greek transcription (second century A.D.) as *Naastabos,* meaning "good luck," or "(my) luck is good." Note in connection with pagan *Naḥash-ṭāb* that *sîmân ṭôb* is synonymous with *mazzāl ṭôb,* "good (astrological) omen" in later Hebrew.

It is most improbable that the words for wine press and oil press ever coincided in Hebrew and Aramaic, since the presses are entirely different in appearance and the processes of extracting oil and wine are as different as possible. Furthermore, wine presses were generally hewn out of solid rock outside a town or village, whereas oil presses were generally found in a town.

It is also noteworthy that the few cases which remain stubborn and from which we cannot learn anything appear only accidentally in the gospels. For instance, Aenon and Salim are mentioned in John iii 23 as places where John the Baptist baptized (probably in Samaria; see *Harvard Theological Review* 17 [1924], 193 f.). Though the places still exist as 'Ainûn and Sâlim, early Christian tradition shifted them both to the middle Jordan Valley, south of Scythopolis, which was swampy and more accessible, though there are no satisfactory sites or names to be found there. In a case like this, where Jesus was not involved at all (only John baptized there), it would not be strange to find the tradition forgotten. In the gospel of John we have memories transmitted through a former disciple of John the Baptist. In any case, there would be no reason why mention of towns connected only with John the Baptist would be remembered in traditions concerned with Jesus.

The case of Gergesa, which also appears as Gadara and Gerasa (see commentary on Matt viii 28), is inscrutable. We have followed the Syriac Gadara, for reasons given in the commentary. How the name became corrupted from *Gergesa* is a mystery. Perhaps the most plausible suggestion is that the original name was *Gergesa,* belonging to a village in Gadarene territory, and later confused in some Greek texts with *Gerasa,* whereas the Aramaic tradition remembered that it was in Gadarene country, since Gadara overlooked the Sea of Galilee directly from the southeast but at a greater distance than the putative Gergesa. In earlier times *Grgš* appears as a personal name in Syria and as an ethnic name in Palestine.

One of the most striking cases is, at first sight, extremely simple. Arimathea appears in the Peshitta as *Rāmethā* (though there may be some doubt as to exact vocalization). The Syro-Palestinian lectionary recension offers instead, as pointed out by M. J. Lagrange in RB 34 (1925), 489 f., *Remṭīs,* which today is pronounced *Renṭîs* by the local population. The spelling *Remṭīs* is in agreement with the Greek *Remphthis* of Eusebius, underlying Jerome's *Remfthis.* On the various forms of the name, see the commentary on Matt xxvii 57. The Peshitta reading is most significant, since it sounds quite different from the Greek and could not possibly have been based on direct translation or transliteration from Greek. It must, therefore, go back to the original tradition as transmitted orally.

In view of the material accumulated in these illustrations, it becomes probable that there are many key Aramaic words and phrases which were preserved by the Syriac recensions in substantially their original form. To be sure, there were undoubtedly dialectal variations, but they were seldom significant about the Christian era. Even centuries later, differences between the Aramaic of Edessa and Dura, on the one hand, and of southern Syria and Palestine, on the other, were seldom serious bars to communication. From the Jewish ossuaries and inscriptions we know that Jewish Aramaic was not divided into really fixed dialects, though there were, of course, differences in the speech of the Aramaic-speaking population in different parts of the continuum Syria-Palestine-Mesopotamia.

We may therefore reasonably suppose that Jewish Christians fleeing from Palestine took with them firmly fixed oral traditions, especially those underlying the so-called "Q" material, and put them into Greek as soon as they could, realizing that they might otherwise be lost.

The contention that Mark was a Roman gospel, compiled around the teaching and reminiscences of Peter, has almost everything to commend it, and it is nowadays generally accepted. But to proceed from there to argue that Mark is the basis, not only of the framework of Matthew and Luke, but also of considerable quantities of material in both, is to carry a historical hypothesis too far. Under the conditions prevailing in Palestine at the generally accepted date of

Mark (ca. A.D. 65), it is hard to imagine that Christians in Palestine were waiting for a gospel tradition from Rome in order to begin writing down their own oral tradition.

Later church speculations about the missionary spheres of the eleven disciples may well reflect traditions about the circumstances of their departure from Palestine. For all the "finished" appearance of the gospels, we must reckon with the serious gaps which they present. There was no information, apparently, from Jesus himself about his early life—presumably reflecting either the death or the dispersal of those few who might have had access to such information. All that we have is a tantalizing glimpse of a visit to Jerusalem recorded by Luke (who seems to have made strenuous efforts to recover what he could). The account of Jesus' reception in Nazareth must raise serious doubts as to how long he remained there after the return from Egypt. There is, besides, the probability that, as a young builder, he had become familiar with much of Palestine and neighboring areas. The Johannine tradition certainly gives the impression that the author knew a great deal more than he recorded, but along with that impression goes the obvious fact that this tradition was far more concerned with preserving knowledge of Jesus' teaching.

There is further confirmation of this when we look more closely at the account of the election of Matthias in Acts i. Examples of choice by lot carried out with inscribed potsherds have been found at Arad and Masada. (On choosing by lot, cf. J. A. Fitzmyer, "Jewish Christianity in Acts in the Light of the Qumran Scrolls," in *Studies in Luke-Acts: Essays Presented in Honor of Paul Schubert*, eds. L. E. Keck and J. L. Martyn [Nashville: Abingdon, 1966], pp. 250 ff.) We have generally assumed that the Greek text of Acts i 21–22 has been transmitted accurately, and that the number of the apostolic band was being made up by including one who had been with Jesus all along. But there is a serious flaw in this interpretation. It is explicitly stated—in the common interpretation—that the proposed candidate should be "one of the men who have accompanied us . . . *beginning from the baptism of John* . . ." (Acts i 22, italics ours). Not only is there possible confusion of names in the lists of the Twelve as we have them (we shall have something to say of this below), but it is clearly stated in our gospels that some of the disciples were called in Galilee after the baptism by John. By the time of the events recorded in Acts i 21–22, there can have been very few who not only had accompanied Jesus right through his ministry, but who also had firsthand knowledge of the ministry of John. We suggest that the Greek of this important section in Acts should read: *oudeis oun*[23] *tōn sunelthontōn hēmin andrōn en panti chronō hō eisēlthen kai exēlthen.* . . . Considering what follows (*martura tēs anastaseōs autou sun hēmin genesthai hena toutōn*) with its emphasis on *hena toutōn,* "one of these," the confusion between *oudeis oun,* "no one, therefore," and *dei oun,* "it is therefore necessary," is easily explained. On our supposition, Peter is represented as saying that there was no one left who had, like Judas, accompanied the inner circle all the way through Jesus' ministry. So the traditional number of twelve (as at Qumran) was restored from "one of these"—i.e., from the company described in i 15. What was required was a witness to the resurrection, *not* someone who had been witness to the whole ministry. If our reconstruction of this reading is correct, then not only is it clear that Paul (who obviously does not fulfill the conditions of i 21 on the usual interpretation) was able to claim apostleship without continued protest from Jerusalem, but it also makes clear how the extension of the term "apostle" to Barnabas could so easily be accomplished.

We have spent some time on this, partly as demonstrating that the number of firsthand witnesses to the ministry of Jesus was not so limitless as is commonly assumed, and partly also as an indication that the conventional number of "the Twelve" probably did not become fixed until the final stages of the ministry. Indeed, it is possible that the number of the inner circle achieved fixed form as a consequence of the saying recorded in Matt xix 28. Students of the Old Testament are familiar with the varying traditions in the OT sources as to the names of the groups subsumed under the title "the twelve tribes." We may assume that some, though by no means all, of the apparent confusion in the list of the Twelve in the gospels and Acts derives from our own assumption that the inner circle must always have consisted of the same persons throughout the ministry.

In any assessment of chronology, authorship, and reliability in the gospels, we are faced with (1) a relatively small number of people who had access to the facts of Jesus' ministry, (2) the early disappearance from the scene of some of the witnesses, and

---

[23] Instead of the obviously haplographic *dei oun* of the present text.

(3) the apparent dismissal by Jesus himself of any recollection of his early years as unimportant. Correspondingly, we must reckon with the desire to record the oral tradition at a comparatively early date, not only on account of a steadily worsening political climate, but also—and more especially—on account of the removal to other spheres of action of many who could provide valuable information. We have no reason to call in question the essential veracity of Luke's statements in the preface to his gospel.

Before we look at these considerations as they may apply to Matthew's gospel, let us pay some attention to a common tendency among many NT scholars. This is the assumption on the part of many writers on NT subjects that there was at some early time a uniform Greek text, which might be reconstructed from the standard recensions, from which all manner of conclusions might be drawn, and upon which all kinds of structural edifices might be erected.[24] Along with this is the tendency on the part of some (often the same) scholars to postulate relatively—in some cases ludicrously—late dates for much NT material. To make these assumptions is to overlook entirely the salient fact that the Hebrew Bible did not become a fixed text until after the fall of Jerusalem in A.D. 70, a fact to which the Dead Sea scrolls are eloquent witness. (Cf. Jan de Waard, *A Comparative Study of the Old Testament Texts in the Dead Sea Scrolls and the New Testament,* Leiden: Brill, 1965; Grand Rapids: Eerdmans, 1966.) There are some examples in our present gospel of Matthew to which we have called attention in the body of the commentary, where a zealous attachment to a so-called fixed text has often completely obscured, or even changed, the original sense (cf., for example, x 34). In the course of writing this commentary it has become increasingly clear to us that we may well be dealing with material which had been transmitted in Aramaic and occasionally in Hebrew. This is a situation which would be much more likely in the third quarter of the first century than at any time earlier or later.

A very strong argument for the originality of the material handed down in Matthew, as well as in the other gospels, is the archaic Jewish-Aramaic in which it was originally composed—whether in oral or written form does not really matter. Thanks to the discovery

---

[24] See against this common assumption Kurt Aland, in *The Bible in Modern Scholarship,* ed. J. Philip Hyatt (Nashville: Abingdon, 1965), pp. 334 ff.

of so much early post-biblical Hebrew and especially of late pre-Christian Palestinian Aramaic among the manuscripts of Qumran, it is possible to reconstruct the original Aramaic of many passages with a close approximation to accuracy in syntax, morphology, and vocabulary—see especially J. A. Fitzmyer, *The "Genesis Apocryphon" of Qumran Cave I,* Rome: Biblical Institute Press, 1966), and CBQ 30 (1968), 417–28. The value of this criterion will become clear in the pages of our commentary, in which we deal with obscurities in the present Greek text which can probably be traced back to Aramaic (or Hebrew). We must not forget that the current Hebrew used in the scribal schools of Palestine in the early first century A.D. was of the type illustrated by the numerous quotations from the early rabbis preserved in the Mishnaic tractate *Pirqê Abôth,* which can now usually be put back into Aramaic of the same period without difficulty. This is naturally also true in reverse: much Jewish Aramaic can be traced back to the late Hebrew of this period. A careful analysis of the proper names in the Syriac recensions of the gospels has also proved very fruitful, and we can now expect some key words and expressions in the utterances of Jesus to be preserved in Syriac (see above).

B

We propose now to examine briefly some of the characteristics of this gospel. Our principal conclusions as to its framework were indicated in Part IV of this Introduction, and will not be repeated here.

The evangelist's use of the Old Testament is not only important in providing him with a biblical framework within which to set the ministry of Jesus, it also gives us some indication of his theological attitudes. The evangelist's eschatology is of the traditional orthodox Jewish type represented especially by the Pharisees. It is important to remember that the evangelist gives new life to traditional concepts such as The Man ("Son of Man") represented in Daniel and Enoch, by seeing them in the light of the ministry of Jesus. If we contend (as we have already done in Part IV above) that Matthew sees the ministry of Jesus in almost exclusively biblical terms, we must at the same time remind the reader that when this gospel was being written there was no agreement as to the exact extent of Scripture beyond the Law and the Prophets (the latter including the earlier historical books and the major and minor prophets). The evangelist shows little interest in any specifically sectarian vocabulary, though he was certainly well aware of it, and not infrequently uses phraseology of the Qumran type. For all the wealth of Christological titles such as "The Righteous One"—and the high estimate placed on the Messianic Community as "Kingdom of heaven"—there is no proliferation of community titles such as one finds at Qumran. Nowhere, for example, is the Community referred to as "the Restored Israel" or "the community of the New Covenant." It is not too much to say that this gospel represents conscious return to Scripture. To that extent, we may be correct in describing the evangelist as in all probability a Galilean, aware of but not inclined toward sectarian theological speculation, and rather "old-fashioned" in his approach to Scripture. As we pointed out in Part IV, the evangelist's *pēsher* method of commentary was in process of being superseded by the Greek hermeneutical methods which had been introduced by Hillel the Elder in the late first century B.C.

C

Traditionally, this gospel was written by Matthew, the tax collector described in ix 9 and x 3, and further identified with the Levi of Mark ii 14 and Luke v 27 (properly, as we shall see, "the Levite"). There are some uncertainties in the NT lists of the Twelve, but the difficulty found in the Levi of Mark ii 14 as a son of Alphaeus, along with a James similarly described in Matt x 3, is more apparent than real. Two sets of brothers are known to us from the lists of disciples, and there is no reason why two sons of Alphaeus should not also have joined Jesus in his ministry, just as there were two Judases and two Simons.

None of this carries us very far, for the main controversy has always centered around the identification of Matthew with Levi in our present texts. (Perhaps the best modern study in short compass is that of Barnabas Lindars, "Matthew, Levi, Lebbaeus and the Value of the Western Text," NTS 4 [1958], 226–32; cf. also Rudolph Pesch, "Levi-Matthäus [Mc 2.14/Mt 9.9; 10.3] ein Beitrag zur Lösung eines alten Problems," ZNW 59 [1968], 15–23.) There is a simple solution to the difficulty, and one which we believe has the merit of doing justice to all available facts. It is that Levi is not (as usually held) a personal name, but the tribal designation of the man who was called by Jesus from his tax collecting. That is to say, the person under discussion is "Matthew the Levite," Gr. *Matthias ho levitēs*. We have called attention in the commentary to the widespread disuse of the definite article in Aramaic in the NT period. It would therefore not be surprising if a translator/scribe, faced with *Levi* in his original, came to the conclusion that this was a personal name—it was, after all, common at this period—and therefore rendered it as such in Greek.

Everything which we judge to be characteristic of this gospel—its conservatism, its interest in the traditional oral law, in lawyers and Pharisees, its traditional eschatology—all this fits admirably into the background of an author who was a Levite. The struggle of the Levites as an order for a firm and lasting place in the ecclesiastical framework of Judaism after worship was centralized at Jerusalem (but especially after the return from Exile) need not detain us here. There are excellent summaries both in *The Jewish Encyclopaedia* and in Kittel's TWNT, ad loc. A Levite of the time of Jesus would normally have been a Pharisee, educated, and from an orthodox (i.e., not sectarian) background. With lower status than the Jerusalem-centered priesthood, more numerous than the temple cult could readily absorb, most Levites would be compelled to seek a livelihood apart from the worship of the temple. If Matthew the Levite found a living as a tax collector for the political authorities—and his education would certainly fit him for such responsibility—then his rejection by his fellow Pharisees would follow inevitably. So too would inevitably follow carefully collected reminiscences of Jesus' attitude to the Law and to those who made their living by oral interpretation of that Law. (It is worthy of mention here that Stendahl, in his *School of St. Matthew* [mentioned above], pp. 30–31, quotes von Dobschütz as suggesting that Matthew was a converted rabbi. However, it is by no means clear what he had in mind in using the term "rabbi," since there were as yet no *ordained* rabbis.

Apart from the fact that church tradition ascribes this gospel to Matthew, what indications are there of anything which may

be called certainty in the ascription? It must be said at once
that there is no single feature to which we can point and say
without equivocation, "This demands that we ascribe this present
work, or the larger part of it, to Matthew the Levite, called by
Jesus from his work as tax collector, and who accompanied
Jesus throughout his ministry." All that we can establish, and
that largely by inference, has been stated in the preceding paragraphs.

We are now at the point where we can examine the strength and
weakness of the early church tradition as to Matthean authorship.
Our earliest testimony as to the author or compiler of the gospel
is Papias, in a quotation by Eusebius, and referred to also by
Irenaeus—again in a quotation in Eusebius. While this sort of evidence is somewhat indirect, it would be unwise to dismiss it out of
hand. Though early church historians such as Eusebius have
often been disregarded by some modern NT scholars as being
inaccurate, the recent discoveries of Gnostic and gnosticizing literature at Nag Hammadi (Chenoboskion)—discoveries which certainly vindicate the accuracy of the descriptions of Gnosticism by
Irenaeus and Hippolytus—give new credibility to these early writers.

It is with such Church Fathers that we must now deal. Eusebius
(ca. A.D. 270–340) quotes Papias (ca. A.D. 130) as saying that
"Matthew compiled (*sunetaxe*) the oracles (or "sayings"—*ta
logia*) in the Hebrew language (*Hebraïdi dialektō*), but everyone
interpreted them (or "translated them"—*hermēneusen d'auta*) as
he was able" (Eusebius *Historia Ecclesiastica* III. 39. 16). Similarly,
Irenaeus is quoted by Eusebius as follows: "Matthew published a
gospel in writing also, among the Hebrews in their own language
(*en tois Hebraiois tō idia autōn dialektō*) while Peter and Paul
in Rome were preaching the Gospel and founding the Church"
(Eusebius V. 8. 2). That Eusebius himself shared the view that
Matthew evangelized Jews and compiled his gospel in "his native
tongue" is clear from III. 24. 5–6. The same writer quotes
Clement of Rome (d. about 101) as stating that the first of the
four gospels which are alone unquestionable (*tas anantirrētous
graphas*) was compiled by Matthew, who was "once a tax collector
but afterwards an apostle." There is no necessity whatever to
suppose that Irenaeus was dependent on Papias for his information
—Irenaeus, on his own showing, was near enough to the same
authorities as those used by Papias himself.

It is not here that the difficulty lies, but in another quotation from Papias, also found in Eusebius. Irenaeus declares Papias to have been a hearer (*akoustēs*) of John, and a companion of Polycarp (the word translated "companion" is *hetairos*). It is worth mentioning here that whenever Eusebius' quotations can be checked from other sources, he is found to be accurate. In the case of Irenaeus, there is a later Latin translation of his *Adversus Haereses* alongside which Eusebius' quotation from V. 33. 4 may be measured. Now Irenaeus declares Papias to have been a man of ancient times (*archaios anēr*), but a recent article takes issue with what it considers to be an attempt to deny Papias dealings with first-generation Christians. C. Stewart Petrie ("The Authorship of 'The Gospel according to Matthew': A Reconsideration of the External Evidence," NTS 14 [1967], 15–32), suggests that Eusebius wished to deny that Papias had contact with first-generation Christians, because Papias was a millenarian (chiliast)—a theological approach which Eusebius deplored—and also because Eusebius was anxious not to have the Apocalypse credited to the apostle John. For all the care which the article takes, we do not think that its author has really disposed of "the elder John," or "John the Elder" as easily as he assumes (NTS 14 (1967), 19 ff.). What is of considerable importance here is the careful distinction which Eusebius represents Papias as making. Papias (Eusebius III. 49. 3–4) declares: "But when someone turned up who had been closely associated with the ancient worthies" (Petrie's translation of *presbuteroi*) "I would enquire about the sayings" (or "discourses") "of the ancient worthies, what Andrew or what Peter had said (*eipen*) or what Philip or what Thomas or James, or what John or Matthew, or any other of the Lord's disciples had said, and also the things which Aristion and the ancient worthy John, disciples of the Lord, were saying." Of interest here is the fact that Papias represents the second John as being still available when he writes, since he is (according to Eusebius) careful to make a distinction between those who *had said,* and those who at the time of writing *were saying.*

We appear to have an important testimony from Papias, through Eusebius, that he was in touch with men who had known the apostle John, and could collect reminiscences as to what the first-generation Christians had had to say about our earliest gospel sources. (See Appendix A.) A careful choice of words is imperative here. Papias' recorded words—that Matthew compiled *ta logia* in Hebrew, and everyone translated as he was able—do not necessarily mean that our present gospel of Matthew must be taken as a mere translation of a whole gospel readily available in Hebrew. So far as we know, several (if not many) honest attempts at translating *ta logia* may have been made, and the phrase is by no means free from considerable ambiguity. It has been taken as a collection of the sayings of Jesus by some, by others as a source which might be roughly equivalent to the elusive "Q," and by yet others to be a kind of collection of OT *testimonia,* or a collection of Matthew's OT quotations. The last may be ruled out, now that we are in possession of whole bodies of *pēsher* (commentary) material from Qumran, which we have found to be represented with such skill in Matthew's gospel.

Much depends on precisely what interpretation we give to Papias' use of *ta logia,* and here the evidence from LXX and other sources is not always clear as to what influences were at work in the New Testament, and therefore (at another remove) in the minds of early Christian authors. Certainly Irenaeus seems to use the phrase *ta logia* as meaning the whole message of the Gospel, and not merely sayings of Jesus. It is interesting that the verdict of Kittel, in the article which appears above his name in TWNT, rejects the notion that Papias' use of the word *logia* ought properly to be confined to sayings, or collections of sayings, of Jesus. Here again, the translation of *hermēneusen* is of interest. There has been (as we saw in Part XI on Parables) an almost inexhaustible variety of interpretations offered of the parables in the light of changing social and religious conditions of Christendom through the ages. But this is strictly a matter of interpretation, however complex the hermeneutic problems may be. Granted that with the movement of the Messianic community from a Jewish milieu into the Gentile, Greek-speaking world, there were certainly problems of translating shades of meaning, it is hard to suppose that what Papias had in mind was a situation where those who first had access to Matthew's work *Hebraïdi dialektō* were left without authoritative interpretation of the message of the Kingdom. It seems to fit the natural sense of the passage from Papias far more easily if we assume that he declares Matthew's gospel to have been *translated* as men were able.

D

Before we attempt to summarize what we have so far said, there is one further puzzle to be investigated—that of the otherwise unknown Matthias, elected to fill the place of Judas (Acts i 15–26). Papyrus and parchment were not in such abundant supply, or so inexpensive, in the first century A.D. as to warrant careless use, and a repeated story or narrative must therefore be treated as being of considerable importance to the writer or compiler. This, we suggest, explains for the repeated account of the conversion of Saul of Tarsus, and of the feeding of the multitude in the gospels. Now, even granted that the writer of Acts considered it necessary to record the election of a man to fill the place of Judas in the Twelve, it must yet be asked why Luke told the story at length, instead of contenting himself with a mere record that the election was duly made. Here we can only conjecture, and it is well to bear in mind that what is being said at this point has only the merit of conjecture and nothing more. Gr. *Matthaios* (Aram. *Mattay*) and Gr. *Matthias* (pronounced *Matyā* in Syriac) are alternative shortened forms of the same Hebrew original *Mattatyahu,* and are also both common names in the period under discussion. It is a possibility to be reckoned with that Luke records the election at some length as being that of a man known to have had some connection with our present gospel of Matthew, whether as compiler of oral tradition, or (being in possession of intimate knowledge of the ministry of Jesus) as supplier of some of the historical framework of the gospel.

Papias' statement that Matthew compiled *ta logia* in Hebrew, and that each translated them as he was able, does not commend our present Greek text as a firsthand translation—indeed, there are indications that by the time our present Greek text took shape there were already serious misunderstandings of the original. It will be recalled that Streeter posited an "M" source as laying the foundation of our present gospel of Matthew, a Jewish-Christian source used by Matthew and then applied later to the finished work which bears his name. (Streeter, *The Four Gospels.* The references to the "M" source are widely scattered through the book, and it is not possible to detail them here.)

The reader has already been warned that there are no firm conclusions to be drawn as to the authorship of our present gospel of Matthew. But there are some things which can rightly be said by way of summary, which may serve to indicate that whatever might be made of Papias' *ta logia,* there is some substance to the supposition that this gospel owes something to Matthew, a Levite, a former tax collector turned disciple of Jesus. We present the summary findings as follows:

1. The author was a conservative-minded Jew, aware of but not inclined to sectarian views.

2. The gospel as we have it preserves material which details Messianic titles (the Prophet, the Righteous One) already archaic in the time of Jesus.

3. The interest of the gospel in the Law, in ecclesiastical matters, in oral interpretation of law and custom, would come most readily from a man trained in the legal disciplines, or from one who had been in constant touch with men so trained.

4. The preservation of sayings of Jesus about the Law, and about some of its interpreters, would be precisely the kind of interest we might expect from a Levite.

5. We do not find Matthew—in spite of much pleading by some commentators—engaging in an attempt to represent Jesus as a "new Moses." To the contrary, we find that the author's interest lies in carefully preserving sayings of Jesus which re-establish the true principles of the Mosaic Law.

6. However interpreted later, Matthew's collection of parables reflects his consuming interest in the spiritual history of Israel as a chosen people. The ministry of Jesus required him to re-examine the theological implications of God's choice of his ancient people.

7. We do not regard Markan priority either in time or as a necessary source, historical or otherwise, of either Matthew or Luke as being in any sense proved.

8. It is too often assumed that traditions grow from nothing, and this unwarranted assumption is often made about the traditional ascription of this gospel to Matthew.

9. If Mark's gospel is accepted as having been written in Rome, around the year A.D. 65, and if it is equally accepted that our present gospel of Matthew is substantially dependent on Mark, then our knowledge of conditions in Syria-Palestine after that date demands not only that Matthew was written far away from a Palestinian

milieu—which may well have been the case—but also that the Matthean Palestinian tradition was dependent on a Palestinian tradition from overseas.

10. Archaic expressions, interest in ecclesiastical matters, carefully recorded statements of Jesus about the Law, a conservative type of eschatology, together with an already dying method of commentary, all serve to convince us that we are dealing with an author or compiler, or both, thoroughly versed in legal commentary, who would have had nothing apart from antiquarianism to inform him if his work was written or compiled at the end of the first century.

The Levite Matthew fulfills the conditions for an author which we have outlined above far better than any other candidate known to us from the New Testament. That there is no certainty to this hypothesis, we readily concede. But it has the merit of taking Papias and those who cite him seriously, and of accepting historical and archaeological evidence of chaotic conditions in Palestine between A.D. 60 and 75. It also saves us from the inherent absurdity of supposing that Palestinian Christians—Jewish Christians at that—would have based the first Palestinian gospel on a recent arrival from Rome. It is very doubtful whether in the thoroughly confused situation which must have immediately preceded the flights of Jewish Christians from Palestine, there would have been time or encouragement for composition of a Palestinian gospel. But the traditions were there, the need of putting them down and translating them into Greek was becoming more obvious every day, so that it can scarcely have taken more than a very short time after the main emigration before our Greek gospel of Matthew emerged from the Aramaic oral and written traditions which had been carried with them by the refugees. Recent suggestions that Matthew was composed in Antioch are not unreasonable in themselves, but cannot be proved.

Precisely what place the Matthias of Acts i had in all this, we may never know. We have merely suggested above that the account of his election in Acts is evidently of some significance in Luke's mind apart from his simply filling the place of Judas.

We have already stated, in the earlier parts of this Introduction, that we do not find it necessary to accept the notion of dependence of Matthew on Mark. And (as has more than once been pointed out by others) it is much simpler to suppose that Luke was in some sense dependent on Matthew, or had access to the same Palestinian traditions as those employed by Matthew, than it is to have recourse to written sources such as the hypothetical "Q." It is perhaps only our own unwillingness to treat oral tradition seriously which has impeded an adequate assessment of Matthew as an independent Palestinian check on the accuracy of Mark's Petrine reminiscences.

One of the most extraordinary historical aberrations is the notion—straight from the German Romantics of the eighteenth century—that Jesus must have been an extremely simple, unlearned man without formal education and inexperienced in the ways of the world. The principal roots of its contemporary manifestations are, first, misplaced emphasis on the Pauline *kenōsis* (from *kenoō*, "to empty out"), according to which Jesus abdicated his divinity so that he could live the life of a mortal. This inevitably led to exaggerated emphasis on his humanity, to the point of denying him any exceptional ability to learn by study or experience. According to this point of view, he lived as a carpenter's son in Nazareth nearly all his life, doing only the humblest jobs open to a carpenter, and then suddenly becoming completely superhuman toward the end of his life. The other, and opposite, point of view, which led to surprisingly similar conclusions, is illustrated by Gerhart Hauptmann's famous novel *Der Narr in Christo, Emanuel Quint* (1910), where we have an account of the short career of a mentally retarded carpenter's son whose one ambition was to live the life of Jesus. He is represented as being capable of imitating Jesus to the extent of his ability, trying to do only good and resisting temptation of all kinds in order to pursue his chosen path. When evil emerged around him it came in spite of his efforts, and the final collapse of his mission was inevitable.

The picture of Jesus that emerges from the four evangelists—properly focused—is quite different. Here we have an exceptionally able man who traveled and studied, one whose range of interest and experience was much greater than that of any of his disciples. This young man was familiar from his own school years, supplemented by further study and wide experience, with the teachings of the Pharisees, as well as with those of his near relative, John the Baptist. Matthew, the ex-Pharisee, was particularly interested in the use by Jesus of early rabbinic case law, corrected when too legalistic by application of the Torah and the ethical teachings of the Prophets. In Matthew we have a systematic effort to collect this material, often without too much attention to context or absolute consistency. In John we have the apostle's recollections of his first leader, John the Baptist, as well as of his second leader, Jesus. They were bound together into sermons whose warp was the common teaching of John the Baptist and Jesus. The resulting theology is that of Jesus, but in terms of the largely Essene vocabulary of John the Baptist. (See Appendix B.) There is no reason to doubt that Jesus used the same vocabulary on occasion, but in the gospel it is too consistently Essene in verbiage to be exclusively the very words of Jesus. There is no means of knowing exactly what words we owe to direct translation of Jesus' vocabulary, what to the Evangelist, and what to the "Elder." (See Appendix A.)

APPENDIX A

The Presbyter John

The article by C. Stewart Petrie, mentioned in Part XIII above, is valuable as further rehabilitation of Papias as a reliable source of information. However, it seems to us that in his anxiety to see justice done to Papias, he has gone beyond the evidence in suggesting that Eusebius was wrong, or even deliberately misleading, in his judgment of Papias. Eusebius affirms that Papias knew John the Elder, and that he was not an eyewitness of the apostles (*Historia Ecclesiastica* III. 39. 2). Irenaeus certainly claims that Papias was a hearer of the apostle John, but there is in reality no conflict between Irenaeus and Eusebius at this point. For Papias' present tense in "what Aristion and John the Elder were saying" must be taken at its face value. Papias may have been a hearer of John the Apostle, but for purposes of his statement, he says only that he was recording what Aristion and the Elder were saying when he began collecting his reminiscences.

Some observations are in order here about Papias' statement. It runs in our present text: . . . *ha te Aristion kai ho presbuteros Ioannēs tou kuriou mathētai legousin,* "the things which Aristion and John the Elder, disciples of the Lord, were saying." But Aristion is totally unknown to us as a disciple, and had he been one for any length of time (such as to make him a definitive witness to the tradition), it is hard to imagine what circumstances could have kept him out of the record. However, if the Greek of Papias originally read . . . *ho presbuteros Ioannēs* <*ou*> *tou kuriou mathētēs,* ". . . John the Elder <not> the disciple of the Lord," then we suggest that the whole context in Papias makes much more adequate sense. (Cf. in this connection John xiv 22, *Ioudas ouch ho Iskariōtēs,* "Judas [not Iscariot].") The incidence of two *ou* endings in the two words preceding *mathētai* in our present text would more than account for the omission of *ou* (a third one), and once that omission had been made it would be necessary to make *mathētēs* a plural. If it is being said that John and Aristion were disciples of the Lord, it is odd (to say the least) that the unknown Aristion takes precedence over the apostle.

It is worth noting here that *Pirqê Abôth* has a chain of transmission of the Law similar to that outlined by Papias. *Pirqê Abôth* assumes that Josh xxiv 31 and Judg ii 7, in speaking of the elders who outlived Joshua and carried on the Mosaic tradition, are, so to speak, the third link in the chain Moses-Joshua-the elders. *Pirqê Abôth* describes the chain as Moses-Joshua-the elders-the prophets-the men of the Great Synagogue. Similarly, we appear to have in Papias, Jesus-the disciples-the elders.

John the Presbyter (or the Elder) is introduced to us in the salutation as author of II and III John, and it may well be that it was he of whom Papias speaks. For a discussion of this John, cf. Brown, *John, i–xii,* pp. LXXXVIII ff., and especially p. XCI.

APPENDIX B

The Gospel of John and Hermetic Literature

In 1953 Professor C. H. Dodd in his book, *The Interpretation of the Fourth Gospel* (Cambridge University Press, 1954), pp. 10–54, considered it possible that the gospel of John had been somewhat influenced by the Hermetic Corpus. This suggestion was carried further by Professor W. D. Davies in his *Invitation to the New Testament* (New York: Doubleday, 1966). At the time when Dodd wrote, he followed G. R. Driver's first view that the Dead

Sea scrolls were very late and historically worthless, as he remarked in the Introduction to his book. He can scarcely be blamed for holding this view, since the late H. H. Rowley was then almost alone among British scholars in accepting their early date. (This was before Cecil Roth and Driver came to the conclusion that the Scrolls were actually much earlier—though they were still too late in their date, as subsequent discoveries have demonstrated.) Dodd later changed his opinion (briefly?) in private correspondence, but Davies followed his teacher in hesitating to connect the phraseology of John with the almost identical phraseology of the Qumran scrolls. (On this, see Brown, *John, i–xii,* pp. LVIII f.)

Two decades ago the Hermetic Corpus, even though extant almost entirely in late mediaeval and even later manuscripts, was believed to be early, and the earlier parts were dated by the leading recent authority, André Festugière, in the second-third centuries A.D., with a possibility that parts were even earlier. The vaguely similar atmosphere of some theological concepts of the Corpus Hermeticum and the gospel of John was exaggerated by both Dodd and Davies. Actually, the Hermetic writings were somewhat influenced by post-Johannine Gnostic writings, such as "The Apocryphon of John" (to be published by Martin Krause), which may have been composed as early as the late first or the early second century A.D.

Besides the mediaeval Corpus Hermeticum (André Festugière, *La révélation d'Hermès Trismégiste,* 4 vols., 1949–54; text edited by A. D. Nock and André Festugière, 1946 [Paris: Librairie Lecoffre, 1955]), there is a Latin treatise of similar character (the *Asclepius*) preserved among the alleged books of Apuleius (second century A.D.), but the attribution to him is not accepted by contemporary scholars. (On the Hermetic treatises from Chenoboskion, see the survey by Jean Doresse, *Les livres secrets des Gnostiques de l'Égypte* [Paris: Librairie Plon, 1958], pp. 256–63, 279–80, and *The Secret Books of the Egyptian Gnostics,* tr. by Philip Mairet [New York: Viking, 1960], pp. 241–48; London: Hollis & Carter, 1960.) (A definitive edition of the new Hermetic material is expected at any moment from the expert hand of Martin Krause.)

The mediaeval Corpus contains a prayer which was called *Tabula Smaragdina,* rendered traditionally "Emerald Table," but properly (green) jasper plaque. A very early form of this prayer is found in Treatise 25 of Chenoboskion. The Coptic treatise, which is related in part to the *Asclepius* (see above), says that the text of the prayer is to be written on plaques of jasper, defended by eight guardians, four with heads of frogs and four with heads of cats. The reference to the eight animal-headed figures naturally refers to the Ogdoad of Thoth at Hermopolis Magna. Nothing is said about these animal-headed divinities from Egyptian mythology in later Hermetic literature. In our earliest Egyptian sources there were eight divinities which together formed the Ogdoad, divided into two groups of creatures with frogs' heads and serpents' heads. Many centuries later, in the Nineteenth Dynasty, they appear in Egyptian syncretism as four male and four female baboons (cf., for instance, the tomb of Sethos I at Thebes). Apparently the cats' heads were a misunderstanding of the "dog-heads," Egyptian baboons (*Papio cynocephalus*). For the symbolism in question see the material collected by R. T. Rundle Clark, *Myth and Symbol in Ancient Egypt* (London: Thames, 1959), p. 55 and *passim;* New York: Grove, 1960. It is perfectly clear that the description of the jasper plaque in the Chenoboskion papyri is itself very late, probably fourth century A.D., when there was no longer an accurate memory of the details of Egyptian mythological iconography. Furthermore, there are too many references in the Hermetic treatises from Chenoboskion to permit any doubt that in the Ogdoad and Ennead there are authentic survivals from Egyptian mythology (confused with the astrological Hebdomad), but that little precise information was availabe when the Hermetic treatises of Chenoboskion were composed. Since the documents are written on papyrus in fourth-century A.D. book hand, they must have been copied in that century. The surprising lack of exact information about Egyptian religion makes it highly unlikely that their composition was any earlier than that same fourth century A.D. But the treatises of the Corpus Hermeticum do not mention these Egyptian mythological representations at all, and they also contain even less reference to pagan Egyptian ideas as well as to Gnostic speculations than we find in the new papyrus codices. In fact, the mediaeval Corpus Hermeticum is permeated with Neoplatonic and specifically Christian ideas (especially post-Johannine). It follows that there is no longer any solid basis for dating any of the previously known Corpus Hermeticum as early as the second or third century A.D., at least in its preserved form. This fits in extremely well with the fact, known to later

Greek compilers of bibliographic data, that among the leading writers on alchemy (to which the Corpus Hermeticum was increasingly devoted) were such figures as Synesius and Zosimus. There has been a general tendency in recent decades to distinguish the "alchemists" Synesius and Zosimus from the well-known polymath, bishop of Cyrene and pupil of Hypatia, and the eminent historian (the first half of the fifth century for Zosimus, and 360[?]–414 for Synesius).

When we bear in mind that Bishop Synesius was himself a Neoplatonist who emphasized the unity of nature like the alchemists and wrote treatises on oneiromancy, astronomy, etc., it should become rather evident that the partly demythologized and neo-platonized Corpus Hermeticum has a later background than the pseudo-Egyptian gnosticizing hermeticism of the new codices.

As for Zosimus, "the Theban," there is no good reason why he cannot be identified with the Egyptian-born historian who was so well informed about the wars of Emperor Aurelian with Palmyra. Zosimus finished his "Decline of Rome" after A.D. 425; the later treatises on the letters *Omega, Kappa* and *Iota* are often attributed to a "Pseudo-Zosimus," or "Zosimus Alchemista." They show an extraordinary mixture of pagan, Jewish and Gnostic names and myths (cf. Doresse, *Secret Books of Egyptian Gnostics,* pp. 99–101, 278, Eng. ed.). It must again be emphasized that there is no good reason to distinguish him from the historian—after all, the greatest scientific genius of modern times, Sir Isaac Newton, hoped to end his career by salvaging as much alchemy as possible. Our attestation of the earliest compositions in the mediaeval Corpus is really no earlier than the fifth century A.D., and the less said about dependence of the gospel of John upon them, the better.

In short, we may safely dismiss modern "critical" scholarly judgments about the figures in question and may date the development of the later Corpus Hermeticum well after the fourth century A.D., when the codices of Chenoboskion were copied. It then becomes impossible to explain anything in John's gospel as derived from the Corpus Hermeticum.

SELECTED BIBLIOGRAPHY

This bibliography represents an attempt to provide suitable material for general readers and does not claim to be exhaustive.

In the course of the last thirty years attention has been paid to Luke-Acts and to John, with continuing work on Mark, to the almost total neglect of Matthew. The search to discover some kind of *Sitz im Leben* for Luke-Acts has been relentlessly pursued, and all kinds of suggestions, probable and improbable, have been made on the basis of the Lukan material. Some of this has been valuable, but none of it has so far faced the outstanding (and in some ways fundamental) question: Why were gospels written at all? To answer it by pointing to an expected early *parousia* (a coming of Jesus in glory, in contrast to the humility of the ministry) does not meet the case at all. For if the early Christian community was anxiously awaiting a return of Jesus to this earth, and this time in recognizable glory and at a very early date, then it is hard to see what motives can have led evangelists to commit the record of the ministry to writing. Similarly, suggestions that the character of our gospel material was dictated by the demands of a lectionary (of a type still unknown outside the gospels) goes far beyond what evidence we have. The primary purpose of narration in the gospels was theological. That is to say, our gospels were compiled around accepted oral tradition concerning the advent of Israel's expected Messiah. The variety of messianic expectation in the time of Jesus, and in the century immediately preceding his ministry, provided enough reason to make the record as accurate as possible in the face of possible misrepresentation and even manipulation. That this latter danger was only too real can be readily seen in later gnosticizing works and in the apocryphal gospels.

I. The Background of the New Testament

Albright, W. F. "Retrospect and Prospect in New Testament Archaeology," in *The Teacher's Yoke* (memorial volume for Henry Trantham). Baylor University Press, 1964. This is a useful supplement to the same author's *The Archaeology of Palestine*, Harmondsworth:

Penguin Books, 1949, and *From the Stone Age to Christianity: Mono-theism and the Historical Process,* Johns Hopkins Press, 1940, 2d ed., 1957; Anchor Books, 1957; Oxford University Press, 1958.

Anderson, Hugh. *Jesus and Christian Origins.* Oxford University Press, 1964. This is an invaluable commentary on, and examination of, modern critical inquiry into the NT sources and the history which may be discovered behind them. The author is quite free of that inhibiting despair which finds itself incapable of discovering historical fact behind the proclamation of the early church.

Black, Matthew. *An Aramaic Approach to the Gospels and Acts.* Oxford University Press, 1954, 3d ed., 1967. It has often been observed that this author tends to overstate his case. Since the time of its publication, it has served as a valuable corrective of those who see Hellenizing or Hellenistic sources behind practically everything in the early books of the New Testament.

Daube, David. *The New Testament and Rabbinic Judaism,* The Jordan Lectures, 1952. London: Athlone Press, 1956. This book, now un-happily out of print, is of great importance for the serious student of the New Testament. It is a gold mine of information, and the author's training in Roman law serves him well in interpreting and evaluating contemporary Jewish sources. The work was produced and the lec-tures given before the study of the Dead Sea scrolls had achieved the paramount importance which it now has.

Davies, W. D. "Reflexions on Tradition: The Aboth Revisited," in *Chris-tian History and Interpretation: Studies Presented to John Knox,* eds. W. R. Farmer, C. F. D. Moule, and Reinhold Niebuhr. Cambridge University Press, 1967. We have had occasion in the commentary to refer frequently to the *Pirqê Abôth,* and Davies' essay is a most useful introduction.

Finegan, Jack. *The Archaeology of the New Testament.* Princeton Uni-versity Press, 1970. This is the first modern attempt to deal com-prehensively with the many recent findings in the field. It is charac-terized by a respect for the traditions preserved by ecclesiastical writers. Although the writer devotes most of his space to sites con-nected with the ministry of Jesus, there is a good discussion of the traditions surrounding John the Baptist and his possible connection with the Essenes.

――――*Handbook of Biblical Chronology.* Princeton University Press, 1964. Reference is made to this work in various places in the Introduc-tion and commentary, and it is an invaluable tool in the hands of the student. It is certainly the finest work of its kind in English.

Finkel, Asher. *The Pharisees and the Teacher of Nazareth.* Leiden: Brill, 1964. This work has the merit of treating Jewish oral tradition seriously, and of setting Jesus against the background of his own time.

Fitzmyer, Joseph A. *Essays on the Semitic Background of the New Testament*. London: Geoffrey Chapman, 1971. This collection of previously published essays by one of the world's leading Aramaic scholars is not directed primarily at the general reader. However, such a reader will undoubtedly profit greatly from a study of this work.

Josephus, Flavius. *Jewish Antiquities*, Loeb Classical Library.

———— *The Jewish War*, Loeb Classical Library.

———— *The Jewish War*, tr. by G. A. Williamson. Harmondsworth and Baltimore: Penguin Books, 1959. These two works are of fundamental importance for our understanding of the New Testament. The rehabilitation of Josephus as an historian is only one of the results of recent archaeological research. It should be noted that all our references to Josephus in this commentary are taken from the Loeb Classics edition of H. St. J. Thackeray, Ralph Marcus, Allen Wikgren, and L. H. Feldman.

MacMullen, Ramsey. *Enemies of the Roman Order*. Harvard University Press, 1967. This is an excellent account of intellectual unrest and disorder within the framework of the Roman imperial system. It is particularly valuable as a study of astrology and then-current popular "philosophy."

McNeile, A. H. *An Introduction to the Study of the New Testament*, 2d ed. rev. by C. S. C. Williams. Oxford University Press, 1953. This is the revision of a work published much earlier in this century, but still a valuable reference source.

Neill, Stephen C. *The Interpretation of the New Testament, 1861–1961*. Oxford University Press, 1964. This is invaluable for the reader who wishes to know the way in which NT scholarship has developed in the century under review.

II. THE NEW TESTAMENT SOURCES

Knox, W. L. *The Sources of the Synoptic Gospels*, ed. H. Chadwick. 2 vols. Cambridge University Press, 1953, 1957. Knox will be remembered by all NT scholars for his painstaking work on the early Church as seen in Acts and the Pauline letters. It is no disparagement of the author's great learning to indicate here that recent archaeological research, together with continuing work on the material from Qumran and elsewhere, has called many of his conclusions in question.

Kümmel, W. G., ed. *Introduction to the New Testament*, 14th rev. ed. of Paul Feine and Johannes Behm, *Einleitung in das Neue Testament* (Heidelberg; Quelle & Meyer, 1965) tr. by A. J. Mattill, Jr. London:

SCM / New York and Nashville: Abingdon, 1966. The great value of this book lies in the very full bibliography, and although the authors of this commentary would wish to dissent from many of the views in Kümmel's work, it is an outstanding work of source material for the student of the New Testament.

Moule, C. F. D. *The Birth of the New Testament*, 2d ed. London: Adam & Charles Black, 1965. This book, for all its comparative brevity, is exemplary in its caution and in its treatment of historical evidence. It is marked by a precision on one hand, and a lack of guesswork on the other, which set it apart from a good deal of current NT writing.

——— *The Phenomenon of the New Testament*. London: SCM, 1967. This short work will give the general reader an insight into what prompted the early Christians to give expression to their faith in the form which we now know as the New Testament.

Sanders, E. P. *The Tendencies of the Synoptic Tradition*. Cambridge University Press, 1969. It is doubtful if what has come to be called "the Synoptic Problem" will ever be fully resolved. This work will be found especially useful to the student of the NT who wishes to be kept informed of some of the current debates on the question.

Stendahl, Krister, ed. *The Scrolls and the New Testament*. New York: Harper, 1957; London: SCM, 1958. The quantity of literature on the Dead Sea scrolls proliferates at an almost alarming rate. It is a tribute to the authors of the articles in this volume that the work still stands as one of the best summaries available of the links between the Qumran scrolls and the New Testament.

Streeter, B. H. *The Four Gospels*. London: Macmillan, 1924, rev. ed., 1930. In spite of the fact that much has been written since Streeter's book, it is fair to say that hardly any book on NT sources can be found which does not at some point refer to it. But cf.

Aland, Kurt, "The Significance of the Papyri for Progress in New Testament Research," in *The Bible in Modern Scholarship*, ed. James Philip Hyatt (New York and Nashville: Abingdon, 1965), pp. 337 ff.

Taylor, Vincent. *The Formation of the Gospel Tradition*. London: Macmillan, 1933. It is still possible, after all these years, to commend Taylor's book as being the most easily understood scholarly statement of the way in which our gospels may have achieved their present form.

It is necessary to indicate here that what has come to be called "the Synoptic Problem" is matter for almost endless debate among NT scholars. No attempt will be made here to guide the reader through what has become a veritable jungle of speculation. All that we can usefully do here is to refer the general reader to the indispensable

Synopsis of the First Three Gospels, 9th ed., eds. Albert Huck and Hans Lietzmann, in conjunction for the Eng. ed. with F. L. Cross. Oxford University Press, 1957. To this we add two books which tackle the problem from quite different angles:

Farmer, W. R. *The Synoptic Problem.* New York: Macmillan, 1964.

de Solages, Bruno. *A Greek Synopsis of the Gospels,* translated from the French by J. Baissus. Leiden: Brill, 1959.

For readers with a knowledge of German and NT Greek, there are two indispensable works in dealing with the New Testament generally and (for our purposes) Matthew in particular. They are:

Kittel, Gerhard et al., eds. *Theologisches Wörterbuch zum Neuen Testament* (abbr. TWNT). Stuttgart: Kohlhammer, 1933– . Translated by Geoffrey W. Bromiley as *Theological Dictionary of the New Testament.* Grand Rapids: Eerdmans, 1964– . For the serious student of the New Testament, Kittel's work is of capital importance. However, not infrequently the theological predilections (not to mention the confessional positions) of the individual contributors are allowed to color what should be an unbiased philological analysis. It is further regrettable that the progress of knowledge since 1933 has not been reflected by publishing supplementary studies bringing the contents up to date.

Strack, H. L., and P. Billerbeck. *Kommentar zum Neuen Testament aus Talmud und Midrasch* (abbr. StB). Six volumes. Munich: Beck, 1922–61. It is necessary to exercise some caution in using rabbinic parallels to gospel material as presented in StB, since the reader must often discover for himself that the parallels quoted sometimes belong to Jewish sources long posterior to the New Testament.

III. On Matthew's Gospel

This bibliography has already called attention to the comparative dearth of recent work on Matthew. We list here only a few books specifically on this gospel.

Allen, W. H. *The Gospel According to St. Matthew,* International Critical Commentary. Edinburgh: T. & T. Clark; New York: Scribner, 1907. Although this work is dated, the student of the New Testament comes back to it time and again, impressed with the author's erudition, caution, and (for his time) perspicacity as to NT sources and tradition. It remains the most valuable commentary on this gospel in English which we possess.

Butler, B. C. *The Originality of St. Matthew: A Critique of the Two-*

Document Hypothesis. Cambridge University Press, 1951. The learned author has more than once been accused of special pleading. It must be said, however, that whatever its defects, the book does effectively challenge the common views as to the priority of Mark.

Kilpatrick, G. D. *The Origins of the Gospel According to St. Matthew*. Oxford University Press, 1946. We include this book because it represents an imaginative attempt, before the discovery of the Dead Sea scrolls, to give some account of the way in which this gospel might be thought to have taken shape.

Stendahl, Krister. *The School of St. Matthew and Its Use of the Old Testament*. Lund: Gleerup, 1954. It is doubtful whether this work has ever received the recognition which it rightly deserves. The author has not only put us in his debt with a very rich bibliography, but has also set Matthew firmly against the background of Jewish life and thought in the mid-first century A.D.

Since it is often asked where a good one-volume commentary on the whole Bible may be found, we suggest two:

Brown, Raymond E., Joseph A. Fitzmeyer, and Roland E. Murphy, *The Jerome Biblical Commentary*. Englewood Cliffs, N. J.: Prentice-Hall, 1968.

Lowther Clarke, W. K. *One Volume* [U. S., *Concise*] *Bible Commentary*. London: SPCK, 1952; New York: Macmillan, 1953. The first has taken full account of recent work on the Dead Sea scrolls; the second has the merit of being the work of one author throughout.

IV. MISCELLANEOUS WORKS ON PARTICULAR THEMES

It will be obvious that much of the content of our Introduction, Parts VI–VIII, is sympathetic to the views expressed by Günther Bornkamm in

Uberlieferung und Auslegung im Matthausevangelium (Neukirchen, 1960), tr. by Peter Scott as *Tradition and Interpretation in Matthew*, eds. Günther Bornkamm, Gerhard Barth, and H. J. Held. Philadelphia: Westminster, 1963; London: SCM, 1964.

Moore, A. L. *The Parousia in the New Testament*. Leiden: Brill, 1966. The whole theme of the "coming" of Jesus (*parousia*) is so interwoven throughout the New Testament that it is not possible to do justice to the books of the New Testament without treating it very seriously indeed. Moore's work is one of the latest dealing with this subject. It has the merit of a very full bibliography. It will be plain from the commentary that the authors of this present work would dissent from many of Moore's conclusions.

There is currently much interest in Jesus' own understanding of himself and his ministry. Two recent studies are valuable here:

Brown, Raymond E., "How Much Did Jesus Know?" CBQ 29 (1967), 315–45, and in *Jesus: God and Man.* Milwaukee: Bruce, 1967.
Fuller, Reginald H., "The Clue to Jesus' Self-Understanding," in StEv, III, No. 2 (1964), pp. 58–67.

Material on the Kingdom in Matthew is almost without limit. We here call attention to a recent article to demonstrate that there is still room for a good deal of argument about Matthew's understanding of the Kingdom:

Walker, William O., Jr., "The Kingdom of the Son of Man and the Kingdom of the Father in Matthew," CBQ 30 (1968), 573–79.

Works on the miracle stories continue to proliferate. There is now available a massive study of the miracle narratives which examines the narratives from every angle, including the medical and the psychological. Among these is

van der Loos, H. *The Miracles of Jesus.* Leiden: Brill, 1968.

No bibliography would be complete without referring to two works of Joachim Jeremias which have bearing on this gospel:

The Parables of Jesus, tr. by S. H. Hooke from the German 6th ed. of *Die Gleichnisse Jesu,* Göttingen, 1962. New York: Scribner / London: SCM, 1963.
The Eucharistic Words of Jesus, tr. by Norman Perrin from the German 3d ed. rev. of *Die Abendmahlsworte Jesu,* Göttingen, 1964. New York: Scribner / London: SCM, 1965.

Nothing illustrates better the contrast between the skepticism of some scholars and the objectivity of others than the current debate about the term "Son of Man." For example:

Tödt, H. E. *Der Menschensohn in der synoptischen Überlieferung,* 2d ed. (Gütersloh, 1963), tr. by D. M. Barton as *The Son of Man in the Synoptic Tradition.* London: SCM / Philadelphia: Westminster, 1965. This work is characterized by an almost complete skepticism as to the genuineness of sayings of Jesus about the "Son of Man." With it, compare:
Jeremias, Joachim, "Die älteste Schicht der Menschensohn-Logien," ZNW 58 (1967), 159–72.
Maddox, Robert. "The Function of the Son of Man according to the Synoptic Gospels," NTS 15 (1968), 65–69. This is a refreshing contrast to much study on this topic, in that the author is prepared to see the

title as being functional, and is therefore quite open to the suggestion that Jesus himself could well have used the term in a variety of ways, all of which are reflected in our sources.

Fitzmyer, J., *The "Genesis Apocryphon" of Qumran Cave I.* Rome, Pontifical Biblical Institute, 1966. Our indebtedness to this work, by an outstanding scholar in the field of Qumran Studies, will be plain both in the Introduction and in the course of the commentary.

The following may be unreservedly commended to the general reader:

Avi-Yonah, Michael. *Illustrated World of the Bible Library*, Vol. V, *The New Testament.* New York: McGraw-Hill, 1961.
————and Emil Kraeling. *Our Living Bible.* London: Olbourne Press, New York: McGraw-Hill, 1962.

Considering the volume of recent publication in German, or in translation from the German, some surprise may be expressed that so little of it is mentioned here or in the body of the commentary. The fact is that during the past fifty years a steadily increasing proportion of German NT scholarship has been devoted to "existentialist" and related types of exegesis, which almost wholly disregard the canons of historical judgment accepted as a matter of course in other historical fields.

A most useful summary of source material for the study of Matthew will be found in

Martin, Ralph P., "St. Matthew's Gospel in Recent Study," ET 80 (1969), 132–35.

There are references to other books and articles throughout the commentary. It is hoped that what has been provided will stimulate the interested reader of the New Testament to make his own way through the bibliographies provided in the works we have mentioned.

V. GREEK TEXTS

Three principal Greek texts were employed in the preparation of the commentary:

The Greek New Testament: Being the Text Translated in the New English Bible, 1961, ed. by R. V. G. Tasker. London and New York: Oxford and Cambridge University Presses, 1964.
The Greek New Testament: (Edition of the American Bible Society) ed. by Kurt Aland, Matthew Black, Bruce M. Metzger, and Allen Wikgren. New York, 1965.
Novum Testamentum graece, ed. Alexander Souter, 2d ed. Oxford: Clarendon Press, 1947.

MATTHEW

1. THE GENEALOGY OF JESUS
(i 1–17)†

I [1] The list of the ancestry of Jesus-Messiah, son of David, son of Abraham.

[2] Abraham was the father of Isaac, Isaac of Jacob, and Jacob was father of Judah and his brothers. [3] Judah was the father of Perez and Zerah (by Tamar) and Perez fathered Hezron, who was the father of Ram. [4] Ram was father of Amminadab, Amminadab of Nahshon, while Nahshon was father of Salmon. [5] Salmon fathered Boaz (by Rahab), Boaz was father of Obed (by Ruth), Obed was the father of Jesse, who was the father of King David.

[6] David was father of Solomon, by the wife of Uriah, [7] and Solomon fathered Rehoboam. Rehoboam was the father of Abijah, who was father of Asa. [8] Asa was the father of Jehoshaphat, Jehoshaphat of Joram, Joram being father of Uzziah. [9] Uzziah was the father of Jotham, Jotham of Ahaz, and Ahaz was the father of Hezekiah. [10] Hezekiah was father of Manasseh, Manasseh fathered Amon, who was the father of Josiah. [11] Josiah was the father of Jechoniah and his brothers, at the time of the deportation to Babylon.

[12] After the deportation to Babylon, Jechoniah fathered Shealtiel, who was father of Zerubbabel. [13] Zerubbabel was the father of Abiud, who was father of Eliakim, and Eliakim was the father of Azor. [14] Azor fathered Zadok, who was the father of Achim, who in turn was father of Eliud; [15] Eliud was the father of Eleazar, Eleazar of Matthan, and Matthan of Jacob. [16] Jacob was the father of Joseph, husband of Mary, of whom

† **Matt i 1–17** || Luke iii 23–38.

was born Jesus who is called Messiah. [17] So there were in all
fourteen generations from Abraham to David, fourteen from
David to the Babylonian Exile, and fourteen from the Babylonian Exile to the Messiah.

NOTES

i 1 (Mark i 1).
i 1. The Greek words *biblos geneseōs* can carry a number of possible
translations, and our own "genealogy" is but one. As it stands, it occurs
in LXX at Gen ii 4, v 1, while *geneseis* is frequently employed to denote
"descendants" in Genesis. But for the first readers of Matthew, it called
attention also to the birth (*genesis*) not only of Jesus, but of the whole
new order to which that birth gave rise.

Jesus. The word is the Greek rendering of a well-known Hebrew
name. It was *Yahōshû* first, then by inner Hebrew phonetic change it
became *Yōshūa,* and by a still later northern dialectal shift, *Yeshūa.*
The first element, *Yāhū* (=Yahweh) means "the Lord," while the second
comes from *shûaʿ* "To help, save." The most probable meaning is "O
Lord, save."

Messiah. By the time of the later Pauline letters, the Gr. *Christos*
(=The Anointed One) was on the way to becoming a proper name
instead of a title; it meant little, as a title, to those without a Jewish
background. We have consistently translated the word as "Messiah." In
this instance we have hyphenated the phrase as *Jesus-Messiah.* In this
period the Aram. *mešīḥā* could equally well mean "a Messiah" or "the
Messiah," since the affixed definite article *ā* came to be used for both
definite and indefinite nouns. See Fitzmyer, *The "Genesis Apocryphon"
of Qumran Cave 1,* p. 200, concerning the varying usage of the Aramaic
article just before the time of Christ.

son of David. G. Dalman, *The Words of Jesus* (Edinburgh: T. &. T.
Clark, 1930), pp. 319 ff., may also be consulted on this. It was suggested
by Yehezkel Kaufmann ("The Messianic Idea: The Real and the
Hidden Son of David," *El Ha'ayin* 5 [1961]), that after the Babylonian
Exile the tradition grew that messiahs were sons-of-David "not because
they were descended from David, but were sons-of-David because they
were messiahs." The same author goes on to suggest that the revelation
of a messiah would carry with it a revelation also of lost genealogical
information. But Kaufmann's view was developed before the Dead Sea
scrolls were adequately assimilated by scholars, and in the light of the
Qumran material his view must be regarded as merely speculative.

There would, moreover, be many families of Davidic descent in first-century Judea wholly unaware of their lineage, though others would have clung tenaciously to the tradition.

son of Abraham. Apart from the emphasis given in the Testament of Levi viii to the descent of the Messiah from Abraham, the appellation has further significance. For all the stress in Matthew on the mission of Jesus to Israel, it was through Abraham that *all* the families of the earth were to be blessed (Gen xii 3), an idea which finds expression in xxviii 19. It was developed extensively by Paul (Rom iv–xi; Gal iii–iv) in defending the status of Gentile Christians as fellow heirs of God's promises.

The genealogy makes use of the OT insofar as that served:

vs. 2   =   I Chron i 34; ii 1
vs. 3   =   I Chron ii 4, 5, 9
vss. 4–6   =   I Chron ii 10–13, iii 5, 10–15
vs. 12   =   (i.e., down to Zerubbabel) I Chron iii 17–19
vss. 13–16   contain names otherwise not known to us in Scripture, but they are names well enough known from Jewish sources of the Hellenistic period, including an increasing number of Aramaic documents. The names are intermediate in character, and in part resemble names in the Edfu papyri (third century B.C.), the names of the translators of the LXX in the Letter of Aristeas, Josephus, Aramaic papyri, and ossuary inscriptions of the first century A.D.

Whatever may have been the original language of Matthew as it was first committed to writing, quotations from the OT in the Greek of the LXX occur. It would seem, however, on the basis of fragments (still mostly unpublished) from the Dead Sea, that what we mainly have in biblical quotations in Matthew is an old Palestinian recension related to the Lucianic text (cf. F. M. Cross, Jr., *The Ancient Library of Qumran* [New York: Doubleday, 1958], pp. 124 ff.).

1. 2–6 (Luke iii 31–34).
2. *Jacob.* The Hebrew of I Chron i 34 has *Israel.*
3. The mention of *Zerah* (in its LXX form of Zara) and *Tamar,* names which have no function in the genealogy, suggests that the author, or an editor, had the LXX in front of him. LXX forms are used for *Hezron* (*Hesrōm*) and *Ram* (*Haram,* I Chron ii 9).
4. LXX forms (*Naassōn* and *Aminadab* from I Chron ii 10–11) are used for *Nahshon* and *Amminadab.*
5. *Rahab* is given as *Rachab* by Matthew, which is not an LXX form, but which does occur in Josephus (*Antiquities,* V. 8, 11, 15) as *hē Rachabē* or *Raabē,* indicating the change of pronunciation which was

beginning in the time of Josephus. LXX forms are used, however, for *Obed* and *Jesse* (*Iobēd* and *Iessai*).

6–7. LXX forms occur here for *Solomon* (*Solomōn*), *Uriah* (*Ouriou*), and *Rehoboam* (*Roboam*).

8–9. *Joram being father of Uzziah.* . . . It is sometimes said by commentators that Matthew omits three kings (Ahaziah, Joash, and Amaziah) for the purpose of tidying up his pattern of three "fourteens." This is not so, however. The evangelist here follows the LXX I Chronicles, which declares (iii 11) that Joram was the father of Uzziah. Matthew continues, *Uzziah was the father of Jotham*, and the LXX has *Joash his son, Amaziah his son, Azariah his son, Jotham his son.* As a result, Matthew has omitted *not* Ahaziah (=LXX Ozeias), but Joash, Amaziah, and Azariah (=Uzziah). The reason for this can be found in the LXX, I Chron iii 11, where the son of *Joram* is called *Ozeia.* Generally, the LXX has *Ochozeias* (in Hebrew, *Ahaziah*), and *Ozeia*=Uzziah (cf. II Chron xxvi 3 ff.). If, therefore, *Ozeia* in I Chron iii 11 is a mistake, it would be natural enough in copying the text to assume that *Ozeia*= *Uzziah* and so pass on to Uzziah's son Jotham, thus omitting three intervening kings by a familiar scribal error known as *homoioteleuton.* It is more than likely that this present genealogy in Greek, with its notes on "fourteen generations," belongs to an editor assimilating Matthew's list to the LXX record.

11. *and his brothers* seems to have been recorded here in line with the list of Jehoiakim's brothers in I Chron iii 15. As it stands, however, the verse is clearly impossible, because Jehoiakim (I Chron iii 15) has been omitted, and it means that in the third division there are but thirteen names, beginning with *Shealtiel.* It can only be presumed that *Jechoniah* (I Chron iii 16) is here an alternative for king *Jehoiakim*, and—as we have suggested—*and his brothers* is due to assimilation from I Chron iii 15, where the names of Jehoiakim's brothers are given.

12. =I Chron iii 17.

How dependent the present form of the genealogy is on the LXX can be demonstrated here. The Hebrew text has Zerubbabel as the son of Pedaiah (I Chron iii 19), whereas the LXX has him as son of Shealtiel. Zerubbabel has apparently been confused with his cousin.

13–15. For the names included in this section, the author was dependent on sources which we do not possess. See NOTE on vs. 1. We have ten names covering over five hundred years, so it is only a fragmentary report. There must have been roughly twice as many names. The names themselves have probably been transmitted correctly; the first six names for the early post-Exilic period are names otherwise attested for that time, and the last four names are characteristic names of the last two centuries B.C. Since there is no trace of the usual papponymy (naming of a son after his grandfather), it follows that some such names may have been dropped from the list in oral transmission. The name Azor belongs to a common type of shortened form (hypocoristicon) of a name like Eleazar or Azariah. Achim is still obscure.

16–17. The genealogy comes to its climax with the birth of Jesus. Modern attempts to find deliberate traces of numerology in the compilation of this ancestry list, in addition to those of the editor in vs. 17, are often ingenious and frequently interesting. They are not, however, susceptible of proof, even when one goes so far as to point to the consonantal value of David's name in Hebrew being fourteen as supporting evidence. Pleas for "six weeks of generations" and the like belong to what has been called the "desk mind" rather than to verifiable historical research. Equally unconvincing is the suggestion that the genealogy can be viewed as reaching one climax in David, declining to the Babylonian Exile, and then climbing to its highest ascent in Jesus the Messiah.

COMMENT

In the first section Matthew's purpose is to demonstrate who Jesus is: the Messiah, God's anointed representative, the expected King. He is also son of David, of the royal house of Judah by descent. Finally, he is son of Abraham, through whom God had promised that he would bless all the families of the earth (Gen xii 3). Beginning with vs. 18 (our §2), Matthew goes on to declare that Jesus was miraculously conceived in the womb of Mary through the agency of the Holy Spirit.

We have no good reason to doubt that this genealogy was transmitted in good faith. There are certainly considerable gaps in its scheme, and there are names which are not known to us from the OT record (vss. 13–15). But the genealogy begins with Abraham, the father of the Jewish people, and the evangelist uses the OT material insofar as this assists his tradition. The inclusion of four women, however, at least three of whom were considered to be Gentiles, and who might otherwise be excluded from such a genealogy (Tamar, Rahab, Ruth, and Uriah's wife), indicates that what we have is no mere conventional genealogy, but one which a Jewish Christian would only have used because tradition compelled him to do so. Such inclusions may also indicate that the evangelist's

tradition saw these women (in their capacity as instruments of
God's providence) as forerunners of Mary.

What we read in this genealogy is what the evangelist's tradition
told him about Jesus, a tradition seen in the light of Israel's history.
What precise historical basis there was for this genealogy is not open
to our inspection; but it would be rash to dismiss lightly genealogies
of the probable period in which Matthew's gospel was written.

Any extensive treatment of the genealogy in Luke's gospel
(Luke iii 23–38) belongs to a commentary on that gospel, but
some attention must be paid to it here. Both Matthew and Luke
claim Davidic descent for Jesus through Joseph, while both at the
same time affirm that the conception and birth of Jesus were
virginal and miraculous. Equally, both claim that this Jesus is to be
equated with a pre-existent "Son of Man" and also with the child
born at Bethlehem. There are divergencies, however. Matthew (i 6)
derives the Davidic ancestry through Solomon the king, son of
David, while Luke's genealogy traces the ancestry through Nathan
—also son of David. The two genealogies coincide again with
Shealtiel and Zerubbabel (Matt i 12, 13; cf. Luke iii 27, 28).
Luke also has more names from the period of the Exile onwards,
and so provides a more probable number of generations than does
Matthew's genealogy for this period of time. The OT material in
Luke from Terah onwards (Luke iii 35–38) is not used by Matthew.

What is being established in both genealogies is a claim to
legitimate Davidic ancestry, even though later Jesus himself is
represented as dismissing the Davidic ancestry as of little moment
(cf. Matt xxii 41–46 in COMMENT on our §81). That there is
formal inconsistency here is not to be doubted: both evangelists
claiming Davidic descent through Joseph, while at the same time
giving us a tradition of virginal conception and birth. To make
charges of dishonesty or to impugn the motives of the writers is—at
this remove of time—perilous. Allowing for the very tenacious
traditions with respect to ancestry among Jews at the time of Jesus,
we are certainly entitled to say that both evangelists were faithfully
recording the traditions which they had received, whatever the inconsistencies.

2. THE BIRTH OF JESUS
(i 18–25)†

I 18 The birth of Jesus-Messiah happened like this: When his mother Mary had been betrothed to Joseph, and before they came together, she was found to be pregnant by the Holy Spirit. 19 Joseph her husband, being a man of character, and unwilling to shame her, wished to divorce her secretly. 20 But as he agonized about this, a divine messenger appeared to him in a dream, and said: "Joseph, son of David, do not be afraid to take Mary as your wife, for what is conceived in her is through the Holy Spirit. 21 She will bear a son, and you shall call his name Jesus, because he will save his people from their sins." 22 All this happened so as to fulfill what the Lord had said through the prophet:

> 23 See, the virgin shall conceive and bear a son,
>   and they shall call his name Emmanuel

(which means, God is with us). 24 When Joseph had awakened from sleep he did the messenger's bidding and took his wife. 25 However, he had no marital relations with her until she had borne a son. He named him Jesus.

† Matt i 18–25 ‖ Luke ii 1–7.

NOTES

i 18. Some late manuscripts and patristic sources omit *Jesus* before *the Messiah*. All early manuscripts and church fathers keep it.

betrothed to Joseph. In the Law (Deut xxii 13 ff.) betrothal was a far more binding step than is our custom of engagement before marriage, and the penalty for fornication with one person while betrothed to another was death for both guilty parties. Cf. vs. 19, where Joseph is described as *her husband*, and vs. 20, where the Greek can be translated "Do not be afraid to take Mary your wife"—i.e., into your home.

(the) Holy Spirit (cf. also vs. 20). In Aramaic at this time there was no differentiation between the definite and the indefinite article. The absence of the definite article in Greek at this point is therefore not significant. The Spirit as the agent of God's creative act is the explanation which Matthew gives here of Mary's pregnancy (cf. Gen i 2; Psalm civ 30), and which Joseph understands in his dream (vs. 20).

19. Joseph's dedication to the Law is indicated in his description as *dikaios*. Contemporary usage in Josephus shows that the Greek means "one obedient to the commands of God, an upright man, a man of character." He decides to divorce Mary secretly—i.e., in the presence of chosen witnesses, without public scandal. *Deigmatisai* (to shame, or disgrace) occurs in the NT only here and at Col ii 15.

20. Only direct revelation, here in a dream, will indicate what is hidden in the purpose of God. Cf. xi 27, xvi 7. For further examples of acts of revelation through dreams in Matthew, cf. ii 12, 13, 19, 22, xxvii 19.

divine messenger. Unless there is plain and inescapable evidence of a visitation by a heavenly being, an "angel," we have translated the Gr. *angelos* by "messenger," which is of course the actual meaning of the Greek. It is worth bearing in mind that in the majority of the cases in which "angels" have appeared to men in the Bible, they have been assumed by the beholders to be human beings.

do not be afraid. . . . According to Jewish law, the betrothal and the taking of the bride to the bridegroom's house were the two parts, the beginning and the ending, of the legal process of marriage.

the Holy Spirit. See NOTE on vs. 18.

Jesus, . . . from their sins. See NOTE on vs. 1.

22. . . . *so as to fulfill.* This is the first instance of Matthew's fulfillment formula, *hina plērōthē*. On its importance, see Part IV of the Introduction. The formula, in varying words, occurs nine times in Matthew: ii 15, 17, 23, iv 14, viii 17, xii 17, xiii 35, xxi 4 (cf. xxvi 56), xxvii 9.

23. *the virgin.* The quotation is from Isa vii 14 and is given in the Greek of the LXX, with the substitution of *they shall call* for *you* (singular) *shall call.* The Greek is (uniquely) *parthenos*, "virgin," for the Hebrew *'almah*, "girl." It is possible on some views that Isaiah was using mythological terms current in his own time to demonstrate an expected deliverer's birth. The LXX translators would appear to have so understood the passage, and only later did Greek translations of the Hebrew appear with the word one would expect, *neanis*, "young maiden" instead of *parthenos*.

Emmanuel . . . God is with us. The sense is of God's active vindication of his people (cf. Ps xlvi 7, 11). The theme of "recapitulation" in Matthew (see Part IV of the Introduction) finds its proper commentary on this verse at Matt xxviii 20.

24. *awakened from sleep* (Gk. *egertheis,* literally "raised up"). On this word, as a Semitic usage, see Dalman, *Words,* pp. 23, 36.

25. *However, he had no marital relations with her.* The Greek imperfect *eginōsken* (literally "did not know her") would appear to militate against the tradition of Mary's perpetual virginity. The verse is commonly cited by Protestants to indicate that Mary had other children, by Joseph. It has been common tradition in both Eastern and Western Christendom since at least the fourth century that Mary was virgin both before and after the birth of Jesus.

One factor is worth mentioning here. One of the men named as a brother of Jesus (Matt xiii 56) is called Joseph. While it was certainly not unknown for sons to be named after their fathers, it was at the same time uncommon. There may thus be some grounds for the view that those described as "brothers and sisters" of Jesus were near relatives (cousins, according to Jerome) and not the children of Joseph and Mary.

COMMENT

The author, from his genealogy linking Abraham and David with the Messiah, has led his readers to expect an unusual birth narrative, and this he proceeds to give. The evangelist's tradition had two elements in it: (a) Jesus was the Messiah, and so he was son of David; (b) Jesus was conceived and born in a wholly miraculous manner, being conceived and born of a virgin without human intervention. Matthew gives expression to the facts as he found them in his tradition, and makes no attempt to reconcile them.

The first part, (a), has been briefly examined already. The second is not open to historical investigation, and we are not called upon to enter realms of faith or theology in a commentary of this nature. Some comment is, however, inescapable.

(a) All through the genealogy, *egennēsen* denotes legal inheritance and descent, not physical. The evangelist could only deal with his material by assuming that Mary's husband was the *legal* father of Jesus.

(b) The tradition of the virgin birth was known to Luke, and also—on one legitimate reading of the Greek—to John (John i 13). It was well known as a polemical battleground in the time of Origen, ca. A.D. 185?–?254 (*Contra Celsum* ii 28, 32, 33, 39), and was also so known to Justin Martyr (106?–?165). Ignatius of Antioch (ca. 112) took the tradition for granted, as did Aristides, (ca. 140). Rendel Harris, in his edition of the *Apology* of Aristides, remarks that ". . . at that period the virginity of Mary was a part of formulated Christian belief." Additional evidence is also to be found in the *Didache* but there is considerable dispute as to the date and importance of this document; we ourselves can only say that we are convinced the work is almost certainly to be dated in the second half of the first century.

(c) The genealogy is certainly no proof that there is an attempt being made by the evangelist to exalt to quasi-divine status the naturally born son of Joseph and Mary. There is not the slightest indication that the genealogy was ever a separate document apart from the gospel; indeed, that genealogy paves the way for vss. 18–25 by informing us that Mary was betrothed to the Joseph of vs. 16.

(d) A Jewish Christian such as Matthew could only deal faithfully with his traditions and set them down as he knew them. If this procedure tells us nothing of the validity of the traditions, it at least tells us something significant about the honesty of an evangelist dealing with what he knew would cause speculation and scandal.

(e) The description of Jesus as "Son of Mary" in Mark vi 3 is possible evidence for a custom known to rabbinic sources of a man being named as "of his mother" when the father was unknown (cf. TB *Yebamoth* iv 13, which speaks of this custom as applied to "the natural son of a wedded wife").

There is a good short discussion of the whole question of the place of the virgin birth in Christian tradition in Reginald H. Fuller's "The Virgin Birth: Historical Fact or Kerygmatic Truth?" *Biblical Research* 1 (1957), 1–8. The reader is warned, however, that the literature on the subject is legion and covers every possible angle. The search on the part of some NT scholars for real or supposed Hellenistic parallels to the tradition of a supernatural birth can be set alongside the sobriety of David Daube's investigation of a similar Jewish legend about Moses (cf. his *New Testament and Rabbinic Judaism,* pp. 5 ff.).

3. THE VISIT OF THE MAGI
(ii 1–12)

II ¹ When Jesus was born at Bethlehem of Judah in the time of King Herod, magi came from the east to Jerusalem. ² "Where," they asked, "is the one who has been born as king of the Jews? For we have seen his star at its rising and we have come to pay him homage." ³ When King Herod heard this he was disturbed, and the whole of Jerusalem with him. ⁴ Having assembled all the chief priests and the scribes of the people, he asked them, "Where is the Messiah to be born?" ⁵ They replied to him, "In Bethlehem of Judah. For it is so written by the prophet:

> ⁶ 'And you, Bethlehem, in the country of Judah,
> are by no means least among the rulers of Judah;
> for out of you shall come a ruler
> who will govern my people Israel.' "

⁷ Then Herod secretly summoned the magi and established from them the time of the appearing of the star. He sent them to Bethlehem with the words ⁸ "Go and search very carefully for the child. When you have found him, tell me, so that I too may come and pay him homage." ⁹ Having listened to the king, they went on their way. The star which they had seen at its rising went before them until it came to rest over the place where the little child was. ¹⁰ Seeing this star, they were joyful with great gladness. ¹¹ On coming into the house they saw the little child with Mary his mother, and prostrating themselves they paid him homage. They opened their treasures and presented gifts to him—gold, incense, and myrrh. ¹² Having been warned in a dream not to return to Herod, they left for their own country by another way.

NOTES

ii 1. *When Jesus was born at Bethlehem.* The actual birth of Jesus is dealt with in this gospel by a simple Greek construction of two words, the genitive absolute, a participial phrase. *Bethlehem* is designated *of Judah* because there was another Bethlehem in Zebulun. Luke's account (Luke ii 1–7) tells how Jesus came to be born in Bethlehem, though subsequently brought up in Nazareth.

in the time of King Herod. Herod reigned from 37–4 B.C. Perhaps the best book on Herod for the general reader is Stewart Perowne's *The Life and Times of Herod the Great,* London: Hodder, 1956.

magi. The RSV perpetuates the unhappy translation of "wise men," where the NEB has "astrologers." We have consistently referred to the visitors as "magi," as being less liable to misunderstanding. It is nowhere said that the magi were three in number, still less that they were kings, and certainly there is no indication that they were Gentiles.

2. To state, as do some commentators, that Jews would not have used the phrase "king of the Jews" is to be ignorant of first-century usage. The phrase was certainly used by the orthodox King Aristobulus I (104–103 B.C.), and in any case "Hebrews" and "Israel" were largely the pre-empted badges of Samaritans and Jewish sectarians respectively. (Cf. Abram Spiro, "Stephen's Samaritan Background," Appendix V, in Johannes Munck, *The Acts of the Apostles,* AB, vol. 31.)

at its rising. Only with difficulty can the Greek mean "in the east"; and it is unlikely that the magi would have said "in the east" rather than something like "in our own land." What we appear to have is a technical expression referring to the beginning of the phenomenon observed by the magi. There is no possessive pronoun ("its") in the Greek, presumably because a copyist at some stage misunderstood the word *rising* (Gr. *anatolē*), assumed the Greek to mean "east," and so omitted *its* (Gr. *autou*) before *rising.* The Greek word refers in pre-Christian literature to the rising of the sun and other stars. All the information which has been thought to be relevant to celestial phenomena in the presumed time of the birth of Jesus is listed in Finegan, *Handbook of Biblical Chronology,* pp. 238 ff.

pay him homage. The word used here and again in vs. 11 (*proskunēsai*) is common in Matthew (thirteen times as against two in Mark and three in Luke). It is a useful indication of style, emphasis, and the homogeneity of a work.

3. *disturbed* (or "frightened"—cf. xiv 26). The same word, with the same meaning of deep agitation, is found at xiv 26 (there used of the disciples). In both instances the fear results from a lack of faith.

5. *In Bethlehem.* On the expectation of a ruler from Bethlehem, cf. John vii 41 ff.

it is so written (Gr. *gegraptai*)="the inspired text runs," a common device in the rabbinic literature.

6. The quotation, from Mic v 1, 3, does not follow the LXX text, and is an independent rendering of the Hebrew. The final clause *who will govern* (literally, be shepherd of) appears to have been assimilated to the form of II Sam v 2.

7. *Then* (Gr. *tote*) is a favorite word of Matthew. He uses it, in all, ninety times.

11. *gold, incense, and myrrh.* All manner of symbolic meanings have been attached to these offerings, under the influence of Isa lx 6 and Ps lxxii 10, 11, 15. Justin Martyr is the first commentator whom we know to have seen the connection between the passages. There is no such connection made in Matthew (but see COMMENT below). Myrrh was certainly suitable for a king, and was used at his anointing (cf. Ps xlv 8). But the gifts were also part of the common stock-in-trade of magi, and magical charms were written with myrrh-ink (cf. K. Preisendanz, *Papyri Graeci Magicae: Die griechischen Zauberpapyri*, Vol. I [Leipzig and Berlin: B. A. Tuebner, 1928], pp. 8, 16, 22, etc.). Regarded as the tools of a trade, offerings of the magi would not be gifts of homage, but a declaration of dissociation from former practices.

12. *they left* (Gr.=withdrew) is a frequent word in Matthew (ten times), and later in Christian literature provided the word *anchorite*, one who withdrew from the society of men to follow the contemplative life. The same word has an interesting secular history, being used in the Roman period to indicate a "flight to the suburbs" to avoid city taxation.

by another way. This same feature—departure by another route—also occurs in Dio Cassius' account of the visit to Nero by Tiridates (*Roman History* LXIII 7).

COMMENT

This account of the visit of the magi to Bethlehem has on the face of it all the elements of historical probability, and yet at the same time elements which appear to belong more plausibly to parable.

It is, for example, well known that not only among Jews was there expectation of a semidivine hero-ruler. "Messianic" hopes were expressed in Virgil's famous fourth Eclogue, and the emperor Augustus was described in inscriptions at Halicarnassus and Priene as the salvation of a new race of men, and as bringing peace on sea and land. The magos Tiridates and some followers came to Naples, and the story of their reception by Nero, and the attendant religious ceremonies, is fascinating. (There are details in Dio Cassius *Roman History* LXIII 1, 7; Suetonius *Life of Nero* 13.) Tiridates was moved to address Nero as "god."

Astrology and the prevalence of magi as a professional class are both very well attested in the contemporary literature. Those Stoics whose works we know were enthusiastic supporters of astrology. Astrology developed early in the Mediterranean, rose to a quasi-science in the Achaemenian period—the earliest Babylonian horoscopes so far known are fourth-century B.C., of the time of Alexander —and was transformed in Egypt into the astrology which we know today. The results of this systematizing are found all over the Middle East, in cuneiform tablets of the Seleucid and Parthian periods, in demotic papyri of the Roman era, and in Greek and Arabic astrological literature. Some astrological texts had a very long life, being preserved in Byzantine Zoroastrian material.

In spite of the frequent condemnation of astrology in the OT, in the intertestamental literature and in the rabbinic writings, Judaism was deeply affected by the phenomenon, as has been demonstrated by Cumont and Bidez.* Josephus (*Jewish War* V. 214) is authority for the statement that the veil of the temple was adorned with stars, and many excavated synagogues in Rome and in Palestine have been found to have the signs of the zodiac depicted in them. Aramaic fragments have been found in Cave IV at Qumran which contain remains of an astrological treatise closely related to a work which circulated in Byzantine times under the name of Zoroaster. The Aramaic fragments may be late first century B.C. or early first century A.D. (cf. David Pingree, *Isis* 54 (1963), for further information).

In the minds of the people at that time, it was inconceivable that the birth of an important personage should go unattended by a stellar harbinger, and such a star is reported to have greeted the birth of Mithridates (ca. 131–63 B.C.). A late Jewish legend ascribes such a star to the birth of Abraham. But for Judaism there was another consideration, and that was the prophetic oracle of Balaam (Num xxiv 17). The promise is that of a "star coming

* Cf. Joseph Bidez and Franz Cumont, *Les Mages hellénisés: Zoroastre, Ostanés et Hystapes d'après la tradition grecque,* Paris, 1938, and Franz Cumont, *L'Egypte des Astrologues,* Brussels, 1937.

from Jacob"; not only would this oracle be well known, but in circles which studied the prophets to find interpretations of the contemporary scene (such as the Essenes) such an oracle could not in the nature of the case have been without fulfillment. A messiah's advent *must* be hailed by a star. (The leader of the patriots in the second Jewish War, A.D. 130–135, Bar Kosba, changed his resistance name, which probably meant "son of a young ram," to Bar Kokhba, "son of a star." This is known from the recently published Murabba'at letters.)

So much by way of background. The historicity of the narrative in ch. ii as it stands is not quite so easily elucidated, and commentators have ranged from dismissing the episode as astrological myth on the one hand to attempting on the other to pinpoint the exact comet or planetary conjunction which first appeared in the assumed year of the birth of Jesus (ca. 9–4 B.C.).

It must be said that the absence of the Matthean clause "that it might be fulfilled" (*hina plērōthē*) in the narrative, either in connection with Num xxiv, or—even more strikingly—Isa lx and Ps lxxii, has to be taken very seriously indeed in any evaluation of the narrative as historical. The absence of the formula would be notable enough if, *pace* some commentators, Matthew's quotations were mere proof texts. If, as we have maintained, his quotations are to be seen in context, then the omission of the formula is striking as casting doubt on how far the evangelist regarded the account as historical.

Historically, there is nothing in the least improbable about magi traveling from Babylon west, or indeed anywhere else in the Mediterranean world. They would find welcome audiences anywhere, from royal courts to market places. Consultation of magi by kings and prominent persons is well attested. With "messianism" of one kind and another in the air almost everywhere—and Herod cannot possibly have been ignorant of the hopes being entertained at Qumran—then the news of magi coming to seek a king would guarantee Herod's calling for them. Herod was constantly concerned with real or imagined usurpers.

It is possible to maintain that Matthew's story was intended as polemic directed against astrology (cf. C. S. Mann, "Wise Men or Charlatans?" *Theology* 61 [1958], 443–47 and 495–500, and later "The Historicity of the Birth Narratives," in *History and Chronology in the New Testament,* London: SPCK, 1965; also W. K.

Lowther Clarke, *Divine Humanity,* London: SPCK / New York: Macmillan, 1936). This may have been the view of Ignatius of Antioch (*Letter to Ephesus* xix. 3) at the beginning of the second century. What seems to us to be wholly inadmissible is the suggestion that Matthew was so anxious to represent Jesus as a new Moses, leading a new Exodus from Egypt (ii 13–15, our §4) into the promised land (i.e., the kingdom—ii 19–23, our §6), that the evangelist has constructed an allegory which includes Gentiles (the magi). There is, however, no indication in the story that we were meant to identify the magi as Gentiles.

If we assume genuine historical reminiscence in the account of the magi, then the omission of the "fulfillment formula," *hina plērōthē,* must also be explained by some means which is valid in historical literary criticism. (E.g., why did the evangelist not quote Ps. lxxii 10, 11 or Isa lx 3, 6, 14?) The one suggestion which appears to carry any weight is as follows: The threat of Gnosticism was very soon felt by the church, as is evidenced by the Johannine letters and by Paul's letter to Colossae. (Cf. also "Simon Magus as 'The Great Power of God,'" by W. F. Albright, Appendix VII in Munck, *The Acts of the Apostles.*) It is probable, therefore, on this thesis that in the midst of the Gnostic struggle within the church or on its periphery a scribe or editor deliberately removed the Matthean formula. Any suggestion that Jesus, through the evangelist's record, even appeared to acknowledge the legitimacy of astrology would have been avidly seized upon by the Gnostics. Plainly, we have no evidence for such editorial or scribal excision, but this suggestion does have the merit of preserving the narrative as broadly historical, and at the same time explaining an otherwise totally inexplicable omission by Matthew.

4. THE FLIGHT TO EGYPT
(ii 13–15)

II 13 When they had made their departure, a divine messenger appeared to Joseph in a dream: "Get up," he said, "take the young child and his mother and flee to Egypt. Stay there until I tell you, for Herod is about to search for the young child to kill him." 14 He got up and took the child and his mother by night and withdrew to Egypt, 15 remaining there until Herod's death. This was to fulfill the Lord's saying through the prophet:

"I have called my son out of Egypt."

NOTES

ii 14. *withdrew.* See first NOTE on vs. 12 (§3).

15. On this quotation from Hosea xi 1 (which is not from the Greek of the LXX), cf. Introduction, Part IV.

COMMENT

Whatever may be the case with the story of the magi, there is no reason to doubt the historicity of the story of the family's flight into Egypt. The OT abounds in references to individuals and families taking refuge in Egypt, in flight either from persecution or revenge, or in the face of economic pressure. Even though Matthew does in fact make the connection, the story of the sojourn in Egypt does not depend necessarily on the reactions of Herod to a consultation with the magi. If we accept the substantial historicity of the Lukan birth narrative, then even a rumor of the events detailed in Luke ii 1–39 would have called forth predictably violent reactions from Herod.

It is certainly not necessary to see in this episode a second Moses fleeing the wrath of another king, preserved against a future Exodus from Egypt. We hope that the Introduction has made it clear that Matthew's OT quotations see Jesus as living, in himself, through the spiritual experience of a whole people, and not as an individual who becomes another Moses.

5. THE SLAUGHTER OF THE CHILDREN
(ii 16–18)

II 16 Then Herod, when he realized that he had been out-
witted by the magi, was furiously angry, and sent men to kill
all the children in Bethlehem and its environs who were two
years old or less, in accordance with the time which he had
learned from the magi. 17 So was fulfilled the saying of the
prophet Jeremiah:

> 18 "A voice was heard in Ramah,
>   crying and loud lament;
>   Rachel weeping for her children,
>   and she refused to be comforted, because they were no
>   more."

NOTES

ii 17–18. The quotation from Jer xxxi 15 is not from the Greek of
the LXX, but represents a translation of the Hebrew. For example, the
LXX does not have *her children* (*ta tekna autēs*), though two versions
of the LXX have *epi tōn huiōn autēs* (*about her sons*).

COMMENT

The slaughter of infants two years old or less in a town of the
size of Bethlehem (population ca. 300) at this time would not
only have been a comparatively minor incident, and so probably
unknown to Josephus, but also completely in line with Herod's
known character.

The evangelist sees the episode as yet another facet of Israel's
whole spiritual experience, summed up in Jesus, and seen against
the context of Jer xxxi. Cf. Introduction, Part IV.

6. RETURN FROM EGYPT
(ii 19–23)

II ¹⁹ When Herod died, however, a divine messenger appeared in a dream to Joseph in Egypt. ²⁰ "Get up," he said, "take the young child and his mother and return to the land of Israel, for those who sought the young child's life are dead." ²¹ So he got up, took the child and his mother and came into the country of Israel. ²² But having heard that Archelaus reigned in Judea in the place of his father Herod, he was afraid to go there. Being warned in a dream he withdrew into Galilean territory ²³ and went to live in a town called Nazareth. So was fulfilled what was spoken through the prophet:

"He shall be called a Nazorean."

NOTES

ii 23. *He shall be called a Nazorean* (*Nazōraios*). There have been many suggestions as to the possible origin of this saying. Some have seen in this evidence that early in his life Jesus was pledged to the life of a Nazirite. But not only is the Greek for Nazirite *Naziraios*—apart from Judg xiii 5 there is no clear OT source from which Matthew might have derived his quotation. If the quotation were simply a "proof-text," then there would be some slight justification for suggesting that what we have here is a text attesting to yet another wonderful birth, somewhat similar to that of Samson. But if the quotation is to be seen in total context, then another and more likely source must be found. The standard Syriac text (Peshitta) of this verse, which follows an earlier and more authentic tradition of Semitic place names, almost everywhere reads *Naṣath* and *Nāṣrāyā*, while the later, more Greek-influenced Christian Palestinian Aramaic has *Nazrath* and *Nazōrāyā*. (Both gentilics are well attested; see W. F. Albright, "The Names 'Nazareth' and

'Nazorean,'" JBL 65 (1946), 397–401. See also J. A. Sanders, "ΝΑΖΩΡΑΙΟΣ in Matt. 2²³," JBL 84 (1965), 169–72.)

We looked for a passage in the prophets where a form of the Hebrew consonants *nṣr* appeared, but where also the meaning had been lost or obscured, both in the Hebrew Masoretic text (MT) and in the Greek of the LXX. Jeremiah xxxi 6 not only appears to be the only such example, but it also provides the necessary context against which the incidents of vss. 19–23 can be measured. The Hebrew MT cannot be correctly vocalized at this point, for it is not grammatically coherent; but with slight modifications in vocalization, the verse could be read: "For there is a day (in which) the guards (Heb. *nōṣrīm*) on Mount Ephraim will call." The LXX probably means, "For there is a day when those who defend (the faith) will proclaim on the mountains of Ephraim." It is clear that the verse in Matthew does not fully conform either to the LXX or the MT; it presumably rests upon a lost "Old Palestinian" recension of a type not infrequent in the NT (see NOTE on i 1), and which may have been vocalized as passive (Heb. *yiqqārᵉū*) to mean: "There is a day when the defenders will be called on Mount Ephraim." Nor was it even necessary for the passive form to appear in the text, since in rabbinic exegesis we frequently have biblical passages interpreted through slightly different grammatical forms, different from anything found in our known texts. Such changes were introduced in the Talmud by the formula: "Do not read . . . , but read . . ." Rabbi Grossfeld (formerly a student in Near Eastern Studies of Johns Hopkins University) has kindly called our attention to Aaron Heimann's Hebrew work, *Treasury of Words of the Wise* (Tel Aviv), pp. 62–65, illustrating this device.

Matthew once more calls our attention, against the context of Jer xxxi, to the role of Jesus and/or his family in the history of the whole people.

This quotation, together with hints and allusions elsewhere in the gospels, may provide us with some indications about Jesus' early life. The Jeremiah context explicitly mentions Mount Ephraim, and there is solid ground for asserting that in the pre-Christian Essene literature (e.g., the Nahum Commentary) the inhabitants of Ephraim were identified in the commentators' own day as Samaritans. (The credit for this discovery is due to the late Abram Spiro, with whom one of us worked through the fragments while in Detroit.) John viii 48 records the hostile supposition that Jesus was in fact a Samaritan, and the burden of the assertion in John viii 33 seems to be that those talking with Jesus were hinting that while they were free-born, and their lineage never in question, he may have come from a people of mixed Assyro-Babylonian lineage, from a line of heretical Jews (cf. also John viii 39, 41). Similarly, Matt xvii 26 has a reference by Jesus to the free-born sons. All this, coupled with the manifest interest in Samaritans not only on the part of Jesus and his disciples (cf. NOTE on x 5), but also on the part of the early Jerusalem church (cf. Acts viii) has to be explained.

Joseph is described as a *tektōn* in our sources (Matt xiii 55; Mark vi 3), which certainly indicates a builder and perhaps even a contractor (cf. NOTE on xiii 55). Equally, our sources agree that his family was Judean, as was that of John the Baptist. The probability is that in the fashion of Mediterranean antiquity Joseph traveled a good deal in the pursuit of his calling, and more than one stay in Samaria is highly likely. Whether Jesus traveled as a child with Mary and Joseph we do not know, apart from the incidents recorded in Matt ii 13–15 and Luke ii 41–51, but it is clear that when Jesus visited his own home territory (cf. Matt xiii 53–58 and parallels) he had been away so long that he was almost unknown. John vii 5 represents members of his own family as being hostile to him.

Jesus' home during all the years before the active ministry remains unknown to us. All that we can say with any certainty is that Jesus and John the Baptist must have spent a considerable amount of time together.

It is possible that the evangelists are silent about the early years of Jesus not only out of respect for a tradition about his birth which might give rise to scandal, but also for reasons which can loosely be termed "spiritual." If the passion and resurrection of Jesus were to have validity outside the confines of Judaism (a matter of pressing urgency in the Pauline ministry), then the Messiah must essentially be identified with all races and peoples and not with any one in particular. Such an explanation may account for the careful hints of doubt and uncertainty about Jesus' origins in the gospels. See also Introduction, Part XIII A.

Richard H. Gundry, whose important book *The Use of the Old Testament in St. Matthew's Gospel* is referred to in Part IV of the Introduction, has a different interpretation. Gundry (pp. 97 ff.) thinks that a connection is necessary not only with Nazareth, but also with the humility and lowliness of Jesus in this quotation. He therefore dismisses the connection between Matthew and Jeremiah, which we think to be essential. A short note by Eugenio Zolli ("Nazarenus Vocabitur," ZNW 49 [1958], 135 f.) came to our notice too late to be discussed in detail, but so far as we are aware it is the first article which deals with the Hebrew of Jer xxxi 6 in connection with the Matthean quotation.

COMMENT

Herod died in 4 B.C. This is a useful dateline in Matthew's gospel, not as elaborate as that given in Luke iii 1–3 (which incidentally has complications unsuspected by the ordinary reader), but one which inevitably puzzles the reader who discovers that Herod's death was "B.C." Unfortunately, the system of dating events in the Christian era which we have inherited was constructed by one Dionysius Exiguus at the beginning of the sixth century. He assumed—wrongly—that the date of Jesus' birth was 753 A.U.C. (*ab urbe condita*), i.e., 753 years after the founding of the city of Rome. Herod died four years before that, in 749 A.U.C., hence we say he died in 4 B.C. Actually, if we assume the accuracy of the events described in vs. 16 above, then the *latest* date for the birth of Jesus must be 4 B.C. (the year Herod died), and it may well have been as early as 9 B.C.

Archelaus ruled over Judea from 4 B.C. to A.D. 6, and Herod Antipas over Galilee from 4 B.C. to A.D. 39.

The whole chronology of the early NT period is beset with difficulty, especially in the light of Luke iii 1–3. For the reader wishing to familiarize himself with the problems involved, there is Jack Finegan's *Handbook,* to which reference has already been made in Part XIII of the Introduction and the third NOTE on ii 2, in which an effort is made to take account of all the available material, biblical and otherwise.

There is interesting, though indirect, evidence for a tradition of the sojourn of Joseph and his family in Egypt. Celsus, an opponent of the early Christian theologian Origen (early third century) was aware of a Jewish tradition that Jesus had worked in Egypt, had there learned the magic arts, and had used them to further a claim to divinity when he returned to Palestine (Origen *Contra Celsum* i 28, 38).

7. JOHN THE BAPTIST
(iii 1–12)†

III 1 In those days John the Baptist came proclaiming this in the Judean desert: 2 "Repent—for the kingdom of heaven is fast approaching." 3 This indeed is he who was spoken of by the prophet Isaiah:

> "A voice crying: 'In the desert
> make ready the way of the Lord,
> make his paths straight.'"

4 This John wore a garment of camel's hair, with a leather belt around his waist. He ate locusts and wild honey. 5 To him there went out Jerusalem, all Judea, and all the territory around the Jordan, 6 and they were baptized by him in the river Jordan, confessing their sins.

7 When, however, he saw many of the Pharisees and Sadducees coming for baptism, he said to them, "You viper's brood! Who warned you to flee from the coming wrath? 8 Bear fruit that befits repentance, 9 and do not presume to say 'Abraham is our father,' for I tell you that God is able to raise up children for Abraham from these stones. 10 Even now, the ax is laid against the root of the trees. Therefore, every tree which does not bear good fruit will be felled and thrown into the fire. 11 I indeed baptize you with water, looking to repentance. There is one coming after me, who is greater than I am, and I am not fit to carry his sandals. He will baptize you with the fire of the Holy Spirit. 12 His winnowing fork is in his hand; he will clear his threshing floor and gather the wheat into his granary. The chaff he will burn with unquenchable fire."

† **Matt iii 1–12** || Mark i 1–8, Luke iii 1–9, 15–17, John i 19–28.

NOTES

iii 2. *Repent.* In contemporary Jewish thinking the place of repentance as a necessary preliminary to the Messianic Age is well documented. Cf. Adolf Büchler, *Studies in Sin and Atonement in the Rabbinic Literature of the First Century,* reprinted New York: Ktav, 1967.

fast approaching. Our translation attempts to capture the urgency of the Gr. *éggiken,* which is lost in such English translations as the "at hand" of the KJ.

3. *the prophet Isaiah.* On the "fulfillment" theme, see Part IV of the Introduction.

"*A voice crying: 'In the desert . . .*'" This is not the customary punctuation of translation from the Hebrew, but it follows Jewish tradition—as pointed out by Dr. Moses Aberbach—and the punctuation has been adopted already by John L. McKenzie in *Second Isaiah,* AB, vol. 20 (New York: Doubleday, 1968), §3.

4. *John wore.* The connection between John and Elijah (cf. xvii 10–13) is here alluded to only by a description of John's clothing (cf. II Kings i 8). See also Mal iv 5; Ecclus xlviii 10.

locusts. A common item of diet among Arabs in the Near and Middle East to this day. The vitamin content of the insect is high. There is no basis for the identification of the word with "carob," the pods of the carob tree, known sometimes as "St. John's bread." Epiphanius (*Heresies* 30. 13) tells us that the Ebionites of his own time (315?–403) changed the word to "cakes" in the interests of vegetarianism, and Tatian (second century) had earlier changed the word to "milk" in the same interests.

5. The great popularity of John is also recorded by Josephus.

6. *were baptized.* There seems no question that John took over the practice of baptism, including the emphasis on repentance, from the Essenes, but gave it a far more profound meaning. There is no certain evidence for the Jewish baptism of proselytes until the end of the first century of the Christian era. Even then, the emphasis was not so much on repentance as on acceptance into a religious heritage. Christian baptism, from the evidence of the Pauline letters, was from the first a twofold rite. It incorporated a man or woman into the covenant people of the Messiah, conceived as one with the Israel of the Old Covenant, and at the same time it was a token of repentance and instrument of pardon. It was interpreted by Paul in terms of the work of the Messiah, as a death to the old life of sin, and a new birth, a rising again, to righteousness. J. A. T. Robinson ("The One Baptism," in TNTS) has

argued persuasively that the once-and-for-all character of Christian baptism derives from the once-and-for-all fact of the passion and death of Jesus. Certainly Qumran's lustrations were regularly repeated as normal ritual, but for the Essenes baptism was a sign of a spiritual state already attained, and there is no indication that they endowed their (self-administered) baptism with sacramental efficacy. John's baptisms may well have been repeated, and there is no indication in the NT material that his baptism was a once-and-for-all rite. It may here be significant that the one still-existing Gnostic sect which consistently traces its origin back to John the Baptist (i.e., the Mandaean sect of the lower Tigris Valley) does repeat baptism as a continuously efficacious rite with quasi-sacramental intention. (Cf. Lady Drower's [E. S. Stevens'] *Mandaeans of Iraq and Iran*, Leiden, 1937 / New York, 1962; and *Canonical Prayer Book of the Mandaeans*, Berlin, 1959 / New York, 1965.)

7. *Pharisees and Sadducees*. In Matthew's account of the ministry, these groups are rather consistently representative of disbelief and opposition to Jesus. It is important for us to be scrupulously fair to these two bodies. (Cf. Introduction, Part IX.) The attitude of this gospel is certainly explained if our suppositions about its authorship are substantially correct.

viper's brood. Jesus uses the same expression in xii 34 and xxiii 33. This was evidently an expression in common use, indicating malice (cf. Gen iii 1 ff.).

the coming wrath. It is important not to equate the wrath of God with the emotion of anger. God's wrath in the Bible denotes the ineluctable condemnation by the all-holy and all-loving God of any sin which defiles his creation and which destroys the dignity of man as part of that creation. The wrath of God therefore always brings judgment in its train, and this is the sense here. Cf. Wisd of Sol v 20; Enoch xc 18, xci 7; Rom i 18, ii 5; I Thess i 10.

9. *Abraham is our father*. John's denunciation of relying upon the privilege of God's choice of Israel is fully in line with the OT prophetic tradition (cf. Rom ii 17–29). In Hebrew the words for *children* (*bānîm*) and *stones* (*abānîm*) are similar and they are here used in a play on words.

10. Cf. Luke iii 7–9. Matthew has the Baptist's words addressed to Pharisees and Sadducees, Luke to the crowds.

11. Baptism, as administered by John, is here contrasted with the forthcoming baptism by the Messiah. John's baptism is symbolized "with water," and "looks to" repentance, is preparatory—i.e., his baptism accepted those who were repentant and desired pardon for their sins.

with the fire of the Holy Spirit. Most English versions translate the Greek as though *fire* and *Holy Spirit* were either antithetical or even exclusive of each other. However, the evidence from the Dead Sea literature makes it perfectly clear that this is a hendiadys (cf. Robinson, "The Baptism of John and the Qumran Community," in TNTS). The imagery is eschatological, looking to the fulfilling of all things in the Messiah. For the Messiah's gift of the Spirit, the intertestamental writings are important; cf. Enoch xlix 3, lxii 2; Ps Sol xvii 42. See also Isa xi 2.

12. This verse emphasizes the role of the Messiah in judgment when he comes with his baptism. Cf. Enoch lxii 2, lxix 27. With these final words quoted from John's ministry, compare the last recorded words of Jesus' ministry in xxv 46.

There is superficial identity between Matthew's and Luke's versions in this account. But there are variations in Matthew at iii 3 (=Luke iii 8), iii 11a (Luke omits *looking to repentance*), iii 11b (=Luke iii 16b), iii 12 (=Luke iii 17) as compared with the version in Luke, and the variations argue against a common written tradition for both.

COMMENT

This section provides a necessary introduction to the ministry of Jesus. It is an interesting example of the—to us—surprising lack of external biographical interest or detail which we might have hoped to find in the gospels. Luke provides us with a good deal of information about John the Baptist's early life and his background. Matthew, like Mark and John, introduces the Baptist almost without explanation. All interest is centered on the ministry and teaching of Jesus, and the other material is included only when it is connected with, or is directly illustrative of, that ministry.

There would seem to be no reason to doubt that John grew up in Qumran. Luke emphasizes the advanced age of his parents. Qumran was probably not more than a long day's walk from his parents' home, and we know that the Essenes were in the habit of rearing boys in their community. We do not know precisely where the home of John's parents was, but it is stated explicitly in Luke i 39 to have been "in the hill country . . . in a town of *Iouda.*" This is almost certainly the same word as Heb. *Yūdāh,* name of the tribe, from which the later name of the larger political entity *Judaia* (Judea) was derived. The long-accepted identification of this *Iouda* with the town of *Yaṭṭa,* (not *Yuṭṭa,* as often spelled) is linguistically impossible and historically improbable, since this place was south of the Edomite capital at Hebron and would, therefore, be in the interior of Idumaea, not in Judea. A late tradition fixes the birthplace of John the Baptist at Ein Kerem, just southwest of Jerusalem. This is quite possible, though there is no early evidence for it.

Far more important, however, is John's choice of words, and the emphasis laid upon an imminent Messianic Kingdom has somehow to be explained. That he learned his Messianism from the Essenes is a thesis advanced and defended by many distinguished scholars, and detailed evidence for this theory may be found in C. H. H. Scobie's *John the Baptist* (Philadelphia: Fortress Press / London: SCM, 1964). There is no evidence whatever for baptistic types of Jewish sectarian activity before the time of John, and the Essenes are the only sectarians we know who practiced ritual lustration. Later on there were many such baptistic sects, including the Gnostics and the Mandaeans. It is possible that John's preaching and ministry arose from an awareness that what he had learned of messianic expectation among the Essenes was nearer to fulfillment than his teachers and associates believed, and that he left the community partly on that account. To this consideration would have to be added the fact that John's language nowhere reflects the absolute predestinarianism of the Essenes. (Cf. here Daniélou, *The Dead Sea Scrolls and Primitive Christianity*, pp. 16 ff., and Brownlee, "John the Baptist in the New Light of Ancient Scrolls," in *The Scrolls and the New Testament,* ed. Krister Stendahl.)

There is roughly a generation between chapters ii and iii, and Luke has a solitary story belonging to those years (Luke ii 41–52). What contact John had with Jesus during those years we cannot know. But here again there are phenomena to be explained, not the least being the vocabulary which John's gospel employs in the discourses of Jesus. There are links with Qumran's sharply contrasting pairs of opposites (e.g., light and darkness, truth and falsehood, etc.), which are not to be explained in terms of later Hermetic writings. Cf. Introduction, Part XIII, Appendix B. Two points of emphasis in Matthew's account should not be overlooked:

(1) This section on John begins with a phrase "Repent—for the kingdom of heaven is fast approaching," which is used to close the whole section at iv 17 with identical words on the lips of Jesus.

(2) The high incidence of the word *anachōrein* (to withdraw) and its congeners in this gospel suggests an awareness on the part of the evangelist of a "withdrawal" into the desert by Jesus in his early years. See Introduction, Part XIII A.

8. THE BAPTISM OF JESUS
(iii 13–17)†

III 13 Then Jesus came from Galilee to the Jordan, to John, to be baptized by him. 14 But John stopped him, saying: "I need to be baptized by you, and do you come to me?" 15 Jesus, however, answered him: "Permit it for now; for thus it is fitting for us to fulfill all righteousness." Thereupon he [John] allowed him [to be baptized]. 16 When Jesus had been baptized he went up immediately out of the water, and—see—the heavens opened and he saw the Spirit of God coming down like a dove and alighting on him. 17 Then came a voice from heaven saying, "This is my Son, the Beloved One, with whom I am well pleased."

† **Matt iii 13–17** ‖ Mark i 9–11, Luke iii 21–22, John i 29–34.

NOTES

iii 13. What is stated in the COMMENT below is emphasized by the Greek construction here. Instead of Mark's *and was baptized* (Mark i 9), Matthew uses *tou* with the infinitive, expressing purpose, this being one of seven such uses of the construction in this gospel. Cf. iv 1 with Mark i 13.

16. *the heavens opened.* Cf. Isa lxiv 1; Ezek i 1, where the Greek verb of the LXX is used in the same sense as Matthew's verb, of heaven opening to reveal God's purpose.

the Spirit of God. Cf. Isa xlii 1. The dove is a symbol of Israel in Hos vii 11, xi 11, and extensively of the bride in the Song of Songs. Rabbi Jose (ca. A.D. 150) on entering one of Jerusalem's ruins to pray recorded that he heard a "divine voice, cooing like a dove" (TB *Berakhoth* 3a).

17. *my Son, the Beloved One.* According to Mark's account of this

incident, the voice is addressed directly to Jesus (Mark i 11); in Matthew, the proclamation is public. *the Beloved One* is not an attributive adjective of *my Son,* but is a separate title, in apposition. Isaac is so described in Gen xxii 2, and the Servant of Isa xlii 1 is *the Beloved.* The first part of the proclamation of sonship appears to be reminiscent of Ps ii 7, speaking of the Messiah. Israel in the OT is described as God's son (cf. Exod iv 22; Hos xi 1). We shall not wholly grasp the full meaning of Matthew's material unless we bear in mind that Jesus in this tradition is at once the chosen, the anointed personal Messiah, and at the same time represents the people of the Old Covenant. On this widespread OT usage, which provided him with the phrase "corporate personality," cf. H. Wheeler Robinson, "The Hebrew Conception of Corporate Personality," in *Werden und Wesen des Alten Testaments,* ed. J. Hempel, *Beihefte zur Zeitschrift für die Alttestamentliche Wissenschaft,* Berlin, 1936. Paul uses other figures to the same end, variously describing Jesus as the new man and the second Adam (cf. Rom v 14; I Cor xv 45, etc.).

COMMENT

The baptism of Jesus by John frequently gives rise to some misunderstanding, the more so when those who seek to understand or explain the event are looking at the incident against a background of Christian baptism. In this connection the words of John to Jesus in vs. 14 tend to reinforce the difficulty. Actually, the difficulty is more apparent than real. It is not necessary to see in the dialogue of vss. 14–15 an attempt by an embarrassed evangelist, still less an embarrassed Church, to provide explanations for an awkward occurrence. If the Baptist's description of himself and his mission in John i 19–28 with its insistent "I am not" is historically accurate, then certainly John would be startled to find the Messiah coming to him for baptism.

The key to the understanding of the incident is in Jesus' reply in vs. 15. "Righteousness" must be seen as the whole purpose of God for his people, and not (as is so often the case in homiletics) as a moral quality only. Ps cxix frequently describes the commandments and ordinances of God as "righteous," and the same sense underlies Jesus' reply. "To fulfill all righteousness" must therefore be seen as meaning the fulfillment not only of the demands of God upon his people, but also the fulfillment of those Scriptures in which those demands are set out—law, prophets, writings. In any event, the baptism administered by John was a direct response to the will of God, and so the Messiah must submit to it. With this in mind, we can understand Matthew's interest in preserving the saying—not, as has occasionally been suggested, in inventing it. First, it was wholly fitting that the Messiah should be completely identified with his people, which is a point constantly made in the NT, however separate from sinners the Messiah might be. Secondly, Matthew's interest in fulfillment can be seen in his emphasis (which he shares with Mark) as Jesus "went up out of the water." We have already called attention in the Introduction (Part IV) to the evangelist's interest in the Servant Songs of Isaiah. Here again we have a key passage to be seen in context: "When you pass through the waters I will be with you" (Isa xliii 2). The narrative both of John's preaching and Jesus' baptism must be seen against the context of Isa xliii. Not only is there considerable ambivalence as to whether the Servant is singular or plural; the privileged position of the Servant is emphasized, as is also his mission and the new event which God is about to inaugurate.

9. THE TEMPTATIONS
(iv 1–11)†

IV 1 Then Jesus was led into the desert by the Spirit, to be tempted by the devil, 2 and after fasting for forty days and nights he was hungry. 3 On coming to him, the tempter said, "If you are God's Son, command these stones to become bread." 4 He answered, "It is written:

'Not by bread alone shall man live,
  but by every utterance from God's mouth."

5 Then the devil took him into the holy city and set him on the pinnacle of the temple and said to him: 6 "If you are God's Son, throw yourself down. For it is written:

'He will give his angels charge of you'

and

'They will bear you on their arms,
  lest perchance you strike your foot against a stone.'"

7 Jesus answered him, "It is also written:

'You shall not test the Lord your God.'"

8 Again, the devil took him to a very high mountain and pointed out to him all the kingdoms of the world and their grandeur. 9 He said to him, "I will give you all these things if you will prostrate yourself and pay me homage."
10   Then Jesus said, "Away, Satan! For it is written:

'You shall pay homage to the Lord your God,
  and him alone shall you worship.'"

11 Then the devil left him, and angels came and served him.

† **Matt iv 1–11** || Mark i 12–13, Luke iv 1–13.

NOTES

iv 1. *to be tempted.* Matthew's use of the infinitive to express purpose is a common device in this gospel. Cf. NOTE on iii 13.

the devil (Gr. *diabolos*). There is a shift of meaning in the Bible as to the way in which evil and temptation are treated, and the material is not easily summarized. The Hebrew figure of the *sātān* appears in the prologue of Job, in chapters i and ii, where he is a member of the heavenly court acting as a kind of legal prosecutor. This material may be as early as the seventh century B.C., and is certainly no later than the fifth century. Similarly I Chron xxi 1 depicts the *sātān* as a kind of opposing counsel, and it embodies a tradition which is older than its late fifth-century date. Ps cix 6, which is certainly pre-Exilic, depicts *sātān* as a prosecutor. A very slight change in emphasis appears in Zech iii 1–2; there the figure is more an active adversary than an accuser. This material (late sixth century B.C.) represents a state of affairs in which the prosecutor can easily become a malign figure. (Here it has to be remembered that the contemporary parallels are innumerable, and the prosecutor can easily become an active adversary when the state is unpopular. In the Persian period this was very likely to be the case to a Jewish writer.)

The intertestamental writings, under the influence of Iranian dualism, see a dominion of God and a beneficent providence sharply contrasted with a dominion of evil, and from this there easily emerges the *mastema* of Jubilees, an active opponent of good. Moreover, in that same literature the *sātān* figure is wholly evil and is no longer a member of the heavenly court. Precisely how *sātān* in Hebrew became "the devil" (Gr. *diabolos*) we cannot say with certainty. But in the NT literature the *diabolos* figure is head of the dominion of evil, bent on destroying man by tempting him. The Greek *diabolē* is "a calumny," and *diabolos* an accuser, calumniator; the LXX uses the word *diabolé* mainly in the sense of "calumny," though occasionally as the equivalent of "enmity." The LXX does use *diabolos* for *sātān*, but rather in the sense of adversary or opponent. Josephus never uses *diabolos* or indeed any other names for Satan. Care must be taken to distinguish *diabolos* from *daimōn* (demon), which can be either good or bad, or even neutral.

Essene theology was developed in direct dependence on Zoroastrianism in some form, and in the Essene system we have a complete dualism which, though ultimately under divine dominion, still placed the good Spirit (i.e., the Holy Spirit) and the evil Spirit (i.e., Satan) in total opposition to each other.

3. The order of events in Luke is different, and there is less verbal agreement with Matthew here. It is reasonable to assume that Matthew and Luke were using independent sources.

On coming to him (Gr. *proserchesthai*). A favorite expression of Matthew, who uses it fifty-two times in all. Similarly the evangelist often uses plurals—in this case *stones*—where Mark and Luke use a singular (cf. Matthew's *crowds* and *mysteries* at xiii 11 with Mark's *crowd* and *mystery,* Mark iv 1 and 11). (On the meaning of mystery/mysteries, see the NOTE on xiii 11.)

God's Son. Cf. Introduction, Part XII, and also Dalman, *Words of Jesus,* pp. 274 f. Matthew, in common with John, sees the passion and death of Jesus as bound up with Jesus' relationship with the Father; cf. xxvii 40, 43; John v 18, 43, viii 15–59, x 31–39.

4. The quotation is from Deut viii 3.

5–10. The historic present verbs in these verses are rendered in our translation in the past tense, but they are an interesting feature of Matthew's Greek, though he uses the device less often than Mark.

5. *the holy city.* As a description of Jerusalem, cf. Dan ix 24; Tob xiii 9; Rev xi 2, xxi 2, 10, xxii 19; Matt xxvii 53.

6, 7. The quotation in vs. 6 is from Ps xci 11–12, and Jesus' reply in vs. 7 is from the LXX of Deut vi 16. Cf. Matt xxvi 53 ff.

8. *very high mountain.* Matthew's account places several significant events in such a setting: the Great Instruction (v 1), the Transfiguration (xvii 1), and the farewell to the disciples (xxviii 16). For the devil as ruler of a world hostile to God, cf. John xii 31, xvi 11; II Cor iv 4; I John v 19.

10. *Away, Satan!* The same abjuration is used to Peter in xvi 23 (cf. Mark viii 33) when Peter, like Satan, attempts to dissuade Jesus from courses of action which would inevitably lead to suffering.

The quotation is from the LXX version of Deut vi 13. Authority derives from God; even the devil's dominion is under sufferance.

COMMENT

The temptation narrative aptly illustrates the NOTE on vs. 17 in the preceding chapter (§8). It is possible to see the temptation scene as illustrating the way Jesus thought his ministry would be fulfilled. To some extent Mark's account of the baptism (Mark i 9–11), with its suggestion that this was when Jesus became fully aware of his vocation, bears this out. Mark tells us that Jesus was "driven" (Gr. *ekballei,* vs. 12) by the Spirit into the desert, there to face the implications of his vocation. On this view, it is permissible to see in both Matthew and Luke the newly baptized Jesus facing temptation as an individual. The first test would be to see if he would identify his mission with what nowadays would be called "social reform," working as a popular leader for the eradication of hunger and poverty. The reality of such a temptation is obvious enough, and the identification of the Kingdom with social programs is well detailed in one chapter of Norman Perrin's *The Kingdom of God in the Teaching of Jesus* (London: SCM, 1963), pp. 37–41, 148–55; Philadelphia: Westminster, 1963. The second temptation in Matthew (vss. 5–7=the third in Luke iv 9–12) would, in this view, be a temptation to trade upon the Messiah's relationship with God, to achieve a reputation as a wonder-worker and so succeed in securing the attention of men. The third test would be to compromise with evil, recognize the devil's dominion to the point of regarding some men, some situations, as beyond hope of redemption.

The view given above is both simple and, in the light of Jesus' ministry, plausible as an account of the way in which such thoughts might have assailed the mind of Jesus. But popular as this theory has been in the past, particularly in homiletics, it has the fatal flaw of looking back at the narrative from the vantage point of an accomplished ministry and of subsequent Christian history. Once again, the OT quotations give us more reliable indications of the meaning of the narrative. They are not, in their own context, addressed to an individual but to a whole covenant-people. The significance of the quotations in the narrative was recognized by Clarke (in *Divine Humanity*) forty years ago—and has received significant recent support from Robinson (in TNTS).

It is not an unreasonable supposition that Jesus thought of his sonship in ethnic terms at the beginning. Israel in the OT is the son par excellence (see above, NOTE on iii 17), and Jesus in the Matthean tradition sees his ministry as a reliving of the spiritual experience of Israel, the experience of sonship being narrowed down to him who is *the* Son, *the* Beloved. Deut viii 2, with its key words of *led, prove* (i.e., try, tempt), *wilderness,* provides the context for the reply to the first temptation, which is Deut viii 3. If Israel had been allowed to hunger, to be humbled, and to be fed with no ordinary food, then ought not he who was repeating that experience also endure the same trials?

Any realization by Jesus that he was alone in his sonship

leads inevitably to the second temptation. If the Messiah was *the* Son (cf. Ps ii 2), then what was his relationship to those who by membership in Israel's heritage addressed God as "Father"? The prophets are witnesses to Israel's constant temptation to presume on sonship, and the nature of Jesus' ministry was such that a temptation to presumption must always have been present. Jesus' reply to the second temptation is from Deut vi 16, with its significant reference to Exod xvii 7. To doubt the presence of God with his own people was to put God to the test.

The third temptation also derives from the experience of Israel, and deals with the promise to Israel in Deut vi 10–15. God gives or withholds at his own good pleasure, and Israel's inheritance was no result of her own effort or moral rectitude. But the lands outside—whose were they? (Cf. Deut xxxiv 1–4.) The story of Israel, as J. L. McKenzie points out (*The Two-Edged Sword: An Interpretation of the Old Testament,* Milwaukee: Bruce, 1956) was a constant struggle between obedience to the claims of the divine imperative and the claims of secular calculation. For Jesus, *the* Son, the same struggle of conscience had to be met, and the dominion of sin could be broken, and its captives freed, only in submission to the Father's will.

(In addition to the material quoted above, see also J. Dupont, "L'arrière-fond biblique du récit des tentations de Jésus," NTS 3 (1956–57), 287–305.

10. THE BEGINNING OF THE MINISTRY
(iv 12–17)†

IV 12 When he had heard that John had been arrested, he withdrew into Galilee. 13 Leaving Nazareth, he went to live in the territory of Zebulon and Naphtali, in Capernaum by the sea, 14 so that what was said by the prophet Isaiah might be fulfilled:

> 15 "The land of Zebulon and the land of Naphtali,
>   the lake road, across the Jordan,
>   Galilee of the nations—
> 16   the people who sat in darkness
>   have seen a great light;
>   and upon those who sat in the land of the shadow of
>   death
>   light has dawned."

17 At that time Jesus began to preach. He said, "Repent, for the Kingdom of God is fast approaching."

† **Matt iv 12–17** ‖ Mark i 14–15, Luke iv 14–15.

NOTES

iv 12. *he had heard.* Cf. xiv 13, another occasion when Jesus' movements were dictated by news of John the Baptist.

14. Is ix 1–2 For the fulfillment formula, and for the quotation in the verse following see Introduction, Part IV.

16. The Greek at this point used to be thought a "composite" text, with elements from three versions of the LXX, but what is important is the total context of the quotation. The evangelist may well be quoting from an Old Palestinian text which we no longer have. (Conflations of

different recensions may point to another proto-Lucianic recension, which has not yet been recovered.) Matthew here uses the past tense, indicating that the prophecy has been fulfilled.

17. Some authorities omit *Repent*. Whether the omission belongs to the original tradition or not, Jesus begins his ministry with substantially the same message as the Baptist.

preach. The verb is *kērussein,* and we shall have occasion to examine it again in the NOTES on iv 23. Properly, the verb is used to mean the proclamation of important news by means of a herald, whose office and person in classical times were inviolate.

COMMENT

Jesus left the Judean desert (iii 1, iv 1) for Galilee, in the district which before the Exile had been the territory of Zebulon and Naphtali, but which was then largely inhabited by Gentiles. Matthew's use of "withdrew" (vs. 12) can hardly be meant as an indication that Jesus was leaving the jurisdiction of Herod Antipas, in which John had been arrested, for Herod held sway over Galilee too. It is possible that Jesus went to Capernaum rather than Nazareth because he wished to be wholly independent of relatives in Nazareth. Moreover, the call of the first disciples argues not a miraculous response to a sudden invitation, but an invitation to those whom Jesus had already met on previous occasions.

11. THE FIRST DISCIPLES
(iv 18–22)†

IV 18 While he was walking near the Sea of Galilee he saw two brothers, Simon, called Peter, and Andrew his brother, casting their nets into the sea—for they were fishermen. 19 He said to them, "Come, follow me, and I will make fishers of men out of you." 20 Then and there they left their nets and followed him. 21 Going on from there he saw two other brothers, James and his brother John, Zebedee's sons, in the boat with Zebedee their father, mending their nets. As soon as he called them 22 they left the boat and their father, and followed him.

† **Matt iv 18–22** ‖ Mark i 16–20, Luke v 1–11.

Notes

iv 18. *Simon.* The Greek form of the Heb. *Shimeon.* It is a common name, found in Ecclus 1 i, in Josephus, and the NT.

Andrew is a Greek name, already known as the name of a Jew from an inscription in Olympus of 169 B.C.

19. *Come, follow me* is a Semitic idiom.

fishers of men. Jesus' phrase is almost certainly a reminiscence of Jer xvi 16. The symbolism of fishing for missionary enterprise is found also in xiii 47 f.; cf. Luke v 1–11; John xxi 4–8; and also Ezek xlvii 10.

20. *Then and there they left. . . .* The gospels constantly emphasize the element of renunciation in the teaching of Jesus, and this element is typified here by the disciples' abandoning their livelihood.

21. *mending their nets.* If the OT background of *fishers* in vs. 19 is significant, then there may be some significance here too in the verb used for *mending.* It occurs five times in the Pauline letters, twice in Hebrews, and once in I Peter, where the sense is "restore," "make perfect." The symbolism of fishing, casting nets, and mending nets may possibly be in the mind of the evangelist as figures of the future ministry of the disciples.

COMMENT

This and the following section introduce the two groups of people who are always sharply distinguished in Matthew: the disciples and the crowds. Both are in mind for the long collection of teaching material which begins in chapter v, though that teaching is represented as being given to the inner circle.

Whatever traditions there may have been about Jesus' first meeting with any of his disciples, the synoptic gospels in their present form emphasize that the initiative in calling them rested wholly with Jesus. Matthew does not offer any explanations for the disciples' *apparently* sudden decision to follow Jesus. He does not satisfy our curiosity as to whether their response to this call came as a result of their having known Jesus previously (cf. John i 19–51).

12. MINISTRY IN GALILEE
(iv 23–25)†

IV 23 He went about the whole of Galilee, teaching in their
synagogues, and proclaiming the Freedom of the Kingdom,
healing every sickness and every infirmity among the people.
24 His reputation so spread through all Syria that they brought
to him all the sick, those afflicted with various diseases and
pains, the demoniacs, the epileptic, and the paralyzed, and he
healed them. 25 Great crowds followed him from Galilee, the
Ten Towns, Jerusalem, Judah, and the territory beyond the
Jordan.

† Matt iv 23–25 || Luke v 17–19.

NOTES

iv 23. *synagogues.* The synagogue as a place of public worship and
teaching is first clearly attested in Egypt in the latter part of the third
century B.C., and in Palestine ca. 200 B.C. (Ecclus li 23). Its origins,
however, are certainly far older even though we are unable to determine
them with any precision. The centralization of worship in Jerusalem
from 621 B.C. onwards, with many Jews thereby denied a share in temple
worship, must inevitably have led to the establishment of non-sacrificial
places of assembly. The Aramaic word for "synagogue" is a Babylonian
loanword which can scarcely be later than the sixth century B.C. Whatever the history of the institution, prophets had been in the habit of
gathering bands of disciples around them, and during the Babylonian
Exile (597–540 B.C.) exiles gathered for prayer and instruction wherever
and whenever this was possible (Ezek viii 1, xiv 1, xxxiii 30 ff.). Cf. John
Bright, *A History of Israel* (Philadelphia: Westminster, 1959), pp. 422 ff.;
London: SCM, 1960.

proclaiming. The verb has already been briefly examined, and its
meaning is well established. Two things dictated our translation of this

verse: (1) The decreasing vitality of the word "gospel" in current English, so much so that it is possible to make any social or political program or idea a "gospel" (cf. "the Marxist gospel"); (2) it was customary for thousands of years, at least from 2300 B.C. and right through the Middle Ages, for sovereigns or rulers on their accession to proclaim amnesties and privileges of various kinds, such as freedom from taxation and/or legal penalty. Paul's description of the "liberty by which Christ has set us free" (Gal v 1) exactly describes the meaning which we have tried to indicate here and elsewhere in our version of the more usual "preaching the Gospel."

the people. The expression is found fourteen times in Matthew, and only twice in Mark. In this gospel it has clear reference in almost every case to Israel, the people of the Old Covenant—i.e., it is an OT usage.

24. *the epileptic.* In Greek this is a rare word, and late, while "the paralyzed (one)" is a NT word, being found in Matthew and Mark. Luke (v 18, 24) uses another and more usual word.

25. *Great crowds.* This is another example of Matthew's predilection for plurals. He uses the expression thirty times, the singular sixteen, while Mark has the plural but once, compared with the singular thirty-seven times.

the Ten Towns. The usual English version, *the Decapolis,* is a transliteration of the Greek. For the history of the region, see any recent Bible dictionary.

COMMENT

In much the same way that Mark gives us a typical day in the ministry of Jesus (Mark i 21–34), whether or not the events so described all happened on the same day, so Matthew here gives us in general terms the scope of the ministry of Jesus. Matthew here uses phrases which in Mark are the basis for whole sections of narrative: iv 23=Mark i 14, 39; iv 24=Mark i 28; iii 10; vi 55–56; iv 25=Mark iii 7 ff. At this stage the evangelist's interest is in the crowds, and the teaching of the inner circle of the disciples comes later. It is to be noted that the ministry is directed primarily to Jesus' own people, and only later are the crowds from Gentile areas affected by his reputation. The descriptions of the ministry are not to be overlooked: teaching, proclaiming, healing. It was concentration on healing in particular which engendered so much misunderstanding on the part of those who came to Jesus. Healing was a sign, an outward manifestation, of the irruption of the dawning reign of God, and Jesus by injunctions to silence on various occasions sought to guard against mistaking sign for substance.

13. THE GREAT INSTRUCTION: THE KINGDOM OF HEAVEN (v 1–12)†

V 1 Seeing the crowds, he went up on the mountain, and when he had sat down his disciples came to him. 2 He began to teach them, in these words: 3 "Fortunate are the humble in spirit, for theirs is the Kingdom of heaven. 4 Fortunate are those who mourn, for they shall be consoled. 5 Fortunate are the meek, for they shall inherit the earth. 6 Fortunate are those who hunger and thirst for righteousness, for they shall be satisfied. 7 Fortunate are the merciful, for they shall have mercy shown to them. 8 Fortunate are the pure-minded, for they shall see God. 9 Fortunate are the peacemakers, for they shall be called children of God. 10 Fortunate are those who are persecuted on account of righteousness, for theirs is the kingdom of heaven.

11 You are blessed whenever men vilify you, persecute you, and falsely charge you with evil for my sake; 12 rejoice and be glad, because your reward in heaven is great, for in the same way they persecuted the prophets before you.

† **Matt v 3–12** ‖ Luke vi 20–23.

Notes

v 1. *crowds . . . disciples.* The Great Instruction is not a public address. In Matthew it represents a collection of material addressed to the inner circle, the disciples. Cf. Part V of the Introduction.

3. *Fortunate.* The word in Greek was used in classical times of the state of the gods in contrast to men. The usual English "blessed" has more and more come to have liturgical or ecclesiastical overtones, and we have chosen "fortunate" as being the best translation available to us. The Heb. *ashrê* originally meant "the good omens of . . ." There is

increasing evidence that the Hebrew originally had the same meaning as the pagan Greek. (Cf. W. F. Albright, *Archaeology and the Religion of Israel* [Johns Hopkins Press, 1942], p. 227.) The meaning is both "they are among the fortunate who . . ." and "fortunate are the . . ." Only the incorrigible pedant can find shades of meaning distinct from each other in e.g. *insulae Fortunatae* and *Fortunatorum Insulae.*

humble in spirit. Those living in uprightness, or "perfection." The phrase occurs in the Qumran material as *'anîyê rûaḥ.* There are two words in Hebrew which would provide us with the background for this saying: *'anavîm* and *'anîyîm.* They are virtually synonymous, and both mean "poor," "afflicted," "humble" (cf. F. Brown, S. R. Driver and C. A. Briggs, *A Hebrew and English Lexicon of the Old Testament* [Boston: Houghton, 1906; Oxford University Press, 1907, repr. 1953, 1957], ad loc.). The Qumran War Scroll (1QM xiv 7), which is Herodian in date, gives us a saying which closely parallels that of Jesus, and may be translated: "Blessed be the Lord God of Israel . . . giving . . . vigor to the shoulders of the bowed, and (. . .) to the lowly spirits; firmness to the melting heart." Unfortunately the script belongs to a period in Hebrew when the letters *yod* and *waw* were not sharply distinguished, and it is possible to read either *'anāv* or *'anî.* However, other occurrences of the letters in the column indicate that the reading should be *'anîyîm* rather than *'anavîm.* It is likely that the original editor felt that the Gr. *ptōchoi* (poor) alone would be misunderstood if left without qualification, and so reproduced the Qumran saying rather than the tradition as it is in Luke (Luke vi 20—"the poor"). The poverty described is that of the man fully conscious of the poverty of all human resource, and knowing his need and desire for God.

for theirs is the Kingdom. The best sense here is "the Kingdom will consist of such as these," bearing in mind the future tenses which characterize the following verses.

4–5. The order of these verses is uncertain in our oldest manuscripts.

4. *those who mourn.* As with vs. 3, the favor of God does not rest upon the state of mourning *as such,* but upon those who lament the sin which mars God's choice of Israel. Cf. Isa lxi 2, referring to those who mourn man's disobedience to God.

5. *the meek.* The meaning here is similar to that of the "humble" or "poor" in vs. 3. The verse is a quotation from Ps xxxvii 11, where possessing the earth is parallel to being admitted to the Kingdom in vs. 3. Cf. also "Whosoever humbles himself, the Holy One, blessed be He, raises him up." (TB *Erubin* 13b. This reference we owe to the courtesy of Dr. Moses Aberbach.)

6. *hunger and thirst.* The OT has many examples of fasting as a form of prayer of desire, and those who are here being commended are they

who pray for the vindication of God's purposes for men. Their reward is that they will be filled (cf. Rev iii 20). The Messianic kingdom as a feast is referred to in viii 11. Cf. also Jer xxxi 25; Isa lv 1; Ps cvii 9.

7. Cf. "Whoever has pity on people will obtain pity from heaven" (TB, *Shabbath* 151b, to which our attention was called by Dr. Moses Aberbach).

8. *pure-minded*. That is, the spiritual equivalent of being ritually pure (cf. Ps xxiv 4). The Aramaic word would here be *dăkhîn*, "broken, humble, contrite" (cf. StB, I, ad loc.). The single-mindedness of the consecrated life as a prerequisite for the vision of God is emphasized in Philo (*On the Contemplative Life* ii 473; *On the Life of Moses* ii 106), and cf. Rev xxii 4. What is here promised is that the sons of the Kingdom will share the vision of God with *the* Son (cf. xi 27). The theme of purity of heart is well attested in the rabbinic literature; cf. "The Holy One, blessed be He, loves everyone who is pure of heart" (Midrash *Rabba* on Gen xl 8), or "R. Jose ben Halafta said to R. Ishmael his son, 'If you seek to see the face of the Shekinah'—i.e., the abiding presence of God—'in this world, study the Torah in the land of Israel'" (Midrash *Shokker Tob* on Ps cv). (Both references by the kindness of Dr. Aberbach.)

9. *peacemakers*. Cf. *Pirqê Abôth* i 12: "Hillel said, 'Be of the disciples of Aaron, loving peace and pursuing it.'"

children of. Often the phrase "son of" or "children of" is equivalent to "belonging to . . . ," and the "sons of the prophets" in the OT can be held to mean those gathered round a teacher, members of a prophetic guild. Here the expression means "those admitted to fellowship with . . ."

The collection of sayings commonly known as the Beatitudes may fittingly be called the spiritual charter of the Kingdom. The form which the individual verses take is well known in the Psalms, Proverbs, and Ecclesiastes. In another form, it can easily be seen as an implied grammatical construction of protasis-apodosis (conditional and result clauses): "If you do this, then that will follow."

What the history of this particular collection may be we cannot know. That the form was well known appears to be certain from an (unpublished) fragment of negative Aramaic beatitudes from Qumran. So far as the difference between Matt v 3–9 and Luke vi 20–26 is concerned, it is not enough to say that Matthew represents another version with some modifications in phraseology. Both versions may be equally valid as recollections of the original tradition, and each version may try to reproduce some variants of that tradition. There is, for example, nothing inherently spiritual about the state of poverty (Luke vi 20), or hunger and thirst (Luke vi 21) and Matthew's "humble in spirit" (vs. 3), and "hunger and thirst for righteousness" (vs. 6) at first sight may strike us as an improvement in meaning. However, it is well to call attention to the fact that poverty *can* save from the often frivolous and frequently ephemeral *desiderata* of a more affluent state. Jesus himself, and the NT writers, and all the ascetical writers, Christian and non-Christian, are unanimous in their warnings against an overinvolvement in worldly goods. Certainly Christianity is never more false to itself than when its institutions are wealthy. The Scriptures are full of warnings against a preoccupation with wealth and possessions.

The two versions of the spiritual charter in Matthew and Luke may well represent two versions uttered by Jesus on two different occasions. Matthew's version, on this interpretation, may be an explanatory expansion given in response to questions. Equally, Luke's version, particularly in the light of the material which follows in Luke vi 24–26, may have been addressed directly to the disciples. What we may have therefore is a direct series of statements to the disciples in Luke and a series of expanded statements in Matthew, though both from Jesus.

10. This statement concludes one group of sayings, for the phrase *theirs is the Kingdom of heaven* began the series and now ends it. This device (called "inclusio") is common in Matthew. Cf. J. C. Fenton, "Inclusio and Chiasmus in Matthew," *Studia Evangelica*, III, 1964.

11. Cf. TB, *Shabbath* 88b: "They that are reviled, but who do not revile, they that hear themselves being put to shame but do not answer back—concerning them, Scripture says 'But they that love him shall be as the sun when he goeth forth in his might' [Judg v 31]."

12. *reward*. It is true that later Jewish theology was a good deal concerned with the theme of rewards and punishments (cf. Wisd Sol ii 22, v 15), but here the idea is not so much a precise calculation of reward for past conduct. Rather it is a contrast between coming pain and persecution, and future blessedness.

It seems appropriate to add here a short comment on the undeniable prominence in Matthew of what is usually called "rewards and punishments," which seems to make many people uncomfortable. In chapter vi (§§22–26) for example, the reward from God for covert good works seems to be an incentive to such works. Sensitive as was contemporary Jewish thought with this kind of consideration, there are ample warnings against overemphasizing it: "Do not be like slaves, who serve their lord in order to receive a reward" (*Pirqê Abôth* i 3, second century B.C.) is one such. Two things may be said very briefly: (1) The whole NT is quite frank in its lack of disinterestedness. What is being held out to men in the NT writings is the salvation which comes from God alone, and —in the NT—is mediated through membership of the Messianic Kingdom which Jesus proclaimed and which he "bought with his blood." Obviously, what is being offered is advantageous to man, and there are responses demanded of man in return for the generosity of God's grace. (2) So far from the reward being "congruent with merit of good works" (to use the mediaeval scholastic expression), the reward is so far beyond anything which men could possibly attain by their own goodness that the very word "reward" has something of irony about it. It would have to be added here that the terms upon which that reward is held to be contingent are in the NT not such as to encourage a light approach to it.

in heaven. It is important not to read into this phrase the notion of "going into heaven," but rather "with God." "Heaven" was a normal Jewish synonym for "God," to save the devout from using even the substitute word *Adonai,* "(my) Lord." On this whole question of "heaven" and "God" with respect to the Kingdom, cf. Introduction, Part VII.

COMMENT

Matthew's putting Jesus' instruction to the disciples in one large group of material was most likely done out of a sense of order, and also to make reference easier for those who would be using the material for teaching. As noted in Part IV of the Introduction, the sayings in this gospel are arranged in forms which ensured their easy committal to memory. In spite of what various commentators have said, it is not likely to have been dictated by considerations of a "second Moses" ascending a "second mountain" to bring thence a "new Law." Such commentators tend to forget that the Great Instruction in Matthew was directed to the inner circle of the disciples, and not to the whole people.

It is well here to call attention to the study of the Elijah-Elisha theme in Mark, as set out by Gerhard Hartmann (*Der Aufbau des Markusevangeliums, mit einem Anhang: Untersuchungen zur Echteit des Markusschlusses,* Münster: Aschendorff, 1936). Hartmann rightly called attention to the fact that in rabbinic sources Elisha is contrasted with Elijah to the advantage of Elisha, and he thought the same considerations to be at work in Mark's gospel with reference to John the Baptist and Jesus.* We call attention to this work here, since we have seen no good reason to suppose that Matthew sees in Jesus a "new Moses." We do wish, however, to suggest that the evangelist *may* have had in mind a parallel between Jesus and Joshua —in any event, the identity of name will certainly not have escaped him. If this supposition is correct, then there is a parallel between

*Our own interest in this theme was renewed by a recent lecture delivered by Raymond E. Brown to a meeting of the Catholic Biblical Association.

John the Baptist and Moses: John the Baptist did not live to see the entry into the Promised Land. Moses was held accountable for his lack of faith on one vital occasion (Num xx 12), and there appears to be a rebuke to John the Baptist for a similar lack of faith in Matt xi 2–6.

Heb iii 2–6 also points to the contrast between Jesus and Moses, and the same work has other points of contrast between the work of Moses and that of Jesus (viii 5, 6, xii 18–24).

Perhaps most telling of all in this connection is the quotation in Matt xi 10 (found in all the synoptic gospels), which is far nearer in the Greek to the LXX of Exod xxiii 20, and refers to the entry into the Promised Land. There is evidently here a whole complex of ideas, and we should be mistaken if we sought to find in our NT sources a ready-made system of parallels or "types." All we are justified in doing is attempting to lay bare the various strands of thought which seem to have occupied the attention of the evangelists from their own Hebraic background. Quite plainly, any discussion of the Law by Jesus—and especially the lengthy report by Matthew in chapters v–vii (our §§ 13–29) must have invited comparison with Moses. But if the evangelist did indeed see Jesus as a "new Moses" it is surprising that he did not introduce specific quotations from the Old Testament to validate the point.

We wish further to add that the significance of Joshua in connection with the Messianic hope in Samaritan sources was continually stressed by the late Abram Spiro in his unfinished studies.

Again it should be pointed out here that nothing is more misleading from the standpoint of Christian history than the assumption that its Founder was engaged in the construction of a new moral code of universal applicability. As suggested in the NOTES above, the Great Instruction is directed to the Messianic Community, first to the disciples, and then to those whom they taught. Any extended application of its provisions to a non-Christian or mixed community, however well-intentioned, is a use of the material which the infant Messianic Community would have found puzzling, to say the least (cf. I Cor v 12).

The whole of chapters v–vii (§§ 13–29) is variously named the Sermon on the Mount, or the Great Sermon, and it has been taken by some as the basis for a universal code of ethics

—so much so that vss. 3–12 of chapter v have been quoted by politicians as a kind of platform. Joachim Jeremias' Ethel M. Wood Lectures for 1961 before the University of London (*The Sermon on the Mount,*) apply a much-needed corrective to this kind of misinterpretation. What follows here is a very condensed summary of those lectures:

Three main views have been held, or are held, about the Great Instruction, as follows: (1) The Instruction is "perfectionist legalism," concerned with the absolute demand of God upon all men, and moreover every bit as demanding in its observance as the Law of Moses. Jesus, on this view, is expressing extreme demands, even though he is at the same time aware that no one can completely respond to them. But "he hopes to bring men to the point where they exert themselves seriously in an attempt to attain part of them" (Jeremias, p. 9). (2) The second view [which according to Jeremias is found among some types of Lutheranism] is that the Instruction represents an impossible ideal. Its proponents argue that Jesus made demands which men could never possibly fulfill completely; but that as men realized their impotence compared to God, they would also come to appreciate the saving love of God. (3) The third view, given formulation by Johannes Weiss (in his *Die Predigt vom Reichen Gottes,* Tübingen, 1892) would have us see the Instruction as an "Interim-Ethik." Jesus, this view maintains, was not propounding a long-term moral structure for his disciples, but was instead facing men with a last opportunity for heroic moral effort before the inevitable catastrophe of the End-time. All is heroic command, calling for heroic commitment. All other considerations are valueless.

There are elements of truth in all three views. Indeed, *any* serious view of the ministry of Jesus must be quite misleading if it does not have *some* element of truth in it. The mistake in all three is that each claims to be final and exclusive as an interpretation. The first view clearly and rightly emphasizes the OT background from which Jesus taught, the background which through the centuries had constantly laid upon Israel the obligation to obey the righteous demands of a righteous God. We ought not to be surprised that so much of the moral teaching of Judaism is to be found reproduced in the Great Instruction. What would or ought to be disturbing would be to find that teaching *absent* from the sayings of Jesus. Nor is this salvation by Law or by works, as

puzzled commentators on Matthew have been known to suggest.
From the Greek philosophical revolution of the sixth-to-fourth centuries B.C., all law was seen by those within the influence of
Hellenism as a response to universal principles of justice thought
to be discernible in the constitution of the universe and the processes
of history, and also a safeguarding of the individual and society
from the evil impulses of men. To that extent, any attempt to
discover a religion without law in Matthew is to pursue a chimera.

The second view is attractive at first sight in that it appears to
provide—as the first apparently does not—for the role of Jesus
as Mediator, as Redeemer to save man from his own impotence.
But this second view, under the influence of the Augustinian interpretations of Paul, wholly fails to do justice to the love and
devotion which the Law evoked, and still evokes, for the devout
Jew (cf. Ps cxix). Whatever impression commentaries on the
Law might convey, no informed Jew of the time of Jesus or
since would suppose that salvation came through observance of
the Law. The OT makes it entirely clear that salvation derives
not from human merit but from God. It was precisely Paul's legal
training which led him to insist on the importance of the grace of
God. We should not lose sight, of course, of his equally great
insistence on man's obedient response to the demands made by that
grace. Moreover, there is not a single sentence in the Great Instruction itself which for a moment suggests that Jesus was propounding an impossible ideal. On the contrary, he clearly expects
from his disciples the most exacting obedience.

The third view certainly emphasizes the element of crisis, of
impending decision-making, in the teaching of Jesus. It is certainly
true that Jesus constantly spoke of the End, and of impending
judgment. But it is exactly this element which is *not* emphasized
in the Great Instruction. "Jesus is no fanatical enthusiast, his
ethic is not an expression of anxiety in the face of catastrophe"
(Jeremias, p. 15). Any interpretation of the Instruction which sees
the teaching as "interim ethics" would have to deny that Jesus
envisaged, made provision for, a continuing community. Such a
denial runs counter to all we know of contemporary messianism
(especially among the Essenes), and it must somehow explain how
the infant community so successfully misunderstood Jesus in so
brief a time as to provide us with the evidence of Acts i–iv.

What is left, if we reject the three views above as in each

case partially if not wholly erroneous? Jeremias declares that what we have is "gospel." We have indicated already in our commentary on iv 23 our interpretation of that verse as "proclaiming the Freedom." What is being propounded to the disciples in chapters v through vii, as to those who must carry the message of this proclamation, is the charter of that Freedom. It is law, it is the Law of the Old Covenant, with a new dimension: the long-expected reign of God is dawning with the presence of Jesus, and the Covenant-law has therefore a new urgency. Stripped of commentary and explanatory gloss, men of the Kingdom are confronted with the demand of God in its starkest form and bidden to obey. Precisely how that demand is to be met in the circumstances of daily living is not the function of a commentary. That function belongs to moral theology, and the beginnings of it in the Christian Church can be seen in the Pauline letters.

14. THE GREAT INSTRUCTION: MARKS OF THE DISCIPLE (v 13–16)†

V **13** "You are the earth's salt. If the salt is of low grade, then how can it be rectified? It is then good for nothing but to be thrown out and trodden underfoot. **14** You are the light of the world; a city on a hill cannot be hidden. **15** And men do not light a lamp and hide it under a container, but they put it on a stand and it gives light to all in the house. **16** In the same way, let your light so shine among men that they may see your good works and give glory to your heavenly Father.

† **Matt v 13–16** ‖ Mark ix 50, Luke xiv 34–35.

NOTES

v 13. The saying as it stands in our English versions makes virtually no sense at all, in spite of all the efforts of the commentators. Sodium chloride does not lose its taste or savor except by dilution. Furthermore, though salts of various kinds are necessary to the fertility of the soil, oversalination can and does effectively render land infertile—as evidenced by the ancient primitive action of sowing an enemy's land with salt; cf. the treatment of Carthage by the conquering Romans in the Second Punic War; or the OT references to a place being "sown with salt," as in Judg ix 45. The Greek word (*mōranthē*) employed by the evangelist and here translated as "low grade" strictly means "to become foolish, imbecile, etc." (*mōrainō* and *mōroomai* are virtually interchangeable in meaning), and Liddell and Scott (*A Greek-English Lexicon*, II, ad loc.) can only adduce this verse in favor of the meaning "to become insipid." We are not entitled to say that Jesus and his disciples knew nothing of the properties of salt, for the saying would hardly have survived unless it had some empirical basis. There is, however, no means of arriving at the choice of this particular Greek verb unless there was something in Aramaic which was misunderstood by an editor or an amanuensis. (The

Aram. *pkh,* "to lose taste, to relax," etc., does not have the meaning of the Greek, and the Syriac here is therefore purely secondary.) In addition, there is the complicating factor that though Greek does distinguish between present and future meanings of the Hebrew imperfect tense, the older Aramaic did not.

Encyclopaedia Britannica (ed. 1960, XIX, p. 897b) asserts that Matt v 13 "refers "simply . . . to the earthy residuum of such an impure salt after the sodium chloride has been washed out." Alfred Lucas (*Ancient Egyptian Materials and Industries,* 3d ed. rev. [London: Longmans, 1948], pp. 304 ff.) mentions impurities such as gypsum (hydrated calcium sulphate), natron, and sodium sulphate.

Our translation is based on the best sense which can be made of the text as we have it. There is no conceivable manner in which salt can be re-salted once it has been diluted. It is the earth itself which is in need of attention. But if salt is of poor quality, of low grade, then the earth itself will suffer loss. This interpretation does have the merit of being far more consonant with the responsibility vested in the disciples. If they are to be light to the world, then they must also accept the equal responsibility of preparing the ground in which the Sower will work.

It is to be noted that the semantic parallel of "low-grade" with imbecile is far closer than might have been expected. Cf. the meanings commonly given to derogatory expressions such as "low-grade citizen," etc.

14. *the light of the world.* Cf. "You [are] the lights of Israel" (Testament of Levi xiv 3, in *The Apocrypha and Pseudepigrapha of the Old Testament,* ed. R. H. Charles, II, p. 312); Philip ii 15. The function of the disciples as light is to be detached from the world, and yet their very existence is such that they cannot but exercise an influence on that world. It is important to beware of using this verse as a kind of proof-text of the often-expressed homiletic concern for "involvement."

Light and *city* were combined by Cicero in a description of Rome as a "light to the whole world" (*Catiline* iv 6).

15. Cf. Luke viii 16, xi 33, xiv 34; Mark iv 21.

16. The *salt, city, light* sayings are united in Matthew, and in combination are eschatological, looking to the end, the purpose and final goal of the disciples' vocation. Moreover, in their Matthean context they emphasize the sacrificial service which the new Kingdom will demand. In Mark there is a "salt" saying (Mark ix 49–50) following a discourse on the demands of discipleship, and Luke (xiv 34–35) has the "salt" saying in similar context. The "light" saying in Mark (iv 21) and Luke (viii 16) follows the parable of the sower, and is joined to a promise that the secrets of the Kingdom will be revealed.

your good works. The emphasis is not on human goodness, but on response to the Father's will, as is made quite clear by vii 21.

heavenly Father. The expression is prominent in Matthew, and is found only once in Mark and Luke. It is erroneous to assert, as is sometimes done, that addressing God as "Father" was unknown to Judaism. Cf. Wisd Sol ii 16, xiv 3; Ecclus xxiii 1, 4. The later literature (Tobit, Jubilees, III Maccabees) uses the expression "our Father" or "their Father," and Allen's ICC *St. Matthew* commentary (ad loc.) lists frequent occurrences of "our Father" in rabbinic literature. Cf. also Dalman, *Words of Jesus,* pp. 184 ff.

COMMENT

The preceding verses in Matthew's scheme set the stage for the material which follows. It progresses from a consideration of the dedication which discipleship demands to a detailing of specific instances—"case law" and interpretation. The scheme is orderly, logical, starting with an outline of general principles and going on to statements about the obligations which Jesus laid on his inner circle of disciples. The final part of the scheme deals with particular points of the Law.

15. THE GREAT INSTRUCTION: THE LAW—FULFILLMENT (v 17–20)

V 17 "Do not suppose that I came to destroy the Law or the prophets. I did not come to destroy, but to fulfill. 18 I solemnly tell you that until heaven and earth pass away not a single letter of the Law shall pass away until all has been fulfilled. 19 Whoever therefore sets aside any prescription of the Law and teaches men accordingly shall be called least in the Kingdom of heaven. But whoever keeps and teaches it shall be called great in the Kingdom of heaven. 20 For I tell you that unless you are more righteous than the scribes of the Pharisees you will certainly not enter the Kingdom of heaven.

Notes

v 17. *destroy . . . fulfill.* This statement by Jesus seems clear enough, but combined with the following verses it might be taken as meaning that the Law is binding on the followers of Jesus to the end of time. It would in that case express the convictions of orthodox Judaism, both Palestinian and Alexandrian, in the time of Jesus (cf. Philo *Life of Moses* ii 136). It should be emphasized that those to whom Jesus speaks at this juncture in the ministry were Jews. There is no shred of evidence that Jesus at any point repudiated his obligation to the Law to which both his birth and his circumcision committed him. Moreover, we know from Acts (xxi 20) that many Jews who embraced the teaching of Jesus nevertheless maintained their adherence to the Law. So far as the Matthean tradition is concerned, Jesus is represented as emphasizing the authority of those to whom the teaching of the Law was committed (cf. xxiii 2 ff.). It is reasonable to assume that those who followed Paul's footsteps during his journeyings were Jewish Christians from Jerusalem who were concerned that Gentile converts should first embrace the Law. Jewish Christians, both residents and non-resident travelers, would have been influenced by rumors of all kinds about the apostle's intentions toward his Gentile converts and also about his own attitude to the Law. (It must be added here that the late Johannes Munck did not subscribe to this view. Cf. his *Paul and the Salvation of Mankind,* London: SCM, 1959, and more recently in *The Acts of the Apostles,* AB, vol. 31, Introduction, Part VIII.)

Much hangs on the meaning of the verb *plērōsai* (to fulfill), and also on the recorded views of the ex-Pharisee and apostle Paul. With regard to the first, the verb can and frequently does convey the meaning of "to clarify the true meaning of" something. Certainly it can be argued that what Jesus is doing in this legal material of Matt v–vii is trying to restore the original meaning of the Law where this seemed to be obscured by the accretions of commentary. But it must also be recognized that the same verb is used in a somewhat different sense in other parts of the NT, even in Matthew. We have already called attention (Introduction, Part IV) to Matthew's use of "fulfill" in his OT contexts. We may legitimately ask whether the experience of the New Covenant in Jesus' blood (Matt xxvi 28) caused some early Jewish Christians to regard the Law as either radically reinterpreted or even abrogated. (Incidentally, this emphasis on the "blood of the Messiah" precisely led to the careful preservation of the tradition. It is quite inconceivable that a devout Jew would have invented the concept of a New Covenant in the blood of the Messiah, while to a Gentile the very idea was monstrous.) Moreover, the verb "to fulfill" in John and some other NT authors certainly can mean "to end, conclude, make complete." Similarly ambiguous is the Pauline phrase calling Jesus the "end" (*telos*) of the Law (Rom x 4).

Perhaps the most we are justified in saying is that two attitudes to the Law are discernible in our sources, and this is precisely what we would expect. Only with the spread of the Gospel to the Gentile world would the two attitudes be brought into sharp contrast.

18. On the validity of the Law in Jesus' view, cf. A. M. Honeyman, "Matthew 5.18 and the Validity of the Law" (NTS 1 (1954–55), 141–42. This saying is certainly hyperbolic for purposes of effect. Paraphrased, it would run like this: "The Law of Moses as an expression of the will of God is permanent, and I came to emphasize its true meaning. No smallest part of it may be eroded or explained away until everything has been accomplished. Therefore (vs. 20) your obedience to the demands of God must be a far more abiding obedience than that given by those who teach and interpret that Law."

not a single letter. The Greek words are *iota* (commonly transliterated by *jot* in the English versions) and *keraia* (given in KJ as *tittle,* and in RSV as *dot*). The *iota* (Heb. *yod*) was certainly employed in the time of Jesus, but *keraia* (small horns attached to some letters to guard against confusion with each other) is another matter. So far as is known

at present, the device only came into use in the Herodian phase of
Hebrew script in the late first century B.C., and it is not possible to
determine what meaning the word might have had at the time of Jesus.
We cannot know whether the Gr. *keraia* referred to the small horns,
with any real certainty.*

COMMENT

General principles having been enunciated, the demands of discipleship clearly laid down, the evangelist begins his collection of
material which deals with the Law. It begins with a prefatory
statement by Jesus as to his mission as it related to the Law.

* Cf. Jehoshua M. Grintz, "Hebrew as the Spoken and Written Language
in the Last Days of the Second Temple," JBL 79 (1960), 32–47.

16. THE GREAT INSTRUCTION:
ANGER
(v 21–26)†

V 21 "You have heard that it was said to the ancients, 'You shall not murder, and whoever murders will be liable to judgment.' 22 But I tell you that everyone who is angry with his brother shall be in danger of (divine) judgment. Whoever insults his brother will answer to the Sanhedrin, while whoever says 'Rebel! (against God)' merits a fiery death. 23 Therefore if you bring your offering to the altar, and there remember that your brother has something against you, 24 leave your offering there before the altar, and go away. First be reconciled with your brother and then come and offer your gift. 25 Come to terms with your accuser quickly, while you are on the way to court with him, lest he hand you over to the judge, the judge hand you over to the jailer and you are thrown into prison. 26 I assure you that you will never come out until you have paid your last cent.

† Matt v 25–26 || Luke xii 57–59.

NOTES

In all that follows, it is important to bear in mind the background of the material as it was discussed in Part IX of the Introduction.

v 21. *it was said*. Cf. the reference in the Introduction (Part IX) to this rabbinic device. We might have expected "It is written," but this would not fit in so well with the later "But I tell you." Furthermore, "said" can refer to scribal interpretation, with quotations from Scripture embodied in the interpretation.

to the ancients. The expression, as referring to men of a past age, is attested in classical Greek. Here it refers to oral tradition in the pre-rabbinic stage, since anything which came after the Torah was by that very fact oral tradition.

You shall not murder. The words as they stand are a quotation and summary of Exod xxi 12, and *liable to judgment* echoes Deut xvii 8. The word we have translated *liable* (Gr. *enochos*) can also mean "guilty," and is so used in xxvi 66. Cf. Rabbi Eliezer (end of first century A.D.): "He who hates his brother belongs to the shedders of blood."

22. This material is admittedly difficult. The verse states simply that intention as well as act comes under the judgment of God, and in asserting this Jesus is appealing to the foundations of divine justice on which the written Law rested. But then we seem to have an ascending scale of judgments for a descending scale of offenses. Moreover, if the Greek (*tē krisei*) means a local court, then we have a different meaning for vs. 21 where it plainly means God's judgment. However, the difficulty may be more imaginary than real. The first case (vs. 21) of the man guilty of murder is simple enough—he will suffer punishment. This verse (22) goes on to deal with an attitude, not an overt act, and here we have kept the meaning of the Gr. *tē krisei* as judgment, or punishment, by putting "divine" in parentheses. Obviously no court is involved here, for unless there is an overt act only God is fully aware of the motions of a man's mind. But the man who insults his brother, presumably in the presence of witnesses, may indeed be brought to judgment before the Sanhedrin. The third instance, that of a man who calls another "Rebel!" is again an accusation made without witnesses, and in such a case judgment is in the hands of God and there is no recourse to any court action.

Whoever insults. The word *rākā* is not Greek but Aramaic; it is a contemptuous mode of address not infrequent in rabbinic writings. It is correctly preserved in the Syriac text, which often transmits the exact Aramaic word used by Jesus. See above, NOTE on ii 23; what is said there of place names applies also to personal names and must often be considered as likely in the case of key words in sayings of Jesus. Cf. James ii 20.

Rebel! (*against God*). Greek *mōre* normally means "fool" but it may have been confused with the Heb. *môrê*, "rebel," in Num xx 10. The epithet is in any case derogatory. It is a value judgment, and as such the man who uses it is attempting to act in the place of God. Legally, the spoken epithet would be a public slander in the presence of witnesses.

fiery death. It is possible that *Gehenna* (the Greek word here employed) was considered equivalent to hell in NT times, but there is no evidence for this, and the equation *Gehenna=hadēs* is never made. The Qumran literature is, so far as known, silent on the matter. The deep cosmic "valley" in I Enoch, designed for the punishment of men, cannot be Gehenna, though it may have some prototype in pagan Canaanite literature (the Baal epic). R. H. Charles's statements (in *Eschatology*

[New York: Schocken, 1963], p. 219 et seq.) are somewhat misleading on this point. The references in the so-called "II Enoch" to the "valley of Gehenna" (liv 1) suggest a "tophet" in a valley, usually southeast of a city, out of the prevailing winds, where trash and garbage were burned, and where human sacrificial victims had been cremated in earlier times (as in Jerusalem and Carthage). Cf. the article in *Theological Dictionary of the New Testament,* the translation of TWNT by G. W. Bromiley (Grand Rapids: Eerdmans, 1964), I, pp. 657 ff. The material in II Baruch and IV Esdras on Gehenna, like that in the usually quoted rabbinic sources, is late and not relevant here. The references sometimes made at this point to Matt xviii 8 are not wholly justified; see NOTE there.

23–24. This is the first application of the preceding statements of principle, and deals with reconciliation before the Day of Atonement. If commentators insist on providing a late date for Matthew's material, they must somehow explain this saying, which refers to a sacrificial system which lasted only until A.D. 70.

25–26. It is possible that some material has been displaced here. At first glance what we have is an injunction that not only must the brother be reconciled, but the accuser too, on the grounds that murder includes anger, and in this sense the word for accuser (*antidokos*) is used at Luke xviii 3. But if this is so, the following half-verse (25b) and verse (26) have no real meaning—for what is apparently being commanded in the rest of this section is not obedience to the demands of a righteous God, but calculated self-interest. We are told to settle with our accuser because otherwise we will wind up in jail! Interpreting these verses as a metaphor for a supposed final confrontation with God on the day of judgment is no help; in that case, either the accuser falls into the background, or Jesus himself must be cast in that role. This would be entirely different from the case law envisaged in vss. 21–24. Luke (xii 58 ff.) has the saying in the context of a crisis in the ministry of the Messiah, and a crisis also in the national life of Israel. In Luke's version, Israel is like an insolvent debtor with one final chance of escaping the legal penalties. (Cf. G. B. Caird, ET 77 [1966], 36 ff.) It is possible that an editor has attached vss. 25b–26 to a saying about an adversary which is now lost to us.

17. THE GREAT INSTRUCTION: THE LAW—ADULTERY
(v 27–30)†

V 27 "You have heard the command 'Do not commit adultery.' 28 But I tell you that everyone who looks lustfully at a woman has already committed adultery with her in his heart. 29 If your right eye causes you to sin, take it out and throw it away. It is better for you to lose one of your members than for the whole of your body to be cast into hell. 30 If your right hand causes you to sin, cut it off and throw it away. It is better for you to lose one of your members than for the whole of your body to be cast into hell.

† **Matt v 29–30** ‖ Mark ix 43–48, Matt xviii 8–9.

NOTES

v 27. *Do not commit adultery.* The prohibition also includes lustful thinking, and the statement in the following verse is a sentiment well known in the rabbinic writings. Cf. "If one gazes"—i.e., lustfully—"at the little finger of a woman, it is as if he gazed at her *pudenda*" (TB, *Berakhoth* 24a). So also with excuses to talk with a woman with the same lustful intent. Cf. Deut v 21; Exod xx 17.

29. This verse is an application of the statement on adultery. Sights which are known to stimulate passion must be avoided—i.e., to quote the moral theologians, "known occasions of sin" are to be avoided.

right eye. This presumably takes its meaning from *right hand*, which is considered to be the more active of the two hands.

30. This is the second application of the principle of vs. 27. Not only must looking be controlled, but also physical contact or occasions which might lead to physical contact. Cf. xviii 8. Deut xxv 11–12 explicitly allows for the punishment of cutting off the hand, significantly in connection with an obscene act by a woman. Rabbinic literature re-

tains expressions denoting that certain acts by the hand deserve the punishment of mutilation (cf. TB, *Shabbath* 88b; Midrash *Niddah* ii 1; both references supplied by Dr. Moses Aberbach).

causes you to sin. The Greek expression "to cause to stumble" is used in the later books of the LXX.

hell. Cf. NOTE on *fiery death* in vs. 22 above.

18. THE GREAT INSTRUCTION: THE LAW—MARRIAGE

(v 31–32)†

V 31 "It is said, 'Anyone who divorces his wife must give her a certificate to that effect.' 32 But I tell you that anyone who divorces his wife, except in the case of adultery, makes her an adulteress, and whoever marries a divorced woman commits adultery.

† **Matt v 31–32** || Matt xix 9, Mark x 11–12, Luke xvi 18.

NOTES

v 32. Cf. Deut xxiv 1, 3; Jer iii 8; Mal ii 14–16. The Greek word *porneia* quite certainly means adultery here, and generally is used of illicit sexual relations, which the school of Shammai held to be the only ground of divorce (Mishnah *Gittin* xc 1: "No one shall divorce his wife unless there is found unchastity in her"). A similar expression is found in Matt xix 9, and it is open to debate as to whether the exceptive clause is editorial, or represents an original tradition. Mark (x 11) and Luke (xvi 18) both represent Jesus as giving a simple prohibition of divorce. Paul's understanding of the matter (I Cor vii 10–11) reinforces this: divorce implies that the woman may well marry again, and in Paul's view (implicitly, too, in Jesus' view) this leads her to adultery. We are not here concerned with the arguments of the moral theologians, still less with the so-called "Pauline privilege" (I Cor vii 12–13). What Jesus is emphasizing is the principle, the foundation, of marriage. In principle, the divorced woman is still the wife of her husband, and the man who divorces his wife makes her an adulteress, on the presumption that she will marry again. The man who marries the divorced woman both shares in her adultery and also commits that offense himself, because in principle—though not legally—the divorced woman is still married to her first husband. The clause "Whoever marries . . . adultery" is omitted by some manuscripts.

19. THE GREAT INSTRUCTION:
THE LAW—OATHS
(v 33–37)

V 33 "Again, you have heard that it was said to the ancients 'Do not make vows rashly,' but 'Be careful to pay any vows made to the Lord.' 34 But I tell you—do not swear at all. Not by heaven, for it is God's throne, 35 nor by earth, for it is his footstool, nor by Jerusalem, for it is the city of the Great King. 36 Do not swear even by your head, for you cannot make one hair black or white. 37 Let your words be 'Yes' and 'No.' Anything more than this is of evil origin.

NOTES

v 33. In its present form, the text is confused. Vows were always accompanied by an oath, and the usual English translations have unhappily reflected the confusions of the Greek, which reads: "Do not swear falsely, but pay your vows to the Lord." It is probable that the translators, being unversed in rabbinic law, misunderstood the Aramaic. A reference to Num xxx 2 shows that the Law stated simply that binding oneself by a vow demanded the performance of the promise. The emphasis is not on the way in which a man binds himself, but on his obligation to perform his promise. Jesus opposes himself to all distinction in oaths, a distinction which a casuist might interpret as determining the relative solemnity of one promise against another. Cf. Lev xix 12 on oaths in God's name.

pay any vows made. Cf. Deut xxiii 21; Ps 1 14; Num xxx 2.

34. God's throne. Cf. Isa lxvi 1.

35. his footstool. Cf. Isa lxvi 1; Lam ii 1.

Jerusalem . . . city of the Great King. Cf. Ps xlvii 2(3H).

37. Jesus tells his disciples to avoid all strong oaths and to content themselves with "Yes" and "No" in dealings between members of the

community. James v 12 has the statement somewhat differently, and that version may be a reminiscence of Jewish legal opinion (TB, *Sanhedrin* 36a) that "Yes" and "No" are oaths if repeated twice. Cf. "Let your 'Yes' be righteous"—i.e., true—"and let your 'No' be righteous" (TB, *Baba Mezia* 49a).

20. THE GREAT INSTRUCTION:
THE LAW—RETALIATION
(v 38–42)†

V 38 "You have heard that it was said 'An eye for an eye and a tooth for a tooth.' But I tell you not to resist one who is evil. 39 But if anyone strikes you on the right cheek, turn the other to him as well. 40 If anyone wants to sue you and take away your tunic, let him have your cape, too. 41 If anyone presses you into service to go one mile, go with him two. 42 Give to him who asks you for a loan, and do not refuse one who is unable to pay interest.

† Matt v 38–42 || Luke vi 29–30.

NOTES

v 38. The *lex talionis* here referred to (cf. Exod xxi 24–25; Lev xxiv 20; Deut xix 21) is often pointed out by modern critics as an example of the savage ruthlessness of the Law of the Old Covenant, contrasted with the "law of charity" of the New Covenant (cf. John xv 12; I Cor xiii 1–13). It should be remembered that the law of retaliation here quoted by Jesus acted, in its own time and for many centuries afterwards, as a much needed check on the widely practiced blood feud. Moreover, the Old Covenant Law provided for recourse to the courts; and however brutal we may think the punishment, it was within set limits and had sanctions which the blood feud did not have. The disciple can have no such recourse in the new community—he must endure anyone who is evil. Jesus then proceeds to outline the limits of its application.

39. *turn the other*. Jesus here speaks of what is still true in the Near East—the most insulting of all physical blows being that of striking the right cheek with the back of the hand. Jeremias (*The Sermon on the Mount*, p. 27) suggests that the allusion here is to the insult offered to one adjudged to be a heretic. Everywhere in the gospels, the members of the new community are subject to persecution and insult by reason

of their attachment to Jesus. The discipleship will bring inevitable suffering and repudiation, and the disciples may not go to law. There appears to be here a reminiscence of Isa 1 6; the disciple is not to expect anything other than what the Servant must endure.

40. An interesting example has been given to us by Dr. Moses Aberbach. TB, *Yoma* 23a, in discussing (with reference to Lev xix 18) the whole concept of revenge as distinct from bearing a grudge, posits two men, agricultural workers, one of whom asks to borrow a sickle and is refused. The one who refused next day asked the would-be borrower for the loan of an ax. He is refused, on the score that he had himself refused the loan of a sickle. That, concluded the judgment, was retaliation, and the cases are wholly congruous. But if one man who has refused the loan of an ax next day asks the would-be borrower if he may have the loan of a garment, and his request is granted with the words "Here it is. I am not like you, who would not lend me an ax," then that is bearing a grudge. This is striking, in that a garment is not a likely object to be loaned or borrowed. The example may well go back in tradition to the first century A.D., and suggests a background of ideas common to both Matthew's tradition and that of the lawyer's casebook.

41. *presses you into service.* The verb is Persian in origin, and the noun (*aggaros,* plural *aggaroi*) denotes men who carried the royal mail. Josephus (*Antiquities* XIII. 52) uses the verb for the compulsory carrying of military stores. Adolf Deissmann, *Biblical Studies* (Edinburgh: T. & T. Clark, 1903), pp. 86 f. points out that the word was used in third-century B.C. Egypt of a boat used for postal purposes.

mile (Gr. *milion*) is found only here in the NT. It is of Latin origin, and occurs in the later Jewish writings.

42. As this verse stands in the Greek and in the standard English versions (cf. RSV, "Give to him who begs from you . . ." and NEB, "Give when you are asked to give . . ."), Jesus appears to be inviting the disciples to allow themselves to be victimized by the unscrupulous. Our translation reconstructs the verse as an assertion by Jesus against prevailing Jewish legal fictions on behalf of the debtors. (This translation is based on the background of the word *danizein,* "to lend at interest," which is translated in RSV by "borrow.") Because although the injunctions of the Law against usury were firm and clear (cf. Deut xxiii 19–20, etc.), certain practices had grown up to circumvent these restrictions, and there were many people whom debt had reduced to a pitiful state. Interest rates were extremely high in the ancient world (often 100, sometimes 200 per cent), thanks to the prevailing hazards of drought, insecurity of travel, the unpredictable rapacity of tax collectors, rebellion, banditry, nomad raids, and warfare of all kinds. While the Law prohibited lending at interest between fellow Israelites,

it said nothing about lending between Israelites and Gentiles—and so it was understood (explicitly in Deut xxiii 20) that interest would be permitted in that case.

In addition to this, the situation in the time of Jesus had led to various kinds of legal fiction in order to circumvent, or at least mitigate, the provisions of the Law on usury. Business and allied financial dealings would have been impossible without long-term loans, which on the letter of the Law had to terminate every seven years in the sabbatical year. There had therefore grown up the Jewish practice of the *prozbul*, which simply demanded a recognition of the indebtedness of the debtor when the debt was legally at an end. Having established that the background of *danizein* was confirmed by the Heb. *sha'al* and the Jewish-Aramaic *she'al*, both of which mean "to borrow," as well as literally "to ask," and in the causative "to lend," on interest, we find that the Syriac similarly translates the Greek of Matthew. It therefore became necessary to look more closely at the Greek of vs. 42. If we can assume that a negative has been dropped before *thelonta*, so that an amended text would read *tone mē thelonta*, then the verse fits into its context with complete clarity. The negative *ouk* with *ethelō* (*mē* with a participle, as here) is common in Greek (cf. Liddell and Scott, *A Greek-English Lexicon*, I, p. 497b; J. H. Thayer, *A Greek-English Lexicon of the New Testament* [Edinburgh: T. & T. Clark, 1888], p. 285), and in the NT. Aristotle (*History of Animals*, 575a 28) makes it clear that the construction *ouk ethelō*="unable," and is the equivalent of *ou dunamai*, being often so used.

21. THE GREAT INSTRUCTION:
THE LAW—ENEMIES
(v 43–48)†

V 43 "You have heard that it was said 'You shall love your neighbor and hate your enemy,' 44 but I tell you to love your enemies and pray for those who misuse you. 45 In this way you will become sons of your heavenly Father, who causes the sun to rise upon both good and evil men, and sends rain to just and unjust alike. 46 If you love only those who love you, what reward have you? Do not the taxgatherers do the same? 47 And if you greet only your brethren, what extra are you doing? Do not the heathen do the same? 48 Be true, just as your heavenly Father is true.

† Matt v 43–48 || Luke vi 27–28, 32–36.

NOTES

v 43. *You shall love your neighbor.* This is a quotation from Lev xix 18, but the remainder of the verse is oral commentary inferred from the distinction drawn in the post-Exilic period between dealings with Jews on the one hand and dealings with Gentiles on the other. All such distinction is here made impossible for the disciple. All men are neighbors to the man who has assumed the responsibilities of discipleship. Cf. Enoch 1 4.

45. *heavenly Father.* See vs. 16.

46. *taxgatherers.* The word is not used specifically of this particular class of men, but rather in the sense employed in the rabbinic writings—i.e., a class of men normally despised, of whatever occupation.

47. *heathen.* The Greek is *ethnikoi,* used in vi 7, xviii 17, and III John 7 to describe Gentiles.

48. *true.* A rabbinic commentary (TB, *Shabbath* 133b), quoting a first-century A.D. authority, paraphrases this as: "Be like him. As he is gracious and merciful, so be you gracious and merciful." The Greek

word *teleios* in this context does not refer to moral perfection, but "truth, sincerity" (cf. Deut xviii 13). In this sense, the Greek word is used in the LXX about Noah (Gen vi 9) and Job (i 1). The Greek word in the LXX is linked with *tāmîm,* and the meaning of the Canaanite-Hebrew word *tām,* "true," is the same in both pagan and biblical literature. There are links in Hebrew between *tāmîm* and *'emeth* (truth), and also in the LXX with the Gr. *alēthinos,* the "true" man. It does not have here the later Greek meaning of being "totally free of imperfection," which is the meaning found in both the KJ and RSV. Cf. also NOTE on x 34, and Appendix to Part IX of Introduction.

22. THE GREAT INSTRUCTION: ALMSGIVING
(vi 1–4)

VI 1 "Take care not to perform righteous deeds in public to be a spectacle to men. If you do, you have no reward from your heavenly Father. 2 When it comes to almsgiving, do not trumpet it abroad, as the overscrupulous do in the synagogues and the market places, so that they may be praised by men. In solemn truth, I tell you that they already have their reward. 3 But when giving alms, do not let your left hand know what your right hand is doing, so that your almsgiving is in secret. 4 Your Father who sees in secret will reward you (openly).

NOTES

vi 1. *reward.* Cf. NOTE on v 12.

2. *overscrupulous.* See the Appendix to Part IX of Introduction for the background of this translation. In face of the evidence nothing can justify the continued use of the word "hypocrite" in our English versions.

3. *in secret.* Cf. "One who does alms in secret is greater than Moses our teacher" (TB, *Baba Bathra* 9b).

4. *(openly).* We have bracketed the word, since it does not occur in all the manuscripts, but the structure of the saying seems to us to require the antithesis for balance (cf. vs. 6).

23. THE GREAT INSTRUCTION:
PRAYER
(vi 5–14)†

VI ⁵ "When you pray, do not be like the overscrupulous, who love to stand in synagogues and public places to pray, so that they may be in plain view of all. In solemn truth, I tell you that they already have their reward. ⁶ But you, when you pray, go into your room, shut the door, and pray to your Father in secret. Your Father who sees in secret will reward you (openly). ⁷ In praying, do not heap up empty phrases as the Gentiles do, for they suppose that they will be heard simply on account of their verbosity. ⁸ Do not be like them; your heavenly Father knows what you need before you ask him. ⁹ Pray like this:

'Our Father in heaven,
   may your name be held in honor.
¹⁰ Let your Kingdom come,
   let your will be done,
   as in heaven, so also on earth.
¹¹ Give us today the food we need.
¹² And release us from our debts
   as we also release our debtors.
¹³ Do not bring us into the final test
   but save us from the Evil One.'

¹⁴ If you forgive men their offenses, your heavenly Father will forgive you, ¹⁵ but if you do not forgive men, neither will your Father forgive your offenses.

† **Matt vi 5–14** ‖ Luke xi 2–4.

NOTES

vi 5. It should be emphasized here that this is no condemnation of praying in a synagogue or public place *as such*.

6. *will reward you*. This does not refer to an answer to prayer, but reward for lack of ostentation.

7. Gentiles. See NOTE on v 47.

verbosity. The Greek word (*battalogein*) can be used of stammering, and so of constant repetition. *Battos* (stammerer) and cognate words suggest constant repetition rather than continually interrupted speech.

9–13. Luke has the Lord's prayer in a shorter form, and in a different context (Luke xi 1–4). Matthew presumably included the prayer here on account of its suitability to his material, and not necessarily because it was given in this context. In Luke the strongly eschatological context is in part absent (cf. the omission of *let your will be done, as in heaven, so also on earth*).

Pray like this. I.e., "in this way," not "in these words." The constant repetition of the Lord's prayer in public worship has steadily eroded the eschatological urgency of the words almost to the vanishing point. To compound this misunderstanding, we have also forgotten that the clauses of the prayer are in a very real sense "headlines," which would have suggested other thoughts, allied considerations. The first three clauses pray for the advent of the Kingdom. When this Kingdom has come, God's name (i.e., his person) will be held in honor, his will performed.

Father in heaven. Cf. third NOTE on v 16. The first hearers would have been reminded of the other titles used of God in the OT—Lord, King, Husband, etc.

may your name be held in honor. The "Name" of God as here used is a thoroughly OT usage. "Knowing the name" of God was equivalent to "fulfilling the terms of the Covenant obligation," because ancient Israelite covenants were solemnly sworn by invoking the name of God. This followed the general practice of royal treaties of the second millennium B.C., in which the gods of the interested parties were named as witnesses. To know, understand, the name of a person was to know the person himself—cf. Gen xxxii 28–29. God's name, his person, suffers outrage in the despoliation of his chosen people, and the restoration of the fortunes of Israel was a sanctifying, an "honoring," of that name (cf. Ezek xxxvi 23). But Israel's sin, which brings upon her the misfortunes which she suffers at the hands of her enemies, is equally a dishonoring of God's name (cf. Isa xliii 25, xlviii 11; Ezek xxxvi 20–22). The juxtaposition of honoring the name of God together with asserting his reign is a common motif, and in its classical form is expressed in the ancient synagogue prayer known as the Kaddish: "May his great name be exalted and sanctified in the world, which he made according to his will. May his kingdom rule, his redemption spring forth, may he bring near his Messiah and save his people, in your lifetime, in your days, in the lifetime of all the house of Israel, quickly and soon. And you shall say, Amen." (Cf. also I Cor xvi 22; Rev xxii 20.)

10. *so also on earth.* The whole tenor of Matthew's gospel (cf. Part X of the Introduction) marks a sharp distinction in his material between "the Kingdom of heaven" and "the Kingdom of God," even though each phrase could be a surrogate for the other. ("Kingdom of heaven" was used in order to avoid use of any word for "God.") This petition in the prayer looks both to the establishment of the Messianic Kingdom in the present age ("Kingdom of heaven" in Matthew's use), and also to the final consummation ("Kingdom of God"). The prayer then passes to petitions proper to those who await the coming of the Kingdom.

11. *Give us today the food we need.* The last two words in our translation are our rendering of an obscure Greek word, *epiousios.* Jerome tells us that the (now lost) Gospel according to the Hebrews had the clause "bread of tomorrow," and this would fit the sense on two counts: (a) the Gr. *hē epiousa hēmera*="tomorrow," and (b) it harmonizes well with the eschatological content of the first part of the prayer. The disciples are to pray for tomorrow's bread today, since tomorrow would be the day of the Messiah (cf. Exod xvi 22 ff.) on which work would not be possible. But this is awkward, for first it would mean that a Greek word was being coined deliberately, when there were already phrases in constant use for "tomorrow," and secondly, on the face of it, it would not harmonize well with "today." The word is found in the papyri in the sense of "ration," and certainly for those waiting for the coming age this sense is appropriate. It is possible that what we have here is a misunderstanding of an Aramaic original which very early was cast into a Greek mold and rendered sacrosanct by use.

12. *release us from our debts.* Luke at this point has "sins." Short of keeping man indentured to him, God could deal with man's debt to him only by his own gracious act. This remission of debt the NT sees as accomplished by the self-giving of Jesus. The cancellation of the disciples' indebtedness, in the face of the dawning Kingdom, must be met by a like service to their debtors. There is close parallel between the Greek of this clause and the LXX Greek of Deut xv 2. Cf. NOTE on v 25–26.

13. *the final test.* Frequently in all the gospel traditions Jesus warns of the distress and tribulation which will mark the end of the present age and the dawning of the Kingdom. The Greek word (*peirasmos*) was used as meaning "the birth pangs of the Messiah," and indicated

a sharp and bitter struggle between men and forces of evil. This theme of conflict is constantly emphasized in the NT, and Jesus saw his work of exorcism as part of this conflict. Cf. the important article of K. G. Kuhn, *"Peirasmos—hamartia—sarx*—im Neuen Testament und die damit zusammenhängenden Vorstellungen," *Zeitschrift für Theologie und Kirche* 49 (1952), 200–22, and also "New Light on Temptation, Sin and Flesh in the New Testament," in *The Scrolls and the New Testament*, ed. Krister Stendahl, London: SCM, 1958.

from the Evil One. Paul's letters give frequent warnings of the heightened intensity of the devil's onslaughts in the time of the Kingdom's inauguration.

The doxology ("for thine is the Kingdom, and the power, and the glory, forever, Amen"), which exists in various forms in different manuscripts, was evidently added by copyists who understood from their own use that such was the customary way to end a prayer. On the Lord's prayer, cf. especially Raymond E. Brown, "The Paternoster as an Eschatological Prayer," in *New Testament Essays*, pp. 217 ff.

14. *offenses.* The word used here, literally meaning a false step, is found only here and in Mark xi 25–26, in the gospels.

COMMENT

The illustrations noted above are collected here by the evangelist to elucidate the injunctions in v 20, which is concerned with the obedient response of the disciple to the will of God. The illustrations are from the familiar duties of prayer, fasting, and almsgiving, all three being areas in which ostentation is a constant temptation.

24. THE GREAT INSTRUCTION:
FASTING
(vi 16–18)

VI 16 "Whenever you fast, do not (like the overscrupulous) look dismal, for they disfigure their faces to make it obvious to men that they are fasting. In solemn truth, I tell you that they already have their reward. 17 But when you fast, anoint your head and wash your face, so that it may not be obvious to men that you are fasting, 18 but to your Father, and your Father who sees in secret will reward you (openly).

Notes

vi 16. On *overscrupulous*, see Introduction, Appendix to Part IX.
17. *anoint your head.* It is possible that this is meant in the sense of, e.g., Ps xxiii 5, that is, of joy and thanksgiving.
18. The Greek of this verse is impossible as it stands ("so that it may not be obvious to men that you are fasting, but to your Father *who is in secret,* and your Father who sees in secret will reward you"). As the Gr. *tō en tō kruphaiō* is plainly dittography, we have omitted the clause in italics. The extant Greek recensions of the verse are all likewise impossible. God may be "hidden"—to use the OT phrase— but it is hard to say how he can be "in secret."

25. THE GREAT INSTRUCTION: WEALTH
(vi 19–21)†

VI ¹⁹ "Do not accumulate wealth for yourselves on earth, where both moth and rust consume, and where thieves break in and steal; ²⁰ but store away for yourselves heavenly treasure, where moth and rust do not consume, and where thieves do not break in and steal. ²¹ Where your wealth lies, there also will be your heart.

† **Matt vi 19–21** || Luke xii 33–34.

NOTES

vi 19–21. Detachment with regard to worldly goods is a constant theme in the NT (cf. last part of third paragraph in second NOTE on v 9). Cf. the following sayings of King Monobazos of Adiabene (A.D. 46–47), who embraced Judaism and in a time of famine gave away all his inherited wealth: "My fathers stored in a place where the hand can reach, but I have stored in a place where the hand cannot reach. My fathers gathered for this world, but I have gathered for the future world." (TB, *Baba Bathra* 11a, *Tosefta Peah* iv 18, references by courtesy of Dr. Moses Aberbach.)

26. THE GREAT INSTRUCTION:
DISCIPLESHIP AND DETACHMENT
(vi 22–34)†

VI 22 "The body's lamp is the eye, and if your eye is healthy then all your body will be full of light, 23 but if your eye is evil, then all your body will be dark. If the light which is in you is dark, then how dark it will be! 24 No one can be the slave of two owners, for either he will dislike the one and prefer the other, or alternatively be loyal to one and despise the other. You cannot be a slave of both God and wealth. 25 Therefore I tell you not to be overconcerned about eating and drinking, nor about clothing. Is not your life more than eating and drinking, and your body more than clothing? 26 Think of the birds in the sky: they neither sow nor reap, and they do not store in granaries, yet your heavenly Father feeds them. Are you not much more valuable than they? 27 Which of you, by worrying, can add anything to his span of life? 28 And why be so worried about clothing? Reflect on the anemones and the way they grow, for they neither toil nor spin, 29 yet I tell you that even Solomon in all his magnificence was not clothed like one of them. 30 If God thus cares for the weeds, which—living today—are used as fuel for ovens tomorrow, will he not much more care for you, men of little faith? 31 Do not therefore be overconcerned with questions such as 'What shall we eat?' 'What shall we drink?' or 'What shall we wear?' 32 for these are pagan worries, and your heavenly Father knows that you need all these things. 33 But seek first of all God's Kingdom and his righteousness, and all these things will be provided for you. 34 Do not be overconcerned about tomorrow, for tomorrow will do its own worrying. Today's misfortune is enough for today."

† Matt vi 22–23 || Luke xi 34–36; 24 || Luke xvi 13; 25–34 || Luke xii 22–34.

Notes

vi 22–23. To lay hold of treasure in heaven, the disciple must have his "inner eye" healthy. The idea expressed here (cf. Luke xi 34) is that just as the body is illuminated by the eye (as though that organ were a window), so there is a spiritual eye, through which the whole spirit of man is either illuminated or in darkness. The two verses might easily be linked with the preceding vss. 19–21, since the "good eye" as a synonym for generosity is well attested in the OT (cf. Deut xv 9; Prov xxii 9, xxiii 6, xxviii 22; Ecclus xiv 10) and in the *Pirqê Abôth* (Sayings of the Fathers) v 15. But it would be a mistake to attribute to vss. 22–23 a preoccupation with wealth and possessions, even though the evangelist uses the word *haplous* (which we have rendered by "healthy"), and which can be translated as "liberal." However, the context of its parallel in Luke xi 34–36 makes it clear that what is under discussion is the generosity, the humility, which is characteristic of freedom from entanglement, whether of wealth or of any other human consideration.

24. The two preceding verses are in our judgment explained by vs. 24. Despite possible echoes from immediately preceding centuries in our own history, we have chosen the translation "slave" at this point, and so all through the gospel. The slave was in Imperial Rome, as in the earlier Hellenistic world, the absolute property of his owner, who had rights of life and death over him. Nevertheless, it is important to emphasize here that—unlike later types of slavery among Christians and Muslims—the slave in Roman and Hellenistic society could often be a person of considerable education and therefore of consequence in a household. In those ancient times, slaves were generally prisoners of war, and the institution had no racial overtones. Slavery was often preferred to freedom, and men made contracts of servitude to ensure food and shelter for themselves and their families. Though flight was possible to slaves under desperate circumstances, masters were under constant economic pressure to treat slaves with some consideration. This did not apply to *state* slaves, who frequently worked in intolerable circumstances. The OT allowed for the institution of slavery, but with very precise safeguards. The apostle Paul could call himself a "slave of Jesus-Messiah" (cf. Rom i 1) to emphasize the absolute rights of the Risen Lord over him, and none would think the expression inappropriate.

25. Rabbi Eliezer the Great (first century A.D.), who was in touch with Christians, quotes a saying of Jesus which is not otherwise attested:

"Whoever has a morsel of bread in a basket and says 'What shall I eat tomorrow?' is one of those who have little faith" (TB, *Sota* 48b).

Therefore. Luke uses this connective in quite different context (Luke xii 22) and we might have expected *therefore* to introduce some conclusion from vs. 24. It is probable that this word gives us an indication that the saying was very early fixed in oral form, and was so reproduced here in Matthew's collection of sayings.

26. The slave cannot serve two owners, and the disciple will be called upon to choose between God and human well-being (wealth, "mammon," vs. 24). If he is single-minded, of "sound eye," he will choose rightly. And if he should ask how he can be assured of human necessities, vss. 25–26 point to God's provident care for nature.

27. The saying is difficult, and may have been conflated. *Pēchus* (cubit) is a measure of space, which we have translated simply by "anything," while *hēlikia* can mean either stature or span of life. Possibly there were two sayings: "Who can add a cubit to his land, or a day to his life?" The confusion is further illustrated by Luke's version (Luke xii 25–26), which adds *elastichon,* presumably referring to "adding to age, or physical growth," and *tōn loipōn,* referring to bodily sustenance and clothing. Whether *hēlikia* be span of life or stature, it is not easy to see how it is "least" compared with the other two as "the rest" (Luke xii 26).

28. *anemones.* See IDB, III, s.v. "lily," fifth paragraph.

30. *ovens* (Gr. *kribanos*). An earthen oven, in which dead weeds were used for fuel (cf. Liddell and Scott, *A Greek-English Lexicon,* ad loc., and Dalman, *Orte und Wege Jesu,* pp. 169, 232).

men of little faith. The word does not occur in Mark, and in Luke only at xii 28. Its use here and at viii 26, xiv 31, and xvi 8 calls attention to faith as trust in the overruling providence of God.

33. Unhappily it needs to be said here that all these lessons in detachment are *not* here summed up by an injunction to assume that discipleship will *ipso facto* produce the necessities of life. This verse, like its predecessors, calls for a searching examination of the disciples' priorities.

to you. The translation of the NEB (". . . all the rest will come to you as well.") at this point is indefensible, resting as it does on an assumption that the prefix in *prostethēsetai* is to be taken literally—a fault common to the KJ also.

enough. The Greek (*arketos*) is late, and is found before the second century A.D.—outside the NT—only in Josephus (*Jewish War* III. 130) and one near-contemporary author.

27. THE GREAT INSTRUCTION: DISCIPLESHIP
(vii 1–14)†

VII 1 "Do not sit in judgment, lest you yourselves be judged, 2 for you will be judged by the same standard which you have used. 3 Why look at the splinter in your brother's eye, if you do not take notice of the beam in your own? 4 How dare you say to your brother, 'Let me take the splinter out of your eye', when all the time there is a beam in your own eye? 5 Casuist! First remove the beam from your own eye, and then you will see clearly in order to remove the splinter from your brother's eye. 6 Do not give what is sacred to dogs, and do not throw pearls in front of pigs, lest they tread them underfoot, and then turn and attack you.

7 "Ask, and it will be given you, seek and you will find, knock and the door will be opened for you. 8 For he who asks will receive, he who seeks will find, and the door will be opened to him who knocks. 9 Who is there among you who will give his son a stone if he asks for bread? 10 Or if he asks for fish, will he give him a snake? 11 If, then, you who are sinful know how to give good things to your children, how much more will your heavenly Father give good things to those who ask him? 12 Whatever therefore you wish men to do to you, do the same to them, for this is the meaning of the Law and the prophets.

13 "Go in by the narrow gate, for the wide gate and the easy path lead to destruction, and many go that way. 14 The narrow gate and the hard way lead to life, and few find it.

† **Matt vii 1–6** || Luke vi 37–38, 41–42; **7–12** || Luke xi 9–13; **3–14** || Luke xiii 24.

NOTES

vii 1. Luke vi 37 connects this verse with the saying "Be merciful," which is a good logical connection of material. Cf. "Whoever accuses his neighbor will himself be judged first" (TB, *Rosh ha-Shanah* 16b).

2. *for you will be judged.* Mark adds this at iv 24b, in a different context. The saying was common in Jewish literature. Unjustifiable condemnation will always call down upon it the just condemnation of God.

3–4. Cf. Rabbi Tarphon (end first century A.D.): "If one says, 'Take the mote from thine eye,' he answers, 'Take the beam from thine own eye'" (TB, *Arachin* 16b), and (from a commentary on Ruth i 1) "It was a generation which judged its judges. If the judge said to a man, 'Take the splinter from between your teeth'"—a variant reading has 'eyes'— "he would retort, 'Take the beam from between your eyes'" (TB, *Baba Bathra* 16b).

5. On *Casuist!*, see Introduction, Appendix to Part IX.

6. This saying is found only in Matthew. Its position in Matthew's tradition belongs to a series of three prohibitions, vi 19–20, vii 1–5.

dogs . . . pigs=alien and heathen people (cf. Philip iii 2; Rev xxii 15), and *pearls* would here stand for religious truth (cf. xiii 46). As it stands it is capable of being interpreted as a Jewish-Christian proscription against evangelizing Gentiles, but one early document (Syrian? second half of first century A.D.?—cf. J.-P. Audet, *La Didaché,* applies it to the Eucharist (*Didache* ix).

7–13. Whatever their original place in any collection which Matthew may have used, the present position of these commands is appropriate, since they follow warnings against the misuse of discipleship.

7–8. Cf. Luke xi 9–10, with identical wording.

9–10. Cf. Luke xi 11–12.

12. This verse seems to be out of place, for Luke has it in a context which deals with duty to others (Luke vi 31). Possibly vss. 7–11 have been at some stage interpolated, and vs. 12 originally followed vs. 6. In negative form, this saying is associated with Hillel the Elder (TB, *Shabbath* 31a), shortly before the time of Jesus.

13–14. This is the second command. Cf. Luke xiii 24. The "two ways" is an OT theme. Cf. Deut xi 26–29 (interpreted in rabbinical tradition as of the "two ways") and Jer xxi 8. The Lukan version is more emphatically eschatological in context than is the position here. But it is likely that we are to see this verse against the context of vss. 22 ff. In this case, *Go in by the narrow gate* will be understood as meaning that entrance into the Kingdom—whether the Kingdom of heaven or the Kingdom of God—is through a narrow gate.

many . . . few. Cf. II Esd viii 3: "Many are created, but few will be saved."

COMMENT

There is no particular logical connection between vi 34 and vii 1, and the material here appears to be a collection of sayings of a moral and quasi-legal character which may have been in current use.

28. THE GREAT INSTRUCTION:
FALSE TEACHERS
(vii 15–20)†

VII   15 "Beware of false prophets, who come to you disguised as sheep; inwardly they are devouring wolves. 16 You will recognize them by their fruits. Are grapes gathered from thorn bushes, or figs from thistles? 17 So, every sound tree bears good fruit, but the decaying tree bears bad fruit. 18 A sound tree cannot bear bad fruit, and a decaying tree cannot produce good fruit. 19 Every tree which does not bear good fruit is cut down and thrown into the fire. 20 Thus you will recognize them by their fruits.

† **Matt vii 15–20** ‖ Luke vi 43–44.

NOTES

vii 16. Cf. Luke vi 44.
17. Cf. Luke vi 43.
18–20. Something of Matthew's method of arranging his material can be seen here. After the warning against false prophets in vs. 15 there is a saying which deals with recognizing such people, a saying which he uses to close the section in vs. 20. But the saying suggested to him familiar sayings about trees and fruit, which he placed at 16b—19. Cf. a similar procedure of using a parable at xx 1–15 to follow on from xix 30, with a conclusion at xx 16 paralleling xix 30.

29. THE GREAT INSTRUCTION:
FALSE DISCIPLES
(vii 21–29) †

VII 21 "Not everyone who calls me, 'Lord, Lord,' will enter into the Kingdom of heaven, but only the man who does the will of my Father who is in heaven. 22 At that time, many will say to me, 'Lord, Lord, did we not prophesy in your name, cast out demons in your name, and did we not perform acts of power in your name?' 23 Then I will declare to them: 'I never knew you. Go away from me, you evildoers.' 24 Therefore everyone who hears these sayings of mine and does them, will be like a wise man who built his house on rock. 25 The rain fell, the river flooded, and the wind blew hard on that house. It did not fall, because it was built on rock. 26 But anyone who hears these sayings of mine and does not follow them will be like a foolish man who built his house on sand. 27 The rain fell, the river flooded, and the wind blew hard on that house. It fell, and its fall was very great."

28 When Jesus had finished saying these things, the crowds were deeply impressed by his teaching, 29 for he taught authoritatively, and not like their scribes.

† Matt vii 21–23 || Luke xiii 25–27; 24–29 || Luke vi 47–49.

Notes

vii 21. Cf. Luke vi 46. Cf. also ". . . strong as a lion to do the will of thy Father who is in heaven" (*Pirqê Abôth* v 22). The phrase "to do the will" is common in rabbinic writings.

22. *At that time* (literally *in that day*) is an expression looking to the end of the present order, i.e., to the judgment. Cf. Luke xiii 26.

23. Cf. Luke xiii 27.

24–27. Cf. Luke vi 47–49.

29. *for he taught* . . . On the scribes, see *Jewish Encyclopaedia,* XI (New York and London: Funk & Wagnalls), p. 123. The origin of the designation "scribe" is far from certain, but what Matthew says here helps to explain the implied criticism. Given any body of law, there will inevitably grow up a whole history of interpretation and reinterpretation of that law in the light of changing circumstances and of a changing social and/or economic climate. Inevitably there will be a corresponding growth in the number of clerks, scribes, and recorders of these interpretations, not necessarily skilled in law, but skilled in recording case-law decisions. Such men, even though not trained lawyers, would exercise considerable influence in forming attitudes to the Law, on account of their known and recognized ability to recall the minutiae of case-law decisions. Even today the influence of "managing clerks" in the United Kingdom in solicitors' and barristers' offices is considerable.

Yet another empirical factor leads to an emphasis on the importance of those who record decisions. This is the observable tendency in all ages and societies to interpret law in a restrictive sense at the beginning, followed inevitably by an equally observable tendency to interpret in a permissive sense. The history of Christian monasticism in the first eight centuries of church history is an interesting example of this tendency, and the same process is discernible in the history of rabbinic commentaries on the Law.

Note: A comparison between the treatment of the material of the Great Instruction in Matthew with parallel material in Luke is not to our purpose in this commentary. The reader will find an excellent and detailed account in Allen's ICC *St. Matthew* commentary, pp. 70–74.

The reader is referred to two works which deal with the Great Instruction. The first, to which reference was made in our COMMENT on vss. 1–12 (§ 13), is Jeremias' *Sermon on the Mount.* The second, more recent—and full-length—work is W. D. Davies, *The Setting of the Sermon on the Mount,* Cambridge University Press, 1964. (This is now available in an abridged paperback, *The Sermon on the Mount* [Cambridge], intended more for the general reader.) This book has the advantage of taking note of the available literature on the subject, however peripheral. Generally, Davies' main arguments may be summarized as follows:

(1) The element of crisis in the teaching of Jesus is emphasized, and for all the careful arrangement of material in Matthew, Davies does not feel that this element has been reduced in the process. Davies, accepting the validity of the "Q" hypothesis, finds his proof in the sayings of that

collection. He rightly points out that the nearest, if not the only, parallel to this "crisis" element lies in the sectarian writings of Qumran, though here—as Davies points out—the Essenes withdrew, in response to this sense of crisis, into rigidly defined groups centered on an exact keeping of the Law. The author—following Kurt Schubert ("The Sermon on the Mount and the Qumran Texts," in *The Scrolls and the New Testament,* ed. K. Stendahl)—finds an anti-Essene element in Jesus' teaching in Matt v. Davies' view that Jesus recalled his disciples to "the essential meaning of the Torah" (p. 432) is substantially our own. He finds Jesus deliberately legislating for the new Messianic age.

(2) Davies, willing to consider the idea that Jesus' words were memorized and transmitted in something like a rabbinic school, sees two divergent traditions resulting: the one, a tendency to treat the words of Jesus as precise regulations, to be used in rabbinic fashion for further interpretation and elucidation; the other, a tendency to draw out from the sayings a single principle from which codes of behavior could be inferred.

(3) Davies considers that the grouping of Matthew's material reflects or parallels the activity of the rabbinical schools, especially under the influence of the scholars at Jamnia (Yabneh) after the destruction of the temple in A.D. 70. Davies regards the Great Instruction as a "formulation of the way of the New Israel" at a time when rabbinical scholars were similarly working on such a formulation for the people of the Old Covenant under changed circumstances. This, the author holds, accounts for the anti-Pharisaism of Matthew, the characteristics of the genealogy, and various details in the Great Instruction.

We would disagree with parts of this last point. Certainly Jamnia was for a time a center of study, but it is by no means certain just what did happen there. There was, so far as we can at present judge, nothing approaching a "council" of scholars. Moreover, it is possible to exaggerate the importance of Jamnia, and the kind of formulation to which Davies calls attention plainly had a far longer tradition of legal debate in oral process than would appear from Davies' book. The widespread and lasting consequences of the Jewish dispersion (the "Diaspora") were such that the sacrificial cultus of the temple was something which affected the majority of Jews only minimally at best. In a very real sense, it was the destruction of Jewish life in Palestine rather than the destruction of the temple which was decisive for Judaism in A.D. 70.

In addition to Davies' view that the events of A.D. 70 were of paramount importance for the formulation of rabbinic tradition, there is allied with this his option for the priority of Mark as a documentary source for Matthew. This is an option for which we find as yet no overwhelming evidence in favor of its final acceptance as an assured result of biblical scholarship.

30. HEALINGS
(viii 1–18)†

VIII ¹ When he came down from the mountain, great crowds followed him. ² A leper, on coming to him, prostrated himself with the words, "Sir, if you are willing, you are able to cure me." ³ Then, stretching out his hand, he said, "I am willing. Be cured." Immediately he was cured of his leprosy. ⁴ Jesus said to him, "Be sure to say nothing to anyone. But go and show yourself to the priest, and make the offering Moses commanded, for proof to them."

⁵ As he was entering Capernaum, a centurion came up to him with the words, ⁶ "Sir, my servant is lying at home paralyzed, in terrible suffering." ⁷ He replied to him, "I will come and heal him." ⁸ But the centurion replied, "Sir, I am unworthy to have you enter beneath my roof. But simply give the word and my servant will be healed. ⁹ For I too am a man under authority, having soldiers under my command. I say to one 'Go,' and he goes, to another 'Come' and he comes, and to my slave 'Do this' and he does it." ¹⁰ Jesus was surprised at hearing this, and said to those who followed him, "I declare to you that I have not found such faith, even in Israel. ¹¹ I tell you that many will come from east and west and will take their place with Abraham, Isaac, and Jacob in the Kingdom of heaven, ¹² while the sons of the Kingdom will be thrown into outer darkness. There will be shrieking and grinding of teeth." ¹³ Jesus said to the centurion, "Go. As you have believed, so let it be." And his servant was cured at that moment.

¹⁴ When Jesus came into Peter's house, he saw Peter's mother-

† Matt viii **1–4** || Mark i 40–45, Luke v 12–16; **5–13** || Luke vii 1–10, John iv 43–54; **14–18** || Mark i 29–34, Luke iv 38–41.

in-law lying sick with a fever; 15 he touched her hand, the fever left her, and she rose and served him.

16 That evening they brought to him many who were devil-possessed. He cast out the spirits with a command and healed all those who were sick. 17 So was fulfilled the saying of the prophet Isaiah:

"He himself took our infirmities
and bore our diseases."

18 When Jesus saw the crowds around him, he gave orders to go across the lake.

NOTES

viii 1. This verse can hardly be anything but a connecting link with vii 28–29, and is not intended to be a chronological note.

2. *leper*. Various skin ailments were often included under the general term leprosy (Gr. *lepra*), and it is important not to see here an indication that one of the three types of Hansen's disease is *necessarily* indicated. The same word would also cover elephantiasis, psoriasis, and vitiligo (depigmentation of skin). Hansen's disease (first isolated in 1871) is certainly the most important, and is the disease to which the term leprosy is now properly applied. (Cf. *Encyclopaedia Britannica*, 1960 ed., XIII, ad loc.) A type of Hansen's disease may well be indicated here, but the Greek word would obviously give us no help. Whatever the affliction in question here, the prescriptions of the Mosaic Law would hold (cf. Lev xiii–xiv). The *Jewish Encyclopaedia*, VIII, ad loc., will give details of the Talmudic regulations.

prostrated himself. See NOTE (on *proskunēsai*) on ii 2.

Sir. The Gr. *kurios* is ambivalent. See Part XII of the Introduction. It is common in this gospel, and in Luke, as a mode of address to Jesus, but is used only twice in Mark.

to cure. The Greek is a late word, and very infrequent outside the LXX and the NT. It is used once in Josephus (*Antiquities* XI. 153).

3. At this point Mark's account represents Jesus as "having pity," and in some manuscripts as "being angry" or "deeply stirred." It might be assumed that Matthew, with Mark's account before him, deliberately omitted the phrase in the interests of reverence for the person of Jesus. But Matthew never mentions human emotion with respect to Jesus except four occasions of his "having pity." It is just as likely that Matthew's account, assuming it to be wholly independent of Mark, may well repre-

sent a tradition which found itself puzzled by what we would call the human personality of Jesus, and so preferred to maintain silence. The assumption that Matthew, having read Mark, revolted against the idea of an emotional Jesus on grounds of reverence makes little sense when seen in the light of the gospel according to John. For if Matthew is late, and John also (as most critics agree), then what is to be said of John xi 28–44? The fact is that the emotions of characters in narrative literature in the ancient world are hardly ever mentioned. It will be recalled that, apart from anger, there are very few occurrences of human emotion recorded of any character in the OT.

4. *for proof to them.* In view of this injunction to silence, lest Jesus' ministry be compromised by a reputation as a wonder-worker, it is important to note that the proof referred to here was not proof of a cure. The priests would certainly assure themselves of a cure before allowing an offering to be made. The proof in question was that of Jesus' allegiance to the Law, and this fact may well have dictated Matthew's placing of the incident here (cf. COMMENT following).

5. *entering Capernaum.* Mark's account of the foregoing incident has the healed man immediately publicizing an account of his cure, embarrassing Jesus to the extent that he was unable to enter any town openly. If Matthew was aware of Mark's account, to have included Mark's ending would have precluded the connection with the next incident. But Luke agrees with Matthew in omitting the man's disobedience and its results. Either (a) Luke shares Matthew's reverential attitude in respect to Jesus and finds disregard of Jesus' command unthinkable, or (b) both Matthew and Luke drew upon a tradition known to both but independent of Mark, or (c) we may see the hand of a copyist or editor at work shaping a future ecclesiastical attitude to the work and ministry of Jesus. If the third option is correct, it is astonishing that Paul should have stumbled so early into this editorial trap (of a reverential attitude to Jesus), even before the tradition was committed to writing. It is well to remind ourselves that (unlike later ages) the evangelists saw no moral or theological question involved in accounts of miracles, and therefore felt entirely free to omit or recount details, to arrange material where it best suited the immediate purpose, or even to omit material altogether. In attempting ingenious guesses as to the motives which led to this, that, or the other item being present or absent in the gospel material, it is well not to try to build a pyramid on its apex.

5–7. The *centurion* was almost certainly a Gentile, though he may have been a God-fearer, and therefore presumably reluctant to bring the sufferer to one whom he knew only as a Jewish healer. In the synoptic gospels the only occasion on which Jesus himself went to the sick is in the case of Jairus' daughter (Mark v 23–24, 35–43; Luke viii 41–42, 49–56).

7. *I will come*. The clause may also be translated as a question: "Shall I come?" Whichever way the translation is made, the essential point is that Jesus is prepared to have dealings with a Gentile, and by implication to enter his house. This was not forbidden by the Mosaic Law, but was certainly not regarded favorably by rabbinic legislation.

8. *servant*. The Greek can also mean "child," but it is definitely "servant" in this context.

9–10. *faith*. Whether the centurion thought that Jesus had effective control over heavenly agencies, and so could heal, is beside the point. For Jesus, the striking thing was the man's faith, the word *pistis* being used here as it is in most parts of the NT as meaning trust and confidence in the power of God.

11–12. For these verses, cf. Luke xiii 28–30. Theologically, the best-known exponent of faith as the one condition by which all men are able to respond to the call of God, and so enter the Kingdom, is Paul in Galatians and Romans. In the synoptic gospels the same concept is embodied in the parable of the prodigal son (Luke xv 11–32). Loyal trust is demanded of the rightful heir (Israel), whereas when the alienated (the Gentiles) demonstrate that faith, that trust, they are given equal place in the Kingdom.

11. *will take their place*. I.e., "will take their place at table with." The usual practice at this time was to recline at table, though sitting at table also had an honorable and lengthy history. The Messianic Banquet was a common Jewish theme (cf. *Pirqê Abôth* iii 20; *Parables of Enoch* xlii 5) and is found in the NT (cf. xxvi 29; Luke xiv 15–24; Rev iii 20, xix 9).

12. *sons of the Kingdom*. I.e., the rightful heirs. Cf. xiii 38. Similar phrases are found in Jewish literature (cf. TB, *Shabbath* 153a; *Pesachim* 8a).

outer darkness. As the just punishment for faithlessness, this expression is found in the intertestamental writings. Cf. Enoch ciii 8; Pss Sol xiv 6, xv 11; Sibylline Oracles iv 43. For the rabbinical references, cf. StB, ad loc.

shrieking and grinding of teeth. This is a common expression in Matthew (xiii 42, 50, xxii 13, xxiv 51, xxv 30) and occurs once in Luke (xiii 28). Cf. also Enoch ciii 8; Parables of Enoch xl 12.

13. *at that moment*. Healing coincidental with the words of Jesus occurs also at ix 22, xv 28, xvii 18.

14–16. Cf. Mark i 29–34. The details which Mark supplies are understandable on the usual theory of Mark's dependence on Petrine reminiscence. The details in Mark i 29 (assuming that Matthew knew them) would be out of place here, since Matthew's scheme takes no account of an incident in the Capernaum synagogue which Mark records.

16. *command*. The Greek is the same as that for *word* in vs. 8.

17. The series of healings is concluded with the quotation from Isa
liii 4. On this, and the whole question of OT quotations in this gospel,
cf. Introduction, Part IV. The quotation here is wholly independent of
the Greek of the LXX.

took . . . bore. The Greek words (*lambanein* and *bastazein*) can be
understood as Jesus' taking away, carrying away, the afflictions of the
person healed, or as taking, carrying vicariously those afflictions. In the
total context of Isa liii, the identification of Jesus with the Servant
would appear to demand far more than a mere removal of suffering.
Indeed, the healings here seem to be a "typical" collection, designed
to illustrate the Servant-Messiah theme of the OT quotations. In that
case, the omission of details, if the evangelist knew them, would be
deliberate, as tending to obscure the empowering act or word of the
Servant-Messiah in his bearing of the sufferings of men.

COMMENT

There are three healings in this section; Matthew's habit of
arranging material in easily remembered groups is a phenomenon
to which attention has already been called (cf. Introduction, Part
IV). There is a parallel in Mark to the first incident, but in
that gospel the healing of the leper is without any details of place
or occasion. So far as Matthew is concerned it may be surmised
that the incident of the leper is placed first because it gives an
indication of the attitude of Jesus to the Law (vs. 4) and is thus
particularly appropriate as following after the Great Instruction.

Any comparison at this point with Mark's order must assume
that Matthew had read Mark and had deliberately changed the
Markan order. (Cf. viii 1–18 and Mark i 29–34, 40–45.) Unless
that assumption is made, then we must suppose that Matthew's
tradition, which had two healings also found in Mark, had those
accounts in no particular order.

31. AN INQUIRER
(viii 19–22)†

VIII ¹⁹ A scribe came to him and said, "Teacher, I will follow you wherever you go." ²⁰ Jesus replied, "The foxes have holes, and the birds in the sky have nests, but The Man has nowhere to lie down."

²¹ Another, (not one) of the disciples, said to him, "Sir, allow me first to go and bury my father." ²² But Jesus replied, "Follow me, and let the dying bury their dead."

† Matt viii 19–22 ‖ Luke ix 57–62.

NOTES

viii 19. Luke's version (ix 57) simply has "someone" (Gr. *tis*), and only Matthew identifies the man as a scribe.

20. *The Man*. It has become increasingly clear in the past two years that the translation *Son of Man*, however accurate as a literal rendering of the Gr. *huios tou anthrōpou*, and however euphonic in English, is inadequate. We have discussed this title more fully in the Introduction, Parts VI and XII, and in the light of a recent work by Fitzmyer (*The "Genesis Apocryphon" of Qumran Cave I*, especially p. 134), we have used *The Man* throughout our translation. It carries more weight as emphasizing the representative character of Jesus' ministry as the evangelist sees it, and certainly is more faithful to the original Hebrew/Aramaic. Cf. recently J. Massingberd Ford, " 'The Son of Man'—A Euphemism?" JBL 87 (1968), 257–67. This article, if its main contention stands, sheds a good deal of light on the title, not only in the NT but possibly also in the intertestamental literature.

21. *Another, (not one)*. The Lukan version of the incident sets the two inquirers in the context of the journey to Jerusalem (Luke ix 51, 57–62). Moreover, in that narrative it is clear that (as in vs. 19 above) a man *comes* to Jesus with a question—i.e., he is not a member of the

company. The same Lukan narrative also refers to *another* posing a
question about obligations to home and family. Alongside the Lukan
narrative, this verse as it stands in the Greek in Matthew is odd. Jesus
would by this time have been fully aware of the home circumstances of
his disciples, the legal requirement of burial within twenty-four hours
would not have posed an intolerable delay in the following of Jesus, and
and the third inquirer in Luke (ix 61) is obviously not of the inner
circle of the Twelve. We therefore come to the conclusion that the Greek
text in Matthew must be defective, particularly in view of the care taken
by the evangelist to confine the word "disciple" to the Twelve. At
present, the text reads: *heteros de tōn mathētōn eipen autō:* "another of
the disciples said to him." Now *de* is a particle which is so frequent
in the NT (nearly 400 times, 51 of them in Matthew) that it is difficult
to decide on occasion whether it is to be ignored or taken note of. But
it is also frequently joined to the negative, as *oude* (26 times in Matthew out of a total of 137 in the NT). We conclude that the Greek must
originally have read *heteros oude tōn mathētōn,* on grounds of haplography between the final syllable of *heteros* and the first of *oude*. The
dropping of *ou* would be relatively easy in times when there were no gaps
between words in manuscripts. Our translation as it appears in the text is
revised to the extent of putting our suggested amendment in parentheses.
We claim that hereby justice is done to the text in three directions: *de*
reads oddly in the present text, and our version renders it explicable; it
is more faithful to the Matthean use of "disciple"; and it is incidentally
more easily reconcilable with the Lukan account.

22. *dying . . . dead.* This is either a proverbial saying otherwise unknown to us, or—again linking the incident with another inquirer in
Luke (ix 61–62)—we are to see in this saying a call to sacrificial
service (cf. xix 29). It is possible, however, that there is yet another
meaning here. The Lukan context (ix 51–62) appears to argue the ending of the old dispensation in the face of the new Kingdom proclaimed
by Jesus. In that event, if Matthew's narrative here has the same
meaning, then the inquirer is being directed to look to the future, to
leave a dying cause behind him. Whether this is meant to refer to the
Israel of the Old Covenant, or whether the inquirers were formerly
adherents of John the Baptist, we are in no position to know. It must be
remembered that in several Semitic languages, including Hebrew / Aramaic, the word for *dead* can also mean *dying,* and we have so rendered
the Greek here.

COMMENT

Three stories of healings are linked with three stories of miracles of power by an interpolated story of two inquirers. The whole cycle—three healings, two inquirers, three miracles of power—would make for easier memorizing of oral tradition.

32. CALMING THE STORM
(viii 23–27)†

VIII 23 When he got into the boat, his disciples followed him. 24 Then a great storm arose on the sea, so that the boat was being swamped by the waves, but he was asleep. 25 They went and awoke him: "Sir, save us, or we are lost!" 26 He said to them, "Why are you afraid, you men of little faith?" Then he stood up, gave orders to the winds and the sea, and there was a great calm. 27 Men wondered: "What sort of man is he, that the winds and the sea are obedient to him?"

† **Matt viii 23–27** || Mark iv 35–41, Luke viii 22–25.

NOTES

In the light of the comments made in the Introduction (Part X) on the subject of the "nature miracles," there is no call for elaboration here. Both Matthew and Luke appear to be working from a tradition which differs from that of Mark. Matthew (vs. 23) and Luke (viii 22) insert a note about embarkation. In Mark (iv 35) Jesus is already in the boat, and there is also verbal Greek agreement between Matt viii 25 and Luke viii 24, as also between vs. 27 and Luke viii 25.

Mark's account is far more vivid, arguing personal reminiscence from Mark's source (especially in details like the cushion in Mark iv 38, and the anguished cry to Jesus in the same verse).

26. *little faith*. Cf. second NOTE on vi 30. The phrase is used four times in Matthew. The Markan version is more forceful (Mark iv 40)

faith. As has already been pointed out, *faith* in the gospels means trust, confidence in the providence of God. It is reading too much into the question to see it as necessarily an appeal for loyalty to, or trust in, Jesus himself.

27. *Men*. In vs. 23 we have *his disciples*, where Mark iv 36 has *they*.

It is possible to assume, as is commonly done, that Matthew used Mark's account, softened its harshness (cf. vs. 25=Mark iv 38; vs. 26=Mark iv 40) and then, unable to have the disciples being "greatly afraid" (Mark iv 41) reverted to "men" here. This kind of revision seems somewhat unnecessary, since whatever the reactions of the disciples (and Matthew seldom tells us much in this regard), men who heard of or possibly witnessed the incident from the shore would certainly be amazed and wonder.

Grammatically, there was a tendency in Koine Greek to overdo the generic article, and it is no wonder that translators misunderstood an original Aramaic in which there was no distinction between the definite and the indefinite article.

33. THE GADARENE DEMONIACS
(viii 28 – ix 1) †

VIII 28 When he came to the other shore, to the country of the Gadarenes, two men who were demon-possessed, on their way out of the tombs, met him, men so fierce that no one could pass on that road. 29 They called out, "What have you to do with us, Son of God? Have you come to torment us before the time?" 30 Now a large herd of pigs was feeding at some distance from them, 31 and the demons pleaded, "If you cast us out, allow us to go into the herd of pigs." 32 He said to them, "Go," and on coming out they went into the pigs, and all the herd rushed headlong down a steep place into the sea and were drowned in the water. 33 The herdsmen fled, came into the city, and told everything and what had become of the demon-possessed. 34 All the city came to Jesus, and on seeing him begged him to leave their district.

IX 1 So getting into the boat he departed and went to his own city.

† **Matt viii 28 – ix 1** ‖ Mark v 1–20, Luke viii 26–39.

NOTES

Matthew's account of this incident is far shorter than Mark's (seven verses against twenty), less detailed, and it is possible that the evangelist is also taking account of an incident recorded in Mark i 21–28 by speaking of two demoniacs instead of one. The same consideration may also account for Matthew's two blind men in xx 30. If the evangelist's tradition was vague where Mark's was detailed, we would expect this kind of combination to occur.

viii 28. *Gadarenes.* There is textual confusion in the Greek here, as there is also in Mark v 1 (though in that instance "Gerasenes" is probably right). The more important Gerasa was thirty miles southeast of the Sea of Galilee, and in Mark (v 1) the adjective Gerasenes is a geographical point of some importance. Matthew has Gadara,* a place only six miles southeast of the lake, and the assumption in this verse is that the incident took place soon after the party landed. Moreover this was Gentile territory (as evidenced by the herd of pigs), and when the meeting took place the herd was *at some distance* (vs. 30), implying that Jesus had walked some way from the shore.

tombs. Ritually unclean (cf. xxiii 27), tombs were regarded as fitting homes for demons and the demoniacs.

29. *What have you to do with us?* Literally in the Greek idiom this is "What is there between us and you?"—i.e., why are you interfering with our proper preserve?

Son of God. The two men, possessed by demons who have spiritual insight, identify Jesus as one possessing healing power, or possibly even using the address as the equivalent of "Messiah."

before the time. According to Enoch xv–xvi, demons have power to torment men until the day of judgment, and the demons ask that they be not cut short before that time.

31. *demons* (Gr. *daimones*). It was pointed out in ch. iv that this word must not be taken as the equivalent of devil (Gr. *diabolos*). Demons were regarded as good, bad, or even neutral, but they could take possession of men and completely change their personality. Some useful modern material—for those who find the NT view too naïve—may be found in William W. Sargant's *Battle for the Mind,* New York: Doubleday/ London: Heinemann, 1957.

31–32. Demons must have some kind of "base of operations" (cf. xii 43), but though they are given leave by Jesus to find such in the herd of pigs, even this fails them, for the pigs are drowned. Such "panic" behavior in many species of animals is well attested, but we have no means of knowing how such a panic might actually have occurred on the occasion to which this incident refers.

33–34. In Mark's account, the city dwellers come out and see the demoniac restored to health (v 14–17), but here it is Jesus who is the center of attention.

begged him to leave. Cf. x 14 f.

* On this, and other place names, cf. Part XIII of the Introduction.

34. THE QUESTION OF AUTHORITY
(ix 2–8)†

IX 2 They brought to him a paralyzed man lying on his bed, and when Jesus saw their faith he said to the paralytic, "Take courage, my child, your sins are forgiven." 3 Certain scribes said to one another, "This man is blaspheming." 4 Jesus, however, discerning their thoughts, said to them: "Why are you harboring evil thoughts in your minds? 5 Which is easier: to say 'Your sins are forgiven,' or to say 'Get up and walk'? 6 But so that you may know that The Man has authority on earth to forgive sin"—he then said to the paralytic—"Rise, take your bed and go home." 7 Whereupon he rose up and went home. 8 Seeing this, the crowds were awestruck and glorified God for giving such authority to men.

† Matt ix 2–8 ‖ Mark ii 1–12, Luke v 17–26.

NOTES

ix 2. In several places, Mark (ii 1, iii 20, ix 28, x 10) has indeterminate references to "a house," which would seem to imply that Jesus had some regular home or lodging in Capernaum. Matthew's version, in all instances where it parallels Mark, has no such reference.

brought (Gr. *prosepheron*). A favorite word in Matthew, who uses it, in all, fifteen times.

your sins are forgiven. The breaking of the power of sin and of the dominion of evil is one of the signs of the dawning Kingdom. See COMMENT on iv 1–11(§9).

faith. Cf. NOTE on viii 9–10.

3. *blaspheming.* Mark's version makes the charge of the scribes explicit: "Who can forgive sins, except God?" (Mark ii 7). The synoptists agree with John that the hostility to Jesus centered principally on his enemies' understanding of what Jesus' words and deeds implied—cf. John v 18, viii 48–59.

5. Jesus' question is not an invitation to watch a demonstration of miraculous power either as a proof of divinity or of his own power to heal. It is a challenge to accept or reject his claim that the reign of God was visibly breaking in. Both healing and forgiveness, even though the former is more dramatically visible, are signs of a restoration of God's order to the disorder in the world. Cf. Introduction, Part X.

sins. Sickness and disease were commonly regarded both in the OT and in the time of Jesus as being the direct result of the sufferer's sins, and it is a belief that should not be completely ignored in considering this passage. In this particular instance we have no means of knowing the circumstances of the case. The sufferer's circumstances may easily have been known to Jesus, for he was by now well known in Capernaum. In addition, our own age has become increasingly aware of the problems posed by psychosomatic conditions.

6. *The Man.* Cf. NOTE on viii 20. It is difficult to see why some commentators have been at pains to wonder whether either Mark (or Matthew) here misunderstood, or an editor misread, his sources, and rendered *The Man* (Son of Man) for a simple "men." What was in dispute was not the obligation of men to forgive each other for wrongs done to each other—every devout Jew was aware of that obligation. What was in question was the authority Jesus claimed *from heaven* to remit the sins of men (cf. Dalman, *Words of Jesus*, p. 261).

8. *crowds.* The contrast is often made in Matthew between the faith, trust, of the disciples and/or the crowds on the one hand, and the unbelief of Jesus' critics on the other.

to men. The Greek construction allows us to read "on behalf of men." In this case, the crowds would be awestruck not only by the healing, but also that to Jesus authority had been given for the sake of man's salvation.

COMMENT

This, the third event in the second group of healings, is of cardinal importance in the Matthean scheme, for it brings clearly into focus the problem of authority which had been briefly raised in vii 29. What had been then a matter of authority in words now passes into a question concerning the authority of the Messiah in action. Whether Matthew's tradition originally had the same details as Mark's, we are in no position to know, but the shorter account which we have here has the effect of emphasizing the rising hostility of the scribes to Jesus. Mark's vivid account to some extent obscures this, for his word picture has the effect of concentrating our attention on the attendant hazards of bringing the paralytic to Jesus and on the faith which overcame those hazards.

There are differences between Mark and Luke also, and agreements between Matthew and Luke against Mark. If these agreements against Mark are to be regarded purely as revision of Mark's work by the other two evangelists, then it is hard to see why Luke should omit the reference to Capernaum (Mark ii 1) by the somewhat clumsy introduction in his own version (Luke v 17–18). The reason for Matthew's omission of any mention of Capernaum by name (ix 1) is obvious enough: he has already established (iv 13) that this town was the center of Jesus' activity. It is simpler to suppose that Matthew and Luke were working from sources wholly independent of Mark.

35. THE CALL OF MATTHEW
(ix 9–13)†

IX 9 As he went on from there, Jesus saw a man called Matthew sitting in the tax collectors' office, and said to him, "Follow me." He arose and followed him. 10 While he was in the house, many tax collectors and non-observant Jews came and sat with Jesus and his disciples. 11 When the Pharisees saw this, they said to his disciples, "Why does your Master eat with tax collectors and non-observant (Jews)?" 12 However, he heard them and replied, "Those who are well have no need of a physician—only those who are sick. 13 Go and learn what this means: 'I desire mercy and not sacrifice.' I did not come to call the righteous, but sinners."

† Matt ix 9–13 || Mark ii 13–17, Luke v 27–32.

NOTES

ix 9. *Matthew.* Greek *Matthaios* reflects Hebrew and Aramaic *Mattay,* a shortened form of *Mattathias* (*Mattatyahu*). Greek *Matthias* represents Hebrew and Aramaic *Matyā,* another shortened form of the same name.

tax collectors' office. Capernaum was on the side of the lake, and the tax office was presumably on the outskirts of the town.

arose and followed. This idiom is common in the Hebrew of the OT.

10. *non-observant (Jews).* The more usual "sinners" obscures the issue, here and in vs. 13. The tax collector was regarded by Jews of that time as a sinner not so much because he was the tool of the occupying power, or because he was regarded by the more rigorous as being a servant of the Herodian house, but more because he had to handle currency with pagan inscriptions and pagan iconography. And since many of these tax collectors were corrupt and regularly accepted bribes, the whole profession had come to have a bad reputation.

sat. Those visiting in the circumstances depicted here would sit on rugs or mats on the floor, with legs crossed, while others would stand. It would be possible to accommodate some thirty to forty people in the small house of a tax collector.

11. It is the *Pharisees,* with their insistence on precise adherence to the letter of the Law as interpreted to cover specific cases, who criticize Jesus. The following verse gives the whole keynote of the NT—later to be given theological treatment in the Pauline letters—that what is demanded of the would-be entrant into the Kingdom is faith, loyal trust. There is no demand for a prior conversion of life and conduct, and entrance into the Kingdom is not a reward for moral rectitude. This emphasis is in marked contrast to the demands of the Essenes, for whom entrance into the community was the result of a righteousness already attained.

13. The quotation of Hos vi 6 in this verse is also found at xii 7, and it is in the words of both the Hebrew and the Greek OT. The reply of Jesus is ironic: it is often those who think they have no need of a physician who really need him most.

to call. The same Greek verb is used of inviting to a feast in xxii 3, 4, 8–9. On the Messianic Banquet, cf. NOTE on viii 11.

righteous . . . sinners. The contrast is common in the Qumran literature, where the words are *ṣaddîq* and *rāshā‘,* both singular, both generic. Here the Greek word *dikaioi* (righteous) does not connote the rejection of the righteous in the sense of those devoted to the Law, but rather the rejection of the self-designated righteous (cf. Gal ii 17).

COMMENT

Here the man whose name is associated with the gospel as author is introduced as though to provide an authentication of his right to record the tradition. The name Matthew occurs only once more, at x 3. Our views on the authorship of this gospel are given in the Introduction, Part XIII.

36. JOHN'S DISCIPLES
(ix 14–17)†

IX ¹⁴ Then the disciples of John came to him with the words, "Why do we and the Pharisees fast often, while your disciples do not fast?" ¹⁵ Jesus said to them, "Can the wedding guests mourn as long as the bridegroom is with them? The time will come when the bridegroom is taken away from them —then they will fast.

¹⁶ No one puts a piece of unworn cloth on an old garment, for the patch tears away from the garment and the damage is made worse. ¹⁷ New wine is not put into old wineskins. If it is, then the skins burst, the wine is lost and the skins are destroyed. But new wine is put into new wineskins, and both are preserved."

† **Matt ix 14–17** ‖ Mark ii 18–22, Luke v 33–39.

NOTES

ix 14. Mark's language at this point (Mark ii 18) suggests that the incident took place during one of the statutory periods of fasting.

15. *wedding guests* (literally "sons of the bridal chamber") is a Semitism.

as long as (Gr. *eph' hōson*). The Greek indicates that the wedding festivities might last some days.

the bridegroom is with them. Here we might have expected some phrase that would indicate the impossibility of fasting during a wedding celebration. But the bridegroom's presence is emphasized as pointing to a time when he will not be there. It is not necessary to see in this a prophecy after the event, inserted by the early community to explain either the crucifixion or the early Christian custom of fasting. Jesus can hardly have been unaware of the well-nigh inevitable consequences of his proclamation of the reign of God. A violent end could safely be predicted for one making such a proclamation, either at the hands of the

Roman authority, or at the hands of a mob (especially a disappointed one).

16–17. Matthew links these two verses with the previous saying by the particle *de,* but the precise connection of these two verses with the preceding is not very clear. The contrast between old and new is obvious enough, but does the verse in its present position intend to suggest that the proclamation of the reign of God and the Messianic Age will expose the weaknesses of Judaism as Jesus found it—i.e., would the proclamation lay bare the dangers of relying upon that literal observance of the Law so characteristic of pettifogging lawyers? Or is there here some quite different material?

Verse 17 carries on the thought of the preceding verse, but this time from the point of view of Jesus' teaching. On the usual interpretation Jesus asserts that superimposing the nascent Messianic Community on Judaism would result in serious harm to Judaism, and equally, to confine the Community to Judaism would do irreparable harm to both. (Cf. here *Pirqê Abôth* iv 20: "Do not look at the jar, but at what it contains. Sometimes a new jar is full of old wine, while an old jar may not even have new wine in it.")

16. *patch.* The patch being unshrunk, will pull away (as it shrinks) from the rest of the garment. The Greek is *plērōma,* the noun from Matthew's verb "to fulfill" (*plēroun*). Rom ix–xi is evidence of the great concern felt about the precise relationship of the Messianic Community to Judaism. On the view that vss. 16–17 are to be regarded as Jesus' teaching on the relationship of his Community to Judaism, then the final clause *and both are preserved* is either editorial comment, or a misplaced saying from another context in an attempt to deal with the question.

But this must be regarded as unsatisfactory. The whole tenor of Jesus' teaching, in all four gospels, makes it hardly possible to suppose that he looked to a continuance of his Messianic Community and Judaism side by side. Certainly, if vss. 16–17 do deal with Judaism, then Luke's tradition is right in calling the material "parable" (Luke v 36). However, it is far simpler to treat the two verses, coming as they do in a context which deals with the disciples of John the Baptist, as a judgment by Jesus on the position of John's followers, now that Jesus has proclaimed the dawning reign of God. There is no evidence anywhere in the NT that Jesus ever had anything but the highest regard for John, and the synoptic record is witness that the death of John affected Jesus deeply. But loyalty to John on the part of those who had listened to him, embraced his message, and attached themselves to him was one thing; it was quite another to suppose that that loyalty and attachment was such as to refuse allegiance to Jesus. Now that the Messianic Kingdom had been proclaimed, John's part had been fulfilled, and there could be no room for the new Community *and* a community of John's disciples, existing together in uncomfortable parallel. (On this point, cf. K. Stendahl, in *Peake's Commentary on the Bible,* eds. Matthew Black and H. H. Rowley [London and New York: Nelson, 1962], p. 782a.)

COMMENT

This section follows on from the last in the sense that it, too, is an implicit discussion of the place of the Law in the dawning Messianic Age. But the assertion that the Messianic Age has already come in the person of Jesus is followed by the warning that the present time of rejoicing is temporary.

37. HEALINGS
(ix 18–34)†

IX 18 While he was talking to them, a ruler came to him, knelt before him, and said, "My daughter has just died. But come and lay your hand on her and she will live." 19 Jesus rose up with his disciples and followed him. 20 And a woman who had suffered from a hemorrhage for twelve years came up behind him and touched the hem of his himation, 21 for she said to herself, "If I can only touch the fringe of his himation I shall be made well." 22 Jesus turned around, saw her, and said, "Daughter, take courage. Your faith has made you well." And from that very hour the woman became well. 23 Jesus came to the ruler's house, saw the musicians and the crowd making a great noise, and said, 24 "Go away, the girl has not died, but is sleeping." They derided him, 25 but when the crowd had been put out, he went in, took her by the hand, and the girl arose. 26 The report of this went all through that district.

27 While Jesus was passing on from there, two blind men followed him crying aloud, "Son of David, take pity on us!" 28 When he entered the house, the blind men came to him and Jesus said to them, "Do you believe that I am able to do this?" They answered him, "Yes, sir." 29 Then he touched their eyes, saying, "According to your faith so let it be done to you." 30 Their eyes were opened, and Jesus said to them urgently, "See that no one knows of this." 31 But they went away and spread his reputation through all that district. 32 As they were on their way a dumb demoniac was brought to him,

† **Matt ix 18–34** ‖ Mark v 21–34, Luke viii 40–56.

33 and when the demon had been exorcized the dumb man spoke; the crowds wondered, saying, "Nothing was ever seen like this in Israel." 34 (But the Pharisees said, "He casts out demons by the Ruler of Demons.")

NOTES

ix 18. In the Markan narrative (v 21 ff.) the first incident takes place when Jesus is surrounded by crowds on the lakeside. Matthew's account has Jesus sitting in a house talking with his disciples. The Matthean account is shorter, and if Matthew's tradition embodied this incident as it is here, set in a series of healings but without detail, then he was free to place the story where he wanted, lacking details which were known (only?) to the Markan tradition.

ruler. Mark (v 22) adds that it was a synagogue official (*ḥāzān=* ruler, functionary) but Matthew assumes that his readers are aware of what is meant. He omits the name of the official (Jairus, Heb. *Yā'îr*, a common name) which Mark supplies.

knelt. Cf. last NOTE on ii 2. Matthew has no equivalent of the details in Mark v 23, 35–37.

20. *himation*. This was an outer garment, a cloak, which in v 40 we translated by *cape*. In essence it was a coat with a girdle, worn over the shirt (Gr. *chitōn*, translated by us as *tunic* at v 40). In all instances from this point onwards we have left the Greek *himation* transliterated.

fringe (Gr. *kraspeda*). Tassels attached to the corners of a garment (cf. Num xv 38; Deut xxii 12). Jesus' accusation (xxiii 5) was that the Pharisees made these ornaments overlarge as a demonstration of piety —though Jesus himself is represented as wearing tassels in xiv 36.

20–21. The woman's illness would make her ritually unclean (Lev xv 19 ff.), and in consequence all that she touched would also be unclean.

It is important to see this kind of ritual impurity in perspective. In an age which knew nothing of distinctions between a blood-flow which caused infection and one which did not, it was safer to bracket all such cases together. The extension of the tabu of ritual uncleanliness arose from a desire to avoid infection or contagion.

23. *musicians* (Gr. *aulētas*)=literally, "flute players." Here Matthew can draw on his knowledge of Jewish custom, which called for "two flutes and one to wail" even for the poorest funerals (cf. *B. Chethuboth* 46b). Mark (v 38) is far more vague.

24. *died . . . sleeping*. The word "sleep" was used in the OT to denote death (e.g., Dan xii 2), and the use is continued in the NT. We are in

no position to determine whether Jesus was saying of the girl that she was dead, and that it was his mission to proclaim that death no longer was to have the tenor of finality, or whether he was asserting that the girl was not dead but in a coma. The evangelist and the witnesses are certainly represented as believing that a miracle of raising the dead had occurred.

Throughout this section the Matthean and Lukan traditions agree in eight instances in Greek verbal detail against Mark.

27. Matthew's account of the healing of the two blind men is of some special interest. There are two healings of blind men in Mark (viii 22–26; x 46–52). The second of these parallels the account here, and it also involves two blind men. In his account of the curing of the leper (viii 2–4), Matthew does not record any cautioning by Jesus that the man remain silent about his cure, though Mark does. Here, however, both Matthew and Mark agree that Jesus urges silence on the cured blind men.

from there. I.e., from the ruler's house.

28. *the house.* I.e., the house in which Jesus was living in Capernaum.

30. *said to them urgently.* The Greek word is emphatic, and is also used of men expressing themselves heatedly.

31. *spread his reputation.* The Greek word occurs in Mark i 45, and Matthew uses it here and again at xxviii 15.

32–34. A somewhat similar story is given by Matt xii 22–24 in a context where we might have expected Matthew's tradition of Mark iii 19–21. But there is no mention here of the casting out of the demon, or of healing, as there is in a somewhat similar account in Matt xii 22–24. The whole order is odd, for these verses would have suited the context of xii 25–30 far better than is the case here. It is also notable that Luke (xi 14–15)—like Matthew—has a tradition of his own in the context of Mark iii 19–21. If we assume that both Matthew and Luke were using Mark, then it is hard to find any reason why at this particular point both evangelists should have deserted the Markan order. On the theory that both Matthew and Luke had access to Mark, then it is necessary to say that Matthew inserted here a story of conflict with the Pharisees which warned the reader that the ministry of Jesus was not met with universal approval. Again, on the same theory, it is necessary to say that when Matthew came to Mark iii 19–21 he substituted xii 22–24 as being a better introduction to the discourse which follows in Mark iii 23. Generally, however, the simplest solutions are preferable, and it is certainly simpler to assume that Matthew and Luke were both independent of Mark, here as elsewhere.

34. Some manuscripts omit this verse, presumably on the grounds that it was thought to be an assimilation to xii 24. However, in its present

position it does illustrate a point which Matthew constantly makes—the welcome of the crowds compared with the hostility of some sections of Judaism.

Suggestions have been made that the whole complex viii 1 – ix 34 contains ten miracles (though ix 18–26 encloses one miracle narrative within another, and so may be counted as one). This, it has been suggested, is in accord with an emphasis on series of ten miracles in *Pirqê Abôth* (v 5, 8). This is ingenious, but it ignores the fact that ten is certainly not, as a number, confined to miracles. Evidence for the use of the number ten in other areas can be found in Allen's ICC *St. Matthew* commentary, p. 94. There is, however, a certain arrangement of material in this section just completed, which deserves some mention.

The Greek verb *sōzein*, "to make well, restore," and—in large areas of the NT—"to save," is used three times in ix 21–22. Attention has already been called to the Messianic work of restoring order and unity to God's creation (Part X of the Introduction); the disciples will be called upon to join in this work in x 7 ff. With this in mind, it is of more than passing significance to read the whole section in the light of Isa xxxv. There we have exhortations to courage (vss. 3–4; cf. Matt ix 22), assertions of God's visitation in order to save (vs. 4; cf. ix 18, 22), demonstrations of the majesty of God (vs. 2; cf. ix 33), and then there are by means of the miracle narratives specific illustrations of the divine work mentioned in Isa xxxv. There are men who receive their sight (vs. 5; cf. Matt ix 27–29), dumb who hear and speak again (vs. 6; cf. ix 32–33), and the ritually unclean are restored to the community (vs. 8; cf. ix 20–22). It is difficult to suppose that this parallel in material should not have been present to the mind of the evangelist when he arranged his material, and from our examination of the OT background of Matthew (Part IV of the Introduction) it is probable that Isa xxxv was a model for the arrangement of this block of narrative.

COMMENT

If we accept Stendahl's suggestion that vss. 16–17 apply to the relationship between Jesus and the disciples of John, then this description of the three healings, dealing as it does with the blind, the deaf, and the dead, anticipates the questions about Messiahship to come in xi 5.

38. MISSION AND DISCIPLESHIP
(ix 35–38)

IX ³⁵ Jesus went through all the towns and villages, teaching in their synagogues, proclaiming the Freedom of the Kingdom, and healing every disease and infirmity. ³⁶ When he saw the crowds he felt deeply for them because they were troubled and helpless, like sheep without a shepherd. ³⁷ Then he said to his disciples, "There is an abundant harvest, but there are few workers. ³⁸ Therefore ask the chief harvester to send workers into his harvest."

NOTES

ix 35. *Freedom.* On this translation, see NOTE on iv 23.

36. *felt deeply.* The Greek word (*splanchnizesthai*) is well represented in the synoptic gospels and in the LXX.

troubled. The meaning of the Greek (*eskulmenoi*) ranges very widely indeed, from being flayed, to being concerned, vexed, bewildered, despondent.

helpless. Literally, "prostrate," either from drunkenness or from a mortal wound.

sheep without a shepherd. Cf. Num xxvii 17; I Kings xxii 17; Ezek xxxiv 5.

38. *chief harvester.* In Aramaic, the phrase *rab ḥeṣādā* means the person responsible for hiring and dismissing harvest workers.

Luke (x 2) has the words of vss. 37–38 at the beginning of the mission of the seventy disciples.

COMMENT

This short section provides both a conclusion to chapter ix and a fitting introduction to chapter x. The evangelist has summarized the teaching of Jesus, placing it firmly in the context of the Old Covenant (chs. v–vii), and has given examples of how the awaited Messiah went about the work of healing and restoration. Now it is time to introduce the inner circle of disciples as the men who will carry on the Messianic activity.

39. THE MISSION OF THE TWELVE
(x 1–15)†

X 1 Calling to him his twelve disciples, he gave them authority to cast out evil spirits, and to heal every disease and every infirmity.

2 The names of the twelve apostles are: first, Simon, called Peter, and his brother Andrew, James and his brother John, sons of Zebedee, 3 Philip, Bartholomew, Thomas, Matthew the tax collector, James (son of Alphaeus), Thaddaeus (called Lebbaeus), 4 Simon the Zealot, and Judas Iscariot, who was to betray him. 5 These twelve Jesus sent on a mission, charging them as follows: "Do not go along the route of the Gentiles, and do not enter a Samaritan town (again). 6 Go rather to the lost sheep of the house of Israel, and 7 as you go, proclaim that the Kingdom of heaven is fast approaching. 8 Heal the sick, cure lepers, cast out demons. You received without paying anything—give without payment. 9 Do not carry gold, silver, or copper coin in your belts, 10 no bag for your journey, nor two tunics, nor sandals, nor a staff. The worker deserves his keep. 11 Find out who is suitable in any town or village you enter, and stay there until you leave. 12 As you enter the house, greet it, and 13 if the house is deserving, then let your blessing rest upon it. If it is undeserving, let your blessing return to you. 14 If anyone will not receive you, or listen to your words, then on your departure from that house or town, shake off the dust from your feet. 15 I solemnly declare to you that Sodom and Gomorrah will be in happier case on the day of judgment than that town.

† **Matt x 1–4** ‖ Mark iii 16–19, Luke vi 12–16; **5–15** ‖ Mark vi 7–13, Luke ix 1–6.

NOTES

x 1. *authority*. Matthew has already spoken of the authority of Jesus (vii 28 f., ix 6) in teaching and in work. Here he depicts Jesus transmitting this authority to the disciples. Cf. also ix 8; xxviii 18.

2. *The names of the twelve apostles are.** This phrase has commonly been held to be editorial, which may or may not be correct. It may well also be a parenthetic note introduced by the author. The word *apostle* occurs only here in Matthew, but the concept of "sending on a mission," from which the noun derives, is common in this gospel; cf. vs. 5 below as a typical example. If our interpretation of Matthew's scheme is correct (see COMMENT following this section), then there would be no call to use the word again, and xxviii 19 gives the commission of the apostles as clearly as does John xx 21.

first. In a list such as we have here, the word is redundant unless it refers to the leadership of the Twelve by Peter.

Simon. See NOTE on iv 18. Note that Matthew arranges all brothers in pairs in this list.

Andrew is a Greek name, like Philip in vs. 3, but this must obviously not be taken to mean that the names indicated that the men were Greeks.

3. *Bartholomew*. This name is Aramaic Bar-Tolmai (Tolmai is attested in South Arabic and Nabataean as normal transcription of Gr. *Ptolemaios*)=son of Ptolemy, indicating that his father had a Greek name.

Thomas (="Twin") is, in Aramaic, *Tōmā*.

Matthew is Hebrew (see NOTE on ix 9), and he is identified with the tax collector of ix 9.

Alphaeus is Aram. *Ḥalfai* (shortened from the common rabbinic name *Ḥalafta*), while *Thaddaeus* is Aram. *Taddai*. It could be a place name, on the basis of quite satisfactory Aramaic etymologies. The manuscript evidence shows that *Lebbaeus* is sometimes substituted for *Thaddaeus*, and we may assume that *called* was added to preserve both traditions. Certainly the names are typical Aramaic shortened forms (hypocoristica). In the list in Luke vi 16, Lebbaeus/Thaddaeus is replaced by Judas=Jude (not Iscariot, John xiv 22), but there is no good reason why the list of twelve apostles should always have been limited to the same persons (until after the defection of Judas).

4. *Simon the Zealot*. For all the discussion in commentaries on the relative merits of the reading *kananaios* (Canaanite) and *kannaios* or

* On the names of some of the apostles, cf. Part XIII of the Introduction.

kanaios (Zealot), the solution certainly lies in the transmission of the Hebrew/Aramaic appellation. In normal transcription the Heb. *qof* was always *k,* while the aspirated *kaph* was always *chi.* The reading can only be *qannāyā, Zealot,* which is the appellation in Luke. The introduction of an extra "a" is very simply explained, for two *n*'s between two *a*'s would very easily produce an extra *a.* If the passage was being dictated, then the confusion between *Kananaios* and *Chananaios* would quickly arise. "Canaanite" seems to us to be a very weak candidate as a description of a disciple of Jesus. It is far more likely that more than one Zealot would have initially been attracted by the teachings of Jesus, and that one of them should have been so identified in this list. Luke (vi 15) reads *Simōna ton kaloumenon Zēlōtēn,* presumably to put the matter beyond doubt (cf. Acts i 13, *Simōn ho* Zēlōtēs).

Judas Iscariot. Attempts to deal with the name *Iscariot* as derived from a place name ("the man from Kerioth"), or as belonging to a leather apron girdle, or bag, or from Judas' later role as traitor, or from a supposed meaning as "assassin," must all be abandoned. *Judas* alone is as useless an identification as would be Muhammed, without a patronymic, in Muslim countries. Harald Ingholt was driven to look for other explanations by the near unanimity in later iconography depicting Judas as red-haired. His technical discussion and full conclusions are to be found in *Studia Orientalia Johanni Pedersen* (Copenhagen, 1953), pp. 152 ff. He demonstrates, on the basis of Palmyrene inscriptions, that "Iscariot" cannot have been a geographical appellation, and suggests that the word derives from the Aramaic root *sqr,* which varies in meaning from reddish-brown to ruddy. What we have therefore in this name is a kenning, or nickname.

The unanimity of all four gospels as to the central place of the Twelve (the title is common in John) tends to obscure the fact that we know very little about this inner circle. It is more than possible that their function (cf. Acts viii 1) may have been almost exclusively within the framework of the Jerusalem community. When Jewish Christianity as a controlling influence came to an end ca. A.D. 65–70, the Gentile communities may not even have known the names of the Twelve with any certainty. The number "twelve," however many there may have been in the inner circle of the disciples, is considered in our gospels to be connected with the twelve tribes of Israel (cf. xix 28; Rev xxi 14). Three significant points must be noticed here:

(a) The OT lists of the twelve tribes seldom agree fully as to the specific identification of all "twelve" tribes.

(b) The emphasis on "the Twelve" in the Qumran community (1QS viii 1–10) is of some importance here. Cf. C. S. Mann, "The Organization and Institutions of the Jerusalem Church in Acts," in Munck, *The Acts of the Apostles,* Appendix IV.

(c) Whatever the original identification of "apostles" and "the Twelve," at least for Jerusalem, the term "apostle" seems to have taken on a wider meaning with the conversion of Paul and the resulting Gentile mission. Cf. Johannes Munck, "Paul, the Apostles and the Twelve," *Studia Theologica* 3 (Lund: Gleerup, 1949).

There are lists of the Twelve also in Mark iii 16–19; Luke vi 13–16; Acts i 13–16. The reader is also referred to our discussion in Part XIII of the Introduction, on authorship and chronology.

5. *sent on a mission.* In Mark's tradition (vi 8–13) this mission is a definite single occasion, and the whole context of the Matthean account supports it.

route of the Gentiles. There were three possible ways in which the disciples could travel to accomplish this mission: (1) along the coastal plain, (2) along the Jordan valley, or (3) along the watershed ridge. It is the first possibility which is being ruled out here. There were few Jewish settlements there at that time, and it would therefore have been extremely difficult for the disciples to obtain ritually clean food (i.e., *kosher* food). The Gr. *hodos* can mean a road or a route, or (as in parts of the NT) a way (of life), a journey. The Heb. *derek* also carries similar meanings.

(again). The present Greek of this injunction is: *kai eis polin Samaritōn mē eiselthēte.* Our translation obviously depends on the supplying of *palin* (again) for *polin* (city) before *eis,* to restore what we believe to have been the original text. If there was here an absolute prohibition against the evangelization of Samaritans, it is hard to imagine why the disciples, immediately after the death of Stephen, should have regarded with equanimity a mission among the Samaritans (Acts viii 2–25). Moreover, the inhabitants of Samaria would certainly have been regarded as being among *the lost sheep of the house of Israel.* Jesus is recorded in John iv as having preached in Samaria and there the surprise of the disciples (vs. 27) is that he was talking with a woman, not that he was talking with a Samaritan. Jesus' prohibition here may have been due to the fact that the disciples, having a Jewish ethnic and religious background, might antagonize the Samaritans unwittingly.

Our restored Greek text is easily understood: *palin eis polin* . . . It would lend itself with great ease to a very natural haplography. *Palin (again)* with the negative imperative is found at II Cor ii 1; Gal v 1; Heb vi 1, 4–6. It is used frequently in the gospels for repeated journeys.

6. *lost sheep.* Cf. NOTE on iii 2.

house of Israel. The contrast sometimes drawn by commentators between the particularism of this verse and the general commission of xxviii 16–20 is not very instructive. For one thing, the commission here

means that those so commissioned are to give absolute priority to those
towns or areas where there are already Jewish settlements (cf. vs. 23),
as areas where the Messianic message would not be foreign. However,
there is the decisive phrase *The Man's coming* in vs. 23, and we have
given reasons for thinking that this "coming" refers to the passion-
resurrection glory of the Messiah (cf. Part VI of the Introduction).
In vs. 23, then, there is a simple statement that the disciples
will not even have time to complete their mission in the Israelite communities before the time of Jesus' glorification. This interpretation assumes independent missionary activity on the part of the inner circle,
and this we know to have been the case (cf. Luke ix 1–6, x 1–20—the
mission of the seventy; Mark vi 7–31; and cf. also John iv 2). The difficulty of interpretation lies partly in Matthew's habit of grouping material into discourses, and the references at the head of this chapter make
it clear that what the evangelist has collected here are groups of sayings
molded into a kind of missionary's vade mecum. The care taken to
preserve all that was known in the oral tradition makes it inevitable that
sayings remained which had validity originally in the immediate ministry
of Jesus and his disciples. On this subject, cf. Jeremias, *Jesus' Promise
to the Nations.*

7. *fast approaching.* Cf. Note on iii 2.

8. *without payment.* Cf. TB, *Nedarim* 37a: "As I taught you free
of charge, so you, too, teach free of charge" (Moses to the Israelites); and "You received without pay, give without pay" (Mishnah
Aboth i 3). The theme is common in a missionary context, and was
emphasized by Paul (cf. I Cor ix 14; II Cor xi 7; I Tim v 18). Hospitality is a common theme, too, and given place in the NT writings (cf. Rom
xii 13; I Tim iii 2; Titus i 8; Heb xiii 2; I Peter iv 9). The possibility of
abuse of the hospitality extended to missionaries did exist, and the first-
century *Didache* (xiii) thought it important enough to establish precise
regulations against such abuse.

9–10. The commands embodied in these verses certainly indicate that
spirit of detachment which is characteristic of the NT writings. Equally,
the injunction may emphasize the extreme urgency of the need to proclaim the Freedom of the Kingdom, and Luke x 4 seems to demand
this sense. The Markan tradition underlines this by prescribing only a
staff for such journeys—anything more would make the missionaries appear as men bent on ordinary business.

10. *The worker deserves his keep.* Luke's version of this statement
(Luke x 7) is quoted in I Tim v 18 as though it were already canonical
scripture.

11. The Matthean version here seems to be a combination of two
remembered sayings, preserved as separate in Luke in two different
contexts. Cf. Luke ix 4; x 5–7.

suitable (Gr. *axios*). This word, in its common English translation of "worthy," may suggest moral rectitude to us, but it would not have done so to the evangelist. Rather the word indicates someone willing to receive an apostle. Cf. the English legal title of "His Worship" (i.e., "his worth-ship") for the mayor or chief magistrate of a town.

12–13. The Lukan version (Luke x 5–6) is manifestly drawing on an independent tradition, and Mark has no parallel to these verses.

blessing. The Heb. *shālôm* does not have the restrictive sense of absence of conflict which our modern political thinking has imposed on the word peace. Rather it has the meaning of "well-being."

14. Mark (vi 11) here has "place," and it is Luke (x 10) and Matthew who use *house* and *town*.

15. *Sodom*. The place is frequently used in the NT as a typical example of the doom reserved for communities that resist the divine will. Cf. xi 23–24; Luke x 12, xvii 29; Rom ix 29; II Peter ii 6; Jude vs. 7; and cf. also Jubilees xxxvi 10.

the day of judgment. The definite article is omitted in Greek, but such omission was not uncommon when a technical term was used. The term as used here means the end of the age, or the end of the temporal order, and in that sense cf. Pss Sol xv 12; Jubilees iv 19; Parables of Enoch xxxix 1.

COMMENT

The scheme of Matthew's gospel has brought the evangelist to the point where, having told how Jesus sees his own work, he must show how provision was made for continuing that work in the future community. Nowhere in Matthew does Jesus' eschatological or apocalyptic language automatically exclude the community which came to be called the Church. Indeed, even if we had no evidence from the OT, the Qumran literature is evidence enough that in contemporary Jewish thinking a Messiah without a Messianic Community was unthinkable. With this in mind, the nineteenth-century "liberal" view that there was a "simple" humanitarian gospel of divine Fatherhood and human brotherhood, later corrupted by the apostle Paul into a full-scale ecclesiastical organization, must be dismissed as a chimera of that same liberal thinking. It is possible that many who held such a view were the victims of various translations of Luke xvii 21: *hē basileia tou theou entos humōn estin:* "God's Kingdom is in your very midst," *not* "within you."

The introduction of the Twelve in this section of the gospel is abrupt, and Matthew has not given us any record of the choosing of the inner circle. The manner of the introduction is explained in part, however, by the designation of the Twelve as "apostles," a title which has reference to their mission in the continuing community after the resurrection. It is also partly explained by Matthew's arrangement of his material. From this point onwards, until the action of the gospel moves to the last week in Jerusalem, all the teaching is concerned with the community and the place of the disciple in it.

40. THE COST OF DISCIPLESHIP:
MISSION
(x 16–25)†

X 16 "See, I send you out like sheep among wolves. Therefore be as prudent as serpents, and as candid as doves. 17 Beware of men. They will hand you over to courts, flog you in synagogues, 18 and you will be hauled before rulers and kings on account of me, to witness to them and to Gentiles. 19 When they hand you over, do not worry about how or what to speak, for at that time what you are to say will be shown to you; and 20 it will not be you speaking, but the Spirit of your Father speaking through you. 21 Brother will hand over brother to death, and the father his child; children will denounce parents and have them killed. 22 On account of my name you will be hated by all, but he who endures to the end will be saved. 23 When they persecute you in one town, flee to the next one, for I tell you truly that you will not have gone through the towns of Israel before The Man's coming. 24 The disciple is not superior to his teacher, nor a slave to his owner; 25 it is sufficient for the disciple to become like his teacher, and the slave to become like his master. If they have called the head of the house Beelzebul, how much more will they miscall those of his household!

† **Matt x 16–25** ‖ Mark xiii 9–13, Luke xxi 12–17.

NOTES

x 16. *sheep among wolves.* The phrase also occurs in Luke x 3, where it is set in the context of the mission of the seventy. It also follows immediately upon fragments of a saying parallel to Luke xi 32 (=Mark xiii 13) in the Gospel of Thomas (xxxix).

The whole previous section (x 1–15), which might be described as ending at vs. 16, illustrates very well the fluid state of the written tradition at the time of the compilation of Matthew, and at the same time the care with which the oral tradition was being preserved. There is a useful parallel here with the careful preservation of the material collected by the schools of Shammai, Hillel, and Yohanan ben Zakkai in rabbinical circles.

The preceding section has much in common with Mark vi 6–11, and Luke ix 1–6 is also parallel to this material. But Matthew and Luke in many instances agree verbally in the Greek against Mark, while at the same time Luke's version of the mission charge to the seventy (Luke x) has material parallel to Matt ix 37–38, x 7, 10, 12–13, 15–16a. The resemblances and the differences can be accounted for somewhat as follows: Mark's charge to the Twelve is in a form which can best be described—like so much of his pre-passion material—as "headlines." Matthew's handling of his material, much fuller and far more systematic, is careful to preserve the distinction between instruction given to the inner circle and that given to a wider audience. Luke is far more concerned, thanks to his emphasis on the results of Paul's conversion, with a wider missionary enterprise than is Matthew. For Luke, "disciple" has a wider meaning than it has in Matthew, and he therefore arranges the missionary charges in his material as addressed to the whole community.

17. *Beware of men.* The evangelist's method of grouping his material is very much in evidence here. The saying about *sheep among wolves,* whether Matthew knew Mark or not, persuaded Matthew to include here remarks about the treatment of the disciples after Jesus leaves them. Mark has the material in xiii 9–13, set clearly in a context which looks to the future of the community. The Matthean material also looks to that future, but with the difference that there are sayings here (vss. 23–25) which could equally well belong to independent missionary activity during the ministry of Jesus.

18. One of the few indications which suggests that Matthew might have been acquainted with Mark (in some form) comes in this verse. Matthew's version ends at *to witness to them and to Gentiles.* In Mark, this clause is divided between two verses, xiii 9–10: "to witness to them. And the gospel must first be preached to the Gentiles." The phrase "And the gospel must first be preached" would certainly be inappropriate in this Matthean context of instruction to the inner circle, if indeed Matthew's oral tradition had it.

19–21. It has more than once been said that these verses are *vaticinium post eventum* (prophecy after the event), reflections added to the sayings of Jesus after the first wave of missionary endeavor. Such a judgment is hard to sustain in the light of what we know of first-century Syria-

Palestine, and the subsequent history of Paul dramatically underlines that knowledge:

(a) Social and religious conditions were such that any proclamation of a Messianic Kingdom as an impending, soon-to-be-fulfilled reality would bring sharply into focus, and into conflict, all the loyalties of Jews, both sectarian and orthodox.

(b) Roman authority could not remain indifferent to such stirrings of passion, whatever the status of Judaism as *religio licita* (lawful religion). Cf. Charles N. Cochrane, *Christianity and Classical Culture* (Oxford University Press, 1940, rev. ed., 1944), especially pp. 100–3.

(c) The language of this section is wholly in keeping with apocalyptic sayings about the last days: cf. II Esdras v 9; Jubilees xxiii 19; Enoch lvi 7, xcix 5, c 1; Apocalypse of Baruch lxx 3.

22. Cf. II Esdras "Whoever remains, that man will be saved, he will see my salvation, and the end of the age" (vi 25); "Everyone who is saved . . . will be preserved" (ix 7–8).

23. Whether this verse is in context is hard to determine. It is wholly in keeping with the teaching of Jesus that the verse should have come to be applied to missionary work in the post-resurrection period. Application is one thing, deliberate invention quite another. Rudolf Bultmann describes the first part of the verse as a "flight-motif" added by the evangelist as a result of persecution endured in the Church's missionary work. This seems to ignore the fact that in contemporary Judaism one sign of the End-time was wandering of people from city to city before the appearing of the Son of David (cf. TB, *Sota* 9.15, *Sanhedrin* 9a). The attention of the reader is again called to Part VI of the Introduction and to the grounds given there for thinking that what we have here in *The Man's coming* is a reference to the exaltation of the Messiah in passion-resurrection. Whatever the length of the public ministry of Jesus, and however extended geographically the independent missions of the Twelve (Matt x 5–15; Mark vi 7–13) and the Seventy (Luke x 1–20), the second part of vs. 23 simply states a truth: *The Man's coming* will supervene before the mission to Israel has been fulfilled.

24–25. It is clear from these verses that Matthew and Luke were working from independent traditions—cf. vs. 24 and Luke vi 40. Similarly for vs. 25; the Lukan version (vi 40) of the saying about teacher and pupil is an illustration of another saying of blind leading blind, of total dependence. Here in Matthew there is a wholly different sense: the treatment accorded to the Master will be the lot of those who carry on his work.

25. *Beelzebul.* The confusion of the Greek text is reflected in the modern English translations. RSV has Beelzebul, and NEB Beelzebub.

The decipherment of the Ugaritic texts, however, makes it clear that the NT form *Beelzebul* is the original Canaanite form rather than the spelling *Beelzebub* found in our Hebrew Bible (II Kings i 2). The name means "Baal the Prince." This was the title of the chief god of Ekron (II Kings i 2 ff.), but in the Canaanite epic of Baal he was *"Zubulu* (prince), Lord of the earth." He later became the chief of demons in early Jewish demonology.

COMMENT

The cost of discipleship to the inner circle is the same as that demanded of the Master. There is, however, a significant difference. Jesus' ministry is addressed to his own people, to Israel of the Old Covenant, as is that of the Twelve initially (cf. vss. 5–6). But while Jesus suffers at the end of his ministry at the hands of those he came to save (cf. John i 12), the disciples addressed in this part of the charge must face suffering at the hands of Jews and Gentiles alike.

It is easy to see, from vs. 23 onwards, how this section came to be understood as anticipating the End, the final judgment. We noted in the discussion of vs. 23 above that in our view, this was not the original meaning of the charge. However, the position of this Matthean material in the Markan "apocalypse" (Mark xiii) *does* place the emphasis on the final judgment. This is not by any means to deny the validity of such emphasis, though in our view this was not the interpretation given by Jesus. On the contrary, it is the universal applicability of large areas of the teaching of Jesus which opens up horizons far beyond the immediate context of that teaching. At the same time, however, it serves to obscure the fact that much of the instruction in our gospels was given only to a small inner circle. Later on, in a wider audience, there was certainly the possibility of expanded interpretation.

41. THE COST OF DISCIPLESHIP: FEAR
(x 26–31)

X 26 "But do not fear them, for there is nothing veiled which will not be revealed, no secret which will not become known. 27 Whatever I tell you in the dark, speak out in the light, and whatever you hear in a whisper, proclaim from the housetops. 28 Do not fear those who kill the body, but who cannot kill the soul; rather fear him who can destroy both soul and body in Gehenna. 29 Are not two sparrows sold for a penny? And one of them does not fall to the ground without your Father's will. 30 Even the hairs of your head are all numbered; 31 therefore do not be afraid—you are worth more than many sparrows.

† Matt x 26–31 || Luke xii 2–7.

NOTES

x 26. *do not fear.* This injunction is repeated twice, cf. vss. 28, 31. This is a device referred to in Part IV of the Introduction.

them. i.e., the persecutors.

It is clear that the saying *nothing veiled which will not be revealed* was a common theme in Jesus' teaching. It finds expression in Mark iv 22; Luke viii 17, xii 2.

27. The application of the saying in vs. 26 differs from that given in Luke. Here there is a plain injunction to make public the instruction now being given in private to the disciples. In Luke, however, viii 17 parallels the present sense, while xii 2 suggests that the proclamation of the Kingdom must not be overlaid by the kind of legal subterfuge characteristic of the Pharisees.

28. *Gehenna.* Cf. NOTE on *fiery death* in v 22.

29. *penny* (Gr. *assarion*). This is the Latin *as*, about $\frac{1}{16}$ of a denarius, less than $\frac{1}{2}$ cent.

30. *hairs of your head*. The stress here is on the hairs, i.e., the insignificant, rather than on "your head."

COMMENT

The section vss. 26–33 is paralleled in Luke xii 2–9, but the differences are notable, even though there is some agreement in language. Two different senses are being used by the two evangelists, and a difference in historical setting as between Matthew and Luke would seem to make reliance on a common written source unlikely.

42. THE COST OF DISCIPLESHIP: ACKNOWLEDGMENT OF THE MESSIAH
(x 32–xi 1)†

X 32 "Whoever acknowledges me before men, I will acknowledge before my Father in heaven; 33 but whoever denies me before men I will deny before my Father in heaven.

34 "Do not think that I have come to impose peace on earth by force; I have come neither to impose peace, nor yet to make war. 35 I have come to divide . . .

> a man against his father,
> a daughter against her mother,
> and a daughter-in-law against her mother-in-law.
> 36 A man's enemies will be members of his own household.

37 The man who prefers father or mother to me is unfitted for me, and the man who prefers son or daughter to me is unfitted for me, 38 and he who does not take up his cross and follow me is unfitted for me. 39 One who grasps at self will lose it, but one who rejects self on my account will gain it.

40 "Whoever receives you receives me, and in receiving me receives him who sent me. 41 Whoever receives the Prophet because he is the Prophet will be rewarded by the Prophet, and so he who receives the Righteous One because he is the Righteous One will be rewarded by the Righteous One. 42 So, whoever gives to one of the most insignificant of these a mere cup of water because he is my disciple will not, I tell you truly, lose his reward."

XI 1 When Jesus had finished instructing his twelve disciples, he went on from there to teach and proclaim in their towns.

† Matt x 32–34 ‖ Luke xii 8–9; 34–39 ‖ Luke xii 51–53, xiv 26–27; 40 ‖ Mark ix 41.

NOTES

x 32. *acknowledges me*. With the preposition *en* with the dative, the expression occurs only here and at Luke xii 8, but without the preposition the same expression, with the same meaning, occurs at John ix 22 and in several other NT books.

33. Vss. 32–33 have a rough parallel in Mark viii 38. Nowhere is the diverse character of the Kingdom's advent seen more clearly than in the severance of family loyalties. The section vss. 34–39, whatever the history of its individual parts, is placed here as following naturally from the thought of what the disciple must endure as the cost of his fidelity.

34. Luke xii 51 has a version of this saying which cannot be said to derive from any written source shared with Matthew.

Here, two expectations of Messiahship are alike dismissed, the one of imposing peace at home by force of arms, the other of asserting the Messianic reign by conquest abroad (cf. Isa lxiii 1). The thought follows logically from vs. 33: Jesus does not come to *impose peace* by kingly rule. On the contrary, his coming will involve painful decisions. He will not interfere with man's freedom. The verse has been the subject of so much controversy, both academic and homiletical, that it is well to spend some time here discussing the linguistic evidence which underlies our translation. Basically, the evidence rests on the play on words in the Gr. *ballō* (Aram. *remā*), together with the Jewish-Aramaic word which lies behind the Gr. *alla*.

(a) The original of the saying, we suggest, was *lā'atēt le-mirmē shlāmā 'ellā ḥarbā*. (The syntax of the Peshitta—*de'armī*—is specifically Syriac and does not directly reflect earlier Jewish-Aramaic.) There is a very good parallel to the verb in the Aramaic "Genesis Apocryphon" (which dates from shortly before the time of Jesus), in col. xxii, line 8, where, speaking of Abraham, it reads, "He fell upon them at night from all four sides," literally, "he hurled" (his troops) "upon them"— *ū-remā 'alēhōn be-lēlyā* . . . Here is good contemporary evidence, then, for the sense behind Aram. *remā*, Gr. *ballō*, for translating *impose* (war), in contrast to the usual translation of "bring."

(b) The Gr. *alla*, usually given as "but" in our English translations, has been inadequately explored by translators. In early post-biblical Hebrew as well as in contemporary Aramaic the construction *lô/ā* . . . *we-lô/ā* and *lô/ā* . . . *'ellā* is common, and there are many examples in (e.g.) the *Pirqê Abôth*. Since *we-lā* and *'ellā* sounded so much alike, there must often have been some confusion in oral transmission into Greek. Here, in this verse, we have precisely this situation, and the

Greek has almost certainly transmitted an oral misunderstanding. What we have, therefore, is not a simple *not peace but a sword* (in spite of RSV), but a *neither . . . nor* saying, with both parts depending on the meaning *impose* for the Gr. *ballō*.

(c) We have translated the Gr. *machaira* by *war*. The Greek is without a definite article, and sometimes can—and in context manifestly does—mean *war* (cf. Jer xv 2). In Hebrew and Aramaic *ḥereb/ḥarbā*, "sword," also means "war," and in Arabic *ḥarb,* which originally meant "sword," is the usual word for "war."

(d) Even when difficulties of translation in vs. 34 have been removed, there is still an awkward transition from this verse to its successor in our versions. Vss. 35–36 speak of division between members of pairs of closely related people. It is hard to know the origin of the common English rendering "set against" as a translation of the Gr. *dichazō,* which means "divide in two." In Greek, the only example given in the lexica for *set against* as a translation of *dichazō* is our passage in Matthew! The translation "divide against" in Liddell and Scott, with this Matthew passage as sole example, is bad Greek and deplorable English. It is in our view most likely that a simple homoioteleuton has allowed a very vital connecting link between vss. 34 and 35–36 to be dropped. Vs. 34 is a denial of Messianic aspirations of various kinds, while vss. 35–36 are a quotation from Mic vii 6 of the results of a coming in judgment. What we have every right to expect in the context of the saying is a statement of true Messianic purpose, and this we do not have in the present text. Our suggestion is that originally the text ran: "Do not think that I have come to impose peace on earth by force; I have come neither to impose peace, nor yet to make war. But I have come to divide the just from the unjust . . . a man against his father . . ." There is important parallel material for our suggested addition in Mal iii 18 (in the middle of a description of the coming judgment); John ix 39; Acts xxiv 15 and II Peter ii 9. Outside both OT and NT there is a text (vii 12) in 1QH, the Thanksgiving Psalms of the Dead Sea scroll material. It reads: "For all my antagonists thou wilt condemn to judgment, in order to separate on my account between the just and the unjust (translation by W. F. Albright, differing only in wording from that of Dupont-Sommer, 1951, and Mansoor, 1955).

There is a further complication. Not only is there homoioteleuton to cause confusion by the repeated *I have come;* the verb *dichazō* simply will not do to govern the Micah (vii 6) quotation in vss. 35–36. The Hebrew original and the Greek of the LXX have the son treating the father with contempt—the division has already taken place. Hence, after "unjust" (in our text above), we have left a blank, and rendered the Gr. *katá* by *against* (*his father*). There has obviously been omission here, but we do not know what it was at this stage—presumably the Micah passage was quoted in full.

(e) Enclosing NT material in quotation marks is not unattended by peril. It is, for instance, by no means clear that John i 34 ought to be enclosed within quotation marks as part of the witness of John the Baptist—that verse may well be the evangelist's own testimony in response to John the Baptist's doubts in vss. 31, 33. (Contrast some commentators at this point.) Similarly, it is not clear from the present context in Matthew whether vss. 35–36 are allusive OT commentary (*pēsher*) on the words of Jesus, in the familiar Matthean fashion, or whether vs. 34 is a saying of Jesus to which Jesus himself gave OT sanction.

35–36. Cf. Mic vii 6. Rabbinic writings also declare that suffering will herald the Messianic Age (cf. TB, *Sanhedrin* 97a, *Sota* 49a).

37. In Luke the sentiment of this verse is expressed differently (Luke xiv 26–27). There, the word translated "hate" in most English versions was changing its meaning from a prevailingly legal sense to one which denoted "opposition to." In the Lukan version, it would be best to render the Greek: "Anyone who follows me, who cannot oppose father and mother. . . .

unfitted for. Cf. NOTE on vs. 11, on *axios*.

38. *take up his cross.* This saying is found in three forms in the synoptic gospels:

(a) Matt xvi 24; Mark viii 34; Luke ix 23, as a positive injunction;
(b) Matt x 38 in negative form;
(c) Luke xiv 27, also in negative form, slightly different.

Both (b) and (c) seem to be derived from a common original. This is the first mention of the cross in Matthew, and from time to time it has been held that the saying is probably not genuine, but more likely another example of prophecy after the event. However, in the climate of the times it is hard to suppose that Jesus did not foresee a violent end to his ministry. It is true that Luke xiv 27 could equally well take "yoke" as a symbol of discipleship (cf. Matt xi 29), since the symbol of the "yoke of the Law" is found in rabbinical writings, as was also "the yoke of the Kingdom of heaven" (cf. *Pirqê Abôth* iiib; TB, *Berakhoth* 13a). But long before the time of Jesus, impaling or crucifixion had become typical of violent death (cf. Plato *Republic* ii. 361; Artemidorus, ii. 56, speaks of the condemned man carrying his cross, and *Bereshith Rabba,* commenting on Gen xxii 6, speaks of bearing the cross). Cf. also J. Gwyn Griffiths, "The Disciple's Cross," NTS 16 (1970), pp. 358–64.

Here, for the disciples, the thought is of being prepared for death in persecution.

39. This saying, like the preceding, comes in varied form in all four gospels:

      (a) Matt xvi 25; Mark viii 35; Luke ix 24;
      (b) Matt x 38;
      (c) Luke xvii 33;
      (d) John xii 25.

It would appear that (a) and (c) are independent translations of the same saying. The saying in (a) and (b) is connected with carrying the cross.

self. The Greek *psychē* is commonly translated either by "life" (RSV) or "soul." (Here, KJ, NEB, and JB all have "life.") The first unnecessarily narrows the meaning, and confines the saying to death by persecution, while the second has all the disadvantages of a scholastic concept little understood by many modern readers. Our translation avoids the second, and also renders the sense in a way which does not confine the cost of discipleship to physical death.

The next short section begins with the disciple (vs. 40) and ends with the disciple (vs. 42), the whole revolving around the person and mission of Jesus in vs. 41.

40. Cf. "He who welcomes his fellow-man is considered as though he had welcomed the Shekinah" (i.e., the divine presence)—*Mekilta,* tractate Amalek, 3.

41. Our translation radically changes the commonly accepted sense of this verse, and makes it a saying about different attitudes to the mission and person of Jesus. It is necessary to examine the linguistic basis upon which our translation rests.

(a) Once it is assumed that there is a connection between this verse and vs. 40, then it becomes necessary to ask "What prophet?" or "What righteous man?" especially as this section reverts in vs. 42 to the links between Jesus and the disciples.

(b) Still unpublished investigation convinces us that the figure of the Righteous One played a decisive part in the evolution of the doctrine of a Messiah among Jews of the NT period. This reaches back into the Dead Sea scrolls and previously known intertestamental writings, with indications of a much earlier OT origin. It also finds expression in the NT, most notably in Acts vii 52.

(c) It is clear that we are dealing in this verse with two titles of Jesus, and at the same time two attitudes to him. These we have clarified by the use of capital letters.

(d) The Greek has no definite article before either *Prophet* or *Righteous One.* This by no means invalidates our translation, for in the Jewish-Aramaic of this period it is context alone which determines the presence or absence of the definite article (in this connection, cf. xiv 33). We suggest that the translation into Greek at this point was scrupulously faithful, but—once the gospel had passed from a Jewish to a Greek *milieu*—later capable of misunderstanding.

(e) As translated by us, the verse depicts Jesus giving recognition to two attitudes to himself: there were those who saw him as The Prophet, Herald of the Messianic Age, and those whose wider perceptions saw him as both Herald and Messianic Righteous One.

42. *because he is.* Here RSV does justice to the Jewish-Aramaic and Syriac (*'al shum* and *'al shem*) behind the Gr. *eis onoma* (literally, "for the name of").

my disciple. Again, there is no definite article or possessive pronoun in the Greek, but the pronunciation of *a disciple* and *my disciple* is the same in the Jewish-Aramaic of this period.

xi 1. *proclaim.* Cf. NOTE on iv 23.

43. JOHN'S QUESTION AND JESUS' TESTIMONY
(xi 2–19)†

XI 2 When John had heard in prison about the deeds of
Jesus, he sent two of his disciples to ask him, 3 "Are you the
Coming One, or are we to look for someone else?" 4 Jesus in
answer said, "Go on your way and tell John the things you
see and hear: 5 the blind see, the lame walk, lepers are cured,
the deaf hear, the dead are raised, and good news is brought
to the humble. 6 Fortunate is the man who does not find me
a stumbling block."

7 When they had gone away, Jesus began to say to the
crowds about John: "What did you go into the desert to look
at? A reed swayed by the wind? 8 But what did you go to see?
A man clad in expensive clothing? Well, those who wear expensive clothing are in kings' houses. 9 But why did you go?
To see a prophet? Yes, I tell you—and much more than a
prophet. 10 He is the one of whom it is recorded:

'See, I send my messenger before your face,
he shall prepare your way before you.'

11 Truly I tell you that no human being has arisen who is
greater than John the Baptist, yet the very least person in
the Kingdom of heaven is greater than he." 12 From the time
of John the Baptist to this moment, the Kingdom of heaven
has been under violent attack and violent men despoil it.
13 For all the prophets, and the Law, up to John, prophesied.
14 If you wish to accept it, he is the expected Elijah. 15 Let
him who has understanding listen.

16 "But to what shall I compare this generation? It is like

† Matt xi 2–19 ‖ Luke vii 18–35.

children sitting in the market place, calling to the rest, [17] 'We piped to you, and you did not dance, we wailed and you did not mourn.' [18] For John came neither eating nor drinking, and they say 'He has a demon.' The Man came, both eating and drinking, and they say, [19] 'See, a drunkard and a glutton, a friend of tax collectors and non-observant Jews.' But wisdom is vindicated by her deeds."

NOTES

xi 2. *in prison.* John's imprisonment has been mentioned already in iv 12. Luke's version coincides with vss. 2a–3.

deeds. Cf. the representative illustrations viii 1–9, 34.

3. *the Coming One.* Cf. iii 11, and also Ps cxviii 26; Dan vii 13; see also Part VII of the Introduction.

5. *lepers.* Cf. NOTE on viii 2, and cf. also x 8.

dead. In the OT and the Orient generally, the expression "dead" can often mean "dying." Cf. NOTE on ix 24.

good news is brought. The Greek verb *euangelizontai* is used only here in Matthew.

6. *stumbling block.* Literally, an occasion of offense, by misunderstanding Jesus' Messianic work.

7. *look at.* The Greek word (*theasasthai*), from which the word "theater" is derived, means to gaze at a show or demonstration. The verb also occurs at vi 1; xxii 11; xxiii 5.

reed swayed by the wind. Either this is ironic (i.e., men did not go out into the desert to look at something perfectly ordinary) or it refers to the hesitancies and doubts which assailed John in prison—which is the interpretation we favor.

8. *expensive clothing.* The desert was no place to look for mere secular show or power. As it was (vs. 9), the reality far exceeded expectation.

10. This quotation, in which Matthew and Luke agree with Mark i 2 as against the LXX rendering, is from Mal iii 1.

before you. This is apparently assimilated from Exod xxiii 20 (cf. Part IV of the Introduction on the OT background of Matthew). However, the quotation, evidently in wide use among early Christian communities, may have belonged originally to a series of "testimonies" associated with John the Baptist. For a full discussion of the problem, cf. Robinson, "Elijah, Jesus and John: An Essay in Detection," in TNTS.

11. *Truly* (Gr. *amēn*). A solemn affirmation of validity. It is common, in repetitive form, in John's gospel.

greater than John. To proclaim the Messiah's advent is to make John's ministry and vocation unique. But those who are incorporated into the Messiah's Kingdom will be greater than John, who will not live to see that Kingdom's inauguration.

very least. The suggestion has been made that this expression refers to the difference in age between Jesus and John, and that Jesus here describes himself. This seems to be somewhat forced, and it is better to take the expression as meaning the newest neophyte in the Kingdom.

12–15. It seems to us probable that these verses do not belong to Jesus. Certainly vs. 14, not found elsewhere, appears to betray something of an uncertainty about the role of John—an uncertainty which was foreign to Jesus—and vs. 15 is a theme verse which occurs also at xiii 9, 43. (On vss. 12 and 13, cf. Perrin, *The Kingdom of God in the Teaching of Jesus,* pp. 171–74.)

But there is more to be said. Luke's version (xvi 16) has the Greek verb *biazetai* in the middle voice, with the plain meaning that men press urgently and even violently into the Kingdom (cf. RSV ad loc.). Certainly the verb *biazesthai* bears this meaning in Koine Greek. But in Matthew's vs. 12 the subject of the verb *biazetai* is *the Kingdom,* and this demands a translation other than Luke's middle voice. (Matthew's verb would seem to demand a translation in passive voice, as we have given.) The evidence seems to suggest that both traditions are edited reminiscences of a saying in which the verb *biazesthai* would be in place. Luke's xvi 16 also indicates that the oral tradition had features which were changed before Luke had access to it. At the same time, the fact that the Lukan tradition in its transposed form makes easier reading both in the Greek and in translation seems to indicate that the original material in the oral tradition was so obscure to both evangelists, and also so important, that both felt compelled to include it, making of it what was possible in each author's arrangement. On the well-known critical principle that there are times when the more difficult reading is to be preferred, we worked almost exclusively on the Matthean version, in the hope that this might yield information which would account for its difficulty. Several points should be considered:

(a) A common *written* source can be ruled out, as Matthew's *heōs* (*up to,* vs. 13) and Luke's *mechri* (xvi 16) are good illustrations of independent translations of an original oral tradition. Cf. Introduction, Part III.

(b) Matthew's *arti* (*this moment,* vs. 12) is decidedly odd in its present position, and it is not explained by the suggestion that at the time of utterance in present context the disciples and Jesus himself were being persecuted. The interval from the death of John to "this moment" is far too short for this saying to be in context, and if it refers to the time after the passion it is meaningless as applied to Jesus.

(c) Verse 13 is not made easier by Luke's "The Law and the prophets were until John" (xvi 16). Not only is there a reversal of the traditional order in Matthew (*the prophets, and the Law*), but the verb *prophesied* abruptly ends the phrase and makes it almost meaningless.

(d) It is possible, by rearranging the material in vss. 12 and 13, to make more adequate sense and at the same time do justice to Luke's version. We suggest that the original reading was more or less as follows:

Apo de tōn hēmerōn tou nomou pantes gar hoi prophētai eprophēteusan . . . heōs Ioannou tou Baptistou . . . (Ap') arti hē basileia tōn ouranōn biazetai kai biastai harpazousin autēn. (From the time of the Law all the prophets prophesied . . . until John the Baptist. From that time the Kingdom of heaven is violently attacked and violent men lay hands on it.)

(e) In such a reconstructed text, it is likely that *eprophēteusan* was followed by *tēn basileian tōn ouranōn,* and its loss is quite easily explained in the transmission of a saying which seemed obscure to the copyist.

(f) We are convinced that the *Sitz-im-Leben* of these verses is explicable only when attention is paid to their present context in Matthew. In the original tradition, the person of John was central to the sayings, as is witnessed by vss. 14 and 15. Moreover, the phrase *until John the Baptist* would seem to indicate a *terminus ad quem* for the circle from which the sayings came. We suggest that the sayings came from a circle of John's disciples, and probably belong to the time after his execution. Such a time seems to be demanded by vs. 12b in the present version. The death of John must have seemed to his disciples to be nothing less than an attack on the Kingdom he had proclaimed. If the saying belongs to the same circle, but belongs in time after the crucifixion of Jesus, then the sayings are even more explicable. The number of John's disciples scattered throughout the Mediterranean is attested by the Acts of the Apostles, and news of the death of John, followed soon after by news of a similar fate in the case of Jesus, must have been a profound shock.

That these verses were a small block of material from Baptist circles, already firmly rooted in oral tradition but belonging outside the gospel tradition proper, is the best explanation for the way in which Matthew and Luke felt compelled to include it. Both were obviously at a loss to know how to deal with some of its obscurities, but in different contexts attempted to do justice to the material.

The work of J. A. T. Robinson, to which reference has already been made, has pointed out the very real difficulties we experience when we attempt to extract and examine Baptist fragments in the gospel tradition. A useful summary of what is possible, on the present reading of Matthew, is to be found in Sherman Johnson's commentary on Matthew in *The Interpreter's Bible* (Nashville; Abingdon, 1951), VII, pp. 382–83.

It is possible to read *the Law* in the sense of oral law as distinct from the Torah. Equally it is at least possible that we have even in the present order of the words a Baptist sentiment. The discovery of the so-called "Temple scroll" confirms the evidence already available, and held by many Jewish and Christian scholars, that the Essene community was formulating a Torah of its own, providing a canon of recognized scripture. The *halakah* of the Damascus Covenant was as rigorous as any Pharisaic teaching. (Cf. Yigael Yadin, "The Temple Scroll," BA 30 [1967].) It must be admitted, however, that this order in Matthew, followed by *eprophēteusan* (*prophesied*), makes very odd Greek.

14. *the expected Elijah*. Cf. Mal iv 5. The coming of Elijah to "restore the tribes of Jacob" is found in Ecclus xlviii 10, and the idea was common in later Judaism. Efforts to introduce here a saying of Rabbi Yohanan ben Zakkai (*B. Edujôth* viii 7)—who was active after the fall of Jerusalem—fail to carry conviction in the light of what we now know of the relation between Essene teaching and that of John the Baptist.

15. This saying comes again in xiii 9, 43; Mark iv 23; Rev ii 7, 11, 17, 29, iii 6, 13, 22, xiii 9. The phrase seems to be a fixed formula, and further complicates the question as to whether vss. 12–15 were ever intended to be understood as being from the lips of Jesus.

16–17. Just as in this allegory children wishing to play weddings or funerals find it impossible to evoke any response to either suggestion from their fellows, so neither the severe asceticism of John (cf. iii 4) nor the more flexible and humane approach of Jesus produces any response. These verses appear to be addressed to the self-conscious rectitude of the Pharisees, and Luke indicates this by his inserted verses in the parallel context (Luke vii 29–30).

The Man. Cf. NOTE on viii 20, on the translation of this term.

19. *a drunkard and a glutton*. Cf. ix 14 ff.

non-observant Jews. Cf. NOTE on ix 10.

wisdom is vindicated by her deeds. This is one of the two versions which the Greek text provides at this point. The other is "children" instead of *deeds*. Here *deeds* is the better attested reading, where Luke vii 35 has a better reading of "children." With these two readings, two interpretations are possible:

(a) *Wisdom* is the divine wisdom of God (cf. Luke xi 49). If we read *deeds*, as here in Matthew, then the saying asserts that God is his own interpreter, and the methods of both John and Jesus have place in God's providence, for all their seeming disparity and seeming failure.

This generation of vs. 16 may be wholly unresponsive to the divine call of John and Jesus, but for those who respond, the wisdom of God is justified in their deeds.

(b) By reading "children," as in Luke, several options are open to us. "Children of wisdom," as an equivalent term for "children of Israel," is attested in Prov viii 32 and Ecclus iv 11, with which we may compare "children of the Kingdom" in Matt viii 12 and xiii 38. In so reading we can interpret the saying as indicating that the *true* children will, by their response, vindicate the divine wisdom and its messengers.

By our translation here—*deeds*—we have attempted to do justice to the aorist tense of *vindicated* (*edikaiōthē*). In Matt xi 27 and xxviii 18 Matthew's use of the tense indicates a pretemporal ordering of events by divine providence, and here indicates that the wisdom of God is eternally vindicated by the course of history. But cf. the recent article by Robert Maddox, "The Function of the Son of Man according to the Synoptic Gospels," NTS 15 (1968–69), 65 f., for a most interesting suggestion.

COMMENT

The three sections which make up chapter xi (our §§43–45) would appear to be an arrangement by the evangelist to summarize Jesus' ministry in relation to three considerations: (a) Jesus' relationship to John the Baptist, (b) the seeming failure of Jesus' ministry, and (c) Jesus' own evaluation of his ministry.

The whole chapter has no parallel in Mark, and the points of similarity with Luke are such that it is very difficult to determine what prompted the arrangement of this material in so divergent a fashion. While it is true that vss. 2–19 are paralleled by Luke vii 18–35, there is very little parallel between vss. 2–3 and Luke's vss. 18–21, even though vss. 4–11 roughly parallel Luke's vss. 22–28. It is at this point—assuming a common source—that the difficulties begin. Here Luke (vss. 29–30), interjects a comment of his own, while Matthew apparently continues with the narrative. The whole tenor of the passage is such, however, that Matthew's vss. 12–15 appear to be derived from another context altogether. Moreover, Matthew's vss. 12–13 are found in Luke's xvi 16, where the order is transposed.

Comparison between Matthew and Luke reveals a pastiche of sayings: Matthew xi 16–19=Luke vii 31–35; Matt xi 20 is obviously an introductory comment, without hint of place or time;

Matt xi 21–23a agrees fairly well with Luke x 13–15, where it is found in the injunction to the seventy disciples. Verse 23b has no parallel in Luke, Matt xi 24=Luke x 12, and then vss. 25–27 are in close accord with Luke x 21–22 (on the return of the seventy). To round off the whole complex, Matt xi 28–30 has no parallel in Luke.

If the two evangelists were working from a common written source, then the arrangement is very odd. Matthew's vss. 20–30 appear to be isolated sayings grouped together for reasons indicated above. But if this is the case, and the source was already formalized, then why does Luke use some sayings from this source in his account of the mission of the seventy? In addition to this, it is impossible to clarify the nature of the relationship between Matt xi 4–11, 16–19 and Luke vii 22–28, 31–35. Both evangelists connect the two pieces of material, but each with an inserted comment which is of a wholly different character in each case. The difficulty of deciding what is, or is not, direct speech in John i 15–18 is well known, and we may have the same difficulty in Matthew's vss. 12–15 in this chapter.

What we appear to have is two groups of sayings dealing with John the Baptist, already fixed in oral tradition when Matthew and Luke compiled their gospels. Both evangelists therefore combined the sayings, but each independently of the other, as is demonstrated by the wholly different connecting material. If both had drawn from a common (written?) source in their editing of the Baptist sayings, it would be hard to say why both evangelists should have felt compelled to intrude comments of their own at exactly the same point. It is far more likely that here we have a common oral tradition, already hardened into blocks of material which the evangelists presented entire. The connecting links between the blocks of material may well represent other facets of the tradition which the two evangelists individually considered especially pertinent. (Cf. NOTES on vss. 12–15 above.)

44. DENUNCIATIONS
(xi 20–24) †

XI 20 Then he began to denounce the cities where most of his acts of power had been done, because they did not repent. 21 "Woe to you, Chorazin, woe to you, Bethsaida! For if the acts of power done in you had been performed in Tyre and Sidon they would long ago have repented in sackcloth and ashes. 22 But I tell you that it will be more tolerable for Tyre and Sidon in the day of judgment than for you. 23 And you, Capernaum—will you be lifted up to heaven? You will be brought down to the underworld, because if the acts of power done in you had been done in Sodom, it would have remained to this day. 24 But I tell you that it will be more tolerable for Sodom in the day of judgment than for you."

† Matt xi 20–24 || Luke x 13–15.

NOTES

xi 20. *Then*. This is not a temporal note; it is simply a connective with the preceding section. Luke's gospel has these denunciations in the mission-charge to the seventy disciples.

21. *Chorazin*. This place is mentioned in the Bible only here and at Luke x 13. It was the nearest town north of Capernaum, an hour's journey distant. We know nothing of any deeds of healing or exorcism by Jesus in Chorazin. *Bethsaida* was north of the Sea of Galilee, and on the east bank of the Jordan.

sackcloth and ashes. As signs of penitence or sorrow, cf. Isa lviii 5; Jon iii 6; Dan ix 3.

22. *Tyre and Sidon*. These were prosperous Phoenician cities in OT times, and the prophets had frequently inveighed against their sinfulness.

23. *Capernaum*. This has already been mentioned as Jesus' temporary

home (iv 13, viii 5, ix 1). It was a flourishing city, but though men might have been proud of its civic achievements, the city had failed to recognize the dawning reign of God in Jesus' teaching and deeds. In spite of its being a Jewish city, its failure to repent, along with its arrogance and pride, doomed it to the fate of *Sodom*, a byword in the OT for sinfulness (cf. NOTE on x 15).

lifted up to heaven. There is an echo here of an oracle of Isaiah (Isa xiv 13 ff.), and Capernaum's fate is compared with that of Babylon.

45. THE SON'S PRAYER
(xi 25–30)†

XI 25 At that time, Jesus said, "I thank you, Father, Lord
of heaven and earth, that you have hidden these things from
the wise and understanding, and revealed them to the childlike, 26 for such indeed, Father, was your gracious will.

27 "Everything has been delivered to me by my Father; no
one knows the Son, except the Father, and no one knows the
Father, except the Son, and anyone to whom the Son chooses
to reveal him.

28 "Come to me, all who labor and are heavily burdened,
and I will give you rest. 29 Take my yoke on your shoulders, and
learn from me, because I am gentle and humble in heart,
and you will find rest for your souls, 30 for my yoke is easy and
my burden is light."

† Matt xi 25–27 || Luke x 21–22.

Notes

xi 25. *I thank you* (Gr. *exomologoumai*). The word is used in the LXX
as being equivalent to "give praise." Cf. II Sam xxii 50; Ecclus li 1.

hidden. Cf. Isa xxix 14. The veiling of God's purposes from the self-
consciously wise is referred to by Paul in I Cor i 19, who also quotes
this verse from Isaiah.

these things. This is a reference to the acts of power which Jesus'
contemporaries could not evaluate as signs of the dawning Kingdom
(vss. 21, 23).

wise and understanding. The leaders of Israel, whose election by God
demanded that she respond to the manifestations of the divine wisdom,
had failed to see the signs of the Kingdom. The children of wisdom, the
childlike, had alone seen and understood.

26. *your gracious will* (literally, "for so it seemed good in your sight"). The phrase is common in later Hebrew/Aramaic as avoiding direct reference to God's will. Cf. TB, *Berakhoth* 17a, 29b, *Taanith* 24b.

27. The two preceding verses are found also in Luke x 21 ff., with very slight differences. This verse has no parallel in the other gospels, and it is this verse which has attracted the most attention from commentators. The difficulty for most writers lies in the implied relationship of Father-Son in this verse, found only here in Matthew, though the relationship is also implied in Luke and is most frequent in John's gospel. The discussion of the passage by Bultmann in Kittel's TWNT (p. 713) predictably argues for a later editorial origin, with Gnostic terminology. Bultmann calls attention to the (hardly surprising) fact that Strack and Billerbeck can find no parallel in the rabbinic literature. To list all relevant literature on this verse would be beyond the scope and purpose of this commentary, and our own conclusions can be summarized as follows:

(a) The argument that speaking of *the Son* in the third person betrays an origin wholly outside the mind of Jesus must be seen against the many occasions on which Jesus speaks of himself as *The Man* in the third person.

(b) Any discussion of vs. 27 must take into account the high incidence of sayings in which Jesus refers to "my Father" or "the Father," and such sayings are by no means exclusively Johannine. Moreover, in many such sayings the plain implication is that Jesus is *the* Son, or *his* Son.

(c) The term "son" as applied to Israel in general and to the anointed king in particular is well attested in the OT, and we have called attention to this both in Part XII of the Introduction and in the COMMENT on iv 1–11 (§9).

(d) In paying the closest and fullest attention to the Jewish background which was Jesus' inheritance, we should not think that Jesus brought no new insights to bear upon that inheritance. This is especially true of Jesus' interpretation of his Messianic vocation. The many and varied facets of Messianic expectation in the time of Jesus are becoming more and more evident, and the complexity of that expectation is now known to us in a way undreamed of thirty years ago. However, the feature of vs. 27 which causes most comment is the implied pre-existence of the Messiah indicated by the Greek aorist tense of *has been delivered* (Gr. *paredothē*). But we have no means of knowing how the original Hebrew or Aramaic text was understood, since the same tense would be used for aorist (past definite), imperfect (past continuous), and perfect (present perfect). This stage of transmission is very early, and translation into Greek meant that verbs took on a fixed tense-meaning which helped make systematic theology possible. It remains to be said that the pre-existence of the Messiah certainly seems to be indicated in Enoch xlviii 3, 6.

(e) Whether the words as spoken by Jesus implied a consciousness of pre-existence we cannot know. But the Markan tradition (Mark xiii 32), along with the passage under discussion, makes it clear that at a very early stage in the primitive Christian community such pre-existence was taken for granted.

(f) In much NT academic writing it is hard to escape the conclusion that commentators think they have found a neatly ordered stratum of primitive Christian belief, wholly self-consistent and with no awkward salients. Against this supposedly definable background they find it possible to contrast the alleged Hellenisms of Paul, hypothetical early Gnostics, and the theologizings of a supposedly late Johannine vocabulary. This familar Hegelian pattern then leads directly to the nascent "catholicism" of the early Church, with elements from the mystery religions introduced to make the usual critical amalgam. This picture, whatever validity it may have been thought to possess thirty or more years ago, has been rendered totally irrelevant by new knowledge from recent manuscript finds in Palestine and Egypt.

28–30. These verses are peculiar to Matthew. Considering the dependence of these verses in the Greek on the LXX of Ecclus li, the search for a Gnostic motif underlying them seems curiously labored (cf. "The Logion of the Easy Yoke and of Rest," by Hans Dieter Betz, JBL 86 [1967], 10–24). The references which bear directly on the Greek are as follows:

$$
\begin{array}{ll}
\text{Matt xi 25—Ecclus li 1, 10} \\
\qquad\text{xi 28—} \qquad\quad \text{li 23, 27} \\
\qquad\text{xi 29—} \qquad\quad \text{li 26, 27}
\end{array}
$$

For the final phrase of vs. 29, cf. Ecclus vi 28; Jer vi 16. The discovery of a first-century B.C. Hebrew text of Ecclesiasticus at Masada should finally put to rest any notions of the supposed dependence of vss. 28–30 on so-called Gnostic sources. Nor is there any evidence for an alleged pre-Christian Gnosticism in any Qumran sources.

29. *my yoke*. The Law is described as a yoke in *Pirqê Abôth* iii 6; and cf. also TB, *Berakhoth* 13a. Pss Sol vii 9 refers to God's service as "God's yoke."

Jesus' own view of his ministry, in the face of apparent failure, is one which involves a *light burden* and an *easy yoke*, for the commitment demanded is that of personal allegiance to himself. An *easy yoke* and a *light burden* are offered in exchange for the arbitrary demands of Pharisaic legalism and the uncertainties of ever-proliferating case law.

COMMENT

Every possible and impossible origin has been suggested for this section, from Gnosticism (usually undefined) to pagan Hellenistic mythology (normally unidentified). Generally, vss. 25–26 are accepted with extreme caution as belonging to an early tradition, while vs. 27 is rejected on the a priori grounds that this could not possibly have been uttered by Jesus. Verses 28–30 are accepted as dependent on Ecclus li 23–27, and probably therefore freely adapted OT themes attributed to Jesus by the evangelist or an editor. Our own comment is given above in the NOTES. We here call attention to the careful analysis of this section by A. Feuillet, "Jesus et la Sagesse divine d'après les Évangiles Synoptiques," CBQ 30 (1968), 573–79. He demonstrates the completely Semitic character and OT background of this section, and his notes and bibliography are excellent.

46. CONTROVERSY OVER THE LAW
(xii 1–15a)†

XII 1 At that time Jesus passed through the grain fields on the Sabbath, and his disciples, being hungry, began to pluck ears of grain to eat. 2 On seeing this, the Pharisees said to him, "Look, your disciples are committing an unlawful act on the Sabbath." 3 He replied, "Have you not read what David did, when he and his companions were hungry? 4 How he went into God's house and ate the bread of the Presence, which was not permitted to him or his companions for food, but was reserved for the priests only? 5 Or have you not read in the Law that on the Sabbath priests in the temple profane the Sabbath and are without guilt? 6 But I tell you that something greater than the temple is here, 7 and if you had known what this means: 'I wish for mercy and not sacrifice,' you would not have condemned the guiltless, 8 since The Man is lord of the Sabbath."

9 Going on from there, he went into their synagogue, 10 where there was a man with a withered hand. They demanded of him, "Is it permitted to heal on the Sabbath?"—so that they might have grounds to accuse him. 11 But he said to them, "What man is there among you, possessing a single sheep, who will not lay hold of it and haul it out, if it falls into a pit on the Sabbath? 12 And how much more valuable is a man than a sheep! Therefore, it *is* permitted to do good on the Sabbath." 13 He then said to the man, "Put out your hand,"

† **Matt xii 1–8** ‖ Mark ii 23–28, Luke vi 1–5; **9–14** ‖ Mark iii 1–6, Luke vi 6–11.

and he held it out, and it was restored, made whole like the other. 14 The Pharisees, however, consulted about how to destroy him. 15ª Jesus, being aware of this, withdrew from the place.

NOTES

xii 1. *At that time.* This is a formula peculiar to Matthew, and most formulae in Matthew appear in close association with each other; cf. "the report of this" (ix 26, 31); a Greek formula of arrival and departure (ii 1, 13, 19); *John came . . . Jesus came* (iii 1, 13); the formula on listening (xiii 9, 43); similar Greek constructions at viii 23, 28, ix 1, 9, xv 21, 29.

Sabbath. The origin of the Sabbath as a compulsory day of rest is obscure, and in the OT it is linked with the creation as an act of God's merciful providence (Gen ii 2 ff.). It is inappropriate to this commentary to provide a lengthy excursus on the development of the Sabbath, since by the time of Jesus the manner of its observance had long become fixed, except for minor cases where changing customs seemed to make adjustments necessary. For fuller information on the Sabbath, cf. Kittel's TWNT, ad loc., and more briefly the appropriate article in *A Theological Word Book of the Bible,* ed. Alan Richardson, London: SCM, 1950; New York: Macmillan, 1951.

to pluck ears of grain. Cf. TB, *Shabbath* 73b. This was one of the thirty-nine kinds of work forbidden on the Sabbath by later rabbinic law.

2–5. Jesus counters the criticism of the Pharisees in two ways. First, the disciples are technically breaking the Sabbath, but out of the pressure of hunger, and Jesus quotes an analogous situation (I Sam xxi 1–6). In addition, the charge is based not on the written Law, which permitted plucking grain which was not theirs (Deut xxiii 25), but on scribal hermeneutics about the Sabbath. Secondly, in this account Jesus cites the example of the temple clergy, who of necessity break the Sabbath law by doing work connected with the offering of sacrifice (Num xxviii 9, 10). It should be noted that this second justification is hardly appropriate, for the work of the temple clergy is not analogous to what the disciples were doing.

The Markan tradition is even more obscure. Mark ii 27–28, in asserting that the Sabbath was given for man's benefit, and therefore man may upon necessity work on the Sabbath, adds: "So The Man is Lord of the Sabbath." But it is the disciples, not Jesus, who are being attacked for Sabbath-breaking. Matthew, if he knew the Markan tradition, places the saying at the end (vs. 8). The formula in Mark ("and he said to them") *may* indicate that the saying is out of context. If so, it is yet another indication of the way in which the evangelists preserved all that was known to them of the oral tradition, though this often meant placing sayings out of context where they could best be accommodated. Matthew's placing of the saying at the end of the incident does not diminish the difficulty, and his repetition of Hos vi 6 (cf. ix 13) reads oddly in the context. Perhaps the best justification for the present position of *The Man is lord of the Sabbath* lies in the fact that there can be no more appropriate day than the Sabbath on which Jesus can fulfill his Messianic work.

6. *something greater than the temple.* Just as the law of the Sabbath must give place to the demands of sacrificial worship, by so much more it may be set aside by the Messiah's activity.

8. *since.* The Greek connective (*gar*) is essential to the argument at this point, if the saying is to remain in this context: the Messiah will be answerable for his community.

The Greek verbal agreements of Matthew and Luke against Mark in vss. 1–8, especially in vss. 1–4, are good illustrations of the dependence of these two evangelists on traditions other than Mark.

9. *Going on from there.* In varying forms, the phrase occurs five times in Matthew.

The Markan version of the incident (Mark iii 1–6) has all the signs of an eyewitness account, presumably derived from Peter.

10. Matthew's tradition says of the onlookers, *They demanded of him,* where the Markan tradition has them observing him with hostility.

11. If works of mercy to animals were lawful on the Sabbath, how much more the Messiah's work of restoration! It is worthy of notice that while Pharisees permitted the rescue of an animal on the Sabbath the Essenes apparently did not.

12. Luke has a similar saying (Luke xiv 1–6) in the context of another miracle. This is a typical case of the principle of *qal va-ḥomer,* arguing by analogy from the less to the greater. This was one of the Greek principles of logical reasoning introduced by Hillel the Elder into Pharisee legal analysis, a generation or two before this episode.

On miracles in general, the reader is referred to Part X of the Introduction, especially the concluding paragraphs.

14. *The Pharisees.* Mark iii 6 adds the Herodians (adherents of Herod) to the plotters.

15. There is a contrast here, continued into vs. 16, between the vociferous Pharisees and the quiet manner in which Jesus goes about his work.

COMMENT

The first section of this chapter is used by the evangelist to give typical examples of opposition to the Messiah. In the treatment of the first example it is interesting to note that both Matthew and Luke view the incident as a minor and insignificant breach of the Sabbath laws. Mark, less concerned with legal interpretation, almost makes the incident an act of idle destruction. Matthew and Luke alone record that the disciples were plucking ears of grain to eat—that is, on a technicality, they were "harvesting."

47. HEALINGS, EXORCISMS, CHALLENGES
(xii 15b–37)†

XII 15ᵇ Many followed him, and he healed them all, 16 ordering them not to make him known. 17 So was fulfilled what was said by Isaiah the prophet:

> 18 "Behold my servant whom I have chosen,
> my beloved with whom I am delighted;
> I will put my Spirit upon him,
> and he shall proclaim judgment to the Gentiles.
> 19 He will neither dispute nor shout aloud,
> nor will anyone hear his voice in the streets.
> 20 He will not break a bruised reed,
> or quench a smoldering wick,
> until he makes judgment victorious.
> 21 And in his name the Gentiles will hope."

22 Then a blind and dumb demoniac was brought to him, and he cured him, so that the dumb man spoke and saw. 23 All the crowds were astonished, and said, "Can this be David's son?" 24 But when the Pharisees heard it, they declared, "This man casts out demons—but only through the agency of Beelzebul, ruler of demons." 25 Jesus, knowing the inflamed state of their minds, said to them, "Every kingdom divided against itself falls into ruin, and no city or house divided against itself will stand. 26 If, therefore, Satan exorcizes Satan, he is thereby divided against himself. How then can his kingdom stand? 27 If I exorcize demons through the agency of Beelzebul, through whom do your sons do it? So they must

† **Matt xii 22–32** || Mark iii 20–30, Luke xi 14–23, xii 10; **33–37** || Luke vi 43–45.

be your judges. 28 But if I exorcize demons through the agency of God's Spirit, then without doubt the Kingdom of God is upon you. 29 How is it possible to enter a strong man's house to plunder his effects, unless one first binds the strong man? Then indeed he may plunder his house.

30 "He who is not with me is against me, and he who does not bring men together scatters them. 31 So then I tell you that every sin and blasphemy will be forgiven to men, but blasphemy against the Spirit will not be forgiven. 32 If anyone utters a word against The Man it will be forgiven, but whoever utters a word against the Holy Spirit will not be forgiven, either in this age, or in the age to come.

33 "Either produce a sound tree, and sound fruit too, or produce a rotten tree and rotten fruit with it, for a tree is known by its fruit. 34 You brood of vipers! Being evil, how can you speak what is good? For it is from the abundance of the heart that the mouth speaks. 35 A good man, out of his store of goodness, produces good things, while an evil man produces evil things out of his store of evil. 36 I tell you that on the day of judgment men will render account for every harmful word they utter, 37 for by your words you will be justified, and by your words you will be condemned."

NOTES

xii 17. *So was fulfilled.* Cf. NOTE on i 22.

18–21. The quotation is from Isa xlii 1–4, but it has little in common with the LXX version. It is clear that what we have here is either a translation of a recension not otherwise attested, but going back to Hellenistic times, or a translation done quite independently for the purpose in hand.

On the place of the quotation in Matthew's scheme, cf. Part IV of the Introduction. The Messiah is the embodiment of Israel's vocation as servant of the Lord.

On the Hebrew background of these verses, cf. John Grindel, "Matthew xii 18–21," CBQ 29 (1967), 110 ff.

18. *chosen.* (Gr. *hēretisa*). The verb *hairetizein* is late, and in I Chron xxviii 6 and Mal iii 17 of the LXX is used the sense of "adopt." On the

aorist tense of the verb, cf. NOTE on xi 27. Interestingly, as an example of the methods of copyists, Isa xlii 4a, b is omitted, as the copyist's eye (or the translator's) moved in the Hebrew text from one occurrence of *mishpāt* (judgment) in xlii 3c to the next occurrence in xlii 4b.

22. Mark has references at this point to a house, and to crowds (iii 20), details which Matthew either omits or does not know. Other instances of this sort of omission include viii 4 (Mark i 45); viii 16 (Mark i 33–34); ix 1 (Mark ii 2); xii 15 (Mark iii 9).

An examination of the relationship between the synoptic gospels at this point will illustrate the difficulty of attaching too definite a shape to the material commonly known as "Q." At the same time it will indicate the relatively fixed state of the tradition from which the evangelists worked.

```
Matt xii 22–23        =          Luke xi 14
         24–26 =Mark iii 22–26=Luke xi 15, 17–18
         27–28        =          Luke xi 19–20
            29 =Mark iii 27    =Luke xi 21–22
            30        =          Luke xi 23
         31–32b=Mark iii 28–30
         43–45        =          Luke xi 24–26
```

Mark's iii 22–30 is omitted where one might have expected it in Luke (vi 19 or viii 4), but as the table demonstrates most of it is found later. Luke combines a request for a sign (which is later in Mark) with the accusation of allegiance with demons. Luke's vss. 27–28 have no equivalent in Matthew, and Matthew's vss. 31–37 have no equivalent in Luke xi. Matthew's vss. 39–42=Luke xi 29–32.

The parallels of Matthew and Luke are in verbal agreement in the Greek against Mark, especially in Matthew's vs. 25 (Luke's vs. 17), and Matthew's vs. 26 (Luke's vs. 18). But even in their parallel to Mark iii 27, Matthew's tradition is far closer to Mark than to Luke. In Matthew there are two incidents, the first as reply to an accusation and the other Jesus' reaction to a demand for a sign; in Luke both are combined, but with interposed material at xi 27–28, without any parallel in Matthew.

The parallels are interesting, but cannot without grave difficulty be met by a presumption that Matthew and Luke had access to both Mark *and* an independent source. Such a presumption, on the evidence before us, calls for an extensive exercise in scissors-and-paste technique. What the situation does appear to demand is fairly rigidly defined blocks of oral tradition, loosely associated with regard to context.

23. *David's son*. On this Messianic title, cf. Part XII of the Introduction.

24. *Beelzebul*. "Baal The Prince." Cf. NOTE on x 25.

25. *city*. This of course included the territory around the city. *House* can also mean family or clan.

26. *Satan*. Cf. NOTE on iv 1.

27–28. Jesus, appealing to current Jewish practices of exorcism, throws the challenge back to his critics. On Jewish exorcism, cf. Acts viii 7, 9–24, xix 13, and Josephus *Antiquities* VIII. 46, 47.

At its best, first-century exorcism was just as effective a form of shock therapy as some experimentally demonstrated methods employed in medical therapy today. At its worst it was no less reliable than some popular forms of contemporary mental therapy.

27. *your sons*. I.e., "you," "your own people."

28. *God's Spirit*. Cf. Luke xi 20, which has "finger," on which cf. Exod viii 19.

Kingdom of God. The term occurs only four times in Matthew (cf. also xix 24, xxi 31, 43), and though the phrase is synonymous in Hebrew usage with "Kingdom of heaven," we have seen reason to find in Matthew a careful differentiation of meaning (cf. Parts VI, VII, and VIII of the Introduction). "Kingdom of God" in the Matthean tradition is applied to the Father's reign after the judgment of the End, and "Kingdom of heaven" to the continuing community of The Man, lasting up to the time of the judgment. Two possibilities may be adduced for the occurrence of "Kingdom of God" here:

(a) Granted the validity of our examination in the Parts of the Introduction to which we have referred, this example of "Kingdom of God" may have been overlooked by the evangelist—or later by a copyist—in assembling the material.

(b) It is also possible that this saying of Jesus was embedded so firmly in the tradition that the evangelist allowed it to stand in this context.

(c) This is the one occasion on which this gospel speaks of the "Kingdom of God" as having come. But it is to be noted that—whatever the origin of this solitary instance—the saying is set firmly in the context of the future judgment (xii 27, 36). Blasphemy against Jesus as The Man may be due to all manner of circumstances—misunderstanding his proclamation, for example—but after the entrance of The Man upon his reign (of which the exorcisms are a proleptic sign) such blasphemy will be against the Spirit who is already manifest in *this age*.

For all the difficulties inherent in this passage as it stands, we are not persuaded by a recent article (W. O. Walker, Jr., "The Kingdom of the Son of Man and the Kingdom of the Father in Matthew: An Exercise in Redaktionsgeschichte," CBQ 30 [1968], 573–79) of the invalidity of the distinction which we have found in this gospel between the "Kingdom of God" and the "Kingdom of heaven." See further C. K. Barrett, *The Holy Spirit and the Gospel Tradition,* New York: Macmillan / London: SPCK, 1947, a work to which Günter Bornkamm draws attention in his *Überlieferung und Auslegung im Matthäusevangelium,* Neukirchen, 1960.

is upon you. The Greek verb *phthanein* occurs only here and in Luke xi 20 in the synoptic gospels; it is a dramatically strong word.

29. *strong man's house.* There is here a striking commentary, in terms of the Messiah's vocation, on Isa xlix 24–26. Cf. also Pss Sol v 4. The very proclamation of the Kingdom was a victory over demonic forces, and the Messiah was gathering the fruits of that victory.

30. If the Messiah was following up an initial victory, then those who opposed him must take sides on what they witnessed. Cf. the reply of Jesus in Luke ix 50; the use of the Messiah's name implies a certain commitment to him.

31–32. The illustrative material from Qumran, and in particular the Rule of the Community (1QS), has provided invaluable control evidence for the ethical dualism of much NT language. This is not confined to the contrasted pairs of the Johannine literature (truth, falsehood; light, darkness; good, evil; etc.). It also gives us firm ground for interpreting this passage. Prior to the discovery of the material now available to us from Qumran, the difficulties of the commentators at this point were understandable.

To speak against *The Man* in *this age* of the Kingdom's proclamation may be due to all manner of misunderstanding, for The Man has not yet entered upon his reign. But speaking against the *Spirit,* either in *this age* of proclamation, or in the *age to come* (i.e., in the time of the Kingdom's inauguration) is the ultimate sin. So with the Messianic work in *this age:* to confuse the Spirit of truth with the spirit of falsehood, to confuse the Messiah's work with that of Beelzebul, is blasphemy.

The principal difficulty always resided in posing the question as: "It is pardonable to speak against The Man, unpardonable to speak against the Holy Spirit." Thus stated, it seemed to be asking too much of Jesus' critics to distinguish between the Messiah acting as such, even though veiled in the humility of mundane circumstance, and the Messiah acting through the power of the Spirit.

32. *The Man.* Cf. NOTE on viii 20. This saying certainly looks to the future of the Messianic Community in the Matthean tradition, for in Matthew "The Man" belongs to a Kingdom inaugurated and in being.

33–35. This is similar in content to vii 17–20 in the Great Instruction. The Lukan tradition (vi 43–45) has more in common with this section than with the similar sayings in ch. vii.

Jesus' critics are being warned of the alternative: either the results of the exorcisms are wholly good, and hence the work of the Spirit, or the results are evil, and so demonic in origin.

36–37. The Syriac text has *"mellā baṭṭālā."* In both Aramaic and later Hebrew, the words from the stem *bṭl* mean both "lazy" and "hurt-ful." Excuses about hasty judgment, speaking on the spur of the moment, cannot be accepted when the subject matter is as serious as good and evil. The sayings look back to the accusation that Jesus was involved in an alliance with Satan.

48. DEMAND FOR A SIGN
(xii 38–45) †

XII 38 Then some of the scribes and Pharisees asked him, "Teacher, we want to see a sign from you."

39 But he answered them, "An evil and adulterous generation seeks avidly for a sign, and no sign will be given to it apart from that of the prophet Jonah. 40 For just as Jonah was in the monster's body three days and three nights, so The Man will be in the heart of the earth for three days and three nights. 41 The men of Nineveh will stand up at the judgment with this generation, and will condemn it, for they repented at the preaching of Jonah. And something more than Jonah is here. 42 The queen of the south will rise up in the judgment with this generation and will condemn it, for she came from the boundaries of the earth to listen to the wisdom of Solomon. And something more than Solomon is here.

43 "When an unclean spirit has left a man, he wanders through dry places, looking for a resting place, but finds none. 44 Then he says: 'I will go back to the house that I left,' and when he returns he finds it vacant, cleaned, and in order. 45 He therefore goes and brings with him seven other spirits more evil than himself, and they enter and take up residence. The last state of that man becomes worse than the first."

† Matt xii 38–39 ‖ Mark viii 11–12; 38–42 ‖ Luke xi 29–32; 43–45 ‖ Luke xi 24–26.

Notes

xii 39. *adulterous*. In contemporary Jewish idiom, this was the equiv-
alent of "idolatrous." Idolatry, all through the OT and in the time of
Jesus, was always identified with sexual excess of all kinds. See W. F.
Albright, *Archaeology and the Religion of Israel*, especially pp. 84–94,
and *Yahweh and the Gods of Canaan* (London: Athlone Press / New
York: Doubleday, 1968), especially pp. 115–52.

39–42. *sign of . . . Jonah*. What is common to *Jonah*, the *queen of the
south*, and *Solomon*, is the uttering of, and a listening to, the word of
God. In the person of Jesus *more than Jonah, more than Solomon* is
among men, for now the sign of the dawning Kingdom of the Messiah
is present.

40. *For just as Jonah*. It is best to describe this verse as editorial,
whether from the hands of the evangelist, or from someone puzzled by
vs. 39. What is being discussed is the sign of proclamation. There is no
indication from the book of Jonah that the Ninevites heard of, and
accepted, the prophet's adventures as a kind of accreditation.

41–42. *the judgment*. I.e., the last judgment. Matthew generally uses
the phrase *the day of judgment* (cf. x 15, xi 22, 24, xii 36).

42. *queen of the south*. I.e., of South Arabia.

43–45. Comment is unnecessary by way of emphasizing the psychological truth embodied in these verses. The reader is referred to Dr.
Sargant's *Battle for the Mind*.

In the Lukan context, the verses are so placed as to appear to be
intended for commentary on the failure of contemporary Jewish exorcism. In Matthew they are commentary on Israel's failure to repent,
and failure to heed the Messiah's proclamation.

43. *dry places*. The ancient belief that desert places are the abode of
evil spirits can be traced back to ancient Mesopotamia, in Babylonian
incantations, and it also finds a place in the OT ritual of the scapegoat
on the Day of Atonement (cf. Lev xvi 8 ff.). Cf. Isa xiii 21, xxxiv 14;
Mark v 10; Rev xviii 2.

COMMENT

The links between this section and the preceding are clear, and
are spelled out verbally in Luke xi 16. Failure to recognize the
signs of the dawning Kingdom in the conflict of the Messiah with
the forces of evil operating in man was but the obverse side of
an attempt to put Jesus to the test.

It is possible to interpret most of this chapter xii as containing
in microcosm the judgment of Jesus on contemporary Israel. The
controversy on the Sabbath laws, ending in the synagogue, is concluded at vs. 15 by *withdrew from the place*. This may be a note
of time and circumstance, but in view of the material in the rest
of the chapter it may also mark a turning point in the ministry.
The Messianic Servant's charter (vss. 18–21) is followed by the
Pharisees' accusations of diabolical alliance when the crowd was
asking about Jesus' possible Messiahship (vss. 22–24). It is therefore possible to see vss. 25–28 in the section above (§47) as
referring to the fatally divided house of Israel: it is the house of
Israel which has been seized upon by evil forces (cf. John viii 44).
If this interpretation is correct, then Jesus came to lay siege to
the strong man's house, to Satan's control of Israel, having first
won a decisive victory against the devil in the desert. Those
who oppose him are on Satan's side, calling good evil, and so failing
to distinguish between the Spirit of truth and the spirit of falsehood
(vss. 30–32). The present section then carries on the argument,
and lines of separation are being drawn even within Israel.

49. THE MOTHER AND BROTHERS OF JESUS
(xii 46–50) †

XII ⁴⁶ While he was talking to the crowds, his mother and brothers were outside, wishing to speak to him. ⁴⁷ Someone said to him, "Your mother and your brothers are outside, wishing to speak to you." ⁴⁸ He answered his informant, "Who is my mother, and who are my brothers?" ⁴⁹ Then gesturing with his hand to his disciples, he said, ⁵⁰ "See—my mother and my brothers. For whoever does the will of my Father in heaven, that person is my brother, sister, and mother."

† **Matt xii 46–50** ‖ Mark iii 31–35, Luke viii 19–21.

NOTES

xii 46. *While he was talking.* There is no indication of place, and his mother and brothers waiting *outside* might apply equally well to a house or to the fringes of the crowd.

his mother and brothers. Apart from chapters i and ii, and the mention of her with Jesus' *brothers* and *sisters* in xiii 53 ff., this is the only occasion in Matthew where Jesus' mother appears. We know nothing of the brothers of Jesus. How old the tradition is we do not know, but it has been commonly held in both eastern and western Christendom, at least from the fourth century, that the brothers here referred to were either cousins, or children of Joseph by an earlier marriage. Matt i 25 can be taken to mean that children were born to Mary and Joseph subsequent to the birth of Jesus.

47. This verse is omitted in some manuscripts, and is also omitted in RSV.

49. The disciples are the beginning of the Messianic Community, and so are members of the Messiah's family.

50. Obedience to the Father's will is the foundation of the community. (Cf. here the prayer of Jesus for the community in John xvii.)

COMMENT

If we accept the interpretation offered in Section 48, then this apparently unrelated instance follows logically. Mere natural affiliation does not determine membership either of Israel or the Messianic community. The only criterion is obedience to the Father's will—a plea wholly in line with the Israelite prophetic tradition (cf. John the Baptist's strictures in iii 9).

50. PARABLES OF THE KINGDOM
(xiii 1–52)†

XIII 1 On that day, Jesus left the house and sat by the sea. 2 Great crowds gathered round him, so much so that he got into a boat and sat there, with the crowds on the beach. 3 He taught them a good deal in parables, as follows: 4 "A sower went out sowing, and in the process some seeds fell along the path and the birds came and devoured them. 5 Some, however, fell on stony ground where they had not much soil, and they immediately grew upwards because there was no depth to the soil. 6 But when the sun rose they were scorched and for lack of roots withered away. 7 Other seeds fell among thorns, and the thorns grew up and choked them. 8 Yet others fell on good soil and produced grain, some a hundredfold, some sixty, and some thirty. 9 Let him who has understanding listen."

10 The disciples came to him with the inquiry, "Why do you speak to them in parables?" 11 He replied, "It has been granted to you to know the mysteries of the Kingdom of heaven, while to them it has not been so granted. 12 For to the man who has, more will be given and he will have abundance, while from the man who has not, even what he has will be taken away. 13 Therefore I address them in parables, since for all their looking they do not see, and for all their hearing they neither listen nor understand. 14 For them is fulfilled the saying of Isaiah the prophet:

'You will certainly hear, but never understand,
and you will certainly see, but never perceive.

† **Matt xiii 1–9** || Mark iv 1–9, Luke viii 4–8; **10–12** || Mark iv 10–12, Luke viii 9–10; **18–24** || Mark iv 13–20, Luke viii 11–15; **31–33** || Mark iv 30–32, Luke xiii 18–21; **34** || Mark iv 33–34.

15 For this people's heart has grown dull,
    their ears sated with hearing,
    and they have closed their eyes,
    lest they should perceive with their eyes,
    listen with their ears,
    and understand with their mind,
    and turn for me to heal them.'

16 But your eyes are fortunate because they see, and your ears, too, for they listen. 17 I solemnly tell you that many prophets and righteous ones have ardently wished to see the things you see, and have not seen them; to hear the things you hear and have not heard them.

18 "Listen then to the parable of the Sower. 19 When anyone hears the word of the Kingdom and does not understand it, the Evil One comes and snatches away what was sown in his heart. This is what was sown along the path. 20 As for what was sown on stony ground, this is the man who hears the word and immediately embraces it with enthusiasm. 21 But he has no root in himself, and lasts only for a time, and when trial or persecution arises because of the word, he immediately falls. 22 As for what fell among thorns, this is the man who hears the word, but worldly worries and care for wealth choke the word and it becomes unproductive. 23 But in the case of what was sown in good soil, this is the man who hears the word and understands it; he certainly produces fruit, making in one case a hundredfold, in another sixty, and in another thirty."

24 He put to them another parable, in this way: "The Kingdom of heaven may be compared with a man who sowed good seed on his land. 25 While men were sleeping, however, his enemy came and sowed weeds in the wheat, and went away. 26 Thus, when the plants came up and bore grain, the weeds also appeared. 27 The householder's servants came and said to him, 'Sir, did you not sow good seed on your land? How then does it happen that it has weeds?' 28 He answered them, 'An enemy has done this.' Thereupon the servants said,

'Is it your wish, then, that we go and gather them up?' 29 But he replied, 'No—lest in gathering the weeds you root up the wheat at the same time. 30 Let both grow together until harvest, and at harvesttime I will give orders to the reapers to gather the weeds first, and bind them in bundles for burning, but to gather the wheat into my granary.' "

31 He put before them another parable: "The Kingdom of heaven is like a grain of mustard seed, which a man (took and) sowed on his land. 32 It is the smallest of all seeds, but when it is grown it is the largest of the shrubs and becomes a tree, so that the birds of the air come and make nests in its branches." 33 He put before them another parable: "The Kingdom of heaven is like yeast which a woman took and put into three measures of flour until it was all leavened."

34 Jesus said all this to the crowds in parables, and he said nothing to them without a parable. 35 In this way was fulfilled the saying of the prophet:

"I will speak in parables,
I will declare what has been hidden since the foundation
of the world."

36 Then he left the crowds and went into the house. His disciples followed him, and asked him, "Explain to us the parable of the weeds on the land." 37 His reply was, "He who sowed the good seed is The Man. 38 The land is the world, and the good seeds are the children of the Kingdom. The weeds are the children of the Evil One, while the enemy who sowed them is the devil; 39 the harvest is the end of the age, and the reapers are angels. 40 As, then, the weeds are gathered and burned in the fire, so will it be at the consummation of the natural order. 41 The Man will send his messengers to gather out of his Kingdom all causes of sin and all evil-doers, and 42 they will throw them into the fire; there will be shrieking and grinding of teeth. 43 Then the righteous will shine as the sun in the Kingdom of their Father. Let him who has understanding listen.

44 "The Kingdom of heaven is like treasure hidden in a

field, which a man discovered and buried, and then in his
joy proceeds to sell all that he has to buy that field. 45 Again,
the Kingdom of heaven is like a merchant searching for fine
pearls; 46 on finding one very valuable pearl, he proceeded to
sell all that he had and bought it. 47 Once more, the Kingdom
of heaven is like a net cast into the sea, which gathered every
kind of fish. 48 When it was full, men hauled it ashore,
sat down and sorted the usable fish into storage, but threw
the unusable away. 49 It will be so at the consummation of
the natural order. The angels will come out, separate the
wicked from among the righteous, 50 and throw them into the
furnace of fire. There will be shrieking and grinding of teeth.
51 Have you understood all this?" And they replied "Yes."
52 He then said to them, "Therefore every scribe who has
been trained for the Kingdom of heaven may be compared
with a householder who produces from his storeroom both old
and new things."

NOTES

xiii 1–9. Cf. Introduction, Part XI, The Parable Audience.
crowds. Cf. second NOTE on iv 3.
4. *sower.* It is not clear in this short section (xiii 1–9) whether Jesus
or the Father is represented as the sower. But the present infinitive of
the verb *to sow* would appear to indicate that this was a continuous
action—i.e., Jesus is continually adding to the Kingdom.
10. *the disciples.* Cf. Introduction, Part V.
At this point, Luke (viii 9) has the disciples "asking him the meaning
of the parable." Mark's Greek is decidedly awkward at this point (iv 10),
and this may be an indication that what follows was fitted in here from a
body of oral tradition.
11. Cf. Mark iv 11, which has a scheme which can be detailed like
this:

The mystery of the Kingdom	Everything
is given	is taught
to you	to those outside
(directly).	in parables.

mysteries. The Kingdom itself, as a Messianic idea, was not only
familiar to the disciples, it was known and awaited with eager expecta-

tion by the Jews. What was granted to the disciples, through their discipleship, was access to the innermost secrets of the Father's providence,
in much the same way that the prophets claimed access to God's heavenly council (*sôd*). Cf. Introduction, Part XI. This meaning of *mystery*, as referring to the prior decisions of God, has been put beyond
question by the work of Raymond E. Brown, largely based on the Dead
Sea scrolls: cf. *The Semitic Background of the Term "Mystery" in the
New Testament*, Philadelphia: Fortress Press, 1968.

12. This idea will be repeated again in xxv 29 in the parable of the
journeying property owner. Cf. Mark iv 25.

The passage is obscure. On the surface the saying deals with spiritual
capacity, with the gift of faith, which—it is implied—the disciples have,
but not the crowds. Hence real or imagined "case law" is taught to the
latter, to enable them to seek the response of faith. However, this is not
very satisfactory, for parable teaching would (vs. 12b) only succeed in
removing from the crowds even the little they have already. It is far
better to interpret the saying as dealing with a spiritual *inheritance,* and
not the capacity for faith. The disciples—Jews, like the members of
the crowd—were humble enough to learn from their inheritance as it was
expounded by Jesus. To them more would be added, i.e., an inheritance
in the Kingdom. To those who had vacated their inheritance by opposition to the proclamation (cf. COMMENT on §48), their reliance on the
Old Covenant would be valueless.

14–17. The introduction of this quotation (from the LXX of Isa vi
9 ff.) does not have the familiar Matthean *hina plērōthē̦*, "so was fulfilled." The total context of the passage in Isaiah determines its place
and meaning here. Cf. Introduction, Part IV, Parables.

16. *But your eyes are fortunate.* The Lukan version (x 23–24) puts
this saying, in a different form, in the context of the return of the
seventy disciples. The *your* is emphatic here (*humōn de*), in contrast
with *them* (*autois, ekeinois*) of vss. 10, 11, 13, 14.

17. *many prophets and righteous ones.* There may be a distinction
drawn here between the two. Attention has already been called to the
fact that *Righteous One* as a Messianic title (cf. Acts vii 52) has a long
and still elusive OT and intertestamental background. It is worth noticing
here that only Noah is described as *the righteous one* without qualification in the OT (Gen vi 9, vii 1), while in the intertestamental material
only Abraham and Simon the high priest are so designated in addition
to Noah (Ecclus xliv 17, 19–21; Josephus *Antiquities* XII. 2, 5). Too
much should not be read into the verse here, which may simply be an
assertion that it was not only prophets who looked for a future revelation
of the hidden divine will. It is equally possible that we have an hendiadys
here—i.e., "the righteous prophets."

18. This verse must be regarded as belonging to a very early stage
of the tradition, but not as coming from Jesus himself. In the first

place, the titles *the parable of the sower,* and the similar *the parable of the weeds* in vs. 36 are the only examples of such titles in the NT. Secondly, even the title here is incorrect, for the parable has more to do with the ground than with the sower. Thirdly, Jesus is rarely recorded as having explained his parables in anything like the detail given here. Fourthly, one must note that the explanation is offered to those (*the disciples,* vs. 10) who have already been told that they are privy to the prior decisions of God and hence have no need of parable instruction. The very confusion between the synoptic gospels here gives us some indication of what has happened. Mark iv 13 represents Jesus questioning the inability of the disciples to understand; Luke viii 9–10 simply says that Jesus explained the parable. It is possible that what we have here, as also in the explanation of the parable of the weeds (vss. 36–43), is uncertainty at a very early stage of the community's history as to what the "coming" of The Man meant. The first explanation has nothing to say about the harvest in terms of The Man's Kingdom, while the second sounds more like the words of Jesus used to describe the Kingdom on quite another occasion.

So far as the present explanation is concerned, it must have been part of the fixed tradition from an early date. It is otherwise impossible to account for its being attributed to Jesus himself. The care taken in preservation of the oral tradition was such as to allow little room for post-apostolic manipulation. Most likely it belongs to a period very shortly after the expansion of the community, when Christians were puzzled by the failure in consecration on the part of some neophytes.

The uncertainty about the interpretation is demonstrated by the confusion which Mark displays between the seed sown (cf. Mark iv 14, 15) which, being the proclamation of the word, may be presumed to be of divine origin, and the state of the ground into which that seed fell. Cf. also the same confusion in Mark iv 16, 17, extended into 18–19. Luke's version (viii 11–15) similarly exhibits confusion between the seed, as word of God, and the ground into which it falls.

It is possible to conclude that there were originally two parables, one concerning seed, and the other about the ground, with a subsequent conflation of content.

24–30. *may be compared* (Gr. *homoiōthē*). Matthew has this regular formula, varied by *homoia esti,* in the customary Jewish manner of introducing any cases which he does not share with the Markan tradition. He has a simpler form at xxv 14 (*hōsper*).

It would appear that Matthew's tradition contained a block of parable sayings (the weeds, the mustard seed, the yeast, the treasure, the pearl, the net) with an ending. The predilection of this gospel for arrangements taken over from the mnemonic devices of oral recitation (in this case two groups of three) would dictate the insertion of a parable explanation at vss. 36–43.

An examination of this block (xiii 24–50) with Mark iv 26–34, on the usual theory that Matthew used, and then rearranged, the Markan material, cannot adequately explain some oddities. Why did Matthew leave aside Mark at xiii 24, then use Mark iv 33–34, and having done so place it after the saying on yeast, rather than leave it where it was in the Markan place after the mustard seed? Moreover, on the usual synoptic theory he omits Mark's iv 21–25 at vs. 31, while the material parallel to the Markan tradition is scattered throughout Matthew. For example, Mark iv 21=Matt v 15; Mark iv 22=Matt x 26; Mark iv 23=Matt xi 15; Mark iv 24=Matt vii 2; Mark iv 25=Matt xiii 12. Even allowing for the diverse manifestations of the oral tradition, this calls more for access to an independent tradition than for a scissors-and-paste technique with an oral tradition already committed to writing.

30. *harvest*. Cf. iii 12. There is no parallel in Mark or Luke to this parable, though Mark (iv 26 ff.) has words in common with Matthew: "were sleeping," "came up," "wheat," "grain," "harvest." The emphasis in the Markan story is different, but the eschatological interest has the same clarity in both by the use of the word "harvest." To explain this parable of Jesus in terms of the opposition to him, as though there is a direct equation between *weeds* and the Pharisees, may indicate the viability of parable as a form of instruction, but by virtually identifying the disciples with the good grain it also identifies them with the elect at the harvest—an identification specifically ruled out in chapter xxiv.

burning. Fire is constantly used in Matthew to describe the judgment (cf. iii 10, v 22, vii 19, xiii 40, 42, xviii 8–9, xxv 41).

31–33. It is a mistaken interpretation which sees in these sayings an assertion of the silent, gradual growth of the Kingdom. In all of them, the emphasis is on the sheer miracle of the growth of the Kingdom.

32. *largest of the shrubs*. The mustard shrub commonly grows to a height of ten feet by the Sea of Galilee.

birds of the air. Cf. Dan iv 21, from which this half of the verse is a quotation. Nebuchadnezzar's kingdom gathered vassal nations; the Kingdom of heaven will also gather men from far off.

There are agreements in the saying about the mustard seed between Matthew and Luke as opposed to Mark. Once again, in this saying it is just as plausible to suppose—on the usual synoptic theory—that Luke used Matthew and Mark, as it is to think that Mathew combined Mark with "Q."

34. It is clear that the above sayings were addressed to the crowds, and not to the disciples.

35. Ps lxxviii 2, from which this quotation is taken, is a rehearsal of Israelite history, in obedience and rebellion, up to the establishment

of the Davidic monarchy. Once more, we emphasize that this is no
mere OT proof text; cf. Part IV of the Introduction.

36. If we may judge from the confusion in the Markan parallel to vss.
18–23, then we may question whether the explanation that follows is
from the lips of Jesus.

37. *The Man*. As we saw in the Introduction (Parts VI and VII), it is
The Man who calls men into his own field, the Kingdom of heaven.

38. *children of the Kingdom*. The phrase was used in viii 12, but there
had the sense of those who had been chosen for the Kingdom, but had
failed in their vocation.

40. *the consummation of the natural order*. This is a constant theme
in Jewish apocalyptic literature. Cf. Testament of Levi x; Apocalypse
of Baruch xiii 3, xxvii 15, liv 21, lxxxiii 7; Enoch xvi 1; Dan xii 13; II
Esdras vii 113. Cf. also Heb ix 26. It is undoubtedly the sense of the
Qumran expression *gemar haq-qēṣ*, where it means "the end of the present age" (i.e., created order). This phrase is repeated in vs. 49. The
Greek phrase can also mean "the end of the present age"—an understanding of the ministry of Jesus characteristic of Pauline thought.

41–43. This illustrates the point made in Part VI of the Introduction:
the Kingdom of The Man is coincidental in time and extension with the
Messianic Community and is temporary. Membership in that community
in no way guarantees inclusion among the *righteous* in the Kingdom of
the Father. Cf. Dan xii 1; Ecclus 1 7.

Let him . . . Cf. NOTE on xi 15.

44–46. These sayings may refer to the mission of Jesus seeking men
for his Kingdom, with a plain statement of the price which must be paid
for that Kingdom's inauguration. Similarly, they may indicate the sacrifice demanded of those who come to the Messianic Kingdom. In the
context in which they were first spoken, they may have reference back
to vs. 11: the disciples are in present possession of a secret, that of the
identity of the Messiah and his impending reign.

Certainly there is a call here for sacrifice and detachment, a steadfast regard for the treasure which the disciples already possess, and
alongside which all else is counted for nothing.

hidden in a field. The practice of hiding valuables in the ground, especially in times of crisis and insurrection, was common enough throughout the Middle East, and has by no means been unknown in Europe
down to our own times.

pearl. Pearls were in great demand in the ancient world, and ranked
with gold as symbols of wealth (cf. vii 6).

There is no parallel to these sayings in Mark or Luke.

47–50. This parable re-emphasizes the theme of the weeds in vss. 24–
30, of separation at the end of the Messianic age.

48. *usable . . . unusable.* This may refer to good or bad fish simply, or—symbolically—to ritually "clean" and "unclean" fish (cf. Lev xi 9 ff.). Mark and Luke have no parallel to this saying, though commentators sometimes refer to John xxi 11, in which connection it is thought that the ancients found the total number of different varieties of fish to be 153.

51–52. The disciples have heard two kinds of instruction in this chapter: the public part in vss. 1–8 and 31–33, and the private explanations and further parables relating to the Kingdom in the remainder of the chapter.

old and new. This may refer to the Law and the Proclamation, or to the new revelation in Jesus of the prior decisions of God, with a reference back to Ps lxxviii 2.

COMMENT

On parables in general, the reader is referred to Part XI of the Introduction.

This section is concerned with the Kingdom which Jesus proclaimed. The presentation of case law to the crowds, followed by the explanations which appear in our present text, altogether makes up an illustration of the way in which parables came to be quoted in various contexts and used to illustrate quite diverse points.

51. UNBELIEF
(xiii 53–58) †

XIII 53 When Jesus had finished these parables, he went away from there 54 and came into his own native town. He taught them in their synagogue, and they were amazed: "Where did he acquire this power and this wisdom? 55 Isn't this the builder's son? Isn't his mother named Mary? And are not his brothers James, Joseph, Simon, and Judas? 56 Aren't his sisters here? Where did he acquire all this?" 57 So they were shocked by him. But Jesus said to them, "A prophet is only without honor in his native town and in his own home," 58 and because of their unbelief he was unable to perform many acts of power there.

† **Matt xiii 53–58** || Mark vi 1–6, Luke iv 16–30.

NOTES

xiii 53–58. The unbelief with which Jesus was faced in the earlier material of this chapter now finds expression in Jesus' own home territory, in Galilee.

54. The last mention of teaching in a synagogue is found here (cf. iv 23, ix 35, xii 9), and Matthew would seem deliberately to have qualified the word *synagogue* with *their* to express the growing rift between Jesus and official Judaism.

55–56. *mother . . . sisters*. Cf. NOTE on xii 46.

builder's son. The Markan tradition (vi 3) has "builder," and it also adds "among his own relatives" (Mark vi 4).

It is important in view of the widespread and romantic notion concerning Joseph's occupation as a "carpenter" that we look at the Greek here. The word *tektōn*, translated by us as *builder*, has a wide range of meanings, from a shipbuilder to a sculptor, but it generally indicates a craftsman of considerable skill. The word can even be used of a physician. It seems clear that so far from Joseph being the simple—and poor—village carpenter making ox yokes or simple plows (which any peasant was capable of producing), he was probably a builder of some consequence, traveling over wide areas of country. So seen, the sacrifice involved in the self-renunciation of Jesus (cf. Matt viii 20) is far more radical than it is when seen against a background of village carpenter. It is worth adding here that our present English "architect," directly derived from the same Greek word, certainly does not mean a man of limited accomplishments.

The Aramaic word *naggārā* covered both a maker of household furnishings or farm tools and a builder. In those days (as had been true for at least two thousand years, to say nothing of more recent times), master craftsmen were generally itinerants traveling alone or with their families from city to city as work became available. This must have been especially true of a builder. In June 1968, an ossuary was excavated in Jerusalem bearing the Aramaic inscription "Simon—he built the temple." In the same way Joseph may have spent much of his working life as a builder in Jerusalem. In view of the implied statement (see also Luke iv 22 and John vi 42) that some of the people of Nazareth did not know Jesus by sight when he first appeared after the beginning of his public ministry, though he must have been by that time at least thirty, it is clear that he had never spent much of his time in Nazareth. Nor presumably had his father.

Nazareth was ideally situated for an itinerant builder, since he could settle his family comfortably within a short walk from the main roads which led to such coastal cities as Ptolemais (Acre) and Caesarea, or Tiberias on the Sea of Galilee and Gadara overlooking the Sea of Galilee from the southeast. All these and many other important towns such as Sebaste (Samaria) could be reached by donkey in a single day. Such cities as Caesarea, Samaria, and Tiberias were rebuilt just before or after the Christian Era.

COMMENT

It is noticeable that from this point onwards the narrative part of Matthew is in fairly close accord with the Markan scheme, though this is not true of the teaching material which Matthew incorporates up to chapter xviii.

There is, however, one clear difference. Mark's scheme works up to the acknowledgment of Jesus as Messiah by Peter, and from that moment Mark strides on rapidly to the passion narrative.

Matthew, however, who has represented the disciples in xiii 51–52 as being in possession of the Kingdom's secrets, has yet to deal with their hesitancies and failures. His scheme provides for side glimpses of Jesus' dealings with Gentiles, for the execution of John, and for the continued and growing hostility of the Pharisees.

52. DEATH OF JOHN THE BAPTIST
(xiv 1–12)†

XIV 1 At this time, the tetrarch Herod, hearing of the fame of Jesus, 2 said to his servants, "This is John the Baptist who has been raised from the dead; that is why these acts of power are working in him." 3 For Herod had seized John and thrown him into prison, over the affair of Herodias, wife of his brother Philip, 4 because John had said to him, 5 "It is unlawful for you to have her." But although he wanted to put him to death, he was afraid of the common people, who regarded him as a prophet. 6 However, when Herod's birthday came round, Herodias' daughter danced before the company and pleased Herod—7 so much so that he promised (under oath) to give her whatever she might desire. 8 Prompted by her mother, she said, "Give me here on a platter the head of John the Baptist." 9 The king was sorry, but on account of his oaths and his guests, he commanded it to be given, 10 and he sent and had John beheaded in prison. 11 His head was brought on a platter to the girl, who gave it to her mother, and 12 his disciples came, removed the body and buried it, and then came and told Jesus.

† **Matt xiv 1–12** ‖ Mark vi 14–29, Luke ix 7–9.

NOTES

xiv 1. *At this time.* Cf. xi 25, xii 1.

Herod. I.e., Herod Antipas, one of the sons of Herod the Great. He is called *tetrarch,* which had come to mean "ruler of a subdivision (of a province)," rather than "king," though vs. 9 in fact uses the title *king.*

2. *acts of power*. This is reference to the miracles of Jesus.

3. In the Markan account, it is Herodias who wished for John's death, and Herod who resisted it out of his regard for John. Matthew lays the blame at Herod's door. Such variations in the tradition give us a perspective which enhances our respect for the independence of the gospel records. If all accounts tallied on every score, then we would have every right to entertain great suspicion that the whole account had been "rigged" or manipulated in the interests of unanimity.

Some manuscripts omit Philip, presumably because it is probable that Herodias was not the wife of Philip but of another Herod who was half-brother of Antipas. For information on the complex and confusing relationships of the family of Herod, cf. Fritz Otto Busch, *The Five Herods,* tr. from the German by E. W. Dickes, London: R. Hale, 1958.

6 ff. Josephus (*Antiquities* XVIII. 5, 2) says that Herod executed John to forestall a possible rebellion, and the same authority bears witness to the enthusiasm for John shown by the common people.

12. *his disciples*. I.e., the disciples of John.

The mission of the disciples of Jesus was not a factor in Herod's decision to rid himself of John.

COMMENT

A comparison of the Matthean and Markan traditions is interesting here. Mark introduces the account of John's death by reference to the missionary work of the disciples (Mark vi 12), which brings Jesus' work to the notice of Herod ("his name became well known"). This induces Herod to say that John ("whom I beheaded") had risen from the dead, and by this means Mark goes on to the account of the execution. Matthew, who does not record this mission of the disciples, introduces his narrative with his indeterminate *At this time*. There is in Matthew's account no explicit explanation of Herod's fear of a John who had come to life again; it is only implied by the unfolding of the story.

53. THE FEEDING
(xiv 13–21)†

XIV 13 Upon hearing this, Jesus withdrew from there by boat to a lonely place by himself, but when the crowds heard of this they followed him on foot from the town. 14 As he went ashore he saw a great crowd, took pity on them, and healed their sick. 15 At evening his disciples came to him with the words: "This is a lonely place, and the day is over. Send the crowds away to go into the villages and buy provisions for themselves." 16 But Jesus said, "There is no need for them to go away; give them something to eat yourselves." 17 They said to him, "We have here only five loaves and two fishes." 18 "Bring them here to me," he said. 19 Whereupon, ordering the crowds to sit down on the grass, he took the five loaves and the two fishes, looked up to heaven, gave thanks, broke, and gave the loaves to the disciples, who gave them to the crowd. 20 They all ate and were satisfied; and they took up twelve baskets full of broken pieces which were left over. 21 Those who ate were about five thousand men, apart from women and children.

† **Matt xiv 13–21** ‖ Mark vi 30–44, Luke ix 10–17, John vi 1–14.

NOTES

xiv 13. *withdrew.* Cf. ii 12 and iv 12. This withdrawal is a direct response to the news of John's death.

14. *took pity.* Cf. ix 36. The pity here springs from the same concern for those lost and shepherdless.

15. *the day is over.* This can be taken to mean that the time for the usual evening meal is already over.

18–19. The Matthean version is terse in comparison with Mark, and Matthew makes no mention of any questions from Jesus.

On vs. 19, see the COMMENT below.

20–21. If the incident, as we contend, was more in the nature of a prophetic symbol, then we may (in the light of John vi 25–59) see the fragments collected as symbolic language from the evangelists. Jesus, who feeds them now in token of the impending Kingdom and the Messianic Feast, will never fail to feed them. There is enough and to spare.

21. *five thousand.* I.e., a good round number. To dismiss the historical accuracy of the event because of exaggeration in numbers is a foolish proceeding. The nature of oral tradition is such that minor details, such as the number of a crowd, almost immediately become subject to exaggeration. Josephus is full of such exaggerated numbers (such as his assertion that towns in and around Galilee had a population of 45,000, about ten times too much), but this in no way reduces his credibility in other historical details.

In 1921 a milk-woman from Lifta came to the American School of Oriental Research in Jerusalem with the news that on the day before, 40,000 Jews had been massacred in Tel Aviv by Arabs. This was the first word of the massacre received by one of the authors; later news reduced the number of deaths to about forty.

By way of conclusion to this material, II Baruch xxix 8 speaks of an expectation of a repetition of feeding on manna in the Messianic Age.

COMMENT

If this account of the feeding (together with its duplicate in xv 32–39) is simply to be regarded as a miraculous multiplication of bread and fish in order to feed the hungry, then it stands alone in the gospels. Aside from the compassion of Jesus, it is plain from all four gospels that Jesus' works of power were not only signs of the Kingdom's advent, but were also instruments by which it came (cf. Introduction, Part X).

In this particular instance it is John's gospel which provides us with some clues as to the real meaning of the narrative. John vi 15 records that after the feeding, the crowds wished to take Jesus by force and make him king. On the face of it, this might be interpreted as the reaction of a weary crowd to one who had suddenly saved its members from hunger—though even this is rather far-fetched. In the ministry of Jesus there is always in the background the issue of Messiahship, and this is the best sense which can be attributed to John vi 15. It is then necessary to ask what there was about this particular occurrence which brought the issue so decidedly to the front. We suggest that the words of Jesus himself, though not recorded for us, indicated that what was being enacted before the people was not a simple feeding, but a dress rehearsal for the Messianic Feast (cf. NOTE on vii 11). That this was the way in which the NT writers understood the occurrence, and also the way in which Jesus interpreted it, can be demonstrated from the occurrence of the key words "took," "gave thanks," "broke," and "gave" in:

> Matt xiv 19, xv 35, xxvi 26
> Mark vi 41, viii 6, xiv 22
> Luke ix 16, xxii 19
> John vi 11 (except for "broke")
> I Cor xi 23–24 (except for "gave").

We are here dealing with a formula of words which was fixed in the tradition at a very early date, as witness their appearance in Paul's account of the Last Supper. If Jesus' "blessing," or "giving of thanks," to the Father had reference to the impending inauguration of the Kingdom, or to the new creation (a constant theme in the Pauline writings), then all the material was at hand for a truly explosive situation, a public declaration by the people of Jesus' Messiahship. Some notes have to be added:

(a) The duplication of the tradition in Matthew and Mark indicates the crucial importance of the incident in that tradition;

(b) The link between the passion of Jesus and the inauguration of the Kingdom is clearly delineated in our gospels, particularly in John, and at this stage of the ministry it will have been abundantly clear to Jesus that the time of supreme trial was not far distant;

(c) The connection between the passion, the Kingdom, the New Covenant and the Eucharist is clearly made in Paul's first Corinthian letter, and he cannot have received this other than from an already existing tradition;

(d) It must not be overlooked that John vi makes this incident the springboard for a discourse on the bread of life;

(e) The Qumran material has provided us with wholly new evidence as to the quasi-sacramental and eschatological character attaching to meals in at least one group in Judaism.

54. THE WALKING ON THE WATER
(xiv 22–36) †

XIV 22 Then he made the disciples get into the boat and precede him to the other side, while he dismissed the crowds. 23 Having dismissed them, he went by himself up into the hills to pray, and when evening came he was there alone. 24 The boat by this time was many furlongs away from the land, being buffeted by the waves, as the wind was contrary. 25 Shortly before dawn he came to them, walking on the sea. 26 But when the disciples saw him walking on the sea, they were frightened. "It is an apparition!" they said, and cried out in fear. 27 But at once he spoke to them: "Take courage—it is I. Do not be afraid." 28 Peter replied, "Sir—if that is who you are—tell me to come to you on the water," 29 and he said "Come." Peter therefore left the boat, and walking on the water came towards Jesus. 30 But giving attention to the wind, he was afraid, and as he began to sink he cried out, "Sir, save me!" 31 Jesus immediately stretched out his hand and caught him, saying to him, "You of little faith—why did you doubt?" 32 When they had got into the boat the wind ceased, 33 and those in the boat reverenced him with the words: "Truly you are the Son of God."

34 When they had crossed over they came to land at Gennesaret. 35 When the men of that district recognized him, they sent word through all that region, and people brought to him all who were sick, 36 desiring that they might only touch the hem of his *himation*, and as many as did so were made well.

† **Matt xiv 22–27** ‖ Mark vi 45–52, John vi 15–21; **34–35** ‖ Mark vi 53–56.

NOTES

The geographical locations are confusing at this point. *The hills* (in Hebrew the singular *har*, "hill/mountain," must often be rendered "hill-country") of vs. 23 in no help (cf. the *hill/mountain* of iv 8, v 1, viii 1, xvii 1, 9, 20, xxviii 16). According to Mark the disciples were sent to Bethsaida, and if the feeding took place at the northeastern part of the lake, then Bethsaida was close by. In addition to this, Mark records only an arrival at Gennesaret (vi 53), as does Matthew in vs. 34.

24. *buffeted.* The verb used (*basanizein*) is found in viii 6 of a man suffering from paralysis, and in viii 29 by the two demoniacs in their complaint to Jesus.

25. *Shortly before dawn* (literally, "in the fourth watch of the night"). The night from 6 P.M. to 6 A.M. was divided by the Romans into four equal "watches."

28–31. The short account of Peter's meeting with Jesus is not found outside Matthew. The tradition here recorded is of importance (against those who maintain that Matthew's gospel always casts the disciples in a favorable light, as compared with the supposedly earlier and harsher Markan account). Matthew stresses the primacy of Peter among the disciples (cf. x 2, xvi 18), but there is no hesitation in recording Peter's weakness under the strain of testing (cf. also xxvi 29 ff.).

31. *little faith.* This is a peculiarly Matthean description. Cf. also vi 30, viii 9–10, 26.

33. *Son of God.* I.e., Messiah. There is no basis whatever in this expression for an assertion that this is a Hellenistic appellation. The phrase is used in the Psalms to describe the anointed king (cf. Ps ii 7).

34–36. The welcome given to Jesus in Gennesaret contrasts sharply with the incidents which follow in ch. xv. On two previous occasions a miracle story in this gospel is followed by examples of the hostility of Jesus' critics (cf. ix 32 ff., xii 23 ff.), in strong opposition to the enthusiasm of others.

COMMENT

Our position on miracles has been made clear in Part X of the Introduction. This—one of the "nature miracles"—commonly gives rise to much difficulty in the minds of many. Attempts to rationalize the story, or to penetrate behind the gospel account for some natural explanation which will not offend "modern" susceptibilities, are rather pathetic. We can never know precisely what happened on this occasion, but the spiritual import is clear.

55. QUESTIONS ON THE LAW
(xv 1–20)†

XV ¹ There came to Jesus from Jerusalem scribes and Pharisees asking, ² "Why do your disciples deliberately flout the tradition of the elders. They do not wash their hands when they eat." ³ He replied to them, "And why do you deliberately flout the commandment of God by your tradition? ⁴ For God said, 'Give honor to father and mother,' and 'Let him who speaks evil of father or mother die.' ⁵ But you say, 'If anyone says to his father or mother: Whatever you might have received from me is consecrated to God, ⁶ he does not dishonor father or mother. So by your tradition you have emptied God's word of meaning. ⁷ Shysters! How well did Isaiah the prophet prophesy of you when he said:

⁸ 'This people honors me with their lips,
   but their heart is far from me;
⁹ they worship me frivolously,
   teaching as divine law what is purely human.' "

¹⁰ Turning to the crowds, he said, "Listen and understand this: ¹¹ What defiles a man is not what goes into his mouth, but what comes out of it." ¹² Then the disciples came to him. "Do you know," they said, "that the Pharisees were shocked when they heard this saying?" ¹³ He answered, "Every growth which my heavenly Father has not planted will be rooted up. ¹⁴ Let them be. They are blind guides, and if one blind man leads another blind man they will both fall into the ditch." ¹⁵ But Peter replied, "Explain the parable to us." ¹⁶ "And are you also without understanding?" he asked. ¹⁷ "Do you not

† **Matt xv 1–20** ‖ Mark vii 1–23.

see that what goes into the mouth passes to the stomach, and so passing on is cast out? [18] But what comes out of the mouth arises from the heart, and this defiles a man. [19] For from the heart arise evil thoughts, murder, adultery, sexual license, theft, perjury, slander. [20] These are the things which defile a man. To eat with unwashed hands does not defile anyone."

Notes

xv 2. The charge against the disciples is not that of breaking the Law, but of setting aside the *tradition of the elders*. No one can deny the hygienic desirability of coming to eat with clean hands; equally no one can deny that such precautions can be carried to extreme lengths.

2–5. Note the parallel framework of the scribes and Pharisees' questions and Jesus' replies in Matthew:

Why do your disciples	*Why do you*
flout the tradition?	*flout the commandment?*
. . . But you say . . .	*God said . . .*

The emphasis on *commandment* in distinction from *tradition* in vs. 3 is very marked.

4. Mark's version (vii 10) has, *"Moses* said, 'Give honor. . . .'" Matthew's version, with *"God* said . . ." makes the antithesis between divine command and human tradition far clearer. It should be noted here that the so-called "Temple scroll" from Qumran also exhibits changes of this character, even altering sayings in the Pentateuch from "God said . . ." to "I said. . . ."

5. *consecrated to God.* Mark uses the technical term *korban* (Heb. *qorbân*). The term is attested in Josephus (*Against Apion* I) and in inscriptions from the middle decades of the first century A.D. Cf. StB, ad loc. By allowing a man to dedicate his property and possessions to the temple, the oral law (*the tradition of the elders*) had in effect permitted a man to escape the obligations of the fifth commandment (Exod xx 12). In this way an oral tradition could *empty God's word of meaning.*

7. *Shysters!* On this translation of *hupokritai*, cf. Appendix to Part IX in the Introduction. What is being condemned is the legalism which robs an otherwise legitimate gesture of all moral content.

8–9. The quotation (Isa xxix 13) is neither from the LXX nor from the Masoretic text. It may derive from the "Old Palestinian" tradition. This source we no longer have, but its existence has been dramatically illustrated by the OT material from Qumran. Cf. Cross, *The Ancient Library of Qumran,* especially pp. 120 ff.

10–11. The preceding incident was a private encounter, as *Turning to the crowds* demonstrates. Matthew's use of *mouth* here clarifies the ambiguities of the Markan tradition ("coming out of a man," Mark vii 16), but the clarification renders the explanation in vss. 17–19 unnecessary. Evidently the oral tradition behind our sources included it.

10. *crowds.* As distinct from *the people;* cf. NOTE on iv 23. *Crowds* may have included Gentiles.

12–14. The shocked reaction of the Pharisees was understandable, since Jesus appeared to be setting aside the legal distinction between ritually clean and unclean food. Certainly Mark (from Peter?—cf. Acts x 1–xi 18) thought that this was the case (Mark vii 19), but Matthew's tradition has no such sweeping conclusion. If we may judge from the controversies which plagued the early community (Acts x, xi, xv; Gal ii 11 ff.) there was no such certainty as that assumed by Mark. Moreover, the controversy with the Pharisees was about a *tradition,* not about the *Law.* It is possible that the use of *the crowds* is of some assistance here. The Matthean tradition uses the word in distinction to *the people* (as indicated in the previous NOTE), and Jesus may well merely have indicated the inapplicability of the Mosaic Law to those outside the Old Covenant. Only the second part of vs. 14 has a parallel outside Matthew; in Luke vi 39 it comes in the context of the Great Instruction.

14. *blind.* The same accusation is brought against the Pharisees in xxiii 16–22, and Paul uses a similar phrase in Rom ii 19. Cf. also John x 39–41.

15. *Peter.* The eminent position of Peter is stressed again here. In Mark (vii 17) it is the disciples who make the request.

parable. Cf. Part XI of the Introduction. The saying of Jesus in vs. 11 was an example of case law.

18. Cf. xii 34.

19. Mark's list has thirteen forms of evil (vii 21 ff.), while Matthew's tradition confines the list to seven, in the order of the Decalogue (cf. Hos iv 2).

20. This verse repeats vs. 11, reversing the order.

COMMENT

The reader is referred to Part IX of the Introduction, on Jesus and the Law. It is important here only to recall our warnings against supposing that Jesus' controversies with the Pharisees and lawyers arose from an intention on the part of Jesus to erect a "new law," or to abrogate the Mosaic Law.

56. THE SYRO-PHOENICIAN WOMAN;
FURTHER HEALINGS
(xv 21–31)†

XV   21 Jesus left that place, and went into the district of Tyre and Sidon, 22 and a Phoenician woman from those parts came to him calling out, "Take pity on me, Lord, Son of David, for my daughter is badly demon-possessed." 23 Not a word did he answer, and his disciples approached him: "Send her away," they said, "for she is calling after us." 24 He replied, "I was not sent, except to the lost sheep of the house of Israel." 25 She, however, came and threw herself before him and said: "Lord, help me." 26 But he replied: "It is not right to take children's bread and throw it to dogs." 27 "Yes, Lord," she said, "yet even the dogs eat the crumbs which fall from their masters' tables." 28 "Woman," said Jesus in reply to her, "your faith is great. Let it be as you wish." Her daughter was made well from that time.

29 Departing from there, Jesus went by the Sea of Galilee, and went up into the hills and stayed there. 30 Great crowds came to him, bringing with them lame, blind, maimed, and dumb people and many others besides. They placed them at his feet and he cured them. 31 The crowds marveled when they saw the dumb speaking, the maimed restored, the lame walking, the blind seeing, and they praised Israel's God.

† **Matt xv 21–28** || Mark vii 24–30.

Notes

xv 22. *Phoenician* (literally, "Canaanite"). The word is clear indication that the woman who came to Jesus was a Phoenician. Otherwise, she would have been called simply a Greek. Phoenician was still spoken, and the native name (*kena'nî*) of a Phoenician was in the Greek *Chananaios*. It is worthy of note that Carthaginian peasants in the time of Augustine (fifth century A.D.) still called themselves Canaanites. Mark's version has "a Greek, a Syro-Phoenician by race."

came to him. The Matthean account has the Gentile woman coming to Jesus when he was in her own home territory, in agreement with Mark (vii 24–25), which states that Jesus was in a house in Gentile country (Tyre).

23–25. These verses are found only in Matthew. Both the silence of Jesus and the near-desperate cry of the disciples are interesting in the light of commentators' assertions that this gospel (in contrast with the supposedly earlier Mark) treats Jesus and his disciples with increased reverence.

26. *children's bread.* Mark's account simply has "Let the children be fed first" (vii 27), which is ambiguous. Matthew's version of Jesus' saying in vs. 24, whether it is in context or not, illuminates this saying about the *children*—they are Israel.

28. *faith.* Once again, trust and confidence has compelled Jesus to extend his mission to a Gentile. Cf. viii 5–13.

29. Mark's geographical details are here more complete, describing as he does a somewhat lengthy journey from Tyre by way of the district of Sidon, in the direction of the Sea of Galilee, then to the territory of the Ten Towns (Decapolis; vii 31). Matthew merely records, after the return, a journey to *the hills,* with a short summary of works of healing.

31. This verse is a reference to Isa xxxv 5, and may provide a sidelight on the way in which the tradition was recorded. Mark (vii 32 ff.) has an account of the healing of a deaf-stammerer (*mogilalōn* in Greek, a word which is found in the LXX of Isa xxxv 6). Matthew simply records the healings in terms of the Isaian passage, where Mark—apparently aware of the same passage—describes a single healing against its background.

COMMENT

The next considerable part of the gospel is marked by a ministry in and around Galilee, and includes teaching by Jesus about his passion and resurrection (xv 21 – xviii 35). This corresponds with vii 24 – ix 50 in Mark, but in Matthew the journeys recorded by Mark are far less detailed (cf. xv 29 and Mark vii 31), while Matthew's record of instruction to the disciples is far more detailed.

The question of clean and unclean having been raised in the previous section, this next encounter naturally follows in sequence, for it deals with the relationship between Jews and Gentiles. Moreover, sayings such as those in x 5–6 would demand explanation when non-Jews began pressing into the Messianic Community.

57. THE FEEDING
(xv 32–39) †

XV ³² Jesus called his disciples to him and said, "I am deeply concerned about the crowd, because they have now been with me three days without eating. I am unwilling to send them away hungry, in case they faint on the way." ³³ "Where," said the disciples to him, "are we to obtain bread enough in this lonely place to feed such a crowd?" ³⁴ Jesus asked them, "How many loaves do you have?" "Seven," they answered, "and a few fish." ³⁵ Commanding the crowd to sit down on the ground, ³⁶ he took the seven loaves and the fish, and having given thanks he broke them and gave them to the disciples, who gave them to the crowds. ³⁷ When they had all eaten and were satisfied, they gathered up seven baskets of the broken pieces left over. ³⁸ Those who thus ate were about four thousand men, besides women and children. ³⁹ Dismissing the crowds, he embarked in the boat, and went to the hills of Magdala.

† Matt xv 32–39 || Mark viii 1–10.

NOTES

xv 32–39. The great importance attached to the account of the feeding is illustrated by its duplication here. The Johannine account of the feeding emphasizes its crucial place in the ministry by the assertion that the crowds wished to make Jesus king. In view of this tradition, and in view of the links suggested between the feeding, the Messianic Feast, the Last Supper and the Eucharist, we are entitled to assume a duplication here.

The assimilation of language in this account to that of chapter xiv reinforces such a view.

39. *Magdala*. The Greek (*Magadan*) is obscure. Magdala, where the hills rise sharply from the sea, would fit the Matthean location admirably.

The Greek mistake arose very simply—*delta, alpha* and *lambda* look alike in uncials (capital letters were used exclusively in the early Greek book hand). The Syriac readings *MGDW* (LXX *Mageddō*=Heb. *Megiddô*), *MGDYN*, etc., may be better, but they would leave us with a quite unknown location.

58. DEMAND FOR A SIGN
(xvi 1–12)†

XVI ¹ The Pharisees and Sadducees came to him, and to test him they asked him to show them a sign from heaven. ² He answered them, "When it is evening, you say 'It will be fair, because the sky is red,' ³ and in the morning, 'Today will be stormy, because the sky is red and threatening.' You know how to judge the appearance of the sky; why then can you not judge the signs of the times? ⁴ An evil generation seeks a sign, but no sign will be given to it, except the sign of Jonah." He left them and went away.

⁵ When the disciples reached the other side, they had forgotten to take bread with them. ⁶ Jesus said to them, "Watch— beware of the yeast of the Pharisees and Sadducees." ⁷ Among themselves they discussed this, reasoning, "We brought no bread," and, ⁸ knowing this, Jesus said, "Why do you discuss among yourselves, you of little faith, the fact that you have no bread? ⁹ Do you not yet understand? Do you not remember the five loaves for the five thousand, and the number of baskets you gathered up? ¹⁰ Or the seven loaves for the four thousand, and the number of baskets you gathered up? ¹¹ How then do you fail to understand that I was not talking to you about bread? Beware of the yeast of the Pharisees and Sadducees." ¹² Then they understood that he was not telling them to beware of the yeast of bread, but of the teaching of the Pharisees and Sadducees.

† **Matt xvi 1–4** || Mark viii 11–13, Luke xii 54–56; **5–12** || Mark viii 14–21.

NOTES

So far from suggesting an uncertainty which they are anxious to dissipate, the critics' request for a sign, an authentication of Jesus' ministry, is represented by the evangelist as a temptation.

xvi 1. *Sadducees.* This is the only place in the NT where the Sadducees are represented as being outside Judea. Their mention here is odd, unless there was some uneasy partnership between a group of Pharisees and a similar group of Sadducees seeking to trap Jesus. See below on vs. 12.
sign. Cf. xii 38.

2–3. While we have a few verbal agreements in the Greek of Matthew and Luke against Mark in vss. 1–4 of this chapter, these two verses are not well attested in the best manuscripts. NEB relegates to a footnote the whole passage *When it is evening . . . signs of the times.* It is possible that the passage is a composition based on the kind of traditional saying which underlies Luke xii 54–56. We have retained the passage in our translation since it is not possible to make any final determination as to authenticity.

4. *sign of Jonah.* Cf. xii 39 and Mark viii 12. Some process of assimilation appears to have been at work here.

5–12. In Mark the conversation takes place in the boat. It is not easy to see what is meant by the Markan (viii 15) "yeast of the Pharisees and of Herod" unless this refers back to Mark iii 6.

6–8. *little faith.* Cf. vi 30, xiv 31. The disciples ought to have realized that Jesus was not referring to mere absence of provisions. *Yeast,* in vs. 6, is a symbol of corruption, as it was commonly known also in the rabbinic writers and in the NT (cf. I Cor v 6–8; Gal v 9).

9–10. The Markan account is fuller, with the disciples answering questions put to them by Jesus, and Matthew here and elsewhere has no tradition (such as that recorded by Mark) of "hardened hearts" on the part of the disciples (cf. Mark vi 52, viii 17).

11. The whole clause *that I was not talking to you about bread* may be an explanatory note by Matthew. It is not in the Markan account.

12. This explanation is hardly satisfactory. The Markan account, as we have seen, speaks of the "Pharisees and Herod," a combination so unexpected that it is likely to be authentic. Matthew, knowing the tradition, and puzzled by it, appears to have substituted *Sadducees* for Herod in vs. 6, and has it also in the odd context of vs. 1. If the Markan tradition is accurate, then the combination of Pharisees and Herod may refer to a common hostility to Jesus, and Matthew's *teaching* is a harmonizing accommodation.

59. PETER'S CONFESSION
(xvi 13–20)†

XVI 13 When Jesus came into the district of Caesarea Philippi,
he inquired of his disciples, "Who do men say that The Man is?"
14 They said, "Some say John the Baptist, others Elijah, and
yet others Jeremiah, or another of the prophets." 15 He said to
them, "But who do you say that I am?" 16 Simon Peter replied:
"You are the Messiah, the Son of the living God." 17 Jesus
answered him, "You are fortunate, Simon son of Jonah, for
this was not revealed to you by human agency, but by my
Father who is in heaven. 18 And I in turn say to you that you
are Rock, and on this rock I will build my community, and the
powers of death shall not overcome it. 19 I will give to you the
keys of the Kingdom of heaven. Whatever you bind on earth
will have been bound in heaven, and whatever you release on
earth will have been so released in heaven." 20 Then he gave
strict orders to his disciples not to tell anyone that he was the
Messiah.

† **Matt xvi 13–20** ‖ Mark viii 27–30, Luke ix 18–21.

NOTES

The graphically described incident of the healing of the blind man,
which prefaces Peter's confession in Mark (Mark viii 22–26), either was
not known to Matthew, or he felt that it was included in the general
statement of xv 29–30.

xvi 13. *Caesarea Philippi.* This was about twenty miles north of the
Sea of Galilee.

The Man. Cf. NOTE on viii 20. It is important to notice here the
difference of treatment between Matthew and Mark. Mark has "Who

do men say that I am?" The Matthean account is, as we saw in Part VII of the Introduction, built around the coming figure of The Man. In Matthew, The Man is a title of triumph, and now that the lines are firmly drawn, opposition to Jesus now overt and hardening, he can ask what the disciples think of The Man-who-is-to-come. The identification with himself is implied, but not explicit until the first question has been answered.

14. The reappearance of dead heroes was a well-known theme in contemporary Jewish thought. On John the Baptist, cf. xiv 2. II Macc xv 13 ff. speaks of Jeremiah and Onias appearing to Judas Maccabaeus, and II Esd ii 18 refers to the coming of Isaiah and Jeremiah. On the coming of Elijah, cf. xi 14.

16. The identification of Jesus with The Man to come is explicit here.

The transliteration of the Gr. *Christos* by Christ in various English versions is inexcusable, and the RSV perpetuates the KJ transliteration. In its original context the question posed by Jesus and answered by Peter as spokesman demanded commitment to Jesus as *Messiah*. The fact that the Greek word is most often without the definite article in NT writings after the Acts must not lead to a too-hasty conclusion that the title Messiah became almost immediately a name, Christ. We have already pointed out that the absence of a definite article, in places where we have every reason to suppose an Aramaic background, makes the article conditional upon context (cf. NOTE on x 41 [d]). The number of occurrences of *Christos* as a name in the Pauline letters may be far less than some commentators have supposed. There is certainly a definite article here in the Greek of Matt xvi 16.

That there was some uncertainty in the primitive Christian community as to the precise nature of Jesus' Messiahship seems certain (cf. Robinson, "The Most Primitive Christology of All?," in TNTS. In addition to this, there was also sectarian speculation about *two* messiahs; the insistence in Hebrews on Jesus' royal *and* priestly Messiahship (e.g., Heb i 5–14, iv 14 – v 10) can best be explained on the basis of a reply to those who had come from such a background.

Son of the living God. Far from this being an explanatory gloss by Matthew, it is perfectly in order in the context of Messiahship (cf. NOTE on xiv 33). "God's Messiah" (in Luke ix 20) makes this quite clear. This was certainly not a Hellenistic concept. Among pagan Aramaeans no later than the ninth century B.C. (but with a far longer prehistory), it was important for a king or dynasty to be the "son" of the tutelary deity of city or state. The use of "Bar" in personal names nearly always had a background of such use. In Hellenistic times the use spread beyond royal personages. Cf. Robert E. Hansen, "Theophorous Son

Names among the Arameans and Their Neighbors," doctoral dissertation, Johns Hopkins University, 1948.

There is some verbal agreement in the Greek of Matthew and Luke against Mark in vss. 13–16 of this chapter, and also between Matthew and Mark against Luke and of Mark and Luke against Matthew. Verses 17–19 are peculiar to Matthew.

17. Simon is *fortunate,* the object of the Father's revelation (cf. xi 25). Cf. also for similar expressions v 3 ff., xi 6, xiii 16, xxiv 46.

Simon son of Jonah. It is possible that the name of Simon's father was *Yohana(n),* which might be transcribed *Iōna* in Greek. "John" was a very common name at this time, while "Jonah" was very rare. However, in view of the Syr. *brēh d'Yōnā,* it is better to assume our sources to be correct here.

human agency (literally, *flesh and blood*). This is frequent in the rabbinic literature, e.g., TB, *Berakhoth* 28b, "a king of flesh and blood" (in contrast with the heavenly King).

18. *Rock* (Aram. *Kēphā*). This is not a name, but an appellation and a play on words. There is no evidence of Peter or Kephas as a name before Christian times. On building on a rock, or from a rock, cf. Isa li 1 ff.; Matt vii 24 f. *Peter* as *Rock* will be the foundation of the future community (cf. *I will build*). Jesus, not quoting the OT, here uses Aramaic, not Hebrew, and so uses the only Aramaic word which would serve his purpose.

In view of the background of vs. 19 (see below), one must dismiss as confessional interpretation any attempt to see *this rock* as meaning the faith, or the Messianic confession, of Peter. To deny the pre-eminent position of Peter among the disciples or in the early Christian community is a denial of the evidence. Cf. in this gospel x 2, xiv 28–31, xv 15. The interest in Peter's failures and vacillations does not detract from this pre-eminence; rather, it emphasizes it. Had Peter been a lesser figure his behavior would have been of far less consequence (cf. Gal ii 11 ff.).

my community (Gr. *ekklēsia*). The use of this Greek word in the Pauline letters antedates the final edition of the Greek gospels by some two decades. It is hard to know what kind of thinking, other than confessional presupposition, justifies the tendency of some commentators to dismiss this verse as not authentic. A Messiah without a Messianic Community would have been unthinkable to any Jew, and how precisely one Jewish group (at least) thought of that Community has been brought sharply into focus by the Qumran literature. The LXX used *ekklēsia* to translate words which denoted an assembly of any character, and it is a word which invariably translated Hebrew equivalents from the stem *qhl.* The character of the assembly in Hebrew is denoted by possessive genitives (e.g., "of the Lord," "of the children of Israel," "of the prophets").

The word used by Jesus may have been *kenishtā,* which in the Syriac versions is used for both *ekklēsia* and *synagogē.* (In this passage the Syriac uses *'edtā*=Heb. *'ēdāh,* "religious community.") Cf. on this subject K. L. Schmidt, TWNT, III, p. 525. When the Church moved into a Hellenistic environment, the Greek carried with it the sense of "assembly of freeborn citizens."

the powers of death (literally, "the gates of Hades"). The community has just been referred to as a building, and here the forces of evil also have a fortress or city, that of Hades, the realm of death. For this concept, cf. Isa xxxviii 10; Job xvii 16, xxxviii 17; Pss ix 13, cvii 18; Wisd Sol xvi 13. The Babylonians had a similar idea about a gatekeeper to the realms of death, and it is the gatekeeper who compels Ishtar to disrobe before entering that realm.

The sense here is that the powers of evil cannot contain or hold in check the new community.

19. Isa xxii 15 ff. undoubtedly lies behind this saying. *The keys* are the symbol of authority, and Roland de Vaux (*Ancient Israel,* tr. by John McHugh [New York: McGraw-Hill, 1961], pp. 129 ff.) rightly sees here the same authority as that vested in the vizier, the master of the house, the chamberlain, of the royal household in ancient Israel. Eliakim is described as having the same authority in Isaiah; it was Hilkiah's position until he was ousted, and Jotham as regent is also described as "over the household" (II Kings xv 5). Significantly, the first Chaldean governor after the deportation of 586 B.C., Gedaliah, is given the same title on his official seal. It is of considerable importance that in other contexts, when the disciplinary affairs of the community are being discussed (cf. xviii 18; John xx 23) the symbol of the *keys* is absent, since the sayings apply in those instances to a wider circle. In John xx 23 the words are used of pardon, and in that context the Greek words *luein* and *kratein* derive from a secondary interpretation of Isaiah's Hebrew.

Kingdom of heaven. The identification of the Community (i.e., the infant Church) with the Kingdom is one which has caused difficulty to some commentators. We hope that Parts VI–VIII of the Introduction will have clarified our position. The Kingdom here is the temporary Kingdom, The Man's Kingdom, as distinct from that of the Father. The objections to the identification of the Kingdom with the Church, with the *ekklēsia* of this passage, can only rest upon a supposition that the Kingdom, as distinct from the Community, is thought to consist of those professing some kind of unschooled enthusiasm for Jesus, while the Church, the Community, has rules which the Kingdom does not have. Unless we are to suppose, in the fashion of some, that the NT material outside the gospels is a perversion of the proclamation of Jesus, then we are bound to find that at no time was the Community which Jesus founded an antinomian society. On the contrary: at the earliest levels open to our inspection commitment in faith to the Messianic proclamation of Jesus carried with it the obligation to submit to that Community's rules of initiation and to continue in the fellowship of that community of The Man's Kingdom, the Kingdom of heaven.

bind. The role of Peter as steward of the Kingdom is further explained as being the exercise of administrative authority, as was the case of the OT chamberlain who held the "keys." The clauses *on earth, in heaven,* have reference to the permanent character of the steward's work. Peter's initiative is well illustrated by the admission of a Gentile to the community in Acts x–xi, under the guidance of the Spirit—an event which the historian considered as meriting a great deal of attention in his work.

whatever. The text here has *ho ean* (whatever), perhaps a scribal error in xvi 19 for *hosa ean* (*whatever*), as appears in xviii 18; the longer reading *hosa ean* is attested at xvi 19 by manuscripts of the Caesarean family. The haplography involved in the corruption of *hosa ean* to *ho ean* is obvious, if it was not originally *ho ean*.

As for the sense of this passage, cf. the gift of the Spirit of truth as counselor, John xiv 16 f., 26. The Latin Vulgate also translates as "will have been bound," "will have been loosed," exactly corresponding to the Greek. It is the Church on earth carrying out heaven's decisions, communicated by the Spirit, and not heaven ratifying the Church's decisions. Periphrastic tenses, though necessary in English, are quite rare in Greek, and therefore the construction at this point must be given its due weight. Cf. the translation and note ad loc. in Charles B. Williams, *The New Testament: A Translation in the Language of the People,* Chicago: Moody Press, 1949; London: Oliphants, 1950.

20. This is not the so-called "Messianic secret" suggested by some earlier scholars. Unless the ministry of Jesus was to be hopelessly compromised and misunderstood, public proclamations of his Messiahship were out of the question. We have already seen the difficulties publicity had caused him.

COMMENT

There is no passage in the gospels which has been more discussed than this, especially with reference to vss. 17–19. The general sense of the passage is indisputable. Jesus asks his disciples who The Man is in popular estimation, and they reply that some suppose him to be John the Baptist, others Elijah, Jeremiah, or one of the prophets.

On being asked who they themselves suppose him to be, Peter answers that he is the Messiah, son of the living God. Jesus calls Peter fortunate, in that this knowledge has not come from human sources, but is a direct revelation from God. He goes on to assure Peter that he (Peter) is the rock on which the new community will be built, and in that community Peter's authority to "bind" or "release" will be a carrying out of decisions made in heaven. His teaching and disciplinary activities will be similarly guided by the Spirit to carry out Heaven's will.

In the Markan account, this acknowledgment of Jesus' Messiahship is central, and it is Peter's confession which prompts Jesus to reinterpret the Messiah's vocation to the disciples in terms of suffering and death. The Matthean tradition has already laid the ground for such reinterpretation by the use of OT quotations from the Servant Songs of Second Isaiah, but Matthew agrees with Mark that it was from this time onward that Jesus spoke openly of his forthcoming passion. There is, however, a significant difference. Having spoken of the founding of the community, Jesus in the Matthean tradition goes on to an extended treatment of matters concerning the community.

Oscar Cullmann's view, that Matt xvi 17–19 should be removed from its present context to an acknowledgment of Jesus by Peter in the Upper Room, has been recently criticized by Robert H. Gundry ("The Narrative Framework of Matthew xvi 17–19," NovT 7 [1964–65], 1–9). Cullmann's view is set out in *Peter: Disciple-Apostle-Martyr*, tr. from the German by Floyd V. Filson, Philadelphia: Westminster / London: SCM, 1962.

60. PASSION PREDICTIONS
(xvi 21–28)†

XVI 21 From that time on, Jesus began to make it clear to his disciples that he must go to Jerusalem and endure many things from the elders, chief priests, and scribes, and be killed, and on the third day be raised. 22 But Peter took him and began to remonstrate with him: "Heaven forbid, Lord! This must not happen to you." 23 He, however, turned to Peter and said, "Get behind me, Satan! You are a stumbling block to me. You are not on God's side, but man's." 24 Then Jesus said to his disciples, "If anyone will come with me, then let him deny self, take up his cross and follow me. 25 For one who grasps at self will lose it, but one who lets go of self on my account will gain it. 26 What profit will a man have if he gains the whole world and loses his own self? Or what will a man give in return for his very self? 27 For The Man is to come with his angels in his Father's glory, and then he will repay every man for his conduct. 28 I solemnly tell you there are men standing here who will not taste death until they see The Man enter upon his reign."

† **Matt xvi 21–28** || Mark viii 31 – ix 1, Luke ix 22–27.

NOTES

The Galilean mission now being ended, Jesus in this gospel devotes himself to the instruction of his disciples, and this particular emphasis can be seen in *his disciples* in vs. 21, in contrast with Mark's *them*. In all our gospels the bewilderment of both disciples and common people, alongside the hostility of official and semiofficial Judaism, is seen as centering upon Jesus' interpretation of his own ministry. In all three synoptic gospels the acknowledgment of Jesus as Messiah is the pivotal point in the ministry, and—again in all three gospels—Jesus speaks with complete candor of the inevitable end of that ministry.

xvi 21. *Jesus.* Some manuscripts add *Messiah.* As we have seen, the Matthean tradition is that the Messiah suffers; The Man is a figure of triumph.

must go (Gr. *dei apelthein*). The synoptic gospels are agreed on Jesus' statement of the necessity of going to Jerusalem, and also on the fact that for Jesus the Messianic vocation necessarily involved suffering.

elders, chief priests, and scribes. This is a very odd order, and its fixed state in the oral tradition is demonstrated by its reproduction in this order in all three synoptic gospels.

third day. So in all the NT writings (Acts x 40; I Cor xv 4; cf. Mark viii 31, ix 31, x 34), reckoning Friday of the crucifixion as the first day.

be raised. The NT writers always speak of Jesus as "being raised" by the Father, or in the power of the Spirit, never that he raised himself. The NT faith is not that of immortality in the sense of continuing existence on earth (which is the meaning of all pagan sources on immortality), but of resurrection, in the sense of God reversing the apparent verdict of nature.

22–23. Peter spoke for the rest in confessing Jesus as Messiah, and here he is their spokesman in protesting the need for the Messiah to suffer and to die.

23. *Get behind me.* Cf. iv 10. Standing in opposition to the will of God is to be on the side of Satan, even to be doing his work.

24. In Mark this is a general saying addressed to the crowd and to the disciples. In context, it is far more likely that the Matthean tradition is correct, and that Jesus begins at this point to spell out the consequences to the disciples of their commitment to him. Further, in spite of his confession, it is plain that Peter has not fully realized that the fate of Jesus involves the fate of the disciples too.

deny self. Cf. NOTE on x 38. To pursue earthly security at this juncture of the ministry is to lose all in the time of The Man's coming. In the light of vss. 27–28, it is important to remember that as originally spoken, this was a plain warning to the inner circle not to become involved in secular calculation, especially in anything which would jeopardize the Messianic vocation. That this warning could be, and certainly was, applied to members of the continuing Messianic Community is evidenced by Mark's *the crowd* and *them* for Matthew's *his disciples.*

25–26. Cf. x 37–39.

self (Gr. *psyche*). Cf. NOTE on x 39.

27. Mark and Luke have a saying (Mark viii 38; Luke ix 26) here, which Matthew has in another context, x 33.

is to come (Gr. *mellein*). This verb will perfectly well serve to indicate either the coming of The Man in exaltation, or his coming to render his Kingdom to the Father at the judgment.

his Father's glory. The background of this saying seems to be that of Enoch—cf. xlv 3, lxi 8, lxii 2, lxix 27—while the phrase *repay every man* is reminiscent of Ps lxii 12 (13H).

28. *solemnly tell you.* Cf. NOTE on ix 11.

men standing here. On vss. 27–28, cf. Parts VI–VIII of the Introduction. It has been observed that Matthew and John see the glory and exaltation of the Messiah (or The Man) in terms of the passion and resurrection of Jesus. There is therefore no call to see in these words of Jesus any belief in his mind that his "coming" was in some sense an expected return to earth in glory, however much this may have been the belief of some in the early Church (including Paul at first). The Markan version (ix 1) speaks of "God's Kingdom coming with power," which is completely at one with the Matthean tradition, when allowance has been made for Matthew's distinction between the two Kingdoms (cf. *The Man,* and God's or the Father's). Cf. x 23; xxiv 34. As it stands, the saying is a factual statement that there were those (either by-standers or of the inner circle) who would not die before the Messiah's passion and resurrection.

II Peter i 16–18 is not without relevance here. It is quite clear that the writer of the letter sees the transfiguration as the fulfillment of Jesus' saying in this verse. This underlines once more our contention that the "coming" of Jesus was by no means without its puzzles to the writers of the NT. It also serves to underline the intense impact of the baptism and transfiguration of Jesus, as later seen in the light of the resurrection.

taste death. Cf. John viii 52; Heb ii 9.

61. THE TRANSFIGURATION
(xvii 1–13) †

XVII 1 Six days afterwards, Jesus took with him Peter, James, and his brother John, and brought them privately to a high mountain. 2 There he changed his appearance in their presence, his face shone like the sun, and his clothing shone as the light. 3 Moses and Elijah also appeared to them, talking with him. 4 Peter said to Jesus, "Lord, it is well for us to be here; if you wish, I will make three tents, one each for you, Moses, and Elijah." 5 He was still speaking when a bright cloud overshadowed them, and there was a voice from the cloud, "This is my Son, the Beloved One; in him I am well pleased. Listen to him." 6 On hearing it, the disciples fell prostrate and were filled with awe. 7 But Jesus came to them and touched them, saying to them, "Get up, and do not be afraid." 8 When they raised their eyes, they saw no one except Jesus. 9 As they were coming down the mountain, Jesus ordered them, "Do not speak of the vision to anyone until The Man is raised from the dead." 10 The disciples asked him, "Why then do the scribes say that first of all Elijah must come?" 11 He replied, "Indeed Elijah comes and re-establishes everything; 12 but I tell you that Elijah has come already, and they did not recognize him, but did to him whatever they pleased. So too The Man will suffer at their hands." 13 Then the disciples understood that he was speaking to them about John the Baptist.

† **Matt xvii 1–13** || Mark ix 2–13, Luke ix 28–36.

NOTES

xvii 1. *Peter, James, and . . . John.* The emphasis on these three figures as a kind of "core" to the inner circle of the twelve is in striking parallel to a similar phenomenon among the Qumran Essenes (cf. Cross, *The Ancient Library of Qumran,* pp. 174 ff.; C. S. Mann, "The Organization and Institutions of the Jerusalem Church in Acts," Appendix IV in Munck, *The Acts of the Apostles*). Cf. xxvi 37.

2. *changed his appearance* (Gr. *metemorphōthē*). The word is ambiguous and capable of being misunderstood. Luke omits it, and his version uses different words. Matthew qualifies the word by the clause following: *his face shone like the sun.* Cf. Exod xxxiv 29; Parables of Enoch i 5, xix 1; II Esd vii 97.

clothing shone as the light. Cf. Enoch xiv 20. Similar expressions occur sixteen times in Revelation to denote heavenly beings, or heavenly things.

3. *Moses and Elijah.* If this account is taken as a dramatically theologized description of the way in which the disciples were beginning to think of the Messiahship of Jesus, then we may take these two names as being the attestation of the Law and the Prophets. Moses and Elijah were both believed to have been translated to heaven.

On Elijah as the Messianic herald, cf. NOTES on xi 10, above, and on vs. 10 below. Cf. also the promise ascribed to Moses, Deut xviii 15, used by the Samaritans as a Messianic prophecy.

4. In Mark the address is "Rabbi," an address which Matthew puts only on the lips of Judas (xxvi 25, 49).

it is well for us to be here. The RSV translation ("it is well *that* we are here") is weak, making of Peter's assertion a remark of surprised accident. Following on the Messianic confession, Peter's desire is to extend the time, evidently thinking that the Messianic New Age is far nearer than he had supposed.

5. *cloud* (Heb. *'ānān*). In the OT, the *cloud* appears very often as that brilliant cloud of glory which hides God from the presence of men (cf. G. E. Mendenhall, in the first of the [unpublished] Lovejoy Lectures, Johns Hopkins University, Baltimore, Maryland, March 10–13, 1967). As a sign of the presence of God, the cloud is primarily associated with the Exodus of Israel from Egypt, and later with the New Age (cf. II Macc ii 8; Exod xl 35).

my Son, the Beloved One. Cf. NOTE on iii 17.

Listen to him. Cf. Deut xviii 15; and also Acts iii 22 ff., vii 37.

6. *filled with awe.* Luke (ix 34) describes this fear as belonging to the

moment when they entered the cloud—a detail of difference which reinforces our belief in the integrity of the independent traditions.

9. *Do not speak.* Again, Jesus regards publicity as a hindrance. Cf. NOTE on xvi 20.

The Man. Cf. NOTE on viii 20.

is raised. Cf. NOTE on xvi 21.

Mark has nothing which corresponds to Matthew's vss. 6–7, and there are certainly indications of independent sources in the treatment of vss. 1–8 by Matthew and Luke. Both Matthew and Luke express a change in Jesus' appearance, and though Matthew uses *metemorphōthē,* he qualifies it where Luke uses other expressions. Both Matthew and Luke record the element of the disciples' fears, though in different contexts. If we assume that Matthew and Luke had a common narrative in addition to Mark (which is the usual theory), then the divergence of traditions (especially Matt xvii 2=Luke ix 29; Matt xvii 4=Luke ix 33 with Luke ix 31–32 standing alone) causes considerable difficulty. On the basis of these divergences it is far easier to suppose that Luke had access to Matthew and modified what he found.

10. The question is posed immediately following the passion prediction and the injunction to silence. Whether as it stands it is in context we have no means of determining. It is possible that the disciples' query about what the scribes said concerning Elijah was placed here because the appearance of Elijah in the vision had caused questioning as to the precise role of Jesus as a suffering Messiah. The editorial comment in vs. 13 would seem to lend support to this view, as also the very obscure comment at Mark ix 12, which would seem to imply that while the advent of Elijah had been prophesied, the same was not true of a suffering Messiah. We suggest that the difficulties in Mark ix 12 can be eliminated if we suppose that the question, "Then how has it been recorded of The Man, that he should suffer greatly and be treated with contempt?" is a second one—from the *disciples* to Jesus. We have (as yet) no clear evidence from intertestamental sources (including Qumran) to indicate any belief in a suffering Messiah. Jesus interpreted Messiahship in terms of suffering, to be sure, but in the framework of OT prophecies on the Suffering Servant.

Elijah. Cf. Mal iv 5 ff. If everything was prepared for the Messiah—and Peter as their spokesman had acknowledged Jesus as such—then what was the place of Elijah in the scheme of things?

11–12. In other words, the prophecy of Malachi was indeed correct, and so was contemporary expectation of a coming of Elijah, but because he had come, and had not been recognized, so neither would The Man be recognized.

12. *Elijah has come already*. This expression is, of course, symbolic, and emphatically not some kind of reincarnation!

The Man. In Matthean usage (to which we called attention in the Introduction, Parts VI, VII, and XII) it is the Messiah who suffers, while The Man is a figure of glory. At first sight what we have nere is an exception to the Matthean scheme, especially when considered alongside vss. 22–23 later in this chapter. However, an examination of the context of the prediction at 12b raises doubts as to the authenticity of the saying here. Verse 12a followed immediately by vs. 13 makes perfectly good sense, whereas the presence of 12b makes vs. 13 read very oddly indeed. Similarly with vss. 22–23: these two verses fit very badly in the context in which they are placed, particularly in view of what follows in vss. 24 ff., whereas the same prediction in the Markan and Lukan traditions is wholly in place. We must therefore reckon with the possibility, in view of the Matthean tradition on The Man, that in both instances (12b and 22–23) we have an editorial addition to the original. The reasons for the insertions, if such they be, can only be speculative. It is fair to assume that the insertions (which are certainly traditional material) were made by someone who failed to understand Matthew's presentation of his material, and assumed that the passion predictions must be added in the Markan context. The presence of vs. 9 probably dictated the addition, though the editor failed to understand that in Matthew The Man's being raised was his glorification, his coming to the Father.

COMMENT

This account is one of the theophany narratives of the NT (cf. also Acts ix 1–19; Rev i 10 ff.). In the OT perhaps the best known is the theophany to Moses in Exod iii 1–6. The supposed distinction drawn in Num xii 6–8 between dream and vision is illusory, but there is a clear difference here between "dream/vision" and the actual seeing of Yahweh "mouth to mouth." Cf. here Albright, *Yahweh and the Gods of Canaan*, pp. 42 ff. The biblical material is such as to make wholly unnecessary an Iranian background (*hvarenah*). For John, the wedding at Cana was a theophany (John ii 1–11), and II Peter i 16–18 regards the present incident as crucial. The tradition as stated in all probability goes back to Peter's own reminiscences. The incident is also linked with the story of Jesus' baptism by the proclaiming of his dignity by a *voice*, the proclamation being the same on both occasions: *This is my*

Son, the Beloved One. On both occasions, the veil of the present is stripped away to reveal Jesus as he is by Messianic calling, and as he will be in glory.

It has been pointed out by several scholars that the account of the transfiguration has words and phrases in common with both the resurrection and ascension stories, especially in Luke. (Cf. G. H. Boobyer, *St. Mark and the Transfiguration Story,* London: T. Clark, 1942; A. M. Ramsey, *The Glory of God and the Transfiguration of Christ,* London: Longmans, 1949; J. G. Davies, "The Ascension in the Third Gospel," JTS 6 [1955], 229–33.) This connection of language and motif we also see in the Apocalypse of Peter (cf. M. R. James, *The Apocryphal New Testament* [Oxford University Press, 1953], p. 519).

The verbal parallels can be seen from the accompanying table:

	Luke	Luke	Acts
	ix	xxiv	i
authority and power	1		2, 8
kingdom	2, 11, 27		3
witness(es)	5		8
John and Elijah	7–9, 18–21		5
returning	10		12
looking (to heaven)	16		11
death and resurrection	22		3
reference to "coming"	26		11
mountain	28		12
white (shining) clothing	29	4	10
two men	30	4	10
glory	31	26	
cloud	34		9

Too much modern NT interpretation has been concerned with finding not only contemporary Jewish eschatological motifs in the accounts, but also cultic and mythological elements (e.g., the "going up" in Acts i 11). In addition, it is sometimes said that what we have in the transfiguration narrative is an attempt to insert a resurrection-appearance into this earlier time of the ministry. The material in the above table is most useful in discussing Luke; but there are certain observations we should make here:

(a) The precision of description in this incident, and the exact detail, make it unlikely that a resurrection-appearance has been placed in this early context.

(b) The crucial place occupied by the account in the tradition of all three evangelists is also evidence that the resurrection-appearance is unlikely. In all three gospels the confession of Peter, with its accompanying predictions of the passion—i.e., the reinterpretation of Messiahship—is followed by this account of the apprehension by three of the disciples of Jesus' glory, their realization of his place in the OT tradition.

(c) If the Lukan account binds together the Messianic Feast, the transfiguration and the glorification of Jesus in a verbal pattern, this ought not to be surprising. Luke as a theologian was dealing with the "glory" of Jesus as men saw it and apprehended it, and a common vocabulary is hardly ground for dismissing the complex as later invention (N.B.: on the ascension, cf. A. M. Ramsey, "What Was the Ascension?" in *Historicity and Chronology in the New Testament,* London: SPCK, 1965).

(d) In whatever terms we explain the phenomena in this narrative, it has been rightly pointed out by Stendahl (*Peake's Commentary on the Bible,* p. 788) that the whole background of the incident is that of the feast of Tabernacles, with its emphasis on the new age of the Messiah and the accompanying Messianic "rest." If we allow that the disciples were full of enthusiasm at the open confession of Jesus as Messiah, rather than occupied with rational explanations of that Messiahship, the incident described in the opening verses of this chapter is precisely what we would expect, in whatever terms described.

62. A LESSON ABOUT FAITH
(xvii 14–21)†

XVII 14 When they were approaching the crowd, a man came up to him, and knelt before him, with the words, 15 "Sir, have pity on my son, for he is an epileptic and suffers terribly, and often falls into the fire or water. 16 I brought him to your disciples, and they were unable to cure him." 17 "Faithless and perverse generation!" Jesus replied. "How long am I to be with you? How long am I to bear with you? Bring him here to me." 18 Then Jesus rebuked it (i.e. the demon), the demon left him, and the boy was cured instantly. 19 Thereupon the disciples came to Jesus privately, to ask, "Why were we unable to exorcise it?" 20 He said to them, "Because of your scanty faith. I solemnly tell you that if you have even the faith of a mustard seed, you will say to this mountain 'Move from here to there,' and it will move, and nothing will be impossible for you. [21 Nevertheless, this kind does not come out except by prayer and fasting.]"

† **Matt xvii 14–21** ‖ Mark ix 14–29, Luke ix 37–43a.

NOTES

The Markan account of this incident is considerably fuller, but also somewhat obscure (e.g., Who was discussing what? Mark ix 16; and Why was the crowd astounded? ix 15). Luke, like Matthew, is far more terse.

xvii 15. *epileptic*. Mark ix 17–18 ascribed the son's condition to demon possession. Cf. NOTES on iv 24, viii 31.

17. For all the brevity of the narrative in the interests of instruction, Matthew notes the saying which suggests the approaching end of Jesus' stay among men. Cf. John xiv 9.

Faithless and perverse generation! Cf. Deut xxxii 5.

20. *scanty faith*. This expression is characteristically Matthean: cf. vi 30, viii 26, xiv 31, xvi 8.

The rest of this verse is similar to Luke xvii 6 and Mark xi 23. On the mustard seed, cf. xiii 31 f.

21. This verse, not found in the best manuscripts, is probably due to later editorial assimilation to Mark ix 29.

63. PASSION PREDICTION
(xvii 22–23)†

XVII ²² While they were gathering in Galilee, Jesus said to them, "The Man will be handed over to men, ²³ and they will kill him. On the third day he will be raised." They were much distressed.

† Matt xvii 22–23 ‖ Mark ix 30–32, Luke ix 43b–45.

NOTES

The second passion prediction occasions no surprise to the disciples, only distress. See NOTE on vss. 11–12 (in §61) above. It is possible, in view of the confusion surrounding the text in Mark ix 9–13, that vss. 22–23 in this chapter are an editorial addition to the original text, with some of the difficulties removed. In that event, we are left with xvi 21 as the first—and so far solitary—passion prediction, a saying which certainly does not imply that it is The Man who suffers.

64. QUESTIONS ABOUT THE TEMPLE TAX
(xvii 24–27)

XVII 24 When they came to Capernaum, the collectors of the half-shekel tax came to Peter, asking, "Does not your master pay the tax?" 25 and he replied "Yes." When he reached home, Jesus asked him first, "How does it appear to you, Simon? From whom do the kings of the earth exact tribute or poll tax? From their citizens, or from the others?" 26 When he replied "From the others," Jesus said to him, "In that case, the citizens are free. 27 However, lest we should cause offense to them, go to the sea and cast a hook, take the first fish that comes up, and when you open its mouth you will find a coin. Take that, and give it to them for me and for yourself."

NOTES

xvii 24. *Capernaum*. In view of the careful organization which surrounded the collection of the tax, this town would have been a natural center in which tax collectors could meet with travelers.

tax (Gr. *ta didrachma*). This word, in the plural, merely means "the two-drachma taxes," and not "half-shekels." Josephus (*Antiquities* III. 194) says that the sum paid was *to didrachmon,* or two Attic drachmas, which corresponds in function to the rabbinic half-shekel temple tax.

25. *How does it appear to you.* This is a common phrase in the latter part of this gospel; cf. xviii 12, xxii 17, 42, xxvi 66.

26. *citizens* (Gr. *huioi*). Literally, *sons,* or *children.* In the light of Allegro's article (cited in the COMMENT below), we must assume this to mean Jesus and his disciples.

27. *cause offense* (Gr. *skandalisōmen*). Cf. NOTE on v 30—something which causes others to sin.

coin (Gr. *statēra*). This coin would presumably be equal to four drachmas, and so was equivalent to the tax for two men. However, the values of these coins were constantly fluctuating. Cf. also the discussion by S. V. McCasland and Sherman Johnson in IB, VII, pp. 96 and 465 f., respectively.

COMMENT

The importance of this narrative to those who were still living within the framework of Judaism, though committed in allegiance to Jesus as Messiah, must have been considerable in the years before A.D. 70. It has been suggested that this passage belongs to the period *after* A.D. 70, when Vespasian diverted the tax to build the temple of Jupiter Capitolinus and so caused a crisis of conscience for Jewish Christians. It may be doubted how many Jewish Christians there were living in Palestine after A.D. 70, since apart from the movement of Christianity into a Gentile milieu, consistent Church tradition was that large numbers of Jewish Christians fled the country during the first Jewish War of 66–70.

In the latter part of the Persian period (which lasted from 525–325 B.C.), Jews resident in Judea were paying taxes for the support of the autonomous priesthood and for the upkeep of the temple. This tax is not mentioned in the Torah, but its existence is established by the archaeological evidence of coins and jar seals. In the rabbinic period the tax was payable by all who had attained twenty years, but slaves and women were explicitly excluded. Gentiles and Samaritans were not allowed to contribute. Great care was exercised in the collection of the tax, both in Palestine and among Jews of the Dispersion, and under Roman domination the tax was accorded state protection and given safe conduct.

Apart from the exceptions already noted, energetic measures were taken to enforce the collection, and provision was made to seize the goods of those who did not pay (cf. *The Mishnah* tr. from the Hebrew by Herbert Danby [Oxford University Press, 1933], p. 152). The currency used in payment varied from time to time, but in the time of Jesus it was the Tyrian shekel, and tables were set up in the temple to deal with the money-changing problems. Exchange brokers made, and were allowed to make, a considerable profit on the undertaking.

We alluded in the first paragraph to the view that this narrative was included in order to deal with Christians and/or Jewish Christians being sued for what was after A.D. 70 a purely pagan tax. But Gentiles were excluded from this peculiarly Jewish tax and Jesus' claim of exemption for the freeborn sons can be construed as claiming exemption from all other taxation. We are faced with the alternative: either (a) the story was adapted to the need of Christians—easily confused with Jews by Roman authority—or (b) the saying of Jesus as it stands had a meaning which in its own context has to be discovered. There are two elements in the narrative: first, the conversation with Peter about the tax, and secondly a seemingly miracle story attached to the conversation and apparently in response to it. These elements will be dealt with in reverse order.

The narrative in vs. 27 is so highly condensed that it is more than likely a much-abbreviated summary of an actual catch of a fish with a coin in its mouth (the *clarias macracanthus,* or "St. Peter's fish," common in the Sea of Galilee, is certainly able to accommodate coins in its ample mouth). Alternatively, the narrative may be the remnant of a parable, much on the lines of folk tales found in the rabbinic tradition of the lost-and-found-again variety. In this case, the parable remnant will have been attracted to its present position by the presence of vss. 24–26.

The incident in vss. 24–26 is not so easily analyzed. It might have answered questions as to the validity of the temple tax for Jewish Christians before A.D. 70—*lest we should cause offense.* But this view gives rise to one serious objection. It casts the *non-*Jewish Christian in the role of "citizen" or "freeborn," and the Jewish Christian in that of slave or subject people. This is the precise opposite of the Pauline view (cf. Rom xi 13–36), even though Paul could call non-Christian Jews "enemies of God." Either Jesus in this narrative is taking sides with the Sadducees (who wanted temple worship maintained by the gifts of individuals) as against a Pharisee interpretation of Exod xxx 11–16, or we must find some other explanation. J. M. Allegro ("An Unpublished Fragment of Essene Halakhah—4Q Ordinances," JSS 6 [1961], 71) seems to indicate that a Qumran fragment suits the present discussion almost exactly. According to Allegro's text, the Essenes linked the once-for-all atonement tax of Exod xxx 11–16 (cf. xxxviii 26) with the valuation tax of Lev xxvii 1–8. He suggests that this unique understanding by the Essenes of the temple tax as being a once-for-all payment was shared by Jesus, and further suggests that this may account for Jesus' hostility toward the taxation officials in the temple. J. D. M. Derrett, "Peter's Penny: Fresh Light on Matthew xvii 24–7," NovT 6 (1963), 1–15, has further suggestions. He asks whether Jesus also was thought to claim exemption on the score that the collectors thought, as did others, that he was a Samaritan. If therefore the tax collectors were claiming from a man not liable, *they* would sin, on the ground that an inferior sinned if he carried out the unlawful commands of his superior. Jesus' saying that "the children are free," not on the ground that he was a Samaritan, but simply because he and the disciples were dependents, living on charity, cf. John xii 6, nevertheless was bound to save the collectors from possible sin. Hence—according to Derrett—the phrase *lest we should cause offense.* (On this tax, see further Hugh Monte-fiore, "Jesus and the Temple Tax," NTS 11 [1964–65], 60–72; L. Finkelstein, *The Pharisees: The Sociological Background of Their Faith,* 2d ed. rev. [Philadelphia: JPS, 1940], 11, pp. 683 ff.)

65. PRECEDENCE IN THE KINGDOM
(xviii 1–9)†

XVIII 1 At that time the disciples came to Jesus asking, "Who is the greatest in the Kingdom of heaven?" 2 Calling a child, he put him in the middle of them, 3 and said, "I solemnly tell you that unless you turn and become again like children, you will not enter the Kingdom of heaven. 4 Therefore whoever humbles himself like this child is the greatest in the Kingdom of heaven. 5 Whoever receives one such child in my name receives me, 6 but whoever causes one of the most insignificant believers to sin, then for him it would be better to have a great millstone about his neck, and to be drowned in the ocean depths. 7 Alas for a world filled with occasions for sin! Such occasions must necessarily arise, but alas for the man through whom they arise! 8 If therefore your hand or your foot causes you to sin, cut it off and throw it away from you; it is better for you to enter life maimed or lame than to be thrown into the fire at the end of the age still having two hands or two feet. 9 And if your eye causes you to sin, then take it out and throw it away from you—it is better to enter into life with one eye, rather than with two eyes to be thrown into the fiery death.

† **Matt xviii 1–5** || Mark ix 33–37, Luke ix 46–48; **6–9** || Mark ix 42–48, Luke xvii 1–2.

NOTES

xviii 1. *At that time.* As the following verses stand they seem intended by Matthew to follow on from the preceding incident, and to answer the question: "Why is Peter reckoned as first?" On the formula, cf. NOTE on xii 1.

3. By the question they have asked, the disciples demonstrate their lack of understanding of the nature of the Kingdom. It is only those who know that they cannot possibly *earn* God's grace who can fully respond to it—in the same way that children know that they can never earn free gifts.

6. *insignificant* (literally, "little ones"). Cf. x 42, and applying here to the apparently unnoticed. The expression is not an indication of any kind of age range. The Markan tradition (ix 42), fuller than Matthew's, makes this point clear. Mark here has two separate sayings about the hand and the foot (ix 43, 45) while Matthew, who here has them together, has a saying about the hand in v 30.

8. *fire at the end of the age.* (See NOTE on v 22.) I.e., better to avoid the occasions of sin than to face a future judgment. The Hebrew equivalent of the Greek adjective *aiōnion* refers to the "(end of) the age" (*qēṣ*) in which men are living. This we now know from the Essene scrolls, where the word is very common in this sense.

COMMENT

Having spoken of his coming sufferings and death on his way to the final encounter in Jerusalem, Jesus here in the Matthean tradition speaks of problems of concern to his community. How much of the material in xviii–xx 28 belongs to the same occasion, we do not know, but it would be natural for the evangelist to group material together in this fashion. Now that the acknowledgment of his Messiahship has been made, it is necessary for Jesus to make provision for the Messianic Community which will continue beyond his death and resurrection. There are some firm indications of the manner in which Matthew has collected the sayings in this section, by making comparisons with Mark ix–x.

Mark ix 37–50 consists of a series of sayings broken by a short narrative at vss. 38–40. But the connection of the sayings is plainly artificial, and the succession of them sometimes very awkward: vss. 42–43 are difficult to connect, and the "by fire" of vs. 49 cannot easily be connected with vs. 48. Certainly there are key words and phrases which would remind Mark of similar sayings (e.g., vs. 37, cf. vss. 38–40, 41; vs. 42, cf. vss. 43–48; vs. 49, cf. vs. 50) and the whole section seems to be contrived by association. Matthew, however, has arranged the material in a thoroughly orderly manner, and makes of Mark's loose association of words and phrases a far more consecutive discourse.

Matt xviii 3–4	=	Mark x 15
xviii 5	=	ix 37a
xviii 6	=	ix 42
xviii 8–9	=	ix 43–47

Mark's ix 37b has already appeared in Matthew's x 40, and the intrusive Markan vss. 38–40 find no place in Matthew. Mark's ix 41 is already in the Matthean tradition at x 42, while ix 50 has a parallel in Matthew's v 13. With Mark ix 48–50 we are not immediately concerned, but those verses with all their attendant difficulties may be fragments of more than two sayings. If Matthew knew them in their present fragmented state, he decided to omit them.

So far as Matthew's vss. 12–14 (§66) are concerned, they have a parallel in Luke xv 3–7; vs. 6 is in Luke xvii 2 in a quite different context, vs. 7 is paralleled by Luke xvii 1, while vss. 15 and 21 (§§67 and 68)=Luke xvii 3 and 4 respectively.

As with so much which has occasionally been used in an attempt to prove that Matthew depends on Mark, the relationships are such that when the Lukan tradition is taken into account, it is far easier to explain similarities and differences on the basis of three independent approaches to the fixed oral tradition.

66. THE LOST SHEEP
(xviii 10–14)†

XVIII   10 "See that you do not treat one of the common
people with contempt, for I tell you that in heaven their angels
always see the face of my Father who is in heaven. [11 The
Man came to save the lost.] 12 What do you think? If someone
has a hundred sheep, and one of them strays, does he not leave
the ninety-nine in the desert and go in search of the stray?
13 If he finds it, I solemnly tell you that he rejoices more over
that one than over the ninety-nine which never strayed. 14 In
the same way, it is not the will of your Father in heaven that
one of the common people should perish.

† **Matt xviii 10–14** || Luke xv 3–7.

Notes

xviii 10. *the common people*. The Greek expression is the same as in vs.
6, literally "these little ones."

their angels. In line with the belief which finds expression elsewhere
in the Bible (Gen xlviii 16; Dan x 11, 20) Jesus asserts that those apt
to be despised because of their status have representatives in the
heavenly courts, just as nations have such representatives (cf. also Acts
xii 15). Such representatives naturally have access to the Father.

11. In view of the meaning which Matthew consistently applies to
The Man, this verse (omitted by some of the best manuscripts) must
be regarded as an editorial assimilation to Luke xix 10, presumably in
the interests of making a transition from vs. 10 to vss. 12–14.

12. It is worth a moment's time to note that the sheep referred to
here and elsewhere are not the fat-tailed, generally lazy sheep often
represented in romantic Bible illustrations. Until recently it was supposed
by some authorities that the broad-tailed sheep (the *Ovis laticaudatus*

of Linnaeus) had not yet been introduced into Palestine at the time of
Jesus. However, see now the study by E. Anati, "Fat-tailed Sheep of
Arabia," in Bibliothèque du Muséon, Vol. 50: *Rock-art in Central
Arabia*, II (Louvain, 1968), especially pp. 1–42. In rock art from
Central Arabia, unknown before the Belgian expedition, we have fat-
tailed sheep represented frequently in carvings from the pre-epigraphic
phase of Arabian history in the early second millennium B.C., going back
probably to the end of the third millennium. We now have cuneiform
records from about 2000 B.C. which mention fat-tailed sheep as being
imported into Babylonia at that time. The Sumerian logogram for fat-
tailed sheep was UDU.KUN.GAL., literally "big-tail sheep." Aside from
a well-known reference in Herodotus (III. 113) and a single early
Babylonian bowl, there was no other known representation or even
mention of this kind of sheep in our ancient sources. Sheep with
relatively fat tails were, of course, well known, and their fat tail was
already called *alyah* in the Pentateuch, just as in Arabic. However, it is
certain that virtually all sheep in representational art from ancient Egypt
and western Asia previously known belong to well-known types of
Mediterranean and Eurasian sheep without fat tails. It is thus quite
possible that the sheep intended by the gospel references were not of
the Arabian fat-tailed type, but perhaps of an intermediate breed with
small fat tails. The sheep of that time were probably more active
than their modern Palestinian counterparts.

13–14. These verses are important as providing evidence of the way
in which Matthew understood the "little ones" of vs. 6. They can
hardly be small children, for in that case it is hard to see how they
could be guilty of the deliberate sin which the *straying* of vs. 12
presupposes. Moreover, putting stumbling blocks in the path of the
recent convert is the kind of problem faced by Paul in I Cor viii and
Rom xiv.

As this whole body of teaching in Matthew concerns life in the
Messianic Community, it seems far more likely that what is envisaged
here is the kind of harm which can be done to the conscience of simple
folk. Paul's first letter to Corinth abounds with examples of unthinking
behavior on the part of the pseudo-sophisticates—the "knowing ones."

67. COMMUNITY DISCIPLINE
(xviii 15–20)†

XVIII ¹⁵ "If your brother sins [against you], go and remonstrate with him privately. If he listens to you, you have gained your brother. ¹⁶ But if he will not listen, take one or two others with you in order that 'by the evidence of two or three witnesses every word may be confirmed.' ¹⁷ If, however, he will not listen to them, tell it to the community, and if then he will not listen to the community, let him be regarded as outside the community. ¹⁸ I solemnly tell you that whatever you bind on earth will have been bound in heaven, and whatever you release on earth will have been released in heaven. ¹⁹ Again, I tell you that if two of you agree on earth about any request you make, it will be done for you by my Father in heaven; ²⁰ for where two or three are gathered in my name I am there in the middle of them."

† Matt xviii 15 ‖ Luke xvii 3.

NOTES

xviii 15. *gained your brother.* Cf. Lev xix 17 ff.; and also Matt v 43, xix 19, and xxii 39. The sayings here concern personal offenses and spring from the same kind of concern as found expression in v 23–24.

16. *But if he will not listen.* I.e., if the offender refuses reconciliation.

by the evidence . . . confirmed may well have been added from the Mosaic law (Deut xix 15) by an editor as apt, though not for an identical situation. What is envisaged is not a court of law, for the *one or two others* are not witnesses to the offense, but to the willingness or unwillingness of the offender to be reconciled.

17. *community* (Gr. *ekklēsia.*). Cf. xvi 18. In the context of the two

men who are out of charity with each other, it is a local community which is here meant.

outside the community (literally, "as a Gentile and a tax gatherer"). Cf. NOTE on v 46, where the expression is similar.

18. This is almost exactly what Jesus told Peter after Peter's confession—cf. final NOTE on xvi 19; cf. also I Cor v 3–5; vi 1–8.

19. It is unlikely that this verse is in its original context, for while vs. 18 dealt with conduct on the part of the community's members, vs. 19 is an exhortation to faithfulness in prayer. Presumably this verse found its way to its present position because of the occurrence of *earth* and *heaven* in both verses.

20. Cf. *Pirqê Abôth* iii 3: "Two that sit together occupied in the Law have the Presence among them."

68. THE QUESTION OF FORGIVENESS
(xviii 21–35)

XVIII   21 Then Peter came to him with the question: "Lord, how many times may my brother sin against me, and I have to forgive him? Seven times?" 22 Jesus replied, "Not 'seven times,' but 'seventy times seven.' 23 For this reason, the Kingdom of heaven may be compared with a king who wished to settle accounts with his slaves. 24 When he had begun the reckoning there was brought to him a man who owed him ten thousand talents, 25 but as he could not pay, his master ordered him to be sold, together with his wife and children and all his possessions, and payment to be made. 26 But the slave threw himself before him, begging him, 'Be patient with me, and I will pay you everything.' 27 The master, pitying him, let him go and forgave him the debt. 28 However, on going out that slave found one of his fellow slaves who owed him one hundred pennies. Seizing him by the throat, he said, 'Pay me the debt.' 29 But his fellow slave knelt before him and begged him, 'Have patience with me, and I will repay you.' 30 He refused, and threw him into prison until he could pay the debt. 31 When his fellow slaves saw what had happened, they were deeply distressed, and went and reported to their master all that had happened. 32 His master then summoned him, and said to him, 33 'You wicked slave! I forgave you all that debt because you begged me; and ought you not to have pitied your fellow slave in the same way that I pitied you?' 34 In anger his master handed him over to the investigators until the debt was paid. 35 So my heavenly Father will deal in the same way with every one of you, if you do not forgive your brother without reservation."

NOTES

There is some discussion in the Babyonian Talmud as to the precise number of times when forgiveness must be unconditionally rendered, with opinions offered that three times is an acceptable maximum.

xviii 22. *seventy times seven.* (It may also be understood as seventy-seven times.) The number merely means an indefinitely great number of times.

24. *ten thousand talents.* The talent was equivalent to six thousand denarii. Two denarii would provide a man and his family with adequate living for one day, and hence the sum named here is tremendous, in contrast with the small sum owed by the other servant in vs. 28.

The lesson of the parable is clear enough, though it is possible that two parables have been merged here into the present narrative. We have a *king* in vs. 23 who appears from the sum involved to be dealing with subordinate officials (who could well be slaves), but the later stages of the narrative read more obviously of a landowner dealing with working slaves.

69. QUESTIONS ABOUT THE LAW
(xix 1–12)†

XIX 1 When Jesus had finished these sayings, he left Galilee and came into that part of Judea beyond the Jordan, 2 and large crowds followed him there, and he healed them.

3 Pharisees came to him with a test question: "Is it lawful to divorce one's wife for any cause?" 4 He replied: "Have you not read that the Creator from the beginning 'made them male and female' 5 and said, 'for this reason a man will leave his father and mother, be joined to his wife, and the two shall become one'? 6 So that they are no longer two persons, but a single body. Therefore what God has joined, let no man separate." 7 They said, "Then why did Moses prescribe 'to give divorce papers, and be rid of her'?" 8 He replied, "Moses allowed you to divorce your wives because of your stubbornness, but it was not so at the beginning. 9 I tell you that whoever divorces his wife, except for unchastity, and marries someone else, commits adultery [and he who marries her who has been put away commits adultery]." 10 The disciples said to him, "If the situation is such between a man and his wife, then it is folly to marry." 11 "Not all men can accept this," he answered them, "but only those to whom it is granted; 12 for there are those incapable of marriage who have been so from birth, others who have been made so by men, and there are yet others who have made themselves so for the sake of the Kingdom of heaven. Let anyone who can, bear this in mind."

† **Matt xix 1–12** || Mark x 1–12.

NOTES

xix 1. *When Jesus had finished.* For this formula, cf. vii 28, xi 1, xiii 53; xxvi 1.

3. *test question.* Divorce was quite legal under Jewish law (cf. Deut xxiv 1–2), but there was some dispute about the reasons for divorce. The followers of Hillel were more lenient in their views than those of Shammai (the evidence can be found in the Mishnah, *Gittin* 90a). The school of Shammai permitted divorce only on grounds of unchastity. It is noteworthy that Jesus makes no reference to Mal ii 14–16.

The differences in this account of the test question as compared with that of Mark are perhaps at this stage incapable of final resolution.

(a) The question of divorce had already been raised (v 31 f.) in the main body of discussion as to the validity of the Law.

(b) It hardly seems adequate to say that this is a test question in the sense that similar tests will be posed in chapters xxi and xxii, and it is quite possible that vss. 3–9, belonging to another discussion on marriage, were attracted to this context by vss. 11–12.

(c) That the Matthean tradition differs from that of Mark can easily be seen here. In Mark the question poses the legality of divorce, and Jesus' questioners, in no doubt about the position of the Law, would not have entertained any doubts on the issue. But the Pharisees, in the light of Mark vii 14–23, might have expected Jesus to call the Law in question on that very point. Whereas in the Markan tradition Jesus demands that they tell him the prescriptions of the Mosaic Law and when they have done so goes beyond that Law to the very purpose of marriage, the Matthean emphasis is quite different. In Matthew there is first the statement of the purpose of marriage, and then another question from the Pharisees, to which Jesus replies that the Mosaic Law was an accommodation. There are two more instructive differences in Matthew as compared with the Markan tradition: (1) According to Mark (x 12), Jesus explicitly accepts the case of a woman divorcing her husband, a provision not made in Jewish law (cf. here Josephus, *Antiquities* XV. 259 for an exceptional example). It is possible to read this Markan provision as an assertion by Jesus of the sinfulness of divorce. (2) In the Matthean tradition in this present chapter Jesus appears, by the exceptive clause in vs. 9, to take his stand with the stricter interpretation of Shammai against Hillel, and in so doing would appear to affirm the permanent validity of the Mosaic marriage law.

We are in no position to make categorical statements at this point. It is possible that Matthew's tradition has here been influenced by a Jewish-Christian view of Jesus as a rabbinic commentator on the Law.

4. Cf. Gen i 27; v 2.

5. *and said*. This is ambiguous. It can refer either to Jesus, or—far more likely—to *the Creator* in the previous verse.

6. *a single body*. The sense is that God created a single man and a single woman, destined for each other, and that the case of a man and a woman in marriage is precisely similar. That is to say, in the purpose of God they are one body, and as such separation is unthinkable.

8. There may be a deliberate contrast in the wording here, between *prescribe* in vs. 7 and *allowed* here. At all events, Jesus describes the Mosaic permission as a departure from the standards presupposed in the creation of a single pair made for each other.

9. Cf. Luke xvi 18; I Cor vii 10–13. Mark (x 10) here represents the disciples as seeking private instruction about this "in the house." For the parallel to this saying, cf. v 32. Mark here has a reference to a woman divorcing her husband—cf. Note c (1) on vs. 3.

except for unchastity. This same exception is found at v 32, but is not found elsewhere in the NT. Commentators have generally taken the position that these words are not part of the saying as originally uttered, but are a community regulation later inserted into the text. It certainly appears to be inconsistent with vs. 6. The precise meaning of *unchastity* is uncertain.

[*and he who marries her* . . .]. These words are not to be found in all the best manuscripts, and may have been added in the light of Mark x 12.

10. *situation* (Gr. *aitia*). The same Greek word is found at vs. 3 (our translation, *cause*). The disciples reason that if unchastity is to be the sole determining factor for divorce, then it is better not to risk marriage.

11. *Not all men can accept this*. Placed where it is, this reply of Jesus is not at all clear. The Greek for *this* (literally, *this saying*) may refer to the following vs. 12, in which case Jesus would seem to be exalting the celibate state as opposed to the married state, in response to the disciples' amazement at the stringency of his pronouncements. Alternatively, *this* may refer to the teaching given on divorce in vss. 4–9, in which case this saying will refer to those unwilling to accept the stricter marriage law of the Messianic Community, and *only those to whom it is granted* will refer to those called by God into that Community. This interpretation removes the burden of supposing that Jesus recommended abstention from marriage for the Kingdom's sake, and the *gar* (for) would support this interpretation better. (It should here be noticed that Paul's advice in I Cor vii 6–8 is in a very

different—Corinthian—context.) In short, Jesus demands of those who come to the Kingdom a standard of marriage discipline at least as stringent as that which applied to Shammai's followers.

It is also possible that the contents of vss. 11–12 are an independent saying which remains obscure. The *gar* would then be an editorial connective.

those to whom it is granted. I.e., by divine grace.

12. In the light of what has been said, it is possible that the saying in this verse has been attracted to its present context as being loosely associated with a discussion on marriage. In reality only two classes of men are being described here—those physically incapable of marriage, either from birth or from being rendered so by others, and those who while at one time physically capable of marriage have renounced that state either by self-mutilation or voluntary celibacy.

The eunuch was for many centuries a well-recognized (and for obvious reasons well-trusted) figure in Near and Far Eastern society. The attitude of the Christian Church to self-mutilation was in the early centuries ambivalent, and though one prominent theologian (Origen, third century) was self-castrated, such a state was a permanent barrier to the ministry. The second class of men described in vs. 12— those who have voluntarily renounced marriage—was well-known to Jesus from the example of some of the Essenes who embraced celibacy. This part of the saying—*who have made themselves so for the sake of the Kingdom*—has been used in Christian history from the earliest times as sanction for the celibate vocation. It is to be noted that the phrase *Kingdom of heaven,* applying as it does in Matthew to the Messianic Community, clearly states the purpose of that vocation.

Let anyone who can, . . . Cf. NOTE on xi 15.

There is quite considerable textual variation and transposition in our manuscripts throughout this section. It is far too technical for discussion in a commentary such as this (vs. 4 is particularly difficult), and the reader who knows some Greek is referred to the note on p. 206 of Allen's ICC St. Matthew commentary.

Some aspects of the question have been dealt with recently by Quentin Quesnell ("Made Themselves Eunuchs for the Kingdom of Heaven [Mt 19:12]," CBQ 30 [1968], 335–58).

COMMENTS

Matthew indicates that a final and definitive stage has been reached in the ministry by the first verse of this section. Although the material in this chapter appears to be made up of loosely connected episodes, it serves as summary of all that has preceded it, and at the

same time as introduction to the final events and concluding teaching
of the ministry.

The evangelist introduced the Galilean ministry with a quotation
from Isaiah (cf. iv 12 ff.) indicating Galilee as a place of special
revelation. That ministry of revelation has now been completed,
and it is fitting that the evangelist should record the departure from
Galilee.

70. BLESSING THE CHILDREN
(xix 13–15)†

XIX   13 Then children were brought to him so that he might lay his hands upon them and pray, but the disciples rebuked them. 14 Jesus, however, said to them, "Let the children come to me. Do not hinder them, because the Kingdom of heaven is for such people," 15 and he laid his hands upon them and went away.

† **Matt xix 13–15** || Mark x 13–16, Luke xviii 15–17.

COMMENT

Here, and in the parallel in Mark, there are indications of the way in which material was collected by the evangelists. There is no immediately obvious connection between this short section and what follows it. The best explanation is that both in Matthew and Mark the incident was placed here because the preceding discussion of marriage suggested this narrative about the children. Luke links the incident to the conclusion of the parable about the Pharisee and the tax collector, as an emphasis on humility. The lesson of the parable is obvious enough—cf. NOTES on xviii 1–14.

71. TRUE RICHES
(xix 16–30) †

XIX   16 Someone came to him with the question, "Teacher, what good thing must I do to have eternal life?" 17 He answered him, "Why question me about what is good? There is One who is good, and if you wish to enter into the life (of the Kingdom), keep the commandments." 18 He said to him, "Which ones?" and Jesus said to him, "You shall not murder, you shall not commit adultery, 19 not steal, not perjure yourself, honor your father and mother, and love your neighbor as you love yourself." 20 The young man declared to him, "I have kept all these; in what respect am I still found wanting?" 21 "If you wish to be true," Jesus said to him, "go and sell all your possessions, give to the poor, and you will have treasure in heaven— and come, follow me." 22 On hearing this, the young man went sadly away, for he was very wealthy.

23 To his disciples Jesus said, "I solemnly tell you, it will be hard for a rich man to enter the Kingdom of heaven. 24 Further, I tell you that it is easier for a camel to go through the eye of a needle than for a rich man to enter God's Kingdom." 25 When the disciples heard this, they were astounded, and said, "Then who can be saved?" 26 Jesus, looking at them, said "For men, this is impossible, but for God all things are possible." 27 Peter then said to him in reply, "See, we have left everything and followed you. What therefore will become of us?" 28 Jesus said to them, "I solemnly tell you that in the new creation, when The Man sits on his glorious throne, you who have followed me will also sit on twelve thrones judging the twelve tribes of

† **Matt xix 16–30** ‖ Mark x 17–31, Luke xviii 18–30.

Israel. 29 And everyone who has left homes, brothers, sisters, father or mother, children or lands, for my name's sake, will receive a hundredfold, and will inherit eternal life. 30 Nevertheless, many who are first will be last, and the last first.

NOTES

Here again we have an example of contextual attraction, in this case the result of a previous saying on conditions for entry into the Kingdom.

xix 16. *Teacher.* Mark's tradition is here common with Luke's; both have the adjective *good* with *Teacher,* as also both speak of *to inherit eternal life.*

17. Occasionally much has been made of a supposed transference by Matthew of *good* from *Teacher* to *thing,* in order (so it is said) to avoid having Jesus make any distinction between himself and the Father. But wherever the adjective occurs, in both traditions Jesus is calling attention to, and calling sharply into question, the presuppositions of his questioner. If Jesus is simply *Teacher,* then he is calculated to know no more and no less than any other teacher as to what actions are deemed "good for" entrance into the life of the age-to-come. If he is *Good Teacher* (as in Mark and Luke), then Jesus will not allow the questioner to use word or ascriptions lightly.

One who is good. I.e., it is not a matter of the *good thing* as if it were some attainable practice or state which, once acquired or accomplished, will guarantee entrance into life. *Good* is a mark of character, pre-eminently of God. God's goodness to man is shown to us in the commandments, and man's loyal response to those commandments is a test of man's goodness.

keep (Gr. *tērein*). The verb is used again in xxiii 3, and there denotes continued action; here it is the urgent aorist imperative.

18. Matthew certainly treats the questioner far less sympathetically than Mark. The question *Which ones?* makes the man appear somewhat stupid, while the *I have kept all these* shows the man's pride.

18–19. *You shall not murder, . . .* It should be noted that neither this NT version, nor the Hebrew text of the Decalogue, provides any foundation for pacifism. What is under condemnation is murder, not killing in warfare.

A comparison of the texts of Matthew, Mark, and Luke in these verses discloses considerable variation, and this is to be expected when access to the LXX provided more than one version by which scribes and others could check the quotations from the Law. By NT times there were several divergent recensions of the Decalogue (cf. A. Jepsen, "Beiträge zur Auslegung und Geschichte des Dekalogs," ZAW 79 [1967], 277–304. Mark (x 19) after "Do not perjure yourself" has "Do not defraud," the provenance of which is uncertain, but which may come from Exod xxi 10; Deut xxiv 14; or Ecclus iv 1. Some manuscripts of Mark omit it, as does Matthew. He has, after *honor your father and mother,* the injunction to *love* (i.e., be loyal to) one's neighbor, taken from Lev xix 18 (cf. also xxii 39=Mark xii 31; Luke x 27). The first four injunctions are from Exod xx 13–16 or Deut v 17–20. Matthew's order is that of the Masoretic text of Exodus and Deuteronomy; but Mark in some manuscripts reverses the order of *murder* and *adultery,* as does Luke in xviii 20, likewise, Philo and one LXX manuscript of Deuteronomy. Matthew incidentally has the imperative future (which is also the Greek of the LXX), literally translating the Hebrew imperfect, which is the negative imperative in Hebrew, where Mark has the subjunctive (which is the aorist prohibitory form).

20. The Markan version of this verse can be read as "Against all these things I have guarded myself."

21. At this point Mark depicts the young man as a lovable character (x 21), but in Matthew, no such attractiveness is to be discerned. We must either conclude with some commentators that Matthew knew the Markan tradition and edited it so as to eliminate all references to human emotion in Jesus, or we must conclude that Matthew's tradition is wholly independent.

true (Gr. *teleios*). I.e., "true to God, true to the Covenant." Cf. NOTE on v 48. This word has frequently been translated as "perfect." Such a translation is unfortunate, because it carries implications of moral perfections to an extent which is not true of either the Greek or the Latin, and certainly not true of the Hebrew which lies behind the Greek. Translated as "perfect," the word has Gnostic implications which are wholly foreign to the Gospel. Mark's "You lack one thing" is not found in Matthew, and the reply of Jesus here is wholly in keeping with the man's character as Matthew sees it. There is no promise of entry into the life of the age-to-come, except in so far as this is implied by *treasure in heaven.* The man who thinks that the life of the age-to-come can be earned by exact calculation is told to abandon all. In so doing he may learn in the community the lessons of humility.

22. Mark here characterizes the young man as being unwilling to obey Jesus' injunction. Luke and Matthew do not use Mark's strong Gr. *stugnasas* ("being shocked, appalled") which denotes this.

The previous incident leads naturally into the next exchange between Jesus and his disciples.

23. *hard for a rich man.* For the rich man the difficulty lies in

making a choice between caring for his wealth and caring for the things of God. Cf. vii 14; it is not that riches per se are a barrier to salvation, it is simply that they pose peculiar temptations to the rich man's spiritual welfare.

24. Mark's x 25 is identical, and in the same context.

it is easier . . . In spite of the attempts of commentators and preachers to find small gates, or even camel-hair, in this saying, it seems certain that this is simply a proverb cast in hyperbolic form.

God's Kingdom. The expression is fully in line with Matthew's tradition, to which we have called attention before. The rich man may indeed enter the Messianic Community, the Kingdom of heaven, but at the judgment a far stricter account will be demanded of him than of others when the Son's Kingdom is given up to the Father. Whether —since Matthew shares the expression with Mark (x 25) and Luke (xviii 25)—the evangelist would have changed the terms if the Messianic Community had been under discussion is a matter which is not open to our inspection.

25. *Then who can be saved?* Presumably the disciples are *astounded,* and ask who then can enter the Father's Kingdom (cf. x 23; xxiv 13, 22), as they had presumed that riches and possessions were signs of God's blessings on a man. This is good OT teaching, from the story of Abraham to that of Job, and is in keeping with the whole empirical approach of ancient Israel. Generally, obedience to law, and diligent work, tend to bring prosperity, and the rich are expected to be generous (though they can often be insensitive to suffering). It is of importance to remember that Jesus' apothegms do not attempt to encompass all reality.

26. Salvation, entrance into God's Kingdom, is the gift of God, and the yardstick of human judgment is inappropriate and misleading. (Cf. Gen xviii 14, Job xlii 2, for the expression *adunaton* which Jesus uses.)

27. Peter's question *may* have reference to the young man: "We have done all that the young man was unwilling to do. What will be our reward?"

28. *the new creation* (Gr. *palingenesia*). The word is peculiar in Scripture to Matthew, though it comes twice in Philo to denote the new world after the flood (*On the Life of Moses* ii. 12) and the restored creation after destruction by fire (*Creation of the World* xv). It is said by some that there is no precise Aramaic equivalent, and that the word must therefore be the evangelist's own. However, it is no more surprising to find here a word common in Stoic circles than it is to find lists of virtues and vices in the Pauline letters which can be paralleled in Stoic material, or to find that the Jewish concept of the Word (probably *Mēmrā,* Gr. *logos*) in the prologue to John's gospel has acquired Greek philosophical overtones. To assume that the occurrence of the word in

the mediaeval *Corpus Hermeticum* indicates a borrowing from magical rites or the mystery religions is to attribute a date to the *Corpus Hermeticum* which is far too early. The finds at Nag Hammadi (Chenoboskion) have demonstrated that the mediaeval work cannot be earlier than the fifth century A.D. in its extant form.* The assumption also fails to take into account the wholesale dissemination of popular Stoic philosophy as a quasi-religious astral determinism in the centuries preceding our present written gospel.

The Syriac version substitutes for this word '*ālmā ḥadthā,* which is archaic in form and might have been used many centuries earlier. In view of the Matthean tradition this is what we would expect. It is more than likely that misunderstanding has arisen about this saying because some commentators have insisted on reading into it the presuppositions of a post-Hellenistic idealist philosophy, presuppositions having to do with the end of the temporal order, rather than seeing in this saying an assertion of the new creation, the new age, to be inaugurated by the exaltation of The Man.

The Man. Cf. NOTE on viii 20.

glorious throne. Cf. Enoch lxii 3, 5. Jesus promises that when the new age of the Messiah is inaugurated in his passion and exaltation, the disciples will share in the administration of the Kingdom.

twelve tribes. As at Qumran, the concern is for the whole assembly of Israel (cf. Rev vii 4), those to whom the Gospel has been proclaimed.

29. Cf. Enoch xl 9. The Markan parallel (x 29–30) lays stress on the new life which the neophyte will enter when he is incorporated into the Messianic Community (cf., e.g., I Cor iii 21). The fact that Matthew does not include, or does not know, Mark's "now in this present time" (cf. Luke xviii 30) ought not to be taken as an indication that for our evangelist all the blessings belong to an eternity divorced from the temporal order. We have called attention before to the thinking which Matthew has in common with John, and this is a case in point. Matthew's *new creation* of vs. 28 says no more than is said by John iii 3–8, and the emphasis here is not on the end of the temporal order, but on the *eternal life* which is the disciple's present inheritance (cf. John vi 35–59). The life of the age-to-come is a common theme in Matthew (cf. v 5, xxi 38, xxv 34), but we must beware of reading into the term meanings which belong to later idealistic and existentialist philosophies.

30. The saying in this verse is repeated in reverse order in xx 16, forming a conclusion to the parable and also making a chiasm, a device often employed by Matthew. At the same time, the meaning of the saying here is not wholly clear. The *first* may refer either to rank or privilege, or to the time at which a man entered the community. It is

* See Introduction, Part XIII, Appendix B.

even possible that in the present context it is a reply to Peter's boast of vs. 27. Luke (xiii 30) has a somewhat similar saying in quite different connection. The saying as used in xx 16 bears a meaning which does not easily fit this context.

It is worth noting here that Matthew and Luke have some textual agreements against Mark in vss. 16–30, but of a minor character.

72. THE KINGDOM:
THE WORKERS IN THE VINEYARD
(xx 1–16)

XX 1 "For the Kingdom of heaven is like a householder who set out early in the morning to hire workers for his vineyard, 2 and when he had agreed with the workers for one denarius a day, he sent them into his vineyard. 3 Going out about nine o'clock he saw other men standing idle in the market place and said to them, 4 'You go into my vineyard, too, and I will give you whatever is right,' and so they went. 5 Going out again at midday, and at three o'clock, he did the same. 6 About five o'clock he went out and found others standing. He said to them, 'Why do you stand here all day idle?' 7 They answered him, "Because no one has hired us.' 'You too go into the vineyard,' he said. 8 When evening came, the owner of the vineyard said to his steward, 'Call the workers and give them their wages, beginning with the last, and so up to the first.' 9 When those who were hired at five o'clock came, they each received a denarius. 10 When the first came, they supposed that they would receive more, but they each received a denarius. 11 On receiving it they grumbled to the owner, 12 'The last only worked an hour, but you have made them our equal, and we have borne the burden and heat of the day.' 13 But he answered one of them, 'My friend, I am not doing you an injustice. Did you not agree with me for a denarius? 14 Take what is yours and go. I choose to give to the last what I also give to you. 15 Am I not allowed to do what I wish with my own property? Or is your eye evil, because I am good?' 16 So the last shall be first, and the first last."

NOTES

xx 1. *early*. I.e., at sunrise, when work began.

vineyard. Isaiah's parable (Isa v 1–7) regards God as the owner of the vineyard, and this parallel adds weight to our contention in the COMMENT below. The vine and the vineyard are common OT figures for Israel.

2. *denarius*. The denarius was the average day's wage, on which an agricultural worker could expect to provide himself and his family with the necessities of life. It was roughly equivalent to the Greek drachma.

3. *market place* (Gr. *agora*). This word, like so many Greek and Latin words, had passed into ordinary Jewish usage.

4. In view of the ending of the parable it is to be noted here that only the first group of workers had any fixed monetary agreement.

6. The scene of the parable is set during the vintage season; there would otherwise be no point in hiring workers so late in the day. Depending on location, the vintage season in Palestine is from July through September.

8. *owner* (Gr. *kurios*). The Greek word here is the one used frequently for God in the NT.

wages (Gr. *misthos*). The same word is translated *reward* in v 12.

beginning with the last. There is no particular significance in the order of payment, except that the method here employed provides the basis for the dialogue in vss. 11 ff.

12. *burden and heat of the day*. Those who came first to the Kingdom, whether disciples or Jewish Christians, might think that they had a claim to preferential treatment by God.

13. *friend* (Gr. *hetairos*). The word is used here, at xxii 12, and xxvi 50, and in all three instances implies a rebuke.

14–15. *Take what is yours*. If we assume that the parable as first used was commentary on an imaginary "case" arising from Israel's choice by God (as Isa v 1–7 certainly is), then the owner (God) grants that Israel's faithfulness has its own just and proper reward. But God may also, of his own free grace, admit latecomers to a life reward. Hence the use of the word *choose*. There is no appeal against God's use of what is his. Cf. Rom ix 14–15; the whole central argument of the Roman letter is concerned with this very question.

15. *evil*. The "evil eye" is one which looks with malice or envy on the supposed good fortune of others.

16. a large number of manuscripts add "Many indeed are called but few are chosen," words which have no meaning in this context, but are certainly in place at xxii 14.

COMMENT

Here again is an example of the way in which blocks of fixed oral tradition were pieced together to form the larger blocks of teaching material in Matthew. The concluding verse of the last section has dictated the presence of the parable about the field workers. Here, too, is an outstanding example of the great flexibility of the parable as a teaching medium. In its primary application we may safely presume that it had to do with God's calling, of Israel first and later the Gentiles, into the Kingdom. But its proximity to vss. 20–28 of the last chapter is equally a warning against any assumption on the part of the disciples that privilege and reward in the Kingdom belong in higher degree to those first called. (Equality of reward does not mean, however, that there will be no differences of position in the Kingdom, as Jesus points out in xix 28.)

Even when allowance has been made for the attraction of this parable to its present position, the evangelist's own understanding of the parable is by no means clear. Does he interpret the parable as a warning against disputed precedence, or against an attitude of exclusive privilege on the part of those who first entered the Kingdom—i.e., Jews? In the light of our examination of parable in Part XI of the Introduction, we believe that the issue of God's choice of Israel is crucial and primary in most parables, and so we believe it was with this parable in its initial use by Jesus. The parable as it stands certainly points to the role of the householder (God) in the judgment (cf. xviii 23, xxv 14 ff. for a similar theme).

73. PASSION PREDICTION
(xx 17–19)†

XX 17 As Jesus was going up to Jerusalem he took the twelve disciples aside, and while they were journeying said to them, 18 "See, we are going up to Jerusalem, and The Man will be turned over to the chief priests and the scribes, who will condemn him to death, 19 and they will turn him over to the Gentiles, to be held up to ridicule, flogged, and crucified. On the third day he will be raised."

† **Matt xx 17–19** ‖ Mark x 32–34, Luke xviii 31–34.

COMMENT

Any way it is seen, this prediction of the passion comes as an interruption of the narrative. The only possible connection with surrounding material—and that by a somewhat far-fetched contextual attraction—would be that Jesus will be *last* in his passion, and *first* in his resurrection-exaltation glory. The obvious connection in this part of the chapter is between vss. 1–15 and 20–28, the two parts broken by this passion prediction.

We called attention earlier (cf. NOTES on xvii 11–12) to another example of an intruding passion prediction, and the arguments adduced there apply equally well here. The reader is referred to the arguments given there for supposing that this prediction, like its predecessors in xvii 11–12, 22–23, is an editorial insertion.

There are verbal agreements in this short section between Matthew and Mark, as well as between Matthew and Luke against Mark, notably *the third day* as against Mark's "after three days." There may be an indication of the editorial intrusion of this passage in the fact that Matthew does not have "the elders" in addition to

chief priests and the scribes (cf. xvi 21), thereby indicating that
this prediction was inserted in Markan context and partly in the
Markan form.

On the prediction of death by crucifixion, found only in Matthew,
cf. NOTE on x 38.

74. PRECEDENCE IN THE KINGDOM
(xx 20–28)†

XX 20 Then the mother of Zebedee's sons came to him, together with her sons, and knelt before him as a suppliant.
21 He said to her, "What do you want?" She replied to him,
"Give orders that these two sons of mine may be seated in
your Kingdom, one on the right hand, and the other on the left."
22 Jesus answered, "You do not realize what you are asking.
Can you drink the cup I am about to drink?" They said to him,
"We can." 23 He said to them, "You will indeed drink my cup,
but to sit on my right hand and on my left is not mine to
grant, but is for those for whom it is prepared by my Father."
24 The ten, on hearing this, were indignant about the two
brothers, 25 but Jesus called them to him and said, "You know
that the rulers of the Gentiles lord it over their subjects, and
their great ones exercise authority over them. 26 Among you,
however, it will not be so. Let anyone who wishes to be great
among you be your servant, 27 while anyone who wishes to be
first among you, let him be your slave, 28 in the same way that
The Man did not come to be served, but to serve, and to give
his life as a ransom for the community."

† **Matt xx 20–28** ‖ Mark x 35–45.

Notes

xx 20. *the mother.* Mark (x 35) represents the two disciples (James
and John) as coming to Jesus directly, a tradition which frequently
leads commentators to suggest either that Matthew's historical tradition
was at fault or that he manipulated the tradition to cast the disciples
in somewhat more favorable light. The suggestion is interesting solely

as an example of ignorance of the ways and manners of mothers anxious for their sons. Since Jesus' replies to the request are in plural form directly to the brothers, it is just as likely either that Matthew knew both traditions, or found his oral source to be as it is here, and for all its abrupt change from mother to disciples, allowed it to stand.

21. *your Kingdom.* Mark has "your glory." The sense is the same.

22. The disciples are not yet aware of the intimate connection between suffering and privilege in the Messianic Community. *Cup* as a synonym for suffering occurs again in xxvi 39. In Ugaritic, *cup* refers to a man's allotted portion or destiny, and is so used in the Psalms (xi 6, xvi 5, lxxv 8) and also in the Apocalypse (Rev xiv 10, xvi 19, xvii 4, xviii 6). Cf. also Isa li 17; Lam iv 21.

If Matthew knew the Markan tradition at this point, then his omission of the Markan "baptism" as a synonym for the death of Jesus is very surprising (cf. NOTE on iii 6 and COMMENT on iii 13–17 [§8]).

"We can." Cf. xxvi 56.

23. *drink my cup.* The martyr's death of James is recorded in Acts xii 2, but there is no certain historical evidence about John's death.

prepared by my Father. Cf. xxv 41.

24. The brothers are not named (cf. also vs. 20) and the evangelist assumes that his readers are well aware of their identity.

25. *exercise authority.* Outside the Covenant Community, greatness is demonstrable by the use of power. In the Messianic Community greatness on the part of those in authority is recognized only by their willingness to share in the humility of the Community's Lord.

28. The model for all who bear authority and responsibility should be Jesus himself.

ransom (Gr. *lutron*). The word is used twice in the NT and denotes the price paid for the manumission of a slave, or a price paid in the market place. In both senses the implication is of great cost, a great price constantly emphasized in the NT (cf. Gal i 4, ii 20; Eph v 2, 25; Col i 14; Titus ii 14; Heb ix 12; I Peter i 18 ff.). The saying emphasizes three points:

(a) the voluntary character of the act of self-giving;

(b) the vicarious character of the act, being done for those who ought to have rendered sacrificial obedience, but who could not (cf. Rom iii 24; Gal iii 13; II Cor v 21);

(c) the universal character of the act (see below). It is to be noted that in Rom iii 24 and I Peter i 18 the two ideas of ransom and sacrifice are juxtaposed when dealing with the meaning of redemption. Cf. further, Vincent Taylor, *Jesus and His Sacrifice* (London: Macmillan, 1937), pp. 99 ff.

Here we have *The Man* in a context of humility, a concept which is deeply rooted in the Markan tradition, but which we have seen reason to think is not part of Matthew's tradition. While we have compelling evidence in other cases to suppose that the association of suffering with The Man is an editorial addition to Matthew's text, there is no such evidence here. The inclusion of this material by the evangelist here must therefore have been of crucial importance. It is not simply that the saying in vs. 28 is the basis and pattern for those in authority in the Messianic Community, though that is obviously of considerable importance. What is vital to Matthew about this critical vs. 28 is that it is the first time in the ministry of Jesus that the whole ministry and future death of Jesus are given an interpretation, and an interpretation moreover which is linked by the phrase *for the community* (the "many") with the New Covenant of forgiveness in xxvi 28 (cf. Jer xxxi 31 ff.).

We must now give closer attention to the whole complex of ideas bound up with *ransom for the community*.

The reader of the NT will be aware that the explanatory clause *for the community* is crucial in the Matthean (xxvi 28) and Markan (xiv 24) accounts of the Last Supper, both in covenantal context. Generally speaking it seems to be assumed that *the community* is in some sense a synonym for *all*, else how explain the Pauline assumption that the sacrificial death of Jesus was of potentially universal efficacy?

So far as our present text is concerned, the phrase *lutron anti pollōn* (*ransom for the community*) is most closely paralleled by Isa liii 10–12. The LXX versions offer some varied readings in this context, and the present confused Hebrew text is not easy to reconstruct. What we have at present is:

> [11] "By his knowledge (?) shall the Righteous One vindicate:
> my Servant shall (. . .) the many,
> he will bear their sins."

The first Isaiah scroll from Qumran has the same reading. If the text originally read in second line above: "My Servant shall redeem the many," the resulting Hebrew scansion would be good.

The same emphasis on "the many" is found in Dan xii 2, 10, a chapter which provides the background for much early Essene literature. Here again in Daniel we have a confused Hebrew text, reflected in the LXX and in the revision by Theodotion of the LXX. Theodotion has: ". . . and from the righteous ones of the many" (vs. 3). What can be derived with confidence from Dan xii 3 is as follows: "And those who vindicate the many (shall be) like the everlasting stars." We have come to the conclusion that in Isa liii 10–12 and Dan xii 2, 10 we have the ultimate and the mediate sources of the Essene concentration on "the many" (*ha-rabbîm*) as background for Matt xx 28, xxvi 28, and Mark xiv 24. Our findings may be summarized as follows:

(a) In our NOTE on x 41 we called attention to the relatively unexplored significance of the Righteous One as a Messianic title, and to our own continuing investigation of it. In Isa liii 10–12 we have a firm correlation of the Servant with the Righteous One in a redemptive context. The LXX revision by Theodotion which renders the Hebrew as "he shall justify the Righteous One who well serves the many" is incorrect.

(b) "The many" of these various texts of Isaiah and Daniel, later given such emphasis by the Essenes as denoting the elect Essene community, has a long and venerable ancestry as a term for the generality of the Covenant people. In Essene usage it clearly meant the elect community of the Essenes. (Their attitude to non-Essene Israelites is still obscure.) It is possible that Matt xxiv 31, where membership of the Messianic Community by no means implies inclusion among the elect, represents a conscious rejection by Jesus of this aspect of Essenism.

(c) In the NT, the Righteous One (=the Servant=the Messiah) will vindicate, redeem, Israel, i.e., *the community*. Herein lies the decisive importance of the interpretation of his death which Jesus offers here (xx 28) and in the eucharistic words of xxvi 28 and Mark xiv 24.

(d) The potentially universal applicability of the sacrificial death of the Messiah was assumed by Paul as axiomatic, however much he may have had cause to spell out its implications to his converts. But it is imperative that we notice in this connection that for all the emphasis laid in the NT generally on the adjective *new* to describe the results of the Messianic work of Jesus, it is never for a moment suggested that there is a "new Israel." To the contrary: men must for their salvation be incorporated into that Messianic Community which is the heir to, and continuous with, the Israel of the Old Covenant. It is clear that *the community* in the interpretative liturgical passage of Matthew xxvi 28 (Mark xiv 24) was sufficient explanation of the redemptive sacrifice of the Messiah.

(e) We have as yet very little firm information as to the liturgical practices of the Essenes, but what does seem clear is that *the community* was a well-established liturgical or quasi-liturgical phrase reaching back to Second Isaiah if not earlier. It was a phrase which had been so hallowed by time that for all the obscurities of the Hebrew text of Second Isaiah, it nevertheless had to be used. Given the Essenes' insistence that they were Israel, then the equation *the community*=Israel is seen to have wider implications than our modern English can hope to convey.

It will be observed that the Gr. *pollōn* has no definite article in the texts under consideration. In a NOTE on x 41 (d) we called attention to the wide variations of use in regard to the definite article in Koine Greek, and the same considerations operate here. The Dead Sea scrolls material is similarly inconsistent in its use of the definite article before *rabbîm:* in many cases the word is simply *rabbîm*, while in many other instances the form is correctly given as *ha-rabbîm*. We are therefore justified in seeing the *pollōn* of our Greek texts in the NT as *the community*, in spite of the fact that grammatically we might have expected *tōn pollōn*.

(f) It is abundantly clear from the rabbinic writings that *ha-rabbîm* was understood as meaning the generality of the Covenant people, and the phrase *reshût ha-rabbîm*, to name but one (=“the public domain,” Mishnah *Shabbath* xi 1) is of very frequent occurrence. (We are somewhat puzzled that a recent article by Mathias Delcor—“The Courts of the Church” in *Paul and Qumran*, ed. Jerome Murphy-O'Connor, Chicago: Priory Press, 1968—fails to make any connection between *ha-rabbîm* and such vital areas as Matt xx 28 and Rom v 15–17.)

(g) In view of the reference of Matt xx 28, xxvi 28; and Mark xiv 24, back to Isa liii 12 and Dan xii 2–3, 10, it is necessary to look at a passage in the *Pirqê Abôth* which can be adduced as control evidence for Jesus' own interpretation of his death as sacrificial. The same passage is also illustrative of the material in Second Isaiah and Daniel. There are variant readings in the Hebrew of *Pirqê Abôth* v 18 (R. H. Charles' translation 5. 21). The contrast there between Moses and Jeroboam is quasi-legal. The work of Moses is said in this passage to have involved the community of Israel, and in the same way Jeroboam (cf. I Kings xiv 16) is said to have involved the community of Israel in his sin. But everything turns on the meaning of the participle *mĕzakkê*. It is commonly assumed by Jewish commentators and their Christian translators that the participle *mĕzakkê* should be rendered by “he made righteous.” But this meaning is at best exceedingly rare, if documented at all. Virtually all occurrences of the verb *ṣdq* in the causative, as well as the late Heb. *zkh*, mean “to declare clear of legal guilt, vindicate” any person on trial. Hence the *Pirqê Abôth* passage must mean literally: “Everyone who clears the community of guilt, sin does not enter by his instrumentality; but everyone who implicates the community in sin, they cannot perform an act of repentance through him. Moses was free of guilt, and cleared the community of guilt; the freedom of the community from guilt was dependent on it, as it is said: ‘The right judgments of Yahweh he carried out with Israel’ [Deut xxxiii 21]. Jeroboam son of Nebat sinned and implicated the community in sin; the sin of the community was dependent on him, as it is said: ‘The sin of Jeroboam the son of Nebat, by which he brought condemnation on Israel for sin’ [I Kings xiv 16].” There is some valuable material in Büchler, *Studies in Sin and Atonement in the Rabbinic Literature of the First Century*, pp. 260 ff.

Absent from the above extract (no author-attribution is made, and the presumption is that it is therefore early) is the Pharisee tradition with its sharp distinction between sinner and righteous, guilty and innocent. What we have here is the same uncrystallized point of view with regard to vindication which we saw to be the case in the passages from Second Isaiah and Daniel.

(h) Two important passages in the Dead Sea scroll material must be mentioned here. The first is from the Community Rule (1QS ix 9): "The men of deceit, who did not cleanse their way of guilt, in order to become separated from evil and go in sincerity of way . . ." (translation by W. F. Albright), reading *lô hizkû.* Similarly, the passage in the Thanksgiving Psalms (1QH) (vii 12, already mentioned under our discussion of x 34) provides evidence for the stricture on Jeroboam in the *Pirqê Abôth.* That king brought condemnation for sin on Israel—it was not that he "caused Israel to sin," as our English versions commonly have it.

(i) Only in a theology where redemption is centered in a single, Messianic, all-embracing figure do the inchoate motifs of redemption, sin, guilt, repentance, and vindication come sharply into focus as a distinctively Messianic work.

(j) Our examination of passages in Matthew and Mark, with control material from elsewhere, makes it abundantly clear that a critical area of Rom v must be examined—and translated—afresh. The "all men" of vs. 12 there is linked with "the many" of vs. 15, and the "trespasses" of vs. 16 are the "trespasses of the many," and it is "the many" in vs. 19 who will be vindicated.

There are other implications to be drawn from this brief survey of the crucial vs. 28, and they cannot be more than cursorily mentioned here. It has already been said that the ideas expressed in Second Isaiah, Daniel, and later in the *Pirqê Abôth* are in large measure inchoate, exploratory, and tentative. But the ideas there given tentative expression were later to blossom into the full flowering of mediaeval scholastic theologizing as to the "imputation" of merit, or of righteousness, to God's people through the redeeming work of Jesus. It is well not to dismiss such ideas too lightly, however much theological speculation sought to reduce them to precise legal patterns. Aware of our common humanity, we realize that human behavior of any kind is not without its universal effects. Paul gave expression to this when he spoke of man being "in Adam," for all that Augustine later thought to render this more precise by asserting that all men were "in the loins" of the first created man. (N.B. The Heb. *'ādām* is both individual and collective, both "mankind" and "a man.") Paul narrowed this concept of being in "Adam," or "solid with" Adam, when he spoke of Israel's relationship with Abraham and then with Moses. The passage in *Pirqê Abôth* to which we have referred seeks to give expression to this kind of metaphysical relationship when it speaks of the effects of Moses and then Jeroboam on Israel; in both cases, the people were in some sense "solid with" Moses and Jeroboam, bound up with them in their work and accomplishments, and even—in the case of Jeroboam—with a man's sin. Paul can find no better expression for the relationship between Christ and the members of his community than to speak of Head, Body, Members. The Christian, through baptism, "puts on" the whole redeeming work of the Messiah, is made "solid with" him in a metaphysical union.

There is one final note to be added here. The Pauline *dikaioun* (=to justify, vindicate) has the same kind of overtones as those which we saw to be true of the Heb. *mĕzakkê* (and also, incidentally, of the verb *hiṣdiq*). It is not that God, through Jesus, makes the member of the Messianic Community righteous by imputing to him moral qualities which he does not possess; but he clears him, vindicates him, justifies him, when all the evidence is apparently against him. With necessary safeguards, there is a sense in which God "imputes" to the Christian— in the Pauline use—a verdict which properly only belongs to Jesus.

After vs. 28 some manuscripts add a version of Luke xiv 8–10.

COMMENT

The connecting theme between this section and Section 72, especially vs. 16, is that of choice and responsibility, whether of individuals or a whole people, with the implication that to be first in the Kingdom carries with it the consequence of being last in secular society, and of sharing in the passion of Jesus. Both here and in the exchange between the two disciples and Jesus, as well as in the parable of the workers, the emphasis on the Father's disposition of his own is clearly marked. The Man will judge his own Kingdom, but the final issues are in the Father's hands. In the meantime, those who throw in their lot with Jesus in the Messianic Community must expect to find the values of secular society completely reversed therein.

75. TWO BLIND MEN
(xx 29–34)†

XX 29 As they were leaving Jericho, a large crowd followed him. 30 Two blind men, sitting by the roadside and hearing that Jesus was passing by, shouted out, "Take pity on us, son of David." 31 The crowd turned on them, demanding that they be silent, but they shouted the more insistently, "Take pity on us, son of David!" 32 Jesus stopped, and called to them: "What do you want me to do for you?" 33 "Sir, let our eyes be opened." 34 Moved by pity Jesus touched their eyes; they received sight immediately, and followed him.

† **Matt xx 29–34** || Mark x 46–52, Luke xviii 35–43.

NOTES

xx 30. *Two blind men.* Mark (x 46) supplies us with the name of a single blind man, "Bartimaeus, son of Timaeus," but this is obviously a conflation of the Greek with the Aramaic, and what we have in effect in Mark is *"son of Timaeus"* repeated. Luke has a single man (Luke xviii 35). It is possible that Matthew's tradition was confused, or that there was indeed a tradition that two men were involved. Matthew also is unaware of the Markan and Lukan "the Nazarene" as an appellation of Jesus (cf. also xxviii 5=Mark xvi 6, but in xxvi 69=Mark xiv 67, Matthew has *the Galilean*).

33. *Sir.* Matthew translates the Aram. *rabbouni,* where Mark preserves it transliterated.

Apart from historical circumstance, the context of this miracle in Matthew may be crucial, as it is in Mark and Luke. The issue of sight and blindness is also crucial in John ix to the understanding of Jesus' ministry, and the same issue may underlie the placing of this incident immediately following upon the apparent failure of James and John to see (understand) the nature of their calling in vss. 20–28. Mark (viii 22 ff.) has a story of a blind man's restored sight immediately before Peter's acknowledgment ("seeing") of Jesus in viii 27 ff. Standing as the narrative does here before the final act in Jerusalem, it pursues the theme of vs. 28: the disciples will be required to see (cf. xxvi 64) the glory of Jesus in death and seeming defeat.

76. TRIUMPHAL ENTRY INTO JERUSALEM
(xxi 1–11)†

XXI 1 As they approached Jerusalem, and came to Bethphage by way of the Mount of Olives, Jesus sent two of his disciples with instructions: 2 "Go into the village opposite you, and immediately you will find an ass tied, with a colt. Loose them, and bring them to me. 3 If anyone asks what you are doing, then say 'The Lord needs them,' and he will send them immediately." 4 This happened in fulfillment of what was said by the prophet:

> 5 "Announce to the daughter of Sion,
> Behold, your king is coming to you,
> humble, mounted on a donkey,
> on a colt, a donkey's foal."

6 The disciples went, did as Jesus directed them, 7 and bringing the donkey and the colt they put their cloaks on them, and he sat there. 8 Most of the crowd spread their own cloaks on the road, while others cut down branches from the trees, and laid them on the road. 9 The crowds which went before and after him shouted out the words: "Hosanna! O son of David! Blessed is he who comes in the Lord's name! (Cry) Hosanna in the heavenly heights!" 10 As he entered Jerusalem, the whole city was stirred up, saying, "Who is this?" 11 and the crowds replied, "This is the prophet Jesus from Nazareth in Galilee."

† Matt xxi 1–11 ‖ Mark xi 1–11, Luke xix 28–38, John xii 12–19.

NOTES

xxi 1. *Mount of Olives.* Cf. Zech xiv 4, where the place is associated with Messianic hope.

with instructions. At first sight, this little incident is full of mystery. This account is one of many in the gospels in which the relevant circumstances were still so well known to the people when the oral tradition became fixed that they were not included. This can be very baffling for the reader in search of exact biographical detail. The high incidence of background information which is assumed or omitted as taken for granted is eloquent proof of the immediacy of the NT material—the transmitters of the oral tradition were not concerned beyond the immediate accuracy of transmission.

3. *he will send.* The subject of this verb is obscure. Mark seems to imply that it is the Lord who will send the animals back to the owners, whereas the sense in Matthew appears to be that anyone questioning the disciples will send the animals without further ado.

4–5. *In fulfillment.* Matthew has two "fulfillment" passages here. The second (from Zech ix 9) had the groundwork laid for it in vs. 2—*an ass tied, with a colt.* The first quotation, *Announce to the daughter of Sion,* is from Isa lxii 11, and the Isaian oracle is cast in a strongly Messianic mold. On fulfillment, cf. Part IV of the Introduction.

5. The last part of the quotation (*on a donkey, [and] on a colt, a donkey's foal*) is Hebrew poetic parallelism. The very ancient picture of the Messiah in Zech ix 9, portraying the Righteous One who will save his people, has a long history. The language with regard to the donkey is identical with that used of a donkey offered in sacrifice in the patriarchal city of Haran. The practice is known to us from the Mari texts (eighteenth century B.C.), belonging to the early patriarchal period. It speaks of the donkey sacrifice as ratifying a treaty between the Apiru (=Hebrews) and various local kings. The figure of the donkey, in the same three words as in the Mari text, occurs again in Gen xlix 11 as well as in the text of Zech ix 9 under discussion.

Attention is drawn to the fact that in the Zechariah text the Messiah is described as the Righteous One (Heb. *ṣaddîq*), a title to which we have referred previously as an ancient Jewish Messianic appellation. The whole Messianic context of Zech ix 9–17 is relevant at this point, and not merely the half verse which the evangelist uses as a kind of anchor. The context in Zechariah looks to the restoration of the people by reason of God's overshadowing providence and of his covenant with the people. The Hebrew parallelism of this verse led a translator to assume that there were two animals involved as he did also in vss. 2 and 3. Mark and Luke know of only one animal.

6. Matthew's account is here considerably shorter than that of Mark, who gives far more eyewitness detail.

7. The NOTE on vs. 5 is applicable here. Jesus could not ride on two animals at once, and the translator has two animals being adorned with cloaks.

their cloaks (Gr. *himatia*, cf. NOTE on ix 20). The placing of cloaks on the back of the donkey implied great respect and honor to the rider.

9. *"Hosanna!"* The word is from Ps cxviii 25–26, and is a prayer for deliverance ("Save now!"); it is not in any way a cry of praise. The absence of indications of quotation in Greek manuscripts has over the centuries, and even into our own times, led to some curious translations of this verse, translations which completely fail to do justice to the Heb. *hôsha'nā*. The translation here must either read: "the crowds shouted . . . Hosanna! to the son of David," or (for reasons next stated) in the way in which we have translated the verse. It is now known that the Heb. *la, lĕ* often introduced a vocative (cf. Pss lxviii 4, 32, 33, 35, and also Mitchell Dahood, *Psalms I, 1–50,* AB, vol. 16 (New York; Doubleday, 1965–66), pp. xxi ff. The meaning of the vocative *la* was misunderstood quite early, and the Greek translation therefore rendered the vocative *O son of David* as "to the son of David," for the Heb. *la, lĕ* is also used to indicate "to," as a dative. What we have here, therefore, is an ancient liturgical text, a cry to the anointed king for deliverance.

son of David. Cf. NOTE on i 1.

he who comes. I.e., the Coming One. Cf. NOTE on xi 3.

in the heavenly heights. This is a translation of the Hebrew of Ps cxlviii 1 (cf. here the Greek with the LXX of the same psalm verse). The meaning of this liturgical prayer is not easily rendered, and our translation renders the best sense in English.

10. *the whole city was stirred up.* Cf. ii 3.

11. *the prophet.* Cf. NOTE on x 41.

There are seven verbal agreements between Matthew and Luke against Mark in this section, but somewhat more agreements between Matthew and Mark against Luke (nine), and somewhat fewer between Mark and Luke against Matthew (five).

COMMENT

The title given to the section rightly describes Matthew's interpretation of the events. It is the entry of the Messianic king into his
own city, the final challenge by Jesus to his own people in his
ministry. It is also the supreme act of obedience of the Son to the
Father (cf. xvi 21).

77. CLEANSING THE TEMPLE
(xxi 12–17) †

XXI 12 Jesus went into the temple, and threw out all who bought and sold in the temple, and overturned the tables of the money-changers and the seats of the pigeon-dealers. 13 "It is written," he said to them, " 'My house shall be called a house of prayer,' but you have made it a robbers' den."

14 The blind and the lame came to him in the temple, and he cured them. 15 But when the chief priests and the scribes saw the wonders which he did, and the young children shouting in the temple the words, "Hosanna! O son of David!" they were indignant, 16 and said to him, "Do you hear what they are saying?" Jesus replied, "Yes. Have you never read, 'Out of the mouths of babes and nurslings you have brought perfect praise'?"

17 Leaving them, he went out of the city to Bethany and stayed there.

† **Matt xxi 12–17** || Mark xi 15–19, Luke xix 45–48, John ii 13–22.

NOTES

xxi 12. *the temple*. Some manuscripts add *of God*.

Matthew used a prophecy of Malachi in connection with John the Baptist (xi 10), and the context of that quoted prophecy announces the coming of the Lord to his temple. The whole complex of this entry of Jesus into Jerusalem implies the fulfillment of that prophecy (cf. Mal iii).

money-changers. Two things must be remembered here:

(a) The incident, however dramatic its implied interpretation of the Lord coming to claim his own (cf. *My house*, vs. 13), probably did not attract much attention apart from its immediate environment. The temple would have been thronged at this time, and Jesus' action, apart from those close to him, may have appeared to be no more than a passing incident.

(b) By acting out this prophetic parable Jesus was attacking a powerful, lucrative, and well-entrenched privilege. All financial transactions in the temple had to be in Tyrian currency, and the money-changers were allowed a substantial discount. The half-shekel was worth two denarii, the denarius being a laborer's wage for a day and two denarii enough for a few days' lodging (cf. Luke x 35).

pigeon-dealers. Cf. Lev v 7; xii 8. Pigeons were a legitimate substitute for lambs for sacrificial purposes. On this last, cf. "The 'Herodian Doves' in the Light of Recent Archaeological Discoveries," by Eliezer D. Oren, *Palestine Exploration Quarterly,* January–June, 1968.

13. *My house.* Cf. Isa lvi 7. Mark's narrative makes explicit what Matthew's abbreviated version implies in the whole context of Isa lvi; the time of ingathering of all God's people, Jew and Gentile, is near.

robbers' den. Cf. Jer vii 11. The prophet predicted the destruction of the temple as punishment for sin. The saying of Jesus indicates a similar judgment; it was Israel's responsibility to know the signs of the times (cf. xi 1–24, etc.), to recognize the time of consummation, but failure to do so involved judgment. Jesus' prophecies of the destruction of Jerusalem and the temple are firmly embedded in the gospel tradition (cf. xxiii 37 ff., xxiv 2, etc.). All but the most superficial acquaintance with the conditions of the time would have led any thoughtful contemporary observer to the same conclusion.

At this point, we call the reader's attention to the variations in tradition between the evangelists as to the chronology of this week:

	Matthew	Mark	Luke
1st day	Entry. Cleansing of Temple. Return to Bethany	Entry. Return to Bethany	Entry. Cleansing of Temple
2nd day	Cursing & withering of fig tree. Teaching	Cursing of fig tree. Cleansing of Temple	Teaching
3rd day	Teaching	Fig tree withered	Teaching

Matthew and Luke appear to shorten the Markan chronology by one day, on the theory that both evangelists used Mark as basis for their work. But even if we allowed that Matthew put the cursing of the tree, and its subsequent withering, on the same day to heighten the dramatic effect, this supposed dependence on Mark is not very impressive when examined. Luke's two days are not even suggested by the evangelist to be consecutive, and Matthew and Luke agree only in recording that the days were engaged in teaching—the material cannot be regarded as parallel. Matthew, far from being dependent on the Markan account (which records the first day as one of teaching), provides us with a first day of activity (vss. 14–15). If Matthew is dependent on Mark, then there is wholesale transference; cf. Mark xi 17 ("he taught") and Matt xxi 23, together with Mark xi 18 and Matt xxii 33.

16. *Out of the mouths.* The quotation is from the LXX of Ps viii 2. Cf. xi 25. The chief priests and the scribes, who from this point on are very prominent in the narrative, appear here for the first time together since ii 4. They were mentioned in the passion predictions of xvi 21 and xx 18—but cf. NOTES on xvi 21 (§60).

Luke has a parallel to this dialogue, connected with the entry into Jerusalem (xix 39–40).

COMMENT

There is an apparent difference in the relative dating of the cleansing of the temple between the Johannine and the synoptic traditions. We have, of course, no external evidence as to whether the event recorded happened once, twice, or even three times, and at present the whole matter is beyond our investigation. All we have is the internal evidence of the tradition, a tradition which links the event with the Messianic prophecy of Zechariah, whose own tradition goes back to pre-Israelite times.

In the Fourth Gospel the cleansing of the temple takes place at the beginning of the ministry (John ii 13–22), and therefore is not associated (as in the synoptic gospels) with the entry into Jerusalem. There are far too many verbal similarities in the Greek between the Johannine and synoptic accounts to make plausible any suggestion that there were two such events. Whether the Johannine account serves a theological purpose, interpretative of the ministry in its present position, or whether John's chronology of events is to be preferred at this point, are matters which the reader will find discussed at length in Brown, *John, i–xii,* COMMENT on ii 13–22 (§8).

We begin here the complex series of events which subsequent usage has called "Holy Week." We must now indicate the problems which are involved.

(a) In broad outline the four evangelists are agreed on the central events of this week from Sunday to Sunday. But there are areas of disagreement in sequence and timing, and it is impossible to determine at this remove which evangelist is factually and chronologically more accurate in his reminiscences. It would cast the gravest doubt on the historical accuracy of the narrative were we to find that there was close and substantial agreement in detail among the four evangelists.

(b) The narratives we have illustrate very well the tenacity of the oral tradition as received by four men, each with his own method of handling that tradition.

(c) It is clear to any intelligent reader of the passion narratives not only that there are discrepancies in the four accounts, but also that the events which immediately lead up to the trial scenes, and the trial scenes themselves, give an impression of haste and confusion. Some of this sense of confusion and haste is fully comprehensible; it is clear that in the final moments of the trial most of the principal eyewitnesses fled. Subsequent reminiscence will certainly have reflected this confusion. Furthermore, the task of determining the precise sequence of events has in recent years been rendered far more difficult, though certainly far more interesting, by discoveries at Qumran. They disclose that at least two sectarian groups used a calendrical system for calculating Passover which was seriously at variance with the official Jerusalem calendar. The Qumran calendar had an older usage historically, and some scholars have insisted that it was this older calendar which Jesus and the disciples used. It is clear that according to this calendar Passover would have fallen on the night of Tuesday-Wednesday, and so would be the night of the Last Supper. This view was first propounded by Mlle. Annie Jaubert in *La date de la céne,* Paris: Librairie Lecoffre, 1957, and it has often been discussed since then. We cannot enter into such discussion here, and the interested reader is referred to George Ogg, "The Chronology of the Last Supper," in *Historicity and Chronology in the New Testament,* for a lucid and convenient summary of the evidence.

(d) It is frequently overlooked that what information we have about Jewish legal procedure, particularly with respect to criminal law as it operated in Roman-occupied Judea, is post-Christian. Our information as to the way in which Roman criminal law operated in the provinces is very limited, but it is known to have been arbitrary and largely discretionary for the non-citizen. We know of no legislation governing the workings of a local prefect or procurator in criminal cases before the second century A.D. (Pliny the Younger). The New Testament, both with respect to the trial of Jesus, and the subsequent trials of Paul and his companions, gives us but one view of the way in which criminal law could and did operate under various Roman officials.

For convenience and for the interest of the reader, we give the sequence of events as the new theory of Mlle. Jaubert explains them:

Official Jewish Calendar		Sectarian (Ancient Priestly) Calendar
Nisan 8 Saturday	Anointing at Bethany	Nisan 11
9 Sunday	Triumphal Entry	12
	Return to Bethany	
10 Monday	Return to Jerusalem	13
	Incident of the fig tree	
11 Tuesday	Preparation for Passover	14
	Passover/Last Supper	
	Arrest of Jesus; Examination before Annas; Jesus taken to Caiaphas' house	
12 Wednesday	Ecclesiastical trial opens	15
13 Thursday	Ecclesiastical trial ends in morning, and Roman trial begins; examination by Herod Antipas	16
14 Friday	Roman trial ends; Crucifixion; official Jewish Passover begins in the evening	17

The merit of this theory is that it accommodates the Johannine tradition, which places the death of Jesus at the time when Passover lambs were being slain in the temple.

Cf. also Finegan, *Handbook of Biblical Chronology,* pp. 290 ff.

78. QUESTIONS ABOUT AUTHORITY
(xxi 18–27)†

XXI 18 Early in the morning, as he was returning to the city, he was hungry, 19 and seeing a single fig tree by the roadside he went to it. But finding nothing on it but leaves, he said to it, "May no fruit ever come from you again!" The tree withered at once. 20 When the disciples saw it they were astounded. "How did the fig tree wither at once?" they asked. 21 Jesus answered, "I solemnly tell you that if you have faith and never doubt, not only will you do what has been done to the fig tree, but if you say even to this mountain, 'Be rooted up and thrown into the sea,' it will happen. 22 Whatever you ask in prayer trusting [God's will] you will receive."

23 When he went into the temple, the chief priests and the elders among the people came to him (as he was teaching), asking: "By what authority are you doing these things? And who gave you this authority?" 24 Jesus answered them, "I too will ask you a question, and if you answer me, then I in turn will tell you by what authority I am doing these things. 25 Whence came John's baptism—from heaven, or from men?" They argued the question with one another: "If we say 'From heaven,' he will say to us, 'Then why did you not believe him?' 26 but if we say 'From men,' we are afraid of the people, for all regard John as a prophet." 27 So they answered Jesus, "We do not know." He in turn said to them, "Neither will I tell you by what authority I am doing these things."

† **Matt xxi 18–22** || Mark xi 12–14, 20–24; **23–27** || Mark xi 27–33, Luke xx 1–8.

NOTES

xxi 18–22. It is impossible to determine precisely what historical background lies behind the narrative in these verses. To describe the fig tree incident as "miracle" would be to demand a re-examination of all other miracles in the gospel narratives. This incident as it is reported to us cannot be regarded as a sign of the Kingdom's coming, still less as a means by which the Kingdom comes (cf. Part X of the Introduction). The connection of the incident with the visit to the temple, both in Matthew and Mark, indicates very strongly that it was a prophetic parable (cf. Acts xxi 11 ff.) looking to an imminent fall of Jerusalem and the destruction of the temple. Some indication that this is the case can be found in Mark, who tells us that the time for fruit to appear had not yet arrived (xi 13). Cf. also Matt iii 10 and the parable in Luke xiii 6 ff. Jesus had looked for faith in his mission and his person, and had not found it (cf. vs. 43).

The spreading of the incident over two days in Mark, as contrasted with Matthew's one day, further complicates the issue. It is not clear whether the saying on prayer in vss. 21–22 belongs to the narrative or not. Mark's version of the saying is considerably expanded (xi 23–25) and has material found in three separate contexts in Matthew (vi 14–15; vii 7–11; xviii 35).

22. *trusting.* The trust indicated here is the response of love and trust called for by God's love for Israel in the Covenant. The words in brackets are added by us to make the point clear.

23–27. This is the first in a series of controversies (xxi 23 – xxii 46) which are conducted in a form well-known in the Talmud. The narrative and the dialogue are alike treated with considerable vigor of expression. The method of question and counter-question may, to our way of thinking, seem like evasion tactics, but it was a common form of debate in Hellenistic and later rabbinic times as well as in Greek practice as early as the fifth century B.C. The form was specifically designed to establish the truth of a matter, and could even involve an opponent in giving an answer which the proponent could not elicit by a direct first question.

23. *these things.* The question about authority revolves round two considerations: the popular cry *"son of David"* and "prophet" (vss. 9–11), followed by Jesus' implicit claim to know God's will for the temple (vss. 12–13). Jesus' reply, as indicated above, is no mere evasion. His questioners had never faced the implications of the popular assessment of John the Baptist.

as he was teaching. This is omitted in some Latin and Syriac manuscripts (cf. Luke xx 1), but cf. the reference to teaching in the temple at xxvi 55.

24. Only those who have submitted to John's call for repentance and baptism can understand the mission of Jesus.

25. *from heaven.* I.e., God-given, as contrasted with *from men,* in the sense of a self-assumed vocation.

believe. I.e., be loyal to, submit to, John's ministry.

27. *"We do not know."* This is a confession of unwillingness to make any commitment either about John or about Jesus.

79. THREE PARABLES
(xxi 28–46)†

XXI   28 "But what do you think? A man had two sons, and he went to the first and said, 'Son, go and work in my vineyard today.' 29 He replied, 'I will not,' but later changed his mind and went. 30 He went to the second and said the same. He replied, 'Yes, sir,' and did not go. 31 Which of the two did as his father wished?" They said, "The first." Jesus said to them, "I solemnly tell you that tax collectors and prostitutes enter God's Kingdom before you. 32 For John came to you in the path of righteousness, and you did not believe him, while the tax collectors and the prostitutes did. Even when you saw that, you did not later change your minds and believe him.

33 "Listen to another parable. There was a householder who planted a vineyard, fenced it, dug out a wine press in it, built a lookout post, and turning it over to tenant farmers, went to another country. 34 When the vintage season approached, he sent his slaves to the tenant farmers to get his fruit. 35 The tenant farmers took his slaves, beat one, killed another, and threw stones at a third. 36 Again he sent some other slaves, more in number than the first, and they did the same to them. 37 Finally, he sent his son to them, thinking, 'They will respect my son.' 38 But when the tenant farmers saw the son, they said to themselves, 'This is the heir. Let us kill him, and we shall have the inheritance.' 39 So they took him, threw him out of the vineyard, and killed him. 40 When therefore the owner of the vineyard comes, what will he do to those tenant farmers?" 41 They said to him, "He will put those wicked men to a miserable death, and will let out the vineyard to other tenant farm-

† Matt xxi 33–46 || Mark xii 1–12, Luke xx 9–19.

ers, who will render him the harvests in season." 42 Jesus said to them, "Did you never read in the Scriptures:

'The stone which the builders rejected,
that same stone has become the head of the corner.
This was the Lord's doing,
and it is a wonderful thing to us'?

43 Therefore I tell you that the Kingdom of God will be taken from you, and given to a people which will be productive." [44 "Whoever falls over this stone will be injured, but as for the man on whom it falls, it will crush him."]

45 When the chief priests and the Pharisees heard his parables they realized that he was speaking about them, 46 but while seeking to arrest him they feared the crowds, because they regarded him as a prophet.

NOTES

There are parallels in this first parable to other sayings of Jesus in quite different contexts—cf. vii 21, xii 50.

xxi 28–31a. The manuscripts have considerable variation as to which comes first in this saying, the obedient or the disobedient son. We have chosen to follow the reading of Codex Sinaiticus and other early authorities, partly on the grounds explained in the NOTE on vs. 30. The NEB has chosen the other reading.

28. *what do you think?* This is a typical Matthean introduction. Cf. xvii 25.

vineyard. Cf. NOTE on xx 1, and below on vs. 33.

29. *changed his mind* (Gr. *metamelesthai*). The word is used only in Matthew in our gospels, and can also mean "repent."

30. *sir* (Gr. *kurie*). Also "Lord"; the connection with vii 21 is apparent. It is the disobedient son who says "Lord, Lord."

31. *tax collectors.* Cf. NOTE on ix 10. It signifies a class of people whose allegiance to the Law was at best suspect.

God's Kingdom. Commentators are occasionally puzzled to know why Matthew, if he was indeed dependent on Mark, did not change this to Kingdom of *heaven*. We have pointed out in the Introduction that the evangelist makes a clear and careful distinction between the two phrases, and it is important to remember that distinction here. What is at issue is not the entrance of Jesus' presently unbelieving hearers into the

Messianic Community (the Kingdom of heaven). We know from Acts that numbers of people who had not committed themselves to allegiance to Jesus in the time of his ministry did so after the first apostolic preaching. The saying looks beyond the present situation, beyond possible entrance into the Messianic Kingdom, to the ultimate possibility of rejected entrance into the Father's Kingdom. Matthew's use here is wholly consistent with what we have observed elsewhere in this gospel. *Enter* is quite indeterminate (Gr. *proagousin*): the tax collectors and the prostitutes "enter," leaving open the question as to whether his hearers do, or do not, enter the final inheritance of the Father's Kingdom.

33. The imagery in the opening of the parable is from Isa v 2. The immediate recognition by the hearers of their own place in the allegory is confirmation not only of the persistent use of the imagery of the vine and the vineyard to describe Israel, but also of the "case law" understanding of parable.

tenant farmers. In the first century, many landowners were absentees, letting out their holdings to tenants. The best parallel in our society is the share-cropping system practiced in various parts of the United States.

34. *approached.* The verb is reminiscent of the words with which Mark opens the ministry of Jesus (i 15); cf. Matt iii 2 and iv 17.

slaves (or servants). The Matthean plural clearly calls for equating the slaves with the prophets, sent as God's representatives.

fruit. The term is constantly used, in one form or another, in both OT and NT, to denote the duty Israel owes to God (cf. Isa v 4).

35–36. Luke has three servants, plus a beloved son; Mark has three servants plus "many others" and a beloved son, while Matthew is more indefinite. Attempts by commentators to fix precise details from the OT to correspond to the precise details of the parables (cf. the stoning of Zechariah, II Chron xxiv 20 f. as an example) must be considered useless; the essential meaning of this parable is clear enough.

37. *his son.* Suggestions occasionally made that this is an ecclesiastical addition to the text are usually vague as to when this post-apostolic manipulation took place, and unless we are to rule out iii 13–17 (cf. Mark i 9–11; Luke iii 21–22; John i 29–34) then it is hard to see what the objection is to the authenticity of this passage. Granted a Messianic consciousness on the part of Jesus, the title "son" was a common designation of the anointed king in the OT. Cf. Part VII of the Introduction.

39. Note that Matthew's tradition here arranges the details in the light of the death of Jesus, who was crucified *outside* the city. Cf. Mark xii 8; Luke xx 15.

41. *They said to him.* In Mark (xii 9) and Luke (xx 15–16) Jesus answers his own question. Matthew has the listeners answer, condemning themselves as they did in vs. 31.

42. The quotation is from Ps cxviii 22–23, and from the text of the LXX. The whole psalm is a vindication of God's purpose, declared as through the agency of a chosen servant. Here again (cf. Part IV of the Introduction) it is the context of the whole psalm which must be taken into account in this quotation. The entire drama of this final week is seen in the light of God's victory snatched from the jaws of defeat, an assertion of the vindication of God's selection of his own. This choice is narrowed into the person of the Son, and with him the nascent Messianic Community. It is against this background that the whole of the psalm should be read at this point.

43. This verse is not found in Mark or in Luke. It is almost impossible to reject the argument that this verse and the one which follows it are secondary commentary. *Kingdom of God,* meaning as it does in Matthew (and in I Cor xv 24–58) the ingathering of the elect into the Father's Kingdom, is inappropriate here. Moreover, the parable makes no judgment of the kind suggested in this verse, and the verse itself interrupts the connection between vs. 42 and vss. 44, 45–46.

44. The builders of Israel's national life, those who might have been expected to welcome the ministry of John and the proclamation of Jesus, had rejected both John and Jesus, and the Messiah would build on another foundation—cf. xvi 18—that of allegiance to himself. This verse, which is not found in all manuscripts, carries the thought a stage further. Jesus, as the cornerstone of the new community, gives offense to those who ought to have welcomed him. The verse has some puzzling features. It is found in Luke, but not in Mark. In both Matthew and Luke the Greek has *sunthlasthēsetai,* ("will be injured") but in view of its rarity and the extraordinary difficulties of pronouncing this word it perhaps ought to be *sumblēthēsetai,* "to be smitten or injured" (which we have translated *will be injured*). Copyists, whether working from a written uncial text, or from dictation, often confused the Greek uncial *beta* with *theta.*

But it is the difficulty of context which is paramount. The connection between vss. 42 and 45 is obvious, and we have already called attention to the very awkward interposition of vs. 43. Since, however, the verse under consideration, 44, is found in two synoptic evangelists, it would seem at first sight as though it is being reported as a saying of Jesus. That the saying about the building stone in vs. 42 exercised considerable influence in early Christian exposition is evidenced by I Peter ii 4–8. At this point, the close parallel between both passages and similar thoughts in Isa viii 5 – ix 1 and xxviii 14 ff. is striking. (Gundry—cf. *The Use of the Old Testament in St. Matthew's Gospel*—thinks the vision of the stone in Dan ii is the background here. This seems to us to be altogether too slender a hypothesis.) Both the Isaian passages are of great significance in determining the place of this saying. In both there is a contrast drawn between the work of God and the attempts of men to deny or frustrate that work. Yet although there is in Isa xxviii an opposition described between the attitude of official Jerusalem on the one hand and God's purposes on the other, it is certain that the background of this verse must be seen in the light of Isa viii. That chapter begins with the refusal of official Israel to put trust and confidence in God's own act, and refers to the conspiracy (historically the Syro-Ephraimite coalition) which blinds men's eyes to God's will.

The *"stone of offense,"* the "rock of stumbling" in Isa viii 13 ff. is God himself, refuge and sanctuary to those who trust, a snare to the faithless. Most significantly, the prophet refers in vss. 16 ff. to the disciples who have understood and will cherish his teaching, and both he and they will be signs from God who dwells on Mount Zion. All that remains for the faithless is distress and darkness (cf. vss. 21–22 and Matt xxiii 37, xxvii 45–51).

It seems clear that this present verse is an allusive commentary by Matthew on the decisive point in the ministry of Jesus which had been reached by his entry into Jerusalem. The public ministry is virtually ended, the disciples have for the most part been instructed, and all that remains is the playing out of the final act in the drama of God's redemptive act. To pursue the Isaian context into chapter ix is to be assured that the future is not in doubt, whatever may lie in the days immediately ahead.

Part IV of the Introduction is concerned with Matthew's use of the OT and Gundry makes much of OT allusions in Matthew. It seems to us that the present vs. 44 is such an allusion. Its present context in both Matthew and Luke provokes questions as to origin and provenance. If it was a saying of Jesus, then it is seriously out of context, and interrupts the flow of the end of this present chapter. If it is a saying of Jesus placed here as commentary on the end of the public ministry of Jesus, then it is yet another piece of evidence for the consuming interest in the prophecies of Isaiah so well known to us from the Qumran discoveries.

One rather tantalizing question remains. The method of OT interpretation which we know to have been commonplace among the Essenes was also Matthew's method, as pointed out first by Stendahl. But it is not that of Luke, who—although having access to hymns which predate the ministry of Jesus—does not use Matthew's allusive commentary methods. We are therefore faced with an intriguing problem of priority in this verse, and the indications would seem to exclude a dependence of Matthew on Luke. Perhaps this kind of text, an allusive reference back to OT material, is the nearest firm indication that we have of a collection of "logia" or sayings of Jesus, from which both Matthew and Luke drew. But it emphatically does not, on the usual documentary hypothesis, explain why this particular verse should have been inserted into the narrative at precisely the same point in Matthew and Luke, and at the same time omitted in Mark.

COMMENT

The three parables (xxi 28 – xxii 14) all have to do with the place of Israel in the purpose of God, seen against the background of the ministry of Jesus (cf. Part XI of the Introduction). If, as we have seen reason to suppose, the incident of the fig tree was "acted parable," or prophetic parable, then the whole complex from xxi–xxii 14 is a unity. Everything in this part of the gospel is concerned with summing up the attitude of Jesus' own people, on the semi-official level, to his ministry and proclamation. It is evident from xxii 15 that to all intents and purposes there is no longer room for argument, and room only for the best way in which Jesus' enemies can accomplish his removal from the scene.

80. PARABLES OF THE KINGDOM
(xxii 1–14)†

XXII 1 Jesus once more addressed them in parables: 2 "The Kingdom of heaven may be compared with a king who gave a wedding feast for his son. 3 He sent his slaves to call those who were invited to the feast, but they would not come. 4 Once more he sent other slaves with the message: 'Tell those who have been invited: See, I have prepared the dinner, my oxen and fat calves have been killed, and everything is ready. Come to the wedding.' 5 But they treated it lightly and went away, one to his own farm, another to his business, 6 while the remainder seized his slaves, treated them brutally and killed them. 7 The king was angry, sent his soldiers and wiped out those murderers and burned down their city. 8 He then said to his slaves, 'The wedding is indeed ready, but the invited guests were unsuitable. 9 So go into the main streets and invite as many as you find to the wedding.' 10 The slaves went out into the streets and collected together all whom they found, both bad and good, and the wedding hall was filled with guests. 11 However, when the king came in to see the guests, he saw there a man without suitable wedding garb, and he said to him, 12 'Friend, how did you get in here without proper wedding garb?' and he was speechless. 13 The king then said to his attendants, 'Bind him hand and foot, and throw him into outer darkness, where there will be shrieking and grinding of teeth.' 14 Many, indeed, are called, but few are chosen."

† **Matt xxii 1–14** ‖ Luke xiv 15–24.

NOTES

xxii 1. *once more*. This is simply an introduction to the material and not a chronological note.

2. *a king*. I.e., God (cf. v 35). In the parable below, which is a separate story (cf. vs. 11) and in xxv 34, it is Jesus who is depicted as king.

wedding feast. The theme is used again to describe the Kingdom in xxv 10. Cf. Rev xix 7 ff.

5–6. Compared with the Lukan tradition, it is more than likely that there has been assimilation to the narrative of xxi 33 ff. The Lukan parable (xiv 18–20) makes it clear that the reasons proffered for absence were not frivolous; they were such as to excuse a man from military service under the Mosiac Law.

10. *bad and good*. This parable deals with the Messianic Kingdom, The Man's Kingdom, and therefore all kinds of people will respond to the invitation.

11. This obviously begins a separate parable. But whatever assimilation may have taken place in vss. 5–7, there seems small justification for saying that it took place when the Church wished to accommodate the parable to the events of the first Jewish War and the destruction of Jerusalem in A.D. 70. It is well to remember that the Zealots were founded shortly after A.D. 8. There is no reason to deny to Jesus in the explosive situation of the second quarter of the first century the insights of an Isaiah or a Jeremiah in like circumstances.

wedding garb. The scene depicted is that of the Son judging his own Kingdom. The man in question had attempted to enter that Kingdom without prior repentance. It is fruitless to discuss whether there was a custom demanding that the giver of a wedding feast had an obligation to provide special clothing. No such custom is known to us, and—cf. Yohanan ben Zakkai's parable in COMMENT below—it is probable that only clean clothes were expected.

12. *Friend*. Cf. NOTE on xx 13.

13. *attendants*. The Greek word is different from the word for "slaves" in previous verses, and presumably in the interpretation means "angels." Cf. the distinction in Hebrew between *'ebed* and *shammāsh*.

Bind him . . . Cf. the similar injunctions in viii 12, xiii 30, 42, 50, xxiv 51, xxv 30.

14. *called*. The Greek is derived from the same verb as "invited" in vs. 3. Many are *called* into the Messianic Kingdom, but few will be finally *chosen* for the Father's Kingdom at the judgment.

Comment

The Lukan reference at the head of this section is not a true parallel, and is given only for the sake of comparison. Both the language and the details are quite different.

There seems to be an attempt to equate this parable to the parable about the tenant farmers (xxii 33–41), as though underlining the lessons of the rejection of Jesus by official Judaism. There would appear to be traditional material behind this present example. There is attributed to Yohanan ben Zakkai a story of a king who invited some servants to a wedding feast, but (purposely?) omitted to supply any details of time. Those with foresight not only dressed in clothes suitable for the occasion, but also waited at the door of the king's house. The unthinking servants, on the other hand, went on with their work. Without warning, the king announced that the time of the wedding had come, and the servants who had been waiting went in to the feast. The unwise, still wearing working clothes, were made to stand and watch the others eat the feast (TB, *Shabbath* 153 a).

81. QUESTIONS
(xxii 15–46)†

XXII 15 Then the Pharisees went to discuss how to trap him in discussion, 16 so they sent to him their disciples, with the Herodians, with the question: "Teacher, we know that you are an honest man, and teach God's will truly, without worrying what men think, for you pay no attention to external appearance. 17 Tell us, then, what you think. Is it lawful to pay taxes to Caesar, or not?" 18 Jesus, aware of their malice, said, "You casuists! Why put me on trial? 19 Show me the tax money." They brought him a denarius, 20 and Jesus asked them, "Whose representation and inscription is this?" "Caesar's," they said. 21 "Then pay to Caesar what belongs to Caesar," he said, "and pay to God what belongs to God." 22 When they heard this, they wondered, left him, and went away.

23 On the same day, Sadducees—who deny the resurrection— came to him with a question. 24 "Teacher," they said, "Moses said, 'If a man dies having no children, his brother must marry the widow so that he can produce children for the brother.' 25 Now there were among us seven brothers; the oldest married, and died without children, leaving his widow to his brother. 26 The same thing happened with the second brother, and then the third, and finally with all seven. 27 Last of all the woman died. 28 Now in the resurrection, of the seven whose wife will she be, for all had married her?" 29 "You are wrong," Jesus answered them, "because you do not know either the Scriptures

† **Matt xxii 15–22** ‖ Mark xii 13–17, Luke xx 20–26; **23–33** ‖ Mark xii 18–27, Luke xx 27–40; **34–40** ‖ Mark xii 28–34, Luke x 25–28; **41–46** ‖ Mark xii 35–37, Luke xx 41–44.

or God's power, 30 for in the resurrection they will neither marry nor be given in marriage, but will be as angels are in heaven. 31 But as to the resurrection of the dead: have you not read God's word to you—32 'I am the God of Abraham, the God of Isaac, and the God of Jacob'? God is not the God of the dead, but of the living." 33 When the crowds heard this, they were greatly impressed by his teaching.

34 The Pharisees, having heard that he had silenced the Sadducees, came together, and 35 one of them (a lawyer) tried to trap him with a question. 36 "Teacher," he said, "which is the greatest commandment in the Law?" 37 He replied, " 'You must love the Lord your God with your whole heart, your whole self, your whole mind.' 38 This is the first and greatest commandment. 39 The second is like it: 'You must love your neighbor as yourself.' 40 The whole Law, and all the Prophets, depend on these two commandments."

41 While the Pharisees were gathered together, Jesus put a question to them: 42 "What do you think about the Messiah? Whose son is he?" They replied, "David's son." 43 "Why then," Jesus asked, "does David in the Spirit call him 'Lord,' when he says:

44 'The Lord said to my Lord,
    Sit here at my right hand,
    until I have put your enemies under your feet'?

45 If then David called him 'Lord,' in what way is he David's son?" 46 No one was able to answer Jesus at all, nor did anyone from that day venture to question him any more.

NOTES

xxii 16. *with the Herodians.* The introduction of the Herodian party makes the question a pointed one. The Herodians were supporters of the family of Herod the Great, ruling only by favor of the occupying Roman authority. Anxious to maintain the *status quo*, the Herodians would certainly have supported the payment of taxes to Rome where the patriotic

Pharisees emphatically would not. *Disciples* of the Pharisees occurs here and at Mark ii 18.

17. *Is it lawful . . . ?* The questioners hope to provoke a reply which will identify Jesus either with the Zealots who refused payment, or with those who had accommodated their life to Roman authority.

18. *casuists.* Cf. Appendix to Part IX of the Introduction.

20. *"Whose representation . . . ?"* The denarius of Tiberius (A.D. 14–37) would carry the emperor's portrait, and also an inscription which accorded him divine honor.

21. *pay to God.* The Greek here (*apodote*) is different from the "pay" (*didonai*) of vs. 17 and has the sense of giving back what is due. The civil rulers therefore receive taxes as a due, not a gift. Similarly, as in xxi 33 ff., God must be given what is his due.

Later Christian attempts to reduce Jesus' statement of principle to exact legislation provided most of the material for the mediaeval conflicts between church and state.

23. *Sadducees.* Matthew provides his readers with minimal information for background, almost as a reminder. It is clear that he assumes that his readers will be fully aware of the main position of the Sadducees. Like the Samaritans, the Sadducees held to the "canonical" status of the Pentateuch, the five books of Moses (=the Law), and placed the rest of the Hebrew Bible on a far lower level or rejected it entirely. The Sadducees must have developed their own case law, but they rejected the oral law which had grown up around the Pentateuch, or any belief which was not clearly held in the Law.

24. *"Moses said . . ."* Lev xviii 16, xx 21 forbid sexual relations with the wife of a brother (referring to adultery); but in some circumstances (Deut xxv 5–10) such a marriage with a brother's widow is imposed on a man as a duty (referring to Levirate marriage).

having no children. This is the LXX version, where the Hebrew has simply "son"—i.e., male children.

28. *in the resurrection.* The imaginary test case, assuming a resurrection, seeks to prove the absurdity of the idea.

29. *"You are wrong . . ."* Jesus' reply is based on two premises: (a) The Sadducees are wrong because they are transferring to the resurrection-life considerations which properly belong only to life before death, a mistake which Scripture, for all its imagery, poetic or homespun, never makes. (b) God, who gave the Law, a Law which contains provisions for the regulation of marriage and the raising of children, cannot be unaware of considerations posed by the test case. On the main question of resurrection, the same two premises apply. The power of God is not confined by the mundane considerations adduced by the Sadducees, and in the resurrection-life marriage and birth are irrelevant to the discussion. Moreover, the fact that the Scriptures acknowledged by the Sad-

ducees do not specifically mention resurrection cannot be said to eliminate all idea of it. The argument of vss. 31–32, perhaps not very cogent
to us, but certainly impressive in its own time setting, is simply that
when God speaks of Abraham, Isaac, and Jacob to Moses in Exod iii
6 he speaks of them as still living.

The question of the extent of belief in a resurrection-life in first-
century Judaism is complicated, as is also the question of the universality
or otherwise of resurrection-life among groups who acknowledged such
a life. The Samaritans denied a resurrection, along with the Sadducees.
The rabbinic writers went so far as to accuse the Samaritans of deleting
possible references to resurrection from the Pentateuch, and the same
writers appeal to the Pentateuch for support for a doctrine of resurrection.

33. This verse might well be found at any point in the teaching ministry. Mark places it (xi 18) after the account of the cleansing of the
temple. The suggestion, sometimes made, that Matthew omitted it in the
Markan context and then later placed it here in his own narrative, is
most unlikely. It not only attaches far too much weight to a single
verse, but it also fails to see that a comment of this character may easily
be out of context in all three synoptic gospels.

34. The Markan framework of this narrative is so different from the
Matthean and Lukan traditions, and is so vivid, that we must assume it
to be an eyewitness account, in contrast with the other two. Matthew
and Luke have an account of the question and its answer, without regard to context or the person(s) involved. Matthew and Luke agree that
the questioner was a lawyer, and we can only surmise that Matthew
placed the incident here in order to gather all the hostile questions into
one part of his narrative. Neither Matthew nor Luke knows anything of
the approbation expressed by Jesus in the Markan narrative. There is
another of Matthew's OT allusions here: *came together* is from the LXX
of Ps ii 2, and is used again at xxvi 3.

37. The first statement is from Deut vi 5, and Matthew's quotation
assimilates to the Hebrew text.

39. This quotation is from Lev xix 18, and is also found in Matt xix
19. In negative form a saying similar to it is ascribed to Rabbi Hillel the
Elder: "What is hateful to you do not do to your neighbor. That is the
whole Law, and all else is commentary" (TB, *Shabbath* 31a).

41–42. The next question is about Messiahship, and begins with Greek
words which reflect Ps ii 2: *gathered together* (vs. 41) and *about the
Messiah* (vs. 42). We are accustomed to regarding this questioning by
Jesus, together with the quotation from Ps cx in vs. 44, as though it
was used by Jesus as proof of his Davidic descent. It is in fact just as
easily interpreted as deliberately casting doubt on the whole idea. That
the expected Messiah would be of Davidic descent was a commonplace in

certain sectors of Judaism and could claim OT support. Among the
Essenes, a kingly Messiah and a priestly Messiah were expected. In
either case, publicly to court a Messianic title was to invite Roman
intervention. In asking this question Jesus compels his critics to question
at least one possible assumption—that he was a nationalist seeking to
rally popular support. By the time our gospels were committed to
writing the events of Holy Week had been overshadowed by the Jewish
revolt against Rome, Jewish Christians had either fled or were under
pressure to declare for or against the nationalist cause, and the Davidic
genealogies of Matthew and Luke were no longer the inflammatory material which they would have been earlier.

42. *David's son.* Cf. Isa ix 2 ff., xi 1 ff., etc. Cf. NOTE on i 1.

43. *David.* The psalms were commonly ascribed to David, though it is
now known that much of the Psalter was written both before and after
David's time. David was, however, the patron of temple music in Israel,
and the musical guilds go back to his time. Cf. Albright, *Archaeology and
the Religion of Israel,* pp. 14 f., 125 ff., etc.

in the Spirit. I.e., by divine inspiration.

44. The quotation is from Ps cx 1, but not in the LXX translation.

45. The answer to the question is implied: that there is far more to
Messiahship than Davidic descent.

46. The conclusion provided by Matthew and Mark emphasizes that
the opposition to Jesus has now taken on far more sinister forms.

On the whole question of Davidic messiahship in this chapter, cf.
now Fitzmyer, "The Son of David Tradition and Mt 22:41–46 and
parallels," in *Essays on the Semitic Background of the New Testament,*
pp. 113–27.

COMMENT

Our interpretation of xxi 44 is in a very important sense the key
to the questions which occupy the remainder of this chapter xxii. In
no way seeking elucidation of the questions posed (and the first was
of crucial importance in the political climate of the times), Jesus'
interrogators were simply seeking a pretext for a criminal charge.

82. WARNINGS AGAINST LEGALISM
(xxiii 1–36) †

XXIII 1 Jesus then spoke to the crowds and to his disciples: 2 "The scribes and the Pharisees are the appointed teachers of Moses' Law, 3 and so you must obey and follow everything they tell you to do, but do not imitate their deeds, for they do not practice what they preach. 4 They make up heavy loads and tie them to men's backs, while they themselves will not lift a finger to help carry the loads. 5 They do everything simply so that people will see them. They make large phylacteries, broaden the hem of their garments, 6 love the best places at feasts and the principal seats in the synagogues; 7 (they love) to be greeted in public places, and to be called 'Teacher' by men. 8 You must not be called 'Teacher,' for you have but one Teacher, and you are all brothers; 9 and you must not call anyone on earth 'Father,' for you have but one Father—in heaven. 10 And do not call anyone 'Leader,' for your one Leader is the Messiah. 11 The greatest among you must be your servant. 12 Whoever makes himself great will be humbled, and whoever humbles himself will be raised. 13 Away with you, you pettifogging Pharisee lawyers! You shut the door of the Kingdom of heaven in men's faces; for you yourselves will not go in, nor will you allow those who are entering to do so.

[14 "Away with you, you pettifogging Pharisee lawyers! You rob widows' houses, and make a show of long prayers. For this, your punishment will be the more severe.]

15 "Away with you, you pettifogging Pharisee lawyers! You

† **Matt xxiii 1–5** ‖ Mark xii 38–40, Luke xx 46–47; **11** ‖ Mark ix 35, x 43, Luke ix 48, xxii 26; **12** ‖ Luke xiv 11, xviii 14; **13** ‖ Luke xi 52; **23–24** ‖ Luke xi 42; **25–26** ‖ Mark vii 4, Luke xi 39–41; **27–28** ‖ Luke xi 44; **29–32** ‖ Luke xi 47–48; **33** ‖ Luke iii 7; **34–36** ‖ Luke xi 49–51.

traverse sea and land to make a single convert, and when you have done it, you make him twice as bad as you are.

16 "Away with you, you blind guides, you who say, 'If a man swears by the temple, it is not binding, but if he swears by the gold in the temple, he is liable.' 17 Blind fools! Which is greater —the gold, or the temple which makes the gold holy? 18 Again: 'If a man swears by the altar, it is not binding, but if he swears by the offering on it, he is liable.' 19 Blind men! Which is greater—the offering, or the altar which makes the offering holy? 20 When therefore anyone swears by the altar, he swears by it and by all the offerings on it. 21 He who swears by the temple swears by it and by him who dwells there, 22 and a man who swears by heaven swears by the throne of God and by him who sits on it.

23 "Away with you, you pettifogging Pharisee lawyers! You give to God a tenth of herbs like mint, dill and cummin, but the important duties of the Law—judgment, mercy, honesty—you have neglected. Yet these you ought to have performed, without neglecting the others. 24 You blind guides! Straining a fly out of your drink, and then swallowing a camel!

25 "Away with you, you pettifogging Pharisee lawyers! You clean the outside of a cup and a plate, but inside they are filled with (thoughts of) robbery and greed. 26 You blind Pharisee! First clean the inside of the cup and plate, so that its outside may be clean, too.

27 "Away with you, you pettifogging Pharisee lawyers! You are like whitewashed tombs, which outwardly look beautiful, but inside they are full of dead men's bones and every kind of ritual defilement. 28 In the same way, you appear outwardly good to men, but inside you are full of casuistry and lawlessness.

29 "Away with you, you pettifogging Pharisee lawyers! You build the tombs of the prophets and decorate the monuments of the righteous ones, saying, 30 'If we had been living in the time of our fathers, we would have had no part with them in the killing of the prophets.' 31 In so doing, you witness against yourselves that you are sons of those who murdered the prophets. 32 Make up, then, what is lacking of what your fathers began.

33 You snakes, you vipers' brood! How will you escape being sentenced to Gehenna?

34 "See, on this account I send you prophets and wise men and scribes, some of whom you will kill and crucify, some you will beat in your synagogues and harry from town to town, 35 so that upon you may come all the righteous blood shed upon the earth, from the blood of Abel the righteous to the blood of Zechariah, the son of Barachiah, whom you murdered between the sanctuary and the altar. 36 I solemnly tell you, all this will come upon this generation."

NOTES

xxiii 2. *appointed teachers of Moses' Law*. Cf. "Every council of three in Israel is like the council of Moses" (TB, *Rosh ha-Shanah* 25a). "Moses' seat" (which is the literal translation) is the name given to the seat in the synagogue from which discourses were given.

3. *everything they tell you . . . do not imitate their deeds*. The oral law, and the inferences commonly drawn from the written Law, came under heavy criticism in xv 1–20, and the same considerations apply here. The verb which we have translated *they preach* carries the implication that the Pharisees did profess to live by the precepts of the Law, but that in effect they made an idol of the Law by often surrounding it with casuistry and cavil, so obscuring real principles (cf. xii 7) and neglecting the very compassion which the Law itself taught (cf. xv 4–5). The minutiae were observed, but God's love, of which the Law was an expression, was easily forgotten.

4. Oral law has a tendency to generate a life of its own, to feed upon itself. The Mosaic Law, given as God's gracious gift to Israel, was more and more obscured by the proliferation of commentary. Experience has shown with what tenacity the traditionalist will defend provisions which have long been irrelevant. In the light of the sayings in xvi 19 and xviii 18 about "bind" and "release," it is possible that Jesus here castigates the legalism which can impose regulations but cannot or will not give relief to the lawbreaker.

5. This is directed against religious ostentation in a common Jewish form.

phylacteries. This is the only mention of them in the New Testament. They were texts of the Law written on sheepskin, enclosed in small containers, and worn on forehead and forearm while praying. Numbers of these have turned up at Qumran.

hem of their garments. I.e., fringes or tassels which were prescribed for the four corners of the outer garment; cf. Num xv 38 ff.; Deut xxii 12.

7–11. *to be greeted.* For the material which follows in these verses, the reader is referred to the essay by Moses Aberbach, "The Relations between Master and Disciple in the Talmudic Age," in *Essays presented to Chief Rabbi Israel Brodie on the Occasion of his Seventieth Birthday,* London, 1965. Here there are examples of the obligation of the disciple to follow a recognized teacher without question, to afford him the highest possible honor; and precise rules were made as to the conduct of a group of disciples when walking with their teacher. (They must never, for example, presume to walk beside their teacher.)

Nothing illustrates better than these five verses (7–11) our contention that what we have in this gospel is a very substantial amount of private teaching addre..ed to the inner circle of the disciples. These five verses are totally misunderstood if they are interpreted as being addressed to the whole community. Aberbach (*ibid.,* p. 13) adduces examples of the warnings given to disciples never to presume to greet their masters, since this implied a certain equality. It is in this sense, and in this sense alone, that the prohibitions in vss. 8–10 must be understood. The relationship of the inner circle of the disciples to Jesus was such that they could not be greeted (*You must not be called 'Teacher'*) as though they were occupying a place which was Jesus' alone. So too with *you must not call anyone on Earth 'Father';* for the inner circle of disciples this would imply the formation of a hierarchy which was not proper during the earthly ministry of Jesus.

12. Cf. Proverbs xxix 23.

13–32. This passage is commonly known as the Seven Woes, from the usual translation of the Gr. *ouai* by "woe." The reader is referred to Part IX of the Introduction, together with its appendix on the word *hupokritai/hupokritēs* (which has, as we pointed out, drastically changed its meaning). It is not necessary to do more than reiterate our warning against reading moral judgments into these verses. Jesus is here concerned with that casuistry which so easily brings law into disrepute. His charge here is that Pharisee lawyers, by their concern for minute analytical commentary on the Law, and for regulating precisely all human conduct under the Law, had made the Law increasingly burdensome.

13. *the door of the Kingdom of heaven.* This is certainly the reading in our text, but Luke xi 52 has "you took away the key of knowledge. You yourselves did not enter, and you prevented those who were going in." In view of the precise interpretation given to *Kingdom of heaven* in this gospel, it may be doubted whether this saying in Matthew is wholly

original. In all other areas of this gospel it is The Man who calls men into his Kingdom, and it is not easy to see what is meant by this saying as it stands. It can only be justified as an accusation that men will be dissuaded from throwing in their lot with the new community by supposing that it is simply another manifestation of Pharisaic Judaism. Certainly the Lukan saying is easier, carrying with it the implication that the Pharisee lawyers' attitude of superior wisdom did not foster love of the Law.

14. This verse is not found in the best manuscripts, and in others it stands after vs. 12. It appears to be a later insertion taken either from Mark xii 40 or Luke xx 47.

15. It is well known that there was widespread interest in Judaism on the part of Gentiles in the NT period. Acts speaks often of "God-fearers" —men who attached themselves to synagogues for worship but who had not taken the final step of submitting to Judaism by formal conversion. Hellenistic literature from Jewish authors is witness to the attempts made by Jews of the Dispersion to attract Gentiles to Judaism. But none of this kind of effort would have commended itself to the extreme legalists here castigated by Jesus. When such legalism does succeed in securing a convert, the history of Christianity and Judaism alike is evidence enough for the extremes to which the zeal of the convert for his new faith may drive him.

twice as bad as you are. Literally, "twice as much a child of Gehenna as you are"—i.e., twice as much subject to condemnation.

16–22. This material repeats in more emphatic form the substance of v 33–37. There is no rabbinic material known which would give us precise evidence for the distinction in oaths which is described here. The purpose of an oath was to bind by something greater than oneself (cf. Heb vi 16 ff.), and as the temple is greater than its treasure, and the altar than its offerings, then oaths taken *by the temple* or *by the altar* are binding. However, the same teaching applies as in the material in chapter v, and distinctions in oaths are to be avoided. Incidentally, the saying in vs. 16 can only have come from a time before A.D. 70, when such oaths as are here described necessarily came to an end with the destruction of the temple.

23. The herbs mentioned were all used in cooking, while dill and cummin were also used for medicinal purposes. On *judgment* cf. Isa i 17; Jer xxii 3; on *mercy* cf. ix 13; on *honesty* cf. Hab ii 4.

24. Cf. Lev xi 41 ff.

25. The judgment of Jesus is not against ordinary cleanliness but against excessive concentration on ritual cleanliness or defilement of eating and drinking vessels.

26. There is here a very obvious difference of tradition between Matthew and Luke (xi 40–41). It is not clear how far the two evangelists saw the polemic of Jesus as directed solely against an excessive concern with ritual cleanliness. Matthew's *its* (literally "its outside," Gr. *autou*) in this verse would have to be omitted if, as in Luke, the reference were to outward legalism contrasted with impure intention. Luke's "your" (literally "your inside") in xi 39 seems to imply such a contrast, whereas in vs. 41 he appears to return to consideration of ritual purity and impurity. Considering the care with which Matthew has preserved his tradition about Jesus' sayings on the Law, it is possible that by the time Luke set his own material in order, the meaning of the saying had become obscure.

27–28. It is important not to read exclusively moral judgments into these verses—an all too common proceeding. Such moral judgments may be proper in a later context and against a background of later concerns. Here in the present context there is a contrast between the *legal* rectitude of those whose principal interest or livelihood lies in a proliferating oral law on the one hand, with lack of respect for the Law which such self-conscious rectitude often produces in others. Of course, self-conscious legal rectitude *can* lead, and often does, to a sinful sense of superiority. Luke's version (xi 44) militates against any theory of a common original source at this point.

29–31. It is not necessary to examine the charges made by the prophets against the official custodians of the Law. (Cf. Bruce Vawter, *The Conscience of Israel: Pre-Exilic Prophets and Prophecy,* New York: Sheed, 1961.) Jesus' charge is that the Pharisee lawyers pay honor to the dead, but this is simply lip service. While condemning their ancestors for persecuting the keepers of Israel's conscience, they nevertheless condemn themselves—they are the sons of "our fathers" (i.e., share their fathers' characteristics).

It should be noted that the parallelism here in Matthew links *the prophets* with *the righteous ones* (cf. xiii 17), a common association in the Dead Sea scrolls and the intertestamental literature. The reader is referred to our discussion of x 41, for in that verse there is no question of any hendiadys. Moreover the titles for the Messiah in that verse appear to have been an archaism or were rapidly becoming so even when spoken, and were almost certainly out of use when our NT sources were committed to writing. While there are more references in the NT to the Righteous One as a Messianic title than is commonly recognized, such lack of recognition is hardly surprising, in view of generally accepted translations of x 41. We shall meet the *righteous ones* again in the account of the resurrection.

The custom of venerating the prophets by paying honor to their grave sites was certainly well established in the time of Jesus, as was also the custom of adorning the graves of pious men with sepulchral monuments. Many tombs of pious men around Jerusalem from the Herodian period have been excavated in recent years. Cf. Joachim Jeremias, *Heiligengräber in Jesu Umwelt*, Göttingen, 1958, and also C. C. Torrey, *The Lives of the Prophets*, JBL Monograph Series, Vol. I, Philadelphia, 1946. (Incidentally, Torrey's contention seems to be wholly correct: that the original was written in Hebrew, and that the place names—irrelevant because abandoned after the fall of Jerusalem—are important evidence for a pre-A.D. 70 date.)

32. The saying is ironical: "Complete what your fathers began."

33. On *Gehenna*, cf. NOTE on v 22.

34. Luke xi 49 ascribes this saying to "the Wisdom of God," which may be an editorial addition to denote Jesus. Alternatively, the words may be a quotation by Jesus in the Lukan tradition, in which case they are from an unknown source. There is no suggestion in Matthew that the words are a quotation.

prophets and wise men and scribes. The missionaries of the new Kingdom are described in Jewish terms, and *prophets* as a function of the early Christian ministry were familiar to Paul. Precise rules were laid down in the (Syrian? second part of the first century) *Didache* for the treatment of prophets (*ibid.*, xiv, xxii, xxiv, xxvi). Cf. also the article by Massey H. Shepherd, Jr., IDB, III (K–Q), s.v. "Prophet in the NT."

35. It might seem natural to see in *Abel* and *Zechariah* the first and the last martyrs of the OT Scriptures (Gen iv and II Chron xxiv 20 ff.). Not only, however, was this Zechariah not *the son of Barachiah* (he was the son of Jehoiada), but Baruch (the shortened version of Berachiah) was a very common name in the end of the OT period. The Zechariah of this passage may well refer to a person of whom otherwise we have no knowledge. It is always possible that two patronymics have been confused in the tradition, but rather than assume such a circumstance, it appears more reasonable to us to assume that this Zechariah was a person of whom otherwise we have no knowledge.

36. Cf. xxiv 34; the "coming" of The Man to the Father will certainly happen in *this generation*, when The Man is exalted in the glory of his passion-resurrection. The coming sufferings Jesus sees as judgment upon official Judaism for its refusal of him and his ministry.

generation (Gr. *genea*). This word may certainly mean "lifetime," and not simply "generation" in our sense of the term. Cf. Donald W. Prakken, *Studies in Greek Genealogical Chronology*, London: Mitre Press, 1944, for the fullest treatment. There is the same fluctuation of meaning in Biblical Heb. *dōr* and Syr. *dārā*.

COMMENT

The relationship of the material in this chapter to similar material found in Luke makes it clear that this is Matthew's own ordering, and that Matthew and Luke did not draw upon a common written source. Luke xi 39–52 contains sayings addressed to a Pharisee (cf. xi 37) or Pharisees, or lawyers, all of whom are found here in Matthew without any distinction as to audience. Matthew's language is considerably different from that of the Lukan material.

The material in this section should be read in the light of the examination made in Part IX of the Introduction on Jesus' attitude to the Law. It would be foolish to assume Matthew is entirely responsible for the critical attitude taken towards the Pharisees in this chapter, and that Jesus himself could not possibly have seriously misrepresented the Pharisees or even caricatured them. Certainly it is possible that early Christians, in the interest of polemics, deliberately changed the character of some of Jesus' sayings; and if Matthew is as late as some think (A.D. 80 or even later), then this may have happened. But it does seem clear that Jesus had strong feelings about the "hypocritical" nature of many of the Pharisees. While Jesus does not condemn all Pharisee lawyers out of hand, he does condemn those who made the Law an end in itself. This chapter does not deny at all that there were many—probably most—Pharisees who were devout, God-fearing men, devoted to Israel, its religion, and its Lord. Nevertheless the chapter stands as clear warning that there are varieties of impiety and idolatry which are not confined to those who fashion graven images. The disciple is just as liable to fall into the sins castigated here.

It is clear that Matthew intended this collection of material to be included in the final section of teaching; it moves from the temple and the crowds to final private instruction to the inner circle.

Most recently, an attempt has been made to see some primitive "wisdom" (Gr. *sophia*) material underlying the "Q" tradition, with the further suggestion that Matthew's use of such material was a crucial factor in primitive Christology. Cf. M. Jack Suggs, *Wisdom, Christology and Law in Matthew's Gospel,* Harvard University Press, 1970. The book has a very full bibliography, and there is obvious room for further discussion on the suggestions which its author advances.

83. LAMENT OVER JERUSALEM
(xxiii 37–39) †

XXIII 37 "O Jerusalem, Jerusalem! You who murder the prophets and stone those who are sent to you! How often did I wish to gather your children together, just as a bird gathers her brood under her wings, but you would not let me! 38 See —your house is forsaken [and desolate]. 39 For I tell you that from this moment you will not see me until you say 'Blessed is he who comes in the Lord's name.'"

† Matt xxiii **37–39** || Luke xiii 34–35.

NOTES

xxiii 37–39. It is not possible to make any firm statement as to whether the sayings in these three verses are in context or not. Luke has them in a wholly different context. Possibly they belong historically to an earlier occasion in the ministry, when Jesus was leaving Jerusalem for the last time before his triumphal entry. In that case we must assume a situation similar to that found in John x 22–39, when some had attempted to stone Jesus. Both mission and message having been alike rejected, Jesus will not visit the temple again (*your house is forsaken*) and they would not see him again until he was greeted with the words of Ps cxviii 26.

38. *your house is forsaken*. Cf. Jer xii 7, xxvi 6. It is possible that Jesus used these words with deliberate reference to the desolation and destruction so vividly portrayed in Jer xii, particularly in view of the *you would not let me* of vs. 37.

39. *from this moment*. The Greek is far stronger than the usual English translations. Cf. also xxvi 64.

84. THE FUTURE OF THE TEMPLE
(xxiv 1–2)†

XXIV 1 Jesus left, and was going away from the temple, when the disciples came to him to show him the temple buildings. 2 He said to them in reply, "You see all these things? I solemnly tell you that there will not be a single stone standing upon another which will not be thrown down."

† **Matt xxiv 1–2** ‖ Mark xiii 1–2, Luke xxi 5–6.

Notes

During the ministry of Jesus the temple of Herod was still under construction. The upsurge of nationalism after the rise of the Zealot movement in A.D. 8 eventually led to the disastrous Jewish revolt of A.D. 64.

xxiv 2. *not be a single stone*. Josephus states that the temple was destroyed by fire. So much for the idea of prophecy after the event, or accommodation by apostolic manipulation to fit the event. (See COMMENT [b].)

Comment

It is a simple matter to lump together the material in chapters xxiv and xxv and label the result "signs of the end," or "the end of the Age." Such a procedure is simple, but wholly fails to do justice to the material. Three distinct matters are dealt with in these chapters xxiv–xxv:

(a) The destruction of Jerusalem in the near future, seen by Jesus as judgment on the rejection of his vocation and ministry by official Judaism;

(b) The persecution of the infant community by authorities and groups inside and outside Judaism;

(c) The continuing life of the Messianic Community, looking to "the End," whether the end of the present age or the end of the natural order.

With regard to (b), it cannot be too strongly emphasized that the rise of the fiercely nationalist Zealot movement in Palestine and throughout parts of the Eastern Mediterranean after ca. A.D. 40 came to face Jewish Christians with exceedingly hard choices. Were they to throw in their lot with the nationalists or remain aloof? Whatever decisions were made would certainly evoke hostility from either Roman or Jews, and often both. We have called attention before in this commentary to the increasingly explosive situation in Palestine in the decades before A.D. 64. Jesus' prophecy of the fall of both city and temple was not an extraordinary feat of prescience, and to write off the saying in vs. 2 as prophecy after the event is wholly unjustified.

The expectation of "the End" is a more difficult matter to cover in a commentary of this size. Not only is there confusion in many commentaries about what Jesus meant when he spoke of the "coming," of The Man, but the confusion is further compounded by reference to xxiv 34. It is not likely to further our understanding of the gospels, still less of the milieu in which the words of Jesus were uttered, to examine every clause and sentence of the sayings of chapters xxiv–xxv for precise prediction, and then attempt to match this with known or supposed events after the passion. Certainly Paul in his earlier letters looked for an early consummation of the natural order and a manifestation of the reign of God over both just and unjust, yet in the later letters (especially if Ephesians is included) we see that he was no longer expecting such a cataclysmic happening in the immediate future. J. A. T. Robinson has argued (in *Jesus and His Coming*) that the expectation of a "return" of Jesus was derived not only from a misunderstanding of Jesus' own words but also from uncertainty about the precise nature of Jesus' Messiahship (cf. *idem.*, "The Most Primitive Christology of All?" in TNTS).

A great deal of the prediction-seeking on the part of NT students has come from a lack of understanding of the forms and imagery of Jewish apocalyptic. It is not very clear why precise prediction should be looked for in Matt xxiv–xxv and allied synoptic material, and not, for example, at the same time in I Thess iv 13 ff., or some of the more imaginative passages in Revelation. It would demand a library of references to list all that has been written on the subject of apocalyptic. Here we can only refer to those works which contain all the relevant information in easily accessible form: H. H. Rowley, *The Relevance of Apocalyptic,* 3d ed., London: Lutterworth Press, 1963, New York: Association Press, 1964; D. S. Russell, *The Method and Message of Jewish Apocalyptic,* London: SCM / Philadelphia: Westminster Press, 1964. The latter, a very important book, takes great care to distinguish between pre- and post-Qumran material, as also does Rowley's work. R. H. Charles's *Eschatology* (1899) is even today a most useful book; its learned author would certainly have appreciated the immense importance of the Dead Sea discoveries to his subject. It must not be forgotten that crisis of any kind in both political and social circumstances tends to produce a particular kind of thinking, speaking and writing; this was the subject of U. E. Simon's *Theology of Crisis,* London: SPCK, 1948.

So far as the present chapter is concerned, we must remind the reader that for all its apparently homogeneous character as a block of material, it is in fact a collection of sayings from different occasions, which reflects the three distinct stages of crisis indicated in the opening paragraph above.

The present collected material represents what would be expected in the process of sifting and ordering an oral tradition. Yet comparison with collections of similar or parallel material in Mark and Luke displays the same process at work—i.e., the collecting under one broad heading of all sayings which reflect the various stages of crisis in, or connected with, or following upon, the ministry of Jesus.

In no area has the confusion been more widespread than in the interpretation given to the "coming" of The Man. This is a point which we have emphasized repeatedly, both in the Introduction and in the commentary. We do no more here than remind the reader of this real danger of confusion. It is necessary to add this: When sayings specifically dealing with the "coming" of The Man are seen in what we hold to be their proper context—i.e., The Man's coming *to* the Father—then the task of interpreting this material is correspondingly far simpler.

There is one matter which must be discussed here, and it concerns the understanding by commentators of the person of Jesus himself. Albert Schweitzer's a priori argument that Jesus expected an imminent cataclysm in which both he and his mission would be vindicated implied, in effect, that Jesus' expectation of "the End" was mistaken and that his hopes were proved wrong by events. On the other hand, there are those who take an ultra-conservative view of the recorded words of Jesus as inerrant, or who force considerations of creedal and conciliar orthodoxy as to the person and/or divinity of Jesus on the NT material. The results have been unhappy. In both cases there has been a failure to do justice to the first-century Jewish milieu in which Jesus spoke, taught, and acted. Allied with this failure has been a tendency to invest each word of the apocalyptic language of Jesus with a precise predictive meaning which would have been alien to orthodox and sectarian Judaism alike. Similarly, both for those committed to a view of verbal inerrancy (in the last analysis depending on the possibility of discovering a "definitive" Greek text), and also for those committed to Nicene and Chalcedonian orthodoxy, there has often been a failure to deal adequately (if at all) with the human nature and human thinking of Jesus. As a result, a good many presuppositions have unconsciously gone into the work of commentators on the material immediately before us.

The work of form-critics distributing all sayings along a line of evolutionary development, from a reconstructed "primitive" preaching, through an assumed "Hellenistic" reordering of the material (on good Hegelian lines), down to the systematic teaching of the Church of the second century A.D., has been very one-sided. The NT writings claim to rest on historical tradition centered on a person.

The history of NT study of the apocalyptic material can be simply stated. From the second half of the nineteenth century onwards it has been generally agreed that the material is composite, gathered from various occasions and contexts. G. R. Beasley-Murray (*Jesus and the Future,* London: Macmillan / New York: St. Martin's, 1954; and *A Commentary on Mark Thirteen,* London: Macmillan, 1956; New York: St. Martin's, 1957) sums up the accepted theory that the whole discourse in Mark (and therefore, on the usual premises, in Matthew also) is based on a "little apocalypse" of Jewish origin. Vincent Taylor (*The Gospel according to St. Mark,* London: Macmillan / New York: St. Martin's, 1952), in our view rightly, argues that the evangelist has grouped together whole series of sayings, not all of which have an apocalyptic content, instead of merely editing a Jewish-Christian apocalypse. It is true that we must somehow account for the widespread belief in the early church in an anticipated early return of Jesus (cf. the third paragraph of this COMMENT). The discovery of an exact, tightly knit, precise body of belief in the primitive Christian community would be most surprising, and it is even more surprising to have writers on the New Testament apparently confident that they have found such a body of belief.

A note of caution must be added here. In order to keep this commentary within reasonable limits it was felt imperative not to place too great a burden upon the general reader. In no case was this more necessary than in the present chapter xxiv. The highly technical nature of the discussion of this material among NT scholars, and the very considerable body of literature accumulated around it, has ruled out any detailed treatment. That Matt xxiv 4–36 (= Mark xiii 5–37; Luke xxi 8–36) is free commentary on Daniel (vii 8–27, viii 9–26, ix 24–27, and xi 21 – xii 13) both in ideas and actual quotations, seems to be generally agreed. Beyond that, there is no large consensus of opinion. The student is recommended to consult Lars Hartman's excellent *Prophecy Interpreted,* Coniectanea Biblica, New Testament Series, I (Lund: Gleerup, 1966), especially Part II. The book has an exhaustive bibliography.

It is hoped that the reader will see the necessity of placing this COMMENT here when reading the NOTES on the ensuing sections.

85. THE COMING PERSECUTION
(xxiv 3–14)†

XXIV 3 As Jesus sat on the Mount of Olives, the disciples came to him privately. "Tell us," they said, "when all this will happen, and what will be the sign of your coming and the end of the age." 4 "Watch," replied Jesus, "and see that no one deceives you. 5 Many will come in my name, declaring 'I am the Messiah,' and they will deceive many people. 6 You are going to hear of wars, and rumors of wars; take care not to be troubled. These things must happen, but the end is not at once. 7 For one people will rise against another, one kingdom against another, and in various places there will be famines and earthquakes. 8 All these things are only the beginning of sufferings. 9 Then men will give you over to punishment and will kill you, and on my account you will be hated by all men. 10 Many will fall by the way, betray one another, hate each other; 11 many false prophets will arise and lead many astray. 12 Because lawlessness is increased, the loyalty of many will grow cold, 13 but the one who stands firm to the end will be saved. 14 This proclamation of the Kingdom will be made throughout the world, as a witness to all nations, and then the end will come.

† Matt xxiv 3–14 || Mark xiii 3–13, Luke xxi 7–19.

Notes

xxiv 3. There is a highly significant divergence in Matthew from the parallels in Mark and Luke. Matthew alone has *the sign of your coming.* Bearing in mind the care which this evangelist takes in ordering his material, this phrase is of considerable importance. It is possible that the disciples' request, especially in view of the Matthean clause, may be in all three gospels a question introduced at this point in the narrative to gather together the apocalyptic and eschatological material. By the time oral tradition began to take fixed form the passion and the resurrection would have been seen in perspective as the pivotal apocalyptic moment of the ministry.

R. H. Fuller (*The Message and Achievement of Jesus,* Naperville, Ill.: A. R. Allenson / London: SCM, 1954) sums this up in the phrase "the cruciality of the cross." There is a further point to be noted. In the rapidly swelling amount of intertestamental writings we find increasing evidence for conventional formulae to introduce the content and sequence of apocalyptic. Such an example is now before us in the request put on the lips of the disciples. Similar devices are found in Revelation and Thessalonians. The Habakkuk commentary from Qumran (1QHab) (vii 1–2, following Habermann's vocalization) supplies us with the following: "And God told Habakkuk to write what things would befall the last period, but the end of the age he did not make known to him." Aside altogether from the fact that Qumran yields the Hebrew background for *the end of the age*—a phrase which some NT scholars have been reluctant to ascribe to Jesus—this is firm evidence of such an introductory formula from Essene practice. Similar phrases occur in the intertestamental writings (preserved in Greek); cf. "the consummation of the times" (Apocalypse of Baruch xiii 3; cf. also xxvii 15, xxix 8, xxx 3, liv 21, lvi 2, lix 8, lxxxii 2, lxxxvii 7, 23). Enoch xvi 1 speaks of "until the day of the consummation . . . in which the age is consummated." The Testament of Levi (x) has "the end of the ages." Cf. also Dan xii 4, 13. Without any question, the Qumran Heb. *gemar ha-qeṣ* is the source of the phrase.

The ensuing sections collect together sayings which bear directly on the fall of Jerusalem, the nationalist uprisings in the period after the passion, The Man's coming, and the end of the age.

5–6. The Qumran discoveries have emphasized just how much Messianic expectation was in the air prior to and contemporary with the ministry of Jesus. Acts v 36 ff. has an account of a Messianic pretender. The position of Jewish Christians, regarded for some time as a sectarian group on the fringes of Judaism, was one of considerable peril. Possible assurances by Zealot and patriotic groups that they were after all acting with Jesus' authority (*in my name*) cannot have made that position easier.

These things must happen. Cf. Dan ii 28. One need hardly be reminded of the frequency with which war and consequent suffering introduce apocalyptic material in the prophetic writings of the OT. We referred in the preceding COMMENT to the widespread nature of Jewish nationalist uprisings, and it was during this time of rumor, of war and doubt that the oral tradition was fixed and committed to writing. The warning *but the end is not at once,* from whatever historical context in the teaching ministry of Jesus, must have taken on added urgency in the days of the infant community's growth. Its place in this collected material is therefore natural.

7–8. Cf. Isa xix 2; II Chron xv 6. Paul's second Thessalonian letter is eloquent proof of the manner in which some members of the early community concluded that "the end" was imminent and abandoned regular habits of work to await its advent.

beginning of sufferings. Literally, the "beginnings of birth-pains," an almost technical term for the sufferings which would immediately precede a new age. (Cf. 1QH iii, the *Hôdayôt*, or Thanksgiving Psalms, from Qumran for similar phrases.) The age of the Messiah's reign, seen in the context of the upheavals which surrounded the spread of the community, was certainly ushered in with much suffering. Cf. Frederick C. Grant, *Ancient Judaism and the New Testament* (Edinburgh and London: Oliver & Boyd, 1960), especially pp. 68–95; TWNT, II, pp. 26–27, 30–31; K. A. Kuhn, "Πειρἀσμος-ἀμαρτία-σαρζ in Nt." ZTK 49 (1952), pp. 200–22; and John Pryke, "Eschatology in the Dead Sea Scrolls," in *The Scrolls and Christianity,* ed. Matthew Block, London: SPCK, 1969.

9–14. These verses adequately underline the way in which one tradition collected sayings as compared with another parallel tradition. There are Markan parallels only in Mark xiii 9a, 13b, 10, and Matthew has the material of Mark xiii 9b–13a (except 10) in his x 17–21.

10. *fall by the way* (literally, "be made to stumble"). Cf. xiii 21. Those looking for an immediate vindication, an immediate triumph of the Messianic Age, will fall by the way through disappointment.

betray one another. This may refer either to divisions within the community, or—in the circumstances of nationalist unrest—to those outside the community reporting believers as traitors.

11–12. Hopes aroused by the proclamation of the Messianic Age, coupled with the upsurge of nationalism, provided all the ingredients necessary not only for self-appointed prophets (cf. Acts xx 30) but also for disappointed hopes and ambitions (cf. I John ii 18). The result in a time of upheaval is a severe strain on faith. Idealistic pictures of the early community need to be balanced by the view recorded in the first three chapters of Revelation.

There are prophecies of apostasy during upheavals and persecution in the intertestamental writings: cf. II Esd v 2; Enoch xci 7. Similarly, the promise of salvation for those who persevere is also found in those writings. Cf. ". . . whoever remains after all these things . . . shall be saved" (II Esd vi 25, ix 7–8).

14. It is simply not possible to refer this saying to the fall of Jerusalem, as do some writers, who then attempt to make sense of a *proclama-*

tion . . . throughout the world. While it is true that the events of A.D. 70 were of cataclysmic dimensions to Jews and Jewish Christians alike, it is equally true that "the end" (*to telos*) in vs. 6 cannot easily be reconciled with the view outlined in the first sentence of this NOTE. Disorder, chaos, and persecution did not end with the sack of the city and the destruction of the temple. Moreover, the Pauline use of *to telos* in I Cor xv 24 specifically refers "the end" to the time of the final judgment. That there is a sense in which any disaster is an "end," and the expectation of it a call to detachment, is clear. Paul's ethical and moral injunctions in I Corinthians were delivered against the background of a call to detachment, against a call for awareness that the believer's final *politeia* ("loyalty," "citizenship"; cf. Philip iii 20, where *politeuma,* a synonym, is used) was in heaven. In the same sense I Peter iv 7 can speak of "the end" being at hand.

Some commentators have apparently fastened upon A.D. 70 and the preceding war as a fixed historical datum. Then, having concluded that the eschatological and apocalyptic material in our gospels all belongs to a single occasion, they attempt to explain the material in question as best they can. This procedure is in direct opposition to the confident assertions of many of the same commentators that the so-called "Sermon on the Mount" is in fact a miscellany.

86. IMMEDIATE SIGNS
(xxiv 15–28)†

XXIV 15 "So when you see the abominable sacrilege, of which Daniel the prophet spoke, standing in the holy place" (let the reader take note), 16 "then those in Judea must go to the mountains, 17 the one who is on the housetop must not go down to take his household property, 18 while the man in the field must not return to get his himation. 19 Alas for those who will be pregnant or nursing children in those days! 20 Pray that your flight is not either in the winter or on a Sabbath, 21 for there will be great suffering, such as has not occurred from the foundation of the world to the present—no, nor ever will be. 22 Unless those days are shortened, no human being can be saved; however, for the sake of the chosen, those days will be shortened. 23 Then, if anyone says to you, 'Look! Here is the Messiah!' or 'There he is!' do not believe it, 24 for pseudo-messiahs and false prophets will arise and show great signs and wonders, so as to lead astray (if it were possible) even the chosen. 25 See—I have told you beforehand. 26 So if they say to you, 'He is in the desert,' do not go out; and if they say, 'Look in the storehouses!' do not believe it, 27 For as lightning comes from the east and flashes across to the west, so will be the coming of The Man. 28 Wherever the carcass is, there the vultures will be gathered.

† Matt xxiv 15–28 || Mark xiii 14–23, Luke xxi 20–24.

NOTES

This section is composed of sayings which have a direct bearing on the impending fate of Jerusalem, others of a more general character, and one which deals with The Man's coming.

xxiv 15. *abominable sacrilege.* Matthew's tradition here makes explicit what is only hinted in Mark, who does not mention the prophetic oracle. In addition, Matthew speaks of the *holy place* and so emphatically refers to the temple. The quotation is from Dan ix 27. Cf. the idol altar of I Macc i 54, 59. With the example of Antiochus Epiphanes in mind, Jesus required neither prescience nor unusual insight to see where the rise of nationalism under Roman occupation would lead. Whether the *abominable sacrilege* refers to actual idolatry, or to the entrance of Roman imperial-eagle standards into the temple area, is immaterial. It was common practice then and for long centuries before, to assert sovereignty over a nation by dethroning its gods and replacing them by those of the conqueror. In the NT writings idolatry of any kind was a warning of distress and judgment to come. Cf. Rom i 25; II Thess ii 3 ff.; Rev xiii 4.

let the reader take note. This is an editorial note and bears the same meaning as a somewhat similar exhortation in Rev xiii 18. It may also indicate to the reader that the Messianic Community must now face a challenge similar to that faced by Israel in the time of the Seleucid kings.

16–20. The sayings here were dramatically illustrated in the time of the war of A.D. 66–70 and again in the revolt of 130–135. How many Christians made their escape in the years before A.D. 70 we do not know. The tradition of Eusebius is that many Christians fled to Pella, and we have no reason to doubt the accuracy of the tradition. Archaeological discovery provides ample evidence for the destruction wrought on Jewish towns by Roman punitive expeditions during the war.

21. This saying is an echo of a similar description of distress in Dan xii 1. Cf. also Jer xxx 7. Those inclined to dismiss the sayings as exaggerated or hyperbolic would do well to bear in mind that crises of a national or international character have been repeatedly described in terms of doom in our own lifetime. Few commentators on this chapter today can fail to recognize the similarity between the premonitions of Jesus and the preoccupations of our own time.

22. Cf. Enoch lxxx 2: "In the days of sinners the years will be shortened."

23–25. We have more than enough evidence to demonstrate the fever pitch of Messianic expectation for a century and a half before

Jesus and in the century following his passion. The crucial test for the disciples, as all the gospels emphasize, is to see the dignity and honor of the Messiah in the circumstances of humiliation and apparent defeat.

26. This saying (which in all probability comes from a quite different historical setting) seems to reject two specific approaches to Messianic expectation. Jesus may be ruling out an Essene view that only *in the desert,* among their communities, could salvation be found. Similarly he may be rejecting the suggestion that his community make common cause with the Zealots (*Look in the storehouses*) in making provision for war.

storehouses. This word may imply storehouses of a military character (as excavated in Masada) which would include weapons as well as food.

27. Given the circumstances of a collection of apocalyptic and eschatological material, the presence of this saying is natural. It is natural also, given the present context of the saying, that there was more than a slight possibility of misunderstanding. The Man's coming will be sudden, with few premonitory signs. The suggestion that *as lightning comes* indicates universal visibility, runs counter to all the warnings in the gospels that men must watch and look for The Man's coming. To what extent primitive liturgical practice shaped common expectations of a "second" coming was nowhere better expressed than by the late Gregory Dix (in *The Shape of the Liturgy* [London: Dacre, 1944], p. 265): "By cataloguing, as it were, the metahistorical and eternal facts (of the resurrection, ascension, session and judgement) side by side with an historic event in time (the passion) the whole notion of the *eschaton* is brought in thought entirely *within time,* and split into two parts, the one in the historic past and the other in the historic future, instead of both in combination being regarded as a single fact of the eternal present. In the primitive conception there is but *one eschaton,* one 'coming', the 'coming *to* the Father' of redeemed mankind, which is the realisation of the Kingdom of God."

28. In context this saying (which may be proverbial in character and origin) appears to have possible reference to two events—either to the prostrate hopes of Judaism after A.D. 70, or to the apparent defeat of the Messiah in his death. Bearing in mind the composite character of this chapter, either interpretation is possible, though we prefer the former.

87. THE MAN'S COMING
(xxiv 29–44)†

XXIV 29 "Immediately after the distress of those days,

'The sun will be darkened,
the moon will not give its light,
the stars will fall from the sky,
and the powers of heaven will be shaken.'

30 Then will appear the standard of The Man in heaven, all the tribes of the earth will then mourn, and they will see The Man coming on the clouds of heaven, with power and great honor. 31 With a loud trumpet he will send out his angels, who will gather his chosen from the four winds, from one end of heaven to the other. 32 Learn a lesson from the fig tree. When its branches become green, and it produces leaves, you know that summer is near. 33 In the same way, when you see all these things, you will know that he is at the threshold. 34 In solemn truth, I tell you that this generation will not pass away until all these things happen. 35 Heaven and earth will pass away, but my words will not pass away. 36 But no one knows that day or that hour—neither the messengers of heaven, nor the Son, but only the Father. 37 The appearing of The Man will be like the time of Noah; 38 for just as in those days before the flood they were eating and drinking, marrying and giving in marriage, until the day that Noah went into the ark, 39 and did not know until the flood came and swept them all away, so will be The Man's coming. 40 Then, two men will be in the field; one is taken and the other left. 41 Two women will be grinding at the mill; one is taken and the other left. 42 There-

† **Matt xxiv 29–31** || Mark xiii 24–27, Luke xxi 25–28; **32–35** || Mark xiii 28–31, Luke xxi 29–33; **36–44** || Mark xiii 32–37, Luke xvii 26–30, 34–36.

fore watch. You do not know on what day your Lord is coming.
43 But realize that if the householder had known at what time
of night the thief was coming, he would have watched and
would not have allowed his house to be broken into. 44 Therefore you also must be ready, for The Man is coming at a time
you do not expect.

NOTES

The material in this section illustrates very well the miscellaneous
character of the sayings grouped together in this chapter. No less than
three separate themes are treated in the first three verses.

xxiv 29. Cf. Isa xiii 10 (natural disorders at the fall of Babylon),
xxxiv 4 (at the downfall of Edom); Ezek xxxii 7–8 (signs attending the
distress of Egypt). Cf. also Joel ii 31. In the intertestamental literature
such natural phenomena are associated with the last times; cf. II Esd
v 4; Enoch lxxx 4. It is important to remember that all these natural
portents in the apocalyptic literature are signs of God's power and overruling providence; they are a terror only to the faithless. The presence of
the following verses, particularly with the prefix *then* (a favorite Matthean device, but no more than a stylistic device) has naturally led to
the supposition that what is being predicted is a period of world disorder, to be followed at once by a return of Jesus in triumph.

The trouble with all rationalizing efforts to arrange the eschatological
predictions in Matthew in a "logical" order and to fit them into subsequent world history is that they were delivered at different times and
under different circumstances, and are apocalyptic, not necessarily addressed to specific events in the future. For this very reason they apply
to many different historical situations and human needs. Millions of
people today find them inexpressibly comforting in world crises which
often seem to foreshadow a final catastrophe to *Homo sapiens sapiens*
and all his works.

30. It is clear, as we shall see later in xxvi 64, that men were asked
to *see* The Man's coming, and we reiterate that this was his coming *to*
the Father in the glorious exaltation of passion-resurrection. The test of
faith is to see all this in The Man's *standard*, the cross. Such is also the
Johannine understanding; cf. John iii 14, viii 28, xii 32.

The second part of the verse is from Dan vii 13—crucial for all
understanding of what Jesus means when he speaks of his "coming."

31. Another theme is introduced in this saying—that of the calling of
the chosen. Reminiscent as it is of Isa xxvii 13 and Zech ix 14, the
saying may be (in the light of OT references) interpreted as The Man

calling men into his Kingdom. However, the use of such words as *his angels* and *his chosen* indicates that this saying refers to the final judgment; cf. Part VII of the Introduction, and also I Cor xv 52 and I Thess iv 16. For the apocalyptic trumpet cf. Isa xxvii 13; Ps Sol xi 1–3.

32–35. These sayings may be taken together, though there is no indication of their original context. The *lesson from the fig tree* bears out the warning of vs. 30: men must be constantly on the alert for The Man's coming. Verse 33 could well be applied as commentary on John xii 34, where Jesus' hearers express doubts both about the "lifting up" and The Man's identity. Only faith alone will recognize the signs of The Man's exaltation by the Father. Seen thus, Matthew's vss. 34–35 are a simple statement of fact. On vs. 34 cf. xvi 28 and on vs. 35 cf. v 18, both of which serve as a warning against treating this chapter as an original unity.

36. Here again is a factual statement, though without indication of its original context. If it is in context at this juncture of the ministry, it is still quite factual. Jesus knew that the testing ground of his ministry had been reached, but the exact timing of its final moments was, of course, unknown to him.

37 ff. Verses 37–41 are paralleled in Luke xvii 26–27, 30, 34–35—yet another indication of the varied historical contexts from which the sayings of this chapter came.

The sayings emphasize again the completely unexpected nature of The Man's coming. Men and women pursue their ordinary occupations, wholly unaware that the decisive moment in the Messianic ministry has been reached in passion-exaltation. Verse 42 summons Jesus' immediate circle to watchfulness; in spite of all their protestations of belief, and all their association with him in his ministry, it is possible for them, too, to miss the decisive moment. At Matthew's vs. 42 the Markan tradition (xiii 33–36) has an exhortaton to vigilance together with the simile of an absent householder. The remainder of this chapter has been attracted into its present context by vs. 43. It is hoped that enough was said in the COMMENT and NOTES to the preceding sections to indicate that, properly understood, we need not accuse the evangelist/various later hypothetical editors of free invention. Nor need we ascribe to Jesus hopes, aspirations, and ambitions destined to be shattered. Even if such were known, they could scarcely have survived the sifting process of oral tradition. It is necessary simply to take The Man's "coming" seriously, as identified with the "coming" of The Representative *to* God in Dan vii 13, as the background for Jesus' sayings.

In this connection, cf. Rev i 7. The emphasis there is that of the *present* triumph of the Messiah Jesus, with its consequences for those who failed to recognize his exaltation in his passion. It also looks to a final judgment and triumph when the reign of the Messiah will be finally declared and made open.

88. PARABLES OF THE KINGDOM
(xxiv 45 – xxv 13) †

XXIV 45 "Who then is a faithful and intelligent slave, whom his master has appointed over his household, to give them their food at the proper time? 46 That slave is fortunate whom the master at his coming finds doing so, 47 for I solemnly tell you that he will appoint him over all his goods. 48 But if the wicked slave begins to say to himself: 'My lord is delayed,' 49 and begins to beat his fellow slaves, eats and drinks with drunkards, 50 the master of that slave will come on a day when he does not expect him, and at a time which he does not know, 51 and will punish him. His lot will be with the timeservers, where there will be shrieking and grinding of teeth."

XXV 1 "Then the Kingdom of heaven may be compared with ten maidens, who took their lamps and went to meet the bridegroom and the bride. 2 Five of them were silly and five sensible, 3 for the silly ones took their lamps, but took no oil with them, 4 but the sensible ones took flasks of oil with their lamps. 5 As the bridegroom was delayed, they all dozed and lay down, 6 but in the middle of the night there was a shout: 7 'The bridegroom! Come out to meet him!' Then all those maidens got up and trimmed their lamps, 8 the silly ones saying to the sensible ones, 'Give us some of your oil; for our lamps are going out.' 9 But the sensible ones replied, 'Perhaps there will not be enough for us and you. It would be better to go to the dealers and buy for yourselves.' 10 While they went to buy, the bridegroom arrived, and those who were ready went in with him to the wedding feast and the doors

† **Matt xxiv 45 – xxv 13** ‖ Luke xii 41–48.

were closed. 11 Afterwards the other maidens came too, with the words, 'Sir, sir, open up for us!' 12 But he replied, 'I solemnly tell you that I do not know you.' 13 Therefore be on your guard. You know neither the day nor the hour.

NOTES

The attraction of the first parable to its present position is explained by vss. 43–44. Such attraction also dictated the presence of the remainder of the final block of parable teaching. The present context of this material is part-cause of a certain ambivalence in Christian belief with respect to the "return," or "second coming," of Jesus. The use of phrases such as *My lord is delayed* (xxiv 48), or *the bridegroom was delayed* (xxv 5), and *the master(of the slaves)returned* (xxv 19) all illustrate this ambivalence. Cf. in this connection II Peter iii 4.

xxiv 45–51. This parable, presumably addressed to the inner circle, is a vivid illustration of the adaptability of this "case law" method of teaching. Warnings against irresponsible use of the disciples' ministry can easily be adapted to serve the wider circle of the continuing community. Cf. I Cor iv 1–5, xii 12–31.

Considering the way in which so many parables are used in Matthew, it is likely that in its original context the story may have been used to illustrate the OT lessons and warnings about Israel's use and misuse of her calling by God. As it stands, the parable is marked by a wide use of specifically Matthean language (much of it used again in the next parable).

Luke has the parable in a wholly different context (xii 41–48), but uses it in practically identical form. This may be an indication that Luke had access to the same Palestinian tradition as Matthew, or even that he knew the parable in Matthew's written form.

xxv 1–13. Here again we are faced with a parable which is capable of almost infinite variation in interpretation. Several commentators have said that this parable is one which deals with the Messiah's return, and this explains why the figure of the bride is missing from many texts. For what bride, it has been said, could the Messiah bring from heaven? In this kind of interpretation, the emphasis is on a triumphant "return" of the Messiah—a concept unknown to subsequent Judaism. The interpretation has only been possible because commentators have been influenced by the present context of the parable. But if we are to be faithful to the OT tradition in which Jesus both lived and taught, then another interpretation is imperative.

The primary meaning of the parable certainly revolves around the figure of the bridegroom. It is a commonplace in the OT to refer to Israel as the bride of Yahweh, a figure used with telling effect by Hosea. A similar figure appears in Revelation to describe the Messianic Community. What is odd in our present text is the presence of attendant *maidens* (vs. 1). Marriage attendants belong to very ancient Near Eastern custom, but they would always have been attendant on the bride, never the bridegroom. We must therefore conclude that the manuscripts which have *and the bride* at the end of vs. 1 represent the original text. The function of these bridal attendants was to await the arrival of the groom when he came to take the bride to his own house.

If we pursue the allegory with Israel being considered *the bride,* then the *maidens* are those whose function it was to keep watch against the time of God's visitation, when God comes to claim his own bride, his Israel. There will then be those who have failed to keep trust (vs. 5) when others have maintained vigilance (vs. 4).

Jesus here unequivocally equates his ministry with God's visit to claim his own; Israel, God's bride, has been badly served by some of her custodians. It is obvious that this parable serves equally well, (in view of the immediate context) no doubt intended by Jesus, as a warning and exhortation to the custodians of the new Messianic Community.

Parables may be capable of almost unlimited adaptation and interpretation, but any interpretation of this parable which makes the maidens attendant on the bridegroom makes nonsense of any known marriage customs of the time of Jesus, or indeed of any other time known to us. Suggestions that this parable has been influenced by, for example, Rev xix 7 or xxi 2 are ingenious and unconvincing. It is not necessary to find the origin of this parable anywhere except in the OT.

There is no parallel in Luke, but cf. Luke xii 35 ff., xiii 23 ff.

2. *silly . . . sensible.* Cf. vii 24 ff.

3. *oil.* This is not only a sign of blessing in the OT, it is also used of repentance in this gospel—cf. vi 17.

12. *I do not know you.* I.e., I will have nothing to do with you.

13. Cf. xxiv 36, 42, 44, 50.

89. PARABLES OF THE KINGDOM (*concluded*)
(xxv 14–30)†

XXV 14 "For it will be like a man going on a journey, who called his personal slaves and handed his property over to them, 15 giving to one five talents, to another two, and to another one, to each according to his ability, and then went away. 16 Immediately, the one who had received five talents put them to work and made five more, 17 as did the one who had two talents—he made two more. 18 But he who had received one talent dug in the ground and hid his master's money. 19 After a long time, the master of the slaves came and settled accounts with them. 20 The one who had received five talents came forward with five other talents. 'Sir,' he said, 'you gave me five talents, and I have made five more talents.' 21 The master said to him: 'Well done, good and trustworthy slave. As you have been trustworthy in a small matter, I will set you over larger concerns. Share your master's prosperity.' 22 There came also the one with two talents. 'Sir,' he said, 'you handed me two talents, and here I have made two more talents.' 23 His master said to him, 'Well done, good and trustworthy slave. You have been trustworthy in a small matter. I will set you over larger concerns. Share your master's prosperity.' 24 Then the one who had received one talent came forward. 'Master,' he said, 'knowing you to be a hard man, reaping where you did not sow, and gathering up where you had not winnowed, 25 I was afraid, and went and hid your talent in the ground. See—you have what belongs to you.' 26 But his master answered him: 'You worthless, lazy slave! You know that I reap where I have not sowed, and I gather where I have not winnowed, 27 so you ought to have

† Matt xxv 14–30 || Luke xix 11–27.

invested my money with bankers, so that when I came again I should have received my own back, with interest. 28 Therefore take away from him the one talent, and give it to the man who has ten talents. 29 For to everyone who has, more will be given, and he will have plenty, but from the man who has nothing even what he has will be taken away. 30 Throw the worthless slave into the darkness outside, where there is shrieking and grinding of teeth.'

NOTES

Here again in the parable of the journeying property owner the emphasis is on the ministry of Jesus as the means by which God called Israel to account. Once more context has determined the customary interpretation, which sees here a parable of a "second coming" or final judgment. In the circumstances of the continuing Messianic Community, an interpretation emphasizing the final judgment seems much more likely than one which sees proof of a "second coming."

xxv 15. The talent was originally a measure of weight, and later a monetary unit of the highest denomination (cf. NOTE on xviii 24). The word passed into English usage in the Middle Ages as a synonym for abilities and/or natural endowments.

18. Cf. xiii 44.

19. *After a long time*. I.e., in the original meaning of the parable the interval between God's choice of Israel and his coming to make reckoning in the ministry of Jesus. Similar phraseology in xviii 23 would certainly reinforce the feeling in the early Christian community that this parable had to do with the final judgment.

29–30. Cf. xiii 12 and also viii 12, xxii 13, xxiv 51.

90. JUDGMENT
(xxv 31–46)

XXV 31 "When The Man comes in his glory, and all the angels with him, then he will sit on his glorious throne. 32 In front of him will be gathered together all the peoples; he will separate them from each other, just as a shepherd separates sheep from goats, 33 and he will place the sheep at his right hand, but the goats on his left. 34 Then the King will say to those at his right hand, 'Come, you who have been blessed by my Father, inherit the Kingdom which has been prepared for you from the foundation of the world. 35 I was hungry and you fed me, I was thirsty and you gave me drink, I was a stranger and you welcomed me, 36 naked and you clothed me. I was sick and you visited me, in prison and you came to me.' 37 Then the righteous will answer him, 'Lord, when did we see you hungry and fed you, or thirsty and gave you drink? 38 And when did we see you as a stranger and took you in, or naked and clothed you? 39 And when did we see you sick, or in prison, and visited you?' 40 'I solemnly tell you,' the King will reply to them, 'that in so far as you did it for one of the most insignificant of these, who are my brothers, you did it to me.' 41 He will then say to those on his left hand, 'You accursed ones! Go away from me into the eternal fire which is prepared for the devil and his agents. 42 For I was hungry and you did not give me food, I was thirsty and you did not give me drink, 43 I was a stranger and you did not welcome me, naked and you did not clothe me, sick and in prison and you did not visit me.' 44 Then they in turn will answer: 'Lord, when did we see you hungry, or thirsty, or a stranger, or naked, sick or in prison, and we did not serve you?' 45 He will answer them, 'I solemnly tell you, that in so far as you did not do this for one of the most insignificant of these, it was to me that you failed to do it.' 46 And they will go into eternal punishment, but the righteous into eternal life."

The theme of judgment in the ministry of Jesus which characterized the previous parables has determined the place of this discourse on the final judgment, a parable found only in Matthew.

If the preceding material illustrates the Johannine theme of Jesus' ministry as judgment (cf. John xii 31, cf. John ix 39), it seems to cover another Johannine theme as well—that of the Father committing the task of judgment to the Son (cf. John v 22, 27). We explored the theme of the Son's judgment in the Introduction, Part VII.

This parable is a fitting climax to patterns of thought which can be traced all through this gospel. This is no indication that this section is public instruction. But if it is instruction to the inner circle, then the climax of a developing series of teaching is striking. For the disciple, covenant-loyalty must far surpass that of the Pharisee lawyers (v 20), a covenant-loyalty which must be manifest in deeds (vii 20). The Man would pass judgment on such deeds (xvi 27), principally upon charity shown or withheld from the insignificant (xviii 5), with his own ministry as exemplar.

Now that the passion narrative is about to be told, Jesus declares his identification with the suffering.

xxv 31. *The Man.* There is a puzzling change in vs. 34 to *the King*. We have no textual evidence to suggest that a change was made from a lost original, to either *The Man* or *the King*. It is permissible to suggest, bearing in mind that The Man's "coming" in all other contexts is bound up with his coming *to* the Father in passion-exaltation, that there is some confusion here. If vs. 31 stands, and is in context, then there appears to follow immediately a picture of the final judgment, when the Son judges his own Kingdom and gives it to the Father (cf. Introduction, Part VII). Verse 31 seems to present an exaltation-enthronement theme, so we may have an assimilation to xvi 27. But it is possible that the change from The Man to the King is not as surprising as may appear.

We begin by restating our position, outlined in Parts VI–VIII of the Introduction, that The Man in Matthew is a figure of glory, and that material which appears to contradict this is in our view later editing.

(a) There is an interesting history behind vs. 31, as a comparison between Matthew (xvi 27, xix 28, xxv 31) and Mark viii 38 and Luke xii 8
demonstrates. Matthew is clear and consistent, and the coming of The
Man in exaltation is what we have learned to expect from the evangelist.
But in Mark, the emphasis is shifted from a consummation of the
ministry to a "second coming." Luke's version seems to hesitate between
the two concepts. It is possible to suggest here that if the Markan gospel
is Petrine in inspiration, the shift in emphasis is explicable. II Peter—
which, judging from the material and vocabulary employed, may possibly have been written by the apostle—betrays an anxiety for a return
of Jesus; a return, moreover, which is evidently expected in a Petrine
speech in Acts (iii 20). Luke not only links Jesus and The Man (me, The
Man) in xii 8—which Matthew never does in a context of the ministry—
but also seems to be capable of an interpretation of a return of Jesus
as The Man in judgment. Was Luke aware of *both* traditions?

(b) It is often urged that what we have in Matthew is a final stage
in a development, from Mark's "glory of his Father with the holy angels"
through Luke's xii 8 to Matthew's The Man coming with his *angels* in
his glory. The argument can be turned almost completely around, and
we maintain that Matthew is faithful to the Hebrew tradition of Dan vii
13 ff., while Mark tries to reproduce his Petrine reminiscences, and
Luke's presentation stands between the two.

(c) Links between the Matthean and Johannine traditions have already
been noted. This dramatic picture of vss. 31–46 serves only to emphasize
the links. The parables of Jesus in the Matthean tradition are almost
totally concerned with the account that Israel must give in the day of
God's visitation—a visitation clearly identified by Jesus with his own
ministry.

(d) There is some confusion on the part of commentators who see in
Matthew a final point in a developing theological theme. Matt xix 28,
for example, is said to represent the end of a working over of the tradition, so that Matthew depicts The Man enthroned, whereas in Mark viii
38 and Luke xii 8 f., The Man is advocate before the throne. This
misses a vital point. Luke xxii 28–30 speaks of a kingdom being assigned
to Jesus by the Father, a kingdom in which the disciples will eat and
drink with him. It is against all the OT evidence, or any evidence
elsewhere in the ancient world, to think of a kingdom in which its
heir is not judge of his own dominion. Once more, we are back to the
tradition of Dan vii 17 f. Here again Matthew is at one with the
Johannine tradition in giving Jesus a judicial role as The Man.

(e) Some critics deny a pre-NT dating for Enoch, but the evidence
now available militates against this view (cf., however, Cross, *Ancient
Library of Qumran*, pp. 202–3). Aside from this consideration though,
there is good reason to think that the parable material in chapters xxiv

and xxv is devoted to God's visitation of Israel, and the background of xxv 31 *may* lie in Zech xiv 5. Certainly it is used by Paul as the background of I Thess iii 13, though in the context (apparently) of a second coming. Now if the background of xxv 31 is Zech xiv 5, with overtones of Enoch (cf. Part VII of the Introduction), then what we have here is Christology of a very developed order. Because it is characteristically pre-rabbinic in type, we maintain that so far from being the *end* of a line of development, it is early, and we suggest that it is Mark and Luke who miss the really incisive nature of their material. To this we may perhaps add, with more hesitation, that the Matthean tradition accurately reproduces the original material.

For some few years we have been working on problems of inter-relationships of Messianic ideas in the early Qumran literature and early pseudepigraphical works such as Enoch, and we have reached the firm conclusion (which will be presented elsewhere) that the so-called Discourses of Enoch are roughly contemporary with the *Hôdayôt* of Qumran (Thanksgiving Psalms—1QH). Cf. Albright and Mann, "Qumran and the Essenes: Geography, Chronology, and Identification of the Sect," in *The Scrolls and Christianity*, ed. Matthew Black, p. 25.

For purposes of present discussion it is quite irrelevant that the Enoch material (*Mêsalê Hanoch*) has hitherto not been found at Qumran—this can be purely accidental. Furthermore, it is simply impossible that Peter's discourses in I and II Peter were uttered initially in Greek, since Peter was an unlettered fisherman. The Greek adaptation, though in a rather sophisticated literary Koine, is the work of hearers who wished to preserve Peter's message for its kerygmatic value.

(f) The language of the whole section is Matthean, though there are parallels in the other synoptic writers. But what has apparently been the cause of continuing debate has been the juxtaposition of *The Man* in vs. 31 with *the King* in vs. 34. One suggestion is that the explanation is simple, and depends on ignoring the *then* of vs. 34, as a word used so frequently in Matthew as to constitute no more than a connective. In this case, however, the real meaning of the connective has not been seen.

(g) Our interpretation, as we have said, depends upon the consistent use by the evangelist of material depicting The Man in glory. This is the case in vss. 31–32. We have also seen that in all cases of The Man's coming in glory, this is to be understood of his exaltation in passion-resurrection.

The scene here, therefore, is The Man's exaltation—but then, why the gathering of *all the peoples* (vs. 32)? If we make this a scene of final judgment, we miss the point entirely. Here again there is a link with John (John xii 23, 31, xiii 1–20). It is precisely in the consummation of his ministry, in the seal of death, and in resurrection-glory, that men will be separated by the response they make, or do not make, to that central, crucial event. This is the real acid test, for both Jew and Gentile.

(h) Coming now to the *then* of vs. 34, it is possible to see how important this apparently insignificant connective is. Far from being a link joining together two apparently disparate pictures of a final judgment, this link emphasizes challenge. Later in this gospel men will be confronted by Jesus with the irony that they will *see* the exaltation of The Man (xxvi 64), in much the same way that in the Johannine tradition Jesus presents his hearers with the reality that they will exalt The Man to his glory (John xii 32). In both traditions the meaning is the same—the exaltation of The Man is to the throne of the cross.

"Then," the Matthean tradition goes on to say, there is a real and continuing connection between one eschatological moment of The Man's exaltation, when all peoples are faced with its challenge, judged as to what their response to that challenge will be, and the final eschatological moment of the last judgment. It is almost as though the evangelist on the eve of the passion "rests his case." One immediate challenge, in which men must see or not see the exaltation of The Man in seeming defeat, and *then* a final challenge, in which The Man whom they have or have not "seen" in exaltation, will be the King in judgment. The first eschatological moment leads to the other. In the humiliation and apparent disaster of the exaltation-glory, the one who suffers and so goes to his glory is still the Shepherd-figure, still the Judge and the Separator. For the time being that function needs the eye of faith by which to discern it—for how can the horror of torture and death be a judgment on those who merely witness it?

We may with justice admire the superb artistry with which Matthew concludes his story of the ministry, and by his own often-used *then* connects two major themes in his tradition. We may also pause to ask why this comparatively simple interpretation of the material in vss. 31–46 has not been recognized for what it is—commentary upon, and summary of, ministry, passion, and final judgment.

Whether the juxtaposition of the material is the result of contextual attraction in oral tradition we are in no position to know. But even allowing for the care and precision which we have come to expect from Matthew, the Johannine tradition is surely enough to warn us against any easy assumption that such juxtaposition is necessarily the evangelist's own. From what we can gather about the mind of Jesus from the gospels, especially as that mind is known to us from John, it is probably not too much to say that the juxtaposition of themes was most likely done by Jesus himself. The expectation of "the End" is part of Christian belief, is founded on the gospels, and is enshrined in credal statements.

The "here-and-now" character of much modern thinking about eschatology, with its roots in the recall to a study of "realized eschatology" earlier in this century, ought not to blind our eyes to the very real emphasis on "the End" in the ministry of Jesus. We have again and again stressed in this commentary the vital links between Matthew and John on the immediacy of the demand upon men which the ministry and passion of Jesus make. That there is real need for a restatement of traditional eschatology, particularly with regard to the imagery with which it is clothed in our gospels, we do not deny. But to attempt to eliminate from the teaching of Jesus any tension between the elements of "now" and "not yet" would be to erode one vital strand of the kerygmatic ministry. The reader is referred to one modern examination of the problems involved, which does justice both to contemporary attempts at restatement, and also to the biblical imagery: U. E. Simon, *The End Is Not Yet,* London: Nisbet, 1964.

31. *angels . . . glorious throne.* Cf. xiii 41, 49, xvi 27, xix 28, and xxiv 30 f.

32. *all the peoples.* Cf. xxiv 14, xxviii 19.

separate. Cf. xiii 49.

33. *sheep . . . goats.* If there is one feature in these opening verses which ought to have cautioned us against seeing here a picture of final judgment, it is the figure of sheep and goats. From remote antiquity sheep and goats have been kept together in Palestine, and the shepherd cares for both. No final disposition is being described here—simply the customary separation by the shepherd at night. What is here described is the separation which inevitably occurs when men are asked to see the cross as a throne of glory.

34. *Then.* The judgment produced by the passion is in anticipation (prolepsis) of the judgment of the End (*eschata*). But now the separation is final, and those *at his right hand*—who may well initially have been "on his left" in the first separation (vs. 33)—are being commended for acting precisely as he demanded within the framework of the Messianic Community. The comparisons in the material which follows bears this out.

inherit the Kingdom. Cf. v 3, 5.

35–36. Cf. x 40, 42, xviii 5; Mark ix 37, 41; Luke ix 48.

40. Cf. x 32; Mark ix 41.

41. Cf. vii 23; Enoch lxvii 13.

eternal fire. Cf. xiii 40, 42, 50, xviii 8.

91. PASSOVER: PLOT TO KILL JESUS
(xxvi 1–5)†

XXVI 1 When Jesus had said all this, he said to his disciples, 2 "You know that in two days the Passover is coming, and The Man will be handed over to be crucified."

3 Then the chief priests and the elders of the people gathered in the palace of the high priest, named Caiaphas, 4 and discussed seizing Jesus by treachery and killing him. 5 They said, however, "Not during the festival, so that it may not cause unrest among the people."

† **Matt xxvi 1–5** ‖ Mark xiv 1–2, Luke xxii 1–2, John xi 45–53.

NOTES

xxvi 1. *When Jesus had said.* Cf. the same formula, vii 28, xi 11, xiii 53, xix 1.

2. *in two days.* In spite of Matthew's specific reference to the date here, there has always been disagreement as to exactly when these events happened. Mark xiv 12 refers to both "Passover" and "Unleavened Bread," and the latter would be three days later, not two. Luke xxii 1 opts for "was drawing near." The connection between the Passover and the impending passion of Jesus is made emphatic—the annual commemoration of the Exodus-deliverance also looked to the deliverance of the last days (cf. Targum on Exod xii 42, on which see NOTE on xxvi 19).

The Man will be handed over. In Greek the tense is futuristic present passive—"is being delivered," translatable "will be delivered." Whatever may be the case with the bulk of sayings about The Man in the remainder of this gospel, here The Man is emphatically a suffering figure. We have previously seen good reason to think that all descriptions of The Man as suffering were editorial except one—that at xx 25 ff. In that instance the tradition, with its vital theological import, controlled the insertion of a saying otherwise outside the evangelist's scheme. The same thing is true here. The saying is included, not solely because Matthew is guided by the earliest oral tradition (that of the passion narrative), but also because vital links must be established between Jesus as The-Man-in-glory, Jesus as The-Man-here-and-now, even in suffering, and Jesus as The-Man-in-kingly-judgment, and most of all because Passover demands all three interpretations. This we shall hope to see more clearly later in the chapter.

3. *chief priests and the elders.* Mark does not have this information, but speaks instead of "chief priests and scribes" (xiv 1), as also does Luke (xxii 2); but all three, together with John (xi 45–53, "chief priests and Pharisees"), speak of secret planning to effect Jesus' removal. Matthew, by emphasizing the place of the meeting—*in the palace of the high priest,* and also the *elders,* appears to be underlining a quasi-official meeting of the Sanhedrin.

Caiaphas. He is mentioned by name in Matthew and John, but not in Mark and Luke. He was high priest from A.D. 18–36, according to Josephus.

4. *by treachery.* If *not during the festival* in the next verse is a correct rendering, then the plan went astray. Some have therefore seen in this verse a possible meaning of "not in the festival crowd." Cf. xxi 46, John xi 53.

COMMENT

We have already observed that the whole subject of the proper dating of the events of this final week of Jesus' life is not only confused by the varying traditions in our gospels, but also, in the traditional pattern of the Last Supper and arrest on Thursday, by almost hopeless overcrowding. We shall not attempt to unravel here the various learned attempts which are currently being made to determine what recent discoveries may do to assist in clarification. This would take us far outside the scope of a general commentary, and would also make this part of the commentary almost as long as the rest of the book. We content ourselves instead by calling attention to two works, easily accessible and in English, in which the reader can see for himself the problems involved: Finegan, *Handbook of Biblical Chronology,* and Ogg, "The Chronology of the Last Supper," in *Historicity and Chronology in the New Testament,* pp. 75–96.

The trial narrative will be dealt with in its own place. For our part, we would be prepared to say that the possibility of Jesus and his disciples' following an archaic calendar known to have been used by sectarian groups in the period immediately before the New Testament, greatly simplifies the chronology of this week.

92. PASSOVER: BETHANY
(xxvi 6–13)†

XXVI 6 Now when Jesus was in Bethany, in the house of Simon the leper, 7 a woman came to him with an alabaster jar of very expensive ointment, and she poured it on his head as he sat at table. 8 But when the disciples saw it, they became indignant. 9 "Why this waste?" they asked. "This ointment could have been sold for a large sum, which might have been given to the poor." 10 When Jesus knew of this, he said to them, "Why do you distress the woman? She has done a beautiful thing for me; 11 for you always have the poor with you, but you will not always have me. 12 She has poured this ointment on my body to prepare me for burial. 13 I solemnly tell you, wherever this proclamation is made in the whole world, what she has done will be told as a memorial of her."

† Matt xxvi 6–13 || Mark xiv 3–9, John xii 1–8.

NOTES

Substantially Matthew's position here, with very minor variations, is that of Mark. The point of the narrative is obvious enough: Jesus knows already that he will die, and knows also that he will be buried without the customary anointing. What is not clear is the connection, if any, between this incident, recorded by Matthew and Mark, the account in John xii 1–8, and the account in Luke vii. In the accounts of Matthew and Mark we have the disciples' anger, in John, Judas' reaction, in all three, the anointing at the table, Jesus' sayings about the poor, his burial, and in Matthew and Mark, the connection of the woman's deed with the Proclamation. Beyond this we have Matthew's and Mark's statement that this happened in Simon's house against John's tradition that Jesus was a guest in the house of Lazarus. These are minor details, however, and in all three gospels the connection with Passover is firmly made. The difficulty lies with the account in Luke vii 36 ff., apparently in Galilee, at the house of a Pharisee named Simon. Of some significance is the omission by Luke of any account of an anointing at Bethany. But the language of Luke for the host at the dinner (cf. "one of the Pharisees," Luke vii 36 and 39, with "Simon," vii 43), in spite of the absence of any vital connection with the future burial (and the unwarranted assumption by later commentators that the Mary of Matthew, Mark, and John was Mary of Magdala) make it entirely possible that Luke's researches misplaced the incident.

6. *Simon the leper*. Cf. NOTE on viii 2.

8. Not only is there indignation on the part of the disciples; it is possible that the evangelist wishes to emphasize that they had overlooked the anointing of kings.

10–11. The woman has made what she can of this opportunity. To see in vs. 11 any blessing of Jesus upon failure to mitigate poverty is outrageous. The NT tradition consistently from the Jerusalem church onwards is emphatic about the obligation to provide for the poor.

12. Mark xvi 1 informs us that three women went to the tomb to perform the customary anointing of the body, but found on arrival that Jesus was already risen (cf. Luke xxiii 55 – xxiv 3). Matthew omits the mention of spices (xxviii 1), as does John (xx 1).

93. PASSOVER: BETRAYAL
(xxvi 14–16)†

XXVI ¹⁴ Then one of the twelve—the one called Judas Iscariot —went to the chief priests. ¹⁵ "What are you willing to give me," he asked, "if I hand him over to you?" They agreed to pay him thirty silver pieces, ¹⁶ and from that moment he looked for a chance to betray him.

† Matt xxvi 14–16 || Mark xiv 10–11, Luke xxii 3–6.

NOTES

Reasons which may be adduced for the betrayal by Judas are as varied and as numerous as commentaries on the gospel. The last previous mention of Judas in this gospel was in x 4, where he was numbered with the disciples. It must be remembered that we have the benefit of hindsight; there must have been features in the character of Judas which commended him to Jesus in the first instance. It is possible that John xii 6 gives us a slight indication of one factor which may have led to the betrayal. In what sense was Judas a thief? We are not told that the money was used for personal gain. The explanation which sees Judas as a secret—and disappointed—Zealot, seeking to force Jesus into an immediate and dramatic public declaration of Messiahship by a contrived arrest, is possible. It must, however, be admitted that there is no proof for this and that we are unable to do more than guess at Judas' motives.

15. *thirty silver pieces.* Cf. Zech xi 12 and its context. This was the traditional purchase price of a slave. The Markan and Lukan traditions speak simply of "money." However accurate or inaccurate Matthew's tradition is at this point, what is important to the evangelist is the way in which the concluding drama of the ministry passes judgment on the false shepherds of Israel. In the final chapters of Matthew there are five allusions to the prophet Zechariah (xxi 5 to Zech ix 9; xxiv 3 to Zech xiv

4; xxiv 30–31 to Zech ii 6; xxvi 28 to Zech ix 11; and xxvii 9 to Zech xi 12–13). If all that we can find here is a "proof text," we fail to understand the use of the OT in the time of Jesus, and certainly its use in this gospel. The accommodation of *thirty silver pieces* to the Zechariah text is of small importance against the background of the entire context of Zech xi and xiii 7–9.

94. PASSOVER: THE LAST SUPPER
(xxvi 17-29) †

XXVI ¹⁷ On the first day of Unleavened Bread, the disciples came to Jesus, asking, ¹⁸ "Where do you want us to make preparations for you to eat the Passover?" He said, "Go to a certain man in the city, and say to him, 'The Teacher says: My time is almost here; I will observe the Passover at your house with my disciples.'" ¹⁹ The disciples did as Jesus directed them, and made preparations for the Passover. ²⁰ In the evening he sat at table with the twelve disciples, ²¹ and as they were eating, he said, "I solemnly tell you that one of you will betray me." ²² They were very sad, and began to say to him one after the other, "Lord, is it I?" ²³ He answered, "One who has dipped his hand in the dish with me—he will betray me. ²⁴ The Man indeed goes, just as it has been recorded of him, but alas for that man through whom The Man is being betrayed! It would have been better for that man if he had not been born." ²⁵ Judas, the traitor, replied, "Is it I, Master?" "The words are yours," Jesus said to him.

²⁶ As they were eating, Jesus, taking the bread and giving thanks, broke it and gave it to the disciples with the words: "Take and eat it. This is my body." ²⁷ And taking the cup, and giving thanks, he gave it to them with the words: "All of you drink from this, ²⁸ for this is my blood of the covenant, poured out for many for the forgiveness of sins. ²⁹ I tell you that from now on I will not drink wine again until that day when I drink new wine with you in my Father's Kingdom."

† **Matt xxvi 17-25** ‖ Mark xiv 12-21, Luke xxii 7-14, 21-23, John xiii 21-30; **26-29** ‖ Mark xiv 22-25, Luke xxii 15-20, I Cor xi 23-25.

NOTES

From its beginnings as a domestic festival, the sacrificing of Passover had for many centuries been centralized for orthodox Judaism in Jerusalem. Our new information about sectarian calendars and places of worship is such, however, that the usual picture of a uniform, centralized Passover celebration in Jerusalem may require drastic revision. In any event, the Jewish colony in Elephantine evidently had no qualms about keeping Passover in exile, and the priestly authorities in Jerusalem, at least at one time, acquiesced in the situation (as we know from the famous Passover Papyrus of 419 B.C.). But how far a sectarian Passover was tolerated in Jerusalem itself we have no means of knowing. We shall have occasion to return to this in the following NOTE on vs. 17.

17. *On the first day of Unleavened Bread.* This would be Nisan 15, the day *after* the Passover, but Matthew certainly means to indicate that the preparations were being made on the day *before* Passover. Josephus (*Antiquities* II. 317) applies the name Unleavened Bread loosely when he speaks of the feast as lasting "for eight days." (But cf. *ibid.*, III. 249.) Perhaps the expression as we have it here is not as simple as it appears. It is possible to translate the Greek by "With reference to the first day of Unleavened Bread . . ."—i.e., the disciples were asking Jesus for guidance as to the procedures to be followed for the next day—or, the term is a generic one for both observances, since both required unleavened bread. The confusion over dating is found also in Mark and Luke. If we are to assume from this notation of time that it was indeed in the afternoon—or even the morning—of the day of the Passover sacrifice, then the interval for preparation seems altogether too short, even allowing for the fact that the *man in the city* (vs. 18) was partly aware of Jesus' intention. Mark, indeed, adds "when they were sacrificing the Passover" (Mark xiv 12). One of the merits—and that not the least—of Mlle. Jaubert's suggestion (in *La date de la cène*) is that the confusion is removed by assuming (a) that Jesus and his disciples followed the old solar calendar, and so kept Passover on a fixed day, Tuesday, and (b) that when the infant Community reverted to the official, orthodox calendar the tradition became confused and remains confused in our sources. John xviii 28 has the death of Jesus taking place at the time when the Passover lambs were being sacrificed—i.e., if the proposed new chronology is correct, then John represents the best historical tradition and the synoptic gospels have tried to adapt one chronology to the other.

18. *My time is almost here.* In Matthew as in John (cf. x 18), Jesus is

always master of events, and here he declares his conviction that the final moments of the ministry are upon him. Mark (xiv 13–15) has additional details here of a prearranged meeting, and the details serve to emphasize the secrecy with which Jesus surrounded his movements before the Supper. If recent suggestions for the chronology of Holy Week are correct, the desire to hold a secret sectarian Passover observance in Jerusalem is understandable. Nothing at this stage was to be allowed to compromise the moment when Jesus would consecrate himself for his sacrificial death (cf. John xvii), nor hinder the inauguration of the New Covenant. (After a lapse of decades, it is still instructive to read Allen's ICC *St. Matthew* commentary, pp. 370 ff. Without any of the indications which we now have from external sources, Allen endeavored to do full justice to the chronology.)

the Passover. Before the current debate on chronology was launched and to some extent even now, much discussion has taken place as to whether the occasion of the Last Supper was a Passover meal or not. Attempts to reconcile the Johannine and synoptic chronologies by making the occasion a quasi-religious meal, said to have been observed by small bands of teachers and disciples, are not convincing. (One such attempt provides the supposed meal with the title *Qiddûsh,* apparently unaware that this was simply the designation of a specific thanksgiving over a meal on particular occasions.)

Any attempt to find in the Last Supper an occasion other than the Passover celebration must accommodate several very awkward realities. Some of the problems are briefly listed here, and will not be argued, since this belongs more properly to a full-scale commentary:

(a) The persistent use of Passover imagery by the Apostle Paul in I Corinthians, together with allusions in other letters, in order to describe the passion of Jesus, is too marked to be overlooked.

(b) The phrase "Lamb of God" in John's gospel, the Apocalypse and I Peter, must be explained if we are to reject the identification of the Last Supper with the Passover. (C. H. Dodd's suggestion that "Lamb" when applied to Jesus means the "bell-wether of the flock" encounters too many difficulties: cf. *The Interpretation of the Fourth Gospel* [Cambridge University Press, 1954], pp. 230 ff.) On the whole complex of ideas thought to be associated with "the Lamb," cf. Brown, *John, i–xii,* COMMENT on §3, specifically on John i 29.

(c) The key phrase *blood of the (New) Covenant,* found in Matt xxvi 28, Mark xiv 24 (Luke xxii 20, added in most manuscripts, making "two" cups), and I Cor xi 25 (source of the addition in Luke), is not easily explained apart from the dramatic rehearsal of the pre-Christian *Haggādā* to give it anchor and meaning. The emphasis given to the same phrase in Hebrews (ix) links it firmly with Sinai but with no other Covenant.

(d) It is not germane to this commentary to discuss the phrase (I Cor xi 24–25 and also Luke xxii 19–20 by accommodation to the Pauline tradition) "for my memorial" (or, "in remembrance of me"). Nevertheless, unless the Last Supper was linked to a celebration which rehearsed God's acts in vindicating his people, it is hard to see why the phrase was already fixed in traditional usage by the time Paul wrote to Corinth. (Cf. here, for the most useful summary in English, Max Thurian, *The Eucharistic Memorial,* tr. by J. G. Davies, Part II, *The New Testament,* London: Lutterworth Press / Richmond: John Knox Press, 1961.) In this connection it is worth a passing note that the Passover *Haggādā* clearly states that the annual commemoration was far more than a mental act of remembering: "In every single generation it is a man's duty to regard himself as if he had gone forth from Egypt. . . ."

(e) R. Le Déant, "De nocte paschali," *Verbum Domini* 41 (1963), 189–95, calls attention to a Targum on Exod xii 42 which speaks of the four nights of Passover commemoration: "The night when God appeared in order to create the world, the night when he promised Isaac to Abraham and Sarah, the night when Egypt was destroyed, and the eschatological night when the world will end." Here again is a link with I Cor xi 25, perhaps also with John xiii 30, and also a link with Essene views of the Covenant.

(f) Attention will be called below to David Daube's important contribution on the links of the Passover meal with the scene in Gethsemane.

21. ". . . *betray me.*" The treachery of the act is underscored by *as they were eating* (vs. 21), which is further emphasized in the Markan tradition; cf. Mark xiv 18; Ps xli 9; John xiii 18. Those who find in Matthew's OT quotations mere proof texts will do well to ask why the evangelist omitted the striking quotation from the psalm, which John includes.

23. *"One who has dipped his hand . . ."* I.e., one who has dipped his hand into the relish of herbs. At first sight this is not very striking to us, and there would appear to us to be no particular indication of treachery on the part of any one of the twelve. But an article by F. C. Fensham ("Judas' Hand in the Bowl and Qumran," *Revue de Qumrân* 5 [1964–65], 259–61), calls attention to some important information from Qumran. The Rule of the Community (1QS vi 1–8) provides that when food has been prepared, there is to be a hierarchic order in reaching out the hands. Fensham suggests that the definitive *with me* indicates that Judas, by not waiting his turn, deliberately denied the leadership of Jesus in the community, and so—to Jesus—marked himself as being in rebellion.

24. *The Man.* Cf. NOTE on viii 20. The passion narrative, it is generally agreed, was the first part of the oral tradition to achieve fixed form, and was in all probability the first part of that tradition to be committed to writing. Mathew is here following that fixed tradition and hence must depict The Man as being in the hands of enemies. Cf. Enoch xxxviii 2.

25. *"Is it I, Master?"* The words are more emphatic than can easily be rendered in English, and perhaps we could here translate rather more freely by "Surely not I?"

"The words are yours." The saying is an ambiguous affirmative, throwing back to the interrogator the responsibility of an answer. Cf. xxvii 11–12, and NOTE on xxvi 64.

26. On the key words (*taking, giving thanks, broke it, gave it*) see COMMENT on xiv 13–21 (§53).

28. Controversy often centers around the supposed impossibility of rendering the words of Jesus (*this is my blood of the covenant*) in Aramaic, but some work by J. A. Emerton has suggested new possibilities about what is, or is not, impossible in Aramaic. Jesus, Emerton suggests, used the rare but perfectly permissible "construction of genitive after a noun with a pronominal suffix, because it avoided any ambiguity" (a very common construction in later Syriac). This, he goes on to emphasize, was to avoid any suggestion that the Covenant was of Jesus' own making; he was but the instrument and the vehicle of its inauguration through his blood—the Covenant was of God's own making. Cf. J. A. Emerton, JTS 13 (1962), 111–17. The construction is also found in Mishnaic Hebrew—if Jesus said the words in Hebrew rather than Aramaic.

covenant. Some manuscripts add the adjective "new," but this is probably by assimilation to the text of I Cor xi 25. Cf. Isa xlii 6, xlix 8; Jer xxxi 31 ff.; and also Oscar Cullmann, *The Christology of the New Testament,* tr. by S. C. Guthrie and C. A. M. Hall (London: SCM, 1957), pp. 64 ff.; Philadelphia: Westminster Press, 1959.

poured out for many. On the crucial importance of this clause, cf. NOTE on xx 28. The Last Supper (at which, according to John xvii, Jesus consecrated himself for his imminent death at the hand of others) is the one occasion in the synoptic gospels where Jesus gives his death a sacrificial interpretation. It is important at this juncture to choose words with care. The "New Covenant" of Jer xxxi 31 ff. does not mention sacrificial blood (cf. StB, I, p. 991), and the conjunction of "blood" and "covenant" in the rabbinic writings is concerned with circumcision more often than with anything else—i.e., the blood of initiation into a Covenant already established. Plainly, several OT concepts underlie this apparently simple declaration of Jesus over the cup, and the basic understanding is that of the Servant who pours out his life for "the many," the community of Israel (cf. Isa liii 10, 12).

We return now to the phrase *for many*. We have emphasized above that never in our NT sources is Jesus represented as inaugurating a separatist movement, and the Pauline letters, for all their insistence on the word "new" to describe God's act in Jesus, never describe the Church as "the new Israel." Jesus, then, voluntarily pours out his life for the community of Israel, and in so doing inaugurates a New Covenant for a Covenant Community already in being. The subsequent admission of Gentiles into the Messianic Community created by this New Covenant was therefore an admission into a community which believed itself to be the true heirs of the promises to Abraham (cf. Rom ix–xi).

Bultmann, in his discussion of Mark x 45, together with the passage now under consideration, dismisses the whole complex as a "Hellenistic-Christian doctrine of salvation" (*Geschichte der synoptischen Tradition*, p. 154).

29. It is impossible to be certain whether this saying is in context, or whether it has been attracted to its present position by *the cup* of vs. 27. Mark xiv 25 does not have the emphatic *from now on* of Matthew, though Luke xxii 18 preserves it (in a parallel form). Perhaps Luke's emphatic assertion that the occasion was a Passover meal (Luke xxii 15), together with I Cor xi 26, provides us with the best meaning which we can achieve at this remove. The words are no solemn farewell, but a looking forward to the perpetual fellowship of the Messianic Age (cf. Enoch lxii 14 and see also Rev iii 21).

There is, however, considerable variation in different traditions. Matthew speaks of *my Father's Kingdom* (which for Matthew looks beyond the Messianic Kingdom), where Mark and Luke speak of "the Kingdom of God." Luke xxii 16 speaks of the Passover as being "fulfilled in the Kingdom of God," and Paul's I Cor xi 26 further complicates matters by speaking of the Lord's Supper as "proclaiming the Lord's death until he comes." With the sources that we presently have, we can make two suggestions: (a) The uncertainty which is reflected in Acts and the earlier Pauline letters about the precise meaning of the "coming" of The Man may be at work in the two sayings as they are recorded in Luke xxii 16, 18. The "coming" of the Kingdom, in the exaltation of Jesus by the Father, certainly would mean the fulfillment of Passover. In I Cor xi 26 there is a shift from this primary meaning to an expected *second* coming of Jesus in glory. (b) Matthew's tradition sees this fulfillment in terms which look beyond the Messianic Kingdom to the Father's Kingdom, a differentiation which we examined in Part VII of the Introduction. Which of the two traditions is more original, we have no means of determining. One further note must be added: the vine as a symbol of Israel is well known throughout the OT. Behind the sayings as we now have them there may originally have been a saying of Jesus which spoke in terms (later misunderstood) of the fulfillment of Israel in the Kingdom, in much the same way that Paul speaks of that fulfillment in Rom xi.

95. PASSOVER: GETHSEMANE
(xxvi 30–46) †

XXVI 30 Having sung a hymn, they went to the Mount of Olives. 31 Jesus then said to them, "All of you will fall away from me tonight. For it is recorded: 'I will strike the shepherd, and the sheep of the flock will be scattered,' 32 but after I am raised up, I will go before you into Galilee." 33 Peter however answered: "Even though they are all ashamed of you, I will certainly not be ashamed." 34 "I solemnly tell you," Jesus said to him, "that this very night, before cockcrow, you will three times deny me." 35 "Even if I must die with you," Peter answered him, "I will not deny you," and all the disciples made similar declarations.

36 Then Jesus went with them to a place called Gethsemane, and he said to his disciples, "Sit here, while I go over there to pray." 37 Taking with him Peter and the two sons of Zebedee, he began to be distressed and very troubled, 38 and said to them, "I am troubled with deadly anguish—stay here and watch with me." 39 He went a little farther, prostrated himself, and prayed: "My Father, if possible, let this cup pass from me; notwithstanding, your will be done, not mine." 40 He went to the disciples, found them sleeping, and said to Peter, "So you could not watch with me for one hour? 41 Watch, and pray that you do not come into the fiery trial. The spirit is certainly willing, but mere humanity is frail." 42 Going away for the second time, again he prayed: "My Father, if it is impossible for this cup to pass away without my drinking from it, your will be done." 43 On his return, he again found them sleeping, for

† **Matt xxvi 30–35** ‖ Mark xiv 26–31, Luke xxii 31–34, John xiii 36–38; **36–46** ‖ Mark xiv 32–42, Luke xxii 39–46.

their eyes were heavy, 44 and leaving them again, he prayed
for the third time in the same way. 45 Then he went back to
the disciples. "Are you still sleeping and resting?" he said to
them. "See, the hour is almost here, and The Man is delivered
up into men's hands. 46 Get up, and let us go. My betrayer is
near."

NOTES

xxvi 30. *Having sung a hymn.* It is of considerable interest here to
take note of a suggestion made by Daube (*The New Testament and
Rabbinic Judaism,* pp. 186 ff.) that the present division of the Passover
Haggādā represents changes which were early made in response to the
interpretation of a new deliverance, wrought by Jesus, being made by
Jewish Christians. Daube, accepting the commonly held view that the
passion narrative was the first part of the tradition in fixed form, suggests that Jewish Christians, maintaining the original order of the Passover meal (ceremonial meal, questions, interpretation of the meal),
so emphasized the changed character of the observance that the whole
order was later deliberately changed by Orthodox Jews. "By relegating
the meal to the end, the Rabbis took the life, or at least any undue
vitality, out of it. . . . The change round was a very clever means of
preventing any fundamentally new significance being attached to the
meal . . ." (pp. 194–95). It is also possible that the emphasis by the
Essenes on their understanding of "covenant" may have served to ac-
celerate the change. The *hymn* referred to here is the *Hallel* (Pss
cxiii–cxviii); it is still sung at the end of the formal Jewish rite, as it was
in the time of Jesus.

they went . . . The Passover celebration was not confined to a single
location. The meal could be eaten in one place, and the recital of
prayers, hymns, etc., could be held in another, always provided that the
company remained together.

the Mount of Olives. Cf. xxiv 3. Jesus quotes from Zechariah xiii 7,
and the mount is mentioned in Zech xiv 4. The concluding part of
Zechariah is much concerned with the failure of the shepherds of Israel.
In ch. xxiv Jesus speaks of such failure, and when he is again depicted
as being in the same place, he once more speaks of the failure of the
future shepherds of his own community in the face of the passion.

36. *Then Jesus went with them.* The Passover celebration was still in
progress for Jesus and his disciples.

36–37. The presence of Peter, James, and John in intimate association with Jesus at critical moments of the ministry is emphasized in all three synoptic gospels.

38–45. Daube (*New Testament and Rabbinic Judaism,* pp. 333–35) reminds us of the rabbinic provision that if during the Passover celebration members of the company fell into a deep sleep, and could not answer at all, then the celebration was regarded as terminated. Distinctions were drawn between a mere doze and deep sleep, and Mark's account of the Gethsemane episode, when Jesus returned the second time, bears this out ("they did not know what to answer him"). Matthew preserves the distinction for us in his words for "sleeping" (vss. 40 and 43) and the addition of "and resting" in vs. 45. Luke's account fails to do justice to this ritual distinction. It was not that Jesus wished merely for companionship in his agony of prayer, but that he did not wish the Passover to be brought to an early close. Only in this light do the repeated visits and inquiries of Jesus make real sense.

39. *this cup.* The expression was commonly used in the ancient world (from Ugarit on) as destiny or fate, and is so found in the OT. As a symbol of suffering, cf. Isa li 17, 22; Lam iv 21; Ps xi 6.

45–46. ". . . *the hour is almost here, and The Man is delivered . . .*" Cf. Note on xxvi 24. Jesus indicates by his *"Get up . . ."* that the Passover celebration is ended.

96. ARREST OF JESUS
(xxvi 47–56) †

XXVI 47 While he was still speaking, Judas, who was one of the twelve, came with a great crowd from the chief priests and the elders of the people, (armed) with swords and clubs. 48 The betrayer had given a sign, telling them, "The one whom I kiss is the man—take him." 49 Immediately he went up to Jesus and said, "Greetings, master!" and kissed him. 50 But Jesus said to him, "Friend, you are here." Then they came up, laid hands on Jesus, and led him away. 51 One of those who were with Jesus reached out his hand, drew his sword, and struck the high priest's slave, cutting off his ear. 52 Jesus then said to him, "Put your sword back in its place, for all who take up the sword will die by the sword. 53 Do you think that I cannot appeal to my Father, who would at once send me more than twelve legions of angels? 54 But then how would the Scriptures be fulfilled, that it must be so?" 55 At the same time, Jesus said to the crowds, "Have you come with swords and clubs to seize me, as you would a bandit? Day after day I sat in the temple teaching, and you did not seize me. 56 But all this has happened so that the writings of the prophets may be fulfilled." Then all the disciples abandoned him and fled.

† Matt xxvi 47–56 ‖ Mark xiv 43–50, Luke xxii 47–53, John xviii 3–12.

Notes

Matthew gives no indication as to when Judas left the group of disciples; John (xiii 30) tells us that it was during the Supper. The impression given here by the evangelist is of a scene of disorder, almost as if an already existing mob had been utilized by the priestly authorities.

xxvi 48. *"The one whom I kiss . . ."* Moses Aberbach has pointed out (see NOTE on xxiii 7–11) that in any group of teacher and disciples the disciple was never permitted to greet his teacher first, since this implied equality. Judas' sign, therefore, was not only a final repudiation of his relationship with Jesus and a signal to the mob, but also a studied insult. We may have an indication in the Johannine account (John xviii 4 ff.), which does not mention the kiss, that those who accompanied Judas were taken aback even at that stage by the treachery of a onetime disciple.

49. *master.* This occasion and that in xxvi 25 are the only ones in Matthew where the title *rabbî* is used, and in both instances it is used by Judas.

kissed him. The verb is a compound form of the one used in the previous verse (Mark's verbs are the same two), and it is possible that it indicates a repeated or emphatic action.

50. *"Friend, you are here."* On *Friend* cf. NOTE on xx 13. The meaning of the phrase in Greek, *eph' ho parei,* is not certain. It may be rendered as a question, "Why are you here?" but this translation seems to make very little sense. By emending the Greek to *aire,* it would be possible to render "Take what you have come to get." Luke's tradition is here quite different.

51. *One of those . . .* I.e., a disciple. Mark has "a bystander," and it is John xviii 10 which identifies Simon Peter.

Luke (xxii 51) adds an account of the healing of the man's ear. Our sources reflect the confusion of the scene, and complete agreement among all four evangelists would destroy our historical perspective. In order to obtain the truest possible idea of what actually happened, we need independent eyewitness reports—the same is true of early oral tradition.

52–54. This incident is described by all four evangelists, so it obviously made an impression on all who witnessed it. The saying quoted by Jesus in these verses has no parallel elsewhere. An article by Hans Kosmala (NovT 4 [1960], 81–95) provides us with some background to Jesus' saying. The quotation is from a Jewish Aramaic Targum (paraphrase) of Isa 1 11: "Behold, all you that kindle a fire, that take the sword: go, fall into the fire you have kindled, and fall by the sword you have taken. From my Word (*Mēmrā*) you have this; you shall return to your destruction." This is, then, not simply a proverbial saying, but a scriptural saying with eschatological meaning. God's will is being fulfilled and nothing can hinder it.

53. To appeal for deliverance at this time (*at once*) would deny to authority its hour, and the purpose of God declared in the Scriptures must be accomplished (cf. Zech xiii 7). Luke xxii 53b preserves a similar meaning—"this is your hour."

55. *Day after day.* Cf. the secret decision to arrest Jesus, in xxvi 4.

56. *the prophets.* Cf. NOTE on vss. 52–54 above, on Isa l 11, and also Isa liii 12, which is quoted in John xvi 32. Cf. also Zech xiii 7.

abandoned him. Perhaps here again there is a reminiscence of Zech xiii 17, but in this case the flock is abandoning its shepherd.

97. JESUS BEFORE THE COUNCIL
(xxvi 57–68)†

XXVI 57 Those who had seized Jesus led him to Caiaphas, the high priest, where the scribes and elders had assembled. 58 Peter, however, followed them at a distance, as far as the high priest's courtyard, and entering, sat with the guards to see the end. 59 The high priest and the whole gathering searched for perjured testimony against Jesus, on which basis they might kill him, 60 but they did not find anything plausible, even though many perjured witnesses came forward. At last two came forward 61 and said, "This man said 'I can destroy God's temple and rebuild it in three days.' " 62 The high priest, standing up, said to him, "Have you no answer to what these men testify against you?" 63 But Jesus was silent, and the high priest said to him, "I charge you by the living God that you tell us if you are the Messiah, God's Son." 64 "The words are yours," Jesus said to him, "but more than that—I tell you that from now on you will see The Man seated at the right hand of power and coming on the clouds of heaven." 65 Thereupon, the high priest tore his himation, with the words: "He has blasphemed! What further need have we of witnesses? Now that you have heard the blasphemy, 66 how does it appear to you?" They all answered, "He deserves the death penalty."

67 They spat in his face, struck him, and some slapped him, 68 with the words, "Show us your prophetic power, you Messiah! Who struck you?"

† Matt xxvi 57–68 || Mark xiv 53–65, Luke xxii 54–55, 63–71, John xviii 12–14, 19–24.

NOTES

xxvi 57. As in vs. 3, Matthew gives the name of the high priest.

58. *Peter*. However refracted, it is possible that much of the information about the trial before the Sanhedrin came from Peter and the beloved disciple (John xviii).

59. *testimony*. Deut xix 15 demands "the evidence of two or three witnesses" to sustain an accusation.

60–61. Evidently witnesses contradicted each other. Two remember Jesus' prophecy of the destruction of the temple (cf. xxiii 38 and xxiv 2). If we may judge from John ii 21, the witnesses combined one prediction of Jesus with a rumor they may have heard of his passion-resurrection sayings. Matthew's tradition is not without difficulty here. In Mark xiv 57–58 the charge of destroying the temple is dismissed because the witnesses could not agree. But Matthew, by emphasizing *two,* seems to indicate that this was part, at any rate, of the evidence used in condemnation in the following verse, 62.

63. Jesus is put under solemn oath to answer to a claim of being the Messiah. Whatever views the ruling party might have on the coming of the Messiah, it should be emphasized that the act of claiming to be the Messiah was not one which was in itself blasphemous. We have no evidence of what view was taken in ruling circles about the use of "God's Son."

64. *The words are yours*. This answer appears evasive in English; however, cf. xxvi 25 and NOTE there. (Mark records unambiguously, "I am!") If the Sanhedrin was to carry a capital charge to Pilate, it had to be such as to leave no doubt in the mind of the governor. John's gospel is clear that it was a charge of making himself a king which constituted the principal accusation, though the point is made far more directly than in the synoptic gospels. There were, in any case, so many theological interpretations of Messiahship, that Jesus' reply does not commit him to one view or another. Cf. for Jesus' answer the reply of Bar Kappara to questions as to whether Rabbi Judah the Patriarch (late second century A.D. and editor of the Mishnah)was dead or not. Bar Kappara, aware that it had been proclaimed that anyone who announced Rabbi Judah's death was to be killed, discovered that the patriarch was dead. He said to the crowd, "Angels and mortals took hold of the holy ark. The angels overpowered the mortals and the holy ark has been captured." To a direct question as to whether that meant that Rabbi Judah was dead, Bar Kappara replied, "You said it; I did not say it."

Messiahship might mean a number of things to Pharisees, to Essenes, and to Zealots, including the possibility of an armed revolt. To Sadducees it clearly meant a threat to their entrenched position. Jesus throughout his ministry saw Messiahship in terms which he had used only in speaking to the inner circle. He could not now make a simple affirmative without compromising his whole ministry and teaching.

from now on . . . The Greek is quite emphatic. Those listening to Jesus are asked to see in the person surrounded by enemies The-Man-in-glory, the cloud rider of Dan vii 13 ff. (cf. also Ps cx 1). In a very real sense this is the climax of all that Matthew's tradition has so carefully preserved for us in the sayings about The Man. Though Jesus does not say "You will see *me*," the identification is plain enough to his hearers.

65. The tearing of one's clothes on hearing blasphemy was well known in this period. In the OT such a gesture was commonly associated with great grief and distress. However, such a gesture was forbidden to the high priest (cf. Lev xxi 10).

He has blasphemed. If Caiaphas was a Sadducee, then aside from Jesus' unspoken claim to be seen as The-Man-in-glory, which he would regard as blasphemy, the mention of angels together with a report of an implied possible resurrection was certainly heretical to him.

66. *"He deserves the death penalty."* There is no suggestion that such a sentence was in fact given by the Sanhedrin, and the scene which follows in vss. 67–68 seems to represent an outburst of angry frustration.

67. Cf. Isa l 6.

68. Cf. xxvii 27–31.

COMMENT

It is now necessary to say something for the general, non-technical reader about current debate on the trial of Jesus. The publication by Paul Winter of his *On the Trial of Christ,* Leiden: Brill, 1961, has in many ways provided the focus for this debate. Broadly speaking, the issues are these:

(a) Was the appearance of Jesus before the responsible leaders of his own people a legally constituted hearing by the Sanhedrin?

(b) Was the Sanhedrin in the time of Jesus legally entitled, under Roman occupation, to pass and carry out the death sentence?

(c) Are the evangelists seeking, for reasons of their own, to exculpate the Roman authorities of any responsibility for the death of Jesus and fasten that responsibility on the Jews?

(d) Are the discrepancies in detail between the gospel narratives such as to cast doubt on the veracity of the whole story?

It is best to dispose of the last question first. If there were solid agreement, item by item and step by step, throughout the whole narrative, then there would be grounds for the gravest suspicion. Luke (who was not a disciple) tells us of the care he took in gathering information (i 1–4). There are items in the traditions of the other evangelists which Luke did not know, while he alone preserved the account of an appearance before Herod (xxiii 6–12). John's version is very widely different, and makes the theological charge the principal burden of accusation. Here again John has details, mainly concerned with Pilate, which the three synoptic gospels do not have or did not even know. What emerges from a reading of all the accounts is an effort by the evangelists to piece together conflicting and puzzling traditions, often preserved in all probability by men who had not close contact with the processes of either Jewish or Roman law, but who clung tenaciously to what they knew or had heard. The atmosphere of noise and confusion, of hurried and secret consultation, is well marked. If this seems to be at variance with the relative calm which we have learned to associate with our own courts, it is well to emphasize not only that few "eye-witnesses" or "special correspondents" can be found to agree in detail even in these days of television reporting, but also that many recent trial scenes have been anything but scenes of calm detachment. In considering the other questions generally raised with regard to Jesus' trial, the reader is referred to an important book, *Roman Society and Roman Law in the New Testament,* by the distinguished student of Roman law A. N. Sherwin-White, Oxford University Press, 1963. His principal arguments are reproduced here, as they apply to the questions we raised.

(a, b) Certainly the Sanhedrin possessed absolute police control over the temple area, including the power to pass sentence of death on Gentiles (even Roman citizens) who were found guilty of violating the innermost temple court. But this was a special case, and is described as such by Josephus (*Jewish War* VI. 2. 4), because of the extreme delicacy of the political situation in Jerusalem. If the Sanhedrin really did have powers of capital jurisdiction, then this explicit Roman provision was quite unnecessary. The mere fact of the provision proves that apart from this instance no power of capital sentence resided with the Sanhedrin at this period. It was precisely under this provision that Paul was accused (Acts xxi 27–29), but even with this special provision the Sanhedrin could not act on its own and had to bring the case to the procurator. In all our gospels the appearance of Jesus before the Sanhedrin is treated very briefly, and it is clear from the accounts that, however solid-seeming the charge of blasphemy, the Sanhedrin could not impose a capital sentence, no matter how great the pressure. The contradiction in the case of Stephen (Acts vii) is only apparent. Sherwin-White observes that there was no permanent civil service to assist the provincial governor, that even in Jerusalem Paul had a narrow escape, and that the only Roman officials of whom we hear in the gospels and Acts, apart from the prefect or procurator, are three centurions and Claudius Lysias (cf. Acts xxi–xxiii—he was military tribune of the cohort in Jerusalem). Essentially, Roman authority in the provinces meant military presence. In the absence of the governor, it was not difficult to evade the law.

(c) John's gospel concentrates all the force of the argument for the condemnation of Jesus on a theological charge, even before Pilate, where Matthew and Mark both emphasize the charge of civil rebellion. Luke's tradition combines both, though with less emphasis on the theological charge before Pilate. Here again Sherwin-White maintains that those who represent the evangelists as seeking to shift responsibility from Roman authority to Jewish mob-violence have missed an essential point. It is that any Roman provincial administrator was entirely free to make his own criminal rules, there being no criminal code for the provinces, and for "trials outside the system" (*extra ordinem*) he could accept or reject charges as he saw fit. Though most governors tended to follow the code as they knew it in Italy, there was no law—only custom—in the procedure to be followed. This demanded that the governor hold trials in public, seated on the tribunal, and that charges had to be made by the interested parties as prosecutors. The accused had an opportunity to defend himself (cf. Acts xxv 16). There was no jury, though the governor usually took the advice of a committee of assessors (*consilium*). The verdict was given, if the charge was proved, by way of sentence to a particular punishment. These procedures were faithfully followed in the Roman trials of Paul (cf. Acts xxi 27–28, xxiv 1–2, xxv 6–7, 10, 12). Roman officials are seen in Acts as refusing to "take knowledge" (a technical law term) of cases concerned specifically with the Jewish Law (cf. Acts xviii 14 ff. and xxv 18 ff.).

We wish to state quite clearly that the above comment is only a brief summary of a very considerable subject, and it would be a mistake to assume that the subject is either basically simple or easily settled. Two final notes may be added. First, we are not in possession of nearly enough material evidence to be as confident as Paul Winter seems to be. Sherwin-White holds that Winter (cf. COMMENT above), though himself trained in Roman law, depends on the mistaken views of two authors—Hans Lietzmann and Jean Juster, in 1931 and 1914, respectively—neither of whom was a professional Roman legal historian. Secondly, if the gospels rest (as we hold that they do) upon early fixed oral sources, then there was absolutely no point in attempting to shift responsibility from the procurator to the Sanhedrin, before the Jewish War of 66–73 posed weighty problems of allegiance. (In this respect, cf. Acts iii 17 ff.) We may reasonably entertain the suspicion that much of the debate about the trial of Jesus, as with so much of the debate about the New Testament, really derives from an a priori assumption that all our sources are late and unreliable, where not tendentious or deliberately untruthful.*

John, with the sectarian sympathies of its author, certainly betrays prejudices against *orthodox* Judaism. The constant reiteration in that gospel of "the Jews" ought to have warned us long ago, but the work of Abram Spiro (cf. Appendix V in Munck, *The Acts of the Apostles*) has made it very clear that sectarian sympathizers sharply distinguished in this period between "Hebrews" (i.e., the Samaritans) or "Israel" (i.e., the Essenes) and "Jews." It is worth adding at this point that neither archaeological finds nor the discoveries at Qumran have contributed anything to our knowledge of the processes of Roman or Jewish law in the time of Jesus. At this time, all we are entitled to say is that our gospels clearly place the responsibility for deciding capital criminal cases upon the Roman imperial authority, in Palestine at any rate. Any exercise of jurisdiction in this area by Jewish authorities could apparently only be undertaken in an interregnum. Mob violence, rather than judicial process, seems to have been at work in the death of Stephen (Acts vii 54–60).

* Cf. most recently *The Trial of Jesus: Cambridge Studies in Honour of C. F. D. Moule,* ed. B. Bammel, Cambridge University Press, 1970.

98. PETER'S DENIAL
(xxvi 69–75)†

XXVI ⁶⁹ Peter sat outside in the courtyard and a girl came up to him, asserting, "You were also with Jesus the Galilean." ⁷⁰ But before them all he denied it: "I do not know what you mean," he said. ⁷¹ Then when he went out to the porch another girl saw him, and said to the bystanders, "This fellow was with Jesus of Nazareth." ⁷² Again he denied it with an oath: "I do not know the man." ⁷³ A short time later the bystanders came up and said to Peter, "Certainly you are one of them, for your accent gives you away." ⁷⁴ He then began to call down a curse on himself, and to swear, "I do not know the man." Immediately the cock crowed. ⁷⁵ Peter remembered Jesus' words, "Before cockcrow you will deny me three times." And he went out and wept bitterly.

† **Matt xxvi 69–75** || Mark xiv 66–72, Luke xxii 56–62, John xviii 15–18, 25–27.

Notes

Unless the figure of Peter overshadowed the early Community to the extent depicted for us in the early chapters of Acts, it is difficult to see why this account of his denial of Jesus should be given so prominent a place in such a comparatively extended form in all the gospels. The differences between the various accounts are minor.

xxvi 70. *before them all*. This is perhaps a reference back to x 33.

74. This probably points to the standard oath formula: "May God dispose of me as he will, if I am not telling the truth." Cf. I Kings xix 2.

75. Cf. vs. 34.

wept bitterly. Cf. II Cor vii 10 for the difference between two kinds of sorrow. Peter's led to repentance, that of Judas led to suicide.

99. JESUS TAKEN TO PILATE
(xxvii 1–2)†

XXVII 1 When day came, all the chief priests and the elders of the people made plans against Jesus to kill him, 2 and putting him in chains they took him and handed him over to Pilate the governor.

† Matt xxvii 1–2 || Mark xv 1, Luke xxiii 1–2, John xviii 28–32.

NOTES

Whether or not the Sanhedrin had the power to pass and carry out the death sentence, its members evidently decided to rely on the discretionary powers of the Roman authority to "take knowledge" of any particular case, and so took Jesus as prisoner to Pilate. The death of Jesus was to be encompassed by some means, and the varying statements of John and the synoptic writers as to the precise charges before Pilate certainly add up to a determination to have the matter dealt with by the occupying power. The governor had discretion in dealing with matters which concerned Jewish internal polity; he also (like Gallio in a later instance) had power to dismiss such things as being peripheral. One difference must be noticed. Gallio (pro-consul of Achaia A.D. 53–?64—cf. Acts xviii 12–17) could afford to dismiss such issues as seemed to arise from internal dissension within Judaism, for he was dealing with a minority group in a largely Hellenistic environment. No such option was open to Pilate. However conflicting the testimony may appear to us as between the synoptic gospels and John, Pilate could not, dared not, ignore an issue which threatened the security of Jerusalem during the tense circumstances of a Passover celebration.

xxvii 2. *Pilate the governor* (Gr. *hēgemōn*). This is the first mention of Pilate in Matthew. He was procurator of Judea from A.D. 26–36. According to Josephus (*Antiquities* XVIII. 4.1 f.), he was recalled because of his cruelty. Contrary to some writers, nothing is proved by the supposed conflict between the description of Pilate as "procurator" in this gospel and the evidence from a recently discovered inscription of Pilate (in Caesarea, which was his capital) as "prefect." This was his own official title, *prefectus judeae*, and we may suppose that the title "procurator" was a later promotion in dignity. In both cases, the powers reserved to the local representative of Rome were the same. Tacitus (*Annals* XV. 44) describes Pilate as "procurator in the reign of Tiberius." It is also possible that the designation was loosely applied; cf. R. M. Grant, IDB, III (K–Q), s.v. "Procurator."

100. DEATH OF JUDAS
(xxvii 3–10)†

XXVII 3 Then Judas the traitor, seeing that Jesus had been condemned, repented and took the thirty silver pieces to the chief priests and elders of the people. 4 "I have sinned by betraying an innocent man!" he said. 5 But they replied, "How does that concern us? That is your affair." Throwing down the silver pieces toward the Most Holy Place, he withdrew and went away and hanged himself. 6 Picking up the silver pieces, the chief priests said, "It is unlawful to put this into the treasury, for it is blood money." 7 Therefore, after coming to an agreement about it, they used the money to buy Potter's Field as a burying place for foreigners, 8 and to this day that field is known as "The Field of Blood." 9 Then there was fulfilled the saying of the prophet Jeremiah:

"And they took the thirty silver pieces,
    the amount the people of Israel had agreed to pay
        for him,
10 and used them to buy Potter's Field,
    as the Lord commanded me."

† Matt xxvii 3–10 || Acts i 18–19.

NOTES

The incident here recorded by Matthew is not paralleled in the other gospels. The account agrees only in part with Luke's tradition in Acts i 18 f. We can merely surmise that there were varying traditions about Judas' death. Matthew's purpose is not to provide information for the sensation monger, but once again to call attention to "fulfillment." The context in Zech xi 13, from which the quotation in vss. 9–10 comes, is important, as are all the contexts in which Matthew's quotations are set. The Shepherd of Israel has been valued at a paltry sum by the rulers, and hence that derisory sum should be cast away.

xxvii 5. *toward the Most Holy Place.* The Greek word here used (*naos*) is that used to denote the Holy of Holies, the innermost shrine of the temple—pagan temples as well as the temple in Jerusalem.

6. *treasury* (Gr. *korbanas*). The word is Hebrew/Aramaic, and is found in Josephus (*Jewish War* II. 175) for the money kept in the temple; it also appears in an Aramaic inscription from Jerusalem from before A.D. 70, though the exact sense is disputed. In place of *yôṣēr*, "potter," in Zech xi 13, the Syriac translates "treasury of the Lord's house," rendering Heb. *'ôṣār;* this reading has been accepted by many modern scholars.

9. *Jeremiah.* The quotation is from Zechariah (x 12–13). The Greek is not that of the LXX, and is a loose translation. We are in no position to determine whether the evangelist's original had Zechariah or Jeremiah. If Allen's suggestion (in his *St. Matthew* commentary, p. 288) is correct, then the confusion may have been introduced by the recollection that Jeremiah purchased a field and also visited a potter (Jer xviii 2 ff. and xxxii 6–15).

101. JESUS QUESTIONED BY PILATE
(xxvii 11–14)†

XXVII ¹¹ Jesus stood before the governor, who questioned him, asking, "Are you the king of the Jews?" ¹² Jesus replied, "The words are yours," but when he was accused by the chief priests and the elders he made no reply. ¹³ Then Pilate said to him, "Do you not hear all the accusations they bring against you?" ¹⁴ But he did not answer, even with a single word, so that the governor was astounded.

† Matt xxvii 11–14 || Mark xv 2–5, Luke xxiii 3–5, John xviii 33–38.

NOTES

xxvii 11. *"Are you the king of the Jews?"* The Sanhedrin had demanded an acknowledgment of Messiahship, and in spite of Jesus' reply seized on this issue as a means to bring the case to the governor. It was a simple matter to explain the term "Messiah" as "king." Pilate was therefore confronted, not only with a possible charge of treason against the Roman imperial authority, but also with a possible claimant to the throne of Herod. Cf. Luke xxiii 2.

12–13. Cf. xxvi 62. Presumably the accusers were making charges of treason, and it is in this sense that John's gospel reports the matter (John xviii–xix).

102. JESUS SENTENCED TO DEATH
(xxvii 15–26) †

XXVII 15 At the time of the festival the governor was accustomed to release for the crowd any prisoner whom they
wished, 16 and they held then a notorious prisoner called
[Jesus] Barabbas. 17 Therefore when they had gathered together, Pilate asked them, "Whom do you wish me to release
for you—[Jesus] Barabbas, or Jesus known as Messiah?" 18 (for
he recognized that they had handed him over out of spite).
19 While he was sitting on the judgment seat, his wife sent to
him the message, "Have nothing to do with that Righteous
One, for I have suffered a good deal in a dream about him."
20 But the chief priests and the elders had persuaded the people
to ask for Barabbas and destroy Jesus. 21 The governor again
said to them, "Which of the two do you want released to you?"
They replied, "Barabbas." 22 "What then," Pilate returned,
"shall I do with Jesus who is called Messiah?" They all said,
"Let him be crucified!" 23 But he said, "Why? What evil has
he committed?" But they shouted all the more "Let him be
crucified!" 24 Pilate, recognizing that he could do nothing, but
rather that a riot was in the making, took water and washed
his hands in the sight of the crowd, with the words: "I am
innocent of this man's death; see to it yourselves." 25 To this
all the people answered, "Let the guilt rest upon us and upon
our children!" 26 He then released Barabbas, and having flogged
Jesus handed him over to be crucified.

† **Matt xxvii 15–26** || Mark xv 6–15, Luke xxiii 13–25, John xviii 39 – xix 16.

NOTES

We know nothing from external sources of the custom described for us by Matthew, Mark, and John, and this account of a (local?) custom has from time to time been used to discredit the whole narrative of the trial of Jesus. Apart altogether from the agreement of three evangelists on this point, it is necessary to emphasize once again how meager and fragmentary is our information on the operation of Roman administration in provincial jurisdictions. Luke speaks of the savage punishment visited by Pilate on some Galileans. It is possible that this was a supression of Zealots or other insurgents. Such insurgent activity must always have posed a problem for any Roman administrator in Palestine, and Mark xv 7 may give us a hint of what lay behind this reported custom of Pilate. It is at least likely that in the explosive and turbulent conditions of the Passover celebration in Jerusalem, the governor thought to assuage the emotions of the crowd by an annual display of clemency to one of their imprisoned countrymen.

xxvii 16. We have preferred the reading *Jesus Barabbas* on the grounds that the dropping of the name "Jesus" by a later editor (or scribe) is far more likely than the addition of that name. It is Mark who gives us the information that Barabbas had been involved in insurrection.

17. Mark depicts the governor as asking whether the crowd wishes him to release the king of the Jews. This scornful attempted dismissal of the issue accords well with vs. 18. Matthew has called attention before to the spite of the native leaders—cf. xxi 15 f. and 45.

19. This incident, reported only by Matthew, has one interesting feature. It is the use by Pilate's wife of *that Righteous One*. We have called attention elsewhere to this old Messianic title, which was becoming archaic by NT times, but we have no means of determining why Pilate's wife is here said to have used the designation. In Acts vii 52 we have the title used by one who may have been a Jewish sectarian, and its use elsewhere (e.g., in the Johannine letters, I John ii 1) may indicate a sectarian background for the author of at least one of the Johannine letters.

20. Mark simply records the demand of the crowd to have Barabbas released. Only Matthew has the added detail of *the elders*.

22–23. The Lukan tradition represents Pilate as having sent Jesus to Herod, and with the result of that abortive examination before him, declares his intention of releasing Jesus. John's gospel tells of the crowd confronting Pilate with twin charges against Jesus of blasphemy and potential rebellion, implying that the release of Jesus would seriously compromise the governor's loyalty to Rome.

We must emphasize again that we are dealing here not with the studied calm of a dispassionate legal examination, but with a mob scene outside the crowded city of Jerusalem at Passover. The recollected traditions preserved in all three synoptic evangelists, as well as in John, must therefore be seen against a confused scene of mounting disorder, in which no single person present could hope to preserve all details.

Let him be crucified! It is difficult to see why the Matthean tradition of the verb (cf. Mark's "Crucify him!") should be thought to place responsibility for the death of Jesus on the mob rather than on Pilate.

24. The possibility of riot in an overcrowded Jerusalem was always present. In such circumstances the governor might all the more readily bow to the demands of the crowd. From his point of view the death of one man was the lesser evil.

washed his hands. The incident is recorded by Matthew alone.

this man's death. Many manuscripts have "I am innocent of the blood of this Righteous One." Cf. NOTE on vs. 19.

25. *Let the guilt. . . .* It is almost certain that this cry was remembered and preserved by tradition because of the events of A.D. 66–70. It was emphatically not remembered as a condemnation of generations unborn, and ought never so to be used. Cf. J. A. Fitzmyer, "Antisemitism and the Cry of 'All the People' (Matt xxvii 25)," TS 26 (1965), 667–71.

103. THE MOCKING
(xxvii 27–31)†

XXVII 27 Then the governor's troops took Jesus into the praetorium, and the whole battalion paraded together before him; 28 they stripped him, put a scarlet robe on him, 29 and plaiting a circlet of thorns they put it on his head, and placed a reed in his right hand. Kneeling before him, they mocked him with the words "Hail, King of the Jews!" 30 They spat on him, took the reed and hit him on the head. 31 When they had made a mockery of him, they stripped him of the robe, and put his own clothes on him, and led him away to crucify him.

† **Matt xxvii 27–31** || Mark xv 16–20, John xix 2–3.

NOTES

There are some minor differences in this account from the tradition as recorded by Mark. Luke's account (xxiii 11 f.) has a tradition of mock-homage by Herod's men.

xxvii 27. *praetorium.* The official residence of the governor.

the whole battalion. I.e., a cohort, about six hundred men, and the tenth part of one legion.

28. *stripped him.* Some manuscripts have the word *endusantes* (*clothed him*). Jesus would have been stripped already for the flogging.

scarlet robe (Gr. *chlamuda kokkinē*). The robe here referred to, the *chlamus,* was usually a military cloak. The word used for "scarlet" does not mean "royal purple," i.e., "deep red," but suggests that a cheaper red cloak may have been substituted for the expensive robe of deep red.

29. It is possible that the *circlet of thorns* was meant as a cheap (and painful) imitation of the radiant circlet depicted on the coins of Tiberius Caesar. The *reed* would similarly correspond to the scepter, which the same coins depict in the emperor's hand.

"Hail, King of the Jews!" Cf. the common contemporary greeting of the emperor, "Ave Caesar!"

104. THE CRUCIFIXION
(xxvii 32–44) †

XXVII ³² As they were going out they found a Cyrenian named Simon, and they compelled this man to carry his cross. ³³ When they came to a place called Golgotha, which means the Place of a Skull, ³⁴ they offered him wine to drink, mingled with gall, but when he tasted it he would not drink it. ³⁵ When they had crucified him, they divided his clothes, casting lots, ³⁶ and then sat down there and watched him. ³⁷ Over his head they placed the charge against him, which read: "This is Jesus, the King of the Jews." ³⁸ Then two bandits were crucified with him, one on his right hand, and the other on the left. ³⁹ The passers-by derided him, shaking their heads: ⁴⁰ "You who would destroy the temple and build it in three days," they said, "save yourself! If you are God's son, come down from the cross!" ⁴¹ In similar fashion the chief priests, with the scribes and elders, mocked him with the words: ⁴² "He saved others, but he cannot save himself. If he is the king of Israel, then let him come down from the cross, and we will believe in him. ⁴³ Does he trust in God? Then let him deliver him now, if he wants him, for he said, 'I am God's son.'" ⁴⁴ The bandits who were crucified with him also heaped scorn on him.

† Matt xxvii 32–44 || Mark xv 21–32, Luke xxiii 26–43, John xix 17–27.

NOTES

xxvii 32. *As they were going out*. This is an allusion to the parable in xxi 39. The position of the traditional site of the crucifixion inside the present city is deceptive, since the present northern city limits are outside those of the city in the time of Jesus.

a Cyrenian named Simon. To this detail of the man's name, Mark (xv 21) is able to add information about his family, presumably because he was known to some Christians and may have become a convert himself.

compelled. The Greek means "pressed into service." The same sense applies as in v 41.

Golgotha. The name may have been given to the place from its resemblance to a skull, or it may have been so named as a regular place of execution.

34. *wine to drink mingled with gall.* The latter was a stupefying drug (cf. Ps lxix 21).

35. *divided his clothes.* The soldiers who carried out the sentence had a right to the clothes of the criminal. Cf. Ps xxii 18 and below on vs. 46.

36. Mark at this point adds the detail that it was about 9 A.M. Matthew's *watched him,* when taken in combination with vss. 62–66, and xxviii 4, 11–15, may be intended to emphasize that Jesus truly suffered physical death and burial. We know from the Johannine letters how early the Docetic belief was propagated that Jesus only appeared to be in the flesh.

37. It was usual for the charge against the criminal to be publicly displayed.

38. *Bandits* are attested in all the gospels. The fact that the execution of Jesus was but one of three underlines the confusion attending the pre-crucifixion scene and the execution itself. Luke's tradition (xxiii 39 ff.) is that one bandit repented.

39. *the passers-by.* Cf. Lam ii 15; Ps xxii 7.

40. Much of the material here is broadly reminiscent of Wisd Sol ii. Cf. xxvi 61.

"If you are God's son," Cf. iv 3, 6.

41. Once again Matthew adds the detail of *the elders.*

43. Although this verse as it stands appears to be part of the crowd's mockery, it is composed of allusions to Ps xxii 8 and Wisd Sol ii 18. It is possible that it reflects the evangelist's meditations rather than the taunts of the crowd.

105. DEATH OF JESUS
(xxvii 45–56) †

XXVII ⁴⁵ From noon there was darkness over all the land until three o'clock, ⁴⁶ and around three o'clock Jesus called in a loud voice, *"Eli, Eli, lema sabachthani,"* which means "My God, my God, why have you abandoned me?" ⁴⁷ Some of the bystanders, when they heard this, said, "This man is calling for Elijah." ⁴⁸ At once one of them ran, took a sponge, filled it with sour wine, and putting it on a reed, gave it to him to drink, ⁴⁹ but the rest said, "Let things take their course; let us see whether Elijah will come to save him." ⁵⁰ Jesus again gave a loud cry, and yielded up the spirit. ⁵¹ Then the curtain of the Most Holy Place was torn in two, from top to bottom, the earth shook, rocks were shattered, ⁵² the tombs were opened as well, and many bodies of the saints who had died were raised, ⁵³ and coming out of the tombs at the time of his resurrection they went into the holy city and appeared to many people. ⁵⁴ When the centurion and his companions who were keeping watch over Jesus saw the earthquake and what happened, they were awestruck, and said, "Truly this was God's son." ⁵⁵ There were also many women, looking on from a distance, who had followed Jesus from Galilee and looked after him. ⁵⁶ Among them were Mary of Magdala, Mary the mother of James and Joseph, and the mother of Zebedee's sons.

† **Matt xxvii 45–56** || Mark xv 33–41, Luke xxiii 44–49, John xix 28–30.

NOTES

45. *darkness over all the land.* Matthew's narrative is here closer in the Greek to Exod x 22 than is that of Mark. Cf. below in COMMENT.

46. The Greek manuscripts of both Matthew and Mark vary in this verse. It is possible that Mark had *Eloi*, which may be an old Hebrew form still used at that time for "my God." In later times the vocalized Hebrew form was *Elohai*, literally "my Gods," used as a plural of majesty, where Matthew has *Eli*, closer to the Hebrew of Ps xxii 1 (2H). It may also be an unusually early case of Aramaic "obscuration" of *ā* to *ō* in normal late Western Aramaic. There are other allusions to Ps xxii in vss. 35, 39, and 43. This is the only utterance of Jesus recorded by Matthew and Mark during the crucifixion. The fact that it was in Aramaic may suggest that Jesus knew and remembered the Psalms in Aramaic.

47. *Elijah.* According to the OT, Elijah did not die but was translated, and the common belief was that the prophet would come to the aid of the distressed. The onlookers misheard Jesus' cry, which in the circumstances is hardly surprising.

48. Matthew's narrative agrees with Mark's against Luke's, which is here obscure: it was one of the onlookers, not a soldier, who ran to Jesus' help.

49. Mark makes it appear that it was the helper who wished to wait and see what would happen.

50. *yielded up the spirit.* This is a very different expression from Mark's "expired," or "breathed his last." In the light of what will be said in the COMMENT, it is important to attempt to penetrate the evangelist's meaning more fully. In the first instance, the only examples in classical Greek for "give up the ghost" in the sense of "to die" and using the formula employed here, seem to be in Euripides and Aeschylus. In those instances there is no definite article before the Gr. *pneuma*. The real background of this expression in Matthew would seem to be Gen xxxv 18 (LXX), though there the word is not *pneuma* but *psychē*. It is clear, however, that the interest of the Genesis account is wholly focused on the fact of a new birth at the time of Rachel's death. Two other OT contexts are also significant—Ps civ 30 and Ezek xxxvii, though Ps civ 30 (LXX ciii 30) has the verb *exapostelēs* and not as in Matthew, *aphēken*. Ezek xxxvii, as is well known, speaks of the renewal of Israel through the "spirit" (or, "breath," Gr. *pneuma*).

Secondly, the NT understanding of God's act in and through Jesus is that those in the Messianic Community are "born through the Spirit," that it is the Spirit who is the "life-giver" in the Kingdom, and who "dwells in" the members of the Community, and who is also the source of truth to the Community.

Without going into details of exegesis, it is vital to call attention to John xix 30 (Gr. *paredōken to pneuma*), which can be—and perhaps ought to be—translated "he handed on the Spirit" or "gave over the Spirit."

Only Luke provides us with an account of both an exaltation (Acts i 1–12; cf. Luke xxiv 50–52) and a gift of the Spirit (Acts ii 1–36; cf. Luke xxiv 49). Certainly Luke xxiv 49 is in complete agreement with John in speaking of the Spirit as the Father's promise, but it is impossible *historically* to reconcile the Acts account with the tradition of the gift of the Spirit in John (cf. John xx 22). This is not the end of our difficulties, for John has Jesus speaking of his "ascension" to the Father at his resurrection (cf. John xx 17). Cf. C. S. Mann, "The New Testament and the Lord's Ascension," *Church Quarterly Review* 158 (1957), 452–65. The exaltation of Jesus is regarded by Matthew and John as being bound up with the cross and resurrection, and in the light of all NT writings (apart from Luke), it is certain that Luke has "theologized" the last appearance of Jesus to his disciples. Moreover, long Christian liturgical usage has not only given the Pentecost narrative of Acts ii a wholly misleading interpretation as the "birthday" of the Community, obscuring the salient fact that the community of the New Covenant was born in the cross and resurrection, it has also given to that local Jerusalem manifestation a universal application which it did not at first possess.

We conclude that Matthew's *aphēken to pneuma* is completely in agreement with the Johannine tradition—i.e., the gift of the Spirit is bound up with the passion and the resurrection. Cf. C. S. Mann, "Pentecost, the Spirit, and John," in *Theology* 62 (1959), 188 ff.

51–53. It is certainly no service to scholarship to find in these verses an imaginative piece of fiction on the part of the evangelist, or simply an attempt to garnish the account of the passion with improbable details. Enough has surely become known in the course of the past fifty years about the language and forms of apocalyptic to evaluate this material seriously. W. G. Essame ("Matthew xxvii 51–54 and John v 25–29," ET 76 [1964–65], 103) is certainly correct in seeing here a dramatiza-tion of a saying preserved in the Johannine tradition. It is worth noting that Essame is following the lead of a much underrated NT scholar, W. K. Lowther-Clarke, who saw the verses as a triumphant assertion in OT language that the resurrection of Jesus was a divine act. The whole complex of these verses is reminiscent of the triumph of the saints described in Dan vii 18, 21, 22, 25, and 27. We call attention here to the NOTE on vs. 50. At the time of the death of Jesus a new community was born.

51. *the curtain of the Most Holy Place.* Matthew and Mark report this detail. In the absence of any firm dating for the crucifixion from external sources, coupled with a lack of historical evidence for an earthquake coincidental to the crucifixion, it is not possible to say whether this detail was intended to be read as history, or whether by this means the evangelists are further pursuing symbolism. Eph ii 14 is the Pauline assertion that in the community of the New Covenant Israel now embraces both Jew and Gentile, while Heb ix 8 ff. expresses the way "opened by the sacrifice of the cross." The position of the saying in Matthew certainly seems to indicate a symbolic meaning. Josephus (*Jewish War* VI. 299) has an account of an earthquake before the fall of Jerusalem, while a letter of Jerome (120.8) recalls that the now lost Gospel according to the Hebrews speaks of a cleavage in the masonry of the temple porch, which might have left the Most Holy Place open to view. The Talmud (TB, *Yoma* 39b) has an interesting story concerned with Rabbi Yohanan ben Zakkai, which reports that the doors of the temple opened of their own accord forty years (*sic*) before the fall of Jerusalem, so portending the end of the temple.

54. *"Truly this was God's Son."* Matthew and Mark both report this saying. Luke xxiii 47 has a saying which may reflect an assertion that Jesus was indeed "the Righteous One," although the Greek is capable of meaning "acquitted." Dr. Garry Wills of the Johns Hopkins University informs us that *dikaios* in classical Greek can only with the greatest difficulty be rendered "innocent." There is a whole new area of exegesis to be carried out in the Pauline letters with respect to this enigmatic word, and it may well be that investigation will prove that the apostle was more concerned with the incorporation of the individual Christian into the community of the Righteous One that he was with the forensic meanings which have often been fathered on it. In the case of the two synoptic traditions, the saying in this verse is not particularly surprising. The centurion would certainly have learned enough from bystanders, both friendly and hostile, to be aware of what had been said about Jesus as the Righteous One, and to have attempted to render this in his own idiom.

55. *many women.* It is John who provides us with most of our information as to what happened immediately before and after the death of Jesus. But all the gospels agree in the tradition that it was the women who had followed from Galilee who also watched to the end. Of the disciples, only the "disciple whom Jesus loved" is mentioned after Peter's denial, and he only in John's gospel.

looking on from a distance. Cf. Ps xxxviii 11. It is Luke (xxiii 49) who makes the allusion to the psalm much clearer in the Greek.

56. The women are mentioned again in xxvii 61 and xxviii 1.
Mary the mother of James and Joseph. Mark has "the mother of
James the younger and of Joses" (xv 40), the "mother of Joses" at
xv 47, and "mother of James" at xvi 1. Though Matthew informs us
in xiii 55 that two of Jesus' brothers were named James and Joseph, it
is quite impossible to determine whether Matthew's second Mary is
meant to imply the mother of Jesus.

mother of Zebedee's sons. Cf. xx 20. Mark supplies the detail that
her name was Salome.

COMMENT

The evangelists say almost nothing of the physical sufferings of
Jesus. Their interests are wholly centered on the way in which this
physical act of crucifixion was used by God to inaugurate the
Kingdom and the New Covenant. The allusions to the Old Testament
in the passion narrative underline the emphasis which is laid all
through the gospels on God's act. Medieval and post-medieval
concentration on the physical agony of the crucifixion steadily obscured the early Christian proclamation of the cross as a "trophy"
and sign of victory. The harm done by such concentration is still
with us. The cry of triumph which John (xix 30) records Jesus as
uttering (*tetelestai*—"it is completed") is unhappily still misunderstood by some as an utterance of patient resignation.

Matthew's quotations from, and allusions to, Pss xxii and lxix, are
calls to understand the passion as Jesus' obedient response to the
Father's will, not the bewildered musings of one caught up in
circumstances beyond his control. The cry from the cross in vs. 46
must be seen in the context of the whole psalm. Ps xxii, for all its
meditation upon immediate suffering, is a triumphant vindication
of the ways of God to a "people yet unborn." (Cf. NOTE on vs.
50.)

There are also allusions to OT expectations in the gospel accounts of the crucifixion. The darkness from noon to 3 P.M. may
be a reference to the darkness over Egypt before the first Passover,
or perhaps a reference to Amos viii 9. In either case, whatever the
historical background of the narrative, the emphasis both with
reference to the darkness of Egypt and to the darkness in Amos
is to God's act. In both cases "the day" belongs to God and not to
the forces of evil.

106. BURIAL OF JESUS
(xxvii 57–66)†

XXVII ⁵⁷ At evening there came a rich man from Arimathea, named Joseph, who was attached to Jesus, ⁵⁸ and he went in to Pilate and asked for the body of Jesus, and Pilate ordered it to be given to him. ⁵⁹ Joseph took the body, wrapped it in clean linen, ⁶⁰ laid it in a new tomb of his own which he had dug out of the rock, rolled a great stone to the door of the tomb, and went away. ⁶¹ Mary of Magdala and the other Mary were there, sitting opposite the tomb.

⁶² On the next day, that is, after the day of Preparation, the chief priests and the Pharisees went to Pilate with the request: ⁶³ "Sir, we recall that that impostor, while still living, said, 'After three days I will rise again.' ⁶⁴ Therefore order the tomb secured until the third day, in case his disciples go and steal him away and tell the people 'He has arisen from the dead,' and the last imposture will be worse than the first." ⁶⁵ "You have a guard of soldiers," said Pilate, "go and make it as secure as you can." ⁶⁶ So they went and made the tomb secure by sealing the stone and setting a guard.

† Matt xxvii 57–66 || Mark xv 42–47, Luke xxiii 50–56, John xix 38–42.

NOTES

xxvii 57. *Arimathea* (Gr. *Arimathaia*). The name of this town appears as *Rāmethā* in the Syriac version (probably the Ramathaim-sophim of Samuel, where the family of the latter lived). The Greek form of the name may stand for an Aramaic *Rāmĕthayyā*, "The (Two) Heights," also called simply *Rāmĕthā* (if correctly vocalized) as in the Peshitta. Later the name was partly Hellenized as *Remtis* (following a common practice; cf. *Emmaus* for *Ḥammātā*) in the Syro-Palestinian recension based substantially on the Peshitta. Hence modern Arabic *Rentîs*. (The native name at the time of Christ may have been *Ḥārematay(in)*, an aramaized Hebrew form.)

Joseph. All our gospels give us an account of this man who had attached himself to Jesus. John xix 38 provides the additional information that Joseph's attachment to Jesus was secret. Similarly, it is John who tells us that in his work of piety he was joined by Nicodemus. Mark xv 43 asserts that Joseph was a member of the Council, while to this information Luke adds that Joseph had not consented to Jesus' death (xxiii 50–51). Mark also adds the information that it was "the Preparation," i.e., Friday. Matthew's *at evening* means before sunset, before the Sabbath began. John xix 14 identifies this Friday with the eve of the (orthodox) Passover. Josephus (*Jewish War* IV. 5.2) informs us that the bodies of crucified criminals were taken down and buried before evening, mentioning this as an example of the care taken by Jews to obey the Law. Cf. Deut xxi 22–23. It is worth noting that the incident reported in John xix 31–33 precisely fulfills the legal requirements of one executed on the eve of the Sabbath. Care was taken that the criminal being executed could not be secretly rescued during the Sabbath period. It was not unknown for those crucified to survive in agony for days. Hence in order to hasten the death of a criminal suffering execution who might still be living, such criminals' legs were broken.

58. Mark adds that the request to Pilate called for courage on the part of Joseph. Pilate is said to be surprised that Jesus is reported as already dead. See NOTE above, and cf. Mark xv 44 ff.

59–60. We are indebted to Matthew alone for the information that the tomb was *new,* that it was *his own,* and that a *great stone* was required to seal the entrance. The last decades of the second temple have provided archaeology with contemporary examples of tombs with a large circular stone rolled in a trough to seal the entrance (notably the tomb of Helen the queen mother from the land of Adiabene, a convert to Judaism). John xix 40 ff. gives additional details about the burial, implying (cf. Luke xxiv 1) the urgency of burying the body before the Feast.

61. Matthew's detail about the women, like that on the guards in the ensuing paragraph, is included to emphasize the identity of the person who died, was buried, and vanished from the tomb.

62–66. There is no parallel to this incident in the other gospels. Matthew has mentioned the Roman soldiers watching Jesus in vss. 36 and 54, the women at the tomb in vs. 61, and now goes even further to make it clear that no deception was possible.

62. *On the next day . . . Preparation.* This is a confusing note of time,

since Matthew could very easily have said "on the Sabbath" or have omitted *after the day of Preparation*. It is possible that we have here an example of the fidelity of the evangelist to his sources. Matthew may well have thought that taking all these precautions on the Sabbath was unlikely but felt that, however unlikely, the tradition must be recorded. Mark xv 42 refers to "the day of Preparation" which Matthew does not have. There is also another possibility with which to reckon, that Matthew's tradition here represents a subsisting uncertainty as to whether Jesus and the disciples did or did not observe the orthodox Jerusalem calendar.

63. *impostor*. The Greek word is from the same root as *imposture* in vs. 64.

65. *You have a guard*. I.e., take a guard—the soldiers would be Roman, not Jewish.

107. THE RESURRECTION OF JESUS
(xxviii 1–15) †

XXVIII 1 After the sabbath, and towards dawn on the first day of the week, Mary of Magdala and the other Mary went to see the tomb. 2 There was a great earthquake, for an angel of the Lord descended from heaven, came and rolled back the stone, and sat on it. 3 His appearance was like lightning, and his clothing was as white as snow; 4 for fear of him the guards were paralyzed with fright. 5 To the women, however, the angel said: "Do not be afraid, 6 for I know that you are looking for Jesus, who was crucified. But he is not here. He is risen, as he said. Come and see the place where he lay. 7 Go quickly, and tell his disciples, 'He is risen from the dead,' and 'He is going before you into Galilee, and you will see him there.' See, I have told you." 8 They therefore left the tomb quickly, with awe and great joy, and ran to tell his disciples. 9 And Jesus met them: "Hail!" he said. They came up, took hold of his feet and worshiped him. 10 Then Jesus said to them, "Do not be afraid; go and tell my brethren to go to Galilee, and they will see me there."

11 While they were on their way some of the guard came into the city to tell the chief priests all that had happened. 12 When they had assembled with the elders and discussed it, they gave money to the soldiers. 13 "Tell people," they said, " 'His disciples came by night and stole him away while we were asleep.' 14 If this reaches the governor's ears, we will satisfy him and keep you out of trouble." 15 They took the money and did as they were told, and this story is told among Jews to this day.

† **Matt xxviii 1–15** || Mark xvi 1–8, Luke xxiv 1–12, John xx 1–10.

NOTES

xxviii 1. *After the sabbath* (Gr. *opse de sabbatōn*). We must remember that the sabbath ended at sunset on Saturday. This phrase appears to be parallel to Mark's *diagenomenou tou sabbatou* (the Sabbath having passed), but Mark then goes on to describe something which happened on the evening after the sabbath (Mark xvi 1) which Matthew does not record. It is hard to understand the opening phrase in this verse as meaning other than "as the sabbath ended," or "when it had ended." In context Matthew goes on to describe events which belong in all the traditions to Sunday morning. Thus, the next clause *towards dawn* must be understood as meaning "when the sabbath had already passed into the next day."

The proliferation of recent studies on the calendar, both sectarian and orthodox, prompts us to add a note of caution here. The Greek phrase which we have translated *the first day of the week* and which is found in all four gospels (*mia sabbatou* or *mia tōn sabbatōn*) is not as obvious an indication of a particular "day" of a "week" as the English suggests. By the time we reach the *Didache* the plural *sabbata* certainly meant "week," and the enumeration of the days certainly makes Sunday the "first day" of the week; cf. *Didache* vi. But the notes of time in our gospels concerning the resurrection, together with the confused chronology of Holy Week, make it hazardous to say with any confidence whether the evangelists wished us to understand Saturday or Sunday at this point.

to see the tomb. Mark, having no tradition of a sealed and guarded tomb, says that the women went "to anoint him."

2–4 Matthew's tradition is radically different from Mark's here. Mark records the women as questioning how the stone over the tomb is to be moved. Matthew and Luke record the women finding the tomb open, while John attributes a similar experience to Mary Magdalene.

2–3. *earthquake.* Cf. NOTE on xxvii 51–53. It is not possible to say whether the evangelists held these three verses as historical, or whether the *earthquake* and the appearance of the angel as *lightning* are meant as symbolic dramatizations of God's act in raising Jesus.

4. *paralyzed with fright.* The expression indicates faces waxen and immobile with fear. Matthew's account of the resurrection appearances is brief compared with those of Luke and John, and his tradition is at variance with that of Mark. Cf. vss. 1–2 and Mark xvi 3. There is no mention of Peter—surprising, in view of the prominence which that disciple otherwise has in this gospel (cf. Mark xvi 7; John xx 1–10).

In Matthew the women obey the angelic injunction, whereas in Mark they are bewildered and afraid.

7. *Galilee*. B. H. Streeter, followed later by L. E. Elliott-Binns (*Galilean Christianity*, Naperville, Ill.: A. R. Allenson, 1956; London: SCM, 1957), argues that the varying emphases in the gospel accounts of the appearances of Jesus in Jerusalem and Galilee provide a key to the later tensions among Jewish Christians. Briefly, the suggestion is that the earlier followers of Jesus in Galilee, including some of the inner circle, were more open and outward-looking than the rather narrower Judaistic Christians centered in Jerusalem around James. Elliott-Binns finds this reflected in the varying traditions of the resurrection appearances, and even in the earlier gospel narratives. He finds contrasts in both earlier narratives and the resurrection narratives as between Mark and material peculiar to Matthew, on the one hand, and John, some parts of Luke, and the early chapters of Acts on the other. If all this is a welcome change from the familiar Hegelian dialectic of the Tübingen school, with its conflict between Paul and the Twelve (especially Peter), it is no freer from arbitrary reconstruction. Streeter, for example, finds some material in Matthew a "later Judaistic reaction against the Petro-Pauline liberalism" (*The Four Gospels: A Study of Origins, Treating of the Manuscript Tradition, Sources, Authorship, and Dates* [London: Macmillan, 1924], p. 512). However, once explain John's polemic against "the Jews" throughout his gospel as perhaps indicating that John had been strongly influenced by Jewish sectarianism, then the related theses of Streeter and Elliott-Binns cease to be persuasive. That there were tensions in the primitive community only the singularly uncritical will deny, and there may well have been much tension between Galileans and Judeans. But in the light of our present knowledge of Judaism in the time of Jesus, it is as well to beware of underestimating the divisions within Judaism, which has become so characteristic of much NT criticism.

9–10. Apart from the final commission in vss. 16–20 (§108), this is Jesus' only resurrection appearance to the disciples in this gospel.

11–13. This tradition is found only in Matthew. The chief priests and the elders used the deception which they expected of the disciples; cf. xxvii 64.

11. *chief priests*. The soldiers (a Roman guard, cf. xxvii 65) presumably reported the matter to the chief priests, because they were aware that this was a matter of some concern to the Jewish authorities.

On the surface, the story appears to be directed against those who did not believe in the reality of the resurrection. But it is equally possible that the tradition in question served only to emphasize the one point on which both believers and non-believers were agreed—that the tomb was empty. Cf. Justin Martyr *Dialogue with Trypho* CVIII.

COMMENT

We are not concerned with theology in this commentary except as required to convey the plain meaning of the words used by the evangelists. This is particularly true when we deal with the resurrection of Jesus. For all the confusing chronology, for the manifest variations in tradition, the one thing upon which all four evangelists are agreed is that the tomb of Jesus was empty. Only Luke and John attempt to explain how the body of Jesus, in his appearances to his disciples, differed from that body as they had known it in the days of the ministry. We are not here immediately concerned with the differences in tradition, but we must use this opportunity to say once more that complete agreement by the evangelists on details and chronology of the story would put the whole NT record under grave suspicion of collusion on the part of eyewitnesses and recorders of tradition or possibly editors of the gospels.

We confine ourselves to the single assertion that the Messianic Community for which Jesus had made provision during his ministry, and for which he was the instrument of a New Covenant, believed not only that the tomb was empty but that God had raised Jesus from the dead. Apart from that faith, there is no understanding of the New Testament.

108. JESUS' FINAL COMMISSION
(xxviii 16–20) †

XXVIII 16 The eleven disciples went to Galilee, to the mountain to which Jesus had directed them, 17 and seeing him they worshiped him, though some were doubtful. 18 Coming to them, Jesus said, "All authority in heaven and on earth has been given to me. 19 Therefore go and make disciples of all peoples, baptizing them into the name of the Father, and of the Son, and of the Holy Spirit, 20 teaching them to observe everything I have commanded you; and I am with you always, to the end of the age."

† **Matt xxviii 16–18** ‖ Mark xvi 14–18, Luke xxiv 36–49, John xx 19–23, Acts i 9–11.

NOTES

Matthew is the only gospel which has anything that can properly be called an ending. The ending of Mark is still a matter of dispute; Luke's gospel looks to its completion in the second part of the author's work, while the ending of John may originally have been at xx 31 (see Raymond E. Brown, *The Gospel according to John, xiii–xxi*, AB, vol. 29A [New York: Doubleday, 1970], COMMENT on §70 [xx 30–31]). This final paragraph of Matthew's gospel looks forward to the continuing work of the Messianic Community, making explicit what has already been hinted elsewhere about a mission to those outside the Old Covenant community of Israel.

xxviii 16. *Galilee*. Cf. the NOTE on vs. 7 (§107). In the light of iv 15 f. it is likely that Galilee here represents *all peoples* in vs. 19; cf. "Galilee of the nations" in Isa viii 23.

the mountain. In spite of various later traditions, the mountain is not identified.

17. *some were doubtful*. Matthew is apparently aware of the tradition

recorded by Luke (xxiv 22 ff. and 36 ff.) and John (xx 8 ff., 11 ff., 24 ff.). Apart from such awareness of other traditions, it is not possible to find any good reason for this assertion, especially in the light of xxviii 8.

18–19. Cf. xxvi 64. Here again Jesus expresses himself in the words of Daniel (cf. Dan vii 14). The mission which had been limited to Israel in the days of his ministry (cf. xv 24) is now extended to *all peoples*.

19. *baptizing them*. In the New Testament *baptizein* (to "baptize," literally used for dyeing of cloth) is the verb used to describe the act of initiation into the Messianic Community. But the verb—and the derived noun "baptism"—includes considerations which are always presupposed in the New Testament. This lustration with or in water assumed (a) repentance on the part of the person being baptized, the baptism itself conveying or implying forgiveness (cf. Acts ii 38); (b) faith in Jesus as Messiah and Lord.

There are two kinds of formal statements about baptismal status in the New Testament, one speaking of baptism "in the name of" and the other "into the name of" the Messiah. Without setting hard and definite limits, we may understand the first formula ("in the name of") as including both the neophytes' expressed faith in Jesus as Lord, and also the ceremonial action which accepted this profession of faith— i.e., the baptismal rite. "Into the name of," however, seems in its various contexts to demand an interpretation which calls attention to the results of the baptismal rite. The neophyte baptized *into the name of* the Messiah thus not only pledges allegiance to Jesus as Messiah and Lord, but is also incorporated into fellowship with him. Hence the expression used in this verse describes an entrance into fellowship with the Father, the Son, and the Holy Spirit.

Father, . . . Son, . . . Holy Spirit. If we approach this verse with a fully developed post-Nicene orthodoxy in our minds, we shall be just as unsympathetic to our sources as are those who find in this verse a highly sophisticated and much later stage of doctrinal formulation retrojected into the text. For all we know, such a saying may have stood in the now-lost ending of Mark. Even apart from such speculation, the concept of God as Father, Son, and Holy Spirit is clearly as old as the Messianic Community as it is known to us in the New Testament. Cf., for example, I Cor xii 4–6; II Cor xiii 14; I Peter i 2; I John iii 23–24. In Mark we have "Father" and "Son" so obviously antithetical that—allowing for Jewish beliefs about "the Spirit"—it plainly opened the way to trinitarian belief. The antithesis Father-Son is found in Matt xvi 27 and is very common in John. But what is also common in John is the emphasis on the Paraclete, clearly represented as being neither Father nor Son.

It seems plain from the early material in Acts that baptism was performed "in the name of" and also "into the name of" Jesus as

Lord and Messiah. The mistake of so many writers on the New Testament lies in treating this saying as a liturgical formula (which it later became), and not as a description of what baptism accomplished. The evangelist, whom we must at least allow to have been familiar with the baptismal customs of the early Messianic Community, may well have added to *baptizing them* his own summary of what baptism accomplished.

It is as well to remember that the *Didache* also has this summary of baptism (*Didache* vii) and its reference to "running water" reflects an earlier Essene preoccupation.

20. *teaching them.* Elsewhere in this gospel Jesus commands the inner circle to *heal* (x 1, 8) and to *proclaim* (x 7). Now that Jesus' ministry is over, the command to *teach* is given.

I am with you always. Cf. i 23 and xviii 20.

to the end of the age. Cf. xiii 39 f. and 49, and xxiv 3. The presence of this old sectarian formula at the end of this passage is additional evidence that the passage belongs to the earliest stages of the tradition.

KEY TO THE TEXT

Chapter	Verse	§	Chapter	Verse	§
xix	16–30	71	xxv	31–46	90
xx	1–16	72	xxvi	1–5	91
xx	17–19	73	xxvi	6–13	92
xx	20–28	74	xxvi	14–16	93
xx	29–34	75	xxvi	17–29	94
xxi	1–11	76	xxvi	30–46	95
xxi	12–17	77	xxvi	47–56	96
xxi	18–27	78	xxvi	57–68	97
xxi	28–46	79	xxvi	69–75	98
xxii	1–14	80	xxvii	1–2	99
xxii	15–46	81	xxvii	3–10	100
xxiii	1–36	82	xxvii	11–14	101
xxiii	37–39	83	xxvii	15–26	102
xxiv	1–2	84	xxvii	27–31	103
xxiv	3–14	85	xxvii	32–44	104
xxiv	15–28	86	xxvii	45–56	105
xxiv	29–44	87	xxvii	57–66	106
xxiv	45–51	88	xxviii	1–15	107
xxv	1–13	88	xxviii	16–20	108
xxv	14–30	89